INSTITUTIONS AND THE PATH TO THE MODERN ECONOMY

LESSONS FROM MEDIEVAL TRADE

It is widely believed that disparities in economic, political, and social outcomes reflect distinct institutions. There is little agreement, however, among economists, political scientists, and sociologists as to what institutions are, what forces influence their persistence and change, why societies evolve along distinct institutional trajectories, and how we can influence institutional development. This multidisciplinary book develops a concept of institutions that integrates seemingly alternative lines of institutional analysis in the social sciences. It advances a unified framework to study institutional origin, persistence, endogenous change, and the impact of past institutions on subsequent ones.

The benefits of this perspective are demonstrated through comparative studies of institutions – particularly those that supported trade – in the late medieval European and Muslim worlds. This comparative analysis of the institutional foundations of markets and polities and their dynamics also provides valuable insights on the functioning of contemporary economies. Indeed, the analysis highlights the possible particularities of the European institutions and why and how they contributed to the rise of the modern economy by supporting impersonal exchange, fostering the rise of effective states, and leading to advances in useful knowledge.

Avner Greif is the Bowman Family Endowed Professor in Humanities and Sciences, Professor of Economics, and Senior Fellow at the Institute for International Studies at Stanford University. He is a recipient of fellowships from the American Academy of Arts and Sciences, the MacArthur Foundation, the Econometric Society, the Canadian Institute for Advanced Research, and the Center for Advanced Studies in the Behavioral Sciences, Stanford. He has published articles in such journals as *American Economic Review, Journal of Political Economy, Journal of Economic History, American Political Science Review, European Review of Economic History*, and *Chicago Journal of International Law* as well as chapters in many edited books. Greif is also a coauthor of *Analytic Narrative* (1998), and some of his works have been published in French, Japanese, Persian, and Spanish editions.

D0916136

POLITICAL ECONOMY OF INSTITUTIONS AND DECISIONS

Series Editors

Randall Calvert, Washington University, St. Louis
Thráinn Eggertsson, University of Iceland and New York University

Founding Editors

James E. Alt, Harvard University
Douglass C. North, Washington University, St. Louis

Other books in the series

Alberto Alesina and Howard Rosenthal, *Partisan Politics, Divided Government, and the Economy*

Lee J. Alston, Thráinn Eggertsson, and Douglass C. North, eds., *Empirical Studies in Institutional Change*

Lee J. Alston and Joseph P. Ferrie, *Southern Paternalism and the Rise of the American Welfare State: Economics, Politics, and Institutions, 1865–1965*

James E. Alt and Kenneth Shepsle, eds., *Perspectives on Positive Political Economy*

Josephine T. Andrews, *When Majorities Fail: The Russian Parliament, 1990–1993*

Jeffrey S. Banks and Eric A. Hanushek, eds., *Modern Political Economy: Old Topics, New Directions*

Yoram Barzel, *Economic Analysis of Property Rights*, 2nd edition

Yoram Barzel, *A Theory of the State: Economic Rights, Legal Rights, and the Scope of the State*

Robert Bates, *Beyond the Miracle of the Market: The Political Economy of Agrarian Development in Kenya*, 2nd edition

Charles M. Cameron, *Veto Bargaining: Presidents and the Politics of Negative Power*

Kelly H. Chang, *Appointing Central Bankers: The Politics of Monetary Policy in the United States and the European Monetary Union*

Peter Cowhey and Mathew McCubbins, eds., *Structure and Policy in Japan and the United States: An Institutionalist Approach*

Gary W. Cox, *The Efficient Secret: The Cabinet and the Development of Political Parties in Victorian England*

Gary W. Cox, *Making Votes Count: Strategic Coordination in the World's Electoral System*

Continued on page following index

INSTITUTIONS AND THE PATH TO THE MODERN ECONOMY

Lessons from Medieval Trade

AVNER GREIF
Stanford University

CAMBRIDGE UNIVERSITY PRESS

CAMBRIDGE UNIVERSITY PRESS
Cambridge, New York, Melbourne, Madrid, Cape Town, Singapore, São Paulo

Cambridge University Press
40 West 20th Street, New York, NY 10011-4211, USA

www.cambridge.org
Information on this title: www.cambridge.org/9780521480444

First published 2006

Printed in the United States of America

A catalog record for this publication is available from the British Library.

Library of Congress Cataloging in Publication Data
Greif, Avner, 1955–
Institutions and the path to the modern economy: lessons from
medieval trade / Avner Greif.
p.   cm. – (Political economy of institutions and decisions)
Includes bibliographical references and index.
ISBN-13: 978-0-521-48044-4 (hardback)
ISBN-10: 0-521-48044-2 (hardback)
ISBN-13: 978-0-521-67134-7 (pbk.)
ISBN-10: 0-521-67134-5 (pbk.)
1. Commerce – History – Medieval, 500–1500.   2. Social institutions.
I. Title.   II. Series.
HF395.G74   2005
381′.09′02 – dc22   2005006468

ISBN-13   978-0-521-48044-4 hardback
ISBN-10   0-521-48044-2 hardback

ISBN-13   978-0-521-67134-7 paperback
ISBN-10   0-521-67134-5 paperback

To the living memory of my father, Dr. Leon Arie Greif

לאבי, מורי, ורבי, סא״ל ד״ר לאון אריה גרייף. תנצב׳א

Contents

Contents

Abbreviations

Annali	*Annali Genovesi di Caffaro e dei suoi Continuatori,* 1099–1240
Bodl.	Bodleian Library, Oxford, England
CDG	*Codice Diplomatico della Repubblica di Genova dal MCLXIIII [sic] al MCLXXXX [sic]*
DK	David Kaufmann Collection, Hungarian Academy of Science, Budapest
Dropsie	Dropsie College, Philadelphia
INA	Institute Norodov Azii, Leningrad
TS	Taylor-Schechter Collection, University Library, Cambridge, England
ULC	University Library, Cambridge, England (exclusive of the TS collection)

Preface

This book grew out of an attempt to gain a better understanding of the causal factors underpinning economic and political outcomes during the late medieval period (circa 1050 to 1350). It was during this period that the Muslim (Mediterranean) World reached what many scholars consider to be the zenith of its commercial integration, whereas expansion of markets in Europe was so pronounced that prominent historians dubbed this phenomenon as "the Late Medieval Commercial Revolution." Gaining a better understanding of this period therefore has the promise of advancing our knowledge regarding why and how effective markets and economically beneficial polities prevailed in some historical episodes but not in others. Although economists have long emphasized the welfare-enhancing implications of market expansion, we know surprisingly little about the source for historical trajectories of market development.

This period is also of interest because it was a point of bifurcation in the histories of the Muslim and European worlds. The Muslim world was probably more advanced economically, technologically, and scientifically than Europe during the late medieval period. Indeed, the Europeans learned a great deal from the Muslim world at the time (e.g., Watt 1987). In subsequent centuries, however, the Muslims developed economically and politically along a different path from the Europeans, and became economically worse off in the long run.

In attempting to understand this period and its implications on subsequent development, I benefited from the training in historical analysis that I received when pursuing an advanced degree at Tel Aviv University. I was particularly fortunate to study under the supervision of Professor Moshe Gil, a specialist in the Muslim medieval world. My training in historical analysis was complemented by further graduate training in economics and economic history at Northwestern University where I had the

xiii

privilege to work under the supervision of Professors Joel Mokyr, John C. Panzar, and William P. Rogerson.

My training in these two disciplines is reflected in this book, which combines historical and social scientific modes of analysis. On the one hand, the book aspires to do justice to historical particularities and processes. Indeed, it argues that they are the keys to understanding distinct outcomes and developments in seemingly identical situations. On the other hand, it also recognizes that a purely historical narrative risks being ad hoc and devoid of general insights.

The analysis conducted here, therefore, also follows the social scientific tradition of relying on explicit theory, using analytical models, and putting conjectures at the risk of being empirically refuted. At the same time, it recognizes the limitations of the social scientific approach: general theory often fails to account for historical particularities; the use of models is restricted by underlying mathematical techniques; and historically specific conjectures often cannot be evaluated using statistical methods.

Historical and social scientific analyses are therefore complements to each other rather than substitutes, as often assumed. My hope is that the studies presented here will demonstrate the necessity, feasibility, and benefit that is derived from integrating these two scientific modes of analysis.

In the course of studying the late medieval period, I realized the need to go beyond invoking different technologies, endowments, or preferences, as classical economic theory directs. To understand the outcomes and processes of interest, I had to incorporate in the analysis the impact of *institutions.* In economics, institutionalists usually identify institutions with either politically determined rules regulating economic activities or contractual and organizational forms chosen by agents interacting within markets. These approaches were too narrow for my purpose because I couldn't take either the political or market orders as exogenous to the analysis. My aim was to examine the endogenous emergence and dynamics of different polities and economies and not merely behavior in them.

To understand the endogenous emergence, operation, and implications of different polities and markets, therefore, I had to go beyond viewing institutions as politically determined rules or as the optimal responses of economic agents interacting within markets. Instead of taking markets and polities as exogenous, I had to consider them as endogenous and study their institutional foundations. To take the analysis to this deeper level, I sought to understand the causal factors influencing behavior in economic and political transactions. Such understanding necessitated going beyond studying rules to consider how systems of rules, beliefs, norms, and organizations (social structures) guide, enable, and motivate behavior in various transactions.

Studying institutions as interrelated systems as rules, beliefs, norms, and organizations turned out to be both challenging and rewarding. By the ad hoc invoking of unobservable beliefs and norms, for example, any outcome can be explained, implying that we have explained nothing of consequence. It is therefore imperative to have a way to restrict the set of admissible institutions. In restricting this set, I found it conceptually sound and empirically rewarding to combine historical and microanalytical – particularly game-theoretic – analyses. Combining historical and game-theoretic analyses enabled me to do justice to the diversity of the possible systems of rules, beliefs, norms, and organizations on the one hand, while analytically restricting and empirically evaluating the set of admissible institutions and outcomes.

Moreover, this approach revealed new ways to advance the study of the thorny issue of institutional dynamics. In what ways do institutions influence trajectories of subsequent institutional and therefore historical development? Economists usually assert that institutional dynamics reflect optimal responses of decision makers to current and expected conditions. Social scientists working in other disciplines and historians, however, assert that institutional dynamics reflect the shackles of history. Each side of this debate captures a potentially important aspect of reality, but neither is satisfactory by itself. By considering institutions from the broader perspective advanced here and combining the historical and the microanalytical frameworks, we can bridge these two approaches. It is possible to better understand when and why an institution persists in a changing environment, how it unleashes processes that lead to its demise, and how past institutions – perhaps even those that are no longer effective in influencing behavior – influence subsequent ones.

The formation and implications of distinct beliefs, norms, and organizations (social structures) have been extensively studied in disciplines other than economics, such as sociology, political science, and cognitive science. Hence, this book builds on analytical and conceptual frameworks developed in disciplines outside economics. It particularly highlights the benefits of merging the study of institutions, as conducted in mainstream economics, with the study of cultural and social factors, as conducted in sociology. By focusing on beliefs, norms, and organizations, which has traditionally been the domain of sociological analysis, this work became a part of the "sociological turn" of institutional analysis in economics.

Sociological variables are invoked to account for the diversity found in institutional forms and development.

My attempt to gain a better understanding of a particular historical episode necessitated attempting to advance institutional analysis. Many social scientists maintain that institutions matter and that institutional dynamics is a historical process. The ability to study institutions and their dynamics is therefore crucial to understanding the reasons for the uneven distribution of welfare among and within different societies and what can be done to improve this situation. The framework outlined in this book attempts to advance our ability to conduct a comparative analysis of the institutional foundations of past and contemporary markets and polities and their dynamics.

Because this book contains an analysis of a particular historical episode and a general framework for studying institutions, it is made up of several overlapping components. The first is a detailed study of institutions that provided the foundations for markets and polities during the late medieval period; the second is a comparative analysis of institutions in the European and Muslim worlds during that period; the third is a conceptual, analytical (specifically game-theoretical), and empirical framework for studying institutions and their endogenous dynamics. Indeed, the analyses of specific institutions are presented in this book as illustrations of the main aspects of this framework.

This book is therefore multifaceted and hence there are many ways to read it. Some readers will read it as presenting a theory of economic and political institutions in which historical case studies illustrate particular theoretical assertions. Some will read it as a statement of why and how we should introduce endogenous dynamics into institutional analysis, or why a context-specific, theoretically informed, case-study analysis is useful. Some will read this book as a comparative study of the institutional foundations of late medieval markets and states in the European and Muslim worlds that fostered our understanding of these particular historical episodes and their dynamics. Others will read it as a study of the interrelations between institutional development and cultural and social evolution, or as a call for expanding institutional analysis in economics by incorporating cultural and social factors. For some it will be read as a confirmation of the applicability of game theory to empirical institutional analysis, while others will read it as social science history. As for myself, the book reflects an attempt to gain a better understanding of a particular historical episode and to learn about institutions in general from this period.

My greatest professional debt in producing this book is to my two teachers: Joel Mokyr and Douglass C. North. Joel and Doug spent many hours inspiring, encouraging, and providing me with detailed comments. Their faith in this project was instrumental in moving it forward. Masahiko Aoki, Randall Calvert, Philip T. Hoffman, Timur Kuran, David Laitin, Steve Tadelis, Barry Weingast, and Oliver Williamson have also provided me with detailed comments on various drafts of this manuscript. This preface seems also an appropriate opportunity to thank Elhanan Helpman who influenced my professional development since my undergraduate days.

While writing this book, I was fortunate to benefit from a particularly favorable work environment at Stanford University. I have greatly benefited from interactions, stimulations, and valuable comments regarding this project from members of the Comparative Institutional Analysis and Economic History groups in the Economics Department, particularly from Masahiko Aoki, Paul David, Marcel Fafchamps, Paul Milgrom, Steve Tadelis, Yingyi Qian, and Gavin Wright. Many other Stanford scholars working on institutions also contributed in many ways to this project. James D. Fearon, John W. Meyer, Stephen H. Haber, Stephen D. Krasner, David Laitin, and Robert Powell were particularly instrumental. Paul Milgrom, Barry Weingast, and David Laitin collaborated with me on projects that grew from or were later incorporated into this book. While I was working on this manuscript, I also had the good fortune to collaborate with and learn from Robert Bates, Margaret Levi, Jean-Laurent Rosenthal, and Barry Weingast while coauthoring *Analytic Narratives* with them.

Several organizations sponsored conferences and seminars where I gained important feedback on the manuscript. These include the Center for New Institutional Social Science at Washington University, the Center for the Study of Economy and Society at Cornell University, the Mercatus Center at George Mason University and the Liberty Fund, and the Canadian Institute for Advanced Research. These events were organized by Itai Sened, Victor Nee and Richard Swedberg, Paul S. Edwards and Brian Hooks, and Elhanan Helpman, respectively. In addition to their comments, I benefited greatly from input by participants, particularly Lee Benham, Peter J. Boettke, Randall Calvert, Bruce G. Carruthers, Stanley Engerman, Philip T. Hoffman, Jack Goldstone, David Harbord, Jack Knight, Michael Macy, Chiaki Moriguchi, Gary Miller, John V. Nye, and Norman Schofield. Avanish Dixit, Thráinn Eggertsson, Steve A. Epstein, Henry Farrell, Judith Goldstein, Peter Gourevitch, Yaron Greif, Leonard

Hochberg, Jeffrey Rogers Hummel, Peter Katzenstein, Margaret Levi, Bentley Macleod, Chris Mantzavinos, Tetsuji Okazaki, Daniel Posner, John Pencavel, Robert Powell, Rudolf Richter, Gerard Roland, Andy Rutten, Kenneth Shepsle, Shankar Satynath, Kathleen Thelen, and Carolyn Warner also provided me with valuable comments.

The able research assistance of Saumitra Jha, Navin Kartik, Na'ama Moran, Lucia Tedesco, and Joanne Yoong contributed much to the research reported in this book. I am similarly in debt for the valuable lessons I received from my students and post docs, particularly Kurt Annen, Gregory Besharov, Ryo Kambayashi, Kivanc Karaman, Aldo Musacchio, Mu Yang Li, Nese Yildiz, and Pai-Ling Yin.

Grants from the National Science Foundation, fellowships from the MacArthur Foundation and the Canadian Institute for Advanced Research, and support from the Stanford Humanities Center and the Center for Advanced Studies in Behavioral Sciences at Stanford gave me both the resources and the time to complete this work. My assistant, Deborah Johnston, provided me with valuable support, going over endless versions of the manuscript among many other contributions. Barbara Karni, through her able editing, contributed much to render the exposition accessible. The editorial team at Cambridge University Press – Lewis Bateman, Brian R. MacDonald, and Eric Schwartz – were similarly of immense help.

The endless energy and impressive intellect of my mother, Koka Lea Greif, has always been a source of inspiration for me. Last, and not least, I am in debt to my wife Esther Greif and our children, Adi, Yaron, and Arielle, who stood by me during the years I worked on this manuscript. They were a constant source of support and motivation, and I greatly appreciate the personal sacrifices they willingly made to enable me to complete this book.

Various chapters in this book build on material previously published by the author.

Chapters 3 and 9 draw on "Reputation and Coalitions in Medieval Trade: Evidence on the Maghribi Traders" (*Journal of Economic History*, 1989), by permission of the Economic History Association; "Contract Enforceability and Economic Institutions in Early Trade: The Maghribi Traders' Coalition" (*American Economic Review*, 1993), by permission of the American Economic Association; "Contract Enforceability and Economic Institutions in Early Trade: Lessons from the Commercial Revolution" (*American Economic Review*, 1992), by permission of the

American Economic Association; and "Cultural Beliefs and the Organization of Society: A Historical and Theoretical Reflection on Collectivist and Individualist Societies" (*Journal of Political Economy*, 1994, copyright by the University of Chicago, all rights reserved), by permission.

Chapter 4 draws on "Coordination, Commitment and Enforcement: The Case of the Merchant Gild" (*Journal of Political Economy*, 1994, copyright by the University of Chicago), by permission. A modified version of Chapter 6 was published as "Theory of Endogenous Institutional Change" (coauthored with David Laitin, *American Political Science Review*, 2004), by permission of the *American Political Science Review*. Chapter 8 draws on "Self-Enforcing Political Systems and Economic Growth: Late Medieval Genoa" (in *Analytic Narratives*, 1998), by permission of Princeton University Press.

Chapter 10 draws on "Institutional and Impersonal Exchange from Communal to Individual Responsibility" (*Journal of Institutional and Theoretical Economics*, 2000), with the permission of Springer Publishing Group; "Impersonal Exchange without Impartial Law: The Community Responsibility System" (*Chicago Journal of International Law*, 2004, 5:1, pp. 109–38), with permission of the journal.

PART I

Preliminaries

1

Introduction

On March 28, 1210, Rubeus de Campo of Genoa agreed to pay a debt of 100 marks sterling in London on behalf of Vivianus Jordanus from Lucca.[1] There is nothing unusual about this agreement – in fact, there is evidence of thousands of such agreements in Europe at the time. But this agreement implicitly reveals why Rubeus lived in a period of remarkable economic growth measured by such proxies as urbanization, population growth, capital investment, and changing patterns of trade.[2]

First, this agreement reflects well-functioning markets. The institutional foundations of these markets were such that merchants trusted agents to handle their affairs abroad, even without legal contracts. Impersonal lending among traders from remote corners of Europe prevailed, and property rights were sufficiently secure that merchants could travel abroad with their riches. Second, it reflects well-functioning polities. The institutional foundations of polities throughout Europe during this time induced policies that were conducive to economic prosperity. Rubeus made his agreement in the Republic of Genoa, which had been established about a century earlier but had already pursued policies that made it a bustling commercial center. To understand why and how such well-functioning markets and polities came about in various historical episodes and what led to their persistence and decline, we have to study their institutional foundations.

Studying institutions sheds light on why some countries are rich and others poor, why some enjoy a welfare-enhancing political order and

[1] Lanfranco Scriba (1210, no. 524).
[2] This economic upturn has been documented by such scholars as and Britnell (1996); Lopez (1976); Persson (1998); Postan (1973); and Pounds (1994).

3

others do not. Socially beneficial institutions promote welfare-enhancing cooperation and action. They provide the foundations of markets by efficiently assigning, protecting, and altering property rights; securing contracts; and motivating specialization and exchange. Good institutions also encourage production by fostering saving, investment in human and physical capital, and development and adoption of useful knowledge. They maintain a sustainable rate of population growth and foster welfare-enhancing peace; the joint mobilization of resources; and beneficial policies, such as the provision of public goods.

The quality of these institutional foundations of the economy and the polity is paramount in determining a society's welfare. This is the case because individuals do not always recognize what will be socially beneficial nor are they motivated to pursue it effectively in the absence of appropriate institutions. A central question in the social sciences and history is therefore why societies evolve along distinct trajectories of institutional development and why some societies fail to adopt the institutions of those that are more economically successful.

This book draws upon detailed historical studies to motivate, illustrate, and present a new perspective – comparative and historical institutional analysis – that goes a long way toward advancing institutional analysis in general and addressing this question regarding the evolution of societies in particular. First, it provides a unifying concept of the term *institution* to integrate the many, seemingly alternative, definitions that prevail in the literature. Second, it studies institutions on the level of the interacting individuals while considering how institutionalized rules of behavior are followed even in the absence of external enforcement. Third, it advances a unified conceptual and analytical framework for studying the persistence of institutions, their endogenous change, and the impact of past institutions on subsequent institutional development. Finally, it argues that institutional analysis requires going beyond the traditional empirical methods in the social sciences that rely on deductive theory and statistical analysis. It then elaborates on a complementary method based on interactive, context-specific analysis. Central to this case study method is the use of theory, modeling, and knowledge of the historical context to identify an institution, clarify its origin, and understand how it persists and changes.

This new perspective makes explicit what institutions are, how they come about, how they can be studied empirically, and what forces affect their stability and change. It explains why and how institutions are influenced by the past, why they can sometimes change, why they differ so much from one society to another, and why it is hard to devise policies aimed at altering them.

This book puts forward the main aspects of this still-evolving perspective and illustrates its applicability by analyzing important issues in medieval economic history. Indeed, the limited ability to address these issues using the common approaches for institutional analysis led to the development of the perspective detailed here. It presents comparative and historical analyses of institutions in the European (Latin) and Muslim (Mediterranean) worlds. The analysis focuses on the late medieval period because the European economy and polity began its ascent to economic and political hegemony at that time. It suggests that even in this early period, institutional difference within Europe and between Europe and the Muslim world developed and directed subsequent institutional outcomes. This analysis leads to a conjecture regarding the institutional origin of the subsequent economic and political European ascendancy and intra-European divergence.

The rest of this chapter is organized in four sections. Section 1.1 briefly reviews the various lines of institutional analysis within economics to present their limitations. It argues that advancing our knowledge of the relationships between institutions and welfare-related outcomes requires mitigating three particular challenges. Section 1.2 provides a glimpse at how comparative and historical institutional analysis addresses these challenges and how it relates to various lines of institutional analysis, particularly outside economics. It also highlights why institutional analysis requires going beyond the empirical methods common in the social sciences and sketches the complementary empirical method developed here. Section 1.3 presents the reason this book focuses on institutional developments in Europe and the Muslim world during the late medieval period. Section 1.4 reviews the structure of the book and the substantive issues addressed in the empirical chapters.

1.1 THE CHALLENGES OF STUDYING INSTITUTIONS

Societies have different "technological" features, such as geographical location, useful knowledge, and capital stock, and these differences impact economic outcomes. Societies also have different "nontechnological" features, such as laws and enforcement methods, ways of allocating and securing property rights, and levels of corruption and trust. It is common to refer to such nontechnological features as institutions. I follow this

5

convention here until I later redefine institutions and their relationships to such nontechnological features.

Economic theory suggests that institutional differences should influence economic outcomes because they affect decisions about work, saving, investment, innovation, production, and exchange. Econometric analyses suggest that they do. Although the results are tentative, they indicate that more-secure property rights, stronger rule of law, and greater trust are correlated with better economic outcomes (R. Hall and Jones 1999; Acemoglu, Johnson, and Robinson 2001; Rodrik, Subramanian, and Trebbi 2003; Zak and Knack 2001).

Econometric analyses and case studies also suggest the historical origins of differences in nontechnological features across societies. These differences were argued to reflect, for example, past cultures, social and power structures, and medieval republican political traditions (Greif 1994a; Glaeser and Shleifer 2002; Putnam 1993). In developing countries, such differences reflect the environment at the time of colonization (Acemoglu et al. 2001), the identity of the colonizing power (North 1981), and the initial wealth distribution (Engerman and Sokoloff 1997).

These findings, however, constitute a beginning, not an end result, for a research agenda aimed at understanding institutions. Understanding the causal mechanism behind these findings requires going beyond identifying correlations between measures of various nontechnological factors and outcomes of interest. It requires examining how the interacting individuals are motivated and able to behave in a manner that manifests itself in these various measures.[3]

It is useful to find out that corruption reduces investment, for example, but this finding does not reveal what motivates and enables people to behave in a corrupt manner. Similarly, discovering a correlation between the security of property rights and outcomes of interest does not *explain* differences in the levels or changes in security; asserting, as is common in economics, that the level of security reflects the function that property

---

[3] Djankov et al. (2003) argued that comparative economics should be used to understand the trade-off between the risk of private and public expropriation of property rights. Institutional arrangements, such as private order, judicial independence, a regulatory state, and state ownership are responses to this trade-off. The absolute level of efficiency possible under each arrangement in a country depends on its residents' capacity to cooperate. The perspective developed here presents a unifying framework with which to study the micro-level operation of such institutional arrangements as well as capacity to cooperate.

rights serve (e.g., efficiency or the interest of elites) does not explain *how* these rights become more or less secure. Understanding how property is secured requires knowing why those who are physically able to abuse rights refrain from doing so. Similarly, discovering correlations between historical events and differences in current nontechnological features does not reveal how and why past institutions influence subsequent institutional development.

Understanding the impact, persistence, and change of nontechnological features requires examining the micro-mechanisms underpinning their emergence, stability, and dynamics at the level of the interacting individuals. This requires, in particular, considering the *motivation* (incentives) of these individuals to act in a manner leading to or manifesting itself in these particular nontechnological features.

The main conceptual and analytical framework used in economic neoinstitutionalism, however, does not focus on this motivation.[4] It often identifies economic institutions with politically determined rules that are imposed "top down" on economic agents by the polity. These rules govern economic life by, for example, assigning property rights and specifying taxes due. Political institutions – rules regulating the election of leaders and collective decision making – and political organizations, such as interest groups and labor unions, are therefore central to the analysis. Political institutions and organizations matter, because economic institutions are established and changed through the political process (North 1981, 1990; Barzel 1989; Sened 1997; G. Grossman and Helpman 2002). Transaction cost economics complements this analysis by postulating that economic agents, responding to rules, choose contracts and, through them, also establish organizations to minimize transaction costs (Coase 1937; O. Williamson 1985, 1996).

This "institutions-as-rules" framework is very useful in examining various issues, such as the rules that politicians prefer and the contractual forms that minimize transaction costs. Yet behavioral prescriptions – rules and contracts – are nothing more than instructions that can be ignored.

---

[4] For recent discussions of neoinstitutionalism in the social sciences, see Eggertsson (1990), Bardhan (1991), Furubotn and Richter (1997), G. Hodgson (1998), and Greif (1996b, 1997a, 1998a, 1998b) in economics; P. Hall and Taylor (1996) and Thelen (1999) in political science; and W. Powell and DiMaggio (1991), Smelser and Swedberg (1994), Scott (1995), and Brinton and Nee (1998) in sociology. The perspective developed here is neoinstitutionalist in focusing on the micro-foundations of behavior.

If prescriptive rules of behavior are to have an impact, individuals must be motivated to follow them.[5] Motivation mediates between the environment and behavior, whether the behavior is rational, imitative, or habitual. By motivation I mean here incentives broadly defined to include expectations, beliefs, and internalized norms.

The institutions-as-rules framework, however, is not well suited for considering the motivation to follow behavioral instructions embodied in rules and contracts. As a first approximation, and for various analytical purposes, it may be sufficient to assert that people follow a rule of behavior because other rules specify punishment if they do not. But this assertion merely pushes the question of institutional effectiveness one step backward, by assuming that those who are supposed to enforce the rules do so. Why would this be the case? Who watches the watchman?

To understand behavior, we need to know why some behavioral rules, originating either inside or outside the state, are followed while others are ignored – something that is not possible within an analytical framework in which motivation is taken as exogenous. A comprehensive understanding of prescriptive or descriptive rules requires examining how the motivation to follow particular rules of behavior is created.

Considering motivation at the level of the interacting individuals as endogenous is crucial to addressing many important issues. It is crucial to understanding what is referred to as "private order" – that is, situations in which order prevails despite the lack of a third-party enforcer of that order. In such situations, the prevalence of order or its absence reflects the behavior of the interacting individuals rather than what transpires between them and a third party. Indeed, order characterized by some security of property rights and exchange sometimes prevails when there is no state, when economic agents expect the state to expropriate rather than protect their property, or when the state is unwilling or unable to secure property rights and enforce contracts. Even in modern market economies with effective states, private order is an essential ingredient.

Because institutions reflect human actions, we ultimately must study them as private order even when a state exists. For some analytical purposes, it is useful to assume – as the institutions-as-rules does – that the state has a monopoly over coercive power and can enforce its rules. But political order and an effective state are outcomes. Political actors can and sometimes do resort to violence and invest in coercive power, the use of

---

[5] I use the term *motivated* (rather than *enforced*) because actions can be induced by both fear of punishment and reward for compliance.

which can lead to political disorder or revolution. Studying political order or disorder requires examining the motivation of political actors to abide by the particular rules. Moreover, the effectiveness of state-mandated rules depends on motivating agents within the bureaucracy and judiciary to enforce them. Understanding the impact of the state requires examining the motivation of the agents involved. In other words, a comprehensive understanding of political order or its absence and of the behavior of the state's agents requires considering the motivation that influences the behavior of the relevant individuals.

Apart from its limited ability to study motivation, the institutions-as-rules approach is also limited in analyzing institutional dynamics. In accounting for institutional stability and change, it focuses only on the important, but partial, impact of politics and efficiency. When institutions are identified with politically devised rules or efficient contracts, institutional change is considered to result from an exogenous shift in the interests or knowledge of the political actors who set the rules or the efficient contracts (see Weingast 1996; O. Williamson 1985). Institutions contribute to change only to the extent that they alter the interests and knowledge underpinning the prevailing rules or contracts.

Institutional persistence has been attributed mainly to frictions in the process of institutional adjustments (e.g., the costs of changing rules) or to the impact of exogenous informal institutions, such as customs and traditions. These informal institutions are considered immutable cultural features whose rates of change are so slow as to be immaterial (North 1990). This leaves much to be explained, because persistence and change are attributed to forces other than the institution under study (O. Williamson 1998, 2000).

Classical game theory has been used extensively to expand institutional analysis to the study of endogenous motivation. Game theory considers situations that are strategic in the sense that the optimal behavior of one player depends on the behavior of others. A game-theoretic analysis begins by specifying each player's set of possible actions and information and the payoffs each will receive given any combination of actions that can be taken by all the players. Given these rules of the game, classical game theory focuses mainly on equilibria in which each decision maker correctly anticipates the behavior of others and finds it optimal to take the action expected of him. (The basic concepts of game theory are explained in Appendix A.) This framework enables endogenously motivated behavior to be considered; motivated by the actual and expected behavior of all other players, each player adopts the equilibrium behavior.

Game theory thus allows the relationship between the rules of the game and self-enforcing behavior to be studied.

Economists, in particular, have used game-theoretic equilibrium analysis to consider why individuals follow particular rules.[6] Such analysis has been applied to the study of private order, particularly one in which property rights are secured and contracts are fulfilled in the absence of an effective legal system administered by the state (O. Williamson 1985; Greif 1989, 1993; Ellickson 1991; Dixit 2004). Related research examines the endogenous motivation to adhere to various contracts despite asymmetric information and limited legal contract enforceability (Townsend 1979; Hart and Holmstrom 1987; Hart and Moore 1999). In the game-theoretic approach, institutions are considered as either equilibria (Schotter 1981; Greif 1993; Calvert 1995), the shared beliefs motivating equilibrium play (Greif 1994a; Aoki 2001), or the rules of the game (North 1990).

When institutions are defined in these ways, however, classical game theory provides an inadequate analytical framework for studying institutional dynamics – that is, the forces leading institutions to change and the influence of past institutions on subsequent ones. Strictly speaking, in classical game theory the present and future behavior of players is a manifestation of a predetermined strategy. All behavior is then forward-looking, although it may be conditioned on past events. Furthermore, because this behavior is an equilibrium, there are no endogenous forces causing institutions to change. Exogenous institutional changes can occur when the rules of the game change – as a result of new technology, for example – but studying endogenous change is inconsistent with the view of institutions as equilibria.

Worse yet, game theory reveals that many equilibria – self-enforcing patterns of behavior – are usually possible in a given game. Attempts to develop a game-theoretic equilibrium concept predicting a unique outcome in all games failed to do so in the repeated situations that are central to institutional analysis. Furthermore, game theory postulates no

---

[6] In political science, the "structure-induced equilibria" approach has enriched the institutions-as-rules approach by studying the motivation of the political actors. It studies politically determined rules as an equilibrium outcome within a game spanned by the rules of the political decision process. It considers structural features of the political decision-making process (e.g., the committee structure of the U.S. Congress) as part of the rules of the game within which political agents interact. An equilibrium analysis identifies exactly what motivates political agents to institute a particular economic rule (Shepsle 1979; Weingast and Marshall 1988; Moser 2000).

relationships between behavior in one game and a historically subsequent one.[7] Any equilibrium in a new game, even if this game is only marginally different from a previous one, is qually plausible, irrespective of what transpired in the previous game. If institutions are viewed as equilibria or beliefs in games, we cannot study the impact of past institutions on subsequent ones.

Beginning institutional analysis with a game – viewing institutions as the rules of the game – and considering the equilibrium behavior within it imply taking as given much that needs to be explained. Why, despite similar technological possibilities, are different games played in different societies? Asserting that a particular game is an equilibrium outcome in a larger – meta – game whose rules reflect only the attributes of the available technology and the physical world is useful yet unsatisfactory, because it simply pushes the question of institutional origin back one step. What is the origin of the meta-game? The theory that enables endogenous motivation to be studied is insufficient for analyzing institutional dynamics.

Finally, specifying and solving a game require strong assumptions about the shared cognitive models of the players and their rationality.[8] Initiating the analysis with a game, therefore, assumes away the possible roles institutions play in creating knowledge and cognition and directing rationality. The importance of the institutions in playing these roles, however, is highlighted in the "old institutionalism" literature. It convincingly argued that the prima facie reason for institutions is that individuals are neither fully rational nor in possession of perfect and common knowledge of the situation (see Veblen 1899; Mitchell 1925; Commons 1924; and Hayek 1937).

Incorporating the old institutionalism's assertions about limited rationality and cognition into the study of institutions and institutional dynamics is central to evolutionary institutionalism (which relies heavily on evolutionary game theory). This approach identifies institutions with attributes of the interacting individuals (behavioral traits, habits, routines,

B. 4.

---

[7] A specific game can have multiple periods, and behavior in later ones can be conditioned on behavior and events from earlier periods. This does not, however, capture the relationships between different games. It captures the relationships between different periods or stages within a given game. Game theory provides mapping from a game to a strategy combination, not a mapping between different games.

[8] Classical game theory models strategic behavior by rational agents in situations whose details are common knowledge. S is common knowledge if all players know S, all players know that all players know S, and so on ad infinitum (D. Lewis 1969).

preferences, and norms) and examines how evolutionary forces, combined with mutation, imitation, and random experimentation, influence the long-run equilibrium distribution of these attributes (Ullmann-Margalit 1977; Nelson and Winter 1982; Sugden 1989; Kandori, Mailath, and Rob 1993; Weibull 1995; Kandori 1997; Young 1998; G. Hodgson 1998; Gintis 2000).[9]

At the cost of dodging the issue of motivation and attributing changes in behavior to evolutionary forces, the evolutionary perspective mitigates the shortcomings of classical game theory in studying institutional dynamics. Its analytical framework, however, limits its applicability. The processes of experimentation, mutation, and learning that drive the process of institutional change are taken as exogenous to the analysis. As David (1994, p. 208) notes, "the exact workings of the evolutionary process...have remained sketchy at best." Furthermore, for technical reasons, the analysis often resorts to extreme assumptions about human nature. Individuals are usually assumed to be completely myopic, unable to recognize those with whom they interacted in the past, unable to choose with whom to interact, unable to coordinate their behavior, and generally incapable of structuring their environment. These assumptions provide unsatisfactory micro-foundations for evolutionary processes in human societies.

Even this short discussion indicates that many definitions of institutions prevail in economics (this is also the case in sociology and political science). These definitions have been considered mutually exclusive. The institutions-as-rules approach defines institutions mainly as rules, organizations, and contracts. Scholars who use classical game theory define institutions as either the rules of the game, equilibria, or shared beliefs motivating equilibrium play, while evolutionary institutionalists identify institutions with equilibrium attributes of the interacting individuals, such as behavioral traits, habits, routines, preferences, and norms.

Furthermore, there is a debate about the degree of choice individuals within a society possess in selecting their institutions. The structural (cultural) view – common in sociology and old institutionalism – emphasizes that institutions transcend individual actors and are immutable cultural features of societies that determine behavior (Sewell 1992; Scott 1995; Dugger 1990). In contrast, the agency (functionalist) view – common in

---

[9] For learning models in which the same players repeatedly interact with one another (rather than random matching), see Schotter (1981); Fudenberg and Kreps (1988); Ellison (1993); Marimon (1997); and Fudenberg and Levine (1998).

economics and neoinstitutionalism – emphasizes that individuals create institutions to serve various functions. Institutions are best studied from a functionalist perspective that recognizes that they are responsive to interests and needs.

Within each of these approaches, scholars differ in their assertions regarding the forces shaping institutions and their dynamics. Among those who adopt the agency perspective, for example, some postulate that institutions reflect efficiency considerations, whereas others emphasize the importance of distributional issues or the desire for social status or political control. Some hold that institutions reflect unintended outcomes of interactions among individuals with limited rationality and cognitive ability, whereas others maintain that institutions reflect intentional responses by rational, forward-looking individuals (Schotter 1981; O. Williamson 1985; North 1991; Knight 1992; Acemoglu et al. 2001).

Considering different definitions of institutions as mutually exclusive and initiating their analysis based on different premises about their nature and the forces shaping them limit the advancement of institutional analysis. Each of these premises captures a different, yet important aspect of reality. It is sometimes appropriate when examining an issue to consider institutions as exogenous structures; other times they are best considered as endogenous to the interacting individuals. In yet other cases it is appropriate to study them as reflecting the actions and interests of some individuals but not others. Therefore it is unsatisfactory to assert that either the structural or the agency perspective is always appropriate for studying institutions.

To advance institutional analysis, we need conceptual and analytical frameworks that integrate diverse lines of institutional analysis and accommodate the factors, forces, and considerations that each highlights.

More generally, the discussion highlights that the institutionalists' attempt to study the relationships between institutions and welfare-related outcomes should meet three interrelated challenges:

- Develop an integrative concept of institutions that benefits from insights and analytical frameworks drawn from seemingly alternative lines of institutional analysis.
- Study institutions at the level of the interacting individuals, while considering motivation to follow rules of behavior an integral part of the analysis.
- Advance a unified conceptual and analytical framework for studying the persistence of such institutions, endogenous institutional

change, and the impact of past institutions on their subsequent development.

1.2 COMPARATIVE AND HISTORICAL INSTITUTIONAL ANALYSIS

This book presents a new perspective aimed at meeting the challenges of integration, motivation, and dynamics, while building on and benefiting from previous lines of institutional analysis.[10] Motivated by the variety in observed trajectories of institutional development, it explores the origin and implications of this variety by combining an explicit analytical framework with contextual, historical information. I refer to this approach as comparative and historical institutional analysis.

To address the three challenges listed in section 1.1, the perspective presented here departs from two practices that have dominated institutional analysis. First, it departs from the practice of defining an institution as a monolithic entity. As we have seen, institutions have been defined in many ways, but all definitions consider an institution as either, for example, rules, the rules of the game, beliefs, norms, or behavioral traits. Instead, the present perspective recognizes that institutions are not monolithic entities but are composed of interrelated but distinct components, particularly rules, beliefs, and norms, which sometimes manifest themselves as organizations. These *institutional elements* are exogenous to each individual whose behavior they influence. They provide individuals with the cognitive, coordinative, normative, and informational micro-foundations of behavior as they enable, guide, and motivate them to follow specific behavior.

Second, the perspective developed here departs from viewing institutions from either a structural, cultural perspective (as common in sociology) or an agency, functionalist perspective (common in economics). Instead, it combines the structural and the agency views. It emphasizes the importance of studying institutions as equilibrium phenomena in which they constitute the structure that influences behavior, while the behavioral responses of agents to this structure reproduce the institution. In studying institutions as an equilibrium phenomenon, I consider neither games nor

---

[10] For earlier and partial expositions of this interpretation, see Greif (1989, 1992, 1994a, 1996b, 1997a, 1998a, 1998b, 2000). This perspective is most closely related to those expressed in Shepsle (1992); Calvert (1995); Gibbons (2001); and particularly Aoki (2001).

institutions as the basic unit of institutional analysis. Rather, I develop a particular notion of transactions and view them as the basic units of institutional analysis.[11]

In other words, institutions are studied from an equilibrium perspective, while recognizing that institutions are not monolithic entities and considering the transaction as the basic unit of analysis. This premise enables me to advance an integrating concept of institutions that reveals why institutions have such a profound impact on behavior and why they exert an independent impact on institutional dynamics. It allows institutional dynamics to be studied as a historical process in which past institutions influence the timing of institutional change, the manner in which they change, and the details and implications of new institutions. Presenting the details of these contributions goes beyond the scope of this introduction; the following merely highlights the basic relationships between the foregoing premise and these contributions.

The integrative definition of institutions advanced here restricts the scope of the analysis, mainly by requiring an institutional element to be an equilibrium outcome exogenous to each individual whose behavior it influences. Because it recognizes that institutions are composed of various components, this definition encompasses many seemingly alternative definitions of institutions (such as rules enforced by the state *or* systems of beliefs) as special cases. It accommodates the fact that institutions have different origins and serve different functions and that they sometimes reflect learning and limited rationality and sometimes reflect forward-looking behavior in well-understood situations. It is therefore possible to build on the insights and analytical frameworks developed in seemingly distinct lines of institutional analysis. The usefulness of the definition advanced here is well reflected in its application in this book to many empirical studies exploring distinct issues.

Similarly, the perspective taken here responds to the challenge of studying endogenous motivation by integrating the agency and structural perspectives. It enables us to study, in the most general case, *endogenous* institutions – those that are *self-enforcing*. In self-enforcing institutions all motivation is endogenously provided. Each individual, responding to the institutional elements implied by others' behavior and expected behavior,

---

[11] The transaction is the basic unit of analysis in transaction cost economics. See O. Williamson (1993), who also discusses alternative units of analysis in institutional economics. The definition of transactions used here is different from that used in transaction cost economics (see Chapter 2).

behaves in a manner that contributes to enabling, guiding, and motivating others to behave in the manner that led to the institutional elements that generated the individual's behavior to begin with. Behavior is self-enforcing in that each individual, taking the structure as given, finds it best to follow the institutionalized behavior that, in turn, reproduces the institution in the sense that the implied behavior confirms the associated beliefs and regenerates the associated norms.

Studying institutions as equilibrium phenomena, while making explicit, as is done here, the forces rendering them self-enforcing, exposes the exogenous shocks that will lead to institutional failure – specifically, the shocks that cause an institution to no longer be self-enforcing. But the perspective advanced here achieves more than that. It enables us to study institutional dynamics as a *historical process*. Institutions can remain stable in a changing environment and can change in the absence of environmental change, while past institutions – even those that are no longer self-enforcing – can influence the details of subsequent ones.

To study stability and change in the same framework, it is necessary to recognize that institutional elements provide the micro-foundations of behavior and that institutions are equilibrium phenomena: this makes it possible to study both institutional persistence in a changing environment and endogenous change in a stable environment. For an individual to choose behavior, he or she needs to have the appropriate information, a cognitive model, and the ability to anticipate others' behavior. Individuals also seek guidance on morally appropriate and socially acceptable behavior. Institutional elements provide these cognitive, coordinative, normative, and informational micro-foundations of behavior. At the same time, retrospective and limitedly rational yet forward-looking individuals respond to the behavioral and normative prescriptions provided by institutional elements based on their private information, knowledge, and innate preferences. In situations in which institutions generate behavior, institutional elements constitute equilibrium phenomena that aggregate these features of the situation.

Under certain conditions, institutions can therefore persist in a changing environment. This is the case because individuals often find it possible, necessary, and desirable to condition their behavior on the cognitive, coordinative, normative, and informational content provided by institutional elements rather than directly on the environment. In other words, in the jargon of game theory, individuals do not play against the rules of the game. Instead, they *play against (institutionalized) rules*. Because these elements are equilibria and do not necessarily correctly aggregate private information and knowledge, they are often more stable than the environment. Behavior will persist in a changing environment. Indeed, behavior can persist even in cases in which if individuals were to condition their behavior on the environment, past behavior would no longer be self-enforcing.

To understand endogenous institutional change, there is a need to study the interplay between the micro-mechanisms through which institutions influence behavior and their implications, behavioral and otherwise. This highlights the ways an endogenous institution – although an equilibrium phenomenon – can *reinforce* or undermine itself. One that is reinforced (undermined) becomes self-enforcing in a larger (smaller) set of parameters. Examining these reinforcing or undermining processes makes it possible, in particular, to study how an institution cultivates the seeds of its own demise, leading to its endogenous change.

The key to understand why and how past institutions influence the direction of institutional change is recognizing the dual nature of the components of which institutions are composed. The interrelated components making up an institution are also characteristics of individuals and societies. Rules, beliefs, and norms inherited from the past constitute and reflect individuals' shared cognitive models; they are embodied in these individuals' preferences and concepts of self; and they constitute commonly known beliefs about expected, normative, and socially accepted behavior. They often also manifest themselves in organizations that have acquired various capacities. There is therefore a *fundamental asymmetry* between institutional elements inherited from the past and technologically feasible alternatives.

Hence, even if the behavior associated with a particular institution is no longer self-enforcing, or if an institution is needed to govern a new transaction, not all technologically alternative institutions are equally likely candidates. Rather, the resulting new institution will reflect the impact of past institutional elements. Beliefs, norms, and organizations inherited from the past will constitute part of the initial conditions in the processes leading to new institutions. Whether such a process is coordinated or not, past institutional elements influence the selection among alternative technologically possible institutions. The past, encapsulated in institutional elements, directs institutional change and leads societies to evolve along distinct institutional trajectories.

The perspective developed here further facilitates comparative institutional analysis over time and across societies by considering the transaction as the basic unit of analysis. We can focus on the same transaction in different episodes and explore the institutions that, as equilibrium systems of their constituting components, generate behavior within that transaction in each episode. Focusing on transactions while studying institutions from an equilibrium perspective closes the gap between two main lines of analysis in neoinstitutionalism. Transaction cost economics (O. Williamson 1985) asserts that institutions are formed to reduce transaction costs; the institutions-as-rules approach considers institutions as determinants of transaction costs (North 1990). The equilibrium perspective I propose allows actors to attempt to improve their lot while simultaneously recognizing that the resulting institution is an equilibrium that determines the transaction costs facing each actor.

Many analytical frameworks can and should be used to study institutions as conceptualized here. The discussion and the empirical studies presented here highlight the benefits of using classical game theory enriched by insights from sociology, cognitive science, learning, and experimental game theory among other fields of study. The usefulness of game theory for institutional analysis has been debated in the social sciences. Many microeconomic theorists, such as Gibbons (1998), believe that it is indispensable, while institutional economists, such as North and Williamson, express reservations. In sociology and political science, a fierce debate has raged over its empirical usefulness (see Hechter 1992; Scott 1995; D. Green and Shapiro 1994; J. Friedman 1996; Scharpf 1997; Bates, de Figueiredo, and Weingast 1998; Elster 2000; and Munck 2001).

Although there is merit in the arguments presented on both sides, the debate often confounds two questions. The first is whether games are the basic unit of institutional analysis and whether game theory provides a theory of institutions.[12] The second is whether game theory is empirically and analytically useful. My own view is that games are not the basic unit of analysis and that game theory does not provide a theory of institutions, although it is analytically and empirically useful.

Furthermore, there is much to learn about institutions from responding to the puzzling observation that game theory has been found useful for institutional analysis, even though it rests on unrealistic assumptions about cognition, information, and rationality. The position taken here is to ask what we learn from the need to impose these assumptions. How

---

[12] By a theory of institutions I mean a theory predicting, based on exogenous features of the situation, the resulting institution. Game theory, however, is a theory of behavior in strategic situations.

18

and to what extent are these assumptions fulfilled in the real world? What do the ways in which they are fulfilled tell us about how and when game theory can beneficially be used to study behavior in real-world situations? As we will see, addressing these questions contributes much to our understanding of institutions.

Because the perspective presented here studies institutions through the lens of a game-theoretic equilibrium analysis, it is sometimes referred to as the *institutions-as-equilibria* approach and the related institutions as *self-enforcing institutions*. These terms capture the spirit of the analysis but not its essence. Institutions are not game-theoretic equilibria, games are not the basic unit of institutional analysis, and game theory does not provide us with a theory of institutions. Indeed, the key to advancing institutional analysis by using game theory is precisely to recognize the difference between game-theoretic equilibrium analysis and institutional analysis.

Both evolutionary institutionalism and classical game theory suggest that the search for a comprehensive, deductive theory of institutions – that is, a theory providing a one-to-one mapping between the observable, exogenous features of the situation and the institutions – may be futile. Achieving a unique equilibrium in evolutionary models requires restrictive assumptions on possible actions, rationality, and the stochastic processes underpinning experimentation, learning, and mutations. Classical game theory indicates that multiple equilibria – and hence institutions – can be self-enforcing. Even under the game-theoretic assumption that individuals are highly rational and the game is common knowledge, multiple equilibria are the rule rather than the exception in the repeated situations central to institutional analysis.

This indeterminacy of institutions challenges our ability to study them deductively. The premise of deductive analysis is that theory can restrict– *predict* – the endogenous outcomes for a given set of the exogenous and observable features of the situation. This prediction should be sufficiently precise to render an empirical analysis meaningful. In the case of institutional analysis, we do not have such a deductive theory able to predict institutions.

Inductive analysis à la Francis Bacon, which identifies and classifies institutions based on their observable features, is similarly deficient for studying institutions while recognizing the need to study motivation. Identifying institutions with such observable features as rules and organizations is misleading, because motivation provided by unobservable beliefs and norms determines whether rules are followed and what is the impact of an organization.[13] While certain components of an institution, such as formal rules, or organizations, such as stock markets or courts, are observable, others, such as norms about honesty in dealing with strangers and beliefs about legal enforcement, are inherently difficult to observe and measure.[14]

Moreover, as game theory and other frameworks reveal, multiple beliefs and norms can be self-enforcing in the same situation, even if we assume that individuals are highly rational and the rules of the game are common knowledge. There is no one-to-one mapping between the observable components of institutions (rules and organizations) and unobservable ones (beliefs and norms). The same rules and organizations can be components of institutions that differ in their beliefs and norms, implying that we cannot study institutions inductively based on their observable components.

Without a deductive theory of institutions or the ability to identify institutions based only on their observable components, the traditional empirical methods used in the social sciences are challenged. These methods rest on twin pillars: the predictive power of deductive theory and the ability to inductively classify outcomes.

The extent of this challenge is reflected in the attempts to evaluate econometrically the effectiveness of institutions while identifying them with their observable features (particularly rules) or implications (particularly the security of property rights). Despite extensive scholarly input and econometric analysis, the debate whether the findings support the assertion that institutions are important still rages (Rodrik et al. 2003; Glaeser et al. 2004). Analyses using quantitative measures of institutions, such as civil liberties and property rights to substantiate their impact on economic growth are similarly not robust (Aron 2000). Even the impacts of political instability and social capital on growth have been difficult to substantiate econometrically (Campos and Nugent 2002; Schneider, Plumper, and Baumann 2000).

These inconclusive results may reflect insufficient attention to the fact that unobserved institutional elements can vary systematically across societies and directly influence the effectiveness of an institution. Two societies with the same formal rules specifying property rights will experience very

---

[13] For this reason, identifying institutions with such observable features as constitutional restrictions on the executive, rules protecting property rights, or an independent judiciary is misguided.

[14] Sources, such as correspondences and surveys that reflect beliefs and norms are sometimes useful. See, for example, Zak and Knack (2001).

different levels of investment if different beliefs about the enforcement of these rights prevail in each. Dismissing such unobservable institutional elements as simply idiosyncratic variations introduces an omitted variable problem that biases any attempt at measurement that fails to account for them explicitly.

As a response to the challenge institutional analysis presents to the traditional empirical methods of social science, the perspective developed here presents a complementary case study method. It is particularly promising given the absence of a deductive theory of institutions, the extent of institutional diversity, the interest in comprehensively understanding particular institutions for policy purposes, and the need to develop general propositions regarding institutions.

This method builds on the argument that institutional elements inherited from the past will influence subsequent institutions and argues the need to use contextual – historical – information in studying institutions. More generally, this book advances an empirical case study method, central to which is an interactive, context-specific analysis that combines contextual knowledge of the situation and its history with theory and an explicit, context-specific model. The method interactively uses contextual knowledge combined with a context-specific model to *identify* the institution; to clarify why and how it established itself; and to understand its persistence, changes, and implications.[15]

By recognizing that institutions are made up of components that are also attributes of individuals and societies, the perspective developed here bridges the divide between studying institutions as rules or contracts (as is common in economics) and studying them as cultural phenomena (as is common in other social sciences).[16] The perspective advanced here recognizes the futility of arguing about definitions of culture and institutions and debating whether one is more important than the other in explaining a particular phenomenon.

Instead, this perspective highlights the large extent to which the "culturalists" and "institutionalists" are fundamentally interested in the same phenomena: the implications of man-made, nonphysical factors that generate regularities of behavior while being exogenous to *each* individual whose behavior is influenced, such as belief systems and internalized

---

[15] This position is in the spirit of Sutton (1991); Greif (1989, 1996b, 1997a, 2000); Scharpf (1997); Bates et al. (1998); Levi (2004); and others.

[16] *Cultural* is difficult to define. As early as 1952, Kroeber and Kluckhohn identified more than 164 definitions of *culture*. For discussions, see DiMaggio (1994, 1997); and Part III.

norms that generate regularities of behavior. This analysis, therefore, highlights the extent and the conditions under which the "cultural" and the "institutional" overlap. Within economics, this implies bringing together institutional analysis and the analysis of social capital.[17]

More important, by recognizing how the institutional and cultural interrelate, the perspective advanced here enables us to study the interaction between them. A significant conclusion of this book is that culture influences institutional development. At the same time, the integration of cultural elements into a society's institutions is a mechanism that leads to their persistence.

Extending the scope of the analysis to include the cultural, social, and organizational implies that the perspective developed here is *socio-economic*.[18] It departs from and complements the institutions-as-rules approach, which studies institutions as determined by economic or political forces. This socioeconomic view reflects and constitutes a "sociological turn" in economic neoinstitutionalism that departs from the institutions-as-rules emphasis on political and economic considerations. The socioeconomic view accommodates but goes beyond these particular considerations.

Indeed, the perspective developed here draws on the main traditions of sociological institutionalism: the tradition associated with Durkheim, which focuses on socially constituted codes of conduct and beliefs; the tradition associated with Parsons, which focuses on normative behavior; the focus on social structures and relationships associated with Wrong (1961), Granovetter (1985), and March and Olsen (1989); and the tradition associated with Weber (1947, 1949), Berger and Luckmann (1967), Searle (1995), and W. Powell and DiMaggio (1991), which concentrates on the cognitive foundations of behavior, organizations, and the social construction of reality. As these sociological notions are also central to old institutionalism (Dugger 1990), expanding neoinstitutionalism to include

---

[17] *Social capital* is often defined as the "features of social organization, such as trust, norms, and networks, that can improve the efficiency of society by facilitating coordinated actions" (Putnam 1993, p. 167). Coleman (1990) and Putnam (1993, 2000) are classic contributions. See also Woolcock (1998); Dasgupta and Serageldin (2000); Sobel (2002); and http://www1.worldbank.org/prem/poverty/scapital/home.htm.

[18] It accommodates the four pillars of the sociological view on institutions, as summarized by Smelser and Swedberg (1994) in the *Handbook of Economic Sociology*. As is now common in economics, the perspective adopted here accepts that preferences and rationality are socially constructed, that social structures and meaning are important, and that the economy is an integral part of the society.

them entails bringing together the two lines of institutional analysis in economics

By addressing institutional stability, endogenous change, and the impact of the past on subsequent institutions in a unified framework, the analysis of institutional dynamics as a historical process complements three lines of research: historical institutionalism in political science, which emphasizes that institutions reflect a historical process (P. Hall and Taylor 1996; Thelen 1999; Pierson and Skocpol 2002); the path-dependence literature developed by David (1985) and Arthur (1988), which emphasizes the stability of historically inherited phenomena; and the study of culture as a "tool kit" for the reconstitution of society in new situations (Swidler 1986).

Equally important is the relationship between the perspective developed here and evolutionary institutionalism. The analysis of institutional dynamics as a historical process is evolutionary in capturing the impact of the past on the rate and direction of change. Indeed, it highlights the micro-foundations of evolutionary processes in institutional development. Existing institutions affect the processes of learning, imitation, and experimentation that lead to new ones; influence the costs and benefits of introducing new institutional elements; and bias new institutions toward ones that interrelate with and do not depart greatly from their elements.

1.3   INSTITUTIONS AND COMMERCIAL EXPANSION DURING THE LATE MEDIEVAL PERIOD

The empirical studies presented in this book compare institutional development both within Europe and between Europe and the Muslim world, primarily during the late medieval period (from about 1050 to about 1350). The words of Sa'id ibn Aḥmad, a Muslim scholar and judge who lived in Toledo in the eleventh century, explain why studying this period is of interest. He compared various nations in terms of their achievements in science, military skills, artistic ability, and craftsmanship. The Europeans – the "barbarians of the North" – did not fare well. They "lack keenness of understanding and clarity of intelligence, and are overcome by ignorance . . . apathy . . . and stupidity" (B. Lewis 1982, p. 68). If one measures development using such criteria as urbanization and the contents of exports, Europe was indeed economically underdeveloped relative to some other regions of the world during the eleventh century.

Sa'id ibn Aḥmad grimly assessed the "barbarians of the North" exactly when the European economy, polity, and society were embarking on the road that led to the Rise of the West, a process that began in the late medieval period with the growth of European commerce (North and Thomas 1973; Rosenberg and Birdzell 1986). Long-distance trade "became the driving force of economic progress, and in the end affected every aspect of human activity almost as decisively as the Industrial Revolution changed the modern world" (Lopez 1967, p. 126).[19] The commercial center of gravity along the shores of the Mediterranean Sea was shifting away from the Muslim world toward Europe.

This book examines various aspects of the institutional foundations of this late medieval commercial expansion and the ensuing political and social transformations. This historical episode lends itself to examining the general nature of institutions, their dynamics, and implications. After all, trade expansion was not, as trade theory would have predicted, a response to changes in endowments or technology. Rather, new institutions, which had provided the foundations for markets and political units, played an important role in initiating trade and creating a complementary process of institutional development and trade expansion.

The historical and theoretical importance of this period has drawn the attention of scholars adopting the institutions-as-rules approach. In their interpretation, once feudal warfare declined, peace enabled the population to grow and to realize the gains from "commerce between different parts of Europe" that "had always been potentially of mutual benefit" (North and Thomas 1973, p. 11). Subsequent institutional development reflects attempts to reduce transaction costs. The "revival of trade led . . . to a host of institutional arrangements [such as insurance contracts and the bill of lading] designed to reduce market imperfections" (p. 12).

This interpretation attributes the revival of trade to exogenous political events that led to institutional development directed by efficiency considerations. This proposition ignores a host of relevant questions, however. Which, if any, institutions curtailed fighting? There was no "state" that could have prevented war between different political entities, and no entity had a monopoly over coercive power even within a political unit. How, then, was peace sustained? During the late medieval period there were no states to provide the institutions required for long-distance trade. Which

---

[19] Scholars such as Herlihy (1958), Lopez (1967), Duby (1974), and Mokyr (1990) emphasize the contributions of increasing agricultural productivity and technological change in this growth. P. Hoffman (1996), G. Clark (1991), and Grantham (1992, 1993) have challenged this claim. For a general discussion of this period, see Pirenne (1939, 1956); Lopez (1976); Hatcher and Bailey (2001); and Cipolla (1993).

24

institutions ensured secure property rights for merchants while they traveled or sent their goods abroad? Which institutions provided the contract enforcement needed for people from various corners of Europe to enter into contracts over time and space?

Was trade expansion a function of only peace and factor endowments, or did institutional elements inherited from the past influence the timing, location, and extent of trade expansion? Why did the emerging institutional arrangements in Europe differ from those in other (technologically similar) economies in response to increased trade? Why did contractual and organizational forms, which early in the medieval period were the same in Europe as in the Muslim and Byzantine worlds, differ by the fifteenth century?

To answer these questions, it is necessary to go beyond regarding institutions as rules and institutional development as an inevitable response to gains from trade and peace. There is a need to examine the origin and manifestation of the institutional elements that generated behavior among the interacting political and economic agents and how they constituted equilibria. In particular, as the historical analysis presented here demonstrates, understanding the late medieval commercial expansion requires considering the institutional foundations of states and markets.

This historical research touches on the question of the Rise of the West. That rise, and the rhythm of history more generally, have recently been attributed to various deterministic forces. Some scholars have subscribed to technological or environmental determinism, attributing Europe's success to the location of coal deposits, ports suitable for trade with the New World, or geography (Diamond 1997; Pomeranz 2000; Sachs 2001; Acemoglu, Johnson, and Robinson 2002). Others have favored cultural and social determinism, asserting that economic and political outcomes reflect the social capital and trust inherited from the past (Putnam 1993; Fukuyama 1995). Another line of research argues that the Rise of the West is a modern phenomenon. Indeed, economic outcomes – measured by food consumption, market integration, and other indicators – may not have been any better in Europe than in other parts of the world until as late as the nineteenth century (Pomeranz 2000; Shiue and Keller 2003). These findings support the conjecture that Europe's success is rooted in such recent events as the rise of the mineral-based economy, colonialism, or the Atlantic economy (Pomeranz 2000; Acemoglu et al. 2002).

The historical research presented here suggests that the West developed distinct institutions as early as the late medieval period. The organization

25

of society in the West was centered on intentionally created institutions. Neither the state nor kin-based social structures, such as tribes and clans, were central to these institutions. Instead, the organization of society was centered on interest-based, self-governed, non-kin-based organizations. These organizations – mainly in the form of corporations – were vital to Europe's political and economic institutions during the late medieval growth period as well as the modern growth period.

Several factors, particularly institutional elements inherited from the past, contributed to the emergence of this societal organization during this period: individualistic cultural beliefs and weak kin-based organizations (which to some extent reflected the church's interests and actions), the institutional weakness of the state, and norms legitimizing self-governance. This historical heritage implied that gains from cooperation could not be achieved by relying on institutions that were based on either kin-based organizations or the state. At the same time, economic and coercive resources were distributed with relative equality so that the resources of many individuals had to be mobilized before the interests of the relatively powerful could be advanced. Interest-based, self-governed, non-kin-based economic and political corporations were therefore established.

Since then, this particular societal organization – centered on self-governed, non-kin-based organizations and individualism – has been behind the behavior and outcomes that led to European-specific economic and political developments. This societal organization is the common denominator behind such seemingly distinct historical phenomena as the late medieval economic expansion, the rise of European science and technology (Mokyr 2002), and the creation of the modern European state, the ultimate manifestation of a self-governed, non-kin-based corporation composed of individuals rather than larger social units (Greif 2004b).

If institutions are central to economic, social, and political outcomes, and institutional development is a historical process, the roots of the eventual success of the West may very well lie in its past political and economic institutions. The tentative nature of this assertion must be emphasized. Surprisingly little is known about past institutions: it may well be that European and non-European institutions had more in common than is currently perceived. Furthermore, the relative efficiency of any particular set of institutions depends on the context. Finally, Western institutions may have undermined themselves in the long run by creating excessive individualism and materialism (see Lal 1998); if success is measured by the share of world population, the West may already have declined. Hence whether the Rise of the West reflects its institutional particularities – or,

26

more generally, whether history is driven by distinct institutional dynamics created by past institutions – remains a question. It is notable, however, that the institutional particularities of the late medieval period are also associated with the rise of Europe in the modern period. The two main periods of economic development in Europe share similar institutional foundations. Claims that the Rise of the West is due to either predetermined factors or recent events must show that the implications of these exogenous factors and these particular events are not reflections of the particularities of European institutions.

1.4 THE STRUCTURE OF THE BOOK

The remainder of this part, Chapter 2, presents the concept of institutions developed here and relates it to other concepts. Part II studies endogenous institutions as equilibrium systems of interrelated components using game theory. It begins with two empirical studies that demonstrate the usefulness of the perspective developed here in considering the institutional foundations of markets. Chapter 3 examines the institution that provided contract enforcement among merchants in the Muslim world, thereby enabling exchange in the absence of legal contract enforcement. Chapter 4 considers the institution that fostered long-distance trade by securing property rights in Europe. This institution enabled a ruler with a monopoly over coercive power to commit to respecting the property rights of foreign merchants.

Chapter 5 delves deeper into the nature of various institutionalized elements and their interrelationships. It articulates what we learn about institutions from the restrictive assumptions required for, and the insights provided by, game-theoretic analysis and what they teach us about the appropriate use of game theory for institutional analysis. The chapter builds on cognitive science, old institutionalism, and sociology, among other fields, and discusses the integration of normative and social considerations in institutional analysis. Appendix B complements this analysis by evaluating whether the assumption that individuals are rational – in the particular sense attributed to the term here – is consistent with the claim that normative and social considerations are important.

Part III studies institutional dynamics. Chapter 6 considers endogenous institutional change, whereas Chapter 7 considers the impact of past institutions on subsequent institutions. The theoretical discussions in Chapters 6 and 7 are illustrated through a comparative analysis of the institutional foundation of the two most successful Italian maritime city-states,

Genoa and Venice. The analysis touches on the critical issues of state building, the endogenous creation of a state with a de facto monopoly over coercive power, and the economically productive use of coercion. Chapter 8 expands on the analysis of institutional success, failure, and dynamics in the process of state building in Genoa. Chapter 9 presents a comparative analysis of institutional and contractual development in two groups of merchants, one from the Muslim world and the other from the European (Latin) world. It emphasizes that cultural beliefs – roughly speaking, shared uncoordinated beliefs – influence the selection of institutions, become integrated into existing institutions, and direct the process of institutional innovations and responses to new circumstances.

Chapter 10 illustrates the benefits of interactive, context-specific analysis. The issue it focuses on – the institutions that provide the foundations of impersonal exchange in the absence of a partial legal system – is of interest for its own sake. The empirical analysis it presents highlights the role of a European institution that endogenously motivated intracommunity, impartial contract enforcement institutions to dispense the partial justice that supported intercommunity impersonal exchange. The long-distance trade that these institutions facilitated in turn influenced the development of intrastate contract enforcement institutions. Chapter 11 generalizes this example to explain why institutional analysis usually requires a combination of deduction and induction. It then presents the mechanics of combining historical, contextual information and explicit models in conducting an interactive, context-specific analysis. Appendix C, which focuses on private-order, reputation-based institutions, complements this discussion by elaborating on the role of theory in delineating general considerations that shape these institutions and hence in identifying the relevant evidence. Chapter 12 concludes by reviewing the assertions and concepts central to the perspective advanced here and elaborating on the general insights provided by the historical studies. It ends by assessing the book's implications for development and institutional design.

To facilitate access by different types of readers, the book is organized so that it can be read while focusing on either the study of institutions or the historical analyses. Readers interested in institutions and their analysis can focus on Chapters 2, 5, 6, 7, 11, 12, and Appendices B and C. Readers interested in the historical material can focus on Chapters 3, 4, 8, 9, and 10 (each of which includes an intuitive discussion of the theoretical results) and Chapter 12. Readers not versed in game theory will benefit from the primer presented in Appendix A.

2

Institutions and Transactions

Scholars in economics, political science, and sociology use various definitions of the term *institution*. Sections 2.1 and 2.2 of this chapter define the term in a precise manner in order to delineate the scope of the analysis. Particular rules, beliefs, norms, and organizations are central to this definition, which helps illuminate why institutions have such a profound impact on behavior and how they should be studied analytically (Part II), why they persist in a changing environment and why they exert an independent impact on institutional dynamics (Part III), and how to study them empirically (Part IV).

The definition presented here encompasses other seemingly alternative definitions. It fosters the development of a unifying concept of the object of study and the integration of insights and analytical frameworks developed in conjunction with various definitions of institutions (section 2.3). The definition also highlights the sense in which transactions are the basic unit of institutional analysis, although this requires defining transactions in a more comprehensive manner than traditionally done in economics. Inter-transactional linkages are central to institutions because, among other reasons, the institutionalized beliefs and norms that motivate behavior in a particular transaction reflect what other transactions were linked to it and in what way, while organizations are reflections of and means for linking transactions (sections 2.4 and 2.5).

While reading this chapter it is useful to keep in mind what it is *not* about. It does not examine the origin of institutions or why and how they change. Later chapters are devoted to these issues. This chapter is concerned only with specifying the object of study: institutions.

2.1 WHAT IS AN INSTITUTION?

An institution is a system of social factors that conjointly generate a regularity of behavior.[1] Each component of this system is social in being a man-made, nonphysical factor that is exogenous to each individual whose behavior it influences. Together these components motivate, enable, and guide individuals to follow one behavior among the many that are technologically feasible in social situations.[2] I often refer to such social factors as *institutional elements*. The institutional elements that this work focuses on are rules, beliefs, and norms as well as their manifestation as organizations. *An institution is a system of rules, beliefs, norms, and organizations that together generate a regularity of (social) behavior.* Each of these elements satisfies the conditions stated previously.

The object of study is restricted by requiring that the institution be composed of man-made, nonphysical factors that are exogenous to each individual whose behavior they influence and generate a regularity of behavior in a social situation. (As we will see, a social situation is one involving a transaction.) Not all rules, beliefs, and norms fulfill these requirements. A legal rule, a constitutional provision, a moral code, or beliefs that do not influence behavior are not components of an institution. The belief that one can buy and sell at the market price is a component of an institution that influences behavior in the market. The "institution of legal enforcement" is not the court but a system of rules, beliefs, norms, and the associated organizations of which the court is just one.

To illustrate what an institution is according to this definition, consider a system of rules, beliefs, and organizations that secures property rights – that is, that generates the behavior of respecting particular rights. In this system, politically determined rules define the relevant properties, assign property rights, identify property owners, define offenses, and specify corresponding (legal) penalties. If the political process is such that each individual cannot unilaterally alter the rules, the rules are exogenous to *each* of them. These rules can be endogenous to all of them, as is arguably the case in a democracy, or exogenous to most of them, as is the case under a dictatorship.

---

[1] I use the term *system* to highlight the interrelations among an institution's various elements, but an institution need not have all of the elements of the system (rules, beliefs, norms, and organizations).

[2] The term *guide* means to provide the knowledge required to take and coordinate a particular action. The term *motivate* means to induce behavior based on external or intrinsic rewards and punishments.

Rules that prescribe behavior, however, do not influence behavior unless people are motivated to follow them. For rules to be part of an institution, individuals must be motivated to follow them. This condition can be satisfied if, for example, it is common knowledge that infringement will be penalized harshly enough to deter abuses. As these beliefs in legal sanctions are common knowledge, they are exogenous to each of the interacting individuals. Although an individual can decide for himself whether sanctions will be forthcoming, each has to take as given that everyone else believes that this is the case.

In this system, behavior is guided by rules and motivated by beliefs in legal sanctions. For these beliefs to be possible, however, organizations constituting the legal system – in the contemporary world, the court and the police – are required. Without them, beliefs in legal sanctions cannot prevail. Clearly, a court and a police force do not necessarily lead to the belief that infringement will be punished because many legal systems are corrupt or ineffective. To study the impact of the legal system, we must therefore also examine the rules, beliefs, and norms that generate behavior among members of its constituting organizations and between them and others. In this sense, organizations also constitute institutions. They have a dual nature: they are components of institutions and they constitute institutions. Organizations are institutional elements with respect to the behavior we seek to understand, but they are institutions with respect to their members' behavior. Organizations also differ from other institutions in that the associated rules, beliefs, and norms lead to differential behavior toward members and nonmembers.

In the institution described here, beliefs about the behavioral responses of others (in the form of legal sanctions) provided motivation.[3] But such beliefs are not the only set of beliefs that can generate a regularity of behavior. Internalized beliefs that reflect cognitive models about the structure of the world around us also influence behavior. For example, the Promethean myth about the gods' disapproval of technological advances reflects (and constitutes a means of perpetuating) such beliefs. Prometheus was punished for delivering – and humanity for accepting – new technology of igniting fire. For the Greeks, who appreciated the benefits of this technology, Prometheus became a hero. The beliefs reflected in the punishment myths, however, once internalized, became a man-made nonphysical

---

[3] Beliefs in other responses can similarly influence behavior. Nee and Ingram (1998) note that social norms and political rules differ mainly in the mechanism for their enforcement.

factor exogenous to each individual that contributed to inhibiting technological advances.

As these examples illustrate, the definition restricts the object of study in several ways and draws attention to the importance of several corresponding factors in studying institutions.

2.1.1   Regularity of Behavior

The object of study is restricted to regularity of behavior, meaning behavior that is followed and is expected to be followed in a given social situation by (most) individuals who occupy particular social positions.[4] Regularity of behavior can be general, such as entering into legal contracts, or specific, such as entering into particular contractual forms. It can transpire often (as paying with a credit card in the United States) or it can transpire rarely (as impeaching a president in the United States). In either case, institutional analysis is about regularities that are robust, in the sense that they are carried out in a broadly defined situation. The focus on regularity of behavior implies that institutional analysis is concerned with recurrent situations between the same individuals over time (e.g., a relationship between a lender and a borrower) or among different individuals (the relationship between drivers on a highway, between a judge and various defendants, or among legislators in the Congress).

Social position specifies one's social identity, which may be defined by a very general factor (such as one's gender) or a more specific one (such as one's occupation or one's history of having defaulted on a debt). Examples of social positions are buyers and sellers, parents and children, lenders and borrowers, and employers and employees. Studying the behavior of individuals occupying social positions entails examining how their behavior is influenced by societal forces rather than individual characteristics.[5]

Diversity of behavior can nevertheless prevail as individuals with distinct social positions (defined over such characteristics as age, gender, or ethnicity) follow different behavior in the same situation. For

---

[4] The association of institutional analysis with the study of social positions is common in sociology. Berger and Luckmann (1967, p. 74) argue that "all institutionalized conduct involves [social] roles," which are commonly known "types of actors." E. Hughes (1937, p. 404) has argued that for the particular case of formal organizations "the conscious fulfilling of formally defined offices distinguishes social institutions from more elementary collective phenomena."

[5] Giddens (1997), Abercrombie et al. (1994), and Zucker (1991) argue that the degree of institutionalization is the degree to which behavior reflects social positions rather than personal characteristics.

idiosyncratic reasons some individuals may hold private beliefs or have particular attributes that lead them to act differently from others in their social position. The focus here is on situations in which such idiosyncracies can be treated as deviations around the mean behavior induced by the shared beliefs and norms. I return later to discuss the role of private beliefs in considering sources for institutional change.

2.1.2 Man-Made Nonphysical Factors That Influence Behavior

Institutional analysis is about situations in which more than one behavior is physically and technologically possible. In considering how regularities of behavior are generated in such situations, the definition focuses on man-made nonphysical factors.

Man-made factors that influence behavior reflect intentional or unintentional human actions. Some man-made factors, such as doors, locks, and barriers, are physical. The focus here is not on these factors but on nonphysical factors, such as religious beliefs, internalized norms, and the expectation that a penalty will follow the violation of a traffic rule. This focus reflects that the physical manifestations of nonphysical factors – prisons, temples, and symbols, for example – have a secondary role in generating institutionalized behavior. Prisons themselves do not make up an effective legal system; rather, corresponding rules, beliefs, and organizations are needed to generate law-abiding behavior.

Alongside physical factors, technology and genetics also influence the set of feasible man-made nonphysical factors. Technology for monitoring workers, such as video cameras, enables the belief that shirking will be penalized. Genetic factors directly contribute to regularities of behavior in various ways, although they are not man-made nonphysical factors. Evolution, however, endowed us with genetic propensities, such as the ability to internalize norms and to seek social status. Within the boundaries determined by this genetic endowment, various man-made nonphysical factors can prevail. Indeed, there is tremendous variety across societies in the ways in which normative behavior and social relationships are structured.

2.1.3 Factors Exogenous to Each Individual Whose Behavior They Influence

The object of study is further restricted by focusing on factors that are exogenous to *each* individual whose behavior they influence. This restriction is a corollary of the assertion that institutional analysis is about factors that enable, guide, and motivate behavior. Factors that come under an individual's direct control (his "choice variables") do not enable, guide, or motivate his behavior.

As discussed in Chapter 5, institutionalized rules and beliefs are man-made yet exogenous to each individual whose behavior they influence. They are exogenous to each individual in the sense that they are commonly known rules and beliefs in situation in which behavior is not technologically determined.[6] In particular, it is known that every member of the society knows these rules and holds these beliefs. That others know these rules and hold these beliefs is exogenous to each individual, even if the response of each individual to these rules and beliefs is part of the mechanism rendering them common knowledge.

It is easier to comprehend why norms are exogenous to an individual whose behavior they influence. After being internalized, norms – the normative rules of behavior that an individual has internalized through socialization – are beyond an individual's control. Indeed, as norms specify the morally appropriate, individuals who have internalized them do not want to change them. Similarly, organizations such as communities, courts, and the police are composed of rules, beliefs, and norms and, as such, are exogenous to those whose behavior they influence.

To provide an example, it is common knowledge that in Britain people drive and are expected to drive on the left side of the road. The rules disseminating this knowledge and the associated expectations are exogenous to each driver, who cannot alter what others think about behavior on the road. In horizontal communities without a leadership structure, the rules, beliefs, and norms influencing membership and behavior toward members and nonmembers are taken as given by each individual. At most an individual can leave the community; he cannot unilaterally alter the related institutional elements.

Institutional elements are social factors as they are man-made, non-physical factors exogenous to each individual whose behavior they influence. This does not imply that institutions are always exogenous to every individual. One individual's choice variable can be part of an institution that influences the behavior of another. Indeed, there is an *institutional hierarchy*, and those higher up in this hierarchy can be said to have *power*

---

[6] When only one behavior is technologically feasible, beliefs about it are likely to be common knowledge but this common knowledge is inconsequential. One course of action does not depend on these beliefs.

over others. Institutional hierarchy, explored in later chapters, provides opportunities for intentional institutional change.

In the economic arena, various institutional elements, such as legal rules and labor unions, influence decisions made by firms about their contractual obligations toward employees. The contract that firms offer their employees is the behavior implied by the institution these firms face. For the employees, however, these contracts specify the rules that are part of the institution that influences their behavior.

Similarly, legal rules are not institutional elements for a dictator, because he is above the law, although his behavior nevertheless generally reflects various institutions, such as those required to elicit control over coercive power. In any case, for his subjects, legal rules are exogenous, man-made, nonphysical factors that, if part of an institution, affect their behavior. Similar to a dictator, a prime minister may also be in a position to change legal rules. Unlike a dictator, however, once they are institutionalized, legal rules influence his behavior because he is subject to the law.

Common to both the dictator and the prime minister is their ability to initiate, in this example, changes in legal rules. In this sense, these rules are not exogenous to them. Each reflects a particular institutionalized way, a set of rules, beliefs, norms, and organizations, generating behavior in the interactions through which new institutions are established.

2.2 INSTITUTIONS AS SYSTEMS OF RULES, BELIEFS, NORMS, AND ORGANIZATIONS

Considering an institution as a system departs from the common practice of considering it a monolithic entity such as a rule.[7] To understand regularities of behavior, in the most general case, we need to study a system of interrelated elements. While I return to discuss the different roles of different institutional elements at length in Chapter 5 to justify this assertion, at this point it suffices to note that various institutional elements – rules, beliefs, norms, and organizations – serve different roles in generating behavior. The various approaches to the study of institutions that have defined them as either rules, beliefs, norms, or organizations highlight the roles that each of these factors plays.

---

[7] Scott (1995, p. 33) advances a different, nonunitary notion of institutions, according to which institutions "consist of cognitive, normative, and regulative structures and activities that provide stability and meaning to social behavior." Chapter 5 clarifies the relationships between the two definitions.

Socially articulated and disseminated rules create shared cognition, provide information, coordinate behavior, and indicate morally appropriate and socially acceptable behavior. They thereby enable and guide behavior by creating a cognitive and normative understanding of the situation and coordinating behavior within it. Although such rules can reflect individualistic learning, they are usually socially articulated and disseminated and can take many forms (formal or informal, implicit or explicit, tacit or well articulated).

Rules correspond to behavior only if people are motivated to follow them. Beliefs and norms motivate individuals to follow institutionalized rules. For example, believing that a reward or penalty will be forthcoming motivates an individual to take or refrain from taking a particular action. The *rule* about driving on the right does not cause us to do so; we are motivated by the *belief* that everyone else will drive on the right and it is therefore best of us to do so as well.

It is useful to differentiate between two kinds of beliefs that motivate behavior: internalized beliefs and behavioral beliefs (expectations). Internalized beliefs are those regarding the structure and details of the world we experience (and potentially other worlds) and the implied relationship between actions and outcomes. They reflect knowledge in the form of cognitive (mental) models that individuals develop to explain and understand their environment. Such beliefs can directly motivate behavior at the individual level. In early medieval Europe, for example, the belief that various deities lived in the forest forestalled land clearing, because people feared divine retaliation if they did so (Duby 1974).

Internalized beliefs also influence behavior indirectly, as individuals who have power – who can influence institutionalization processes – act on their convictions. In the age of mercantilism, for example, policy makers believed that international trade was a zero-sum game. They believed that a nation's economic success, particularly in exporting goods, came at the expense of the success of other nations. Through regulations, policy makers attempted to institute rules and beliefs that fostered their nation's competitiveness in world trade.[8]

Behavioral beliefs are beliefs about the behavior of others in various contingencies, whether or not the behavior actually occurs. An individual's beliefs about others' behavior directly influences his behavioral choices. The belief that everyone else will drive on the right motivates an individual to do likewise. These beliefs are about behavior – driving

---

[8] This line of causation is central to the argument in North (2005).

on the right – that actually occurs given these beliefs. Behavioral beliefs regarding behavior that does not actually transpire given these beliefs can also influence behavior. Believing that a policeman will arrest a person who commits a crime and that the legal system will penalize the offender reduces the motivation to commit a crime. If these beliefs are sufficient to deter crimes, criminal activity will not occur. Beliefs about the policeman's response in a situation that does not actually transpire influences behavior. Finally, internalized norms are socially constructed behavioral standards that have been incorporated into one's superego (conscience), thereby influencing behavior by becoming part of one's preferences.

Different institutional elements have distinct roles, each of which contributes differently to generating regularities of behavior. Rules specify normative behavior and provide a shared cognitive system, coordination, and information, whereas beliefs and norms provide the motivation to follow them. Organizations – either formal, such as parliaments and firms, or informal, such as communities and business networks – have three interrelated roles: to produce and disseminate rules, to perpetuate beliefs and norms, and to influence the set of feasible behavioral beliefs. In situations in which institutions generate behavior, rules correspond to the beliefs and norms that motivate it, while organizations contribute to this outcome in the manner mentioned previously.

How, for example, do the rules of the road produce regularities of behavior among drivers? They create a shared cognitive understanding of the symbols drivers encounter (red lights, yield signs) and the definition of various concepts and situations (passing, yielding, having the right-of-way). The rules also include prescriptive instructions on expected behavior in various situations by law enforcement officials, pedestrians, and other drivers. Believing that others will follow these rules of behavior motivates most drivers most of the time to follow them. Departments of motor vehicles and law enforcement agencies are organizations that generate and disseminate these rules and facilitate the creation of the corresponding beliefs. To understand the behavior of drivers requires studying these three institutional elements, which constitute the interrelated components of an integrated system in which rules correspond to beliefs about behavior and the behavior itself.

Table 2.1 provides examples of the interrelated roles of various institutional elements: describing the foundations of regularities of behavior requires describing multiple institutional elements. Chapter 5 examines these institutional elements in depth.

Table 2.1. *Institutions as Systems*

Rule	Organizations	Beliefs and Internalized Norms	Implied Regularity of Behavior
Rules of the road	Departments of motor vehicles and law enforcement officials	Beliefs that other drivers and law enforcement officials will behave in a particular way	Driving according to the rules
Rules regulating the payment of bribes such as the amount paid, how, and to what effect	State administration, police, courts of law	Belief that the response of the state, police, and courts to bribe taking renders it profitable to take; beliefs that paying the bribe is the least costly way to advance one's interest	Corruption
Rules regulating use of credit cards and prosecution of defaulters	Credit card companies and legal authorities	Belief in the credit card company's ability to screen cardholders, impose legal punishment, and damage one's credit history	Impersonal exchange without cash among sellers and holders of credit cards
Rules governing membership and behavior toward members and nonmembers	Community of Jewish traders in New York	Belief in community members' ability and motivation to punish cheaters, thereby making cheating unprofitable	Exchange without reliance on legal contracts
Behavioral rule of not clearing forests	None	Internalized beliefs about retaliation by forest deities	Avoidance of forest clearing
Rules legalizing and governing slavery in the United States	White communities, state and federal legislators, legal authorities in the South	Internalized norms justifying slavery; beliefs in particular behavior by other whites, African Americans, and legal authorities	Slavery

2.3 AN INTEGRATIVE APPROACH TO INSTITUTIONS

Considering institutions as systems of interrelated rules, beliefs, norms, and organizations, each of which is a man-made, nonphysical social factor, encompasses the definition most widely used in economics, which states that institutions are formal and informal rules together with their enforcement mechanisms (North 1990). The definition presented here, however, places motivation to follow rules – and consequently beliefs and norms – at the center of the analysis.[9] It highlights the need to study rules and motivation to follow them in an integrated manner. Taking the reasons that people follow rules as exogenous to the analysis, as North's institutions-as-rules approach does, is clearly useful for various purposes, but it is limiting to consider motivation as exogenous. It implies that there is no one-to-one relationship between rules and behavior, namely, between the explanatory variable and the outcomes we wish to understand. Rather than assuming that people follow rules, we need to explain why some rules are followed and others are not.[10]

More generally, the definition advanced here encompasses many of the multiple definitions of the term institutions used in economics, political science, and sociology. These include defining institutions as the rules of the game in a society (North 1990; Ostrom 1990; Knight 1992; Weingast 1996); as formal or informal organizations (social structures), such as parliaments, universities, tribes, families, or communities (Granovetter 1985; R. Nelson 1994); as beliefs about others' behavior or about the world around us and the relationship between actions and outcomes in it (Weber 1958 [1904–5]; Denzau and North 1994; Greif 1994a; Calvert 1995; Lal 1998; Aoki 2001); as internalized norms of behavior (Parsons 1990; Ullmann-Margalit 1977; Elster 1989b; Platteau 1994); and as regularities of behavior, or social practices that are regularly and continuously repeated, including contractual regularities expressing themselves in

---

[9] Another difference is that, for North, organizations are not a part of an institution but players in the political game through which institutions – politically determined rules – are established. I return to elaborate on a more subtle view of organizations as integral parts of institutions.

[10] Indeed, motivation is central to institutional analysis in sociology. Parsons's (1951) analysis centers on the normative foundations of behavior. The recent cognitive turn in sociology asserts that individuals follow rules because they are motivated by concern about their self-image, which is socially constructed, and about others' feelings toward them (see, e.g., Scott 1995 and March and Olsen 1989). For reviews, see Ellickson (1991); Scott (1995); and P. Hall and Taylor (1996). In the terminology developed here, these considerations reflect institutionalized beliefs and norms.

organizations such as firms (Abercrombie, Hill, and Turner 1994, p. 216; Berger 1977; Schotter 1981; O. Williamson 1985; Young 1998).

Recent important works on economic institutions either refrain from defining them or adopt one definition at the expense of others.[11] Considering different definitions of institutions as mutually exclusive is counterproductive, however, and it curtails advancing institutional analysis. As the discussion of the various roles of institutional elements highlights, seemingly distinct definitions are complements rather than substitutes, and they have more in common than meets the eye. My reading of the literature is that, whatever the theoretical approach or disciplinary affiliation, students of institutions ultimately study regularities of behavior generated by man-made nonphysical factors that are exogenous to each individual whose behavior they influence. Various lines of institutional analysis concentrate on one such factor at the exclusion of others. The definition adopted here takes advantage of their commonality to build on the insights and analytical frameworks developed in many lines of analysis. It is thus an encompassing concept.

The main approaches to institutional analysis, however, differ in more than just their definitions. They also differ in their basic assertions and premises about the nature, dynamics, and origins of institutions. These assertions and premises are used to restrict the scope of analysis and gain analytical leverage. Identifying institutions with politically determined rules, for example, restricts them to outcomes of the political process. Relying on different premises to restrict the scope of the analysis, however, comes at the cost of limited ability to integrate the insights and analytical frameworks developed in conjunction with various definitions. The definition advanced here fosters such integration by limiting the object of study by focusing on institutional elements and regularities of behavior.

A major fault line in institutional analysis separates those who adopt an *agency perspective* of institutions from those who adopt a *structural perspective.* According to the former, individuals shape institutions to achieve their goals; according to the latter, institutions transcend individual actors.

The agency perspective places the individual decision maker at the center of the analysis. It studies institutions as reflecting the objectives of the individuals who established them. Institutions therefore reflect the

---

[11] See, for example, North (1990); Eggertsson (1990); Ostrom (1990); Furubotn and Richter (1997); Weingast (1996); Young (1998); and Aoki (2001). Many students of institutions have noted the need for, and the potential benefit of, integrating various lines of institutional analysis. See, for example, Coleman (1990) and Ostrom (1990).

interest of their creators and are postulated not to endure beyond the conditions that led to their emergence. Politicians, for example, aspire to create rules that best serve their political and economic objectives. If either the objectives or the political process of rule formation changes, so will the resulting rules. The point of departure for such institutional analysis is, therefore, at the (micro) level of the individuals whose interactions in a particular environment give rise to an institution.

The structural perspective emphasizes that institutions shape rather than reflect the needs and possibilities of those whose behavior they influence. Institutions structure human interactions, mold individuals, and constitute the social and cultural worlds in which they interact. Institutions therefore transcend the situations that led to their emergence; beliefs, internalized norms, and organizations are part of the structure in which individuals interact, and this whole is larger than the sum of its parts. The point of departure for such institutional analysis is therefore at the (macro) level of the structure in which individuals interact.

Economists have traditionally adopted the agency perspective, emphasizing that institutions are intentionally designed to constrain behavior. Economics is the "study of how individual economic agents pursuing their own selfish ends evolve institutions as a means to satisfy them" (Schotter 1981, p. 5). Institutions are "the humanly devised constraints that structure political, economic, and social interactions" (North 1991, p. 97). But even among economists, there are many who examine institutions from a structural perspective (e.g., Hodgson 1998).

In contrast, sociologists tend to employ a structural perspective, postulating that institutions transcend individual actors and shape their interests and behavior. Institutions, according to them, are exogenous to all individuals. They are the properties of societies that "impose themselves upon" individuals (Durkheim 1950 [1895], p. 2) and consist of "structures and activities that provide stability and meaning to social behavior" (Scott 1995, p. 33).[12] But even among sociologists, those who follow Weber's (1949) tradition often examine institutions from an agency perspective.

These two seemingly contradictory views on institutions – the structural and the agency perspectives – must be bridged because each captures an important feature of reality. An institution is sometimes a structure beyond the control of the individuals whose behavior it influences,

---

[12] For an illuminating discussion of these differences in political science, see P. Hall and Taylor (1996).

whereas at other times it is an outcome reflecting their actions. For some analytical purposes it is useful to consider an institution as a given structure, whereas for other purposes it is useful to study it as a product of those whose behavior it influences or other individuals. It is therefore imperative to have a concept of an institution that does not exclude either case. More generally, as has long been recognized in sociology, there is a need to study institutions while combining the structural and agency perspectives because institutions influence behavior while being man-made (e.g., Coleman 1990).

The definition advanced here combines both the structural and agency perspectives by recognizing the dual nature of institutions as both man-made and exogenous to each individual whose behavior they influence. The benefits of capturing this dual nature are many. It enables us to advance a unified framework for studying institutional persistence, endogenous change, and the impact of institutions on institutional development (Part III).

Various approaches have also adopted different premises about the related issue of institutional origin and functions. For Hayek (1973) institutions emerge spontaneously and unintentionally. They reflect human actions but not intentions, because individuals have limited knowledge and rationality.[13] For many others (O. Williamson 1985; North and Thomas 1973; North 1990), intentional attempts by individuals to improve their lot underpin the processes through which institutions emerge. In political science the rational choice approach examines them as instrumental outcomes, while historical institutionalism emphasizes that institutions reflect a historical process (see Thelen 1999).

Other approaches to institutional analysis assert that institutions fulfill a particular function. For North and many others, "the major role of institutions in a society is to reduce uncertainty" (North 1990, p. 6). For Williamson and many others, they foster efficiency. They are the "means by which order is accomplished in a relationship in which potential conflict threatens to undo or upset opportunities to realize mutual gains" (O. Williamson 1998, p. 37). For Knight (1992), the main function of institutions is to affect the distribution of gains.

Different approaches to the study of institutions rest on contradictory assertions about human nature (see P. Hall and Taylor 1996). Parsons (1951), for example, assumes that individuals are capable of internalizing

---

[13] See also Sugden (1989); Knight (1992); G. Hodgson (1998); and Young (1998). See Scott (1995) regarding the main fault lines in sociological institutionalism.

rules and that institutions are behavioral standards that have been internalized; for O. Williamson (1985), however, individuals are assumed to act opportunistically unless constrained by external forces. For Young (1998) and Aoki (2001), institutions reflect humans' limited cognition; others, such as O. Williamson (1985) and Calvert (1995), assume that individuals have a comprehensive knowledge of the environment within which they interact.

The definition advanced here does not commit to any of these premises. It does not dispute that institutions can be established, emerge, or impose themselves on members of a society nor does it claim that they serve a particular function, such as providing incentives, reducing uncertainty, enhancing efficiency, or determining distribution. By focusing on regularities of behavior, the definition recognizes the need to study the relationships between institutions and various outcomes such as the war of all against all that Hobbes envisioned in the absence of a state and the institutions that secure property rights in some states and not others.

Similarly, the definition also does not assert that institutions reflect either intentional decision making by forward-looking agents or unintentional evolutionary and learning processes reflecting limited cognition. The definition of institutions neither depends on a particular assertion about whether motivation is provided by economic, moral, social, or coercive means nor subjects the analysis to a particular analytical framework.[14]

A definition that does not depend on such assertions and premises is useful for advancing institutional analysis, because institutions fulfill a variety of functions, emerge through various processes, influence behavior in situations that are and are not cognitively well understood, and rely on different motivational factors. Defining institutions, for example, based on their function as the incentive structure in a society (North 1990) is analogous to saying that a car transports people rather than calling it a "vehicle moving on wheels," as the dictionary does. Transporting people is one of the many things a car can do, but it is not what a car is. Similarly, defining institutions while assuming that individuals are motivated solely by either internalized norms or external incentives is partial at best. Whether individuals act "morally" or opportunistically depends

---

[14] See, for example, the definition provided by Sugden (1989), which subjects the analysis to a particular institutional framework. An institution (*convention* in his terminology) is an evolutionary stable strategy in a game with multiple evolutionary stable strategies.

on a society's institutions – whether or not, for example, they lead to the internalization of particular norms. Assuming that individuals do or do not act morally ignores the need to examine the institutional foundations of such types of behavior.

The definition used here distinguishes between what institutions are, what they do, and what they imply. Institutions are systems of factors that are social in being man-made, nonphysical, and exogenous to each individual whose behavior they influence; what they do is generate regularities of behavior. What they reflect – how they came into existence – and what they imply should not be assumed a priori or used deductively to restrict the set of permissible institutions but should be analytically and empirically examined.

Why is it so common to define an institution as fulfilling a particular function, having a particular origin, or reflecting a particular motivation? Such definitions are used to pin down either the scope of the analysis or the forces directing institutional change. If one asserts that institutions are politically determined rules serving the interest of the polity, the scope of the analysis is thereby limited to politically determined rules, the origin of institutions is limited to the political arena, and the forces leading to institutional change are limited to changes in the political process or the objectives of the political actors. These restrictions come, however, at the cost of taking as exogenous such potentially important issues as beliefs and internalized norms, which directly influence behavior and hence should be part of the analysis. In contrast, the definition presented here limits the scope of the analysis by concentrating on recurrent situations, regularities of behavior among individuals with particular social positions, and the requirement that institutional elements be man-made nonphysical factors exogenous to each individual whose behavior they influence.

This perspective highlights both the need and the ability to integrate various analytical frameworks. When studying the relationships among organizations and rules, for example, it allows us to take advantage of the analytics and insights developed in the study of the political economy of rule formation. In studying the relationships between organizations and internalized norms, the analysis can benefit from the analytics and insights developed in sociology and political science. As for the relationships among rules, organizations, and behavior, the analysis can benefit from the analytics and insights offered by transaction cost economics in exploring how decision makers try to lower these costs. At the same time, the definition advanced here, and hence the implied analysis, is not bound by the premises underpinning various analytical frameworks. It allows for considering institutions as, for example, means to reduce transaction costs but does not impose that every institution achieves this outcome.

2.4 EXTERNAL EFFECTS AND TRANSACTIONS

Motivation provided by beliefs and norms exogenous to each individual whose behavior they influence is the linchpin of institutions, as it mediates between the environment and behavior. For such beliefs and norms to exist, someone must be able to take actions that directly affect the well-being of individuals whose behavior is generated by the associated institution from taking various actions.[15] If this is not the case, their behavior cannot be motivated by social factors – institutional elements – which, by definition, have to be exogenous to each of them. In other words, if nothing that others have done, are doing, or are expected to do has any impact on one's well-being from taking various actions, then one's behavior cannot be influenced by man-made factors exogenous to that individual. Robinson Crusoe lived in a noninstitutionalized world (except for the norms and beliefs he internalized before arriving on the island). His behavior may have exhibited regularities, but those regularities reflected factors such as his preferences, knowledge, habits, or laws of nature, not institutions. There was no society external to him.

The past, present, or expected future actions of others that are of interest here are those which have *external effects*: one person's action directly and unavoidably influences another's. The one whose behavior is generated by the institution cannot choose whether to be exposed to the impact of other people's behavior.[16] One does not choose the norms his parents instilled in him or the police's expected behavior. Such external effects can occur through pecuniary rewards, physical punishments, social sanctions, praise, or socialization to particular internalized norms; they can even reflect role models provided by others that influence one's aspirations and identity and hence well-being from taking various actions.

Saying that in any institution someone's action must have an external effect implies that transactions are central to institutions.[17] A *transaction*

---

[15] Such actions include those leading to the internalization of beliefs and norms.

[16] Sometimes people can choose whether to become involved in a situation in which they are exposed to external effects. See, for example, Ensminger (1997), who explains religious conversion as an attempt to alter relevant external effects.

[17] Transaction cost economics, advanced particularly by Williamson (1985, 2000), studies contractual and organizational responses to the attributes of transactions. I complement that approach by emphasizing the role of intertransactional linkages.

is defined here as an action taken when an entity, such as a commodity, social attitude, emotion, opinion, or information, is transferred from one social unit to another.[18] These social units can be individuals, organizations, or other entities (such as God or the spirits of ancestors) that are considered actors by those whose behavior we study. Transactions can thus be economic (such as the provision of a pecuniary reward), political (such as a vote in the Congress), or social (such as the provision of social approval); transactions can involve inflicting pain or sharing emotions (such as the expression of sympathy). Nothing in this definition assumes a particular reason for or form of transacting. It can be voluntary, as economics often assumes it is, but it can also be involuntary or forced; it can be legal or illegal, unidirectional (where only one side transfers something to the other), bidirectional, or multidirectional.

Transacting renders a situation social, and the focus here is on transactions that entail external effects by directly affecting the well-being, knowledge, internalized beliefs, or norms of at least one of these social units (henceforth referred to as *individuals*). For example, transactions associated with legal sanctions, social sanctions, the transfer of property, and praise directly affect well-being. Transactions that provide information about an individual's credit history influence knowledge; transactions that provide opinions, such as sermons or lectures, influence internalized beliefs; and transactions associated with the socialization process influence norms.

One's behavior is influenced by another's past, present, or future action only if such transactions are involved. A necessary condition for one's behavior to be influenced by man-made nonphysical factors exogenous to him is that something (such as money, praise, or a penalty) reflecting someone else's behavior was, is, or is expected to be transferred to him. Institutionalized internalized beliefs and norms reflect transactions. They reflect the socialization process through which one's world view, identity, and norms were developed and beliefs (in, e.g., holy scriptures and creation myths) were formed. Similarly, institutionalized behavioral beliefs are about transactions, because they are concerned with one's response

---

The attributes of the central transaction, however, influence the implications of various linkages.

[18] Although many scholars have emphasized the importance of transactions in institutions (see, e.g., Coase 1937; O. Williamson 1985; and the review in Furubotn and Richter 1997), no single definition of the term dominates the literature. The most commonly used definition is that a transaction "occurs when a good or service is transferred across a technologically separable interface" (O. Williamson 1985, p. 1).

to another's behavior. The threat of punishment by the court for reneging on a contractual obligation, for example, generates the regularity of behavior of adhering to contracts. The potential external effects of legal sanctions induce behavior in the economic transaction; the belief that individuals will adhere to contractual obligations in the economic transaction is achieved by conditioning actions in the legal transaction on what has occurred in the economic one.

Note that, in this example, the legal transaction between the court and an individual is *auxiliary*, in the sense that it facilitates the generation of beliefs about behavior in yet another transaction – namely, the one between contracting individuals. The transactions leading individuals to internalize particular beliefs or norms are auxiliary transactions with the same impact. An auxiliary transaction can also be part of an institution generating regularities of behavior in actions other than transactions. When the fear of legal punishment prevents an individual from taking illegal drugs, for example, the auxiliary transaction influences behavior not in another transaction but in a situation in which one can either act or refrain from doing so.

When an institution generates behavior in a transaction, we can refer to the transaction as *central*. For ease of exposition, I concentrate on institutions that generate behavior in central transactions, but the analysis applies equally to cases in which the regularity of behavior relates to actions other than transactions (e.g., smoking or diets). Similarly, for simplicity of exposition, I do not differentiate between actual and potential transactions. *Potential transactions* are actions that can be taken to transfer an entity between individuals, thereby directly affecting the well-being or information of at least one of them. If the threat of punishment by a court, for example, is sufficient to deter cheating, no transaction will take place between the court and the individual, who is induced to respect the law by his belief in the court's response. The potential transaction that induces this behavior is an auxiliary transaction.

2.5 INTERTRANSACTIONAL LINKAGES, INSTITUTIONS, AND ORGANIZATIONS

Once we recognize the distinction between auxiliary and central transactions, we can develop a more nuanced view of institutional elements. Some institutionalized beliefs and norms constitute, or create, intertransactional linkages in that they link an auxiliary transaction with a central transaction. Belief in a court's response – rather than a response by the extended

47

family or the mafia, for example – to a contractual breach, links the (central) economic transaction between economic agents with the (auxiliary) legal transaction between each agent and the law. The belief that God will punish a cheater links the economic transaction with the transaction that is perceived to exist between human beings and the divine. Norms create transactional linkages between the superego and the ego or id.[19]

The behavioral beliefs which are possible in a central transaction depend on the beliefs and norms that create intertransactional linkages. When it is believed that courts will sanction cheaters, it becomes possible to believe that people will not cheat because they fear these sanctions. If it is common knowledge that enough people have internalized the fear of God or the norm of honesty, then it becomes possible to believe that they will be honest in a central, economic transaction. Institutionalized beliefs and norms, which directly generate behavior in central transactions, reflect the particular transactions that have been linked in a society.

At the same time, as was mentioned in the previous section, interactions in auxiliary transactions are an important source of institutional elements. Actions in auxiliary transactions – transactions other than the central one under consideration – generate institutional elements. Institutionalized rules reflect the information that was transmitted through transactions; institutionalized internalized beliefs and norms reflect the knowledge and actions that were taken in the transactions through which education, socialization, and indoctrination transpire and role models are provided; and institutionalized behavioral beliefs often have similar origins.

Noting the importance of auxiliary transactions also provides a more nuanced view of organizations. Organizations are the arenas in which actions in auxiliary transactions take place. As such, organizations fulfill multiple roles. They produce and disseminate rules, information, and knowledge, perpetuate beliefs and norms, and influence the set of feasible beliefs in the central transaction. This last role of organizations, which reflects their impact on the set of feasible intertransactional linkages, merits further elaboration here.

---

[19] According to Sigmund Freud, a child is born with an id. The id is based on the pleasure principle, meaning that it desires whatever feels good at the time, without consideration for others. By the age of three, a child develops the ego, which is based on the reality principle. The ego understands that other people have needs and desires and that sometimes being impulsive or selfish can cause harm in the long run. It's the ego's job to meet the needs of the id, while taking into consideration the reality of the situation. By the age of five the child develops the superego that constitutes our moral principles. The superego (conscience) dictates our beliefs in right and wrong and the ego functions as an intermediary between it and the id.

Courts must exist before a belief in legal punishment can motivate a particular behavior (e.g., honesty) in an economic transaction. In other words, courts are a necessary condition for believing that the behavior in the (auxiliary) legal transaction is linked to behavior in the (central) economic transaction. Similarly, the existence of a community is a necessary condition for believing that communal sanctions will motivate economic behavior. Organizations are a manifestation of and a means for intertransactional linkages and thereby they alter the set of possible behavioral beliefs in the central transaction.[20]

To see the point and the generality of the argument, consider, for example, the case of institutions that facilitate exchange. Because all exchange is sequential, the party that moves second has to be able to commit ex ante not to renege on its obligations ex post.[21] Generically, commitment is achieved by linking this central (exchange) transaction with other transactions so that it will be possible to believe that individuals will not renege. A linkage can be achieved without a supporting organization. Conditioning entry to future exchange relationships on past conduct links present and future transactions. If the value of this future exchange is sufficiently high relative to the gains from currently reneging, belief in good conduct can be sustained.

Organizations that link the central transaction to other transactions extend the set of possible behavioral beliefs in the central transaction beyond those possible though such bilateral and intertemporal linkages. These organizations can have different origins and take many forms; they can be formal or informal, intentional or unintentional. Examples include communities, social networks, courts, firms, credit bureaus, escrow companies, and credit-rating companies, all of which are institutional elements that change the set of possible beliefs in the central transaction by linking it to others.

Credit bureaus, credit card companies, Moody's, VeriSign Inc., and TRUSTe are organizations that extend the set of possible beliefs between partners in various economic exchanges. Within communities, social exchange is linked with various other economic and social transactions. The court system links transactions between economic agents with the legal transactions between each of them and the law. In religious

---

[20] Chapter 5 defines the term *possible* as it is used here. The relevant game is contingent on the transactions that were linked. Organizations change the set of self-enforcing (equilibrium) beliefs in the central transaction.

[21] The basic game is the one-sided prisoner's dilemma (also known as the game of trust). See discussions in Appendixes A and C.

49

communities, transactions between members are linked with the perceived transaction between each member and a deity. Political parties link transactions between political activists and voters.

In any of these cases, organizations that are institutional elements are mechanisms for, or a reflection of, the ways in which a central transaction is linked with others.[22] Information provided by such organizations as credit bureaus and communities makes possible the beliefs that future partners to exchange will condition their behavior on past conduct. Organizations that, for example, coordinate actions, provide common interpretations of events, and monitor behavior have a similar effect. Organizations can be infinite-horizon players with better ability for intertemporal linkages among transactions, and they can similarly better link transactions over space (e.g., as hotel chains do).[23] Organizations thereby alter the set of possible behavioral beliefs (and more generally norms) in the central transaction.

It is now possible to clarify the remark made earlier that organizations are both components of institutions and institutions. Organizations are institutional elements vis-à-vis the central transaction under consideration, but they are also institutions – systems of rules, beliefs, and norms exogenous to each individual whose behavior they influence – that generate behavior among the organization's members. Whether we consider an organization an institution depends on the issue being studied. In Chapter 3, for example, understanding the behavior in the central transaction requires first understanding why members of a merchants' community were motivated to retain their membership and transact in information.

Whether we study the organization only as a component of an institution or also as an institution, we still may need to consider its behavior as endogenously determined. Understanding the nature and impact an organization has on beliefs in the central transaction requires considering the choice of its relevant actors (e.g., a judge or policeman). To understand the impact a court has on beliefs about behavior in an economic exchange, it may not be necessary to consider it as an institution and study

---

[22] Greif (1989); Milgrom, North, and Weingast (1990); Greif, Milgrom, and Weingast (1994); Greif (1993); Aoki (2001); Tadelis (1999, 2002); and Ingram (1996) discuss these roles of organizations.

[23] If such an organization is not an institutional element, it cannot change beliefs and behavior in the central transaction. If an economic agent can dismiss the court at will or control its operation, the threat of legal sanctions will not be part of the institution that influences this agent's behavior.

the rules, beliefs, and norms that generate behavior among the decision makers within it or provide it with the capacity to penalize. But studying the judge's motivation for executing justice rather than collecting bribes is necessary. In other words, it is necessary to understand how the court linked the central economic transaction with the legal transaction rather than the private transaction between the judge and the parties to the dispute in which a bribe exchanged hands.

This view of the relationship between institutions and organizations departs from that of the three perspectives that dominate the study of these relationships.[24] They view organizations as either arenas for political rule making, players in the political rule-making process, or private responses to the incentives that institutions entail.

The institutions-as-rules perspective that dominates economics and political science considers organizations as bodies for collective decision making, such as parliaments. Institutions are defined as rules specified by the members of these organizations. The second perspective defines an organization as a group of individuals bound by some common purpose to achieve objectives (Arrow 1974; Olson 1982; North 1990; Thelen 1999). Organizations such as interest groups, courts, and labor unions influence politically determined rules by participating in the political decision-making process. Organizations often reflect existing rules that motivated their beneficiaries to organize in the first place in order to ensure that the rules would persist.

The third perspective, from organizational theory, holds that organizations are "collectivities oriented to the pursuit of relatively specific goals," such as production (Scott 1998, p. 26). But it maintains that they reflect the options and constraints implied by institutions, conceptualized as systems of meaning and regulatory processes (enforcement mechanisms). The sociological branch of organizational theory emphasizes that organizations reflect the meaning, objectives, and identities provided by institutions (see, e.g., Scott, Meyer, et al. 1994; Scott 1995). The economics branch of organizational theory emphasizes that institutions affect the costs and benefits of various organizational forms. Organizations are optimal – transaction-cost-minimizing – responses to these incentives (Coase 1937; O. Williamson 1985, 2000).[25]

---

[24] With few exceptions (such as Bowles and Gintis 1976), the economic literature has neglected the important role organizations play in perpetuating internalized rules and beliefs. I touch on this issue in Chapter 5.

[25] I integrate the insights of these perspectives in the historical analyses. For example, the Maghribi traders' group (Chapter 3) was an unintentional response, and the

None of these perspectives is concerned with motivation; for them organizations either determine institutions or are determined by them. Motivation enters the analysis only in considering the incentive to choose a particular institution (rule) or respond to it in a manner leading to a particular organization. In contrast, the perspective advanced here emphasizes that an organization can also be an institutional element, a component of an institution that motivates behavior in various transactions. Organizations are a means for and a manifestation of the way a central transaction is linked with other transactions. By creating this linkage, organizations change the set of institutionalized behavioral beliefs that can motivate behavior in the central transaction. In institutionalized situations, the behavioral beliefs that can motivate behavior are contingent on linkages among transactions, and organizations are instrumental in creating them.

The distinction between organizations and institutions highlights the role of symbols and signs (such as contracts, bills of exchange, the marriage ceremony, and shaking hands) in the functioning of institutions. They are means to communicate one's social position to the relevant organizations (and individuals). A legal loan contract signifies the debtor's social position in the court of law; a handshake between members of a business network signifies to other members of the network that the two have assumed particular obligations toward each other; the marriage ceremony signifies to the legal authorities and the community the social positions of two individuals. How one will live up to the behavioral rules – rights and obligations – associated with this social position, in turn, determines the behavioral response of others; the expectations that this will be the case, in turn, influence the behavior of that individual.[26]

Because different transactions can be linked to the same central transaction, rules, beliefs, internalized norms, and organizations can take many forms, which reflect the related intertransactional linkages. A borrower may repay a loan, for example, because he is motivated by the belief that, if he does not, he will be fined by the court, beaten by a Mafia thug, or ostracized by the community. These various manifestations of the same

merchant guilds (Chapter 4) an intentional response to the lack of legal institutions that ensured contract enforcement and security of property rights.

[26] In studying self-enforcing institutions, symbols and signs can be studied themselves as equilibrium outcomes, similar to the way in which we treat social positions. The symbol influences behavior because individuals condition their behavior on it and each individual's best response to the conditioning of others is to follow suit. See also Calvert (1995).

institutional element can potentially replace or complement each other in influencing behavior in a given central transaction.

2.6 CONCLUDING COMMENTS: SELF-ENFORCING INSTITUTIONS

The definition of institutions advanced here says nothing about the conditions under which a particular institution is effective in generating a particular behavior or how we identify which institution is relevant in a particular situation. It highlights what has to be studied and points out that, in the most general case, we need to study institutions as endogenous in the sense that they are *self-enforcing*: responding to the institutional elements implied by others' behavior and expected behavior, each individual behaves in a manner that contributes to motivating, guiding, and enabling others to behave in a manner that led to the institutional elements to begin with. In explaining such institutions, the analysis does not invoke as exogenous other institutions (e.g., political institutions) to explain them. Nor does the analysis rest on the assumption that institutions are determined by their function or environmental forces. Instead, it recognized that the structure – institutional elements – that each individual takes as given enables, motives, and guides the individual to take the actions that, at the aggregate level, contribute to creating the structure itself.

Various analytical frameworks can be employed for studying different aspects of institutions in general and those that are self-enforcing in particular. This book builds on game theory to accomplish this task.

PART II

Institutions as Systems in Equilibria

Definitions direct analytic attention and confine the scope of an empirical study; conducting a study requires an analytical framework. An analytical framework is required to reveal the conditions under which a particular institution is effective in generating a particular behavior, to expose causal relationships, to generate predictions, and to evaluate arguments. An analytical framework is particularly important in studying institutions, because beliefs and norms are unobservable.[1]

Central to the analytical framework used here is classical game theory. Because the proof is in the pudding, this book contains five empirical studies that attest to its usefulness in studying institutions as defined here. These studies use an empirical method that combines detailed contexual knowledge of the situation and its history with explicit, context-specific modeling. This case study method uses contexual knowledge to develop a conjecture regarding the relevance of a particular intertransactional linkage and the related institution. It then uses an explicit (and in this work) game-theoretic model to evaluate this conjecture. This empirical method is employed in all the historical analyses presented in this book. It is elaborated on in Part IV.

The empirical studies presented here consider the institutional foundations of markets. Doing so departs from a long tradition in institutional analysis that goes back to Adam Smith and considers markets as primitives that need not be explained. According to this view, markets emerge

[1] Indeed, as W. Powell and DiMaggio (1991, p. 2) note, promising institutional research that attempted to go beyond the institutions-as-rules and agency views – from Veblen and Commons in economics to Parsons and Selznick in sociology – "fell into disfavor, not because they asked the wrong questions, but because they provided answers that were either largely descriptive and historically specific or so abstract as to lack explanatory punch."

spontaneously when and where there is an opportunity for profitable exchange. As O. Williamson put it, "in the beginning there were markets" (1975, p. 20).

The failure of markets to emerge, particularly in transition economies, revealed the fragility of this assertion. Markets do not necessarily spontaneously emerge in response to opportunities for profitable exchange. For exchange to transpire, institutions that protect property rights and provide contract enforcement must be in place. By determining who can exchange and what products can be exchanged, these institutions determine the scope and scale of the market.[2]

The next two chapters demonstrate the usefulness of the perspective developed here for empirically studying the institutional foundations of markets. Chapter 3 considers private-order institution for contract enforcement. Chapter 4 presents an institution that secured the property rights of alien traders. By dealing with distinct institutions, these analyses lend empirical support to the claims made in Chapter 2. In analytically studying institutions, it is imperative to examine intertransactional linkages and the interrelated institutional elements rendering this linkage effective and generating regularities of behavior.

Chapter 5 reflects more generally on the relationship between game theory and institutions as defined here. It seeks to gain insights about institutions by learning from the unrealistic assumptions that are required to make game theory a useful tool for studying behavior in strategic situations. The discussion first highlights what classical and learning game theory teach us about the role of institutionalized rules in providing the cognitive, informational, coordinative, and normative micro-foundations of behavior. It then proceeds by exploring the implications of this better understanding of rules and their relationships to beliefs about the appropriate use of game theory for institutional analysis.

When presenting and analyzing institutions, it can be cumbersome to adhere to the terminology presented in Chapter 2. It is easier to note, for example, that a community provides a network for information transmission than to say that linkages of information-sharing transactions within the community imply circulation of information. It is easier to note that members of a community shared the expectation that a cheater would be collectively punished than to say that the

---

[2] For related research, see Greif (1989, 1992, 1994b, 1997a, 2000, 2004b); Milgrom et al. (1990); Stiglitz (1994); Greif and Kandel (1995); Aoki (2001); McMillan (2002); and Fafchamps (2004).

institutionalized beliefs for collective punishment prevailed within the community. Similarly, it can be easier to state that a particular (institutionalized) rule of behavior prevailed than to say that beliefs and norms motivated behavior corresponding to these rules. For ease of exposition, therefore, I often adopt the simpler rather than the more precise terminology.

3

Private-Order Contract Enforcement Institutions

The Maghribi Traders' Coalition

In premodern trade, merchants had to organize the supply of the services required for the handling of their goods abroad, because goods were sold abroad only after being shipped to their destination (De Roover 1965; Gras 1939). A merchant could either travel with his merchandise or hire overseas agents to handle his affairs abroad. Employing agents was efficient, because it enabled merchants to avoid the time and risk associated with traveling and to diversify their sales across trade centers. Despite their efficiency, however, agency relations are not likely to be established unless supporting institutions are in place, because agents can act opportunistically and embezzle the merchants' goods.

This chapter examines the reputation-based economic institution – which can be referred to as a coalition – that enabled the Maghribi traders, a group of Jewish traders in the Mediterranean in the eleventh century, to deal with the contractual problem inherent in the merchant-agent transaction. In reputation-based institutions, future rewards or penalties in (auxiliary) economic or social transactions are made conditional on conduct in a central transaction. When effective, this intertransactional linkage enables an individual to credibly commit himself ex ante not to behave opportunistically ex post. In the case of agency relationships, the agent can commit to honesty and hence be trusted. Examining the operation of such institutions requires studying the institutional elements that create the intertransactional linkages and allow future utility to be conditioned on past conduct. In particular, such examination has to identify which transactions are linked to create sufficiently large sanctions or rewards, how information about past conduct is generated, and why inflicting sanctions or providing rewards is credible. (Appendix C presents the analytics of such institutions.)[1]

Two intertransactional linkages were central to the Maghribi traders. First, the agent-merchant transaction was linked with information-sharing transactions among the merchants. The resulting network provided merchants with the information required to evaluate the conduct of faraway agents. It supported the institutionalized beliefs that opportunistic behavior is likely to be detected. Second, the agency transaction between each merchant and agent was linked with future transactions between that agent and every other merchant in the group. Every merchant in the group was expected to hire only member agents and never to hire an agent who had cheated another member.

A credible threat of collective, multilateral punishment supported the beliefs that the short-run gain from cheating today was less than the long-run benefit of being honest. Because this situation was common knowledge, merchants perceived that the agents could not do better by cheating. A member agent acquired a reputation of being honest, and the merchants could trust him while a set of rules – known as merchants' law – defined what actions constituted appropriate conduct. The Maghribis' code of conduct was a social norm, a rule that is neither promulgated by an official source, such as a court or a legislator, nor enforced by the threat of legal sanctions but is nevertheless regularly complied with (Posner 1997).

The organizational manifestation of this institution was an informal organization – a business network of members who belonged to the same ethnic and religious community. It was a reflection of and a means for creating an intertransactional link that changed the set of self-enforcing beliefs in merchant-agent transactions. It was the manifestation of the institutionalized beliefs that individuals with a particular social identity – those who belonged to the community – would share information and collectively punish a cheater. Indeed, the existence of this community and the personal familiarity and information flows within it facilitated the rise of the coalition. At the same time, the benefits of transacting with other community members were greater than those each trader could have realized by establishing agency relations based on a reputation mechanism outside the group. Each member was therefore motivated to maintain his communal affiliation, thereby perpetuating this social entity.

---

[1] In the game-theoretic setting, a player's reputation is defined as a function from the history of the game to a probability distribution over his strategies.

Analysis of the Maghribi traders is based on a historical source found in Fustat (Old Cairo) known as the *geniza* ("depository" in Hebrew). It contains about a thousand contracts, price lists, traders' letters, accounts, and other documents that reflect eleventh-century trade in the Muslim Mediterranean.[2] These documents were written by the Maghribi traders, who lived initially mainly in the western basin of the Mediterranean. (The *Maghrib* is the Arabic word for the Muslim world's *West*.) For religious reasons, these traders deposited every document written in Hebrew letters in the *geniza* of a synagogue in Fustat. Because they conducted their commercial correspondence in Judeo-Arabic – an Arabic dialect written in Hebrew letters – it is reasonable to conjecture that the documents found in the *geniza* contain a representative sample of their commercial correspondence (Goitein 1967, p. 149).[3]

In the first section of this chapter, I provide information on the context and the Maghribi traders and describe their pattern of behavior in agency relationships and its purpose. Then, in section 3.2, I discuss the commitment problem inherent in the merchant-agent transaction and evaluate the historically derived conjecture that a multilateral reputation mechanism mitigated the associated commitment problem. Section 3.3 models the commitment problem in order to determine whether the institution postulated here could have constituted an equilibrium and why. Section 3.4 uses the model to generate predictions that further substantiate the claim that agency relations were governed by a coalition. It discusses the role of the merchants law in coordinating collective responses among the Maghribi traders. In section 3.5, I consider the implications of the analysis.

---

[2] For an introduction to the *geniza*, see Goitein (1967, introd.). The documents were purchased by various libraries. Documents referred to here are denoted by the library in which they are located and their registration number. When the reader is directed to specific lines within the document, the side (a or b) and the lines are also indicated. The list of abbreviations used here appears at the beginning of the book. Many of the documents have been published by Goitein, Gil, and others. For published, translated, or quoted documents, I cite the published source after the reference to the document. For example, TS xx.xxx, a, ll 24–25, Goitein (1967, p. 727) is a reference to document xx.xxx in the Taylor-Schechter collection, side a, lines 24–25, published in Goitein 1967 on page 727.

[3] On Judeo-Arabic, see Blau (1961, 1965). This chapter is based on Greif (1989, 1993). The analysis is based on about 250 documents contained in Greif (1985), Michael (1965), Gil (1983b), and Ben-Sasson (1991). These documents are the only ones available regarding trade between Egypt, Sicily, and Israel during the mid-eleventh century and the trade of Naharay ben Nissim, a Maghribi trader who lived in Fustat earlier that century.

3.1 COMMERCE, OVERSEAS AGENTS, AND EFFICIENCY

The Maghribi traders were descendants of Jewish traders who left during the tenth century the increasingly politically insecure surroundings of Baghdad and initially emigrated to Tunisia in North Africa – part of the Muslim West, the Maghrib – which was controlled by the Fatimid Caliphate. Toward the end of the century, the capital of the Fatimid Caliphate moved to Cairo. The Jewish traders that followed from the Maghrib became known in Egypt as the Maghribi traders, those whose place of origin is the Maghrib.

The Maghribi traders were a minority, with a distinct social identity, within a much larger Jewish population. We do not know how many Maghribi traders operated during the eleventh century, but we do know that the number was not trivial: in 175 documents, 330 different names are mentioned.[4] Most of the Maghribi traders invested in merchandise worth several hundred to several thousand dinars – substantial sums at a time when the monthly expenses of a middle-class family in Fustat were two to three dinars.[5]

The *geniza* documents indicate that eleventh-century Mediterranean trade was free, private, and competitive. They show that there were few official restrictions that fettered migration or the transfer of raw materials, finished goods, or money across the Mediterranean.[6] Within each trade center, commercial transactions were conducted competitively. But trade was characterized by uncertainty over such factors as prices, the duration of the ship's voyage (and whether the ship would reach its destination at all), the condition in which the goods would arrive, and the cost of storage.[7]

To cope with the uncertainty and complexity of trade, the Maghribi traders operated through overseas agents. An overseas agent is anyone who supplies the services required for a commercial venture and shares the capital, profit, or both with a merchant located in a different trade

---

[4] These letters are all those available regarding the trade with Sicily and Israel during the mid-eleventh century and the trade of Naharay ben Nissim. They are a subset of the documents specified in the previous footnote.

[5] See Goitein (1967, pp. 214–17); Gil (1983b, 1:200–8); Greif (1985, pp. 73–6). For expenses, see Goitein (1967, p. 46) and Gil (1983a, p. 91).

[6] Customs, however were imposed. See Gil (1983b, 1:257–8); Goitein (1967, pp. 29–35, 157, 187, 192ff., 266–72); and A. Lewis (1951, pp. 183–224).

[7] See, for example, Dropsie 389, a, lines 4–5, b, lines 27–8, Gil (1983a, pp. 113–25). See also Goitein (1967, pp. 148–64, 200–1, 273–81, 301); Stillman (1970, pp. 70–82); and Greif (1985, pp. 3, 69–78, 92; 1989, 1993).

center. (Henceforth in this chapter and Chapter 9 the term *merchant* is used to denote a person who receives the residual revenue after the agent receives his compensation. The term *trader* refers to both agents and merchants.)

Agents provided merchants with many trade-related services, including loading and unloading ships; paying customs, bribes, and transportation fees; storing the goods; transferring the goods to the market; and deciding when, how, and to whom to sell the goods and at what price and on what credit terms (Goitein 1967, p. 166). Agency relations enabled the Maghribi traders to reduce the cost of trade by better allocating risk by diversifying, by benefiting from agents' expertise, and by shifting trade activities across trade centers, goods, and time. Agency relations enabled merchants to operate as sedentary traders, thus saving the cost and risk of sea journeys. They also enabled traveling merchants to rely on agents to handle their affairs in their absence (Goitein 1967; Greif 1985, 1989).

The efficiency gain from operating through agents is impossible to assess quantitatively. But scholars have recognized the superiority of premodern trade systems in which cooperation through overseas agents prevailed over those in which it did not.[8] That the Maghribi traders themselves saw operating through agents as crucial for business success is reflected both in the extent to which they established agency relations and in their statements. "All profit occurring to me comes from your pocket," wrote one trader to his overseas agent. "People cannot operate without people," wrote another.[9]

3.2 THE COMMITMENT PROBLEM AND THE REPUTATION-BASED COMMUNITY ENFORCEMENT MECHANISM

Transacting in agency services is characterized by a commitment problem. Letting an overseas agent conduct business with capital he does not own increases efficiency, but once the capital is in the agent's possession, the agent can embezzle it. Without a supporting institution, merchants, anticipating this opportunistic behavior, will refuse to operate through agents, and mutually beneficial exchanges in agency service will not be

---

[8] De Roover (1965, pp. 43–6, 70–5); Postan (1973, pp. 66–71); Lopez and Raymond (1955, p. 174).

[9] DK 22, b, line 18, Gil (1983a, pp. 97–106); TS 13 J 25, f. 18, Goitein (1967, p. 164). For the extent of agency relations through business associations, see Stillman (1970) and Michael (1965).

carried out. To surmount this commitment problem, there is a need for an institution enabling an agent to commit himself ex ante, before receiving the merchant's capital, to be honest ex post.[10]

The historical records implicitly indicate the existence of such an institution among the Maghribis, as agency relations were the rule rather than the exception. The *geniza* documents indicate that agency relations were characterized by trust. Despite the many opportunities for agents to cheat, only a handful of documents contain allegations of misconduct (Goitein 1973, p. 7).[11] How was the merchant-agent commitment problem resolved?

It was not resolved by using only family members as agents: in the sample used for this study, less than 12 percent of agency relations involved family members.[12] In some situations, a legal system can surmount a commitment problem inherent in a central transaction by linking it to a coercive (legal) transaction. Beliefs in legal sanctions deter misconduct. But the historical evidence suggests that this was not the case among the Maghribi traders. Many, if not most, of the agency relations reflected in the *geniza* were not based on legal contracts. Only a few documents indicate that commercial disputes between merchants and agents were brought before a court, and the operation of the court in these cases seems to have been expensive and time-consuming.[13]

---

[10] Were a merchant to sell the venture to an overseas agent, he would have to become the agent. Selling it to a local agent meant losing the advantages of an overseas agency.

[11] Misconduct is mentioned in less than 5 percent of the documents examined for this study.

[12] The evidence – commercial correspondence – is not likely to be biased against reflecting intrafamily overseas agency relationships. Information on specific merchants indicates that they hired nonrelatives. Naharay ben Nissim, a prominent merchant in Fustat, used more than 90 different agents. In the sample of contracts studied here, each merchant averaged 3.3 agents (excluding the two merchants with the largest number of agents – 90 and 27 – the average number of agents per merchant was 2.5 agents). This figure represents a lower bound, however, because many merchants probably had agents about whom no record was preserved. It is not possible to calculate the share of capital sent through agents who were family members. The evidence suggests, however, that such an evaluation would not alter the foregoing conclusion.

[13] See discussion in Greif (1989). On the cost of litigation, see Bodl. MS Heb., a3, f. 26, Goitein (1973, p. 97); TS 10 J 4, f. 4, Greif (1985, appendix, pp. 5–7); Bodl. MS Heb., f. 42, Poznanski (1904, pp. 171–2); TS 20.152, Bodl. MS Heb., a3, f. 9, Gil (1983b, 2:724–32). Jews living in the Muslim world at the time could use the Jewish and the Muslim legal systems. The Merchants' correspondence used here is equally likely to reflect the use of either system.

The court also faced difficulties tracking down agents who had emigrated, and it was not structured to collect the information required to adjudicate disputes among traders regarding events that took place months before the trial, in faraway places (Greif 1989, 1993). Several months after the event, for example, a court could not verify the condition of goods upon their arrival, the price received for the goods, the amount of the bribe paid at the port, the cost of delivery, or whether the goods were stolen from the agent's warehouse. Moreover, Jewish law restricts the ability to sue agents. An agent entrusted to buy certain items cannot be sued for "bringing [to the merchant] an item worth 1 [dinar] for [which he charges the merchant] 100 [dinars]."[14] Indeed, in 1095 an agent who received 70 dinars reported having lost all but 20 dinars. The furious merchant, certain that he had been cheated, was unable to sue the agent, because his claim did not have any legal basis.[15]

The conviction of the furious merchant that the agent had cheated him was probably based on information that enabled him to monitor the agent only imperfectly. For diversification, traders were associated with many traders residing in different trade centers. It was customary for merchants to supply their business associates with trade-related information, which was crucial to business success.[16] Reciprocity probably prevented "free riding" on these information flows.[17] Within the Maghribi traders' group, these information flows, together with merchants' experience, reduced the asymmetry of information possessed by merchants and agents, enabling the merchants to monitor agents.[18]

---

[14] Maimonides (1951, p. 208). See discussion in Greif (1989).

[15] TS 13 J 2, f. 5, Goitein (1967, p. 176).

[16] A Sicilian merchant, Jacob ben Isma'il, had at least five business associates in three different trade centers (see Greif 1985, p. 133). An important sedentary merchant like Naharay ben Nissim of Fustat had business relations with dozens of merchants from Spain to Syria (see Michael 1965 and letters to Naharay published in Gil 1983b, 3:96–330).

[17] Trade-related information, including prices, ship arrivals and departures, and the general economic and political situation, appears in many *geniza* documents. See, for example, TS 20.76 and 13 J 15, f. 9, Goitein (1973, pp. 113–19, 320–2); TS 10 J 11, f. 22, a, lines 11–12. Cf. Goitein (1967, pp. 195, 201ff.) and additional references in Greif (1985, p. 95, n. 60). For the importance of information flow for commercial success, see Dropsie 389, a, lines 2–4, Gil (1983a, pp. 113–25); Michael (1965); Gil (1983b, 3:96ff.).

[18] For examples of such information, see DK 22, a, lines 11ff., Gil (1983a, pp. 97–106); ULC Or. 1080 J 42, Gil (1983b, 3:300); TS Box Misc. 28, f. 225, Gil (1983b, 3:96–101).

These information flows also enabled agents to signal that they were honest. Just as modern firms hire auditors to establish the legitimacy of their financial statements, eleventh-century Maghribi agents generally conducted important business in the presence of other coalition members. In their reports they included the names of witnesses the merchant knew, thus enabling the merchant to verify the agent's report.[19]

The ability to monitor, however, was imperfect; a merchant could mistakenly conclude that an agent was dishonest. For example, around the middle of the century Maymun ben Khalpha of Palermo sent a letter to Naharay ben Nissim of Fustat. Discussing a conflict that Naharay had with one of his agents, Maymun makes clear that, in contrast to Naharay, he contends that the agent was honest and should not be accused of cheating.[20]

Ability to monitor agents is a necessary condition for surmounting the commitment problems by intertemporally linking merchant-agent transactions between a particular merchant and agent. Information regarding cheating is necessary for the merchant to adopt the strategy of hiring an agent each period as long as he is honest and never rehiring him if he ever cheats. Belief in this strategy can endogenously motivate the agent to be honest out of the desire to retain his position. To make the prospect of future employment sufficiently attractive to deter cheating, however, the merchant must create a gap between the expected lifetime utility the agent receives from working for the merchant and the agent's best alternative elsewhere. To do so, the merchant must provide the agent a per period premium; for example, he can pay him more than what he can earn elsewhere. Given these beliefs and premiums, a dishonest agent earns a short-run gain until he is caught, whereas an honest agent reaps a long-run gain by earning a premium each period.

This bilateral reputation mechanism relies on intertemporally linking merchant-agent transactions between the same parties.[21] Whenever the relationship between a merchant and an agent is expected to be terminated for exogenous reasons even though the agent was honest, more agency relationships in more situations can be entered into by linking transactions

---

[19] On the use of witnesses, see DK 13, sect. G; ULC Or. 1080 J 48; Bodl. MS Heb., a2, f. 17, all published in Goitein (1973, pp. 32, 92–93, 103). See also the discussion in Goitein (1967, pp. 168, 196) and Greif (1985, p. 143). In certain circumstances, Jewish law requires eyewitnesses. See Maimonides (1951, p. 214).

[20] See DK 22, b, lines 5ff., Gil (1983a).

[21] See discussion of reputation mechanisms and references in Appendix C.

between different merchants and agents. Central to the associated reputation institution is an organization – a group of traders with a specific social identity ("coalition members") – who share information about agents' conduct. Members of this network share the beliefs that coalition merchants will employ only member agents and that each of them will reward his agent enough to keep him honest.[22] All coalition merchants, however, are expected never to employ an agent who cheated while operating on behalf of any coalition member.[23]

More agency relationships in a greater number of situations can be entered into in this case because, other things being equal, these beliefs reduce the premium that a merchant must pay an agent to keep him honest. These beliefs reduce the premium, because they lower the probability that a cheater will be able to earn the premium elsewhere. In addition, these beliefs enable merchants to employ agents for assignments that both parties know ahead of time will be of short duration. Because an agent who considers cheating a particular merchant risks his relations with all coalition members, the agent's lifetime expected utility is robust with respect to the length of his associations with a particular merchant. Hence the premium required to keep an agent honest is unaffected by the expected duration of the agent's dealings with a particular merchant.

Theoretical considerations can generate many hypotheses; evidence is required to verify any postulate. The *geniza* contains direct evidence of the operation of a coalition. It suggests that a multilateral reputation mechanism governed agency relations; merchants conditioned future employment on past conduct, practiced community punishment, and ostracized agents who were considered cheaters until they compensated the injured party. The *geniza* further suggests that agents were ready to forgo current gains in order to sustain their good standing in the merchants' group.

Evidence of collective punishment within the coalition is found in two letters dated 1055. Abun ben Zedaka, an agent living in Jerusalem, was accused of (although not legally charged with) embezzling the money of

---

[22] The coalition, however, was not a monopsony in the usual sense of the term, since, as described later, a Maghribi trader usually operated simultaneously as a merchant and an agent.

[23] Chapter 9 extends the analysis to enable agents to be merchants. If an agent who is caught cheating operates as a merchant, coalition agents who cheat in their dealing with him are not expected to be considered by other coalition members to have cheated.

a Maghribi trader. When word of the accusation reached other Maghribi traders, merchants as far away as Sicily canceled their agency relations with him.[24]

In the first decade of the eleventh century, Samhun ben Da'ud, a prominent trader from Tunisia, sent a long letter to his business associate, Joseph ben 'Awkal of Fustat. The letter reflects the traders' awareness of the importance of the prospect of future relationships as a motivating force. Joseph made this point clear when he made his future dealings with Samhun conditional upon his record: "If your handling of my business is correct, then I shall send you goods."[25] The letter reveals that future relations were conditioned upon past conduct – the essence of the reputation mechanism.

The same letter reveals the use of economic, rather than social, sanctions and the expectations for collective punishment among coalition members. Believing that Samhun had not remitted his revenues on time, Joseph imposed economic sanctions on him by not providing him with agent's services. He ignored Samhun's request to pay two of Samhun's creditors in Fustat and failed even to inform them of Samhun's request. By the time Samhun found out about it, "their letters filled with condemnation had reached everyone." The letters caused Samhun to complain that "my reputation [or honor] is being ruined."[26]

The letter also reveals why agency relations were established and sheds light on their nature. It shows that economic interdependence, not internalized norms regarding mutual help or altruism, motivated the parties. Samhun cited two reasons for acting as Joseph's agent. The first was his desire to receive the agent's share of the profits. "You did not think that I should have a profit through you of even 10 dinars. Although you have made through me ten times as much." Elsewhere he mentions that he sold Joseph's pearls for 100 percent profit and added, "Should I not have taken one quarter of the profit?"[27]

The second reason why Samhun sought to maintain relations with Joseph was to increase the expected value of his capital. "What I do need is the benefit of your high position and for you to take care on my behalf," he writes. "It is my desire to avail myself of your high standing

[24] TS 13 J 25, f. 12; TS 12.279. See also TS 8 J 19, f. 23. These letters are published in Gil (1983b, 3:218–33).
[25] DK 13, a, line 41, Stillman (1970, pp. 267ff.).
[26] DK 13, a, lines 26ff., Stillman (1970, pp. 267ff.).
[27] DK 13, b, lines 12–13, 20–21, Stillman (1970, pp. 267–75).

for those things which I send to you."[28] Note that the merchant is able to create a gap between the future utility stream of an honest agent and that of a cheater by controlling the expected income stream from the agent's capital. This correspondence thus suggests that agents received both a wage premium and a capital premium.

The deterrent effect of fearing the loss of one's reputation is clear from an incident described in a letter sent from Mazara, Sicily, in 1059. The writer had sold flax illegally (before the ships had arrived and the trading season officially opened) in Sfax, Tunisia, receiving an average price of thirteen dinars a load. By the time the ships arrived, the price had dropped to eight dinars a load and the buyers refused to pay the agreed-upon price. Eventually, the buyers paid, solely out of fear of harming their reputations. As the seller wrote, "We were lucky ... if not the [for their fear of losing their] honor ... we wouldn't have received a thing."[29]

A letter sent around 1050 from Maymun ben Khalpha of Palermo to Naharay ben Nissim of Fustat also suggests that relations between a particular agent and merchant were of concern to other coalition members. Discussing a conflict that Naharay had with one of his agents in Palermo, Maymun writes, "You know that he is our [the Maghribi traders'] representative [so the conflict] bothers us all."[30] Another letter, sent around 1060, confirms the deterrent effect that fear of jeopardizing future relations had on opportunistic behavior. In this letter an agent justifies his actions, which caused some loss to the merchant, on the ground that he did not want people to say that he had contradicted the merchant's instructions.[31]

A letter sent in the middle of the eleventh century from a merchant in Palermo to Yeshu'a ben Isma'il in Alexandria further reveals the importance of reputation within the coalition.[32] The merchant describes how he handled the sale of two loads of pepper, one belonging to himself and the other belonging to his partner. The pepper price was very low: "I held [the pepper] until the time when the sailing of the ships approached in the hope [the price] would rise. However, the slump got worse. Then I was afraid that suspicion might arise against me and I sold your pepper to Spanish merchants for 133 [quarter dinars]. ... It was the night before the

---

[28] DK 13, a, line 32 and a, line 43, Stillman (1970, pp. 267–75).

[29] Dropsie 389, b, lines 22ff., Gil (1983a, pp. 113–25). See also Bodl. MS Heb., a3, f. 26 and ULC Or. 1080 J 42, Goitein (1973, pp. 97, 92–5).

[30] DK 22, b, line 5ff., Gil (1983a, pp. 97–106).

[31] Bodl. MS Heb., d66, f. 60, a, margin, lines 7–9, Gil (1983b, 3:216).

[32] Bodl. MS Heb., a3, f. 13, Goitein (1973, p. 123).

sailing of the ships . . . pepper had became much in demand . . . [because] boats [with buyers] arrived. . . . Thus, [the pepper] was sold for 140–142. I took collateral for the sale of my pepper at 140–142. But brother, I would not like to take the profit for myself. Therefore, I transferred the entire sale to our partnership." The merchant decided to share the profits in order to maintain his reputation, even though he did not intend to do business with the partner in the future. "Settle my account with yourself and give the balance to my brother-in-law," he wrote, "for you are a very busy man." The merchant acted honorably solely to maintain his reputation with other coalition members.

The operation of a coalition is based on uncoordinated responses of merchants located in different trade centers. Hence it critically depends on a common cognitive system that ascribes meaning to various actions, particularly actions that constitute cheating. In other words, for the threat of collective punishment to be credible, "cheating" must be defined in a manner that ensures collective response. If some merchants consider specific actions to constitute "cheating" while others hold a different opinion, the effectiveness of the collective threat is undermined.[33] The required coordination can be achieved by specifying an agent's obligations in an explicit contract, ideally a comprehensive contract. But given the state of communication technology and the uncertainty and complexity of trade during the eleventh century, detailed contracts entailed a high negotiation cost. If a merchant and an agent had had to agree on a contract before goods could be shipped to an agent, trade through agents would have been impractical.[34]

Indeed, the *geniza* reflects the extensive use of incomplete contracts, usually in the form of letters with instructions that involved no negotiation. "Do whatever your propitious judgment suggests to you," wrote Musa ben Ya'qub from Tyre, Lebanon, to his partner in Fustat some time in the second half of the eleventh century.[35] Merchants often authorized their agents to do whatever they deemed best if none of the prespecified contingencies occurred.

---

[33] For relevant theory, see Banks and Calvert (1989).

[34] The inappropriateness of comprehensive contracts in long-distance medieval trade is reflected in the difference between the Maliki and the Hanafi schools of law in Islam. See Udovitch (1970, pp. 208–9). For theoretical considerations of the inability to specify comprehensive contracts, see Hart and Moore (1999); Grossman and Hart (1986); O. Williamson (1985); and I. Segal (1999).

[35] ULC Or. 1080 J 42, Goitein (1973, p. 94). For a similar situation in Europe, see Gras (1939, p. 80).

Incomplete contracts, however, undermine the operation of a coalition, because they do not define which actions represent cheating and allow agents to act strategically to take advantage of the incompleteness of the contract.[36] Theoretically, hierarchy (authority) relations may be used as a substitute for an ex ante comprehensive contract by assigning the merchant with the right to make all (ex post) decisions (O. Williamson 1985). Alternatively, culture may substitute for comprehensive contracts by specifying ex ante systematic rules of behavior.[37] Cultural rules can indicate what members of the organization should do after an unforeseen state of nature occurs. Hierarchy does not require ex ante learning of rules, but it does require ex post transmission of information between the parties; culture requires ex ante learning of the rules but no ex post communication.

Given the state of communication and transportation technology in the eleventh century, it is not surprising that the Maghribi traders did not rely on hierarchy.[38] Instead, they employed a set of cultural rules of behavior – merchants' law – that specified how agents needed to act to be considered honest in circumstances not mentioned in the merchant's instructions. The merchants' law was a commonly known rule among the Maghribi that served as a default contract between agents and merchants. Agents who were known not to have followed the merchants law were considered cheaters.

The importance of the merchants' law in determining expectations about and attitudes toward an agent's behavior is reflected in the letter written by Maymun ben Khalpha to Naharay ben Nissim. In discussing the conflict between Naharay and his agent, Maymun justified the agent's actions by arguing that the agent "did something which is imposed by the trade and the communication [system; what you asked him to do] contradicts the merchants' law." (Another way to translate the term used is as "the way of the trade.)" In another letter, a "very angry" merchant accused his business associate of taking "actions [that] are not those of a merchant."[39]

---

[36] Such behavior is reflected in Dropsie 389, Gil (1983a).

[37] See discussion in Camerer and Vespsalaninen (1987) and Landa (1988). Cf. Kreps (1990b).

[38] See DK 22, a, lines 9–11, Gil (1983a, pp. 97–106) for explicit statement indicating that it was impractical for an agent to await new instructions when an unspecified contingency occurred.

[39] DK 22, b, lines 5ff., Gil (1983a, pp. 97–106); TS 12.434 l.7, Goitein (1967, p. 202, n. 50). See also Goitein (1967, p. 171).

Little is known about the content of the merchants' law. The most convincing evidence for its existence and the process by which it emerged is found outside the *geniza*. In the middle of the twelfth century, Maimonides, an important Jewish spiritual leader who lived in Fustat, wrote in his legal code, "If [an agent] enters a partnership with another without specifying any terms, he should not deviate from the custom current in the land in regard to the merchandise they deal with" (Maimonides 1951, p. 223).[40] Similarly, the early medieval Islamic legal literature contains numerous instances in which systematic legal reasoning is suspended because of the "custom of the merchants" (Udovitch 1970, pp. 13, 250–9). Unfortunately, neither the legal literature nor the *geniza* documents reflect exactly how the merchants' law was formulated and changed.[41]

Within the Maghribi traders' coalition, the merchants' law promoted efficiency by providing a coordination device necessary for the functioning of the coalition, economizing on negotiating cost, and enabling flexibility in establishing agency relations. The merchants' law also imposed rigidity on the system, however, as the process of adjusting it was probably impeded by agents' concerns about what others would think about their actions rather than what the outcome of their actions would be. This is reflected in the words of Joseph ben Yeshua, an eleventh-century agent who wrote to a merchant that he could not act without written instructions, because he did not wish that "people will . . . say that I did something that I was not ordered."[42]

The historical record indicates the importance of a reputation-based institution. Informal, community-based contract enforcement mechanisms enabled the operation of a market in agency services. The historical evidence, however, raises many questions. Why was the community punishment self-enforcing? Why was the boycott of cheaters not undermined by agents' ability to seek employment with non-Maghribis? Why was the merchants' commitment to future employment of honest agents credible despite their ability to hire non-Maghribi agents?

---

[40] By that he did not mean a particular partnership form but partnership in general. This may indicate that the merchants' law was not specific to the Maghribi traders' coalition but was shared by a larger group. In the *geniza*, see DK 13, b, lines 7ff., Stillman (1970, p. 272); Dropsie 389, b, lines 22–23, Gil (1983a, pp. 113–25); TS 20.26, sect. I, Goitein (1973, p. 117).

[41] See, however, DK 22, on the a. margin, Gil (1983a, pp. 97–106); Goitein (1973, pp. 111–12); and Greif (1985, p. 136).

[42] Bodl. MS Heb., d66, f. 60, a. margin lines 7–9, Gil (1983b, 3:216).

3.3 THE MODEL: THE AGENT COMMITMENT PROBLEM AND
THE MULTILATERAL PUNISHMENT STRATEGY

The questions raised in section 3.2 can be addressed using an explicit model. The analysis evaluates the claim that such a coalition was possible and furthers our understanding of its operation. Constructing a model with which to examine the functioning of a contract enforcement institution in a specific historical episode presents a methodological problem. Should the model's assumptions be restricted only to those reflected in the historical records? Or is any assumption about the model that does not conflict with the evidence legitimate? The position taken here (for reasons elaborated in Part IV) is that, to the extent possible, the model should be based on assumptions that are justifiable by the historical evidence, and it should account for the phenomena under consideration using the fewest additional assumptions.

The model presented here therefore does not impose the assumption that generates perhaps the most intuitive explanation for collective punishment – that merchants perceive an agent who cheated to be a "bad type" who will continue to cheat in the future.[43] There is no evidence to justify such an assumption, directly or indirectly, by indicating that an agent who had proved honest in the past was considered to be more likely to be honest in the future. On the contrary, there is evidence suggesting that merchants were likely to participate in collective punishment even when they believed that the agent was honest. In a letter quoted earlier, Maymun makes clear that he believes that Naharay's agent was honest and "should not be accused [of cheating]." Maymun feared that if the agent were openly accused, it would affect his relations with the agent, presumably since Maymun would have to participate in collective punishment.[44]

A model based on agents' types seems unable to provide a satisfactory explanation for some historical phenomena. For example, as discussed later, the Maghribis did not maintain agency relations with Jewish traders from Italy, although, ignoring agency cost, the Maghribis perceived such relations as very profitable. A model based on agents' types can account

---

[43] See discussion in Appendix C. Institutions with information sharing and collective punishment can also reflect such asymmetric information (see Kali 1999 and Annen 2003).

[44] DK 22, b, lines 5ff., Gil (1983a, pp. 97–106). Similar considerations led to the rejection of a model in which costly participation in collective punishment is motived by punishing individuals who failed to punish a cheater (see Pearce 1995 and Kandori 1992).

for this behavior, but it requires either making strategies contingent on social affiliations or assuming that members of one group could not verify whether a particular member of the other group ever cheated (implying that a non-Maghribi could not free-ride on the information generated by the Maghribis by observing their actions). Neither possibility is appealing. There is no reason to believe that various Jewish traders "discriminated" against one another, and whether a particular individual was serving as an agent could easily be observed, because merchants could examine a ship's cargo, ownership, and destination (see Goitein 1967, pp. 336–7).

The model used here, which is based on the historical evidence, reveals another mechanism that can support collective punishment and account for other historical phenomena. In this model, collective punishment is feasible due to the availability of information; it is self-enforcing due to the link between expectations about future hiring and the stream of rent required to keep an agent honest. To simplify the presentation, the model ignores the possible importance of imperfect monitoring.[45] The model is aimed at capturing the essence of intertransactional linkages and the associated institutional elements that generated behavior among the Maghribis.

Consider a perfect and complete information economy in which there are M merchants and A agents, each of whom lives an infinite number of periods. The Maghribi traders did not, of course, enjoy infinite life-spans, but relatives were considered morally responsible for one another's business dealings, and traders' sons became traders, serving as their parents' old-age insurance policies.[46] Hence the value of one's reputation did not diminish with old age. In considering the conditions under which reputation induces honesty, it therefore seems appropriate to assume an infinite horizon.

---

[45] To capture the asymmetry and imperfectness of information, as well as commercial uncertainty, the model presented here can be extended as follows: revenue is observed only by the agent and is a random variable x with domain $[a, b]$. The agent reports a revenue realization $y \in [a, b]$. A wage is a contract that is a function of the agent's report, $w{:}[a, b] \rightarrow [a, b]$, $w(y) \leq y \; \forall \; y$. The merchant observes the actual realization with probability $f(y, x)$, where $1 > f(.) > 0, \forall \; y \neq x$ (information asymmetry), and $f(.) > 0$ when $x = y$ (imperfect monitoring). The path of play in imperfect monitoring models is characterized by episodes of noncooperation; in some periods the agent is punished for perceived cheating by not being hired (see Appendix C, section C. 2.7).

[46] See Goitein (1973, p. 60). Goitein (1978, pp. 33ff.) notes that "both the government and public opinion were prone to hold a father, or brother, or even more distant relative responsible for a man's commitments, although strict law, both Islamic and Judaic, did not recognize such a claim."

Assume (in accordance with the historical evidence) that there are less merchants than agents, M < A.[47] Agents have a time discount factor δ, and an unemployed agent receives a per period reservation utility of w̄ ≥ 0. In each period, an agent can be hired by only one merchant and a merchant can employ only one agent. Matching is random, but a merchant can restrict the matching to a subset of the unemployed agents made up of agents who, according to the information available to the merchant, have previously taken particular sequences of actions.[48]

A merchant who does not hire an agent receives a payoff of κ > 0. The gross gain from cooperation is γ. A merchant who hires an agent decides what wage (W ≥ 0) to offer the agent. Because an employed agent held the merchant's capital, it is appropriate to assume that an agent is ensured of receiving his wage. An employed agent can decide whether to be honest or to cheat, and his actions are public information. If the agent is honest, the merchant's payoff is γ − W, and the agent's payoff is W. If he cheats, his payoff is α > 0 and the merchant's payoff is γ − α. It is assumed that γ > κ + w̄ (cooperation is efficient); γ > α > w̄ (cheating entails a loss, and an agent prefers cheating over receiving his reservation utility); and κ > γ − α (a merchant prefers not to hire an agent and to receive κ over being cheated or paying a wage as high as the amount the agent can cheat him by).

After the allocation of the payoffs, each merchant can decide whether to terminate his relations with his agent. There is a probability τ, however, that a merchant is forced to terminate agency relations. The need to shift commercial operations over places and goods – and the high level of uncertainty of commerce and life during the eleventh century – curtailed a merchant's ability to commit himself to future wages or employment. Hence the model assumes a stationary wage scheme (which was indeed practiced among the Maghribis) and a limited ability to commit to future employment.[49] Finally, wages were neither politically nor legally determined, and there is no evidence of collusion in wage determination.

---

[47] More specifically, the historical evidence indicates that merchants were not deferred from terminating agency relationships due to fear of being unable to hire an alternative agent.

[48] The following assumes that the probability of rematching with the same agent equals zero for all practical consideration.

[49] For an efficiency wage model in which this result is derived endogenously, see MacLeod and Malcomson (1989). Their approach could be utilized here as well; it is omitted to maintain simplicity. Levin (2003) has established that self-enforcing contracts in repeated settings with moral hazard will generally be simple and stationary.

Accordingly, the analysis assumes that no subgroup is organized in a way that affects wage determination.

Analyzing this model – a version of a one-sided prisoner's dilemma game – highlights why the collective punishment was self-enforcing among the Maghribis. Consider a multilateral (collective) punishment strategy combination according to which a merchant offers an agent a wage W^*, rehires the same agent if he was honest (unless forced separation occurred), fires the agent if he cheated, never hires an agent who has ever cheated any merchant, and (randomly) chooses an agent from among the unemployed agents who never cheated if forced separation occurred. An agent's strategy calls for being honest if paid W^* and for cheating if paid less than $\dot{W}^*$. Is a multilateral punishment strategy a subgame perfect equilibrium? Will a merchant punish an agent who did not cheat him?

To address these questions it is necessary to consider the factors determining the wage, W^*, that will be offered by the merchants. Let h_h denote the probability that an unemployed honest agent (i.e., an agent who was honest when last employed) will be rehired. Let h_c denote the probability that an unemployed cheater (i.e., an agent who cheated when last employed) will be rehired. Proposition 3.1 presents the relationship between the model's parameters, these probabilities, and the lowest wage for which an agent's best response is to be honest.[50]

Proposition 3.1: Assume that $\delta \in (0, 1)$, $h_c < 1$. The *optimal wage*, the minimum (symmetric) wage for which, if offered by all merchants, an agent's best response is to be honest, is $W^* = w(\delta, h_h, h_c, \tau, \bar{w}, \alpha) > \bar{w}$, where w is monotonically decreasing in δ and h_h and monotonically increasing in h_c, τ, $\bar{w}$, and α.[51] (Proof is given in annex 3.1.)

Under a multilateral punishment strategy, what motivates an agent to be honest is the carrot of receiving a premium over his reservation utility and the stick of being fired. If the difference between the present value of the lifetime expected utility of an unemployed cheater and an employed agent is higher than the one-period gain from cheating, an agent's best response is to be honest. The optimal wage thus decreases if an honest

---

[50] This specification enables the optimal wage under both the multilateral and bilateral punishment strategies discussed later to be examined.

[51] More precisely, this monotonicity is weak at some neighborhoods of the extreme values of the parameters.

agent is more likely to receive future wage premiums (higher h_h), can gain less by cheating (lower α), is more likely to remain employed if he is honest (lower τ), has worse opportunities elsewhere (lower $\bar{w}$), and has a smaller chance of being hired if he cheats (lower h_c). Further, the optimal wage decreases as an agent values future income more (higher δ), because rewarding for honesty and punishing for cheating is done in the future.

For a multilateral punishment strategy to constitute a symmetric sub-game perfect equilibrium, each merchant should find it optimal to hire agents. On the equilibrium path, this condition means that the wage is set low enough – that is, $W^* = w(., h_c, h_h) \leq \gamma - \kappa$, where $h_c = 0$, and $h_h = \tau M/(A - (1 - \tau)M)$.[52] Assume that this condition holds. Will a merchant find it optimal to punish an agent who did not cheat him? When switching agents does not impose any cost – as assumed here – merchants may as well punish a cheater; hence the multilateral punishment strategy is a subgame perfect equilibrium. Having the credibility of multilateral punishment rest on a knife-edge result, however, is unsatisfactory. Clearly, Maymun be Khalpha considered that punishing the Sicilian agent was costly. Therefore, a more relevant question is whether the multilateral punishment strategy motivates a merchant *strictly* to prefer hiring an honest agent over a cheater.

As proposition 3.2 demonstrates, a merchant strictly prefers to hire an honest agent under the multilateral punishment strategy merely because a cheater is not expected to be hired by other merchants. An honest agent is expected to be hired in the future, but an agent who has ever cheated is not. Because the optimal wage decreases in the probability of future hiring, a cheater's optimal wage is higher than an honest agent's wage. Hence each merchant strictly prefers to hire an honest agent. The uncoordinated response of all the merchants and the interrelations between their expected future behavior and an agent's optimal wage as perceived by an individual merchant ensure solidarity of incentives. The possibility of forced separation links the optimal wage a particular merchant has to pay his agent and the agent's expected future relations with other merchants. This link increases the optimal cheater's wage above an honest agent's wage, because punishments are independent of the agent's past conduct while rewards are not. Hence merchants find it optimal to follow the multilateral punishment, *despite* the fact that the agent's strategy does not call for cheating any merchant who violated the collective punishment,

---

[52] These probabilities are induced by the strategies.

and *despite* the fact that cheating in the past does not indicate that the agent is a "lemon." Hence it is reasonable that Maymun was concerned about Naharay's interpretation of his agent's actions, because open accusation would have initiated an uncoordinated response that would have affected Maymun's business with that agent.[53]

> **Proposition 3.2:** Assume that $\delta \in (0, 1)$ and $h_c < 1$. Under a multilateral punishment strategy, a merchant *strictly* prefers to hire an honest agent. (Proof is given in annex 3.1.)

3.4 THE MAGHRIBI TRADERS' COALITION: THEORY AND INDIRECT EVIDENCE

The historical anecdotes presented in section 3.2 suggest that contract enforcement among the Maghribis was achieved by collective punishment. The model and its equilibrium analysis lend support to the conjecture about the importance of this reputation mechanism by indicating that it is logically consistent. But we can do better than that. It is possible to substantiate the hypothesis further by considering the model's implications. A coherent explanation of historical observations can be advanced based on the assertion that a coalition governed agency relations. Predictions based on this assertion can be generated and confirmed by historical records.

The record is rich in facts that should be explained. The Maghribis were the descendants of merchants who lived in the 'Abbasid Caliphate, centered in Baghdad until the first half of the tenth century. Military conflicts and political instability caused these merchants to emigrate during the tenth century, mainly to Tunisia, which prospered at the time, under the control of the Fatimid Caliphate. With time these traders extended their trade from Spain to Constantinople. While the agency relations required for this expansion could have been established with non-Maghribi traders (Jewish or Muslim), evidence of such relations is rare. Instead, members of the Maghribi traders' group emigrated to Spain,

---

[53] One document (Bodl. MS Heb., a2, f. 17, sect. D, Goitein 1973, p. 104) also reveals another, related way through which the expectations for collective punishment rendered it self-enforcing. Because traders usually acted as both merchants and agents, they maintained "open accounts" with other traders – that is, accounts that were cleared only periodically. When an agent was rumored to be in trouble, traders feared that he would not be able to pay his debts. As a preventive measure, they ceased sending him goods and held on to the money they owed him.

Sicily, Egypt, and Palestine. For generations members of these colonies maintained agency relations with the descendants of other Maghribi traders.[54]

Because the Maghribis lived in the Arab world for centuries, they adopted its customs and language. Hence, emigration outside the Arab sphere of influence was culturally and materially difficult. Indeed, the Maghribis did not emigrate to the emerging trade centers of Italy, despite their perception that trade with the Christian world was very profitable.[55] This perception is reflected, for example, in the words of a merchant from Palermo, who complained around 1035 that even the Rums (in this case, Christians from the Latin world) were not ready to buy the inferior black ginger.[56] Arguably, it was often easy to sell them inferior goods for prices no one else was willing to pay. Despite the perceived profitability of this trade, Maghribi traders did not establish agency relations with Jewish traders from Italy who were active during this period. The communities within which the Maghribi traders operated maintained communal ties with the Italian Jewish communities, and no political restrictions hindered cooperation between the Maghribis and the Italian Jews. Yet there is no evidence of agency relations between the Maghribis and Jewish traders from the Christian world.

In the trade centers to which the Maghribi traders emigrated, a well-established Jewish community already existed, into which the Maghribi traders integrated. But as long as they were active in long-distance trade, they preserved a separate social identity. This identity is reflected in documents in which they refer to themselves as "our people, the Maghribis, the travelers (traders)."[57]

The Maghribis operated in the Mediterranean Sea during the eleventh century, until the Italian and more generally European military and commercial ascendancy in that area drove merchants from the Muslim world away. The Maghribis then turned to the Indian Ocean trade, until the end

---

[54] Goitein (1967, pp. 156–9, 186–92); Gil (1983b, 1:200ff.); Greif (1985, pp. 124–7).

[55] See, for example, TS 8 Ja I, f. 5, Goitein (1973, pp. 44–5); Goitein (1973, p. 211); and Greif (1989).

[56] Dropsie 389, b, lines 6ff., Goitein (1973, p. 45). See also Bodl. MS Heb., c28, f. 11, lines 11–13.

[57] Gil (1971, pp. 12–15; 1983b, 1:215, 223); Goitein (1967, pp. 30–4, 148–9, 157); Greif (1985, p. 153, n. 32); and see, for example, DK 13, sect. G, F, Goitein (1973, p. 32); TS Box Misc. 25, f. 106, a, line 9, Gil (1983b, 2:734); TS 13 J 26, f. 24, b, lines 3–5; TS Box Misc 25, f. 106, line 9, Gil (1983b, 2:601, 734).

of the twelfth century, when they were forced by the Muslim rulers of Egypt to withdraw.[58] At that point they integrated with the larger Jewish communities and vanished from the stage of history.

These historical observations raise intriguing questions. Why did the Maghribis not establish seemingly profitable agency relations with non-Maghribis? How can the governance of agency relations by a coalition and the possibility of establishing an agency with nonmembers be reconciled? The possibility of hiring nonmember agents seems to undermine the member merchants' commitment to hire honest member agents in the future, and it seems to undermine the effectiveness of collective punishment, because agents can potentially forge agency relations with nonmember merchants. What ensured the closeness of the coalition? Why was it self-enforcing and hence sustainable?

To support the hypothesis that a coalition governed agency relations, these issues should be explained in a way that is consistent with the assertion that agency relations were governed by a coalition. Furthermore, theoretical insights consistent with this assertion should be able to tie the Maghribis' immigration to Tunisia with the emergence of the coalition, as well as account for the fact that the Maghribis retained their social identity only as long as they were active in long-distance trade.

To address these questions, we need to examine the relations between coalition and efficiency. A coalition increases efficiency relative to a situation in which agency relations are governed by the bilateral punishment strategy. This bilateral strategy is identical to the multilateral punishment strategy, except that merchants do not condition their hiring on past conduct (because they do not have information regarding past actions, they do not expect others to make hiring conditional on that information, or they do not observe the wage paid to the agent and believe that cheating reflects underpayment).

Under a bilateral punishment strategy, merchants do not hire agents in situations in which they would hire agents under a multilateral punishment strategy. Consider, for example, the case in which each merchant can commit himself to hire an agent for only one period ($\tau = 1$). Under this condition, in a bilateral punishment strategy, for any finite wage agents will cheat. Agents are thus never hired. In contrast, under a multilateral punishment strategy, an agent takes into account the implications of cheating a particular merchant on his future employment with other

---

[58] For the Maghribis' trade in the Indian Ocean, see Fischel (1958).

merchants. The optimal wage will be finite and may be low enough to support cooperation.

Indeed, agency relations among the Maghribis were extremely flexible, as merchants operated through several agents at the same time and even at the same trade center. Agency relations were initiated and canceled with ease, depending on merchants' needs (Stillman 1970; Greif 1985).

Proposition 3.3 indicates that in general a multilateral punishment strategy supports cooperation when a bilateral punishment strategy fails to do so, due to the limited ability of each merchant to commit himself to rehire an honest agent by decreasing the probability that a cheater will be rehired, h_c.

Proposition 3.3: For ease of presentation, suppose that the agents' time discount factor approaches one ($\delta \to 1$). Define a as the ratio of agents to merchants, $a = A/M$. Recall that $\bar{w} < \alpha$ and $a > 1$. Given a, cooperation is feasible for all $\tau \in [0, 1]$ if and only if $\gamma - \kappa \geq (a - 1)\bar{w} + \alpha + \epsilon, \forall \epsilon > 0$ under a bilateral punishment strategy but if and only if $\gamma - \kappa \geq a\bar{w} + \epsilon, \forall \epsilon > 0$ under a multilateral punishment strategy. Given τ, cooperation is feasible for all $a \geq 1$ if and only if $(\gamma - \kappa) \geq \alpha + \epsilon, \forall \epsilon > 0$ under a bilateral punishment strategy but if and only if $(\gamma - \kappa) \geq \bar{w} + \epsilon, \forall \epsilon > 0$ under a multilateral punishment strategy. (Proof is given in annex 3.1.)

A multilateral punishment strategy enhances efficiency, because it enables cooperation when the ability of each merchant to commit to hire an agent in the future is limited. As long as the ability of a merchant to commit to hiring an agent in the future is less than perfect, a coalition decreases the wage, W^*, relative to the wage that prevails when a bilateral punishment strategy governs agency relations. This reduction reflects a decrease in the probability that a cheater will be hired, (h_c), and an increase in the probability that an honest agent will be hired (h_h). This wage reduction enhances efficiency by making agency relations profitable in situations in which the total gain from cooperation is relatively low (γ is small). Although in such cases cooperation is efficient, it will be initiated only if it is profitable to a merchant, that is, $W^* \leq \gamma - \kappa$. Because the wage under a multilateral punishment strategy is lower than under a bilateral punishment strategy, more cooperation will be initiated. The wage reduction and the enhanced efficiency imply that organizing agency relations in a coalition increases member merchants' profits and may increase the lifetime expected utility of an honest agent who is a coalition member relative to that of an honest agent under a bilateral punishment strategy.

Efficiency gains generated by a coalition encourage its emergence; the coalition rewards member merchants and agents in a manner that encourages agency relations among coalition members. Hence by affecting efficiency and profitability, the beliefs that members will hire and be hired only internally can be self-enforcing: member merchants are motivated to establish agency relations with member agents, and member agents are better off being employed by member merchants.

Additional factors also contribute to this result. Expectations with respect to future hiring, the benefits provided by the network for information transmission, and strategic considerations discouraged members from initiating agency relations with nonmembers, and they discouraged nonmembers from initiating agency relations with members.

To see the impact of these factors, consider an economy with two identical coalitions. By definition, coalition members are not expected to establish intercoalition agency relations. Will these expectations be self-enforcing? A merchant will initiate intercoalition agency relations only if it is expected – that is, the institutionalized beliefs hold – that the other coalition's merchants will employ a multilateral punishment strategy against a member agent who cheated a nonmember merchant. Otherwise, the merchant strictly prefers to establish intracoalition agency relations because the optimal wage in intercoalition agency relations is $w(., h_c = h_h > 0)$, which, by proposition 3.1, is strictly higher than the optimal wage in intracoalition agency relations, $w(., h_c = 0, h_h > 0)$. For this wage differential to exist, it is sufficient that the merchant be uncertain about whether a multilateral punishment strategy will be applied in intercoalition relations.[59]

A merchant is likely to be uncertain about whether a multilateral punishment strategy will be applied in intercoalition relations due to information barriers between coalitions and strategic considerations. The fact that within a coalition each trader is known to others enables informal information flows, which the agent does not control, to facilitate monitoring

---

[59] The formal analysis of this argument is presented in propositions 9.4 and 9.5, which consider a more general issue – the implications of different beliefs regarding behavior off-the-path-of-play on the motivation to establish intereconomy agency relations.

and to inform traders about cheating. This mechanism does not function in intercoalition agency relations. Furthermore, coalition members are strategically motivated to ignore an outsider's accusations concerning the conduct of a coalition member agent. If the coalition members simply take the word of an outsider, an agent is vulnerable to blackmail by nonmembers, which reduces his lifetime expected utility as an honest agent. This reduction comes at the expense of member merchants, because it increases the optimal wage. Hence coalition members find it optimal to ignore outsiders' accusations. In contrast, insiders' accusations are not likely to be ignored, because they can be assessed more accurately and an insider merchant puts his own reputation on the line in accusing an agent. Khalluf ben Musa seems to have regretted ignoring insiders' accusations when he wrote to his partner in response to the accusation that he had retained revenues received for the partner's goods, "had I listened to what people say, I never would have entered into a partnership with you."[60]

As a multilateral punishment strategy does not apply in intercoalition relations, the wage required to keep an agent honest in intercoalition agency relations is higher than the intracoalition wage. Merchants are thus discouraged from establishing intercoalition agency relations, and the expectations that intercoalition agency relations will not be initiated are self-enforcing. Note that this result holds even in some situations in which these intercoalition relations are more efficient. More precisely, intercoalition agency relations will not be established if the increase in the gains from cooperation does not compensate a merchant for the wage increase.

Expectations with respect to future hiring, the nature of the networks for information transmission, and strategic considerations ensure the self-enforceability of a coalition. These factors encourage member merchants to hire only member agents and discourage member merchants from hiring nonmember agents. They enable member merchants to commit to hire only member agents, even if efficient agency relations can be established with nonmembers. At the same time, these factors make collective punishment effective, by discouraging nonmember merchants from hiring member agents, thus enabling member agents to commit themselves not to enter agency relations outside the coalition. By discouraging intercoalition

[60] Bodl. MS Heb., a3, f. 13, sect. B, Goitein (1973, p. 121). See also DK 13, sect. G; ULC Or. 1080 J 48; Bodl. MS Heb., a2, f. 17, Goitein (1973, pp. 32, 92–93, 103); Goitein (1967, pp. 168, 196); Greif (1985: 143).

agency relations, these factors contribute to making the beliefs on which the coalition rests self-enforcing. Hence once a coalition is formed through some historical process, agency relations will be established only among the traders about whom expectations were initially crystallized.

These theoretical observations suggest that the informal social networks for information transmission, which became available to the Maghribis in the process of immigrating to Tunisia, enabled them to support agency relations based on a multilateral punishment strategy.[61] This immigration process determined the social identity (position) of the individuals with respect to whom expectations of collective punishment and future hiring were established. Within the resulting coalition, information regarding the circumstances an agent faced was essentially free, because it was obtained as a by-product of commercial activity and passed on along with other commercial correspondence. The fact that the marginal cost of obtaining this information was essentially zero is important, because it made credible the merchant's claim that he would monitor his agents. Without such monitoring, the reputation mechanism could not have functioned.[62]

Once these beliefs were institutionalized – once the Maghribi traders' coalition was formed – only descendants of Maghribis were perceived by others to be members, and hence only they could become members. The factors that encouraged intracoalition agency relations and discouraged agency relations with nonmembers made membership a valuable asset. For this reason, the descendants of Maghribi traders continued to be active in long-distance commerce as members of the Maghribi traders' coalition. This, in turn, implied that each trader had a horizon long enough to render a reputation mechanism effective, because his children could have been punished if he defaulted.

As the Maghribis expanded the geographical scope of their trade, the profitability of intracoalition agency relations became high enough to encourage emigration and the establishment of colonies in other trade centers. Because Maghribi merchants were motivated to employ other coalition members, they were able to commit themselves to future employment of Maghribi agents. This ensured the emigrants that they would be

---

[61] It was a necessary but not sufficient condition. See Chapter 9 regarding the importance of cultural beliefs in leading to the coalition.

[62] According to the theory advanced here, agents do not cheat. Thus, if monitoring agents is costly, it is not credible. Knowing that the merchants will not monitor, agents will cheat. Anticipating this, a merchant will not employ agents to begin with.

compensated for the cost of emigration. Emigration to Italy was more difficult culturally and therefore forgone. Nonmember Italian Jews were not employed as agents, despite the common religion and the potential gains from trade with Italy, since the additional gains from establishing agency relations outside the coalition did not compensate for the relatively high agency cost.[63]

The Maghribi traders' social structure was an organization that provided them with the initial information-transmission mechanism required for the emergence of an economic institution – the Maghribi traders' coalition. This economic institution for the governing of agency relations provided the interactions required to sustain the social structure, while the Maghribis' social identity provided the means to coordinate expectations required for the functioning of the coalition. When the Maghribis were forced by the Muslim rulers to cease operating in long-distance trade and their coalition ceased to function, the motivation for social interactions diminished, their social structure lost its vitality, and the Maghribi traders assimilated into the broader Jewish community.

The discussion of the credibility of the collective punishment and endogenous information flows suggests that as long at the Maghribi traders coalition survived, its functioning crucially depended on maintaining an appropriate size. The credibility of collective punishment rests on the coalition being sufficiently large that one agent can be used as a substitute for another if the latter cheats. But, everything else being equal, a larger coalition implies a slower circulation of information and hence delayed punishment (which can be captured in the model by making the time discount factor an increasing function of the coalition size).

The conjecture about the operation of a multilateral reputation mechanism gains further support from illuminating the rationale behind patterns of bookkeeping and employment of agents among the Maghribi traders.

---

[63] Goitein (1967) conjectures that the lack of evidence of such relationships reflects selection bias, as the correspondents did not pass through Egypt. Yet the *geniza* is rich in documents reflecting agency relationships with agents in North Africa, Sicily, and Spain. In many cases, we learn about trade in Spain from communication with agents in Sicily, and this island was also en route to Italy. Consistent with the argument advanced here, the Maghribis did integrate with other communities in matters unrelated to agency relationship. Such non-agency-related relationships are well reflected in the *geniza* (Goitein 1967). Yet agency relationships rarely appear. For example, in the letters of Naharay ben Nissim, the most important Maghribi trader in Fustat in the mid-eleventh century, only two of the ninety-seven different traders mentioned were Muslims (Michael 1965).

Agency relations among the Maghribis resembled the relations between a modern firm and its workers in that typically no explicit legal commitment governed the length of the relationship. When a commitment was made, it was for a short period of time. The duration of agency relations varied from a single season to several generations, with sons replacing their fathers as agents.[64] The Maghribi traders used a per trade venture rather than multiventure accounting system, in which the income and expenses associated with each trade venture were detailed (Goitein 1967, pp. 178, 204–9).

These trade practices are consistent with the operation of a reputation mechanism within a coalition. Whenever a reputation mechanism is employed, a merchant may prefer short-term contracts, because the shorter the contract, the sooner the merchant can discover deviation and the less he will have to pay to keep an agent honest. A per venture accounting system is more efficient than a multiventure accounting system whenever a reputation mechanism is employed, because it facilitates comparing agents' reports with any relevant information.

The historical evidence presents other puzzling questions. Why did most Maghribi traders operate as both merchants and agents? Why did the Maghribis employ agents through particular contractual forms? Why did different practices prevail among other comparable traders' groups, such as the Italians, who also operated around then? Were efficiency and profitability sufficient to lead to the emergence of the coalition? These questions are better addressed in the context of a comparative study between these groups, presented in Chapter 9.[65]

3.5 CONCLUDING COMMENTS

The Maghribi traders' coalition mitigated problems of contract enforceability and coordination that arose in complex trade characterized by asymmetric information, slow communication technology, inability to

---

[64] Goitein (1967, pp. 169–70, 178) and Greif (1985, p. 133). In the Italian trade cities, *commenda* relations were also of short duration (see, e.g., Lopez 1952, p. 323). Sons did not inherit their fathers' businesses per se, but members of the younger generation began providing agency services to each other.

[65] The historical evidence presents another puzzling question: why did Maghribi agents not cheat and begin to operate as merchants? The model presented here ignores this issue by assuming that an agent consumes whatever he appropriates. I address this issue in Chapter 9.

specify comprehensive contracts, and limited legal contract enforceability. Within the coalition, information flows enabled monitoring and made cheating known, while a merchants' law coordinated responses. The multilateral punishment, the value of the information flows for commercial success, and the importance of the merchants' law as a substitute for comprehensive contracts generated wage and capital premiums. Receiving these premiums was conditional on past conduct, while intergenerational transfers ensured a horizon long enough to support the operation of a reputation mechanism. Because the present value of the premiums was larger than what an agent could gain by cheating, agents could credibly commit themselves to be honest, and merchants could trust them.

The coalition reflects intertransactional linkages and institutional elements exogenous to each individual whose behavior it influenced. It illustrates the importance of going beyond the confines of classical contract theory in economics (surveyed in Hart and Holmstrom 1987), which explores how bilateral contracts mitigate contractual problems. The analysis of the Maghribis highlights the importance of the social context in mitigating bilateral contractual problems. The Maghribi traders' group was a means of linking information-sharing transactions among merchants and fostering the personal familiarity required to render a threat of collective punishment credible. Beliefs about future hiring and collective punishment among the members of this organization linked each merchant-agent transaction with agents' future transactions with all Maghribi traders. The Maghribi traders' group and the commonly known beliefs in collective punishment were exogenous to each individual trader, while each member's best response to them was to maintain his affiliation with the group and to participate in collective punishment. Hence the coalition was self-enforcing and the threat of collective punishment credible. The commonly known merchants' law lent credibility to the threat of collective punishment by providing the unified interpretation of actions and facilitating a coordinated response.

The institution that supported trust among the Maghribi traders was composed of several interrelated social factors, rules, beliefs, and organizations. Together, these institutional elements enabled, guided, and motivated a particular regularity of behavior, namely, the intragroup hiring of agents and honesty. Rules provided the common cognition, coordination, and information that enabled and guided behavior in the related transactions. They enabled traders to make informed decisions by providing micro-foundations of behavior. Rules specified, for example, the structure of the situation, who held membership in the Maghribi traders' coalition, how one gained relevant information, which actions constituted cheating, how one complained about it, and what behavior was expected of merchants and agents if cheating transpired.

Beliefs motivated the traders to follow the behavioral instructions provided by these rules. It was common knowledge that the prevailing internalized and behavioral beliefs were that merchants would hire only Marghribi agents and would participate in collective punishment, and that agents would not be employed by nonmembers and would be honest. Given this, it was optimal for most traders, in general, to follow the behavioral instructions provided by the rules. The Maghribi traders group constituted a means for rules to be specified and information generated and disseminated. In particular, information flows within the group and the common interpretation of agents' actions increased the set of situations in which agents could credibly commit to be honest.

The origin and size of the coalition do not reflect the function it served. Rather, they reflect the relationships between an immigration process, the resulting social group, and, as elaborated in Chapter 9, historically inherited cultural beliefs. The social identity of and network for information transmission within an immigrant group determined the coalition's initial size. In the resulting coalition, the original social identity served as a signal that coordinated actions and expectations. By promoting agency relations and information transmission among a particular group of individuals, the economic institution that governed agency relations preserved the initial social structure, which in turn determined the boundaries of the economic institution.

By reducing agency costs and other transactions costs, the coalition promoted efficiency and profitability among its members. It provided the foundations for the operation of a market in agents' services, enabling merchants to operate through agents even when the cost of establishing agency relations between a particular merchant and an agent in isolation would have been prohibitively high. The merchants' law economized on negotiation cost, governed the transmission of information and the provision of services, and substituted for comprehensive contracts between particular agents and merchants.

Despite these advantages, the coalition seems not to have been an optimal institution in the sense of enabling all gains from agency relationships given the period's enforcement, communication, and production technology. Specifically, the coalition was not dynamically efficient. The same factors that ensured its self-enforceability prevented it from expanding in response to welfare-enhancing opportunities.[66] The merchants' law potentially introduced another distortion, as its modification seems to have been done in a manner that did not ensure optimal changes. Within a coalition, agents are more concerned about the interpretations of their actions by other members than about the outcomes of their actions. Hence their actions, while aiming to maximize their expected utility, do not necessarily maximize total profit. The introduction of some form of leadership might have mitigated these distortions, albeit possibly at the cost of introducing others.

The analysis of the Maghribi traders' coalition illustrates the importance of contract enforcement institutions in the operation of markets. This nonmarket institution provided the foundation for a market in agency services, thereby contributing to the integration of interregional product markets. The nature of nonmarket institutions affects the cost, and possibly the feasibility, of trade, thereby affecting the ability to exchange and the process of market integration. As market integration is commonly believed to be a key to economic growth, institutional analysis of nonmarket institutions, their relationships to social and business networks, and their relations to market integration is a key to advancing our understanding of the processes of economic growth.

Social networks and ethnic groups play an important role in facilitating contract enforcement in the absence of the law in the East and the West, as many sociologists, anthropologists, and economists have noted (Macaulay 1963; Furnivall 1956; Landa 1978; Granovetter 1985; Homans 1961; Nee and Ingram 1998). These analyses, however, tend to take the social network and the credibility of punishment within it as a given. The analysis of the Maghribis highlights that fully understanding the nature and implications of economic institutions related to these networks and groups requires understanding the dynamic interplay between the social structure and the related economic institution. Understanding this interplay in various historical periods and economies is likely to provide an important supplement to the study of the institutional foundations

---

[66] In general, networks with collective punishment can be inefficient, particularly when entailing negative externalities on nonmember merchants. The magnitude of the effect depends on how the contractual problem that the network mitigates would have been resolved in its absence. For relevant theoretical analyses, see, for example, Kali (1999) and Dasgupta (2000).

of markets provided by the state and the interrelationships between the two.[67]

Proof of Proposition 3.1

For a given h_c and h_h, to show that playing honest is optimal for the agent, it is sufficient to show that he cannot gain from playing cheat one period if offered W^*. Accordingly, let V_h denote the present value of the lifetime expected utility of an employed agent who, whenever hired, plays honest, V_h^u denote the lifetime expected utility of an unemployed honest agent, and V_c^u the lifetime expected utility of an unemployed cheater (who will play honest in the future if hired). Note that the last two expressions take into account only income from the next period and on (i.e., the first period of unemployment). These lifetime expected utilities are:

$$V_h = W^* + \delta(1 - \tau)V_h + \tau V_h^u, \quad V_i^u = \delta h_i V_h + \delta(1 - h_i)(\bar{w} + \delta V_i^u) \quad i = h, c.$$

Cheating once yields $\alpha + V_c^u$. An agent will thus not cheat if $V_h \geq \alpha + V_c^u$. Substituting and rearranging terms show that an agent's best response is playing honest if and only if $W \geq (T - \delta\tau H_h)[\alpha/(1 - \delta H_c) + \delta\bar{w}(P_c/(1 - \delta H_c) - \tau P_h)] = W^*$, where $T = 1 - \delta(1 - \tau)$; $H_i = h_i/(1 - \delta^2(1 - h_i))$, $i = h, c$; $P_i = (1 - h_i)/(1 - \delta^2(1 - h_i))$, $i = h, c$. The properties of w can be derived directly from this expression by using the fact that $h_c \leq h_h$. Q.E.D.

Proof of Proposition 3.2

Under a multilateral punishment strategy, the probability that an agent who has ever cheated will be rehired if he cheated or was honest this period and became unemployed is $h_c^c = h_c^h = 0$. The same probabilities for an agent who never cheated are $h_c^c = 0$ and $h_h^h = \tau M/(A - (1 - \tau)M) > 0$. The optimal wage for a cheater is $W^* = w(., h_h^c = 0, h_c^c = 0)$, and the optimal wage for an honest agent is $W_h^* = w(., h_h^c > 0, h_c^c = 0)$.

[67] For important recent contributions and surveys of such findings, see Rauch (2001); Casella and Rauch (2002); McMillan and Woodruff (1999); Kranton and Minehart (2001); and Chwe (2001). See Greif (1994b) and McMillan (2002) regarding the relationships between private and public contract enforcement institutions.

Hence, because $h_c \leq h_h$ for cheaters and honest agents, proposition 3.1 implies that $W_c^* > W_h^*$.   Q.E.D.

Proof of Proposition 3.3

Take the limits of W^* as δ goes to 1 and use the facts that $h_c = h_h = \tau M/(A - (1 - \tau)M)$ under a bilateral punishment strategy and $h_c = 0$ and $h_h = \tau M/(A - (1 - \tau)M)$ under a multilateral punishment strategy. Use the relations between W^* and the appropriate parameters as specified in proposition 3.1 to take the appropriate limits.   Q.E.D.

4

Securing Property Rights from the Grabbing Hand of the State

The Merchant Guild

One of the central questions about the institutional foundations of markets concerns the power of the state. The simplest economic view of the state – as an entity that enforces contracts and property rights and provides public goods – poses the following problem: a state with sufficient coercive power to do these things also has the power to withhold protection or confiscate private wealth, undermining the foundations of the market economy.

In the medieval era, before a trading center was established a ruler might pledge that foreign merchants would be secure and their rights respected. Once trade was established, however, the ruler faced the temptation to renege on his pledge – by failing to provide the promised protection or by using his coercive power to abuse the merchants' property rights.[1] Before the emergence of the nation-state, foreign merchants could expect little military or political aid from their countrymen. Without something tangible to secure the ruler's pledge, foreign merchants were therefore not likely to frequent a trading center – an outcome that could be costly for both the ruler and the merchants. What institutions, if any, mitigated this problem?

Trade relationships between a particular merchant and ruler consist of a potentially long sequence of trading visits, during each of which the merchant may pay tax to the ruler. Intuitively, one might conjecture that a particular reputation-based institution could have enabled the ruler to commit himself. Central to this institution is an intertemporal linkage of the central transaction of respecting rights with the auxiliary transaction of tax payment. The belief that the ruler will respect a trader's property

---

[1] Unlike in Chapters 3 and 9, in this chapter I use the terms *merchants* and *traders* interchangeably.

rights could be supported by conditioning future trade – and hence tax payments – of the trader on the ruler's past conduct. The Folk theorem of repeated games (presented in Appendix A) lends support to this conjecture. It suggests that if the ruler sufficiently values gains from future trade relative to his gains from abusing rights, such a reputation mechanism can mitigate this commitment problem.

Yet the historical record indicates that, by and large, ruler-merchant relations were governed by neither bilateral reputation mechanism (in which a merchant whose rights were abused ceases trading) nor informal multilateral reputation mechanism (in which the cheated merchant and his close associates cease trading). The records reflect the importance of formal organizations – administrative bodies rooted outside the ruler's territory. These organizations held certain regulatory powers over member merchants in their own territory, supervised the operation of these merchants in foreign lands, and coordinated their responses to a ruler's conduct. What roles could these organizations – and the associated intertransactional linkages – theoretically play in overcoming the ruler's commitment problem? What roles did they actually play?

The thesis advanced here is that these organizations – merchant guilds – were manifestations of and a means for creating additional intertransactional links to change the set of self-enforcing beliefs in the ruler-trader transaction. Such intertransactional linkages were necessary because the intertemporal linkage of the central transaction of respecting rights with the auxiliary transaction of tax payment between each merchant and the ruler, enabled the ruler to commit to respect rights only when the volume of trade was low. These organizations and the intertransactional linkages they reflect were responses to the failure of the simple reputation mechanism modeled as an exchange of protection in return for tax payment by each merchant and his close associates.

This failure reflects two interrelated factors. First, the ruler could discriminate among merchants. Because protection of rights was a private good rather than a public one, a ruler could respect the rights of some merchants but not others. Second, unless merchants could credibly commit to retaliate collectively, it was optimal for the ruler to abuse the rights of some merchants once trade had expanded, because expansion reduced the value of the future tax payment of each individual merchant. Securing merchants' rights based on a reputation mechanism therefore required that the threat of collective retaliation following a transgression against any merchant be credible.

In the absence of appropriate organization and the implied intertransactional linkages, this threat, however, could not have been credible at the efficient level of trade for two reasons. First, collective punishment requires coordination. Second, rendering a threat of collective punishment credible required that all (or sufficiently many) merchants must be motivated to participate. Providing such motivation, however, presented a problem. Paradoxically, abusing the rights of some merchants fostered the ruler's ability to commit to respect the rights of the remaining merchants, whose future tax payments became more valuable to him. The enhanced ability of the ruler to commit undercuts the credibility of the threat of collective punishment. Fostering this credibility required that merchants be able to motivate one another to participate in collective punishment. The linkage of information-sharing and coercive transactions among them was necessary. The intertransactional linkages that the merchant guild organization reflects rendered the threat of collective retaliation credible.

The merchant guild organizations linked information-sharing and coercive transactions between merchants in order to render credible their threat to retaliate collectively following transgression against any merchant. These organizations provided the monitoring, coordination, and internal enforcement required to credibly commit to retaliate collectively following an abuse. The merchant guild organizations exhibited a range of administrative forms, from a subdivision of a city administration to an intercity organization.[2] All of these forms served the same function: they linked each transaction between the ruler and merchant (the central transaction) with the information-sharing and coercive transactions of all the merchants (the auxiliary transactions). By enabling coordination and motivating each merchant to participate in collective retaliation, the merchant guild organizations changed the set of self-enforcing behavioral beliefs in the transaction between each individual merchant and the ruler. The merchant guild organizations rendered self-enforcing the belief that rulers would respect merchants' rights as trade expanded.

---

[2] This definition of merchant guild organizations is based on their function and applies to a wider range of merchant organizations than those usually labeled *merchant guilds*. The argument does not concern craft guilds, which economists have long associated with the monopolization of a given craft within a particular town. For a recent economic analysis of craft guilds, see Gustafsson (1987); Hickson and Thompson (1991); S. A. Epstein (1991); S. R. Epstein (1998); and Richardson (2002).

The merchant guild organization was thus an institutional element in the merchant guild institution that was based on a multilateral reputation mechanism, mitigated the ruler's commitment problem, and facilitated the expansion of trade. These merchant guild organizations, the associated rules that coordinated actions and specified what actions were abusive, and the associated self-enforcing behavioral beliefs together constituted a system of institutional elements, the merchant guild institution. (To simplify the presentation, I use *merchant guild* to refer to the merchant guild organization and *merchant guild institution* to refer to the institution.)

Viewing merchant guilds as supporting trade is complementary to the more common view among economic historians that they emerged to reduce negotiation costs, administer trade and taxation, extract privileges from foreign cities, and redistribute rents in their own cities (Gross 1890; Thrupp 1965; North and Thomas 1973). While the existence of merchant guilds could affect the distribution of rents in addition to enhancing the security of agreements, the unadorned theory of merchant guilds as cartels presents a puzzle: if the purpose of the guilds was to create monopoly power for the merchants and increase their bargaining power with the rulers, why did powerful rulers during the late medieval period cooperate with foreign merchants to establish guilds in the first place? What offsetting advantages did the rulers enjoy? The puzzle is resolved if the power of the implied merchant guild institution enabled trade to expand to the benefit of merchants and rulers alike.[3]

To present this argument, section 4.1 describes the problem faced by trading centers and merchants in providing security for merchants and their goods, and demonstrates that the guild organization had the features theoretically required to resolve the problem. It then recounts milestones in the evolution of the guild among German traders and the related expansion of trade. Section 4.2 formalizes the analysis, presenting a game-theoretic model that allows us to explore the incentives of traders and cities and to explain why a guild organization was sometimes able to support an efficient level of trading activity when a simple reputation mechanism could not. Section 4.3 concludes by considering the transformation and decline of the merchant guild associated with

---

[3] De Roover (1965, p. 111) asserts that the guild's role "was, of course, to provide collective protection in foreign lands, to secure trade privileges, if possible, and to watch over the strict observance of those already in effect." He did not explain how the guilds could provide protection and ensure the observance of rights by local rulers in foreign lands in which the ruler had a preponderance of military force.

the rise of the state and suggests other applications of the theoretical framework.

4.1 THE COMMITMENT PROBLEM AND THE ROLE OF MERCHANT GUILDS

This section not only presents the historical evidence on the merchant guild institution but intuitively introduces the main theoretical assertions. The historical evidence reveals the concern of medieval merchants with protecting their property rights abroad. Theory suggests the possible role played by the merchant guild institution in fostering trade. Historical analysis supports the conjecture that this institution prevailed.

4.1.1 Institutions and Commitment

Long-distance trade in late medieval Europe was based on the exchange of goods brought from different parts of the world to central cities or fairs located in geographically or politically favorable places. The combination of gains from trade and of suitable locations for conducting exchange does not necessarily imply that exchange could occur without institutions securing foreign traders' property. Rulers' concerns about providing such security is reflected in the words of King Edward I, who noticed in 1283 that because foreign merchants' property rights were not well protected in England, "many merchants are put off from coming to this land with their merchandise, to the detriment of merchants and of the whole kingdom."[4]

His words must be understood against the background of events such as the one that occurred in Boston, England, in or shortly before 1241. A Flemish merchant accused an English trader of not repaying a commercial loan. The result was

an uproar on all sides and the English merchants assembled to attack the Flemings, who retired to their lodging in the churchyard. . . . The English threw down the pailings, broke the doors and windows and dragged out [the lender] and five others, whom they foully beat and wounded and then set in the stocks. All the other Flemings they beat, ill-treated and robbed, and pierced their cloths with swords and knives. . . . Their silver cups were carried off as they sat at table, their

---

[4] *English Historical Documents*, 3:420. The recognition that unprotected foreign merchants would not come to England is also expressed in the Carta Mercatoria of 1303 (see ibid., 3:515).

purses cut and the money in them stolen, their chests broken open and money and goods, to an unknown extent, taken away.[5]

Such incidents were not peculiar to England; they mark the history of long-distance medieval trade.[6] During the twelfth century, insecurity often hindered commercial relations between the Byzantine Empire and the Italian city-states. Pisans attacked the Genoese quarter in Constantinople in 1162, killing at least one merchant and forcing the others to flee to their ship, leaving all their valuables behind. In 1171 the Venetians attacked and destroyed the same Genoese quarter. About ten years later, a mob destroyed all the Italian quarters in Constantinople during the "Latin massacre" of 1182 (Day 1988).[7] Merchants abroad needed protection from coercive power.

In light of the theory of repeated games, one might conjecture that a ruler's commitment problem could be solved by a bilateral reputation mechanism in which individual merchants whose person and property were not protected by a local ruler would refuse to return with their goods in the future. The ruler might reap short-run gains by ignoring a merchant's rights, but he stood to lose the future stream of rents from the cheated merchant's trade. Beliefs linking conduct in the central transaction (protection of rights of a particular merchant) with behavior in an auxiliary one (future tax payments by that merchant) can support the beliefs that rights will be secured.

As section 4.2 demonstrates formally, this intuition omits some important considerations. In particular, at the level of trade that maximizes the total net value of trade – the efficient volume of trade – a bilateral reputation mechanism cannot resolve the commitment problem. At the efficient volume of trade, the value of the stream of future rents collected by the ruler from an individual marginal merchant is almost zero – less than the value of goods that can be seized or the cost of services that can be withheld. The same conclusion holds even at lower volumes of trade if the frequency of visits by an individual trader is low. As long as ruler-merchant relations are governed only by a bilateral reputation mechanism, theory holds that trading volume cannot expand to its efficient level.

[5] Curia Regis, 121, m.6, published by Salzman (1928).
[6] In all of the cases described here, abuses took place despite the relatively high level of ability of the ruler to secure rights.
[7] For other examples, see Kedar (1976, pp. 26ff.); Lane (1973, p. 34); and de Roover (1963, p. 61).

This discussion and the formal model presented in section 4.2 allow only one kind of sanction for cheated merchants: withdrawal of trade and hence tax payment. Military action against a polity or a town in response to abuses, although sometimes used, was not generally a viable option. In the late medieval period defensive technology was superior to offensive technology, and the costs and risks of offensive military action at distant ports limited the credibility of threats of military action in response to trade violations.[8]

A multilateral response by all merchants to transgressions against any subgroup of merchants is a possible means of increasing the punishment and hence deterring abuses. Conditioning behavior in many ruler-merchant transactions on the ruler's conduct in any such transaction increases the punishment following an abuse. Beliefs in such a linkage can therefore render self-enforcing the belief that a ruler will not abuse rights in a wider set of circumstances.

Indeed, the history of relations between trade centers and foreign merchants presents several examples of multilateral retaliations against rulers who reneged on their contractual obligations. Around 1050 the Muslim ruler of Sicily imposed a 10 percent tariff (instead of the 5 percent tariff specified by Islamic law) on goods imported to Sicily by the Maghribi traders. The traders responded by imposing an embargo and sending their goods to the rival trade center, Tunisia. The embargo was effective: after a year the Sicilian ruler removed the extra tariff.[9]

Incidents like this one suggest the relevance of a *multilateral reputation mechanism* in which the ruler is deterred from abusing the rights of any merchant by the threat that many others will cease trading following such an abuse. Conditioning future transactions between the ruler and many merchants on his conduct toward a particular merchant may be able to surmount the commitment problem without the aid of any formal organization. In Sicily, as in the other examples cited, merchants imposed collective punishment on the city that included participation by merchants

---

[8] As Parker (1990, p. 9) notes, "After the proliferation of stone-built castles in western Europe, which began in the eleventh century . . . [in] the military balance between defense and offense, the former had clearly become predominant." This situation changed only during the "military revolution" of the fifteenth century. Military sanctions did sometimes occur, however, particularly among commercial entities in the Mediterranean Sea.

[9] DK 22, a, lines 29–31, b, lines 3–5, Gil (1983a, pp. 97–106); TS 10 J 12, f. 26, a, lines 18–20, Michael (1965, 2:85).

who had not been directly injured. The offenses reflected in these cases were often against an entire group of merchants. But rulers could also discriminate among merchants, abusing or not protecting them selectively, by confiscating the belongings of or withholding legal protection from some merchants without directly harming other merchants. Indeed, the Sicilian ruler increased the tariff only on Jewish traders; and in Constantinople, during two attacks on the Genoese quarter, other Italian merchants were not harmed.

These examples suggest two interconnected reasons why, without a supporting organization, a multilateral reputation mechanism may be insufficient to surmount the commitment problem at the efficient level of trade. The first involves contractual ambiguities and asymmetric information. The second reflects the distinct incentives among different merchants generated by a multilateral response.

Long-distance premodern trade took place in a highly complex and uncertain environment. Unanticipated events and multiple interpretations of existing agreements were always possible under these circumstances, implying that the definition of a "contract violation" was often ambiguous. Different interpretations of facts by merchants, information asymmetry, and slow communication implied that without an organization that coordinated responses, merchants as a whole were not likely to respond effectively to the abuse of any group of merchants. Section 4.2 demonstrates formally that if the fraction of merchants who detect and react to an abuse against any group of merchants is only proportionate to the number abused, then a multilateral reputation mechanism is ineffective at the efficient volume of trade for the same reason that a bilateral reputation mechanism is ineffective: a threat by a group of marginal traders to withdraw their trade is barely significant once trade has expanded to its efficient level.

Expanding trade to the efficient level in the medieval environment required an organization that supplemented the operation of a multilateral reputation mechanism by *coordinating* the responses of a large fraction of the merchants. Only when a coordinating organization exists – when it links the ruler-merchant transactions with information-sharing transactions among merchants – can the multilateral reputation mechanism potentially overcome the commitment problem. Formally, when a coordinating organization exists, there is a perfect equilibrium in which traders come to the city (at the efficient level of trade) as long as an embargo has never been announced and do not come if an embargo has been announced.[10] The ruler respects merchants' rights as long as an embargo has never been announced but abuses their rights otherwise. Thus, when a coordinating institution exists, trade may expand to its efficient level.

Although these strategies correspond to a perfect equilibrium, the theory in this form remains unconvincing. According to the equilibrium strategies, when a coordinating institution organizes an embargo, merchants are deterred from disregarding it because they expect the ruler to abuse violators' trading rights. But are these expectations reasonable? Why would a city not *encourage* rather than punish embargo breakers? Section 4.2 verifies that this encouragement is potentially credible, in the sense that beliefs that embargo breakers' rights will be protected are self-enforcing. During an effective embargo, the volume of trade shrinks and the value of the marginal trader increases; it is then possible for bilateral reputation mechanisms to become effective. That is, there may exist mutually profitable terms between the city and the traders that the city will credibly respect. This possibility limits the potential severity of an embargo and, correspondingly, potentially hinders the ability of any coordinating organization to support efficient trade.

To support the efficient level of trade, a multilateral reputation mechanism may need to be supplemented by an organization with the ability both to *coordinate* embargo decisions and to *enforce* them, by applying sanctions on its own members. In other words, such an organization links information-sharing and coercive transactions among the merchants themselves. This organization and its expected actions are beyond the control of the ruler; his best response to them is to respect traders' rights. Traders will therefore correctly believe that their rights will be protected and hence trade. These beliefs, however, critically depend on the fact that the actions of the guild organization are beyond the control of each trader.

---

[10] More precisely, the equilibrium is a Markov perfect equilibrium. In studying complex environments, as is done here, it is sometimes useful to restrict attention to equilibria in a smaller class of "Markov" or "state space" strategies, in which the past influences current play only through its effect on a state variable that summarizes the direct effect of the past on the current environment. Hence, in the preceding equilibrium, players condition their actions on the state "embargo." Every Markov perfect equilibrium is also a subgame perfect equilibrium (see Fudenberg and Tirole 1991, pp. 501–2, regarding Markov equilibrium and see Appendix A regarding subgame perfect equilibrium).

This is exactly why the traders can credibly commit to respond to abuses collectively.

4.1.2 Evidence of the Role of Formal Organizations

The discussion has so far focused on showing that guaranteeing the security of foreign merchants and their goods was problematic in medieval Europe and that both historical evidence and theoretical reasoning suggest that a simple reputation mechanism could not completely resolve the problem. This subsection provides direct evidence to support the claim that the merchant guild institution secured rights. It provides evidence that merchants and rulers recognized the need to provide believable assurances of security for traders and their goods and negotiated trading arrangements that often included a role for formal organizations. The subsection also presents evidence regarding the coordination and enforcement roles that these organizations played, the strategies they adopted, and the expansion of trade in cities that negotiated these agreements with merchant guilds.

The historical record repeatedly bears out the fact that medieval rulers and merchants recognized the need to secure foreign merchants' property rights before trade could expand. Christian traders, for example, did not dare to trade in the Muslim world unless they received appropriate assurances of security. Within Europe, merchants did not trade in locations in which security agreements were not in place. The Italians began traveling to other European cities and to the Champagne fairs, and the Germans began traveling to Flanders, England, and the Slavic East, only after negotiating appropriate security agreements.[11]

Security agreements and the associated formal organizations appear to have been crucial to trade expansion. The trade of Catalan merchants expanded "within only a few months" after 1286, when they received privileges and the right to have a consul in Sicily (Abulafia 1985, pp. 226–7). The trade of German merchants in Bruges expanded after they received privileges and the right to have a *Kontor* (establishment or office) (Dollinger 1970, p. 41). Italian trade with Flanders flourished only after merchants were allowed to establish local organizations, called *nations* (de Roover 1948, p. 13).

Genoese trade with North Africa provides an instructive illustration of the relative importance of security agreements in contributing to trade

---

[11] See, for example, de Roover (1965); de Roover (1948, p. 13); and Dollinger (1970).

expansion. In 1161 the Genoese legate, Otobonus d'Albericis, and the local ruler of North Africa, Abd alMumin, signed a fifteen-year agreement securing the property rights of the Genoese. The agreement specified a 2 percent reduction in the 10 percent customs fee, a rather negligible reduction given that the average expected gain from goods that reached North Africa was more than 26 percent. Nevertheless, trade expanded dramatically after the agreement. Before 1160 Genoese trade with North Africa never exceeded 500 lire a year. After the agreement, it more than doubled, to 1,057 lire per year, and remained at this higher level in later years. The central feature of the agreement seems to have been provision of security.[12]

Indirect evidence also suggests that the parties recognized the importance of an *institutionalized commitment* to security rather than mere promises. Muslim rulers provided European traders with *aman* – a religious obligation to secure the merchants' rights. Some cities in England went so far as to elect a foreign merchant as mayor.

Yet it seems that a specific institution, the merchant guild, was the most common success. The core of this institution was an administrative body, the merchant guild organization, which supervised the overseas operation of merchant residents of a territorial area and held certain regulatory powers within that area.[13] In England, for example, the merchants of a town were granted the right to establish a society of merchants that retained specific commercial privileges in the internal and external trade of the town and usually had representation in the trade centers in which its members traded. On the European continent, many towns were controlled by the mercantile elite, who organized a merchant guild to advance their interests. In some Italian and German towns, the merchant guild organizations were virtually identical with the town's government, while in some Italian cities, the merchants' operations were supervised by the city (Gross 1890; Rorig 1967; Rashdal 1936, pp. 150–3).

Guilds provided merchants with the leadership and the information-transmission mechanisms required for coordinated action. The guild

---

[12] Krueger (1933, pp. 379–480); Krueger (1932, pp. 81–2). The agreement was self-enforcing because Genoa and the North African ruler were political allies.

[13] This is not to argue that guilds were always established to secure property rights abroad. On the contrary, they were often established for other purposes, such as imposing taxes, governing the city, and organizing commerce. As emphasized in Chapter 7, organizations that were established or emerged in the context of one institution provide the initial conditions in processes leading to new institutions and often are integrated in them.

decided when to impose a trade embargo and when to cancel it. The trade center usually provided the guild with the right to obtain information about disputes between its members and the center's authorities or between its members and other traders. The guild's regulations facilitated the collection and transmission of information among its members.[14]

The Italian cities often performed the functions of a merchant guild on behalf of their resident merchants. The city's role in coordinating embargo decisions is well reflected in the relationship between Genoa and Tabriz, a vital city on the trade route to the Persian Gulf and the Far East. In 1340 Tabriz's ruler confiscated the goods of many Genoese traders. Genoa responded by declaring a commercial embargo (*devetum*) against Tabriz. In 1344 Tabriz's ruler sent ambassadors to Genoa promising to indemnify the traders for everything that had been taken from them and to provide favorable treatment in the future. As a consequence, the *devetum* was removed and Genoese traders flocked to Iran. But the ruler of Tabriz did not keep his promise to protect their rights – the Genoese traders were robbed, and many of them were killed. Material damage reached 200,000 lire, an immense sum. When a subsequent ruler of Tabriz invited the Venetians and Genoese to trade, he "could not give them the guarantees they required, [hence] the Italian merchants, eager as they were to recover their prosperous trade in Persia and to reopen the routs to India and China, felt it was unsafe to trust a mere promise" (Lopez 1943, pp. 183–4).

An incident that occurred during the Genoese embargo of Tabriz confirms the historical importance of enforcement within the merchant group and shows that merchant guilds assumed this enforcement role. In 1343, during the *devetum* against Tabriz, a Genoese merchant named Tommaso Gentile was en route from Hormuz to China. Somewhere in the Pamir plateau, he became sick and had to entrust his goods to his companions and head back to Genoa along the shortest route, which passed through Tabriz. When knowledge of his journey through Tabriz reached Genoa, Tommaso's father had to justify this transgression with the "Eight Wisemen of Navigation and the Major [Black] Sea" – that is, Genoa's board of overseas trade. These officers accepted the father's claim that

---

[14] Guild members were required to travel together, to live and store their goods throughout their stay in quarters that belonged to the guild, to examine the quality of one another's goods, and to witness on another's sales (see, e.g., Moore 1985, pp. 63ff.). As de Roover (1948) notes, the "main purpose of the consular organization [of the Italians in Bruges] was . . . to facilitate the exchange of information" (p. 20).

Gentile had been forced to travel through Tabriz by an act of God and acquitted him, inasmuch as he had traveled through Tabriz without merchandise (Lopez 1943, pp. 181–3).

The merchant guild's strategy of conditioning future trade on adequate past protection, its use of ostracism to achieve security (rather than to achieve privileges or low prices), and the relationship between acquiring information, coordinating action, and being able to boycott are reflected in the agreement made in 1261 between Flemish merchants from Ghent, Ypres, Douai, Cambrai, and Dixmude who purchased English wool. "For the good of the trade" they decided that "if it should happen that any cleric or any other merchant anywhere in England who deals with sales of wool deals falsely with any merchant in this alliance . . . by giving false weight or false dressing of the wool or a false product . . . and if they do not wish to make amends, we have decided that no present or future member of this alliance will be so bold as to trade with them." To make their threat of an embargo functional, they "decided that there will be in each of these cities one man to view and judge the grievances, and to persuade the wrongdoers to make amends" (Moore 1985, p. 301).

The credibility and force of a coordinating organization's threat to impose an embargo crucially depended on curtailing the ruler's ability to undermine an embargo by offering special terms to violators. Theoretically, because the marginal gains from additional trade rise during an embargo, a bilateral reputation mechanism can potentially enable a ruler to commit to these terms. The fact that guild organizations needed to take special measures to prevent shipments to the embargoed city are confirmed by the historical evidence. In 1284 Norwegians attacked and pillaged a German trading ship. In response, the German towns imposed an embargo on Norway, prohibiting the export of grain, flour, vegetables, and beer. To prevent German merchants from smuggling food to Norway, the German towns posted ships in the Danish Straits. According to the chronicler Detmar, "There broke out a famine so great that [the Norwegians] were forced to make atonement." The particular geographical situation of Norway seems to have made the embargo particularly effective (Dollinger 1970, p. 49).[15]

The fact that the success of a trade embargo depended crucially on obtaining the support of virtually all merchants involved was clear to the

---

[15] See also Dollinger's description (1970, p. 48) of the embargo on Novgorod. The punishment for breaking the embargo was death and the confiscation of the smuggled goods.

cities on which the embargo was imposed. When, in 1358, the German towns imposed an embargo on Bruges, the city attempted to defeat the embargo by offering extensive trade privileges to merchants from Cologne (Dollinger 1970, pp. 65–6).

Physically preventing ships from entering a strait and imposing fines were two ways of countering a merchant's temptation to break an embargo. The evidence, however, suggests that the credibility of the threat to carry out an embargo was often sustained by a different means. Credibility was established by endowing guilds with the ability to impose commercial sanctions on their member merchants. In England and elsewhere in Europe, a local guild usually had exclusive trade privileges in its own town. These privileges typically included monopoly rights over retail trade within the town; exclusive exemption from tolls; and the right, under certain circumstances, to exclude members from the guild (Gross 1890, pp. 19–20, 38ff., 65; de Roover 1948, pp. 18–19).[16] These guild organizations were therefore able to provide their members with streams of rents in their hometowns. Receiving these rents, however, could have been made conditional on following the recommendations, rules, and directives of the guild organization. These rents could therefore tie a member to the guild by making change of residence costly and ensuring solidarity among the guild's members.[17]

The argument advanced here suggests that the guild's monopoly rights in its home locality may have been instrumental in advancing trade with other localities. These monopoly rights generated a stream of rents that depended on the support of other members and so served as a bond, allowing members to commit themselves to collective action in response to a ruler's transgressions.[18]

---

[16] Exclusive commercial rights for the guild organization should not be confused with monopoly rights. Entry into the organization was permitted during the period under consideration. The German *Kontore* were established by the merchants who traveled abroad to trade. In England, even individuals who did not live in a particular town could join its merchant guild, and each member had to pay an entry fee (see, e.g., Dollinger 1970 and Gross 1890). By imposing a cost for entry and providing rents subsequently, such a system motivates each merchant to adhere to the guild rules, including honoring guild-sponsored embargoes. As shown later, this permits a higher volume of trade than would be possible without the entry restrictions.

[17] This is not to claim that this was the chief role of these rents. The analysis examines the role of the merchant guild in the expansion of trade between, not within, political units.

[18] This is not to argue, however, that this function was necessarily the main reason for these local monopoly rights. These were often given for taxation reasons.

The Flemish regulations of 1240 illustrate the role of rents in providing the appropriate incentives. A merchant who ignored the ban imposed by the guild on another town was expelled, losing his rent stream: "If any man of Ypres or Daouai shall go against those decisions [made by the guild] ... for the common good, regarding fines or anything else, that man shall be excluded from selling, lodging, eating, or depositing his wool or cloth in ships with the rest of the merchants. ... And if anyone violates this ostracism, he shall be fined 5 shillings" (Moore 1985, p. 298).

4.1.3 The Evolution of Guild Organizations

The evolution and operation of the institution that governed relations between German merchants, their towns, and the foreign towns with which they traded may provide the best example of the guild's contribution to fostering the growth of trade. Because of the relatively small size of the German towns, to achieve the necessary coordination and enforcement for the reputation mechanism to operate effectively, a means was needed to influence the behavior of merchants from different towns. This led to the rise of an interesting form of guild organization known as the German Hansa.[19]

Several extensive studies have mined the abundant historical records of the Hansa (such as Weiner 1932; Dollinger 1970; Lloyd 1991). They enable us to examine its evolution in light of the theoretical analysis. These studies emphasize episodes in which conflict occurred and trade was affected. In purely theoretical terms, conflict can be explained as an equilibrium phenomenon when information about the behavior of the parties is imperfect, as it surely was in this period. The historical episodes examined here, however, are ones in which conflict was followed by organizational and hence institutional change. It seems implausible to model these as equilibrium outcomes. Instead, the episodes can be considered as disequilibrium outcomes and the resulting changes adaptations to changing circumstances or improvements based on accumulated experience.[20]

For historical reasons, membership in the basic organizational unit that coordinated the activities of German merchants abroad – the *Kontor* – was not conditional on residency in a particular town. Any German

---

[19] The Hansa is not usually referred to as a guild. I refer to it as one here, because the discussion is concerned with the function of the organization rather than its official name. I do not claim that the efficiency attributes of the Hansa were sufficient for its emergence.

[20] Chapter 7 refers to such changes as "institutional refinements."

merchant who arrived in a non-German city could join the local *Kontor*. A *Kontor* had the same function as the guild organization in coordinating the responses of German merchants in disputes with the town. It lacked the ability to punish merchants in the towns in which they resided, however, weakening its ability to enforce sanctions against its members. If this theory is correct, the difference between the German *Kontore* and other guild organizations should have made the *Kontore* less effective and led to changes in or the dissolution of that form of merchant organization.

The history of the contractual relations between the city of Bruges, the local *Kontor*, and the German towns provides a clear illustration of this evolution. In 1252 a *Kontor* of German merchants obtained extensive trading privileges from Bruges, and a permanent settlement followed (Weiner 1932, p. 218). The *Kontor* was led by six aldermen elected by the German merchants present in the town. Two of the aldermen were from Rhenish towns, two from Westphalian-Wendish towns, and two from Prussian-Baltic towns, reflecting the range of origins of the participating German merchants (de Roover 1965, p. 114; Dollinger 1970, p. 86).

The trading privileges given to the foreign merchants in Bruges were continually abused, eventually causing riots. A document dated 1280 reported that "it is unfortunately only too well known that merchants traveling in Flanders have been the objects of all kinds of maltreatment in the town of Bruges and have not been able to protect themselves from this."[21] Together with most of the other foreign traders who operated in Bruges, the German merchants retaliated in 1280 by transferring their trade to Aardenburg. After two years of negotiation, a new agreement was reached and the *Kontor* returned to Bruges.

Seemingly successful, the embargo failed to guarantee the property rights of the German merchants, as Bruges simply ignored its agreement with them (Dollinger 1970, pp. 48–51). Bruges did respect the rights of other foreign merchants who frequented the city, however. The present analysis points to the reason for that discrimination. The embargo was not imposed by the German merchants alone but by all foreign merchants in Bruges, including the important and well-organized Italian and Spanish *nations*. While the lesson for Bruges from that episode was to respect the rights of those well-organized groups, it became clear to the city that the German merchant organizations were different. The *Kontor* proved incapable of imposing its decisions on its members. Because the *Kontor*

[21] Urkundenbuch der Stadt Lubeck, I, no. 156, p. 371, translated by Dollinger (1970, p. 383).

encompassed only the German merchants actually present in Bruges – rather than all the potential German traders who might want to trade during an embargo – its threat of sanctions was not credible. As a result, for a time, German merchants had to accept inferior treatment.

Another embargo, from 1307 to 1309, was required to force Bruges to respect its contractual agreements with the Germans. In this embargo, only they participated. What had changed between 1280 and 1307 was the ability of German traders from different towns to coordinate their responses and enforce their embargo. A milestone was passed in 1284, when the Wendish German towns imposed an embargo on Norway. After merchants from Bremen refused to cooperate in the embargo, the other German towns excluded Bremen's merchants from all German *Kontore*. The German towns had achieved the coordination needed to expel one of their members. The act of expelling a city came to be referred to by a special word, *Verhansung*, indicating the importance of this achievement.[22]

After 1307 the ability of the German merchants to commit themselves to coordinate their actions and to enforce their decisions on individual merchants and towns was rather advanced, thus guaranteeing Bruges's adherence to its contractual obligations. The belief that Bruges would respect property rights became self-enforcing. Indeed, Bruges respected the charters agreed upon in 1307 and 1309. As a result, Flanders's trade flourished, expanding for the next fifty years (Dollinger 1970, p. 51). As the theoretical analysis indicates, once the ability of the German *Kontor* to coordinate and impose its decisions on its members was well developed, the contract enforcement problem could be resolved and trade expanded.

It was not until the middle of the century, when the cost of providing security around Bruges rose drastically, that a new level of cooperation among the German towns was needed to force Bruges to provide the security required to support efficient trade. The Hansa's relations with Bruges deteriorated around 1350, mainly because Bruges was not ready to compensate the Germans for their damages in Flanders from the war between England and France. The Hansa responded by strengthening its internal organization. In 1356 the German Hansa held its first Diet, which determined that the *Kontor* of Bruges should be operated according to the Diet's decisions. Apparently recognizing the need for coordination among towns, the *Kontor* accepted this decision. Dollinger, the prominent historian of the Hansa, emphasizes the importance of this change. "In law,

---

[22] Dollinger (1970, p. 49); Weiner (1932, p. 219).

and not only in fact," he writes, "the towns, acting through the general Diet, were establishing their authority over their merchants in foreign ports" (Dollinger 1970, p. 63).

A Hanseatic embargo of Bruges followed in 1358. Any disobedience, by a town or an individual, was to be punished by perpetual exclusion from the Hansa. Bruges attempted to defeat the embargo by offering trade privileges to individual cities, including both non-Hanseatic ones, such as Kampen, and a Hanseatic one, Cologne. The theory suggests that by offering these privileges it hoped to undermine the effectiveness of the new leadership. Although the non-Hanseatic cities accepted Bruges' terms, Cologne refused to cooperate. The embargo proved a success, and in 1360 Bruges came to terms with the Hansa. This time, reflecting the parties' more complete understanding of the range of circumstances in which the city would have to provide services, the privileges were written "in much detail as to prevent any one-sided interpretations."[23]

The institution of the German Hansa was now crystallized. It was a system of institutional elements – rules, beliefs, and organizations – that linked various transactions among merchants, their towns, and foreign cities to advance exchange. The Hansa's organizational structure provided the coordination and enforcement between German merchants and their towns that were required to alter the set of self-enforcing beliefs in the relationship between each merchant and foreign cities.

Trade in Northern Europe prospered for generations under the supremacy of the Hansa. Although the trade embargo of 1360 was not the last, later trade disputes seemed to center on distributive issues, such as the provision of trade privileges. Commitment for security was no longer an issue.

It is illuminating to contrast the development of the Hansa among German towns with the rather different organization among the Italian merchants. The solid internal political and commercial organization of the Italian cities and their prominence in trade enabled them to overcome the coordination and internal enforcement problems. Collective action among the merchants from Italian cities was ensured. Because they were sufficiently large – none of the cities was a marginal player in the ports in which they traded – coordination among the cities was unnecessary.[24] In

---

[23] See Dollinger (1970, pp. 63–6) and Weiner (1932, p. 220).

[24] Bairoch, Batou, and Chèvre (1988) contains information on the relative sizes of Italian and German cities. Some intercity cooperation was practiced in Italy, with smaller cities "affiliating" themselves with larger ones.

contrast, the German *Kontor* was a local organization lacking the ability to impose its decisions on its members, who came from various German towns. The German towns were small, and before the establishment of the German Hansa, most were relatively insignificant in large trading centers like Bruges.

Interestingly, size matters here, just as it did for the Maghribis. Among the Maghribis, too small a coalition would have reduced the credibility of the punishment by increasing the cost of inflicting it, whereas too large a coalition would have undermined the information flows required for the credibility of the punishment. Similarly, for the Hansa to be effective, it had be sufficiently large to ensure that the German merchants would not be marginal.

The timing of the emergence of guilds was therefore related to population growth and the processes that lead to the formation and internal organization of cities. In Southern Europe the major Italian city-states grew large because of social and political events around the Mediterranean. Italian trade expanded because each city functioned as a merchant guild of sufficient size that its traders were not marginal. Their property rights were hence secured.

Although the potential gains from trade in the Baltic Sea were substantial as well, that region's settlement pattern – influenced by the Germanic military expansion eastward – produced small towns that could not ensure the safety of their traders abroad. Only after a long process of urban expansion and institutional evolution were these towns incorporated into an intercity merchant guild, the German Hansa, that enabled Baltic trade to prosper.

Although the guild was a precondition for trade expansion, its rise in Europe was not caused by the new gains from trade. Rather, its rise in various localities reflects the nature of institutional dynamics as a historical process. The ways in which the various guilds were organized and the timing of their rise – and hence of trade expansion – were determined by social, economic, and political processes through which institutional elements and other conditions required for a guild's functioning were crystallized.

This historical analysis supports the hypothesis that the merchant guild organization was at the center of an institution that overcame the ruler's commitment problem and facilitated trade expansion. Although these organizations exhibited a range of administrative forms – from subdivision of a city administration (such as that of the Italian city-states) to the intercity organization of the Hansa – their functions were the same: to provide the coordination and internal enforcement required to enable the beliefs required to surmount the commitment problem. The actions taken by rulers and traders, their strategies as reflected in their regulations, and the expansion of trade that followed the establishment of guild organizations all confirm the importance of this role of the guild organization.

4.2 THE FORMAL MODEL

The theoretical modeling is kept simple and directed to analyzing the potential of various plausible mechanisms for overcoming the ruler's commitment problem. Each of the mechanisms examined explicitly captures a particular intertransactional linkage and might feasibly permit commitment by the ruler at some level of trade. The focus is on the growing need for more sophisticated mechanisms as the level of trade rises and approaches the efficient level.

The environment in which trade takes place has two kinds of players, a city and individual merchants. The merchants, identical and large in number, are identified with the points on the interval $[0, \bar{x}]$. The city – a potential trading center – has the following trading technology: if the number of traders passing through the city in a single period is x, the gross value of trade in that period is $f(x)$. In addition, suppose that there is a cost of $c > 0$ per unit of value traded incurred by the city for the services it provides and a cost $\kappa > 0$ per unit of value incurred by each trader, so that the net value of trade is $f(x)(1 - c - \kappa)$. Assume that trade is profitable, that is, $c + \kappa < 1$. Also assume that f is nonnegative and differentiable, that $f(0) = 0$, and that f achieves a maximum at some unique value $x^* > 0$, which is referred to as the *efficient volume of trade*. In this model the city funds its services and earns additional revenues by charging a toll or tax of $\tau \geq c$ per unit of value passing through its ports, so that its total tax revenues are $\tau f(x)$. If it provides the services contracted for, its net revenue for the period is $f(x)(\tau - c)$. If the city breaches its contract by failing to provide services to a fraction ϵ of the traders, it saves $\epsilon c f(x)$, so its payoff for the trading period is $f(x)(\tau - c(1 - \epsilon))$.[25] Traders who are not cheated each earn profits, net of costs, tolls, and taxes, of $(1 - \tau - \kappa)f(x)/x$. Traders who are cheated pay taxes and incur costs κ but receive no revenues; each earns $-(\tau + \kappa)f(x)/x$.

---

[25] This formulation captures the gains to the ruler from either abusing rights directly or neglecting to provide merchants with costly protection.

This game is repeated period after period. The players' payoffs from the repeated game are the discounted sum of the periodic payoffs using a discount factor of δ. Thus the city's payoff when the trading volume is x_t in period t is given by:

$$\sum_{t=0}^{\infty} \delta^t f(x_t)(\tau - c(1 - \epsilon_t)). \tag{1}$$

The payoffs of the individual traders are determined similarly, as the discounted sum of their periodic payoffs.

The specification of the model captures the idea that merchants are substitutes as far as the ruler is concerned and each merchant is relatively "small."[26] The historical observation that rulers could discriminate between traders is captured through the specification of the ruler's strategy. In discussing the Maghribi embargo on Sicily, we have seen that competition among alternative centers can sometimes constrain abuses. Yet, abstracting from the issue of competition among alternative trade centers in general seems appropriate. The essence of medieval trade was that it was based on exchange of goods brought by traders from several regions to a particular trading place. Thus, by and large, without the cooperation of traders from other regions, the threat by a group of traders from a particular region to switch permanently to an alternative potential trade center was not credible.

The specification of the merchants' payoffs is based on the historical observation that merchants were most likely to trade abroad when they perceived that their rights were secure. The specification of the ruler's payoff reflects the fact that a ruler could gain from abusing rights or allowing his subjects to do so. Although the model equates the gains from abusing rights to the protection costs saved, one can think of gains from abuse as reflecting the gain from the ruler's confiscation of merchants' goods. The ruler's and the merchants' payoffs are specified to allow a conceptual and analytical distinction between distribution and efficiency. This specification treats the tax rate as given and hence refrains from examining the process through which the gains from trade are allocated. Any losses to the merchants above the agreed-upon rate of taxation are defined as abuse.

Analytically, this specification implies that any first-best outcome is characterized by the level of trade x^* in every period and the absence of

---

[26] Each merchant is small in the sense that he can be considered as marginal in the model.

cheating by the city. Different first-best utility allocations are achieved by setting different tax rates τ. Technically, this conclusion reflects the assumption that some value is lost when the ruler fails to provide protection. This is consistent with events such as those described earlier, in which failure to provide protection led to the destruction of goods and loss of value. Whatever the merchants were willing to pay the ruler – that is, all issues of transfer – are modeled here as part of the tax.

Game 1: Informationally Isolated Traders: Bilateral Reputation Mechanism. The first model represents the situation of merchants who travel alone or in small groups with no social or economic organization. The traders remain unaware of how the city has treated other merchants. Only intertemporal linkages between each ruler-merchant transaction are considered. Although this model is surely too extreme to be fully descriptive, it highlights the difficulties faced by individual merchants negotiating with the city on their own but able to condition their future transactions on past conduct.

In this game, knowing only the history of his own decisions and his own past treatment by the city, a trader must decide whether to bring his goods to the city in each period. A strategy for the trader is a sequence of functions mapping this history into decisions about whether to offer his goods for trade in that period. Similarly, the city must decide the property of which traders to abuse under various conditions. A strategy for the city is a sequence of functions identifying a (measurable) subset of the current traders for the city to abuse as a function of who shows up to trade currently and the full past history of the game.

Readers familiar with either the economics of reputations or the theory of repeated games will recognize that the repetition of the interactions between the city and the individual traders creates the possibility for reputations to be created that enforce good behavior by the city. The idea is that a trader who is abused once might refuse to return to the city, reducing the city's profits. The effectiveness of this threat depends on both the frequency of trade and the periodic value of the individual merchant's trade in the city. If the frequency of trade is sufficiently high and the volume sufficiently low so that the value of the repeat business of any individual trader to the city is high, the simple reputation mechanism can be effective in providing the city with incentives to protect individual rights. In the analysis, however, when the volume of trade rises to the efficient level, the value of repeat business falls to zero, so the usual conclusions of the Folk theorem of repeated games do not apply at the efficient level.

Proposition 4.1: No Nash equilibrium of game 1 can support honest trade ($\epsilon_t \equiv 0$) at the efficient level ($x_t \equiv x^*$), regardless of the levels of c, τ, κ, or δ.

Proof: Suppose there were such an equilibrium and consider the payoff to the city if it deviates from the equilibrium strategy and cheats a fraction ϵ of the first-period traders. In the initial period its payoff is $f(x^*)(\tau - c[1 - \epsilon])$. In subsequent periods the informational assumptions of the model imply that the play of at most ϵ traders is affected. Consequently, at least $1 - \epsilon$ traders come to the city in each future period, and the city's payoff from treating them honestly is, in present value terms, at least $\gamma(\tau - c)f(x(1 - \epsilon))$ (for convenience define $\gamma = \delta/(1 - \delta)$). So the city's total payoff from cheating a fraction ϵ of the traders in the first period and adhering to the purported equilibrium thereafter is at least

$$f(x)(\tau - c(1 - \epsilon)) + \gamma(\tau - c)f(x(1 - \epsilon)), \qquad (2)$$

and this expression coincides exactly with the actual payoff when $\epsilon = 0$, that is, when the city adheres to the purported equilibrium. The derivative of expression 2 with respect to ϵ at $\epsilon = 0$ and $x = x^*$ is

$$cf(x^*) - \gamma(\tau - c)x^*f'(x^*) = cf(x^*) > 0, \qquad (3)$$

because $f'(x^*) = 0$. This establishes that the city has a profitable deviation – that is, the specified behavior is not a Nash equilibrium. Q.E.D.

No mechanism based only on sanctions by those who are cheated can support honest trading at the efficient level, x^*, because when trading is conducted at that level, the marginal trader has zero net value to the city. By cheating a few marginal traders, the city loses nothing in terms of future profits but saves a positive expense in the present period. There is no institution in which the ruler's belief in a merchant's retaliation enables him to commit at the efficient level of trade. The belief that the ruler will respect rights at the efficient level of trade is not self-enforcing. To support the efficient level of trading, some kind of collective action among merchants is needed.[27] Rendering collective action feasible, in turn, requires additional intertransactional linkages.

The proposition is stated in terms of the Nash equilibrium because it is a negative result: even with the most inclusive of noncooperative equilibrium concepts, the efficient volume of trade cannot be supported. For positive results, stronger, more-convincing equilibrium concepts are used.

Game 2: Informationally Isolated Small Groups of Traders: An Uncoordinated Multilateral Reputation Mechanism. Information in medieval times was slow to spread by modern standards, but it was available. If a merchant was abused, even in the absence of any organization for diffusing information, some of his peers were likely to learn of it. Can this limited, uncoordinated diffusion of information reflecting informal linking of information transactions among merchants enable the ruler to commit not to abuse merchants at the efficient level of trade?

Suppose that an incident in which the city cheats a group of traders always becomes known to a larger group of traders. Formally, whenever a set T of traders is cheated, there is a set of traders $\hat{T} \supset T$, each of whom learns of the event. Assume that there is some constant K ($1 \leq K < \infty$) such that if the number of traders cheated is $\mu(T)$, then the number who learn about the event, $\mu(\hat{T})$, is no more than $K\mu(T)$: if few traders are cheated, then proportionately few discover that the event has occurred. Each trader makes his decisions to bring goods based on history of his actions and relationships with the city and the behavior of the city known to him toward other merchants. Cheating could then lead to a withdrawal of trade by a group many times larger than the group that was cheated. Even if this could be realized, however, it would not suffice to support an efficient volume of trade.

Proposition 4.2: No Nash equilibrium of game 2 can support honest trade ($\epsilon_t \equiv 0$) at the efficient level ($x_t \equiv x^*$), regardless of the levels of c, τ, κ, or δ.

---

[27] This result is not an artifact of the specification of costs. If the costs borne by the city include some fixed costs per trader (possibly in addition to the proportional costs), the city would have an even stronger incentive to reduce the number of traders, because it bears only a fraction τ of the resulting loss of value but saves all of the service costs. Making costs proportional to value minimizes the distortion in the city's incentives, but it still leaves the city tempted to seek short-term gains by cutting services at the expense of individual traders when only the bilateral reputation mechanism is at work.

The proof is essentially the same as for the first proposition, except that the bound on the number of traders who decline to trade in the future is multiplied by K. Expression 3 is replaced by

$$cf(x^*) - \gamma K(\tau - c)x^*f'(x^*) = cf(x^*) \geq 0.$$

Violations against a few merchants that are noticed only by proportionally few merchants cannot be deterred by a threat of retaliation by those with firsthand knowledge.

The real situation faced by traders is considerably more complicated than that modeled in games 1 and 2. One important missing element concerns informal and word-of-mouth communication. Although game 2 allows that some traders are informed when the city cheats any trader, it also assumes that traders know nothing about who else is currently trading. This assumption is a device to rule out endogenous communication among the traders in the game, by which one trader may infer that another was cheated because he did not show up to trade. In theory, this kind of communication can be significant (Kandori 1992). Both word-of-mouth communication and some inferences of this kind could take place, but the model disallows them on the assumption that they were of minor importance for enforcing contract compliance. To the extent that informal communications and indirect inferences could provide effective information, the need for organized communication and coordination is reduced.

Game 3: Guild Organization with Coordinating Ability. We have seen that it is impossible for the city and traders to sustain an efficient level of trade based only on sanctions applied by small groups. Given the historical evidence of the existence of organizations that governed the relationships between traders and the city, it is natural to examine whether these could contribute to trade expansion. If these organizations, as conjectured here, linked information sharing transactions among *all* merchants, could they have supported the efficient level of trade? Could they have rendered self-enforcing the beliefs that no right will be abused in the efficient level of trade?

A crucial characteristic that separates formal organizations such as guilds from informal codes of behavior is the creation of specialized role (positions), such as those of the guild's aldermen to make decisions on behalf of the guilds' members. Determining how the guild organization selects its aldermen, identifying the private interests those merchants may have, and modeling how the guild organization manages the principal-agent problem of controlling the aldermen are complex issues that merit close analysis. Modeling the guild organization in this manner implies explicitly considering it as an institution in addition to an institutional element. Doing so and including these issues in the model here would only obscure the main point, however. For this reason these issues are set aside for future research, and the guild organization is modeled as a mere automaton. By considering different intertransactional linkages and hence assigning information and capabilities to the guild, it is possible to evaluate its contribution to trade expansion.

This subsection examines the role of the guild as an *organization* for communication and coordination. Assume that if the city cheats a set of traders, T, the guild discovers the event and announces an embargo with probability $\alpha(T) \geq \mu(T)$. This specification means that the more merchants were cheated, the more likely the guild organization is to realize that cheating had occurred. It does not imply, however, that the guild organization has better information than that which was available to merchants under the uncoordinated reputation mechanism examined in game 2. It implies only that if the guild discovers cheating, it can communicate it to all merchants.

In this game, the guild organization makes embargo announcements mechanically and without any means of enforcement. Traders learn of the guild's announcement each period, but they are not forced to heed it. The announcement simply becomes part of the information available to them and to the city. In all other respects, the game is the same as game 1. Despite the guild organization's lack of enforcement ability, the mere change in information alters the set of equilibria.

Proposition 4.3: Suppose that $\tau + \kappa \leq 1$ and

$$c \leq \gamma(\tau - c). \tag{4}$$

Then the following strategies form a Markov perfect equilibrium of game 3. The city does not cheat unless an embargo is announced by the guild organization leader; after an embargo is announced, it cheats any trader who offers to trade. Traders offer to trade in a given period if and only if no embargo has been announced.[28]

---

[28] This is a Nash equilibrium of the game with the properties that the player's strategies at any period depend only on whether an embargo was announced and each player's strategy at each period maximizes his payoff from that time onward, given the equilibrium strategies of the other players.

The formal proof is by direct verification. Condition 4 implies that what the city stands to gain by cheating a trader, which is proportional to $cf(x^*)$, is less than the average future profits from each trader, which is $\gamma(\tau - c)f(x^*)$. With group enforcement, average trading profits rather than marginal profits determine the city's incentives. This accounts for the continued effectiveness of group sanctions even at the efficient level of trade.

In the institution captured in this equilibrium analysis, the city's behavior is motivated by the beliefs that abuse will lead to an embargo while respecting rights after an embargo is announced will not cause the resumption of trade. The expectation that their rights will be respected motivates traders to trade; the expectation of being abused motivates them not to trade after an embargo is announced. As these beliefs are commonly known, each side takes the other side's expected behavior as given, and each merchant and the city find it optimal to act as expected of them.

The equilibrium strategies contain a counterintuitive element: the city cheats any trader who offers to trade during an embargo. Traders' unanimous expectations that the city will behave this way cause all of them to honor the embargo. But why should the city not welcome traders during the embargo rather than cheat them? In a Markov perfect equilibrium, the city can be expected to cheat embargo-breaking traders only if it is in the city's interest to do so once the embargo has been announced. Given the specified strategies, if y traders violate the embargo and offer their goods, the city expects a payoff of $(\tau - c)f(y)$ in the current period and zero in future periods if it acts honestly. If it cheats, it expects $\tau f(y)$ in the current period and zero in the future. Cheating is therefore optimal.

Although the strategies described in proposition 4.3 constitute an equilibrium, the expectations and behavior that they entail seem implausible. The equilibrium requires, for example, that, no matter how desperate the city may be for renewed trade relationships, once an embargo has been announced, it nevertheless cheats anyone who trades with it. In addition, traders expect that behavior. By the equilibrium logic, the city behaves in this manner because it expects the embargo to take full hold in the next round whatever it does, so it anticipates that any cooperation it offers will be fruitless.

This equilibrium behavior does not match the historical facts very well, and it is of doubtful merit even as theory, because it supposes that the city and potential embargo breakers play the equilibrium with the lowest possible value for themselves. Scholars – notably Farrell and Maskin (1989), Bernheim and Ray (1989), and Pearce (1987) – have leveled similar criticisms at the equilibria of other repeated-game models.

None of the alternative concepts that these authors suggest applies directly to the model presented here, but all suggest that it is more reasonable to suppose that some cooperation may be achieved between traders and the city even after an embargo is announced. As an example, consider the possibility that mutually profitable *bilateral* agreements between the city and individual traders may be reached even during an embargo. It will be apparent from the logic of the arguments that any other kind of cooperation would lead to qualitatively similar conclusions.

Suppose that if some traders agree to trade with the city despite the embargo, they cannot rely on the threat of a group embargo to enforce their own claims against the city. What, then, can enforce honest behavior by the city during the embargo? A cheated trader can, for example, threaten to withdraw his own future trade. Proposition 4.1 established that the efficient level of trade, x^*, cannot be supported by such an equilibrium, but it leaves open the possibility that some inefficiently low level of trade can be supported. It is thus natural to ask, What is the highest level of exchange, x', that can be supported in this way?

Proposition 4.4: Assume that f is concave. Consider the strategies in which the city cooperates in each period only with traders whom it has never cheated and each trader offers to trade in each period if and only if he has not been cheated before. These strategies constitute a subgame perfect equilibrium of game 1 when the volume of traders is x and the taxes are τ if and only if for all $y \leq x$

$$0 \geq cf(y) - \gamma(\tau - c)yf'(y). \tag{5}$$

A sufficient condition is that $0 \geq cf(x) - \gamma(\tau - c)xf'(x)$ and the elasticity $e(x) = d\ell nf(x)/d\ell n(x)$ is a decreasing function of x.

Proof: The traders' strategies are obviously best replies to the strategy of the city from any point in the history of the game, so only the optimality of the city's strategy needs to be proved. Beginning with x current traders, consider the subgame achieved after $x - y$ traders depart, when $y \leq x$ traders remain. By cheating a fraction ϵ of the y current traders, the city's payoff will be $g(\epsilon;y) = (\tau - [1 - \epsilon]c)f(y) + \gamma f(y[1 - \epsilon])(\tau - c)$. A necessary condition for the optimality of $\epsilon = 0$ is $\partial g(\epsilon;y)/\partial \epsilon \leq 0$ at $\epsilon = 0$. An easy calculation verifies that this is the same as condition 5, so the latter condition is necessary for all y.

By the optimality principle of dynamic programming, it is sufficient to show that there is no subgame in which the city would do strictly better by setting $\epsilon > 0$ in the initial period and then adhering to its equilibrium strategy thereafter, given the strategies of the others. If f is concave, then for all y, $g(\epsilon;y)$ is concave in ϵ, so a sufficient condition is that for all y, $\partial g(\epsilon;y)/\partial \epsilon \leq 0$ at $\epsilon = 0$, which is again equivalent to condition 5, proving sufficiency.

The elasticity can be rewritten as $e(x) = xf'(x)/f(x)$. Condition 5 is that $e(y) \geq c/[\gamma(\tau - c)]$ for all $y \leq x$, which follows from $e(x) \geq c/[\gamma(\tau - c)]$ and the hypothesis that $e(\cdot)$ is decreasing.   Q.E.D.

Let x' be the largest solution to condition 5. The equilibrium described by proposition 4.4 suggests an interesting interpretation of the levels of trade, x', observed during boycotts, and it explains why some merchants continued to trade and others did not. According to the theory, additional traders, beyond the number x', would be cheated by the city and would be unable to exact retribution for their losses. Alternatively, if one thinks of the level of trade $x < x^*$ during the embargo as being determined by factors outside the model (such as existing alliances or other interests), then condition 5 implies that the minimum tax rate necessary to deter cheating is lower the lower x is. This confirms the intuition that an embargo breaker may be able to negotiate an unusually attractive deal, both because the value of trade per trader $(f(x)/x)$ is higher when x is small and because the minimum tax rate τ necessary to prevent cheating is lower for small x.

Proposition 4.4 implies that in the absence of a strong guild organization – one that can impose the embargo on its members – the guild cannot credibly threaten to reduce the city's income to less than $f(x')$. This threat may or may not be sufficient to support honest trade, depending on the parameters γ, τ, and c. That is, an embargo that leaks may or may not be enough to deter the city from violating its agreement. If this kind of embargo is not sufficient, mutual gains may be achievable by strengthening the guild organization and enabling it to make a more powerful threat. The force of any potential embargo depends not only on $f(x')$ and $f(x^*)$ but also on the net rate of profit, $\tau - c$, earned by the city. Incentives for honest behavior by the city are stronger when taxes and tolls are high, because the city then has more to lose from an embargo. A strong guild organization can make it feasible to offer lower taxes and tolls while still promoting honest behavior by the city that, in a richer model, could lead to additional advantages in terms of increased value of trade.

A guild with coordination and enforcement abilities may be central to enabling trade expansion. It creates and reflects intertransactional linkages among all ruler-merchant transactions and the ruler's conduct in each transaction. The guild links information-sharing and coercive (and sometimes also economic) transactions by merchants with the ruler-merchant transaction. By also linking economic and coercive transactions, the resulting institution mitigates the deficiency of the institution described in game 3. The power of the guild enables it to render credible the belief that an embargo by all merchants will follow cheating.

Game 4: The Guild with Coordination and Enforcement Abilities. The last variant is a game in which the guild has the ability to force individual traders to comply. No formal analysis of this case is presented, because the only role of enforcement by the guild against member merchants in the formal model is to prevent trade during boycotts. Accordingly, the results are the same as in proposition 4.3, but traders participate in the boycott because they are required to do so, rather than because they expect participation to serve their individual interests.

4.3 CONCLUDING COMMENTS

Like all models in economics, the model presented here is stylized, abstracting from inessential details in order to highlight particular points. It enables us to capture a historically derived conjecture about the importance of particular intertransactional linkages and how they enabled securing foreign merchants' property rights. The central transaction between a ruler and a merchant – in which the ruler provided protection in return for taxation – was linked to other transactions, namely, information-sharing and coercive transactions among the merchants themselves and transactions between the ruler and all merchants. This linkage – which manifested itself in, and was created by, the merchant guild organization – changed the set of self-enforcing beliefs in the central transaction in a way that rendered credible the ruler's commitment to respect rights as trade expanded.

Several interrelated social factors – rules, beliefs, and organizations – constituted the merchant guild institution. Together, these institutional elements enabled, guided, and motivated a particular regularity of behavior: tax payment and respect of property rights. Rules provided the cognition, coordination, and information that enabled and guided behavior in the related transactions. They enabled merchants and rulers to make

120

informed decisions by providing the micro-foundations of behavior. Rules specified, for example, the structure of the situation, who held membership in the guild, who was the legitimate tax collector, which actions constituted an abuse of rights, and how one went about filing a complaint against abuse. They also defined who had the authority to announce an embargo, what was expected of merchants during one, and the consequences of failing to adhere to expected embargo behavior.

Beliefs motivated individuals to comply with behavioral instructions provided by these rules. It was common knowledge that the prevailing internalized and behavioral beliefs were that merchants would pay tax and rulers would respect property rights. The merchant guild organizations produced and disseminated the rules, perpetuated the associated beliefs, and increased the set situations in which the beliefs supporting trade were self-enforcing. These organizations increased the set of self-enforcing beliefs by verifying actions, disseminating information, providing coordination, and credibly threatening to punish embargo breakers.

Unlike the theory of the merchant guild organization as an instrument of monopoly by a local ruler, the theory presented here predicts that rulers will *encourage* the establishment of merchant guild organizations of foreign traders with specific rights and an effective organization. Such encouragement would not be expected if the sole purpose of guild organizations was to shift some of the fixed gains from trade from rulers to merchants, unless the encouragement itself reflected the merchants' ability to coerce rulers to shift rent in merchants' favor. The historical evidence reveals that even when merchants could not coerce rulers by the threat of an embargo and even when the privileges provided to merchants did not entail any shift in rent, rulers did grant merchants various rights, including the rights to organize, hold courts and assemblies, elect their own consuls, and serve on juries when merchants were being tried.[29]

Unlike a cartel theory of guilds, which suggests that guilds form to reduce trade in goods in order to drive up relative prices, this analysis predicts that establishment of these guild organization rights expands trade. At least during the late medieval period, the historical evidence is consistent with this prediction. Although it is likely that the merchant guild organizations sought to advance the merchants' interests in many

---

[29] See also Carus-Wilson (1967, p. xviii) and *English Historical Documents*, 3:515–16. In Bruges the role of the guild in securing rights rather than achieving privileges is suggested by the city policy to provide all nations with the same rights (see de Roover 1948, p. 15).

ways, including negotiating for rights to control prices, these rent-seeking activities cannot account for the patterns identified here.

As centuries passed and trade gave impetus to political integration, larger political units emerged, taking upon themselves the functions that the merchant guilds had performed. The political, commercial, and military relations among rulers enabled all rulers to commit to ensuring the safety of the foreign merchants frequenting their realms. Illustrative are such acts as those of the English kings, who made agreements and enforced embargoes to provide the English Merchants of the Staple and the Merchant Adventurers with security in their dealings with the Hanseatic League. As states evolved, the need for the merchant guild institution to secure merchants' rights declined.[30]

Merchant guild organizations did not disappear, however. Some became fiscal instruments that hindered trade expansion. Others consolidated their political power and, after securing their members' rights, turned to limiting the rights of their competitors. For example, although the establishment of the German Hansa enabled Northern European trade to flourish, once organized the Hansa's concern was not efficiency but profitability. In its constant efforts to preserve trade rights and supremacy, the Hansa crushed other traders' groups, without consideration of their comparative efficiencies (Greif 1992). Thus a merchant guild that had facilitated trade in the late medieval period was transformed into a monopolistic organization that hindered trade expansion during the premodern period.

Although this chapter focuses exclusively on the role of the merchant guild institution at a particular time and place, the principles that applied then may help explain the emergence of other organizations and institutions in other places and times. The analysis explains why a powerful party might find it advantageous to help weaker powers organize themselves into entities that can exert countervailing power, in order to allow itself to commit to certain mutually beneficial arrangements. This explanation seems relevant and warranted regarding other issues. For example, French kings developed an elaborate system to help secure their borrowing and thereby enhance their ability to borrow.[31] The features of this system – which used the officer corps to aggregate loans and help borrowers coordinate and relied on the parliament to authorize the legality

---

[30] On the later relations between the Hansa and England, see Colvin (1971) and Postan (1973).

[31] For details, see Root (1989) and P. Hoffman (1990).

of royal edicts – suggests that the kings were trying to create organizations capable of collective action to enforce their fiscal promises.

The analysis also highlights the need to examine protection of property rights as private goods. At least since the time of Hobbes, scholars have considered the security of property rights as public goods provided to all or none. But protection can and often is a private good, as in the case of the merchant guild (Greif et al. 1994). In contemporary economies without the rule of law, protection is often awarded by the politically powerful to some – those who can reciprocate through their economic activity or political support – but not to others (Haber, Razo, and Maurer 2003).

More generally, this chapter highlights the fact that in order to understand whose property rights protection matters to economic prosperity, knowledge of the particularities of the economy is required. Understanding whether, how, and why such protection will or will not be forthcoming requires going beyond the prevailing political economy framework, which considers protection provided by such means as the division of power and constitutional protection. This chapter illustrates the need to examine the extent and the ways in which property rights are secured from coercion by institutions based on countervailing economic, political, social, and military powers (Greif 2004b).

5

Endogenous Institutions and Game-Theoretic Analysis

Chapters 3 and 4 illustrate that restricting the set of admissible institutionalized beliefs is central to the way in which game theory facilitates the study of endogenous institutions. Durkheim (1950 [1895], p. 45) recognized the centrality of institutionalized beliefs, arguing that institutions are "all the beliefs and modes of behavior instituted by the collectivity." But neither Durkheim nor his followers placed any analytic restrictions on what beliefs the collectivity could institute. Because beliefs are not directly observable, however, deductively restricting them, as game theory lets us do, is imperative. The only beliefs that can be instituted by the collectivity – that can be common knowledge – are those regarding equilibrium (self-enforcing) behavior. Furthermore, the behavior that these beliefs motivate should reproduce, not refute or erode them.

Game theory thus enables us to place more of the "responsibility for social order on the individuals who are part of that order" (Crawford and Ostrom 1995, p. 583). Rather than assuming that individuals follow rules, it provides an analytical framework within which it is possible to study the way in which behavior is endogenously generated – how, through their interactions, individuals gain the information, ability, and motivation to follow particular rules of behavior. It allows us to examine, for example, who applies sanctions and rewards that motivate behavior, how those who are to apply them learn or decide which ones to apply, why they do not shirk this duty, and why offenders do not flee to avoid sanctions.

The empirical usefulness of the analytical framework of classical game theory is puzzling, however, because this theory rests on seemingly unrealistic assumptions about cognition, information, and rationality. For example, the analysis requires a common knowledge of rationality and that the players have a complete and closed model of the situation. It is possible to respond to this puzzle by taking comfort in the empirical usefulness of the theory. It works. But it is beneficial to go beyond this position. Accordingly, this chapter asks what is revealed about endogenous institutions by the need to impose various unrealistic assumptions when studying behavior in strategic situations?

Similarly, the chapter asks what do we learn about institutions from the game-theoretic insight that coordination problems are common? In strategic situations, each individual is better off playing the strategy that is the best response to the particular equilibrium strategies others are following. Yet game theory shows that multiple equilibria usually exist in the repeated situations central to institutional analysis. This multiplicity of equilibria implies that one will seek ways to coordinate his behavior because deduction alone – knowledge of the structure of the situation – is insufficient for finding one's best response.[1]

The aim of this chapter is to address these questions to better understand institutions and the extent to which game theory can be used to study them. Doing so requires examining the cognitive, coordinative, normative, and informational micro-foundations of behavior, how institutions provide them, and how the implied behavior then reproduces these institutions. In conducting such an examination, the chapter draws particularly on learning and experimental game theory, cognitive science, and sociology.

Section 5.1 emphasizes the importance of socially articulated and disseminated rules in providing individuals with the cognitive, coordinative, and informational micro-foundations of behavior. These social rules provide an individual with the information and the cognitive model (also referred to as a mental model or internalized belief system) required to choose behavior. (Henceforth I will use the terms cognitive model, mental model, and internalized belief system interchangeably.) Similarly, social rules coordinate behavior by providing a public signal regarding the behavior that is expected of individuals in various circumstances. In short, social rules constitute the heuristics that enable and guide behavior by helping individuals to form beliefs about the world around them and what to expect from others.

Commonly known social rules enable and guide behavior, and retrospective individuals with limited rationality and cognition respond to these rules. On the one hand, each individual takes the cognitive,

---

[1] Indeed, coordination problem is a characteristic of every game that is not dominance-solvable.

125

coordinative, and informational content of institutionalized rules as given; he responds to (or plays against) the rules, taking them as given. On the other hand, because each individual responds to these rules based on his private information and knowledge, such rules aggregate information and knowledge and distribute it in a compressed form.

The only social rules that can be institutionalized – that can be common knowledge, can be expected to be followed, and correspond to behavior – are rules that each individual finds optimal to follow, given his private information, knowledge, and preference. In situations in which institutions generate behavior, institutionalized rules and the associated beliefs correspond to self-enforcing behavior. Finally, because behavior corresponds to the institutionalized rules and the associated beliefs, these rules and beliefs are reproduced – not refuted – by behavior.

In situations in which institutions generate behavior, institutionalized rules, the corresponding internalized and behavioral beliefs, and the behavior that these beliefs motivate constitute an equilibrium. A structure made up of institutionalized rules and beliefs enables, guides, and motivates the self-enforcing behavior that reproduces it. Most individuals, most of the time, follow the behavior that is expected of them.

Section 5.2 employs this understanding of institutions to highlight why the game-theoretic analytical framework, which rests on seemingly unrealistic assumptions about cognition, information, and rationality, has been a useful tool for positive institutional analysis. Understanding why this is the case is essential to knowing when game theory can be usefully employed and to what extent.

The section argues that the game-theoretic analysis, which assumes a complete model and common knowledge and focuses on equilibrium strategies played by highly rational individuals, corresponds to a situation in which institutionalized rules that aggregate private knowledge and information provide shared cognition, information, and coordination. The game-theoretic analysis restricts the set of admissible rules, beliefs, and behavior to those in which each limitedly rational individual, responding to the cognitive, coordinative, and informational content of the institutionalized rules, follows the behavior expected of him.

In situations in which an institution generates behavior, the knowledge and information that are compressed into the institutionalized rules enable and guide individuals, despite their limited perception, knowledge, and computational ability, to act in a manner that leads to behavior and reflects the constraints on admissible beliefs and behavior that the game-theoretic equilibrium analysis captures. Classical game theory can

126

be usefully employed to study situations in which it is reasonable to assert that social rules were institutionalized.[2]

For simplicity of presentation, sections 5.1 and 5.2 ignore norms and social considerations. Section 5.3 supplements their discussions by elaborating on how to integrate normative and social considerations into the analysis. Indeed, a promising aspect of game theory is its ability to provide a unified analytical framework to study the cognitive, coordinative, normative, and informational foundations of behavior while capturing the response of individuals to both social, normative, and materialistic considerations.

Distinguishing between the object of study (institutions) and the analytical framework used to study it (game theory) is central to this chapter. This distinction is also the focus of studying the dynamics of endogenous institutions, the topic of Part III. To lead into this topic, section 5.4 explains why it is appropriate to study institutions without examining their origins. It also notes that legitimacy is crucial to the institutionalization of intentionally created institutions. Different societies can and do have distinct norms regarding legitimacy, each entailing a distinct institutional development. The different sources of legitimacy that established themselves in late medieval Europe and the Islamic world still prevail today. Section 5.5 summarizes the chapter's argument and delineates directions for further development.

The argument made in this chapter rests on a particular notion of rationality, maintaining that when institutions generate behavior, socially articulated and disseminated rules span the domain that people understand and within which they can act rationally. At the same time, the chapter recognizes that individuals are motivated by social and moral considerations. Are these two premises consistent with each other? Is it appropriate to consider individuals as strategic while recognizing that social and normative considerations influence their behavior? Appendix B presents evidence supporting the claim that although individuals have social and normative propensities, they are nevertheless rational in the sense just given.

Before proceeding, it is important to emphasize what this chapter *is not* about. The chapter is about institutions and not about their dynamics. It

---

[2] The discussion in Aoki (2001, pp. 13–14, 235–9, 412–13) is closest to the one developed here. He argued that institutions provide "summary representation" of situations and that the set of summary representations is constrained by individuals' responses to them.

focuses on regularities of behavior in the population as a whole while ignoring forces and factors that direct particular individuals to act differently, thereby sometimes leading to institutional change. I return to this important issue in Chapter 6.

5.1 INSTITUTIONALIZED RULES, INSTITUTIONS, AND EQUILIBRIA

The behavioral choices an individual makes require both a cognitive model and a sufficient amount of the right information (see Hayek 1937; Savage 1954; and North 2005). Cognitive models constitute one's understanding of the causal relationship between actions and outcomes. Although they are usually incomplete, they underlie rational as well as habitual and mimetic behavior (see Denzau and North 1994; Eysenck and Keane 1995; Clark 1997a, 1997b; and Mantzavinos 2001).[3] In addition, however, behavioral decisions require appropriate information about the particularities of the situation. For example, if one's model asserts that sufficiently religious people can be trusted, acting on this premise requires knowing the extent of peoples' religiosity.

Classical game theory is mute regarding the sources of the cognition and information required for behavior. But the analysis requires a strong and unrealistic assumption about players' cognition and information, calling attention to how, whether, and to what extent this requirement is met in the real world. The analysis requires that players have a complete and closed model of the situation and correct common priors.[4] It assumes that it is common knowledge that each player has complete information about the details of the situation, including causal relationships, other players' preferences, and the magnitude of various parameters. When such information is missing, the players assign the correct prior probabilities to all possible values of the unknown parameters. Each player assumes that

---

[3] Indeed, it is part of human nature to seek a rationale for actions ex post and to try to explain and develop a cognitively coherent account of past experiences to guide future behavior.

[4] The discussion here counters the assertion that game theory is inappropriate for institutional analysis because it assumes that the rules of the game are common knowledge, although common knowledge is neither necessary nor sufficient for the Nash equilibrium condition to hold (see Aumann and Brandenburger 1995). Nash can prevail or be reached in evolutionary and learning games without common knowledge, while common knowledge is sufficient only for the weaker equilibrium notion of rationalizable equilibrium (Bernheim 1984; Pearce 1984), the essence of which is the iterated elimination of dominated strategies.

his opponents are rational, that they model the game exactly as he does, and that they assign the same correct priors. Even after making these assumptions, the computational complexity required to find an equilibrium is daunting, even in moderately complicated games. How, then, can we expect real-world actors to reach an equilibrium when, as is common in complex situations, they lack a complete model? How can we assert that individuals can rationally calculate their way through games that are difficult even for the modeler?

Behavioral choices in social situations also rest on a player's ability to coordinate his behavior with that of others. Whether it is best to drive on the right or the left depends on what others are doing. Even in simple, repeated strategic situations, such as the prisoners' dilemma game, multiple equilibria usually exist (see Appendix A). Because there are multiple equilibria and because the behavior that serves one best depends on the particular equilibrium behavior others are following, rationality alone is insufficient to guide one how to behave. One faces a coordination problem. In the case of the Maghribi traders, for example, the strategy calling for merchants not to hire agents and for agents to cheat is also an equilibrium. Multiple equilibria imply that ex ante deduction is insufficient for choosing behavior (see, e.g., Schelling 1960; D. Lewis 1969; and Sugden 1989). Yet, one seeks to know – because it is beneficial for one to know – what particular strategy is followed by others. How do individuals choose behavior given that, even in the simplified world captured in the game-theoretic models, rationality alone is insufficient for making choices?

To solve a game there is a need to impose restrictive assumptions, such as the assumptions that individuals are highly rational, that they have the same cognitive understanding of the situation, and that all this is common knowledge. The analysis reveals the importance of coordination, as it indicates that multiple equilibria exist in strategic repeated situations. What does the need to impose such assumptions tell us about the real world? How can we assert that an analytical framework based on such unrealistic assumptions is useful for positive analysis? How and to what extent are these assumptions met in the real world?

Economists responded to these challenges by exploring whether learning by individuals with limited knowledge and information can lead to self-enforcing regularities of behavior.[5] The theory of learning in games asks if a rule of behavior corresponding to a Nash equilibrium can

---

[5] These models generally focused on learning about others' strategies or various parameters of the models. The lack of a theory to account for the emergence of endogenous

reflect individualistic learning. It turns out that reaching Nash equilibrium requires replacing the very demanding assumptions of classical game theory with a set of other demanding and unrealistic assumptions.[6] Learning models often require that individuals be completely myopic, implying unreasonable behavior, such as not performing a costly experiment no matter how high the resulting expected return might be. These assumptions are very restrictive, but not imposing them makes the analysis too complicated to provide a convincing account of how individuals learn.

Focusing on individualistic learning, however, ignores the social context within which institutionalized behavior takes place. In this context, socially articulated, disseminated, and commonly known rules provide individuals with the cognitive, coordinative, and informational foundations of behavior. In order to act, each individual needs a cognitive framework, information, and the means to coordinate his behavior. Individuals seek these micro-foundations of behavioral choices at the social level at which it is provided in the form of social rules. Sociologists have long noted that when taking actions, members of a society are aided by rules providing "socially sanctioned facts of life . . . that any bona fide member of the society knows" (Garfinkel 1967, p. 76). Decision making at the individual level is done in the context of commonly known social rules that provide a cognitive system, information, and coordination.

These rules are shared by members of a society: everyone knows them, and everyone knows that others know them. The rules can emerge spontaneously (e.g., in the form of social norms) or deliberately (through a political process); they can be formulated quickly or over a long period of experimentation and social learning. Social rules are transmitted in diverse forms, through laws, regulations, customs, taboos, conventional rules of behavior, and constitutions. They are articulated and disseminated by such socializing agents as parents, teachers, peers, priests, tribal elders, and CEOs; they become identical and commonly known during the socialization process, during which they are unified, maintained, and communicated. They are transmitted by myths, fables, holy scriptures, educational systems, public announcements, manuals, and ceremonies and

cognitive systems based on individualistic learning lends support to the assertion made later about the importance of social rules.

[6] Schotter's (1981) seminal work pioneered the application of learning game theory to institutional analysis. Regarding learning, see Marimon (1997); Fudenberg and Levin (1998); Rubinstein (1998); and Young (1998). Evolutionary game theory was another response to justifying the use of Nash equilibria. Chapter 1 argues that it suffers from drawbacks similar to learning game theory.

disseminated by various carriers, such as parents, teachers, priests, and regulatory agencies.[7]

Such socially articulated and transmitted rules contain a cognitive system that embodies, transmits, and propagates knowledge and information reflecting the accumulated experience and innovativeness of past and present members of the society. A cognitive system provides the terms for describing socially recognized and created items, ideas, actors, events, and possible actions to which the system also imputes meanings. It articulates the objectives and capabilities of various actors and the outcomes associated with various circumstances; those who speak publicly against a dictator suffer, for example, and those who are honest in per period profitable exchange prosper. A cognitive system constitutes a shared cultural understanding (a script or interpretive frames) of the way the world works (Zucker 1983, 1991; Meyer and Rowen 1991; DiMaggio and Powell 1991a; Dobbin 1994; Scott 1995) and provides typification, classifications, and meanings, using symbols such as words and signs. In a sports game, for example, the cognitive system enables us to communicate and comprehend various physical items (such as a basketball), ideas (winning), events (fouls and free throws), actors (a captain and coach), and the set of events or actions that fall into a particular category (such as those that entail winning) (see D'Andrade 1984; Searle 1995; and Scott 1995).

Using the typification, categorization, and cognition provided by the cognitive system, the "behavioral rules" component of social rules specify what is expected of individuals with particular social positions in various circumstances: members of the two basketball teams have to stand in particular positions during a free throw, a driver must stop at what is cognitively defined as a stoplight, and a Maghribi merchant is expected to hire only an honest Maghribi agent and to reciprocate in sharing information. Social rules also specify the objective function of the team (winning). Social rules define, articulate, and disseminate social positions, objectives, causal relationships, and expected behavior. By providing commonly known cognition, information, and coordination, they delineate causal relationships and expected intertransactional linkages, behavior, and outcomes.

---

[7] See, for example, K. Davis (1949, in particular pp. 52ff., 192ff.) and Bandura (1971). Even the form of circular seating in organizations for collective decision making – from the ancient Native American councils to the U.S. Congress – is aimed at making decisions common knowledge (Chwe 2001).

Analyses of the necessary conditions under which learning leads to equilibrium behavior reveals the behavioral implications of commonly known social rules. These analyses indirectly indicate that the properties of learning guided by commonly known rules are very different from those based on individualistic learning. Reaching self-enforcing regularities of behavior requires neither the restrictive conditions of classical game theory nor those of individualistically based learning models. Indeed, reaching regularities of equilibrium behavior rests on intuitive assertions.

Kalai and Lehrer (1993a, 1995) considered learning in a repeated game in which individuals share a cognitive system but each knows only his payoff matrix and discount factor. In other words, the players have the same cognitive understanding of the situation, they do not know the relevant parameters of the model, and the objective of each is to maximize his payoff. Observing the outcomes of the game, each player can develop his own subjective evaluation of these parameters and others' strategies. The analysis also assumes that individuals are subjectively rational, in the sense that they start with subjective beliefs about the strategies used by each of their opponents. There is no assumption that each player believes the others are rational. Each individual then uses these beliefs to compute his own optimal strategy.

Analyzing the process of learning reveals that one of the main requirements for convergence on regularities of behavior is a restriction on each player's initial subjective beliefs about other players' strategies. If each player's initial subjective beliefs assign a positive probability to the events that will indeed occur in the play of the game, then eventually learning will lead each player to be able to predict the behavior of the others. Furthermore, these players will converge in finite time to play a Nash equilibrium of the real game.[8] Subjectively developed beliefs converge on

---

[8] Specifically, they will learn to play an equilibrium that satisfies the Nash restrictions or those of the epsilon–Nash equilibrium, but such details are not important here.

Although the argument in Kalai and Lehrer (1993a) is intuitive, the technical analysis rests on the assumption that individuals use Bayesian updating in response to new information. In fact, people may not update their beliefs based on Bayesian reasoning. If they do not, however, social rules specifying other players' behavior are arguably even more important in leading to regularities of behavior. Indeed, a sufficient condition for a Nash equilibrium is that every individual should have an accurate prediction of what others will do rather than knowledge (or common knowledge) of the rules of the game (Aumann and Brandenburger 1995). The intuition is that a Nash equilibrium is a strategy combination in which each player's strategy is optimal for him, given the strategy of the others. If each player knows what others will play and nevertheless finds it optimal to behave as expected of him, the rule of behavior must satisfy the Nash condition.

equilibrium beliefs. An initial "grain of truth" regarding others' behavior is thus sufficient for individuals to learn independently how others will play and for convergence on an equilibrium.

The implication regarding the role of social rules in leading to regularities of behavior is clear: an initial "grain of truth" regarding others' behavior provided by social rules is sufficient for individuals to learn independently how others will play and for convergence on a (Nash) regularity of behavior. *Social rules help individuals form beliefs – represented by probabilistic estimates – about the situation and what others will do.*[9] As long as subjectively rational individuals accept the behavior associated with the social rule as possibly correct and respond based on their private knowledge and information, learning will lead to a regularity of behavior (specifically, to a Nash equilibrium).[10] Furthermore, a social rule that correctly informs each individual about how others will actually play is a sufficient condition for a Nash equilibrium, even if the player has neither a complete model nor the ability to make the necessary calculations to find the equilibrium set. If the rule is correct, it must be the case that each player, responding to the rule based on his private information and knowledge, finds it optimal to follow the rule.

In situations in which institutions generate behavior, social rules correctly inform each individual how others will behave because of their dual nature as exogenous to each individual whose behavior they influence but endogenous to all of them. They are exogenous to each individual in the sense of being commonly known. But because each individual is playing against these rules, they aggregate private information and knowledge through each player's response to them.[11] In situations in which institutions generate behavior, social rules and the associated beliefs therefore constitute an equilibrium. Each individual, relying on the social rule to enable and guide his behavior – to form beliefs about

---

[9] See Schotter (1981, p. 52) on the informational role of norms. See D. Lewis (1969); Sugden (1986, 1989); and Young (1993, 1998) on the informational role of conventions. These analyses focus on individualistic learning rather than the role of institutionalized rules in guiding behavior.

[10] One should not confuse formal rules with institutionalized ones. The formal rules of the road set speed limits, but after watching how fast experienced drivers go, new drivers usually do not adhere to these limits for long. The formal rule helps drivers form beliefs, which they update based on observed behavior.

[11] "Playing against the rules" means neither playing in accordance with nor playing in violation of the rules. It means that each individual takes the commonly known social rules as exogenous and bases his behavioral choices on the content of these rules as well as his private knowledge, information, and preferences.

others' behavior and his best choice of action – finds it best to follow the rule.

In such situations one does not need to know more than this social rule, because *institutionalized rules aggregate private information and knowledge and distribute it in compressed form.* If, for Hayek, institutions constitute a "device for coping with our ignorance" (1976, p. 29), this device manifests itself in institutionalized rules. Institutionalized rules are a useful device because they provide the cognition, information, and coordination required for choosing behavior. They span the domain within which one can make rational decisions. At the same time, institutionalized rules aggregate the knowledge and information of the interacting individuals. In doing so, they direct individuals to play an equilibrium outcome.

This role of institutionalized rules is well recognized for the particular case of market prices. They aggregate market participants' private information and correspond to an equilibrium outcome. Taking market prices as given, each economic agent responds based on his private information. Hence unless prices already incorporate all of this private information, they cannot be in equilibrium. The response of economic agents will cause the quantity demanded to differ from the quantity supplied, causing prices to change. In equilibrium, prices provide a sufficient statistic for each individual to make an informed, optimal decision. At the center of the argument is the relationship between a public signal and each individual's response to it.

A similar relationship between a public signal – institutionalized rules – and each individual's response to it is at work in situations in which institutions generate behavior more generally. Institutionalized rules provide coordination, and they aggregate and disseminate knowledge and information. The only social rules that can correspond to actual behavior are those in which each individual, basing his decision on his private knowledge and information, finds it optimal to follow the rules. Hence, in an institution, institutionalized rules aggregate the private knowledge and information of all agents, providing each with a sufficient statistic to make an informed decision.[12]

Behavior in competitive markets theoretically aggregates information correctly; this is not necessarily the case for institutionalized rules in

---

[12] This is not to argue that rules precede beliefs in the process of institutional emergence; as the discussion in Part III emphasizes, beliefs often precede rules. Similarly, there is not necessarily a process of learning and a convergence, as the issue of choosing which side of the road to use when driving reveals. The argument here is about the system of rules and beliefs that can be institutionalized.

general. When information is revealed through behavior in social interactions, the information aggregation process depends on the prevailing self-enforcing behavior, which, in turn, depends on the available information. If the players believe that the time discount factor cannot support cooperation in a repeated prisoners' dilemma game, for example, they will not cooperate and therefore never find out that this is not the case. Although one knows his discount factor, others' discount factors are not revealed to him by their behavior.[13]

In situations in which institutions generate behavior people are motivated to acquire the relevant public signal – social rules – just as they are motivated to learn about prices in market situations. In the market each individual is motivated to discover what are the prevailing prices because of their informational value. More generally, individuals interacting in situations in which institutions generate behavior have an incentive to discover the prevailing rules of behavior, because they reflect an equilibrium and hence following them is one's best response. In deciding how to act and when forming beliefs about others' behavior, individuals respond to socially transmitted rules that they believe come from a reliable source. Doing otherwise is costly, and at times the implications are even irreversible: one may not have many opportunities to find out if individuals are expected to drive on the left or the right or how others will act at an intersection.[14]

The Maghribi traders and the German merchants whose behaviors were examined in Chapters 3 and 4 did not have to solve the mathematical models we now use to study their institutions – nor did they have the information required to do so. Yet each trader or merchant was motivated to learn and was guided by a simple socially transmitted rule of behavior to which he responded based on his private information and knowledge. Game-theoretic analysis is useful in considering this feedback, because it captures the response of each individual to the shared beliefs – created by social rules – about how others will play and restricts the set of these beliefs to be an equilibrium.

---

[13] Kuran (1995) emphasized that private information is often distorted in situations in which institutions generate behavior. Individuals are deterred from correctly revealing information about their preferences given the information about others' preferences revealed by this behavior. An individual is motivated to falsify the public representation of his preference as this is the best response to the information revealed by the rules.

[14] This is not to say that institutions do not endogenously change and people do not seek to alter the prevailing equilibrium. I return to this issue in Part III.

We can thus see how institutionalized rules and the beliefs they help form enable, guide, and motivate most individuals to adopt the behavior associated with their social position most of the time.[15] An individual adopts the appropriate behavior because other members of the society condition their behavior on the individual's social position; given the others' expected behavior, an individual's best response is to behave in the way others expect him to.[16] Socially constructed characteristics – social positions – have behaviorally meaningful implications, because equilibrium behavior and expected behavior are conditioned on them.[17] The king's strength comes not from his army but from the beliefs held by each member of the army that everyone else will obey the king's orders and that the best response is also to obey. In situations in which institutions generate behavior, rules of behavior are both prescriptive and descriptive; institutionalization is complete when the behavior associated with the institutionalized rules becomes routine, habitual, and taken for granted.[18]

Whether the private or social propagation of rules will better prevail – and hence be more likely to prevail – depends on the structure of the situation. When this structure is such that an individual who does not know the relevant rules imposes an externality on others, rules are better propagated socially through a dedicated public organization. Because society does not want every new driver to figure out the rules of the road through experimentation, it mandates that a public organization establish the rules of the road and disseminate them. When there is no such externality, rules

[15] The reasons for and the role of deviators is discussed later in this chapter and in Part III.

[16] In situations in which institutions generate behavior, individuals are seemingly *rule followers*; they follow the rules associated with the social positions they occupy. March and Olsen (1989) argue that peoples' tendency to adopt the behavior associated with their position does not reflect an instrumental logic that asks, "What is my interest in this situation?" Instead, this tendency reflects a "logic of appropriateness," which asks, "Given my role in this situation, what is expected of me?" March and Olsen argue that individuals behave "appropriately" out of a sense of social obligation rather than the promise of reward or the fear of punishment. Such intrinsic motivation is critical, as I discuss later and is easily integrated in the framework developed here. But the mere observation that people seek to find out and then follow the behavior associated with their roles does not reveal the logic behind it.

[17] As Calvert (1995, p. 59) notes, if "the underlying game ... does not set apart any individual players as having special opportunities or powers, then such role differentiation can be maintained only as part of an equilibrium."

[18] In sociology, institutionalization is considered the process in which social practices become sufficiently regular and continuous to be described as institutions (Abercrombie et al., 1994, p. 216).

are more likely to be propagated privately, based on the incentives of individuals to study or transmit them. Among the Maghribis, fathers taught their sons the appropriate rules. When institutionalized rules serve the interest of particular social units – parents, the state, the church, priests, corporate CEOs – they will labor to propagate these rules.

Public propagation of institutionalized rules also takes place because the role of many institutions is deterrence, and actual punishment is socially costly. Furthermore, complex institutions of this sort often rely on the coordinated response of many to a deviation. In situations in which it is the expected reactions of the many that influence one's decision how to act, it is imperative that the understanding of the circumstances under which individuals have to act be common knowledge. It is imperative that many individuals attribute the same meaning to an objective situation or action.

This role of rules was already noted in Chapter 3, which argued that the credibility of the threat in collective punishment among the Maghribis would have been undermined without a merchants' law that defined a common, shared, ex ante understanding of what actions constituted cheating (Greif 1993, p. 542). The study of the Hanseatic League also reflects the importance of a shared understanding of the meaning of various actions. Institutional failures in this case led to organizational changes; as Chapter 4 showed, the embargo of 1360 ushered in a long period in which no conflict occurred between Bruges and the Hansa. This outcome was due partly to a change in the underlying cognitive foundation. The merchants' privileges were written "in much detail as to prevent any one-sided interpretations" (Dollinger 1970, p. 66). Fearing the responses of many merchants, agents and rulers did not cheat or abuse property rights. The shared meaning of various actions was therefore crucial to making this collective response credible.

Rules specifying the meanings of various actions (i.e., whether a transgression has occurred or not) are general features of situations in which the threat of collective responses influence actions. Social pacts, customary laws, constitutions, and traditions are among the manifestations of rules that, by creating common knowledge, lend credibility to such threats.[19]

---

[19] Shared meaning and the collective responses that such meaning renders possible also provide the institutional foundation of the state. The Magna Carta offers an example of how institutionalized rules provide the institutional foundations of the state by creating the shared meaning required for beliefs that political agents will collectively respond to a transgression of their rights by a ruler. For analyses in this spirit of modern political systems, see Hardin (1989); Prezworski (1991); and Weingast (1995, 1997), among others.

In situations in which institutions generate behavior, rules disseminate a shared cognitive system (including the specification of social positions and states of nature), which is needed to specify and transmit behavioral rules whose information content and coordination functions help individuals form beliefs about what others will do and hence choose their behavior. Each individual, seeking guidance for behavior at the social level, is motivated to learn them. Each individual responds to these rules based on his private knowledge and information, leading to the aggregation of knowledge and information. In situations in which institutions generate behavior, each individual finds it best to follow these rules, and because each individual behaves as expected, no information is generated to cause individuals to change their behavior. Regularities of behavior prevail, and players hold accurate beliefs about others' behavior, even though they lack a complete model or the ability to deduce others' behavior.

5.2 GAME THEORY AND MODELING ENDOGENOUS INSTITUTIONS

We can now see why and to what extent game theory is a useful tool for studying behavior generated by institutions. The game-theoretic assumption that the rules of the game are common knowledge captures the cognitive and informational roles of social rules. The focus on strategies – plans of behavior – that are common knowledge captures the coordinative role of social rules. The game-theoretic analysis captures the idea that in situations in which institutions generate behavior, social rules provide players with a common cognitive model, information, and coordination that enables each individual to form beliefs about others' behavior. It restricts the rules that can prevail to those that are self-enforcing, where each individual, expecting that everyone else will follow the rules, finds it optimal to follow them as well.

The games used to study the Maghribis' coalition and the merchant guild embodied cognitive aspects, such as traders, merchants, agents, cheating, rulers, territory, money, penalties, cities. The models also assumed that the players had the required knowledge to condition their actions on these cognitive aspects – that the Maghribi traders knew how to recognize each other and shared a common understanding of what behavior constituted cheating, for example. The analysis of the merchant guilds assumed that the merchants were informed about aspects of the situation, such as the territorial area of a ruler, who the representative of the

Kontor was, who a merchant from a particular town was, and so forth. Simple rules of behavior enabled and guided the behavior of merchants, agents, and rulers.

At the same time, game-theoretic analysis restricts the set of admissible social rules that can be common knowledge and correspond to behavior exactly by demanding that these rules aggregate private knowledge and information. The game-theoretic analysis restricts the set of behavioral beliefs that can be common knowledge, correspond to behavior, and are not refuted by it. The analysis achieves that by considering possible equilibria. When beliefs that the interacting individuals hold are commonly known, and each player plays his best response to them (and is rational in this limited sense), the set of beliefs is restricted to those associated with an equilibrium behavior. In other words, admissible behavioral beliefs and the corresponding coordinative rules are those that are self-enforcing (Greif 1994a, p. 915).[20] Nash equilibrium analysis restricts beliefs about behavior on the equilibrium path – that is, in circumstances that can transpire with positive probability given the expected behavior. Equilibrium refinement concepts, such as subgame perfection, restrict beliefs about behavior off the equilibrium path – that is, in circumstances that will not transpire given the expected behavior. Using the subgame perfection equilibrium concept has the intuitive appeal of restricting expected promises and threats off the equilibrium path to those that are credible. The Nash restriction (on behavior on the equilibrium path) also limits the set of admissible behavioral beliefs, and hence institutionalized rules, to those that are reproduced, not refuted, by the implied behaviors. Nash equilibrium requires that individuals correctly anticipate one another's behavior, and hence they do not encounter behavior that refutes their expectations.

---

[20] Formally, in a complete-information, extensive-form game, denote by P a path of play, and define $S(P)$ to be the set of all strategy combinations for which the path of play is P. Denote the beliefs of player i by $B_i(S(P))$, defined as a probability distribution over $S(P)$. Note that the possible probability distributions differ only in the weight they place on different behaviors off the path of play. Concentrating on this probability distribution thus captures the notion that the player has to hold the beliefs generated by the observation that a particular path of play is followed. Denote by $B(s^*)$ the shared beliefs that strategy combination $s^* \in S(P)$ will be played. That is, $B_i(S(P)) = \{\text{Probs}^*(P) = 1\} \; \forall \, i \text{ for } s^* \in S(P)$. When $U_i(s_i, B(s^*)) \geq U_i(s_i, B(s^*))$ $\forall \, i$ and $\forall \, s_i \in S_i$ (i.e., following this strategy is the best response given the beliefs), then s^* is a Nash equilibrium. Hence $s^*(P)$ is an equilibrium, and the associated beliefs are self-enforcing.

Game-theoretic equilibrium analysis restricts the set of institutionalized behavioral rules and beliefs (including beliefs about intertransactional linkages) that guide and motivate behavior given the cognitive content of the institutionalized rules. At the same time, it restricts the set of admissible internalized beliefs – the cognitive content of institutionalized rules – to those that are reproduced, not refuted, by the resulting behavior. Applying the Nash restriction does not directly limit the cognitive structure imputed in the rules of the game. Indeed, there is no theory that deductively restricts the admissible set of cognitive structures in a given situation.[21] Yet because such an analysis exposes the relationships between the rules of the game and possible outcomes, we can restrict admissible models to those in which the implied behavior reproduces – does not refute – the cognitive models imputed in the game.[22]

The logic of reproduction of the cognitive model – its confirmation by the observed outcomes – must have been on the mind of the prophet Elijah when he challenged the pagan priests of Baal to call upon their idol to light a fire on his altar on Mount Carmel. Their failure to demonstrate their idol's ability in this way cost them their lives and convinced the Israelites to return to worshiping God. The repeated failure of the merchant guilds to protect the property rights of the German merchants in Bruges refuted the merchants' beliefs that rights would be respected. Institutional change followed.

A game-theoretic analysis therefore evaluates whether, given our perception of the objective structure of the situation, the assertion that a particular institution – consisting of particular rules and beliefs – is logically consistent. The analysis restricts institutionalized rules by limiting the set of admissible beliefs and behavior to those that are self-enforcing and reproducing. (For simplicity I henceforth refer to such institutions as self-enforcing and denote reproduction separately only when the distinction between the two concepts is important.)

---

[21] Reviewing the vast literature in cognitive science, Mantzavinos (2001) argues that we are not likely to develop such a theory. Kaneko and Matsui (1999) and Aoki (2001) developed inductive game theory, which explores whether purely individualistic behavior can generate regularities of behavior when each of the interactive individuals inductively develops his own subjective understanding of the situation.

[22] As is well known, individuals tend to interpret evidence in a way that confirms their prior beliefs. Part III considers the implications of this tendency for institutional change.

Technically, presenting a situation as a game entails specifying the rules of the game, the relevant actors, their actions, the information available to each when choosing behavior, and the outcomes associated with various behavioral choices. The discussion presented here, however, highlights that conceptually, when we present a situation as a game, we are making a statement about our own understanding of the objective features of the situation, our perception of the relevant intertransactional linkages, and the cognitive and informational content of the prevailing institutionalized rules. A model constitutes a statement about the players' understanding of the situation (Rubinstein 1991).

When interpreting the analysis, therefore, we have to keep in mind that while we study games, real-world actors do not play against the (commonly known) rules of the game but against commonly known institutionalized rules.[23] The Maghribi traders' coalition was studied as if each individual played against the rules of the game. The analysis indicates that there could have been a cognitive model of the situation consistent with our understanding of it and beliefs about the various unobservable features of the situation (e.g., time preferences and outside options) that could have rendered self-enforcing the beliefs in the rules of intragroup hiring, honesty, and punishment. Clearly, each Maghribi trader did not solve this game-theoretic model, directly observe the factors that were important to others' decisions, or necessarily understand the nature of the institution as an equilibrium outcome. But the analysis substantiated that each trader could have found it optimal to adhere to the associated behavioral rules while responding to the social rule.

Such analyses can be used to capture, when appropriate, the direct and indirect influences on behavior of the actors' (internalized) belief system regarding the natural and supernatural worlds around them. These internalized beliefs influence the perceived utility of taking a particular action and thereby directly influencing it. Notice that these beliefs may be unverifiable on the path of play. If enough members of a society internalize the belief that God will send a cheater to hell, they may behave honestly. The Aztecs internalized the belief that the world would end if human blood was not shed in the evening. The belief could not be refuted by observable outcomes, because it motivated the Aztecs to shed blood every evening. Outcomes that could have refuted the beliefs were off the path of play and the existence of alternative possible institutions was not revealed.

---

[23] The game-theoretic implications of this distinction are not yet well developed.

Internalized beliefs indirectly influence institutionalized behavior by changing the set of self-enforcing behavioral beliefs. If the internalized belief that God sends blasphemers to hell is an institutional element, a borrower can credibly commit to pay his debt by taking an oath to be honest, because breaking the oath would show contempt for God and entail divine punishment. Of course, there can be uncertainty over who internalized such a belief. Such uncertainty is captured in incomplete information models, which reveal that even if the actual number of true believers in the population is small or even zero, it can nevertheless have a large impact on behavior, because nonbelievers find it beneficial to pretend to be believers (see Kreps et al. 1982; Appendix C; and Kuran 1995).

Although institutions generate regularities of behavior, there are usually some individuals who, for idiosyncratic reasons, will not follow the behavior expected of people in their positions. The implied responses to such deviations are important in reproducing institutionalized rules and beliefs regarding behavior off the path of play. Game theory restricts the analysis of this deviation-as-confirmation mechanism in two ways. First, this mechanism operates only if the threats that follow deviations are credible. Behavior and expected behavior have to correspond to a subgame perfect equilibrium that restricts the threat of behavior off the equilibrium path to be credible. Second, game-theoretic learning models explicitly incorporate how individuals update their beliefs about others' behavior in the specification of the game, thereby enabling a study of the limits of the deviation-as-conformation mechanism.

Ironically, the more effective an institution is in preventing deviations, the more individuals are likely to maintain that different rules of behavior will prevail off the equilibrium path. More generally, "semi-institutionalized" situations are those in which there is no uniformity of expectations regarding actions that will be taken off the equilibrium path. On-the-path-equilibrium behavior (where there is uniformity of beliefs) is still self-enforcing and reproducing, and each individual's best response is to follow the behavior expected of him.[24]

---

[24] Subjective game theory (Kalai and Lehrer 1993b, 1995) and self-confirming equilibria (Fudenberg and Levine 1993, 2003) provide an appropriate analytical framework in this case. Roughly speaking, in equilibrium an individual can hold any beliefs about the behavior of others that is not contradicted by the observed implications of the actual behavior and still generates the equilibrium path behavior. For an empirical analysis of such a semi-institutionalized situation, see De Figueiredo, Rakove, and Weingast (2001).

5.3 INSTITUTIONAL RAMIFICATIONS OF SOCIAL AND NORMATIVE BEHAVIOR

The discussion so far has ignored the social and normative foundation of behavior.[25] Everything else being equal, people seek to act in a manner that generates positive social responses by the people they know, elevates their social status and esteem in the broader society, provides them with identity, and is consistent with their (internalized) norms.

In modern sociology the argument over the behavioral importance of social exchange, beliefs in others' social responses, or losses of esteem following a particular action is associated with Homans (1961), Wrong (1999, 1961), and Granovetter (1985). Another line of research, associated with Talcott Parsons (1951), emphasizes the importance of norms in motivating behavior by influencing the intrinsic utility from it.[26] Internalization of norms, or the incorporation of behavioral standards into one's superego, essentially means the development of an internal system of sanctions, one that supports the same behavior as the external system.[27] In this theory, "values and norms were regarded as the basis of a stable social order" (Scott 1995, p. 40).[28]

Recent work in experimental game theory has convinced even skeptical economists of the importance of the social and normative foundations of behavior. Some individuals do act altruistically – (that is, they are willing to decrease their own material welfare if it increases that of others

---

[25] Sociologists have explored this foundation (for reviews, see Wrong 1961, 1999 and Scott 1995). Its importance has also been stressed by many prominent economists, including Becker (1974); Arrow (1981); Hirshleifer (1985); Akerlof (1986); Lal (1998); North (1990); Platteau (1994); Samuelson (1993); and Sen (1995). Evolutionary models of the origin of social and normative propensities can be traced back to Wilson (1975). For recent contributions, see Güth and Yaari (1992); Güth (1992); Bowles and Gintis (1998); Huck and Oechssler (1999); Bester and Güth (1998); Kockesen, Ok, and Sethil (2000a, 2000b); Ely and Yilankaya (1997); Dekel, Fudenberge, and Levine (1999), and the reviews and contributions in Field (2002) and Gintis (2000). Some evolutionary models, such as Kandori (2003), cast doubt on the long-run sustainability of normative behavior, pointing out that they are likely to be eroded.

[26] Psychologists define an intrinsically motivated act as one that is taken despite the lack of any reward from doing so except for the value of the action itself (see the review in Frey 1997, pp. 13–14).

[27] On norms and their transmission, see K. Davis (1949); Cavalli-Sforza and Feldman (1981); Bandura (1971); Witt (1986); Shapiro (1983); and Elster (1989a, 1989b).

[28] A finer sociological distinction is that between values specifying the preferred or the desirable (e.g., winning the game) and norms specifying the legitimate means of achieving these goals (e.g., winning by playing fair). To simplify the discussion, I use the term *norm* to include both.

(Andreoni and Miller 2002; Charness and Grosskopf 2001; Kritkos and Bolle 1999). Knowing another person – even just by sight – alters how altruistic one is willing to be toward that person.[29] Some people exhibit inequality aversion, expressed as concern about the equality of the pay-offs between themselves and others.[30] Many individuals reciprocate the behavior of others, even if doing so reduces their material well-being. They respond to "fair" behavior, for example, with actions that raise others' material payoffs.

Such social and normative behavior is *situationally contingent*: whether a particular action insults others, how status is acquired, who is deserving of altruism, and what constitutes fair behavior depend on the time and place. As sociologists and anthropologists have long argued, a wide range of behavior is socially and normatively sanctioned. Findings in social physiology (see, e.g., Ross and Nisbett 1991) lend support to this observation.[31] Game-theoretic experiments conducted by E. Hoffman, McCabe, Shachat, and Smith (1994), Henrich et al. (2001, 2004), and Roth et al. (1991) among others reach the same conclusions.[32]

The social and normative foundations of behavior can have institutional ramifications. "Institutions are something beyond us and something

---

[29] Consider the dictator game experiment in Bohnet and Frey (1999), in which the "dictator" can impose any division of ten dollars between himself and another player. Only 25 percent of dictators divided the money equally when the game was played anonymously, but 71 percent did so when the two players were identified to each other. See also Dawes and Thaler (1988); E. Hoffman, McCabe, Shachat, and Smith (1994); E. Hoffman, McCabe, and Smith, (1996a, 1996b); and Ostrom (1998).

[30] Fehr and Schmidt (1999) survey relevant experiments; see also Loewsenstein, Bazerman, and Thomson (1989) and Bolton and Ockenfels (2000). Some individuals are willing to make inequality-increasing sacrifices when they are efficient and inexpensive.

[31] For theoretical support, see Andreoni and Miller (2002). They note the failure to find a general model of social preferences and conclude that "many things other than the final allocation of money are likely to matter to subjects. Theories may need to include some variables from the game and the context in which the game is played if we are to understand the subtle influence on moral behavior like altruism" (p. 20). The axiomatic approach for social preferences led to similar conclusions (Segal and Sobel 2000).

[32] Platteau and Hayami (1998) and Platteau (2000) have argued that environmental factors influence norms. Different norms manifest themselves even in current laws. For empirical evidence from the United States, see Young and Burke (2001). Distinct notions of who is responsible for acting altruistically toward whom are reflected in social welfare policy. Until very recently, the Japanese Civic Code Article 877 specified that family members within three lineal generations had an obligation to pay for the living costs of a disabled family member. This is not the case in the United States, where family members have no such legal responsibility.

in ourselves," wrote Durkheim (1953, p. 129). They are "something in ourselves" when beliefs associated with social responses and expected normative behavior generate regularities of behavior. Studying the institutions within ourselves amounts to studying particular intertransactional linkages. Considering the institutional ramifications of social exchange amounts to examining the linkage between social and economic transactions; studying norms amounts to examining the "transaction" between an individual's superego and his ego or id.

A way to study such social and normative intertransactional linkages analytically using the game-theoretic framework is to take norms and beliefs associated with social exchange as given and integrate norms and social sensitivities in the specifications of actions and payoffs. Such games allow one, for example, to take a "social" action, such as displaying spite, and to specify the players' preference to be conditional on such actions. The behavioral beliefs and behavior that can prevail as an equilibrium outcome in this extended game are then studied; self-enforcing behavioral rules and beliefs will reflect the actual or perceived social responses of others' reactions to various actions and the psychological cost of acting in ways that are not consistent with one's internalized norms.[33]

We can go farther and use game theory to study the simultaneous determination of behavior and its social and normative foundations. The situational contingency of social and normative considerations implies that people seek social and normative guidance about what is socially acceptable and normatively appropriate. They find this guidance at the society level in the form of social rules that define the means for gaining status, the reasons to resent others, the behavior that is normatively sanctioned, and the normative frame to use in particular situations.[34] Which of these commonly known beliefs about social responses and which norms that motivate behavior can be self-enforcing? What factors influence whether socially appropriate and normative behavior is a cultural phenomenon that does not correspond to behavior or institutionalized rules that do?

[33] There is much related economic research (mainly theoretical and focusing on contractual and organizations issues), reviewed in Fehr and Schmidt (1999). Cole, Mailath, and Postlewaite (1992) analyzes the growth implication of how societies bestow social status upon their members. See also Fershtman and Weiss (1993) and Benabou (1994). The difference in normative dispositions among individuals (indicated by experimental game theory) can be incorporated in the analysis using incomplete information games. See Kreps et al. (1982).

[34] A framing effect (Tversky and Kahneman 1981) is a change of preferences between options as a result of a change in the formulation of the issue or problem.

Game theory is flexible enough to allow players' preferences to be specified in a way that captures their sensitivity to others' social responses and the dependency of their norms on the extent to which others adhere to them. At the same time, this specification can and should capture the material costs that such behavior can entail. It thus allows us to model the simultaneous determination of behavior and its social and normative foundations through feedback between each individual's choice of behavior and aggregate behavior. Using game theory, we can identify the factors that influence socially appropriate and normative behavior by considering which social and normative rules of behavior can be common knowledge and correspond to an equilibrium behavior while each individual responds to them while taking into account the material cost of following them whenever appropriate.

As an example, consider the analysis of Höllander (1990), who integrates social exchange theory in examining voluntary cooperation in the provision of public goods.[35] He assumes that individuals respond to emotionally prompted social approval and that the desire to gain social approval influences economic behavior. When choosing behavior, each individual considers the economic cost of contributing a particular amount to the public good as well as the social approval and disapproval associated with doing so. The social approval or disapproval that a particular action implies is determined by the actions other individuals have taken. Specifically, the social approval or disapproval is proportional to the difference between one's contribution to the public good and the others' average contribution. In the game-theoretic equilibrium, an individual's behavior is influenced by self-enforcing behavioral beliefs about how much others will contribute and the implied trade-off between the desire for social approval and the cost of providing a public good.[36] Annex 7.1

---

[35] His analysis therefore examines the implication of linking an economic transaction with a social one. As noted below, institutions also influence whether a contribution to a particular public good confers esteem or not.

[36] Psychological game theory (Geanakoplos, Pearce, and Stacchetti 1989) studies endogenous psychological motivations, such as anger and pride, by assuming that utility functions are belief dependent. "The players' payoffs depend not only on what everybody does but also on what everybody thinks" (p. 61). Equilibrium beliefs correspond to reality and deviation from expected equilibrium behavior can trigger an emotional response. One's behavior is influenced by self-enforcing beliefs about others' emotional responses, and these beliefs are reproduced by the implied behavior. Applicability is limited by the problem of multiple equilibria (see Rabin 1993; Fehr and Schmidt 1999; and Charness and Rabin 2002; for a game-theoretic evolutionary approach to norms, see Frank 1987).

in Chapter 7 provides an example of a game-theoretic analysis of social exchange.[37]

As this discussion illustrates, a useful feature of game theory is that it allows us to study all intertransactional linkages – economic, coercive, social, and normative – simultaneously using the same analytical framework. Such an integrative framework responds to the concerns of the eminent sociologist Dennis H. Wrong (1999), who argues that taking the social and normative foundations of behavior as exogenous is too simplistic. We cannot, according to Wrong, "dispense with the venerable notion of material 'interests' and invariably replace it with the blander, more integrative 'social values'" (p. 43). Recognizing the importance of normative considerations "does not mean that...[they] have been completely molded by the particular norms and values of their culture" (pp. 45–6). What is needed is an integrative framework that captures the fact that various factors – social, normative, and materialistic – can simultaneously influence behavior. Game theory provides such a framework, one in which social exchange, norms, and materialistic considerations (regarding money, power, and other materialistic rewards and sanctions) can easily be integrated.

In a game-theoretic analysis, payoffs can be conditioned on the actions taken to reach a particular outcome and the players' beliefs regarding appropriate and emotional responses. This attribute of the game-theoretic framework renders it useful for studying the normative and social foundations of institutionalized behavior. These considerations can be incorporated in the rules of the game to examine their impact on behavior and behavioral beliefs. They can also be derived endogenously as equilibrium outcomes.

5.4 LEGITIMACY AND THE ORIGIN OF INSTITUTIONS

Because institutions are equilibrium phenomena, it is conceptually sound and analytically useful to discuss them without examining their origins. Whether an institution evolved spontaneously or was established intentionally, whether it reflects individualistic learning, evolutionary pressure, or social design, its equilibrium nature is the same. I touch on some aspects of institutional origin in Chapter 7. Here the discussion focuses on the way rules are mapped into beliefs, as it is such mapping that differentiates

---

[37] Aoki (2001) provides a game-theoretic analysis of social exchange in premodern Japan.

social from institutionalized rules. Social rules are commonly known, whereas institutionalized rules are social rules that are commonly believed to be followed.

For an institution to be established by decree, it is necessary that a sufficiently large number of those who are supposed to follow the rule believe that others will follow it. Each individual must believe in the cognitive content and coordinative impact of the rules and/or believe that its declaration will affect social exchange and norms. If individuals do not hold these beliefs, they will not follow the rules, even if the rules correspond to an equilibrium (i.e., specify self-enforcing beliefs, norms, and behavior). Unless a rule leads to beliefs that it will be followed, the behavior it prescribes will not be followed. The legitimacy of those who issue rules is therefore central to institutionalization. Indeed, in the absence of individuals or organizations with such cultural authority, institutions would never emerge by decree. All institutions would emerge from individualistic learning processes, which economists model well (see, e.g., Chamley 2004). Arguably, however, complete inability to coordinate by decree is not optimal.[38]

In most societies some social units have the legitimacy required to alter institutions. One universal source of legitimacy is the observation that rules issued by the social unit in the past have been followed. The individuals and organizations with legitimacy, however, differ across societies and situations reflecting initial conditions including organizational heritage and internalized beliefs. Once established, a social norm conferring legitimacy constitutes an equilibrium: if it is expected that a new legitimately issued (equilibrium) coordinating rule will be followed, it will be. The more such new rules are followed, the more they will confirm the legitimacy of those who issued them. Because different legitimate authorities are likely to have different objectives and because societies differ in terms of their legitimate authorities, institutional development is likely to vary across societies.

Legitimacy is therefore central to institutional development. But contemporary students of institutions in economics, political science, and economic sociology have little to say about it.[39] Accordingly, I note here

---

[38] I am not familiar with general analyses exploring the trade-off between inability to coordinate and the influence of the coordinator on the efficiency of the resulting institution. Hayek (1979) stresses the importance of rules issued by decree.

[39] The term *legitimacy* has only six index entries and receives very little coverage in the *New Handbook of Political Science* (Goodin and Klingemann 1996). The *Handbook of Economic Sociology* includes no index entries for *legitimacy* (Smelser and

only that the late medieval period was crucial in Europe in terms of the development of legitimacy norms. During this period, rulers were well aware of the value of legitimacy in facilitating their rule and preventing challenges. Legitimacy is at the heart of the Bayeux Tapestry (1092), for example, which depicts how the Normans, led by William, conquered England in 1066. The tapestry was ordered by Odo, William's half brother and the bishop of Bayeux. Its opening scene shows Edward the Confessor, the last Saxon king, bestowing the kingdom upon William, thereby establishing William's legitimacy. After conquering Sicily and southern Italy, other Normans sought legitimacy by giving the area to the pope and ruling as his vassals.

These examples reflect the struggle between the secular and the religious regarding the source of legitimacy of rulers and rules in medieval Europe. During the late medieval period, the church was in the process of losing its bid to become the ultimate source of legitimate rules governing the practical aspects of the polity, society, and economy, either by nominating rulers or issuing rules. The beliefs in the appropriateness of man-made customary law embedded in Roman law and customary German law, which suited the interests of traditional secular leaders who therefore cultivated it, played an important role in this process. The failure of the church to prevent its members from strategically using their canonical position for their material benefit may have been instrumental as well by undermining the moral foundations of the church legitimacy (Ekelund et al. 1996).

During the late medieval period, legitimacy norms increasingly rested with the state and corporations in Europe. Rules were legitimate if issued by rulers with the hereditary right to the throne, conferred through a participatory process of selection, or issued through a participatory process of rule making. The Magna Carta, the elected monarchy in Germany, the Swiss confederacy, the Italian city-states, and the French Estates-General are among the many manifestations of this process, which reached its zenith with the modern democratic state.[40] In the West today, the state

Swedberg 1994), although Weber (1947) studied it. Levi (1988) indirectly touches on the issue by discussing "consent" for taxation. The discussion here builds on Greif (2002).

[40] The participatory nature of these bodies may directly contribute to their legitimacy. Ostrom (1998, p. 7) surveys experimental evidence indicating that when people can communicate and agree on rules of behavior, they behave in the way that is agreed upon, even if it is not in their material best interest to do so. Stewart (1992) notes that legitimacy confers normative value. In his comparative study of rules regulating

and participatory professional associations are the main sources of legitimate rules (DiMaggio and Powell 1991b; Scott 1995).

In the Muslim world the opposite process was taking place regarding legitimacy norms. Early on rulers were legitimated by virtue of being closest to the prophet. Later a ruler's legitimacy increasingly became faith-based, conditional on the ruler respecting, advancing, and promoting Islam. Failure to do so legitimized the use of force to overturn the ruler. As one of the period's most esteemed Muslim jurists, al-Mawardi (d. 1058), declared, one should not obey even a caliph if his orders contradict the teachings of Islam. The state, however, had only limited legitimacy as an interpreter of the Shari'a, the Islamic code of law. By the late medieval period the *'ulamạ*, the religious scholars, had already became the legitimate interpreters of the Shari'a. Even a caliph had no such legitimacy. Ever since, Islamic rulers have attempted, with various degrees of success, to create a state-controlled *'ulamạ*. Rulers were particularly successful to influence rules regarding matters that concerned them the most such as taxation and fiscal policy (e.g., Sonn 1990; B. Lewis 1991; Abou El Fadl 2001; Crone 2004; Kuran 2005).

Yet, the need to circumvent, evade, or confront this source of legitimacy influenced institutional development in the Islamic world. Indeed, even when monarchies, republics, and dictatorships were established in the Arab Middle East after the demise of colonialism, the traditional sources of legitimacy still held sway. Even these relatively secular polities found it necessary to signal their adherence to the Shari'a. The constitution of the Egyptian monarchy, established in 1922, for example, declared the Shari'a as the source of law. The 1971 constitution of the Arab Republic of Egypt defines Egypt as a socialist democratic state but declares that the principal source of legislation is the Shari'a.

5.5 CONCLUDING COMMENTS

This chapter uses insights from classical and learning game theory to better understand the roles and interrelationships between various institutional elements and the merit, manner, and limitations of the game-theoretic framework for studying endogenous institutions. These insights highlight the importance of institutionalized rules that enable and guide behavior

the donation and selling of human blood, he notes that where legal rules prohibit the sale of human blood for medical purposes but encourage donations, stronger norms exist against selling blood.

150

by helping individuals form beliefs about the world around them, about what others will do, and about what is morally appropriate. They create shared cognition, provide information, enable coordination, and indicate morally appropriate and socially acceptable behavior. Individuals seek guidance regarding the situation and how to behave in it; social rules provide this guidance. Social psychologists have convincingly argued that evolution has fine-tuned the human brain's capacity to take actions in situations in which individuals are guided by social rules (Tooby and Cosmides 1992).

At the same time, because retrospective individuals respond to social rules based on their private knowledge and information, institutionalized rules – social rules corresponding to regularities of behavior – aggregate private information and knowledge. The only social rules that can be institutionalized are ones that, if they are expected to be followed and to specify the morally appropriate course of action, are indeed followed and are not refuted by the outcomes these rules, beliefs, and norms generate. An institution can therefore be defined as comprising cognitive, coordinative, informational, and normative social elements that jointly generate a regularity of (social) behavior by enabling, guiding, and motivating it.

Game theory is a useful analytical tool in situations in which institutionalized rules prevail, because such rules correspond to the game-theoretic assumption regarding common knowledge. The analysis then restricts the set of admissible social rules that correspond to behavior to those that are self-enforcing: every individual, believing that others will follow the rules, finds it best to do likewise, given his private knowledge and information. The set of admissible institutionalized rules is thereby restricted. Indeed, self-enforceability in the Nash sense also implies that behavior reproduces – does not refute – the beliefs and does not subvert the norms that motivated it. Social rules that are self-enforcing are the only ones that can be institutionalized. The ability to restrict the set of admissible beliefs is thus central to the way game theory proves useful for institutional analysis.

The argument developed in this chapter requires further development in many ways. The analytical tools for deductively restricting internalized beliefs (mental models) and norms are limited. Also undeveloped is the argument that people play against (the cognitive and informational content of) rules rather than against the rules of the game. More broadly, as Simon (1955) argued, the substantiative implications of limited cognition and rationality are yet to be fully worked out. Further development may benefit from linking strategic behavior with that of the individual seeking to "satisfice" rather than optimize.[41]

Social psychologists argue that behavior is also psychologically motivated, because acting in a way that is at odds with one's conception of one's self is psychologically costly. Moreover, individuals tend to develop identities that correspond to what others expect of them. An honest person develops an identity that renders cheating more difficult; an individual who is expected to be an entrepreneur derives satisfaction from being one. The behavior generated by institutions and the beliefs motivating it therefore lead to corresponding identities and psychological motivation to follow this behavior. Further exploration of the interrelationships between external and intrinsic motivations along these lines seems promising.

Yet, even without these developments, it is imperative to understand the basic interplay between rules, beliefs, norms, and behavior in situations in which institutions generate behavior. People seek cognitive models and information on which to base their behavioral decisions; they seek a means to coordinate their behavior and search for guidance on what is socially acceptable and normatively appropriate. Socially distributed and disseminated commonly known rules provide these micro-foundations, enabling an individual to gain cognitive understanding of the situation and information, determine the morally appropriate and socially accepted behavior, and form beliefs about others' behavior. Each individual, however, responds to the commonly known rules based on his private information and knowledge, implying that institutionalized rules aggregate and disseminate such information and knowledge. In situations in which institutions generate social rules, beliefs, norms, and behavior constitute a system in equilibrium. The game-theoretic framework is a useful tool for institutional analysis because it captures this interplay between rules, beliefs, norms, and behavior, thereby enabling us to restrict the admissible set of institutions.

---

[41] Simon (1955) uses the word *satisficing* (a blend of *sufficing* and *satisfying*) to characterize algorithms that deal with conditions of limited time, knowledge, or computational capabilities. He postulates that an individual will choose the first alternative that satisfies his aspiration level rather than calculate the probabilities of all possible outcomes and choose the best alternative. For a recent survey, see Conlisk (1996). Gilboa and Schmeidler (2001) present an analytical framework for studying *satisficing* behavior.

PART III

Institutional Dynamics as a Historical Process

How does an institution persist in a changing environment? How do exogenous changes and the processes that an institution unleashes lead to the institution's demise? How do past institutions – perhaps even institutions that are no longer effective in influencing behavior – affect the direction of institutional change? Why do societies evolve along distinct institutional trajectories, and why is it so difficult to alter institutional dynamics to induce better outcomes?

These questions have long bedeviled institutional analysis in economics, political science, and sociology. Addressing them requires a framework that can accommodate both stability and change – a framework that can account for an institution's persistence and stability in a changing environment on the one hand and endogenous institutional changes and the limit on institutional persistence on the other. The framework must also facilitate studying why, how, and to what extent past institutions influence subsequent ones.

Since the 1970s economists have developed two perspectives – the intentionally created perspective and the evolutionary perspective – to study institutional dynamics. The intentionally created perspective postulates that institutions are intentionally established by forward-looking individuals to serve various functions. Institutional dynamics are best studied as reflecting responses to the functions the institutions serve (e.g., North 1981; O. Williamson 1985).[1] Political economy models were found

---

[1] Institutions reduce uncertainty (Sugden 1989; North 1990), influence distribution (Olson 1982; Knight 1992), maximize groups' welfare (Ellickson 1991), and minimize transaction costs (O. Williamson 1985). Such functionalist analysis is persuasive only when it is possible to delineate the mechanism linking the origin of the institution and its presumed effect (Stinchcombe 1968, pp. 87–93; Elster 1983; and Fligstein 1990).

to be particularly useful in studying processes through which institutions are established and changed. Economic institutions (which in political economy models are defined as formal rules regulating economic activities) are outcomes of political processes; they therefore change following exogenous changes in the decision-making process or the political actors' interests (for surveys of this literature, see Weingast 1996 and Peters 1996).[2]

In the intentionally created perspective, the past per se does not constrain institutional changes that forward-looking agents would initiate. The cost of change, rather than the shackles of history, limits institutional adjustments. Institutions fail to adjust in response to exogenous changes, due mainly to sunk costs, coordination costs, and network externalities (North 1990); the costs of overcoming the objections of those who benefit from the existing institutions (Olson 1982); and the difficulties associated with co-opting potential losers (Fernandez and Rodrik 1991; Kantor 1998).

To further the limited ability of this perspective to account for the lack of institutional change, scholars have invoked the stickiness of informal institutions. The argument is that informal institutions – defined mainly as customary rules of behavior, social relationships, or norms – cannot be changed by fiat, and this limits the effectiveness of changing formal rules (North 1990, 1991; Mantzavinos 2001; Aoki 2001).[3] This position is unsatisfactory, however, because, as O. Williamson (2000) notes, it accounts for institutional change by using one analytical framework, whereas it accounts for the lack of change by invoking forces outside that analytical framework. Invoking the constraints imposed by informal institutions on the process of institutional change is appropriate only when the forces contributing to the persistence of these informal institutions are explicitly integrated into the analysis (as in Greif 1994a and Ensminger 1997).

Evolutionary Institutionalism, which is rooted in Old Institutionalism and Austrian Economics (Menger 1871 [1976]; Hayek 1937), presents another approach for studying intertemporal relationships among institutions. It usually defines institutions as patterns of behavior reflecting the

---

[2] Transaction-cost economics (following O. Williamson's seminal 1985 contribution) also considers institutions (which are identified with contracts and organizational forms) to be determined by their function.

[3] The general conscription introduced by Britain during World War I exempted the Irish, whose anti-English norms implied that the cost of enforcing conscription and effective military service would be too high (Levi 1997).

unintentional consequence of interactions among individuals with limited rationality. It rejects the forward-looking and functionality premises of the intentionally created perspective.

In formal models capturing this idea, mutation, selection, and inertia link the behavior of limitedly rational individuals with institutions.[4] Each individual is endowed with a trait that dictates his behavior. The relative payoff to a trait depends on the environment and the population distribution of behavioral traits. Selection and the exogenous introduction of new traits – mutation – alter the population distribution of behavioral traits. Over time, more successful traits increase their proportion in the population.

While mutation and selection influence the direction of change in the distribution of traits, inertia determines its rate. The proportion of more successful traits increases only over time. It takes time for selection, operating through imitation or a higher reproduction rate, to transpire. The analysis considers the conditions under which a stable distribution of traits – an equilibrium – is reached.

Stability and change can be studied within the same analytical framework in such evolutionary models, but their micro-foundations are restrictive, as noted in Chapter 1. The framework postulates that individuals are not forward-looking; at best they are retrospective. The social level is ignored, as individuals are assumed to be unable to coordinate, communicate, or collectively alter the environment within which they interact. Processes of mutation that drive institutional change are taken as exogenous, while inertia, which determines the rate of change, is assumed rather than derived endogenously.

Chapters 6 through 9 outline another perspective on institutional dynamics. The *institutional dynamics as a historical process* perspective makes explicit the forces contributing to institutional persistence in a changing environment. It exposes when and why institutions endogenously change and how past institutions influence subsequent ones. This historical-process perspective bridges the gap between the Old Institutionalism evolutionary perspective and the New Institutionalism intentionally created perspective. It incorporates the Old Institutionalism's recognition of the evolutionary and undesigned nature of institutional development and New Institutionalism's concern with intentionality. Unlike the

---

[4] See, for example, R. Nelson and Winter (1982); Frank (1987); Sugden (1989); Young (1993, 1998); G. Hodgson (1998); Kandori et al. (1993); and Macy (1997) and the surveys in Kandori (1997) and Gintis (2000).

intentionally created perspective and like the evolutionary perspective, the historical-process perspective seeks to account for an institution's emergence, stability, and change by exploring the forces that render it an equilibrium. Unlike the evolutionary perspective, it places the social level (institutional elements) at the center of the analysis and considers processes of change and the micro-foundations of inertia to be endogenous. It thus extends the study of the intertemporal relationships among institutions to situations that cannot be captured in political economy or evolutionary models.

By bridging the gap between the evolutionary and intentionally created perspectives, the historical-process perspective contributes to the development of both. In contrast to the evolutionary perspective, which takes institutional inertia, mutation, and experimentations as exogenous, the perspective developed here explores the micro-foundations of institutional inertia and captures the fact that mutation and experimentation depend on existing institutions. It enriches the intentionally created perspective by recognizing that individuals look forward through the prism implied by past institutions, that an institution's equilibrium nature limits responses to functional needs, and that different institutions imply distinct institutional trajectories.

Perhaps more important, the historical-process perspective presents a new direction in social-sciences-oriented historical research. This research has long followed in the footsteps of such giants as Marx and Malthus in seeking a deterministic theory of history. The flow of history reflects the shackles of such inescapable forces as geography, class struggle, and demography. The historical-process perspective suggests an alternative: history unfolds based on the nondeterministic impact of past institutions on outcomes in general and institutional dynamics in particular.

Although the analytical development of the argument is still in its preliminary stages, Part III introduces the broad argument and empirically demonstrates its merit. Chapter 6 presents a theory of endogenous institutional change. Chapter 7 discusses the influence of past institutions on the direction of institutional change. Chapters 8 and 9 present empirical studies of institutional dynamics, showing how different societies embarked on distinct institutional trajectories. These studies do not capture all the aspects of the argument advanced in the theoretical chapters, but they illustrate various aspects of it.

Specifically, Chapter 8 focuses on the dynamics of the institutional foundation of polities, examining the Republic of Genoa. Understanding political order and disorder requires departing from a long tradition of studying these issues while focusing on the relationships between political institutions defined as rules governing political decision making, political order, and economic prosperity (see, e.g., Przeworski 1991). The analysis here considers polities as self-enforcing institutions whose details generate the behavior leading to political order, disorder, and economic outcomes. Rules governing political decision making are only one component of these institutions. Understanding political order, disorder, and its impact on the economy requires studying the polity as a self-enforcing institution.

Chapter 9 focuses on the dynamics of economic and social institutions. It compares the organizational, contractual, and institutional development of the Maghribi and Genoese traders. Economists often assume that such developments are influenced by efficiency considerations reflecting, in particular, attempts to reduce transaction costs (O. Williamson 1985). The comparative analysis of developments in these two societies, however, establishes the importance of past institutional elements in directing them. Furthermore, these distinct institutional elements reflect cultural influence on institutional selection. Initial cultural and social factors influence institutional selection, integrate into the resulting institutions, reproduced by them, and thereby exert a lasting influence on institutional, organizational, and contractual development.

6

A Theory of Endogenous Institutional Change

A prerequisite to studying endogenous institutional change is recognizing the mechanism that causes institutions to persist in the absence of environmental changes and to exhibit stability despite environmental changes. Sociologists such as Berger and Luckmann (1967), Searle (1995), and Giddens (1997) have long noted the importance of studying the mechanisms causing an endogenous institution to persist once it has prevailed. But sociology has not offered a satisfactory analytical framework with which to study the phenomenon. As Scott notes, "The persistence of institutions, once created, is an understudied phenomenon [in sociology].... The conventional term for persistence – inertia – seems on reflection to be too passive and nonproblematic to be an accurate aid to guide studies on this topic" (1995, p. 90; see also DiMaggio and Powell 1991a, p. 25; Thelen 1999, p. 397).

In economics the study of institutional persistence is usually referred to as the study of institutional path dependence (North 1990; David 1994; Greif 1994a). The idea of path dependence was originally developed to study technology (David 1985; Arthur 1988, 1994). It postulates that "the present state of arrangements" requires examining the "originating context or set of circumstances and ... [the] sequence of connecting events that allow the hand of the past to exert a continuing influence upon the shape of the present" (David 1994, p. 206).

The game-theoretic analytical framework and the view of institutions developed in the previous chapters highlight a particular mechanism for institutional persistence. In situations in which institutions generate behavior, beliefs motivate it, and observed behavior confirms the relevance of these beliefs. Taken together, self-enforcing (and reproducing) beliefs and behavior are in a steady-state equilibrium: The observed behavior reproduces the beliefs that generated it, because it confirms each individual belief that others will behave in a particular manner, and given these beliefs, it is optimal for each individual to do so. By revealing which beliefs and behavior can be self-enforcing in a given environment, the game-theoretic perspective highlights the limit of this mechanism. It exposes which exogenous change would cause the current behavior to no longer be self-enforcing and hence to change.

Studying endogenous institutional change, however, seems particularly difficult when institutions are viewed as equilibrium phenomena. In an institution, each player's behavior is a best response. The seemingly inescapable conclusion is that change in a self-enforcing institution must have an exogenous origin, because no one has an incentive to deviate from the behavior associated with the institution. As P. Hall and Taylor note, studying institutions as equilibria "embroils such analysis in a contradiction. One implication of this approach is that the starting point from which institutions are to be created is itself likely to reflect a Nash equilibrium. Thus it is not clear why the actors would agree to change in existing institutions" (1996, p. 953). Endogenous institutional change appears, then, to be a contradiction in terms.[1] Indeed, the analysis of institutional change using game theory has concentrated mainly on the dynamics triggered by changes in parameters exogenous to the institutions under study.

In this chapter, I argue that the equilibrium approach can be integrated with the study of endogenous institutional change. Recognizing the distinction between institutions and game-theoretic equilibria allows two related concepts to be introduced: *quasi-parameters* and *institutional reinforcement*. Before discussing these concepts, it is important to note the distinction between parameters and variables in a game-theoretic framework. Parameters are exogenous to the game under consideration. If they change, the implied new equilibrium set needs to be studied. In contrast, variables are determined endogenously as outcomes in the game. Institutional analysis using the game-theoretic framework typically concentrates on a single transaction (e.g., abusing or protecting property rights by a ruler) and examines as variables possible related

---

[1] Although this criticism of the game-theoretic contribution is fundamentally fair, it should be noted that ex ante creation of institutional arrangements can be predicated on variables that are not realized until later. Once such a realization occurs, the institution can change as part of a dynamic equilibrium (see Muthoo and Shepsle 2003 for an example). The discussion in this chapter of stability in the face of parametric shifts notes that it is appropriate and realistic to model institutions when the long-term implications of a shift in variables are not foreseen ex ante.

self-enforcing behavior (e.g., security of property rights) for a given set of parameters.

In contrast, this chapter asserts that it is conceptually sound and analytically tractable to consider some aspects of a situation as parametric when studying self-enforceability but as variables subject to change when studying institutional dynamics. It is appropriate to inquire whether the institution, analyzed as a game-theoretic equilibrium, endogenously affects aspects of the situation apart from behavior in the transaction under consideration. The argument advanced here is that some such aspects should be considered as parametric in studying self-enforceability in the short run but as endogenously determined – and thus variable – in the long run. Parameters that are endogenously changed in this manner and with this effect are referred to here as quasi-parameters. Marginal changes in quasi-parameters do not lead to a change in the behavior and expected behavior associated with this institution.

Equilibrium analysis fosters the study of quasi-parameters by making explicit the factors that make a particular behavior an equilibrium. The distinction between a parameter, a variable, and a quasi-parameter is not rigid; it is based on empirical observation. If self-enforcing outcomes affect the values of one or more parameters supporting the observed equilibrium in a manner that would lead only to long-term behavioral change, these parameters are best reclassified as quasi-parameters.

An institution is reinforcing when the behavior and processes it entails, through their impact on quasi-parameters, increase the range of parameter values (and thus situations) in which the institution is self-enforcing. If an institution reinforces itself, more individuals in more situations will find it best to adhere to the behavior associated with it.[2] When they are self-reinforcing, exogenous changes in the underlying situation that otherwise would have led an institution to change fail to have this effect. An institution would be self-enforcing for a wider range of parameters. But such reinforcing processes can fail to occur. The processes an institution entails, can undermine the extent to which the associated behavior is self-enforcing. The behavior an institution entails can cultivate the seeds of its own demise. Whether this change is gradual or sudden, marginal or comprehensive, depends on the nature of these processes.

Considering endogenous institutional change as reflecting undermining processes ignores the impact of institutions on the incentive to invent or

---

[2] More specifically, any combination of more individuals in the same situation and the same number of individuals in more situations.

160

adopt new institutional elements or to bring about new situations. These important issues are left to the next chapter.[3]

Historical Institutionalism in political science represents the line of research that particularly focuses on institutional change (see P. Hall and Taylor 1996; Thelen 1999; Pierson and Skocpol 2002). It stresses the importance of historical processes in shaping institutions but offers no theory able to study the interrelationships among stability, processes, and change. As Pierson (2000, p. 266) notes, an important obstacle for furthering Historical Institutionalism has been that institutional changes "are usually attributed, often ex post, to 'exogenous shocks.' We should expect, however, that these change points often occur when new conditions disrupt or overwhelm the specific mechanisms that previously reproduced the existing [behavior]." Bridging the game-theoretic and historical perspectives – by examining the relationships between factors implying that an institution is self-enforcing, the processes this institution implies, and the implications of these processes on the institution's self-enforceability – enriches both perspectives (see Greif and Laitin 2004 for a discussion of the relationship between Historical Institutionalism and the perspective developed here).

In this chapter, sections 6.1 and 6.2 examine institutional persistence and stability. Section 6.3 introduces the concepts of quasi-parameters and reinforcement. Section 6.4 illustrates how self-enforcing institutions can be either self-reinforcing or self-destroying by studying political institutions in early modern Genoa and Venice. Section 6.5 presents a model of institutional reinforcement. Section 6.6 focuses on reputation-based institutions and explains why institutions may exhibit a "life cycle" in which they are first reinforced and then undermined. Section 6.7 considers the argument's further development.

6.1 PERSISTENCE

As already noted in Chapter 5, in order for an institution to persist through time, it must be *reproduced*. An institution is reproduced when the rules and beliefs that enabled, guided, and motivated an individual's actions are not refuted by observed behavior or outcomes. Thus, observed behavior and outcomes confirm the rules and beliefs that enabled, guided,

---

[3] Similarly, for simplicity of presentation, this chapter focuses mainly on beliefs rather than on norms. Extending the argument to the case of norms is possible, however, building on the discussion in section 5.3.

and motivated the original behavior, as expectations are consistent with outcomes.

D. Lewis (1969, pp. 41–2) beautifully expresses the idea of the reproduction of beliefs by behavior in equilibria: "Each new action in conformity to the regularity [of behavior associated with this equilibrium] adds to our experience of general conformity," he writes. "Our experience of general conformity in the past leads us, by force of precedent, to expect a like conformity in the future.... And so it goes – we're here because we're here because we're here because we're here. Once the process gets started, we have a metastable, self-perpetuating system of preferences, expectations, and actions capable of persisting indefinitely." The structure generates behavior that, because it is self-enforcing, reproduces that structure.

This mechanism for persistence rests on intuitively appealing propositions. Individuals are forward-looking: they look before they leap and take into account what others are likely to do. They are also retrospective, evaluating their beliefs based on observable outcomes.[4] This mechanism for persistence is captured by the Nash condition, which requires each individual to hold the correct beliefs about others' behavior (see Appendix A and Chapter 5). Any institution that is self-enforcing in the Nash sense also reproduces itself by the behavior it generates.

The historical examples of the previous chapters illustrate the relevance of the causal mechanism for institutional persistence that the Nash restriction captures. The persistence of the Maghribis' coalition, for example, reflects the self-enforceability of correct behavioral beliefs and behavior. Each trader's best response to the belief that everyone will follow a particular behavioral rule was to follow it as well. The observed behavior of hiring only member agents and honesty, in turn, reproduced (confirmed) these beliefs.

Game theory thus captures the conditions under which, and the mechanism by which, the structure – commonly known rules and beliefs – generates behavior that reproduces this structure. The distinction between game-theoretic and institutional analysis, however, is worth recognizing. First, game-theoretic analysis assumes that players have common knowledge of the rules of the game; institutional analysis recognizes that individuals play against the (institutionalized) rules and learn about

---

[4] Because this mechanism regards the relationships between beliefs and behavior, it is applicable to all transactions (economic, information-sharing, coercive, legal, political, social).

various aspects of the situation through social rules, others' behavior, and similar observable outcomes. As I show later, this implies that some individuals may not recognize underlying changes in various aspects of the situation and will therefore not change their behavior accordingly. In such cases, institutions can and often do persist despite parametric changes.

This mechanism for institutional persistence also contributes to the persistence of what is often referred to as a society's cultural and social (organizational) features. Institutionalized rules, beliefs norms, and organizations are components of institutions that generate behavior. At the same time, they are also part of the society's cultural and social features, because they imply social positions, are embodied in individuals' preferences, and constitute internalized and other beliefs that are commonly known societal features. The overlap between institutional features on the one hand and cultural and social features on the other implies that the described mechanism for institutional persistence contributes to the persistence of a society's cultural and social features.

The Maghribis' social structure – the Maghribi traders' group – was an integral part of an institution that fostered the welfare of the groups' members. The different behavior toward members and nonmembers that this institution implied reproduced this distinct social identity. The merchant guild organizations were reproduced in a similar manner. This reproduction process implies that the endogenous processes that render a particular institution no longer self-enforcing also imply that its overlapping cultural and organizational features can no longer be reproduced by the behavior the related institution entails.[5]

6.2 STABILITY IN THE FACE OF AN ENDOGENOUS PARAMETRIC SHIFT

Game-theoretic analyses of institutions have traditionally focused on studying the relationships between the rules of the game and equilibrium behavior – cooperation, wars, political mobilization, social unrest – in the transactions captured in the game. Such analyses make explicit the dependency of possible equilibria, and hence institutions, on various parameters (such as payoffs from various actions, time discount factors, risk

---

[5] The mechanism for persistence discussed here, however, is not the only one that propagates cultural and social features. They can also be maintained based on other mechanisms such as the transmission of norms through socialization or individuals' desire for social identity.

preferences, wealth, and the number of players) of the underlying game. The framework highlights the conditions under which an exogenous change in parameters will render an institution no longer self-enforcing.

Focusing on regularities of behavior in a particular transaction for a given set of parameters diverts attention from other possible ramifications of an institution that go beyond this behavior. Institutions influence factors – such as wealth, identity, ability, knowledge, beliefs, residential distribution, and occupational specialization – that are usually assumed as parametric in the rules of the game. Although it may not be possible to prove that institutions generally have such ramifications, it is difficult to think of any institution that in the long run does not have implications beyond the behavior in the transaction it governs. In the game-theoretic framework, such influence implies a dynamic adjustment of variables that, had this influence been ignored, would have been considered parameters in the stage game (i.e., a game repeated every period; see Appendix A).

In the game-theoretic framework, such changes would not necessarily lead to behavioral change. The Folk theorem of repeated games (presented in Appendix A) exemplifies the general game-theoretic insight that, for a given parameter set, a multiplicity of equilibria usually exists. The theorem also highlights a corollary to this insight: a particular equilibrium can usually be sustained over a broad range of parameters. If a strategy combination is an equilibrium, it is usually an equilibrium in some parameter *set*. Game theorists have long recognized that game theory does not predict behavioral change following a parametric change. Moriguchi (1998) refers to the set of parameters in which a particular strategy set is an equilibrium – and hence the associated institution can prevail – as "institutional support."

Indeed, there are good reasons for individuals to continue to follow past patterns of behavior even under conditions of marginal parametric change. This is the case for various interrelated reasons, such as knowledge and coordination, which were touched on in Chapter 5. Other reasons, such as attention and habit, are introduced here.

6.2.1 Knowledge and Playing against the Rules

In Chapter 5, I argued that institutionalized rules provide the cognitive, coordinative, and informational basis for behavior at the individual level. Institutionalized rules of behavior aggregate cognition, knowledge, and information in a compressed form and direct individuals to play an equilibrium strategy in the game thereby constructed. Individuals play against the (institutionalized) rules rather than against the commonly known rules of the game.

Hence past behavior can reign, and an individual will continue to follow past institutionalized rules of behavior despite marginal parametric changes. This outcome occurs because institutionalized rules learned in the past convey these cognitive models, provide aggregate information, and guide behavior. As long as the behaviors of others (the causal underpinnings of which one may not understand) do not reflect that these models are mistaken or that the parameters have changed, an individual will not change his behavior if it is still in his best interest to follow it while responding to the cognitive and informational content of the prevailing institutionalized rules. In other words, the fact that actors play against the rules implies that changes in various aspects that are incorporated into the rules of the game influence behavior only when those who observe them reveal them through their behavior.[6] If they do not, behavior continues to reproduce beliefs, and the institution persists.

6.2.2 Coordination

Schelling's (1960) seminal work on focal points highlights the importance of coordination in choosing behavior in strategic situations characterized by multiple equilibria. The related argument made here is that the need for coordination implies that individuals continue to follow past patterns of behavior, even under conditions of observed marginal parametric change. They do so because they face a situation in which rationality alone is insufficient to select a behavior (because of multiple self-enforcing outcomes). They therefore rely on institutionalized rules to guide them. Under these circumstances, behavioral rules learned in the past are the best predictor of future behavior, even when some individuals and organizations have the ability to coordinate on new behavior. For many reasons, such coordination may fail to transpire even when it is beneficial. Sunk costs associated with coordinating change, free-rider problems, distributional issues, uncertainties, limited understanding of alternatives, and asymmetric information may hinder coordination on new behavior. In the terminology developed here, the need to coordinate on one out of many possible

---

[6] Chapter 3 discusses models of incomplete information that explore one's motivation and ability to reveal his information to others. For a general discussion, see Fudenberg and Tirole (1991).

behaviors implies that even observed marginal changes in the rules of the game are not likely to cause behavioral changes, because past behavior constitutes a focal point.

6.2.3 Attention

What an individual sees, knows, and understands in a given situation reflects the amount of attention he devotes to the task. Attention is a scarce resource (Simon 1976); institutionalized rules allow individuals to choose behavior in complicated situations while devoting their limited attention to decision making in noninstitutionalized situations. People do not consider their optimal response to every choice they make in life (DiMaggio and Powell 1991a). In particular, they do not consider such responses in situations in which institutions guide their behavior. In such situations, parametric shifts that might have been noticed if more attention had been devoted to observing them may go unnoticed, contributing to the lack of behavioral change. Moreover, those who observe the parametric shift and can bring it to the attention of others may not have the incentive to do so. Limited attention capacity implies that even potentially observable changes in the rules of the game may go unnoticed and hence not influence behavior.

6.2.4 Habit and Scarce Cognitive Resources

Judgment and habit are interrelated in influencing behavior (Margolis 1987, p. 29).[7] But once a particular pattern of behavior has been institutionalized, individuals tend to rely more on habits and routines than on reason and calculations. We follow institutionalized behavior habitually because of the scarcity of cognitive resources (see Clark 1997a, 1997b; R. Nelson and Winter 1982; R. Nelson 1995; March and Olsen 1989). Habit enables people to devote scare cognitive resources to other tasks. When individuals are guided by habit and routine and rely less on judgment, past behavior reigns despite marginal parametric changes.

---

[7] The analysis of habit and institutions can be traced back at least to Simon (1976). Berger (1977) and Kuran (1993) argue that institutionalized behavior has become the social equivalent of an instinct. Margolis (1994) and G. Hodgson (1998) identify habits with institutions.

6.3 QUASI-PARAMETERS AND REINFORCEMENT

Many features that are usually taken as parameters in the repeated-game formulation share two properties: they can gradually be altered by the implications of the institution under study, and marginal changes to them will not necessarily cause the behavior associated with the institution to change. These features do not cause the behavior associated with the institution to change because, ex ante, people do not recognize, anticipate, directly observe, understand, or pay attention to the changes in these features and the ramifications of those changes for the institution. Even when this is not the case, because of ex post coordination problems, these changes do not cause the behavior associated with the institution to change. These features are neither parameters (as they are endogenously changed) nor variables (as they do not directly condition behavior); they are quasi-parameters. Because the actors do not recognize changes in quasi-parameters or their implications, quasi-parameters must be considered as parametric – exogenous and fixed – in studying the self-enforcing property of an institution in the short run but as endogenous and variable when studying the same institutions in the long run.[8]

Changes in quasi-parameters implied by an institution can reinforce or undermine that institution. An institution reinforces itself when, over time, the changes in quasi-parameters it entails imply that the associated behavior is self-enforcing in a larger set of situations – a larger set of other parameters – than would otherwise have been the case. A self-enforcing institution that reinforces itself is a *self-reinforcing* institution. A self-enforcing institution can also undermine itself when the changes in the quasi-parameters it entails imply that the associated behavior will be self-enforcing in a smaller set of situations.

Central to endogenous institutional changes are therefore the dynamics of self-enforcing beliefs and the associated behavior. A change in beliefs constitutes an institutional change; it occurs when the associated behavior is no longer self-enforcing, leading individuals to act in a manner that does not reproduce the associated beliefs.[9] Undermining processes can lead

---

[8] Institutional elements and their attributes (e.g., the size of a community) can be quasi-parameters. An institutional element is part of a system that generates behavior, implying that each of the notions – an institutional element and a quasi-parameter – highlights a distinct characteristic of a social factor.

[9] The focus here is on endogenous institutional change due to self-reinforcement and undermining, but the observations about the nature of institutions, institutionalized

previously self-enforcing behavior to cease being so, leading to institutional change. A sufficient condition for endogenous institutional change is that the institution's implications constantly undermine the associated behavior. Conversely, a necessary condition for an institution to prevail over time is that the range of situations in which the associated behavior is self-enforcing does not decrease over time: the institution's behavioral implications have to reinforce it, at least weakly. Hence unless an institution is (weakly) self-reinforced, eventually the behavior associated with it will not be self-enforcing, and endogenous institutional change will occur.

Considering reinforcement highlights the importance of another, indirect way in which an institution endogenously influences its change – by affecting the magnitude and nature of the exogenous shocks necessary to cause the beliefs and behavior associated with the institution to change. When an institution reinforces itself, the behavior associated with it does not change, but the reinforced institution is nevertheless more robust than before. The behavior associated with it becomes self-enforcing in situations in which it previously would not have been. Reinforcement implies institutional hysteresis; the institution will be self-enforcing in situations in which, prior to its reinforcement, it would not have been. The opposite holds in the case of an institution that undermines itself. By reinforcing or undermining itself, an institution indirectly influences its change by determining the magnitude of an external change in parameters required to render behavior associated with it no longer self-enforcing.

Institutions can change due to endogenous processes, exogenous shocks, or combinations of both. The mechanism that brings about institutional change once the behavior associated with an institution is no longer self-enforcing depends on the nature of the quasi-parameters that delimit self-reinforcement. If these changes in quasi-parameters are unobservable, uncertain, and unrecognizable, the mechanism of institutional change is likely to reflect individuals' willingness to experiment and risk deviating from past behavior or the emergence of individuals with better knowledge of the situation, who, through their behavior, reveal a new

rules, and beliefs allow us to extend the analysis easily to address related issues, such as intentional coordinated action to change others' beliefs, to draw attention to change, to coordinate actions by some to influence others' optimal behavior, and to establish organizations that foster or halt reinforcement or undermining. Some of these issues are discussed later.

institutional equilibrium.[10] In either case, learning is slow, and it may take a long time for self-undermining to be reflected in new behavior.

When the undermining that leads to the institutional change is not foreseen ex ante but many individuals recognize ex post that following past behavior is no longer optimal, the change will be manifest by the sudden abandonment of past behavior.[11] Institutional change can thus be characterized by punctuated equilibria (Gould and Eldrege 1977; Krasner 1984; Aoki 2001), in which change is actually evolutionary but appears to be abrupt. Such abrupt change is typically associated with a crisis that reveals that the previous behavior is no longer an equilibrium.

An institution can also cease to be self-enforcing due to changes in quasi-parameters that are observable and whose importance is understood. When the impending change in behavior becomes progressively more recognizable, decision makers will realize that past behavior is becoming less self-enforcing, and the mechanism directly leading to institutional change will be intentional and is likely to be gradual. Alternative behaviors, specification of new rules through collective decision making, and intentional introduction of organizations are common manifestations of this mechanism. Such institutional change often manifests itself in intentional reinforcement – the preemptive introduction of reinforcing institutional elements – which is likely to occur gradually. Institutional change in this case will take the form of restoring the prechange behavior but supporting it with different institutional elements. We have seen just that in considering the organizational evolution of the merchant guild institution.

Like intentional reinforcement in the face of anticipated self-undermining, the prevalence of a particular institution can induce coordinated actions aimed at undermining it and instituting other self-enforcing behavior. Such coordinated undermining reflects the fact that, although no individual dissatisfied with the prevailing institution can change it, individuals acting collectively may be able to do so.[12] They can undermine it

---

[10] Game theory highlights the importance of uncertainty in these processes. If the eventual collapse of the institution is known and expected to prevail at a particular time, the transaction has to be modeled as a finite game. The set of behaviors that is self-enforcing in these games is much smaller than the behaviors that can prevail in an infinitely repeated game. If the eventual collapse is not expected or its timing is uncertain, the equilibrium set is much larger (see Appendix A).

[11] Gradual processes of institutional change are discussed later in this chapter and in Chapter 7.

[12] I discuss the role of leadership in institutional change in Chapter 7.

by, for example, aggregating their resources and using them to increase the payoffs others receive from following the behavior they want to institute. Resources are needed, because the institutionalized behavior is everyone's best response, and inducing someone to adopt a so-far-noninstitutionalized behavior requires changing motivation (by, e.g., changing beliefs regarding its consequences). Once the behavior of a sufficiently large number of people has shifted to a new self-enforcing behavior, the best response for all others is to adopt the behavior as well. The previous institution has been undermined, and a new behavior becomes institutionalized. Once it is, it may no longer be necessary to devote resources to inducing this behavior.

6.4 SELF-REINFORCEMENT: A TALE OF TWO CITIES

To illustrate this dynamic approach to institutional change, I examine the experiences of late medieval Venice and Genoa, analyzing the political regime of each city as an institution made up of the following elements: the organization of the governing structures; the rules for choosing leadership positions and behavior; and the norms, rules, and beliefs shared by their citizens.[13]

The residents of the settlements around the Venetian lagoon established Venice as a political unit in 697; residents of Genoa organized themselves into a commune around 1096. By the mid-fourteenth century, Venice and Genoa had become the two most commercially successful maritime city-states in the Italian peninsula.

The rise of both cities reflects opportunities for commercial expansion made possible by the naval and military decline of Muslim and Byzantine forces around the Mediterranean, particularly during the eleventh century. During this century, however, both cities found themselves in a political vacuum, as neither the Byzantine Empire (which claimed sovereignty over Venice) nor the Holy Roman Empire (which claimed sovereignty over Genoa) was in a position to interfere in local political developments.

As result of the decline in central authority, clans and lineages became the prominent unit of social organization in both cities (D. Hughes 1978). As Herlihy notes, "The corporate or consortial family was better able than the nuclear household to defend its wealth and status ... [increasing]

---

[13] For a general discussion of Venetian and Genoese history, see Lane (1973) and Epstein (1996) respectively. The analysis here builds mainly on Greif (1995, 1998c). For an illuminating analysis of the Venetian polity as a self-enforcing institution, see González de Lara (2004).

family solidarity, at least among the aristocratic classes" (1969, p. 178). In both Genoa and Venice, the strongest clans agreed to cooperate politically in order to advance their economic interests.[14] The resulting political institutions governed a particular transaction: motivating members of the cities' strong clans and families to delegate decision-making power and resources in return for political order and the economic benefits of collective action.

The political organizations of Genoa and Venice were seemingly identical. Both cities were governed by oligarchies, their political leaders were de jure elected by the citizenry as a whole and subject to the law. At the top of Venice's political system was a doge and the Ducal Council. Genoa was governed initially by consuls and, after 1194, by one or more executives – called the *podestà* (power) – and a council of rectors. The political institutions that prevailed in Venice and Genoa from the late eleventh century were both able to support interclan cooperation that initially fostered commercial expansion and political order.

Despite these similarities, the histories of the two cities differ greatly. Venice was able to maintain political order in a changing economic environment and to mobilize resources to sustain its economic prosperity even following the decline of its trade with the Far East. Throughout its history, its members' social attachments to the clan structure gradually declined. In contrast, in Genoa political order often broke down, contributing to the city's economic decline, and the social and political importance of clans grew.

How can we account for these different trajectories in cities that faced similar initial conditions, outside opportunities, and basic political structures? To understand these histories and their long-term implications, I examine these cities' institutions. The origins of Genoa's and Venice's two distinct institutions are not the focus of the analysis. Yet the institutional differences that account for Venice's relative success probably reflect the institutional heritage of the post of the doge, its less unequal

---

[14] An agreement for interclan cooperation does not imply that clans were unwilling to use force against one another to advance their own interests. Indeed, the historical records are rich with evidence indicating that moral considerations – internalized constraints – were not sufficient to deter one Genoese clan from using force against another and that clans aspired to achieve political dominance (Greif 1998c; Tabacco 1989). Genoa's two dominant viscountal clans were a product of the feudal world, in which the objective was to become a lord within one's domain. At the same time, the tight internal organization and military and economic resources of these clans were such that, for each, gaining control over a city was not out of reach.

initial distribution of interclan military might and wealth, and a series of able leaders who coordinated on and developed elements of Venice's institutions.

Both Genoa and Venice initially developed political regimes that were sufficiently self-enforcing to sustain interclan cooperation and economic prosperity. But Genoa's institutions were self-undermining, whereas Venice's were self-reinforcing. To develop this argument, I consider quasi-parameters, such as the wealth of the cities, the strength of the *popoli* (roughly speaking, the nonnobles), and the social identities of the clans. Understanding these cities' subsequent histories requires examining the dynamics of these quasi-parameters in two different institutional equilibria. Changes in the quasi-parameters in Genoa undermined political order, making its institutions sensitive to relatively small exogenous shifts in clans' strength, trading opportunities, and level of external threat. Changes in the quasi-parameters had the opposite effect in Venice.

6.4.1 Genoa

During its first hundred years (1096–1194), elected consuls were Genoa's political, administrative, and military leaders. These consuls were representatives of the main Genoese clans (D. Hughes 1978, pp. 112–13). Control of the consulate enabled clans to gain economically from the city's resources and power. The behavior of these consuls and the clans they represented was guided by the belief that clans would challenge one another militarily if the opportunity arose to gain political dominance over the city. The self-enforcing institution that governed the clans' interrelationships was thereby based on mutual deterrence: each of Genoa's two main clans expected the other to use its military might to gain political and economic dominance over the city, but each was deterred from doing so by the other's military strength. Hence each of Genoa's two main clans was motivated to mobilize its resources for interclan cooperation to advance Genoa's economy, albeit only to the extent to which its ability to deter other clans from militarily challenging it was not weakened.

Initially, the relatively high gains from the joint mobilization of resources implied that interclan rivalry did not hinder interclan cooperation. But because interclan cooperation advanced Genoa's economic prosperity (an endogenous change in a quasi-parameter), it rendered political control over the city a more rewarding objective and intensified the competition over political and economic dominance in the city. Fearing that any temporary decline in their relative power would constitute an opportunity that the other clan would exploit, clans became engaged in an "arms race," which led to yet other endogenous changes in quasi-parameters: the purchase of land, which clans fortified to dominate particular quarters; the establishment of patronage networks; and the socialization of clan members to internalize loyalty to the clan and the norm of revenge to protect clan honor.

A foreign threat constituted an exogenous shift in parameters that sustained interclan cooperation. For a period after 1154, attempts by the emperor Frederick Barbarossa to regain de facto control over northern Italy rendered mutual deterrence self-enforcing in a larger set of parameters. This external threat did not alter clan members' beliefs about what other clans would do if the threat receded, but because the clans expected the threat to last, every clan had a reduced incentive to challenge another clan militarily. The result was that the Genoese clans jointly mobilized their resources, acquired overseas commercial possessions, and expanded commercially, as Genoa's economic structure was transformed into one based on long-distance commerce.

This commercial expansion and structural transformation undermined interclan mutual deterrence by making it self-enforcing for a smaller range of parameters. Greater economic prosperity, which increased the gains from controlling the city, implied a smaller set of parameters for which mutual deterrence was self-enforcing in the absence of an external threat.

In 1164 civil wars in Germany diverted the emperor's attention from Italy. As a result, the level of external threat facing Genoa substantially declined, possibly returning to its pre-1154 level. But the quasi-parameter of wealth was now higher than it was before, and with beliefs remaining stable, the previous mutual-deterrence equilibrium among the clans was no longer self-enforcing. The commune sank into a lengthy civil war, during which various clans gained the upper hand for a time, only to be challenged when exogenous conditions changed. As a twelfth-century Genoese chronicler observed, "Civil discords and hateful conspiracies and divisions had risen in the city on account of the mutual envy of the many men who greatly wished to hold office as consuls of the commune" (*Annali* 1190, vol. II, pp. 219–20). The fighting was particularly devastating between 1189 and 1194, when it endangered the city's very existence.

These events reflect more than just the shift in exogenous conditions. They reflect the fact that endogenous changes – increasing commercialization and prosperity, the clans' past investments in military ability and patronage, and perhaps the fomenting of individuals' identities as clan members – made Genoa's institution self-enforcing for a smaller set of parameters. The city that was peaceful despite the absence of a threat by an emperor before 1154 became embroiled in a civil war during the emperor's absence after 1164. An exogenous situation that previously would not have led to the collapse of Genoa's institution now had a devastating effect.

In 1194 the Holy Roman Emperor, who needed the assistance of Genoa's navy, had an interest in ending the civil war. By promises of rewards and threats of war, the emperor induced the Genoese clans to agree to alter Genoa's political institutions by introducing a self-enforcing organization that restored interclan mutual deterrence and cooperation.

At the center of Genoa's new institution was a non-Genoese *podestà*. The *podestà* was selected by a committee of representatives from the city's neighborhoods, a committee that was large enough that no clan dominated it. Hired for a year to serve as Genoa's military leader, judge, and administrator, the *podestà* was supported by the soldiers and judges he brought with him.

The *podestà* and his military contingent fostered the clans' ability to cooperate by creating a military balance among them. The threat of intervention by the *podestà* deterred each clan from attacking the other to gain control over the city. Because the *podestà* was paid at the end of his term, the threat was credible, because if a clan took control of the city, there was no reason why it should pay the *podestà*. This reward scheme also made it in the *podestà*'s interest not to alter fundamentally the balance of power among the factions. The *podestà* could thus credibly commit to be impartial and to retaliate only against individuals who broke the law rather than against an entire clan.

For a while, the *podesteria* fostered interclan cooperation – and thus political stability and economic growth. It was a self-enforcing institution, as the self-enforcing belief in the futility of gaining political dominance by using force deterred clans from trying. The belief that all clans could gain from cooperation without risking their economic position through military confrontation also motivated cooperation.

Yet, like the consular system that prevailed prior to the *podesteria*, the *podesteria* was not reinforcing – indeed, it contained the seeds of its own destruction. Specifically, because the *podesteria* was based on a balance of military strength among the clans and each clan wanted to be militarily prepared in case of need, it contained but did not eliminate interclan rivalry. Each clan was still motivated to strengthen itself militarily with

174

respect to the others, and clan members' main identification was still with their clan and not the city.

The creation of the *alberghi* and the rise of the *popolo* as a faction during this period were further manifestations of the lack of reinforcement of the institutional equilibrium. *Alberghi* were clanlike social structures whose purpose was to strengthen consorterial ties among members of various families through a formal contract and the assumption of a common surname, usually that of the *albergo*'s most powerful clan (D. Hughes 1978, pp. 129–30). By the fifteenth century, about thirty *alberghi*, each containing five to fifteen lineages, dominated political and economic life in Genoa. At the same time, each clan's attempt to develop a patronage network and the access of all city residents to Genoa's lucrative overseas trade implied that over time the *popolo* acquired the resources, organization, and recognition of their common interests to form a political faction that disrupted the noble-controlled equilibrium.

Under the *podesteria*, peace was maintained. But Genoa's institutions motivated clans to establish patronage networks (thereby mobilizing the *popoli*), to indoctrinate their members to internalize the norms of revenge and adopt identities through the *alberghi*) as clan members, to fortify their residences, and to acquire the military ability to attack other clans. These changes did not render the *podesteria* ineffective in the short run; it remained self-enforcing. But over time these changes caused Genoa's political structure to become self-enforcing in a smaller range of situations, leading to its eventual demise. In the long run, a *podestà* could not constrain the balance of power incentives among Genoa's rival clans, and the system collapsed.

6.4.2   Venice

The early history of Venice parallels that of Genoa. After an initial period of interclan cooperation, interclan rivalry developed, with the goal of capturing the office of the doge (Lane 1973; Norwich 1989). Originally, the doge was a Byzantine official, but shortly after Venice was established (in 679), the post became that of an elected monarch with judicial, executive, and legislative powers. For the next few hundred years, clans fought for control over the doge's post. As in Genoa, economic cooperation was hindered by the lack of an institution able to contain interclan rivalry.

Changes around the Mediterranean increased the cost of such confrontations. Toward the end of the eleventh century, the decline of

Byzantine naval power increased the gains to the Venetians of forming a political institution that enabled cooperation. They responded by establishing a new self-enforcing institution that this opportunity made possible. At its center was the belief that every clan would fight against a renegade clan that attempted to gain political dominance over the city and its economic resources.[15] This belief and the behavior it fostered may have helped forge a common Venetian identity that reinforced this belief. In any case, a set of institutionalized rules guided the behavior of the Venetians toward this self-enforcing belief and generated the conditions required for these beliefs to be self-enforcing. The rules limited the doge's power to distribute economic and political rents, curtailed the clans' ability to influence the outcome of the election of a doge (or any other officer), established tight administrative control over gains from interclan political cooperation, and allocated these rents among all the important Venetian clans so that all had a share in them regardless of clan affiliation. This allocative rule did not provide clans with incentives to increase their military strength to prepare for interclan military conflict. Because these rules were being developed at a time when the Byzantine and Islamic naval powers were on the decline and cooperation was most beneficial, Venetians were able to make the most of this opportunity.[16]

Beginning in 1032, the doge's authority was limited through the establishment of advisory councils until it was de facto altered from an elected monarchy to a republican magistracy. In 1172 the Venetians, through their representative organizations, established that a doge should never act contrary to the advice of his councillors. To inhibit the ability to use a clan's political machine and popular support to influence the election, the selection of the new doge was entrusted to an official nominating committee, which was selected and formed through an elaborate process based on both lotteries and deliberation. The (partially random) process began in the Great Council, in which all adult members of the powerful clans were eligible to participate. From this council a committee of thirty was chosen by lottery, and its role was to propose a list of candidates for the post of the doge. The selection of candidates proceeded through an additional nine steps of deliberation and selection by lot until the proposed candidate was brought before the Venetian assembly for approval. The

---

[15] How these beliefs were formed remains unclear.

[16] Muslim naval power particularly declined during the eleventh century following the political disintegration of Muslim Spain, the crumbling of centralized control over North Africa, and the military conflict between the Fatimid Caliphate centered in Egypt and the 'Abbasid Caliphate in Baghdad.

importance of clans and their patronage network was reduced by these processes and rules requiring that only one family member could be on any committee and that a delegate had to recuse himself when a relative was being considered. The process was designed to reach a quick decision, thereby reducing the ability to manipulate the system.

Similar, albeit less elaborate, selection processes were used to select other officials. Their numbers were relatively large and their time in office relatively short, so that members of many clans could hold a particular office in a given period of time. Nominating committees for many posts were selected by ballot in the Great Council in a way that gave every person present an equal chance of being on a nominating committee. To prevent officials from reaping unlawful gains, the conduct of all officials (including the doge) was subject to scrutiny by committees.

The belief that clans would join together to confront another clan that attempted to use military power to change the rules was self-enforcing because all clans benefited from these rules. The rules and associated beliefs were also reinforcing, because they provided clans with few incentives to invest in fortifying their residences or establishing patronage networks. By weakening the importance of clans and linking one's prospects to the city's rules and success, the system fostered norms of loyalty to the city. By weakening the clans, over time Venice's republican magistracy increased the range of situations in which this political institution was self-enforcing. This institution also prevented the endogenous formation of a political faction among the *popoli*, because the magistracy as an institution did not motivate clans to establish patronage networks that would have channeled rents from political control over Venice's overseas possessions to nonnoble clans.[17]

6.5 FORMAL REPRESENTATION OF INSTITUTIONAL REINFORCEMENT

Repeated games are games in which the same stage game is repeated each period (Appendix A). Such games would appear to be less promising for the study of institutional dynamics than dynamic games, in which the game can be changed each period. In fact, as argued earlier and evident from the success of repeated-game theory to facilitate empirical studies, the theory of repeated games captures important ways in which people

---

[17] This group was extended several times to absorb emerging nonnoble families. The system therefore had the flexibility required for its perpetuation.

view their environment and make decisions. This theory does not impose the unrealistic informational requirements or involve the computational complexities of dynamic games, which render such games unrealistically demanding as a basis for a general theory of institutional change. For these reasons, I model endogenous institutional dynamics using the framework provided by the theory of repeated games.

This section provides a formal representation of a game in which there is the possibility of an endogenous shift in one of the parameters of the game (the payoffs).[18] It illustrates how quasi-parameters and reinforcement processes can be incorporated into standard repeated-game-theoretic models. To illustrate the generality of the illustrative discussion, I relate it to the empirical analyses already discussed.

The game-theoretic framework makes explicit the parameters delineating the extent of self-enforceability of various beliefs in a game that is conditional on the relevant intertransactional linkages. Building on this framework allows us to study institutional dynamics by combining what the analyst understands about the situation – particularly regarding processes that reinforce or undermine (quasi-) parameters – with a conjecture about what decision makers understand, know, and observe.

To grasp the implications of this formulation, consider the infinitely repeated prisoners' dilemma game presented in annex 6.1. In order to focus on the relationships between self-enforcing institutions and reinforcement, this model considers only one institutional element, that of shared beliefs of mutual cooperation (the outcome of the strategy (c, c) in equilibrium over repeated play).[19] This game has four parameters: the initial cooperative payoff for each player (b_0), the sucker's payoff (k), the

[18] The force of the argument about the importance of self-enforcing and undermining processes is not limited to the particular game structure or equilibrium refinement. It rests on the difficulties individuals normally face when having to think their way through strategic situations.

[19] In asserting that the players are engaged in the prisoners' dilemma game, I am asserting that particular institutional elements are or are not relevant. A legal system is implicitly assumed to exist and to be able to commit to taking particular actions in response to a prisoner's action. This implicit assumption is reflected in the game's payoff, which captures the prisoners' beliefs that cooperation reduces punishment. Potentially relevant organizations such as the Mafia are assumed not to exist. The game thus assumes away the possibility of beliefs that a prisoner who defected would be penalized by such an organization. The analysis also assumes away the possible influence of norms, such as that of honor among thieves, which the prisoners may have internalized before their arrest. Internalization of such norms would affect the prisoners' payoff from cooperating or defecting.

additional payoff for defecting while the other player cooperates (e), and the discount factor (δ). In this representation, (b_t) is a quasi-parameter.

This game differs from the standard repeated-play prisoners' dilemma model in that it allows for neutral, positive, and negative feedback from past behavior to the quasi-parameter that lead to neutral, positive, and negative self-reinforcement (undermining), respectively. In a positive feedback situation, the payoff b after any (c, c) outcome increases by ϵ for the next round of play, reinforcing the institution. In a negative feedback situation, the payoff b after any (c, c) outcome decreases by ϵ for the next round of play, undermining the institution. The cooperative payoff changes depending on the outcome in the previous round of the game. In the case of positive reinforcement, over time the range of δ for which (c, c) will be self-enforcing increases: the institution of cooperation is thus not only self-enforcing but self-reinforcing. It is an equilibrium in the short run that, in the long run, is an equilibrium for a wider range of discount factors and other parameters.

Conversely, in the case of undermining, cooperation is self-enforcing but not self-reinforcing, as the range of δ for which (c, c) is self-enforcing decreases over time. At some t in the future, cooperation will no longer be self-enforcing, and (d, d) will become the behavior associated with the new institution.

In this game, reinforcement and undermining processes do not depend on players' knowledge of the feedback mechanism. But whoever possesses this knowledge determines the institutional ramifications of these processes. Consider first a situation in which the actors are fully aware of the reinforcing (undermining process) (case 1). In this case, positive reinforcement extends the set of parameters (δ, e, $-k$, b_0) in which cooperation is self-enforcing (claim 1). Cooperation would be more fragile to exogenous shocks earlier in the process. Indeed, Venice's political institution faced its most challenging moments in its early days. Alternatively, negative reinforcement reduces the set of parameters in which cooperation is possible, and cooperation, due to unraveling, would never be an equilibrium outcome.

In reality, other responses to foreseen undermining processes are often possible. The study of Genoa reflects two of them. First, cooperation led to undermining, by increasing wealth and hence the temptation to capture it. Each Genoese clan was motivated to cooperate with other clans only to the extent to which its gains from additional wealth outweighed its expected increase in deterrence cost. The response to undermining was thus behavioral: ceasing cooperation while retaining the institutions of mutual deterrence.

A second possible response is organizational, altering the organizational component of the institution to restore its self-enforceability. In 1194 the mutual-deterrence equilibrium was no longer self-enforcing, but its costs to both clans increased as a result of the emperor's threat to intervene. The response was organizational: the introduction of the *podestà*, an organization designed to restore mutual deterrence and cooperation that reflected a process of learning.

In case 2 the relevant players do not recognize the reinforcing and undermining processes. In the prisoners' dilemma game, ignorance of undermining would imply cooperation for several periods until the players recognized that the situation had changed and responded by defecting. But the dynamics can take other forms, reflecting more complex situations. Even if an undermining process is recognized, the incentives implied by the self-enforcing institution may imply that players will not effectively respond to it.

Often those who observe a process of undermining have little incentive to reveal it to others. Such one-sided knowledge regarding undermining leads to the collapse of the previous institution only once the person who possesses the knowledge begins acting in a manner that reveals his knowledge. This collapse can then be followed by institutional refinement and redesign aimed at restoring a desired outcome, given new knowledge about the situation.

6.6 THE INSTITUTIONAL LIFE CYCLE

Institutions may have "life cycles" as suggested by Genoa's history. Initially, institutions tend to reinforce themselves, but undermining processes assert themselves as time passes. Initial reinforcement reflects, among other factors, the role of institutions in providing the cognitive, coordinative, and informational foundations of behavior. In the processes of institutionalization, each individual faces some uncertainty as to whether the behavior in the process of institutionalization will or will not be followed and to what effect. Basing one's actions on beliefs about what others will do is not foolproof. Others' actions are not known with certainty ex ante, and, as stressed in Chapter 5, many factors influencing other peoples' behaviors and outcomes are not directly observable. The ex ante expected value of goal-oriented behavior may be high, but these strategies could still fail ex post. When these behaviors work ex post, uncertainty is resolved – the mechanism for institutional persistence sets in – and the value of continuing to use them is higher than it was ex ante. The fact that a particular behavior led to particular results reinforces the belief that the strategy adopted by the relevant decision makers will produce the same results in the future, making it more likely to be followed.[20]

Furthermore, institutions shape individuals in ways that tend to reinforce these institutions by making the cost of deviation from the behavior these institutions generate emotionally or socially costly. Institutionalized behavior and the associated outcomes lead to reinforcing norms, senses of entitlements, identities, self-images, thinking patterns, and ideologies.[21] Regularities of behavior tend to become the normatively appropriate and fair way to behave; they gain legitimacy, lead to the development of congruent personalities, and are incorporated in individuals' identities. Once this happens, subsequent socialization further reinforces the institution. This social and psychological reinforcement implied by an institution tends to lead to political activities aimed at reinforcing it through laws and regulations. Similarly, those who economically benefit from existing institutions tend to have the means and influence required to pursue such activities (Olson 1982; North 1990; Mahoney 2000; Pierson 2000).[22] Finally, institutions motivate the establishment of reinforcing organizations and the acquisition of complementary capabilities, knowledge, and human and physical capital that reinforce them (Rosenberg 1982; R. Nelson and Winter 1982; North 1981; David 1994).

Once this initial stage of reinforcement occurs, undermining may set in, although the conditions under which this might occur are not yet clear. No general theory identifies attributes of institutions that lead to undermining.

Reputation-based institutions, however, undermine themselves when the implied behavior decreases the expected value of future rewards or

---

[20] One way to integrate this argument formally in the models presented here is to extend them to reflect incomplete information (see, e.g., the discussion in Fudenberg and Tirole 1991). Individuals have some beliefs over the "type" of others and hence their responses in various situations. There is thus a distinction between ex ante and ex post beliefs about their actions.

[21] K. Davis (1949); Homans (1950); Berger and Luckmann (1967); Scott (1995); March and Olsen (1989); Mead (1967 [1934]); Sugden (1989); Rabin (1993, 1994); Fudenberg and Levine (1993); G. Hodgson (1998); Kuran (1995, chaps. 10–14; 1998); Ben-Ner and Putterman (1998); and Akerlof and Kranton (2000) present economic analyses of such features and processes.

[22] The extent to which the political system maps the public's preferences into political outcomes depends on its institutional details.

sanctions (see Appendix C). This decrease renders the beliefs that motivate the behavior associated with the institution self-enforcing in a smaller set of parameters. This is the case because, in reputation-based institutions, the fear of losing rewards or being sanctioned motivates the institutionalized behavior. If this behavior undermines these rewards and sanctions and the incentives they imply, the institutionalized behavior eventually ceases to be an equilibrium.

This mechanism through which private-order, reputation-based institutions undermine themselves is reflected in three empirical studies in this volume: the evolution of the merchant guild, discussed in Chapter 4; the undermining of Genoa's political institution, discussed in Chapter 8; and the decline of an institution that provided contract enforcement in impersonal exchange, discussed in Chapter 10. In the case of the merchant guilds, the related institution fostered the expansion of trade based on rulers' concerns about losing their reputation for protecting the rights of foreign traders. Rulers valued this reputation because they gained from custom duties paid by the traders. Expansion of trade, however, reduced the value of customs paid by the marginal merchant. Initially, the reputation-based institution that motivated rulers to respect the rights of German merchants was based on the threat by the abused merchant and his close associates to cease trading. As trade expanded, however, the reduction to the ruler in the value of the future customs of the marginal merchant undermined the operation of this institution. Additional supporting organizations that rendered credible retaliation by a sufficiently large number of merchants were required.

This historical episode illustrates how the fact that actors play against the rules creates quasi-parameters; changes in various aspects that are incorporated into the rules of the game influence behavior only when those who observe them reveal them through their behavior. At no stage in the process of institutional undermining did merchants directly observe changes in the benefits and costs to rulers of abusing them. Only when a ruler's behavior revealed to the merchants that the institution was no longer self-enforcing did they act to introduce a new institutional element to reinforce the failing institution.

6.7 CONCLUDING COMMENTS

By analyzing reinforcing processes, this chapter examined why and how the behavior induced by self-enforcing institutions influenced their long-term stability. Behavior in equilibrium can gradually alter quasi-parameters in a way that causes institutions to be self-enforcing in a larger or smaller set of situations. Hence institutional equilibria are subject to endogenous change, both indirectly and directly. They do so indirectly by making them more or less sensitive to exogenous shocks. Institutional behaviors directly influence rates of institutional change, for unless a self-enforcing institution is (weakly) reinforced, it will change in the long run. Either the associated behavior will no longer be self-enforcing or new institutional elements will be required to support it.

Endogenous change in this perspective is driven by marginal shifts in the value of quasi-parameters. Such shifts make the institution more or less sensitive to environmental changes, and they can render an institution no longer self-enforcing in a given environment. Analytically, one can combine the study of self-enforcement and reinforcement by first examining an institution's self-enforceability while considering quasi-parameters as fixed and exogenous, then examining the implied reinforcing processes, and finally examining the long-term implications of these processes on the institution's endogenous rate of change.

Several methodological and substantive extensions to these insights into the study of endogenous institutional change are called for. First, the analysis relies on the repeated-game framework, but furthering the analysis of self-reinforcement will benefit from a more explicitly dynamic analytical framework that is only hinted at by the formal model presented here. Second, statistical tests may strengthen the contextually based game-theoretic analysis of institutional change. Unless the observable implications of models of reinforcement are statistically validated over a range of cases outside the set of cases from which the theory was developed, there will remain a tautological residue on those models. However, statistical tests of the observable implications of the model on aspects of the society that were not analyzed in the formation of the model further lend support to the analysis's validity. For example, an observable implication of the model of the two Italian city-states is that over time there would be more interclan exogamy in Venice than in Genoa. Showing that this was the case would help overcome charges of tautology. Furthermore, statistical tests will also allow us to assess the relative importance of endogenous versus exogenous sources of institutional change. Third, the analysis emphasized the importance of quasi-parameters but only began to explore the features of institutions that foster reinforcing or undermining changes in quasi-parameters in various situations.

Substantively, much work remains. The theory presented here concentrates mainly on beliefs (albeit noting the importance of norms in reinforcing institutions); a parallel theory has to be developed regarding norms. The relevant issues are many: Under what conditions is behavior internalized as morally appropriate and hence reinforced? What determines the relative weights in preferences between one's normative behavior and behavior that is materially beneficial? Addressing this question is central to understanding when economic (materialistic) considerations will or will not undermine normatively appropriate but economically unrewarding institutionalized behavior.

More generally, we have no theory to explain the factors that determine the extent and speed of reinforcing processes. What factors, for example, determine the extent of intentional and habitual behavior? What organizations respond to the risks implied by playing against the institutionalized rules rather than the rules of the game? What determines the ability of individuals to manipulate institutionalized rules?

By introducing and elaborating on the concepts of quasi-parameters and institutional reinforcement, this chapter provides a framework for integrating the study of self-enforcing institutions with that of endogenously induced institutional change. This approach can be extended, as it is in the next chapter, to examine why and how self-enforcing institutions influence the direction of institutional change.

ANNEX 6.1: A MODEL OF INSTITUTIONAL REINFORCEMENT

Consider an infinitely repeated prisoners' dilemma game in which the period $t = 0, 1, \ldots$ stage game actions and payoffs to the two players are:

1 \ 2	c	d
c	b_t, b_t	$-k, b_t + e$
d	$b_t + e, -k$	$0, 0$

where $b_0, k, e > 0$, and players share a common discount factor $\delta \in (0, 1)$. The model has four parameters: $\delta, b_0, k,$ and e. b_t, is a quasi-parameter, since it can be affected by the institution in place. The institution we are interested in is the one generating cooperation, that is, stage-game play of (c, c).

Definition: Cooperation has a positive (negative, neutral) reinforcement if play of (c, c) in period t implies $b_{t+1} - b_t > (<, =) 0$.

184

Standard models of repeated prisoners' dilemma take cooperation to have neutral reinforcement. For simplicity, I assume that the change in cooperation payoffs under any reinforcement mechanism is fixed over time.

Assumption: For all t, $b_{t+1} - b_t = \epsilon$ with $\epsilon > (<, =)$ 0 under positive (negative, neutral) reinforcement. In what follows, the equilibrium notion is subgame perfect Nash equilibrium. To avoid introducing complicating notation and terminology, the presentation is somewhat informal.

Case 1: Knowledge about Reinforcement

Consider the case in which players are aware of the reinforcement mechanism.

Claim 1: The cooperation institution is self-enforcing over a larger range of discount factors under positive reinforcement than under neutral reinforcement.

Proof: Fix the period as τ. It is easily seen that cooperation can be a self-enforcing institution under neutral reinforcement if and only if

$$\delta \geq \frac{e}{b_\tau + e}. \tag{1}$$

Suppose there is positive reinforcement. Recall that $\epsilon \equiv b_{\tau+1} - b_t > 0$ under Nash reversion (specifically, playing defect every period). If players follow Nash reversion, then on the equilibrium path their payoffs will be strictly larger than $b_\tau + (b_\tau + \epsilon)\frac{\delta}{1-\delta}$, while deviating yields $b_\tau + e$. Hence cooperation is incentive compatible if $e \leq (b_\tau + \epsilon)\frac{\delta}{1-\delta}$, which can be rewritten as

$$\delta \geq \frac{e}{b_\tau + e + \epsilon}. \tag{2}$$

Because $\epsilon > 0$, the right-hand side of expression (2) is strictly smaller than the right-hand side of expression (1), which proves the claim. Q.E.D.

Claim 2: Under negative reinforcement, cooperation is not a self-enforcing institution.

185

Proof: The proof is straightforward by backward induction, given that payoffs from mutual cooperation decrease by ϵ every period if players have cooperated in previous periods.

The institution of cooperation can thus be self-enforcing only under neutral or positive reinforcement. Under positive reinforcement, the institution is positively reinforcing, because the right-hand side of expression (2) decreases over time (because b_t increases), causing the equilibrium to hold for a larger range of δ over time. By similar reasoning, the institution is neither positively nor negatively reinforcing under neutral reinforcement, because the range of δ over which it is self-enforcing is identical in any period t.

Case 2: Ignorance about Reinforcement

Now consider the case in which players are unaware of the reinforcement mechanism. In each period players observe b_t and imagine that this value remains fixed in all future periods regardless of their actions. If cooperation can be supported in equilibrium, it can be done with Nash reversion. In any period τ, this is incentive-compatible if and only if $b_\tau + e \leq \frac{b_\tau}{1-\delta}$, or equivalently, if and only if

$$\delta \geq \frac{e}{b_\tau + e}. \tag{3}$$

The right-hand side of expression (3) is strictly decreasing in b_τ. Hence, if cooperation produces positive reinforcement, the range of δ for which Nash revision is self-enforcing increases over time (i.e., the institution is positively self-reinforcing). If the institution is self-enforcing in some period τ, it will be self-enforcing in all periods thereafter.

If cooperation produces negative reinforcement, the institution is negatively self-reinforcing. Indeed, with negative reinforcement, for any δ and any starting value b_0, there is some (possibly large) t such that cooperation is no longer self-enforcing at period t. At t the institution changes to defect, defect. The gradual erosion of the gains from cooperation implies that at some point, the future gains from cooperation are smaller than the present gain from defecting.

7

Institutional Trajectories

How Past Institutions Affect Current Ones

Societies face new situations when an institution that governed a transaction is no longer self-enforcing, when it is perceived to be losing its self-enforcing characteristics, or when technological, organizational, and other changes bring about new transactions. Do past institutions – perhaps even institutions that are no longer effective in influencing behavior – affect the direction of institutional change? If they do, why and how?

The intentionally created perspective on institutions, which often views them as rules, emphasizes that new institutions reflect the interests and inductive reasoning of economic or political agents. Evolutionary institutionalism emphasizes the importance of environmental – structural – forces and the lack of deductive reasoning. To explain the impact of past institutions, these perspectives commonly invoke as exogenous one set of institutions to explain subsequent ones. In studying economic institutions as rules, for example, it is common to study the formation of the rules while considering either political or informal – culturally determined – institutions as given. This position, however, amounts to pushing the question of institutional impact one step back.

In contrast, this chapter explores why and how the past, encapsulated in institutional elements, directs institutional change and leads societies to evolve along distinct institutional trajectories. Exploring the properties of the social elements that make up an institution is the central focus of this argument. These properties imply a *fundamental asymmetry* between institutional elements inherited from the past and technologically feasible alternatives. Because of fundamental asymmetry, beliefs, norms, and organizations inherited from the past influence subsequent institutions by constituting the default in new situations; they are part of the initial conditions in the processes that influence selection among alternative new institutions. This is the case even if these elements originally emerged as components of an institution that is no longer self-enforcing.

The fundamental asymmetry, as will be further articulated later, reflects that institutional elements are not only attributes of institutions but attributes of individuals and the social and cultural worlds they know and share. Institutional elements reside in individuals' memories, constitute their cognitive models, are embodied in their preferences, and manifest themselves in organizations; they are what individuals bring with them when they face new situations. Institutional elements inherited from the past are the default in providing the micro-foundations of behavior in new situations; creating alternative, technologically feasible institutional elements requires action. History matters.

When considering the forces that shape institutional development, this historical-process perspective is less permissive than the intentionally created agency perspective in allowing agents to change institutions; agency (the pursuit of institutional change by goal-oriented actors) is limited by the shackles of history. At the same time, the historical-process perspective recognizes that the past influences the future, not because agents are passive but because they find it necessary, useful, and desirable to draw on the past. They do so to determine how to behave in new situations when intentionally pursuing institutional change, and when contemplating the development or adoption of institutional and organizational innovations. The perspective developed here is therefore more permissive than the evolutionary or other structural perspectives in allowing for intentional institutional change and recognizing the role of agency.

The historical-process perspective thus recognizes that history's influence on the direction of institutional change complements rather than substitutes the role of agency. This mitigates the analytical difficulties in studying new institutions as reflecting either historical forces or agency. History is central to the sociological approach to institutional analysis, which argues that culture provides a "tool kit" that facilitates the reconstitution of a society facing new situations (Swidler 1986). Social networks inherited from the past provide the foundations of new institutions (Granovetter 1985, 2002; Greif 1989), while past cognitive models shape the way new situations are perceived (DiMaggio and Powell 1991a). Yet history is littered with cultural, organizational, and cognitive models that ceased to influence behavior (see Thelen 1999). To be meaningful, the assertion that the past matters requires delineating its limitations. Without a discipline imposed by a deductive framework, purely historical analyses of institutional dynamics risk being ad hoc.

At the same time, the ability to study the direction of institutional change deductively while adopting an agency perspective is also limited. Game theory highlights the fact that in situations central to institutional analysis – strategic repeated situations with a large action space – multiple equilibria, and hence institutions, usually exist (see Appendix A). We cannot satisfactorily limit the set of admissible institutions deductively by requiring that an institution be self-enforcing.

Recognizing the importance of the fundamental asymmetry and the role of agency in influencing the direction of institutional change highlights a way to and the usefulness of combining historical and deductive analyses. It is conceptually sound and analytically useful to rely on *contextual refinement* in studying the direction of institutional change. The force of history is limited by recognizing that the new institution has to be self-enforcing. The set of admissible self-enforcing institutions is also limited, however, by relying on the knowledge of the context – specifically, knowledge of institutional elements inherited from the past. Such knowledge rules out possible yet contextually irrelevant institutions. Institutional elements inherited from the past constitute part of the initial conditions in the processes that lead to new institutions. History and theory discipline one another. The analysis is far less permissive (in allowing intertemporal links among institutions) than the standard historical analysis, and it is also far less permissive (in terms of the set of admissible institutions at each point in time) than the standard game-theoretic equilibrium analysis.

In presenting this argument, section 7.1 elaborates on the fundamental asymmetry between institutional elements inherited from the past and technologically feasible alternatives. Section 7.2 discusses the implications of this asymmetry on new institutions while sections 7.3 and 7.4 discuss the role of agency and institutional innovations respectively. Section 7.5 presents the contemporaneous implications of the fundamental asymmetry and illustrates them by considering the history of slavery in Europe and the Muslim worlds. Section 7.6 summarizes the argument and presents the concept of contextual refinement.

7.1 THE FUNDAMENTAL ASYMMETRY BETWEEN INSTITUTIONAL ELEMENTS INHERITED FROM THE PAST AND TECHNOLOGICALLY FEASIBLE ALTERNATIVES

In new situations, no institutionalized rules guide behavior, and forward-looking individuals have a limited ability to deduce how to behave.

Individuals seek a cognitive framework, information, normative guidance, and a way to anticipate what others may do to coordinate their behavior with their responses. In seeking these micro-foundations of behavior, individuals draw on institutional elements inherited from the past, even those that were part of institutions that are no longer self-enforcing. Past institutional elements are attributes of both institutions and the social world individuals know, share, and remember. They reside in memories, constitute cognitive models, embody preferences, and constitute commonly known behavioral beliefs.

Alternative institutional elements can also provide these micro-foundations of behavior – new organizations or behavioral beliefs can coordinate behavior in new situations, for example – but past institutional elements are the default. Introducing other technologically feasible institutional elements and rendering them effective in new situations requires action: generating new knowledge, changing commonly known beliefs about what others can and will do, and replacing internalized beliefs and norms. There is therefore a fundamental asymmetry between a society's institutional heritage and alternative institutional elements. One reason for this asymmetry is that creating new institutional elements involves bargaining, coordination, search, and learning costs. Moreover, the results of such actions and the implied institutional change are likely to be uncertain, take time to transpire, and have unknown and uncertain welfare and distributive implications. Often such actions also imply the provision of a public good, by setting standards, providing a unified interpretation of past events, or establishing new organizations such as a court of law. Hence they are plagued with collective action, free-rider problems, and strategic manipulations. These transaction costs of institutional transition contribute to the asymmetry between institutional elements inherited from the past and alternatives.

The fundamental asymmetry between institutional elements inherited from the past and technologically feasible alternatives reflects more than just the cost of introducing alternatives. It reflects the cognitive, informational, coordinative, and normative contents of past institutional elements. These contents, in turn, result from poorly understood and often unintentional processes of socialization, internalization, learning, and experimentation, as well as the acquisition and diffusion of capacities and knowledge by individuals and organizations. Hence past institutional elements constitute what individuals believe about their environment, what they believe others believe about what action will be taken in various circumstances, and what they consider morally appropriate. Past institutional elements represent what is expected, and what is perceived as true and morally correct.

The rules against which individuals play embody a cognitive model of and information about the nature and the details of various observable and unobservable aspects of the situation, such as the physical environment, discount factors, attitudes toward risk, and the objectives of various decision makers. New, alternative rules of behavior are devoid of such content (see Chapter 5). Developing an alternative model – a new set of internalized beliefs – and gaining new information is a lengthy, costly, and uncertain endeavor. Even more fundamental is the fact that as long as individuals hold a particular model to be true, they will not attempt to develop an alternative one but will try to use the existing model – perhaps slightly modified – to direct behavior in a new situation. For atheists, for example, contract enforcement institutions based on the fear of God are not viable.

The incentives to develop a new model (internalized beliefs) are further dulled by the common-knowledge feature of existing models. Even if one recognizes the existence of a better model, as long as others follow the behavioral instructions embodied in a different one, the best response may be to follow that model as well.[1] Existing institutional elements constitute the environment within which new institutions will establish themselves, because they represent the domain within which individuals can make decisions.

Cognitive dissonance – the mental conflict that occurs when beliefs or assumptions are contradicted by new information – further contributes to the asymmetry between past and alternative mental models (internalized beliefs). To avoid mental conflicts and preserve order in one's concept of the world, an individual uses various defensive measures, such as confirmatory bias and avoidance of conflicting evidence.[2] Past institutions and institutional elements provide much of what individuals wish to preserve by constituting, generating, and maintaining internalized norms, beliefs, and their related behavior. Responses to the demands of a new situation are characterized by an attempt to retain the beliefs and norms constituting the institutional elements inherited from the past.

[1] The conditions under which this is true have not been worked out. Clearly, having a different model can leave an individual better off. Kuran (1995) examines the conditions under which others' expected negative (social or coercive) response motivates people to refrain from revealing their true model.
[2] I am not aware of an analysis of the factors influencing when people will or will not use such defensive measures.

Consider, for example, the experience of the Jewish people after the destruction of the First Temple and their exile in the sixth century B.C.E. How could the Jews reconcile such a military defeat with their belief in an almighty God who had promised to defend his followers? To eliminate cognitive dissonance, the biblical prophecies argued that the defeat had been a punishment for the Jews' failure to follow God's ordinances. Reality was explained in a manner consistent with the internalized beliefs inherited from the past. Furthermore, when most people are expected to do so, each individual is less motivated to rely on the new information.

The fundamental asymmetry of behavioral beliefs reflects the limited ability to rely on deduction in guiding behavior in recurrent strategic situations. As game theory highlights, in these situations there is a multiplicity of self-enforcing behavior. People use behavioral beliefs inherited from the past to direct their actions and to predict others' behavior. They rely on past behavioral beliefs because there is a fundamental asymmetry between institutional elements inherited from the past and alternative ones. Those inherited from the past are commonly known: each individual knows that everyone else knows them. Changing what everyone believes everyone else believes is inherently difficult.

The fundamental asymmetry of norms inherited from the past reflects the fact that once internalized, they constitute a part of individuals' identities or concepts of themselves that is transferred to a new situation. A norm constitutes part of one's identity that influences his or her behavior in new situations. While preferences in economics are defined over outcomes (in such forms as goods and services), norms differentiate among such outcomes by the process of reaching them. Norms imply that the welfare an individual derives from one dollar may well depend on whether it was stolen or earned. Changing one's identity or concept of oneself is psychologically costly. Eradicating existing norms and creating new ones requires time-consuming processes, such as socialization, indoctrination, and observation of others' behavior as well as rationalization of why the old norms are not applicable in the new situation.[3]

Asymmetry also exists between past organizations and alternative ones. The rules, beliefs, and norms that govern behavior among the organization's members and between them and nonmembers are part of their

---

[3] While intuitive, this argument does not explain which past internalized beliefs and norms will be effective in a particular new situation. Should, for example, the internalized norm of not stealing from one's neighbor also apply to a traveling merchant?

192

historical heritage. Furthermore, organizations have a dual nature, as both institutions and institutional elements (Chapters 2 and 5). They are institutions with respect to transactions among their constituting members and possibly between them and outsiders (e.g., transactions among police officers and transactions between the police and other members of the society). Organizations are components of institutions generating behavior in other transactions (e.g., the police alter the set of self-enforcing beliefs in transactions among criminals and law-abiding citizens). Because organizations are also institutions, they do not instantly cease to be self-enforcing, even when the institution in which they were elements is no longer self-enforcing. It is often useful to think of this argument as follows: an organization encompasses self-enforcing behavior and beliefs in a subgame, while the institution to which it belongs encompasses behavior and beliefs in the entire game.

Organizations inherited from the past have various capacities that they acquired through their operation: routines, information, and other assets, such as legitimacy; intraorganizational personal relationships and communication codes; information-processing capacities; technological know-how; and human, social, and physical capital.[4] These assets increase their ability to accomplish various tasks. Hence once an organization begins to operate, positive feedback contributes to the asymmetry between it and alternative organizations (David 1994). Organizations inherited from the past are also in a position to advance their interests in processes that lead to new institutions. Organizations that do not yet exist have neither voice nor the ability to take action.

The extent of the fundamental asymmetry depends on institutional elements inherited from the past, which determine the transaction costs of institutional transition. In a theocracy, for example, attempts to change the rules associated with the religious dogma in a noninstitutionalized manner

---

[4] The importance of such assets in providing initial conditions in processes that lead to a new institution has been recognized in economics, political science, and sociology. See Greif (1989); North (1990); Rothstein (1996); and Granovetter (1985, 2002). Greif (1994a); Banerjee and Newman (1993); and Galor and Zeira (1993) provide some explicit analyses of such dynamics. The accumulation of such assets can also render a new institution possible in a given situation. As notaries in ancien régime France gathered sufficient information over time, they created new contract enforcement and matching institutions (P. Hoffman, Postel-Vinay, and Rosenthal 2000). Modern credit bureaus exhibit a similar process (Klein 1996). Legitimacy is often acquired gradually as past successes of a leader or an organization in influencing behavior lead others to expect such success in the future.

can be psychologically costly and may imply social, economic, and coercive sanctions. In an effective democracy, individuals have much less to lose by forming lobbies that attempt to change various rules governing economic behavior. Indeed, effective democracies are geared toward facilitating changes. The transaction costs of institutional transition – the cost to an individual of taking actions motivated by such considerations as efficiency, greed, or fairness and aimed at introducing new institutional elements – is a function of institutional elements inherited from the past.[5]

To sum: That actors play against rules that encompass cognition and knowledge, search for coordination drawing on the past, and seek consistency of behavior with internalized norms and beliefs implies a fundamental asymmetry between institutional elements inherited from the past and alternative ones. The extent of this asymmetry is a function of the institutional elements inherited from the past.

7.2 THE IMPLICATIONS OF THE FUNDAMENTAL ASYMMETRY

The fundamental asymmetry implies that institutional elements inherited from the past are part of the initial conditions of processes that lead to new institutions. Processes leading to new institutions reflect agents' responses to the cognitive, informational, coordinative, and normative content of past institutional elements. Institutional elements inherited from the past, rather than technologically feasible alternatives, provide the means to cognitively order new situations, obtain information, coordinate behavior, identify one's interests, and receive normative guidance. Institutional heritage matters and new institutions bear its imprint.

The fundamental asymmetry manifests itself through four implications on the relationships between past institutional elements and new institutions. As further discussed in this section, the first implication is that in response to institutional failure, new institutions are not created de novo but emerge or are established by marginally altering elements inherited from the past. New institutions reflect this *institutional refinement.* Other implications of the fundamental asymmetry are the *environmental, coordination, and inclusive* effects. Institutions more compatible with the environment spanned by existing ones, those reflecting the coordinating

---

[5] The beliefs and norms governing the standard of proof of one's argument regarding what is correct and appropriate are particularly important (Mokyr 2002). In the late medieval period, Europeans began adopting beliefs about the appropriateness of scientific (analytical and empirical) standards of proof. During this period, the Muslim world emphasized relying on statements by past scholars.

influence of past institutional elements and incorporating institutional elements inherited from the past, are more likely to result.

Institutional change is characterized by institutional refinement, that is, attempts to reinforce failing institutions rather than create new ones. Such reinforcement takes the form of marginally altering their elements or adding new ones to render them self-enforcing. The failure of an institution that governs a particular transaction to deliver an expected outcome will usually also not lead to a completely new institution. The response is to build on the knowledge that the failure generated and mitigate the institution's deficiencies by reinforcing it. Reinforcement also takes place when an institution is recognized as being bound to fail or having undesired limitations or implications. Reinforcement, rather than creating a new institution, transpires when and because institutional failure and expected failure highlight the difficulties of effectively devising institutions due to limited cognition, knowledge, information, and coordination. More generally, the fundamental asymmetry implies that an institution that emerges or is established in new situations is more likely to be a refinement of an existing institution or to be reconstituting existing institutional elements.

The history of the Hanseatic League (Chapter 4) reflects such institutional refinement. To prevent rulers from abusing their rights, merchants needed to coordinate a response. Initially, such coordination among German merchants was provided by a local organization that included only the merchants who were present at the center where the abuse occurred. The growth of trade that this institution enabled, however, exposed its limitations: it could not support trade expansion beyond a relatively low level and hence abuses continued to occur. In response, the institution was reinforced by shifting coordination to an intercity organization, the Hansa, which coordinated actions by merchants in a particular trade center and other merchants. The knowledge generated by an existing institution led to its adaptive refinement.[6]

Intentional, wholesale institutional change tends to follow an institutional crisis when the outcomes associated with past institutions are perceived to be so deficient that, despite the fundamental asymmetry, comprehensive change is initiated. Such comprehensive changes are more

---

[6] The institutions-as-rules approach (discussed in Chapter 1) emphasizes the important point that those who lose from an institutional failure attempt to reinstitute it by trying to retain the *outcomes* associated with past institutions. The argument here is different. It regards retaining the *form* (institutional elements) inherited from the past in a new institution.

likely to be attempted if there is a "role model," a known alternative institution with better outcomes whose operation reduces some of the fundamental asymmetry.[7] The major military defeat of the Ottoman Empire in the modern period by Western powers and the economic and technological decline it reflected motivated comprehensive institutional reform. Not surprisingly, the reforms tried to imitate many of the institutions that prevailed in the West.

Institutions inherited from the past exert an *environmental effect* on new institutions by constituting part of the exogenous, albeit socially constructed, rules of the game within which interactions leading to new institutions occur. This is clearly the case with respect to institutions exogenous to *all* the decision makers relevant to the process leading to the new institution:[8] I considered the institutions that enabled the emperor to mobilize an army against Genoa as exogenous because they were beyond the Genoese control.

Some institutions endogenous to the relevant decision makers also exert an environmental effect. One reason why this is the case is that these institutions are exogenous to each decision maker. Because they constitute an equilibrium, and due to the fundamental asymmetry, each agent finds it optimal to follow the behavior expected of him and expects that others will do the same. In addition, in noninstitutionalized situations, decisions regarding behavior have to be made without the assistance of institutionalized behavioral rules and the cognitive model and information they embody, aggregate, and disseminate. In these situations, a decision is facilitated by economizing on scarce cognitive resources (Simon 1987 [1957]). This is achieved by taking existing institutions as a given, which reduces the complexity of the problem and restricts it to a more manageable size. Taking existing institutions as given also reduces the extent of coordination required to lead to new institutionalized behavior.

Although this assertion is probably not controversial, it is difficult to state analytically which institutions should be considered exogenous in a particular study. If, however, the environmental effect reflects attempts to reduce the cognitive and coordinative loads of decision making in a new situation, then the farther away a transaction is from the central transaction under consideration, the more the interacting individuals are

---

[7] At the same time, the fundamental asymmetry implies that adopting such institutions is likely to be difficult without adjustment to local conditions (see Chapter 12).

[8] North (1990) refers to institutions within which others establish themselves as the *institutional environment*.

likely to take the related institutions as given. The analytical problem is how to measure the distance between transactions. Nevertheless, common sense can take us a long way toward recognizing institutions appropriately taken as exogenous. In studying the transition to the *podesteria*, for example, I considered as exogenous institutions that were endogenous to the Genoese yet remote from political transactions, such as their language and institutions governing marriage. The environmental effect implies that new institutions establish themselves within the structure provided by existing ones.

The *coordination effect* reflects the impact of past institutional elements on selection among the multiple institutions that can be self-enforcing given this structure. In seeking to coordinate their behavior with that of others in the new situation, individuals seek guidance in past institutional elements, such as formal coordinating organizations, past behavioral rules, and behavioral beliefs. In Genoa, the consulate – an institutional element – coordinated the transition to the *podesteria*. The governing bodies of various cities coordinated in establishing the Hanseatic League. I show in Chapter 9 how distinct culturally determined behavioral beliefs inherited from the past coordinated on different institutions among two groups of medieval traders. All else being equal, new institutions are more likely to be those that reflect the coordinating impact of past institutional elements.

The environmental and coordination effects imply that, all else being equal, new institutions are likely to complement those that already exist. One institution *complements* another if it extends the set of parameters in which the other is self-enforcing or if the benefits to those who can coordinate on that institution are larger when the other institution exists.[9]

The Maghribis' coalition was complemented by the institutions that provided secure property rights created by the Fatimid Caliphate, which was interested in increasing revenues within the empire. The implied increase in the expected value of trade increased the net present value of being honest to a Maghribi trader (Chapter 3). Clans restricted the set of

---

[9] Aoki (1994, 2001) and Okazaki and Okuno-Fujiwara (1998) present a related concept of institutional complementarities. Building on Milgrom, Qian, and Roberts (1991), this concept conditions complementarities on supermodularity. Roughly speaking, payoffs from a particular equilibrium behavior in one game increase because a particular equilibrium behavior is followed in another game. For various empirical analyses, see Greif (1994a, 1996a, 1998a); Baliga and Polak (2004); Moriguchi (1998); Yang (2002); and Pagano and Rossi (2002).

parameters in which democracy could have been self-enforcing in Genoa. (Chapters 6 and 8). The community responsibility system extended the set of parameters for which the *podesteria* was self-enforcing (see Chapter 10). Under that institution, a member of a community present in another's territory was held liable for contractual default by any member of his commune against a member of the local commune. Every Genoese traveling abroad could have been held liable for the failure by the Genoese commune to pay the *podestà* at the end of his term. This increased Genoa's ability to commit to pay a *podestà*.

All else being equal, a new institution is more likely to include institutional elements that were crystallized in the past than those that were not. This *inclusion effect* reflects the fundamental asymmetry and people's response to it. In Genoa the inclusion effect manifested itself by including the same norms, beliefs, and organizations in the institutional foundations of the state under the consulate and the *podesteria*. As discussed in Chapter 8, the *podesteria* incorporated the existing clan structure, norms justifying the use of force to achieve political aims, and the belief that one clan would challenge another if the appropriate opportunity emerged. These institutional elements were part of the initial conditions in the process leading to the new institutions – as part of the rules of the game and beliefs in it – and the resulting institution incorporated them.

Like the coordination effect, the inclusion effect influences selection among alternative self-enforcing institutions. Although conceptually distinct, at times the two effects overlap. Past behavioral beliefs, for example, can coordinate on new behavior and become an integral part of the resulting new institution. The relationships between the consulate system and the *podesteria* in Genoa, discussed in Chapters 6 and 8, reflect this overlap. An integral part of Genoa's political foundations under the consulate were the cultural beliefs that each clan would attack the other if the opportunity arose. These beliefs coordinated on expected behavior under the new institution, which included the *podestà* and became an element in the resulting institution.[10] The distinction between the coordinating and inclusion effects is nevertheless conceptually beneficial, as some institutional elements can coordinate on new institutions without becoming part

---

[10] Chapter 9 presents an elaborated example of this overlap. It discusses how cultural factors inherited from the past led to cultural beliefs associated with a particular self-enforcing behavior in a new situation.

of them. The Genoese consulate was an organization that coordinated on the *podesteria* system but did not become a part of it.

7.3 AGENCY AND HISTORY

The refinement, environment, coordination, and inclusion effects reflect the impact of the fundamental asymmetry on actions leading to new institutions. These effects reflect agents' responses to the cognitive, informational, coordinative, and normative challenge of choosing behavior, through reasoning or by default. The influence of past institutional elements on the trajectory of institutional change is therefore intermediated through agents' responses to the opportunities and constraints these elements entail in pursuing their interests.

Indeed, the influence of past institutional elements implies that agents can have a larger impact on institutional selection than otherwise would have been the case. Institutional elements inherited from the past provide them with common cognition, shared beliefs, similar norms, and the organizations required to influence institutional selection.[11] Furthermore, the role of institutional entrepreneurs in influencing institutional selection is facilitated, because new institutions do not require a wholesale systemic change. They can be created by changing, introducing, or manipulating past institutional elements.

Consider first the case in which the past seemingly exerts the least influence on new institutions, namely, the case in which there is an institutionalized way to reach a new institution. By an institutionalized way to reach a new institution, I mean that there is a system of institutionalized rules, beliefs, norms, and organizations regarding how to reach a new institutional equilibrium. In particular, there is a social entity – a leader or an organization for collective decision making – that sets the rules to guide behavior in the new situation. For this guidance to be effective in leading to new institutionalized behavior, for that entity to have power

---

[11] Even meanings, symbols, terms, and gestures associated with past institutions, such as "signing a contract" or "the crown," influence institutional selection. They constitute commonly known external representations of encapsulated knowledge (Zhang 1997) on which individuals condition their behavior. Sociologists have long emphasized the importance of a shared cultural understanding (script, cognition, or interpretive frames) in constraining the behavior that leads to new institutions by determining what actors can conceive (see Zucker 1983, 1991; Meyer and Rowen 1991; DiMaggio and Powell 1991a; Dobbin 1994; and Scott 1995).

three conditions must hold. First, the announcer has to have the legitimacy to convince a sufficiently large number of people to believe that others will follow the announcement or the ability to render the announced behavior a best response of those who are supposed to follow it.[12] Second, the announcer has to have the organizational capabilities to disseminate the rules and render them common knowledge. Third, the rules must specify self-enforcing behavior.

Because of the fundamental asymmetry, the beliefs, norms, and organizations inherited from the past are those that confer legitimacy and imply power; determine the ability to disseminate rules; and, by constituting part of the rules of the game and coordination devices in them, influence whether a particular behavior is self-enforcing. They determine who has the ability to coordinate on new institutions, in what environment, and to what extent. The resulting institutions therefore reflect the coordination, environmental, and inclusion effects.

Consider, for example, the transition to the *podesteria*, which was coordinated by the consulate, although, as I discuss further in Chapter 8, it also reflected the intervention of the emperor. The consulate had the power to effect the transition because it was a legitimately elected body and, more important, its members were the representatives of Genoa's leading clans. It also had the formal organizational capacity, developed when it governed the city, to inform the Genoese of the transition. The new institution reflected the coordinating effect of institutional elements inherited from the past.

The *podesteria* also reflected the constraints the consuls faced in the form of institutional elements inherited from the past. These constraints influenced the set of self-enforcing institutions on which the consulate could coordinate. Specifically, the consuls were constrained in their choices by the existence of clans, their internalized norms, and their behavioral beliefs. The set of institutions on which the consulate could coordinate was restricted to those incorporating these institutional elements.

In modern societies, institutional elements inherited from the past similarly entail constraints and provide opportunities when new institutions are selected in an institutionalized way. The failure of the prohibition of alcohol in the United States between 1920 and 1933 reflected more

---

[12] On legitimacy, see section 5.4. Power reflects institutional hierarchy (see section 2.1) in which a particular institutionalized behavior can be dictated. There is a social entity with the ability to make this behavior the best response of those whose behavior the institution influences.

than the love of drink. It reflected beliefs that individuals had the right to consume alcohol and that the government had no legitimacy in regulating such consumption. The same prohibition is much more effective in some contemporary Muslim countries, in which different beliefs and norms prevail.

Past institutional elements provide opportunities as well as constraints in the process of institutional change that able coordinators take advantage of. Franklin D. Roosevelt's insistence that the U.S. Social Security system be defined as an insurance and not a welfare system involved more than semantics. Framing the issue in a way that linked the system to beliefs associated with the institution of insurance (the belief that one has the right to be paid after paying one's premiums) was intentional. Roosevelt knew that this would render Social Security self-enforcing in a larger set of circumstances in the future (see Romer 1996).

The demand for coordination in new situations can lead to the development of new coordinating organizations, but these new organizations often draw on past ones and the associated beliefs and capacities. The need for better coordination among actual and potential merchants in foreign lands made it beneficial to create the Hanseatic League. The actions of institutional entrepreneurs, the mercantile elite who governed German cities, led to the establishment of an assembly – a diet – of the cities' members in the Hanseatic League. The diet emerged through a process that built on institutional elements inherited from the past – specifically, the institutions of self-governance in the German cities. Drawing on organizations and associated beliefs inherited from the past, agents engaged in actions that led to a new coordinating organization. It therefore reflected the coordination and inclusion effects. The diet was made up of representatives of the cities; the beliefs and organizational capacity rendering these cities' self-governance effective also served the league.

Institutional entrepreneurs who attempt to coordinate on new institutions also operate outside the institutionalized process for selecting new institutions. Indeed, some of the most dramatic and important institutional changes throughout history have been brought about by leaders, prophets, and visionaries who were successful in creating new institutions without relying on institutionalized means to do so. Indeed, the changes they brought about were revolutionary exactly because they brought them about without relying on the existing institutionalized means for creating new institutions. Their choice of actions was nevertheless influenced by the constraints imposed and the opportunities afforded by past institutional elements. These institutional entrepreneurs relied on institutional elements inherited from the past to mobilize resources, predict responses to their actions, frame the new situation, and influence what individuals considered to be their interest or the morally appropriate response.

As an institutional entrepreneur, Muhammad established a new religion and polity without relying on an existing institutionalized way of creating new institutions. He was nevertheless constrained by and took advantage of existing institutional elements and their implications. Consider the case of Mecca, which before the rise of Islam had already been a center of commercially profitable religious pilgrimage focusing on the Kaaba.[13] Beliefs about the religious importance of such a pilgrimage and the Kaaba were later integrated into the Muslim system of beliefs, and it is toward the Kaaba that Muslims face in their prayers. Not contradicting the behavioral manifestations of previous beliefs may have facilitated the propagation of the new system of beliefs. It also alleviated the fear by Mecca's commercial elite that the new religion threatened its prosperity (B. Lewis 1991). The ability of institutional entrepreneurs to coordinate on a particular outcome relies on manipulating past institutional elements even if they do not rely on institutionalized ways to reach a new institution. Hence, even new institutions that emerge in such "revolutionary" ways, often include past institutional elements.[14]

In the absence of a coordinated response, the process of selecting among possible institutions is a spontaneous, individualistic one that reflects the combined impact of the actions of many individuals. In this case as well, institutional elements inherited from the past provide opportunities and constraints, which manifest themselves in the inclusion and coordination effects.

Annex 7.1 provides an example in which economic agents, in an uncoordinated manner, acquired membership in existing organizations,

---

[13] The Kaaba (*cube* in Arabic) is the central, cubic stone structure, covered by a black cloth, within the Great Mosque in Mecca, Saudi Arabia. The sacred nature of the site predates Islam, and pre-Islamic Meccans used it as a central shrine to house their many idols. Also known as the House of God, it is the center of the circumambulations performed during the *hajj* (the pilgrimage to Mecca). The circumambulations also have a pre-Islamic origin.

[14] In advocating passive resistance in India's fight for independence, Mohandas Gandhi took advantage of the predictability of responses that past institutions entailed. His strategy built on institutional elements inherited from the past, namely, the internalized norms of the British regarding the appropriate coercive response to civil resistance. Bates et al. (1998) argue that one cannot understand responses to violent political actions without understanding the historically determined meaning of the object under attack.

thereby enabling new behavioral beliefs to be self-enforcing and leading to a new contract enforcement institution. It examines the case of U.S. traders in Mexican California, who intentionally integrated into local communities, enabling them to trigger social sanctions against community members who cheated them.[15] These traders retained their affiliation with a reputation-based economic institution that enabled exchange among long-distance traders from the United State who operated in Mexico and beyond. The local U.S. traders became intermediaries in credit relationships between community members and the long-distance U.S. traders. They rendered effective a new, two-tier contract enforcement institution that supported exchange among the local population and the long-distance traders from the United States. A U.S. long-distance trader could lend to a member of the local community holding that, in case of need, the local U.S. trader would be able to recover the debt. The local U.S. trader was able to commit to provide this agency service to the long-distance trader, because cheating entailed losing his reputation among the long-distance traders.

In uncoordinated processes leading to new institutions, past institutionalized norms and beliefs provide individuals with a means of forming expectations about others' behavior and hence deciding on their own behavior. When a new situation is similar (by whatever criteria) to an old situation, individuals expect that others will behave in the new situation as they did in the old one. Self-enforcing beliefs formed in one context constitute a *focal point* (Schelling 1960) that coordinates behavior in a new one.

7.4 KNOWLEDGE, INSTITUTIONAL INNOVATIONS, AND THE DIRECTION OF INSTITUTIONAL CHANGE

Different institutions generate different observable outcomes and hence different knowledge, implying that institutional learning is local in the sense of being specific to that institution. The implied local knowledge influences the direction of institutional change by shaping perceptions about possibilities and interest.[16] The failure of the Genoese consular system in a civil war in 1164 revealed its fragility in the absence of an external threat. Despite an enhanced external threat, in 1194 the

---

[15] This discussion builds on Langum (1987) and Clay (1997).

[16] The literature has emphasized the importance of knowledge that institutions imply about the activity (e.g., piracy or farming) it generates (see North 1990).

clan that had lost the civil war refused to cooperate under the consular system.

Different institutions also provide different incentives for developing and adopting various contractual forms, ways to organize information, and organizations. These distinct innovations influence the subsequently possible set of self-enforcing institutions and other outcomes. The reputation-based institution that governed agency relationships among the Maghribis implied that per venture accounting was sufficient, as it enabled a merchant to compare his agent's report on a venture with information obtained from other sources. In contrast, in Venice the state gathered the information required to monitor agents (Gonzalez de Lara 2002). As merchants did not have to organize their information on a perventure basis, they were better motivated to devise an accounting system that better reflected their overall financial situation. The result was the invention of double-entry bookkeeping (or the Venetian system, as it was known at the time).

The separation between ownership and control in medieval merchant and craft guilds led to the invention of auditing and the creation of the profession of external auditors (Watts and Zimmermann 1983). Double-entry bookkeeping and auditing played important roles in the eventual rise of the modern business corporation, in which ownership is separated from control, because these procedures enable owners and investors better evaluate the performance of managers and firms.

The impact of institutional elements on institutional innovations and on the adoption of such innovations is more subtle. Institutional elements affect organizational, contractual, and procedural innovations by shaping expectations regarding the implications of pursuing them. Past institutional elements influence what one expects will happen in new situations brought about by adopting such innovations. A necessary condition for organizational change is that those who are able to initiate it expect to gain from it. Their expectations depend on existing institutional elements – particularly culturally determined behavioral beliefs – that enable them to form these expectations. Different institutional elements thus lead to different trajectories of organizational development.

The distinctiveness of each trajectory is reinforced by the process of modifying and refining "microinventions," which follow an "organizational macroinvention."[17] Diverse paths of organizational development, in turn, further affect the historical process of equilibrium selection.

---

[17] Mokyr (1990) introduced these terms with respect to technological change.

Once a specific organization is introduced, it influences the rules of historically subsequent games and hence the resulting institutions.

In Chapter 9, I present an extensive analysis of this influence, arguing that the collective punishments practiced by the Maghribis entailed disincentives to invent and adopt institutions to support impersonal exchange. This was not the case among Genoese merchants, among whom a bilateral reputation mechanism supported by the legal system governed agency relationships.

7.5 INSTITUTIONAL COMPLEXES: THE CONTEMPORANEOUS IMPLICATIONS OF INSTITUTIONAL DYNAMICS

The intertemporal relationships among institutions that the fundamental asymmetry implies affect the contemporaneous (contemporary) relationships among institutions. The environmental, coordination, and inclusion effects imply that institutions will cluster in *institutional complexes*. Within a complex, institutions complement one another, reflect the influences of the same coordinating factors, or share the same institutional elements. These synchronic relationships among institutions further influence selection among alternative institutions in new situations, as well as the timing of institutional change.

Institutional complexes differ from each other along various dimensions such as the following: which institutions are grouped within the same complex, the degree of institutional complementarities within it, the extent to which a particular element is shared by many institutions, whether coordination is based on explicit decision-making organizations, what combination of reward and punishment provides motivation, and what the objectives are of those who administer it. The details of a society's institutional complexes affect the transaction costs of institutional transitions.

To see the relationships among a complex's details and the cost of institutional change, consider one of the most profound institutional changes that occurred during the late medieval period: the de facto elimination of slavery within Europe. The practice was, of course, later reintroduced in the European colonies, only to be abolished de jure and de facto around the mid-nineteenth century. The elimination of slavery in Europe was "one of the great landmarks in labor history" (Duby 1974, p. 40). It may have been a major factor contributing to the changing long-run trend of European economic growth: while growth was slow during the millennium of Roman control and negative during the five hundred years that followed Rome's collapse, it rose during the following millennium, which began with the decline of slavery. The change may suggest that slavery provides worse incentives than freer labor and enterprise to produce and innovate productivity-enhancing technology. Indeed, the origin of "labor-saving power technology, which has been one of the distinctive character-istics of the Occident in modern times," began in the late medieval period (White 1964, p. 79; see also Mokyr 1990).

This profound change – the early endogenous elimination of slavery – did not occur in Muslim countries, many of which retained legal slavery until after World War II. Some Muslim countries abolished slavery as late as 1962, and the institution still exists de facto in various contemporary Muslim countries (B. Lewis 1990; R. Segal 2001).

Why was the Christian world ahead of the Muslim in abolishing slavery? The explanation has to do with the two civilizations' distinct institutional complexes. The historical root of this distinction dates back to the rise of Christianity within the Roman Empire. Because the Roman Empire had a unified code of law and a rather effective legal system, Christianity did not have to provide a code of law governing everyday life in creating communities of believers. Christianity developed as a religion of orthodoxy and proper beliefs; in earthly matters, Christians followed Roman law and later other secular laws. During the late medieval period, this legacy enabled the new European states to reassert control gradually over civil legal matters, including slavery.

Islam rose through a very different process, in which Muhammad established both a religion and a political, economic, and social unit. Islam therefore had to provide, and emphasize the obligation of adher-ents to follow, the Islamic code of law, the Shari'a. Like Judaism, therefore, Islam is a religion that regulates its adherents' behavior in their everyday, economic, political, and social life.

The holy scriptures of both Christianity and Islam discuss behavior toward slaves, thereby giving it moral legitimacy (see, e.g., Leviticus 25:46, Ephesians 6; Qur'an 16:71, 4:36, 30:28). But in each civilization the institutions governing slavery were part of distinct institutional com-plexes. In the Christian world, laws governing slavery fell within the insti-tutional complex, at the center of which were legal and political organiza-tions. Given the European tradition of man-made law, abolishing slavery did not alter the organization, beliefs, or norms central to Christianity.

This was not true in the Islamic world, where slavery was part of an institutional complex at the center of which were beliefs in the holiness of religious law. The legal tradition in Islam considers law as "the moral status of an act in the eyes of God" while "assessing the moral status of human acts was the work of the [religious] jurists" (Crone 2004, p. 9). The Shari'a recognized slavery; abolishing it thus implied an action that contradicted a central internalized belief of Muslims – that the Shari'a is a sacred law sanctioned by God. Abolishing slavery challenged the faith's moral authority, the legal authority of the Shari'a, and the stature and power of those responsible for administrating it.[18] A difficulty in abolishing slavery was that "from a Muslim point of view, to forbid what God permits is almost as great an offense as to permit what God forbids – and slavery was authorized and regulated by the holy law" (B. Lewis 1990, p. 78). The institutional elements relevant to slavery were central to Muslim religious beliefs.

Institutions within a complex reinforce one another, rendering institutional change more difficult than otherwise would be the case. Institution A reinforces institution B if A implies changes in quasi-parameters that make B self-enforcing in a larger set of parameters. Because an institution that is undermined by another will either vanish or require further reinforcement, institutions within an institutional complex will eventually be the ones that are mutually (weakly) self-reinforcing. It is therefore more difficult to replace one institution in the complex, if such replacement requires undermining an institutional element common to other institutions in that complex, because these institutions will reinforce this element.[19]

Institutional complementarities also increase the cost of institutional transition. These complementarities imply that one institution extends the set of parameters in which the other is self-enforcing or that the benefits to those whose actions lead to that institution are larger when the other institution exists. In the case of the merchant guild, the institution that generated behavior in the ruler-merchant transaction was complemented by the institutions that governed the relationships among the merchants themselves. Such complementarities imply that changing one institution renders the other self-enforcing in a smaller set of situations

---

[18] I do not argue here that the laws specified in the Shari'a were static and immutable. This definitely was not the case. The argument made here is that different constraints and opportunities for legal changes exist in societies with and without religious laws. More broadly, legal dynamics are distinct amoung systems in which laws have different normative contents and different decision makers influencing legal development.

[19] For the appropriate analytical framework, see Milgrom and Roberts (1990); Milgrom et al. (1991); Milgrom and Shannon (1994); and Topiks (1998).

or provides fewer benefits to those whose actions led to this institution to begin with. Intentionally changing an institution will therefore be more challenging.

The details of a society's institutional complex also influence the nature of institutional change – that is, the nature of the processes leading to new institutions. Institutional change can be gradual or sudden, local (encompassing a few institutions) or comprehensive (encompassing many); it can reflect intentional and explicit decision making or spontaneous evolution.

To exemplify the relationships between the details of an institutional complex and the nature of institutional change, consider the case in which an institutional complex is characterized by mutual reinforcement and institutional complementarities. Mutual reinforcement implies that institutional change is not likely to occur often, but complementarities imply that once one institution is no longer self-enforcing, many other complementary institutions are likely to cease being self-enforcing as well. Institutional change is thus less likely to occur, but when it does, it is likely to be comprehensive and include many institutions.

The same holds when many institutions in a society share the same institutional element. A change in this fundamental element implies a comprehensive institutional change that will affect many institutions. Once it is no longer self-enforcing, the resulting institutional change will be "revolutionary": it will rarely happen, but when it does, it is likely to be comprehensive, influencing many institutions and reflecting actions by a large number of people. If an institutional complex is characterized by relatively weak interrelatedness among various institutions, institutional change is likely to be gradual and affect only a few institutions at a time.

Because once particular institutions prevail they influence subsequent institutions, the sequence in which institutions established themselves is significant. Particularly important in directing subsequent institutional developments are periods or events when an institution or an institutional element establishes itself and gives rise later to an institutional complex.[20] The adoption of the Roman legal tradition in Europe and of the Shari'a

---

[20] This idea is closely related to that of *critical moment* in Historical Institutionalism (see Collier and Collier 1991; Pierson and Skocpol 2002). Collier and Collier define *critical moments* as "major watersheds in political life . . . [which] establish certain directions of change and foreclosure of others in a way that shapes politics for years to come" (1991, p. 27). But as Thelen (1999, p. 397) notes, developing this argument requires delimiting the events constituting a critical moment and the details of subsequent institutional development. The perspective here advances toward this goal.

in the Muslim world were both such times.[21] These distinct legal tradi-tions influenced the subsequent development of commercial and political institutions (see, e.g., Kuran 2004 and Chapter 10).

7.6 CONCLUDING COMMENTS

What are the implications of the arguments made here regarding the way we should study the dynamic of endogenous institutions? What more should we learn to further our understanding of the impact of past insti-tutions on new ones? After summarizing the main assertions made in this chapter, this conclusion turns to address these two questions.

7.6.1 *Institutional Trajectories and the Influence of the Past*

The past, encapsulated in institutional elements, leads societies to evolve along distinct institutional trajectories. The details of new institutions and the capacity of institutions to change are functions of history, because there is a fundamental asymmetry between institutional elements inher-ited from the past and technologically feasible alternatives. Institutional elements inherited from the past provide and reflect what is understood, what is expected, and what is conceived to be morally appropriate. As such, these elements, although components of institutions, reside in indi-viduals and groups. They are embodied in preferences and memory and provide shared cognition and beliefs. Even elements that were part of an institution that is no longer self-enforcing – norms, beliefs, and organi-zations – still prevail, at least for a while, as a cultural and social her-itage. Institutional elements inherited from the past are part of what indi-viduals bring with them to new situations; creating alternative, techno-logically feasible institutional elements requires action and a process of learning, experimentation, and socialization. Past institutional elements thus constitute part of the initial conditions in processes leading to new institutions.

Whether or not the process leading to new institutions is coordinated, it reflects the historical heritage encapsulated in institutional elements. New institutions reflect institutional refinement – the marginal alternation of

---

[21] By the Roman legal tradition I mean that of explicit, man-made, secular laws (Stein 1999; Kelly 1992). Although the Islamic legal tradition drew greatly on the Roman and other codes of law, it obscured these origins and emphasized those that were divine. For discussion, see Crone (2002, chap. 1), Rahman (2002, chap. 6).

existing institutions – and the environmental, coordination, and inclusion effects of past institutional elements. The institutions that are more likely to establish themselves are those that the institutional elements inherited from the past render self-enforcing for a larger set of parameters, reflect the coordinating influence of these elements, and incorporate them. Using the jargon of game theory, institutional elements inherited from the past constitute part of the relevant rules of the game in a new situation, coordinating devices given these rules, and factors influencing the cost of taking actions leading to new institutional elements. Institutional elements inherited from the past influence subsequent games and equilibria in them.

Does the final outcome – the resulting institutions – depend on which institutional elements are inherited from the past? Game theory suggests that it does. In strategic situations, the set of possible self-enforcing outcomes – equilibria – depends on the details of the relevant rules of the game. A particular outcome can be self-enforcing if some rules of the game and not others are relevant. Even small differences in rules can have a significant impact on the equilibrium set. Furthermore, for given rules of the game, multiple equilibria – and hence institutions – are usually possible. The details of the institutional elements influencing selection among different outcomes therefore matter.

The past also affects the details of new institutions because the environmental, coordination, and inclusion effects lead institutions to form institutional complexes. Institutions within a complex are interrelated, complementing and reinforcing one another and sharing institutional elements. Moreover, past institutional elements influence the process of institutional, organizational, and contractual innovations, as they influence expectations about behavior and outcomes following the introduction of these innovations.

It is therefore difficult to alter institutional dynamics to induce better outcomes. New rules can be declared and organizational forms can be established, but their impact on behavior still depends on institutional elements inherited from the past. Declaring new rules and establishing new organizational forms do not necessarily lead to new institutions and, in particular, do not necessarily lead to the institutions whose effectiveness inspired the change. Adopting new institutions requires more than adopting new rules and organizations. It requires a transition from one set of self-enforcing institutions to another, despite the fundamental asymmetry. Doing so is difficult, however, particularly because it requires changing norms and beliefs inherited from the past. Altering what people believe is right and what people believe others believe is not an easy task.

Because of the fundamental asymmetry, it is particularly difficult to change institutions without taking into account the constraints and opportunities provided by past institutional elements, or recognizing the details and implications of institutional interrelatedness. Institutional entrepreneurs do just that when influencing institutional selection. In pursuing institutional change, entrepreneurs are aided by the fact that institutions are not a unitary entity. Creating new institutions does not require a wholesale systemic change: they can be created by refining existing institutions or building on and recombining institutional elements inherited from the past. Agents can therefore have a big impact on institutional selection. Institutional dynamics is not predetermined by past institutions.

7.6.2 Endogenous Restrictions on the Direction of Change: Contextual Refinement

Game theory, as already noted, highlights the fact that in situations pertaining to institutional analysis – strategic repeated situations with a large action space – multiple equilibria, and hence institutions, usually exist (see Appendix A). We cannot satisfactorily limit the set of admissible institutions deductively in a given situation by requiring that an institution be self-enforcing. We can do better than imposing only theoretical restrictions on the set of admissible institutions, however, by considering the influence of history on subsequent institutional development.

History influences the direction of institutional change by providing relevant initial rules of the game and coordinating mechanisms within the resulting structure. The impact of institutional elements inherited from the past both reflects and is restricted by agents' responses to them. Indeed, when institutional elements inherited from the past are not integrated into a new institution – when they are not self-enforcing and (weakly) self-reinforcing in the new situation – they will gradually decay and vanish.[22]

---

[22] This is true unless they are propagated by mechanisms, such as socialization, that are distinct from the one captured here. More generally, institutional elements will propagate if members of the society are motivated to propagate them through interactions in the relevant transactions. In particular, propagation of cultural features through direct socialization reflects the internalized norms and beliefs of the socializing agents; propagation through indirect socialization (through schools, activities of political parties, and other means) reflects the interests of those who control them. Recall (from Chapter 5) that self-enforcement also includes the requirement that the institution be self-reproducing in the sense that the related beliefs and norms are not refuted or weakened by the institution's observable implications.

We can therefore study the selection of new institutions by using contextual refinement – by refining (restricting) the set of admissible institutions based on knowledge of the historical heritage (encapsulated in institutional elements), recognizing that it influences the relevant rules of the game and provides coordination within them by requiring that the resulting institutions be self-enforcing. We can use knowledge of the past to eliminate theoretically possible but contextually irrelevant institutions, and we can use the analytical power of game theory to restrict the impact of the past by requiring that only institutional elements that are self-enforcing ex post can be part of the new institution.

Contextual refinement constitutes a departure from game theory that is larger than just restricting the set of admissible institutions based on historical knowledge. In game theory, the rules of the game are taken as given, and beliefs and behavior are determined endogenously. The argument advanced here recognizes the possible importance of the reverse line of causality. Beliefs and norms inherited from the past are part of the initial conditions in the process leading to a new institution. Relevant games – and hence institutions – are constructed around the beliefs and norms inherited from the past by establishing supporting rules and organizations.

7.6.3 *Taking Stock and Looking Ahead*

The discussion in this chapter is preliminary; its further development requires addressing the many questions it raises. What institutional factors determine the extent of the fundamental asymmetry? What are the characteristics of institutions with low institutional transition costs, which also imply transitions to new welfare-enhancing institutions? These questions are paramount, because no institution is efficient under all circumstances; the ability to change flexibly to accommodate new needs is at least as important to long-term success as static efficiency.

The argument that past institutionalized beliefs and organizations shape the direction of institutional change also merits further analytical development. Individuals employ past beliefs in subsequent strategically similar situations. But what determines similarity?[23] What determines the

---

[23] Sugden (1989) notes that individuals choose behavior in a new situation by analogy, but the question raised here is how to identify what makes two situations analogous. A similar problem arises in the context of case-based optimization (Gilboa and Schmeidler 2001).

mapping of beliefs from one situation to another? Are framing effects, analogy, or structural similarities important?

These questions notwithstanding, Chapters 8 and 9 present empirical analyses that support the assertions made here regarding why and how history leads societies to evolve along distinct institutional trajectories and the empirical benefit of using contextual refinement. They establish the importance of organizations and cultural beliefs inherited from the past in influencing selection among alternative institutions, becoming an integral part of the resulting ones, and influencing the subsequent trajectory of institutional evolution.

ANNEX 7.1: INTENTIONAL USE OF PAST INSTITUTIONAL ELEMENTS IN THE DEVELOPMENT OF UNCOORDINATED INSTITUTIONS: THE CASE OF U.S. MERCHANTS IN MEXICAN CALIFORNIA

This annex illustrates the intentional use of past institutional elements in the development of uncoordinated institutions. It also provides an example for linking institutions based on social exchange and economic reputation. Social relationships within communities were central to contract enforcement in Mexican California during the nineteenth century.[24] They were intentionally used to form a new economic institution that supported trade between these communities and traders from the United States. Social and economic transactions were linked to change the set of self-enforcing beliefs in yet another economic transaction.

Mexican California was a remote part of a vast country in which, in the early nineteenth century, communication and transportation were slow. Communities were small – by 1840 the largest settlement in what is today California was Santa Barbara, with eighteen hundred residents – and the hand of the state was invisible in contract enforcement. The local judicial officer, the *alcalde*, drafted contracts and maintained an archive of them, but the state did not enforce commercial contracts (although it did attempt to enforce the law in criminal matters). In Monterey, the capital, 65 percent of the 374 civil suits filed between 1831 and 1846 were for debt collection or recovery of damages. None of these cases ended in the seizure of the debtor's assets to satisfy the judgment. As one observer from the United States remarked at the time, these courts were "inefficient, at times unpredictable, and they lacked

---

[24] This discussion builds on Langum (1987) and, in particular, on Clay (1997).

any semblance of effective enforcement techniques" (Langum 1987, pp. 115, 123).

That observers from the United States perceived the courts as ineffective does not imply that social order did not prevail or that the courts played no role in creating it. As Langum (1987; see also Clay 1997, pp. 504–7) notes, contract enforcement and social order in these small Mexican communities was based on social control: the expected social responses of others motivated members of these communities to adhere to customary behavioral conduct. The *alcalde* was a locally elected, unpaid, community official who did not rely on a written code of law. Indeed, he did not need to be literate.

The legal process reflected the role of social control. Before filing a suit, the plaintiff and the defendant participated in a mandatary reconciliation hearing, in which two local "good men," selected by each party to the dispute and the *alcalde*, listened to both sides and proposed ways to resolve the dispute. About 85 percent of cases were resolved in this way (Langum 1987, chap. 4). The court was used to inform the community of who was at fault. It did not impose punishment if reconciliation was achieved. The expectations of the social consequences of failing to reconcile once a decision had been made induced reconciliation.

The small size of these communities, the high cost of emigrating from them, the large number of interactions among community members, and presumably the transmission of information through gossip provided the conditions for motivating behavior based on social relationships. The immobility of residents implied that they had to take the community and their membership in it as exogenous. At the same time, the community was an organization that altered the rules of the game relevant to each of the interacting individuals while remaining endogenous to the actions of all of them. The court was an organization that provided a public signal regarding who was at fault in cases of dispute.

During this time, the economic benefits of linking these local communities to the larger economic system around them were increasing. California was rich in hides, tallow, furs, horses, and lumber, which the United States, Mexico, Hawaii, and China sought. As the supply of these goods declined, as a result of political unrest in Latin America, demand for them rose.

Traders from the United States became increasingly involved in international shipping of goods in and out of California. They bought goods ahead of time, providing credit to local producers, in order to ensure that when they reached California they would have goods to export. But establishing credit relationships with the local population presented a contractual problem. The legal system did not enforce civil suits, and the social control institution that was effective within a local community was not extended to the traders from the United States. The local community had no incentive to punish those who cheated outsiders; an outsider's threat of punishing the community as a whole for failing to punish one of its members was not credible, given the small number of settlements and the high sunk cost of coming to trade. Morever, the community of the U.S. traders lacked an effective means of coordinating and ensuring the collective punishment of a community.

A new institution was required to facilitate long-distance trade. The solution that emerged involved a strategic manipulation of the social control system. Traders from the United States integrated into the local community in settlements that were important to their trade. They married into local families, converted to Catholicism, became Mexican citizens, spoke Spanish, and raised their children as the locals did. By becoming members of the community, these traders gained access to the local contract enforcement institution. Trade between traders from the United States and the local community was channeled through these "Mexicanized" traders, who received credit from other merchants from the United States. When a trader from the United States had a collection problem in a community in California, he called on a "Mexicanized" expatriate for help.

How could these Mexicanized traders commit to be honest in their dealings with other U.S. traders? Among the U.S. traders (Mexicanized or not), honesty was maintained through a multilateral reputation mechanism based on economic sanctions. An agent who cheated a trader was punished by all the others. Such punishment was costly to the Mexicanized trader, because of the sunk costs he had invested in settling in Mexico. At the same time, his local connections implied that punishing him was relatively costly to the other traders. The optimal punishment was a gradual one, in which some trade partially ceased after the first instance of cheating and ended completely after the second instance (Clay 1997).

The U.S. traders used their extensive network of commercial correspondence to disseminate information about the conduct of various individuals. Their relatively small number ensured the personal familiarity required for the threat of collective punishment to be possible.

Among the Mexicans the *alcalde* and other communal leaders provided the public signal required to coordinate punishments. Their decisions were based on customs that had evolved over time. Merchants from the United States lacked such a coordination device, and they lacked a long tradition of customary behavior. Instead, they relied on common law to specify appropriate behavior. An institutional element that was part of a formal institution was also part of the historical heritage these merchants brought with them and integrated into a new, private-order institution.

8

Building a State

Genoa's Rise and Fall

Many contemporary countries face the challenge of building states that effectively promote political stability, curtail political violence, and foster economic prosperity. Late medieval Europe witnessed a wave of attempts to create such states, particularly in the form of the city-states of northern Italy (see, e.g., Waley 1988). No microanalytical examination of this process of state building has been conducted, and its lessons have not been uncovered.

This chapter examines the state-building process in the city-state of Genoa, which emerged from obscurity to become one of the wealthiest cities in Europe but whose history was characterized by frequent intracity political violence and later also by relative economic decline. This chapter provides a microanalytical examination of the historical process of state building in Genoa, explicitly studying the polity as an equilibrium outcome in which actors can choose between predatory and economic behavior.

Two perspectives dominate the study of the relationships between political institutions and economic prosperity, neither of which adequately accounts for Genoa's experience. The first perspective assumes the existence of a predator-ruler, a ruler with a monopoly over coercive power. According to this view, promoting prosperity entails building institutions that enable the ruler to credibly commit to respecting property rights.[1] This perspective cannot be applied to the city-state of Genoa, which had no de facto ruler with or without a monopoly over coercive power at the time it was established.

---

[1] See, for example, North (1981); Levi (1988); North and Weingast (1989); Root (1989); Olson (1993); Greif et al. (1994); Barzel (2002); and Greif (2004b).

The second, neo-Hobbesian, perspective on state building assumes that the state reflects attempts by economic agents to advance their interests, as "the state produces order" and provides other public goods that benefit them (Hardin 1997, p. 23). Achieving these benefits requires institutions that mitigate the agency problems inherent in relationships between the economic players on the one hand and politicians and bureaucrats on the other (see Buchanan 1999; Barzel 2002).

Economic historians have implicitly invoked the latter perspective to explain the rise of the Italian city-states that were established as republics. The prevailing view, articulated by Robert Lopez, the great historian of the commercial expansion of the late medieval period, is that these city-republics were "governments of the merchants, by the merchants, for the merchants" (1976, p. 71). Yet the political violence that was endemic in late medieval Italian cities often occurred among those who were otherwise engaged in economic activity (Martines 1972; Tabacco 1989). This suggests the limitations of this view. Why the residents of these city-states traded rather than fought, is something to be explained rather than taken as given. We need to study the process of building an effective state as one of institutional development that causes individuals who can engage in either economic or predatory behavior to become merely economic agents.

Genoa's experiment in state building suggests the importance of recognizing that those processes entail a transition from one set of self-enforcing institutions to another. State building usually does not begin with a clean institutional slate. Rather, it arises from a situation in which existing institutions influence the behavior of potential and actual political actors, that is, actors who can muster coercive power. Often central to these institutions are political actors organized in such forms as clans, tribes, aristocracies, religious groups, castes, communities, and armed groups. These organizations – social structures – and the rules, beliefs, and norms that generate political and other behavior within and among them constitute institutions that influence political behavior. The institutions that generate behavior within and among social structures inherited from the past are part of the initial conditions in state-building processes.

To simplify the analysis, this chapter focuses on the institutional elements that influence the behavior of such social structures, treating each as a monolithic entity. It argues that in the initial stages of the state-building process, the state does not have independent resources and must rely on the support of social structures inherited from the past. The challenge then for building an effective state is to motivate these social structures to mobilize their economic and military resources to accomplish the tasks the state must undertake to foster political stability and economic prosperity.

The difficulty in providing such state-coordinated motivation is that joint mobilization of resources to tasks that were not undertaken before may well undermine the self-enforcing institutions that govern the relationships among these social structures. It can undermine them without providing a Pareto-improving institutional alternative, particularly because once cooperation increases the available economic resources, these resources can be used to muster military ability. Anticipating or fearing this outcome, the social structures are willing to mobilize their resources only for tasks that will not reduce their welfare, given the existing institutions. The resulting *coordinating state*, in which each social structure can decide whether to mobilize its resources for the state is weak. Its ability to act is limited, because a social structure will contribute only to tasks that do not alter the capacity of others to use their coercive power ex post to expropriate the resulting gains or gain additional powers and resources, thereby leaving the relevant social structure or its leaders worse off.

Without countervailing considerations or an institutionalized commitment to their welfare, the initial social structures will be only limitedly motivated to mobilize their resources jointly for tasks that have not been undertaken before. Hence building an effective state requires creating new institutions that empower it to impose an ex post allocation of gains.[2] Yet a powerful state can alter the distribution of resources and shift institutional and other powers away from the social structures inherited from the past. If these social structures are to help the state gain this power, they must believe that the state's power will not be used ex post to reduce their welfare. Even if the resulting state is effective and promotes order and prosperity, it does not necessarily mean that particular social structures will benefit. Thus it is necessary to create a limited state or government.

Social scientists have long recognized the problem in creating a *powerful yet limited* government, one that is given sufficient power to institute behavior but is prevented from abusing its power. The experience of Genoa indicates that creating even a limited government with power over the social structures inherited from the past is insufficient for creating a stable, effective state. Achieving this goal requires a strong yet limited

---

[2] Recall that those higher up an institutional hierarchy have power over others in the sense of being able to dictate the institution that generates behavior among them. See section 2.1.3.

state whose institutional foundations undermine the capacity of the social structures inherited from the past, or new ones that the state's functioning entails, to use coercive power against it or capture it for their benefit.

Genoa's success in mobilizing resources, promoting prosperity, and containing political violence depended on the extent to which its spontaneous and designed institutional foundations influenced responses to this challenge. Genoa's institutional foundations – that is, institutions that generated behavior among actual and potential political actors – reflected the constraints implied by institutional elements inherited from the past on the set of new self-enforcing institutions and the degree to which they motivated and enabled social structures inherited from the past to mobilize their resources and create a limited government.

The dynamics of the institutional foundations of Genoa were shaped by exogenous shocks, the degree to which these institutions were self-undermining, and local learning that led to their refinement. Initially, under the consular system, Genoa was a coordinating state with a limited ability to mobilize resources among its clans. Indeed, the institutional foundations of this state were self-undermining. Particular historical circumstance and learning induced and enabled the Genoese to create a more effective and powerful, yet limited, state. Economic prosperity and political stability were the result. Yet Genoa's institutions were still self-undermining, because the system of clans inherited from the past was reinforced and motivated to retain extrastate coercive power.

Economic historians hold that the economic growth of northern Italy's city-states during the late medieval commercial expansion had a lasting impact on the economic development of Europe. "[W]estern wealth began with the growth of European trade and commerce, which started in the twelfth century in Italy" (Rosenberg and Birdzell 1986, p. 35). Although the economic aspects of the growth of these cities have been examined by Robert Lopez and others, its political foundations, by and large, have been ignored (although see Greif 1994c, 1998c). The Genoese experience, examined in this chapter, however, indicates that we cannot understand this growth and, more generally, economic, political, and social outcomes in these cities without studying their institutional foundations.

Genoa's rich historical records, dating back to the republic's establishment, facilitate this analysis. Annals written by contemporaries offer a detailed account of the period, beginning with the First Crusade (1096–9). The *Codice Diplomatico della Repubblica di Genova* (CDG) contains numerous political and commercial documents from as early as 1056. Cartularies of scribes, which include private contracts, such as commercial agreements, real-estate transactions, wills, and marriage contracts, are also available from this period. Together, these primary sources provide unusual resources for analyzing Genoa's history. I used them extensively, along with the many excellent secondary sources.[3]

In addition to providing important historical details, section 8.1 describes the importance of two clans, the Manecianos and the Carmadinos, to Genoa's state-building process. Section 8.2 then provides a model of interclan relationships aimed at exploring possible institutions that could have governed these clans' relationships. Section 8.3 combines the model's insights with the historical evidence to analyze the consular system, which provided the institutional foundation of Genoa from 1099 to 1154. Section 8.4 discusses the endogenous dynamics and the exogenous factors that first reinforced and then undermined this system between 1154 and 1194, leading to prolonged periods of civil war. Sections 8.5 and 8.6 examine the subsequent institution of the *podesteria*, which restored interclan cooperation in the short run but undermined political order in the long run. In concluding, section 8.7 reflects on the European and Muslim worlds' experiments in state building in the Genoese mirror. To facilitate the presentation, technical details are relegated to annexes 8.1, 8.2, and 8.3.

8.1 CONTRACTING FOR A STATE

During the late medieval period, Genoa emerged from obscurity to become one of the largest and wealthiest cities in northern Italy.[4] Initially, Genoa's economy was based mainly on piracy (including organized large-scale raids). Later its economy was based on "privileged" long-distance trade, an important source of growth and prosperity in the premodern world. This trade was privileged in the sense that the Genoese merchants benefited from commercial privileges abroad, in the form of

---

[3] Regarding the value of Genoa's historical sources, see in particular Face (1980); Abulafia (1977, pp. 6–24); Epstein (1984, pp. 5–24); and the introduction to Giovanni Scriba (1154–1164). The excellent work by Genoa's historians, including Gabriella Airaldi, Eugene Byrne, Franco Cardini, John Day, Gerald W. Day, Steve Epstein, Richard D. Face, Diane Owen Hughes, Hilmar C. Krueger, and Teoflio Ossian de Negri, has contributed much to our knowledge of Genoa. This chapter builds on but at times disputes their analyses. See Greif (1994c, 1995, 1998c, 2004a) for these disputes and the many important details omitted from this chapter.

[4] Genoa's rise, like that of northern Italy in general, cannot be accounted for by technological and economic factors (Pryor 1988; Reynolds 1929, 1931; Krueger 1987; Greif 2004a).

ports, quarters, customs reductions, and legal rights that reduced the risk and costs associated with trade and provided the merchants with a competitive advantage over other merchants.

Rulers along the Mediterranean shores gave privileges to political units whose naval and military forces merited their support or neutrality.[5] Gaining support or neutrality in this manner became common in the eleventh century, following the decline of the Muslim and Byzantine military and naval forces that had dominated the Mediterranean. As a result, to gain privileges abroad and achieve commercial success, merchants depended on their state's ability and motivation to provide the necessary military power.

In eleventh-century Genoa, there was no state to organize forces to protect the city's merchants from piracy or to obtain privileges for them abroad. Although Genoa was part of the Holy Roman Empire, for various reasons, including the civil war in Germany, the empire was in no position to provide the Genoese with naval or military support.[6]

The residents of Genoa stood to benefit from organizing themselves politically and mobilizing their own military and naval forces. They had much to gain from appropriate governance of a (political) transaction: mobilizing economic and military resources in order to benefit from the provision of a public good in the form of public order and privileges. Indeed, shortly after 1096 the Genoese organized themselves politically and established a commune – a temporarily sworn voluntary association – headed by consuls who were elected in the *parlamentum* (the gathering of all Genoese with "full rights") for a limited period of time (*Annali* 1099, vol. I, p. 9).[7]

The historical records reveal the economic motivation beyond this social contract. A consul had to swear "not to diminish the honor of [the] city, nor [its] profit[s]" and to labor for "our city, with regard to movable and immovable goods" (*CDG*, vol. I, no. 20).[8] The Genoese

---

[5] See Heyd (1868, 1885); Lopez (1938); Luzzatto (1961, pp. 73ff.); Hicks (1969, pp. 49–50); G. Day (1988, pp. 5–6); Jacoby (1997); and Greif (2004a).

[6] See Tabacco (1989, chap. 4); Schumann (1992, chap. 4); and Airaldi (1983).

[7] See Hyde (1973, pp. 29–52); Donaver (1990 [1890]); Lopez (1937); Vitale (1951, p. 17; 1955, 1:3ff.); de Negri (1986, pp. 232–4); D. Hughes (1978); and G. Day (1988, pp. 72–3). Genoa's bishop (later an archbishop) lost his de facto political autonomy shortly after the commune was established (S. A. Epstein 1996, pp. 33–4).

[8] Regarding the Genoese consulate, see Vitale (1955); de Negri (1986); Pertile (1966); and S. A. Epstein (1996). Waley (1988, pp. 35ff.) presents a general discussion of the city-republics in northern Italy. The choice of a republican system governed by elected consuls may have reflected ideas and beliefs inherited from the Roman

annals provide detailed information on Genoa's economic gains from having sent a fleet and an army for the First Crusade (*Annali* 1101–2, vol. I, pp. 20–1). That economic considerations motivated establishing and joining the commune is reflected in the fact that the ultimate punishment for refusing to participate in its activities was exclusion from its overseas trade (*CDG*, vol. I, no. 285).

In evaluating the effectiveness of the commune in promoting Genoa's economy, one has to identify the institutional foundations that generated behavior among Genoa's political actors. Doing so, as I argued in Chapter 7, benefits from identifying the institutional elements inherited from the past that may have exerted environmental, coordination, and inclusion effects on these institutions. In the case of Genoa, clans and their beliefs and norms were the institutional elements around which new institutions emerged.

By the late eleventh century, clans became important economic, social, and political entities in northern Italy following a long period of decline in central authority (Herlihy 1969, pp. 174–8). Two viscountal clans, the Manecianos and the Carmadinos, were particularly important in Genoa. These clans, descended from a tenth-century feudal viscount of the area, had the economic and military resources needed to build a state in Genoa. In the early days of the commune, they had the resources required to launch large-scale piracy raids and obtain commercial privileges abroad.[9] The commune gained privileges on a substantial scale only when these clans cooperated and mobilized their resources toward that end.

The historical records suggest that members of these clans internalized the norms and shared the beliefs of the feudal era. During this time nobles aspired to become independent lords reigning over a particular locality;

---

period. "Italian city-dwellers, by the close of the eleventh century, had had enough of classical learning and legal training to conceive of themselves as the Roman people in minatory, to call their chosen officers consuls, and to claim rights of self-government as their lawful heritage" (Hearder and Waley 1963, p. 43).

[9] On the genealogy of these clans, see Olivieri (1861); Belgrano (1873, tables XIX–XXVI and XIX ff.); Byrne (1920, pp. 200–1); Cardini (1978); and G. Day (1988, p. 74). The Maneciano clan comprised the Spinula, Castro, Embriachi, Bruscus, and Vicecome families. The Carmadino clan comprised the Piper, Ususmaris, Lusis, and Carmadino families. Genoa's third viscountal clan, the delle Isole (Belgrano 1873, table XXXVIII) was not active politically. Other clans allied themselves with these clans and sometimes even assumed leadership. These clans were thus often at the center of political factions. For simplicity, I ignore these issues here but discuss them at length in Greif (2004a).

they considered military force a legitimate means of achieving this goal. Various Genoese nobles became independent lords outside Genoa, often through force provided by their clans (Greif 1998c, 2004a).

To what extent did these institutional elements curtail commercially beneficial cooperation in Genoa? If the clans mobilized their resources for the sake of profit, each of them would have been unwilling to do so unless it expected to gain. In the absence of third-party enforcement, and the commitment it enables, an allocation of gains agreed upon ex ante had to be self-enforcing ex post, although clans could use force to break agreements. Did the need for self-enforceability limit Genoa's commercial expansion?

8.2 A MODEL OF MUTUAL DETERRENCE

A model of mutual deterrence is useful for addressing these questions. (The detailed model appears in annex 8.1.) Assume that, consistent with the historical evidence, there are two clans with infinite life-spans and that at the beginning of a period each clan decides whether or not to cooperate in piracy. These decisions are made simultaneously. Piracy raids cannot be launched against a polity from which Genoa had already gained privileges. (Privileges were given to prevent such raids; the credibility of Genoa's commitment not to raid was achieved in a manner detailed later.) This implies that gains from cooperation in piracy declined with the number of privileges. To capture that long-distance trade was the key to economic prosperity, the model assumes that gross income increases as the number of privileges rose.

Whether or not the clans cooperated in piracy, they shared the income from cooperating in piracy and from Genoa's privileges possibly in an unequal manner. After obtaining this income, each clan decides *in turn* how much of it to divert to sunk investment in military strength (which would last until it is that clan's turn to invest again in the next period).[10] Past investment in military strength becomes obsolete only when the new investment is made (so the military strength of the second clan that invests in a particular period still prevails when the first clan to invest makes its decision). Military strength is public information and can be used to defend one's clan or to attack another clan in order to gain control of the

---

[10] The investment is assumed to last one period, because it supported a clan patronage network. For simplicity, I ignore military investment for piracy.

city. Immediately after investing in military strength, a clan can decide whether to attack the other.[11]

An attack is costly. If neither clan attacks, each obtains a payoff equal to its share of the income minus its expenditure on military strength, and this stage game is repeated.[12] If a clan attacks, each clan's probability of winning increases with its relative military strength. A winning clan becomes a "controlling" clan, which receives all future income from privileges, but both clans lose any gains from future joint piracy.

The commune was peaceful for many years following its establishment. There are thus historical reasons to consider initially subgame perfect equilibria in which interclan conflicts do not occur. There are also theoretical reasons to consider such equilibria, as we are interested in evaluating whether Genoa's clan structure hindered building a state that was effective in promoting political order.

Examination of the set of subgame perfect equilibria in which an interclan attack does not transpire indicates that mutual-deterrence can maintain interclan peace. In mutual-deterrence equilibria, each clan is deterred from attacking the other by the self-enforcing belief that an attack will not pay, given the other clan's military strength, the cost of the attack, and the implied loss from forgoing future joint piracy.[13]

Interestingly, peace based on mutual-deterrence equilibria provides a disincentive to acquire privileges. To show why this is the case, I extend the model to allow the number of privileges to be determined endogenously. Specifically, because acquiring privileges required the clans to cooperate, I assume that the number of privileges is the largest that both clans agreed to acquire and then ask if this number of privileges is smaller than the efficient (joint income-maximizing) number.

Analyzing this game indicates that under a mutual-deterrence equilibrium, peace comes at the price of economic prosperity. The number of privileges that each clan finds optimal to acquire if the mutual-deterrence equilibria are characterized by a positive investment in military strength is less than the efficient number of privileges (proposition 8.1). Intuitively,

---

[11] Sequential moves are at the center of Powell's (1993) work on mutual deterrence. The assumption made to capture that clan's moves were obviously uncoordinated.

[12] The subsequent analysis is strengthened if either of the following historically reasonable assumptions is made: a clan reaps nonpecuniary benefits from gaining control of the city, and a defeated clan gets a positive continuation value.

[13] Many mutual-deterrence equilibria can prevail, each of which entails a different allocation of gains from piracy and privileges.

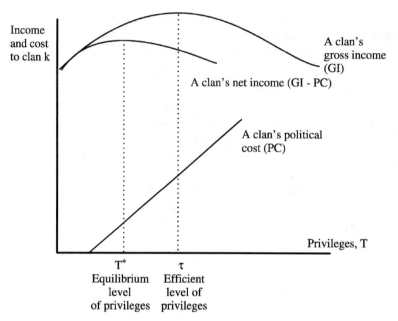

Figure 8.1. Equilibrium and efficient levels of privileges

when considering acquiring an additional privilege, a clan must take into account the implied additional expense (political cost) required to ensure deterrence. Everything else being equal, the additional privilege increases each clan's benefit from attacking the other. There is more to gain by capturing the polity but less to lose from forgone future cooperation in piracy. Hence the investment in military strength required to deter the other clan from attacking before gaining this additional privilege would no longer be sufficient.[14] Therefore, the optimal number of privileges for each clan is not one that equates the marginal economic benefit with the marginal economic cost (which, for simplicity, I assume to be zero). Instead, a clan's optimal number of privileges – the number that maximizes its net income – equates the marginal economic cost with the sum of the marginal economic and political costs.

A mutual-deterrence equilibrium with the efficient number of privileges maximizes each clan's *gross* payoff but does not maximize its *net* payoff (Figure 8.1). A mutual-deterrence equilibrium with fewer privileges is

[14] A clan has more to gain and more to lose if it attacks another clan after gaining additional privileges. In cases in which the clan was previously indifferent to attacking or not (as indicated by the other clan's need to deter attack by having a military force), everything else being equal, the increase in gain will dominate.

optimal for a clan. In this mutual-deterrence equilibrium, the marginal economic gain from additional privilege equals the marginal political and economic costs. This result holds whenever the mutual-deterrence equilibrium at the efficient level of privileges requires a positive military investment.[15]

8.3 THE CONSULAR SYSTEM, 1099–1154

If interclan mutual-deterrence equilibrium indeed prevailed in Genoa, its institutional foundations reflected the coordination and inclusion effects of past institutional elements. Furthermore, the model suggests that the rise of an effective state was curtailed by clans' inability to commit to each other. Was this the case? Does the empirical evidence confirm the predictions of the model presented here? This section considers this evidence and establishes that the rise of an effective state in Genoa from 1099 to 1154 was hampered by the inability of the city's clans to commit to one another.

If a mutual-deterrence equilibrium prevailed, the analysis predicts that Genoa's economy would be biased toward piracy and away from privileged commerce, despite the contractual nature of the Genoese commune and the profitability of long-distance trade. Indeed, a contemporary traveler, Benjamin of Tudela, noted that the Genoese have "command of the sea and they build ships which they call galleys, and make predatory attacks upon Edom [the land of the Christians] and Ishmael [the land of the Muslims] and the land of Greece as far as Sicily, and they bring back to Genoa spoils from all these places" (1987, p. 62).[16] Privilege-based commerce was, in the words of the historian Gerald W. Day, "unusually slow to develop" (1988, p. 6). Caffaro, the contemporary author of Genoa's annals, attributed this slowness to the clans' disincentives to mobilize their resources. According to him, "the city was asleep and was suffering from apathy and was like a ship wandering across the sea without a navigator" (*Annali* 1154, vol. I, p. 48).

Comparing Genoa's history with that of Pisa, Genoa's smaller neighbor to the south, provides more tangible evidence of the claim that the Genoese

---

[15] Analytically, the results hold only at the efficient level of privileges. For ease of exposition, however, Figure 8.1 portrays the result as holding everywhere.

[16] Otto the bishop of Freising noted that the strength of the Genoese was "naval warfare" (1152–8, p. 126). For evidence of piracy, see *Annali* 1133–4, 1137–8, 1147–9, vol. I, pp. 36, 38, 105–19. *CDG*, vol. I, no. 75.

acquired fewer privileges than were possible and profitable because of their need to sustain a self-enforcing political order.[17] Like Genoa, the Pisan commune was established at the end of the eleventh century, but by 1154 it had already acquired privileges throughout the Mediterranean, from Byzantium to Spain. Genoa at the time had privileges only in the Crusader states, Sardinia, Barcelona, perhaps Valencia, and some principalities in Provence. There is no indication that Genoa had any privileges in the important trading areas of Byzantium, Egypt, Sicily, or North Africa.[18]

This difference cannot be attributed to exogenous factors, such as opportunity, geography, or endowments. Pisa's location was not superior to Genoa's, and throughout the twelfth century Pisa's population was no more than 60 percent of Genoa's (Bairoch et al. 1988). Nor can the difference between Genoa and Pisa be attributed to "first mover advantage," that is, the fact that the Pisans began to acquire privileges earlier than the Genoese. The question is why Pisa moved first, not what transpired as a result.

Whereas Genoa's commercial expansion was curtailed by interclan mutual deterrence, this was not the case in Pisa. Consistent with the argument that mutual deterrence provides disincentives to acquire privileges, Pisa's polity was dominated by a single clan, the Visconti, composed of just three families. Until 1153 this clan held 65 percent of Pisa's known leadership posts (consuls and vicecomes). Almost every year one or more of its members led the commune, and Pisa's consuls had the right to nominate their own successors (Rossetti et al. 1979; Christiani 1962).[19] In Pisa the Visconti could have acquired privileges without worrying about how these additional privileges would have affected the intracommune balance of military power.

---

[17] For the history of Pisa, see Heywood (1921); Duffy (1903); and Rossetti et al. (1979).

[18] Pisa had privileges in Corsica (since 1091); Sardinia (before 1118); the Crusader states (since the First Crusade); Byzantium (since 1111); Spain (in Catalonia since 1113 and in Almeria since 1133); North Africa (in Bona, Tripoli, Sfax, and Bugia since 1133); Egypt (including a bazaar in Cairo since 1153 and a bazaar in Alexandria, where it had acquired rights much earlier); and probably several principalities in Provence (since 1113) (Heywood 1921, pp. 46–82, 108–15). On Genoa's privileges, see *CDG*, vol. I, and *Annali*, various years, vol. I. In 1116 some Genoese consuls obtained private privileges in Sicily (*CDG*, vol. I, no. 27).

[19] The record of consular holdings is incomplete. In any case, the Visconti provided one or more consuls or vicecomes each year before 1155 (Heywood 1921, pp. 8, 253–4; Waley 1988, pp. 35–6).

Internal peace prevailed in Genoa from 1099 to 1154. But as early as 1143, clans invested heavily in building fortifications to protect themselves from one another (*CDG*, vol. I, no. 128). They bought land and constructed walls and houses to form fortified enclaves with defensive towers.[20] Each clan established networks in which clients provided military and political assistance in return for economic and political patronage.[21] This seemingly wasteful behavior in a peaceful period was logical if interclan relationships were governed by a mutual-deterrence equilibrium. Clans invested resources to maintain the interclan military balance. As Genoa's wealth increased, each clan had to invest more to maintain this balance.

The well-preserved information on Genoa's consular holdings provides a measure of the extent to which clans mobilized resources to gain privileges. Consuls were elected by members of the Genoese commune, most of whom were not members or clients of the main clans. The number and military ability of these humbler Genoese made them a politically relevant force, as reflected, for example, in their right to approve taxation (*CDG*, vol. I, no. 111). The economic interests of these commoners favored expanding privileged commerce. Yet in the early days of the commune, these Genoese were too weak – organizationally, economically, militarily, and politically – to pursue this objective without the leadership and resources of Genoa's main clans. They did have a say in electing consuls and, given their interests, only clans willing to mobilize their resources to gain privileges could be expected to participate regularly in the consulate.

If this was the case, the conjecture that a mutual-deterrence equilibrium governed interclan relationships suggests that initially Genoa's two main clans would jointly serve on the consulate. Theoretically, as long as the number of privileges is below what each clan finds optimal (T^* in Figure 8.1), both clans will find it advantageous to mobilize their resources to gain more privileges. Once a particular clan reaches the optimal number of privileges, it will cease cooperating in mobilizing its resources. The institution discourages such a clan from pursuing a welfare-enhancing policy. It would therefore not be represented in the consulate.

---

[20] See, for example, Giovanni Scriba (1154–64, nos. 342 and 505); Krueger (1957, pp. 270–1); and D. Hughes (1977, pp. 99–100; 1978). A contemporary traveler, Benjamin of Tudela (1159–73), who visited Genoa between 1159 and 1173, described the use of the tower in interclan conflict (1987, p. 62). See Greif (2004a) for the reasons why other clans also built towers.

[21] For example, *Annali* 1164, vol. II, p. 16; 1179, vol. II, p. 192; 1192, vol. II, p. 227.

Asymmetry in the optimal number of privileges for a clan, in turn, is more likely to prevail if gains from existing privileges are also asymmetrically distributed. To see why this is the case, consider, for simplicity, the case in which one clan expropriates all the rent from existing privileges but expropriates nothing from any new ones.[22] This clan's payoff will decline if new privileges are acquired, because it will have to increase its investment in military strength to maintain deterrence.[23]

Does the historical evidence confirm these predictions? Did the Genoese clans cooperate initially? Did the clan that gained more from existing privileges cease mobilizing its resources? The historical evidence indicates that this was indeed the case. Between 1102 and 1105, members of both the Maneciano and the Carmadino clans served on the consulate. Their joint mobilization of resources to acquire privileges is reflected in official documents.[24] About this time, Genoa participated in the First Crusade, thereby gaining privileges in the East.[25]

After the initial acquisition of privileges, interclan cooperation ceased until 1154 (although Pisa's actions suggest that acquiring more privileges was profitable). The Manecianos dominated the consulate until 1122, while the Carmadinos dominated it from 1123 to 1149 (Table 8.1).[26]

---

[22] Formally, according to proposition 8.1, λ^k equals one with respect to existing privileges and zero with respect to additional privileges.

[23] Formally, using the notations developed in annex 8.1, the increase in gross income implies a higher investment in military strength (i.e., ICC^k implies that $\partial \psi^{-k}/\partial (I(T) + R(T)) > 0$) and thus clan $-k$'s higher investment induces clan k to increase its number of supporters (i.e., ICC^{-k} implies that $\partial \psi^k/\partial \psi^{-k} > 0$). Not cooperating in the acquisition of privileges is optimal for a clan that prefers the current equilibrium over an equilibrium with more privileges but prefers the equilibrium with more privileges over challenging.

[24] See, for example, *CDG*, vol. I, nos. 24, 30. During this period Genoa sent piracy expeditions as well, but we do not know if the two clans jointly mobilized their resources to do so.

[25] On conquest by the Genoese, see Caffaro, *Libro della Liberazione delle Città d'Oriente*, which is part of the *Annali*, vol. 1, particularly pp. 155–60. The Maneciano held more consular posts during this period than any other clan; Ido de Carmadino, a member of the Carmadino clan, was consul in 1102–5, 1118, and 1119 (Table 8.1). For the Ido clan's affiliation, see Belgrano (1873) and G. Day (1988, p. 71). On privileges, see *CDG*, vol. I, nos. 15, 16, 17. For a discussion of this period, see Heyd (1885, 1:149–50); Byrne (1920, 1928); and G. Day (1984).

[26] Before 1122 the Manecianos held more consular posts than any other Genoese clan (18 percent of the total); after 1122 the Carmadinos provided more consuls than any other clan (13 percent of the total). This change from domination by the Manecianos to domination by the Carmadinos was associated with a broader change in the composition of the consulate, suggesting that when either of these main

Table 8.1. *Rank Order of Families or Clans That Together Provided at Least 50 Percent of Consuls*

Family or Clan	1099–22	1123–49
Maneciano (clan)	1	
Rustico (family)	2	
Platealonga (family)	3	
Rufus (family)	4	
Roza (family)	5	
Pedicula (family)	6	
Carmadino (clan)		1
della Volta (clan)		2
Caschifellone (family)		3
Mallonus (family)		4
Gontardus (family)		5
Bellamutus (family)		6
Number of consuls	102	111

Note: The results are not sensitive to the choice of years (see Greif 2004a).

Source: Annali, various years; Olivieri (1861).

That the Manecianos practically abandoned the consulate after 1122 is consistent with the conjecture regarding the importance of mutual-deterrence equilibrium if they also gained disproportionally from existing privileges. Indeed, after the First Crusade, members of the Maneciano clan were left to govern Genoa's ports, quarters, and towns in the East on the commune's behalf. Over time they gained de facto control over these territories. Throughout the twelfth century, they increased their independence, refusing to pay an annual lease to Genoa or to return the holdings to the commune for reinvestiture.[27] The Manecianos had little motivation to acquire additional privileges for Genoa. The Genoese responded by transferring the consulate to the Carmadinos.

If the transfer of the consulate to the Carmadinos reflected different incentives to acquire privileges due to the Manecianos' control of privileges in the East, then the Carmadinos would have been likely to attempt to gain privileges in the western Mediterranean. This was indeed the case,

---

clans dominated the consulate, smaller clans in their patronage networks served on the consulate as well.

[27] *Annali* 1099, vol. I (also quoted in *CDG*, vol. I, no. 9); *CDG*, vol. I, no. 47, 170, 246–8. For a discussion, see Heyd (1868, 1885); Rey (1895); Byrne (1920, pp. 202–5; 1928); Cardini (1978); and Face (1952).

although trade with the East was more lucrative. This accounts for an otherwise puzzling shift in policy in Genoa, which participated in the First Crusade (circa 1099) but not in the Second Crusade (1147–9). Instead of sending its navy and army to the East, the Genoese sent them to the West to gain privileges in Spain. Genoa's policy depended on whether the Carmadinos or the Manecianos controlled the consulate: the Carmadinos concentrated on the West because of the Manecianos' de facto control over Genoa's privileges in the East. Without the Manecianos' support, Genoa failed to acquire significant new privileges throughout this period, a result that is consistent with the argument that acquiring privileges required interclan cooperation.[28]

Genoa's self-enforcing polity under the consulate thus had three main characteristics. First, the beliefs associated with mutual deterrence governed the relationships between the two viscountal clans. Each was deterred from challenging the other militarily by the cost implied by the other's military strength and the lost benefits from future joint piracy. Second, the consulate itself constituted a means to coordinate clan behavior through their representative and mobilized the resources of the common Genoese to support Genoa's policy. Third, this consular system maintained peace and political order at the cost of commercial expansion. Because acquiring privileges decreased the gains from future joint piracy, it implied political costs – either the breakdown of political order or additional military expenses by each clan to maintain the balance between them. Too few privileges were therefore acquired during this period; the city-state of Genoa was no more than a "coordinating state" without power over the clans.

8.4   EXOGENOUS CHANGES, UNDERMINING, AND INSTITUTIONAL FAILURE, 1154–94

Although trapped in an institutional equilibrium with a low level of privileges, Genoa's main clans nevertheless returned to cooperating in acquiring privileges after 1154. The change transformed Genoa's economy into one based on privileged commerce. Theoretically, this renewal of cooperation could happen even in the absence of an institutional change if the Genoese faced an unexpected parametric change – for example, increases

---

[28] *Annali* 1143, vol. I, p. 41; *CDG*, vol. I, nos. 122, 124, 125. Regarding the failed expedition to Spain, see Caffaro, *Storia della Presa di Almeria e di Tortosa*, which is part of the *Annali*, vol. 1, and Krueger (1949).

in external military threats, which reduce the value of becoming a controlling clan (by reducing the gains from winning an interclan military confrontation).[29] Such a reduction implies that a new mutual-deterrence equilibrium with a higher number of privileges is now optimal for both clans. Intuitively, a threat shifts the clan's net income line in Figure 8.1 upward (proposition 8.2).

Italians of the late medieval period recognized that an external threat could foster cooperation. An eleventh-century Milanese chronicler remarked that when his fellow citizens "lack external adversaries they turn their hatred against each other" (cited in Waley 1988, p. 117; Riker 1964 makes a similar observation in the modern context). The point here – that an external threat enables cooperation in dimensions other than (joint) confrontation of the external threat – is different.

In 1154 Genoa was subjected to an unexpected external threat from a German emperor. In that year, Frederick I Barbarossa's accession to the throne ended the civil war in Germany. The emperor, who was Genoa's de jure ruler, crossed the Alps with a large army, explicitly declaring his intention to reimpose the empire's control over the northern Italian cities.[30] A contemporary drawing in the *Annali* displaying the devastation imposed by Barbarossa on the city of Tortona in 1155 suggests how the Genoese perceived the emperor's intentions. Quickly they began building walls around their city.[31]

If mutual deterrence hindered interclan cooperation in acquiring privileges, theory suggests that this new external threat would have led to the interclan mobilization of resources to gain privileges. Indeed, in 1154 members of the Carmadino and Maneciano clans served jointly on the consulate for the first time in forty-nine years; between 1154 and 1162 the two clans held nearly the same number of consular posts (*Annali*, various years; Olivieri 1861). Furthermore, both clans were directly and jointly involved in acquiring privileges. Between 1154 and 1162 Genoa gained privileges in all the main trade centers around the Mediterranean. It reaffirmed its privileges in the Crusader states and acquired more in Spain, North Africa, Byzantium, Sicily, and several cities on the French

---

[29] For simplicity, the basic mutual-deterrence equilibrium analysis ignores this issue.

[30] See Munz (1969, pp. 119–20); Waley (1988, pp. 88–97). Otto of Freising (1152–8, pp. 126–8).

[31] *Annali* 1154, 1155, 1158, 1159, vol. I. Deterring an external threat was not necessarily costless, as assumed in the model, but including such costs would not have altered the model's main results.

coast.[32] For the nine years after 1155, the value of Genoa's long-distance trade was higher than in that initial year and its record was fourteen times its initial level.[33]

History confirms the relationships between an external threat, joint mobilization, and commercial expansion that are predicted by the conjecture regarding the centrality and implications of mutual deterrence in the consular system. The greater external threat increased the number of privileges for which political order was self-enforcing and increased each clan's optimal number of privileges. The external threat was a substitute for the value of gains from future joint piracy and lower gains from capturing the city in maintaining mutual deterrence in Genoa. It thereby enabled Genoa's economy to transform itself structurally from one based on piracy to one based on privileged commerce.[34]

Despite its apparent success, the consular system was self-undermining. The system implied endogenous changes in various quasi-parameters that rendered the mutual-deterrence equilibrium self-enforcing for a smaller set of parameters. Additional privileges reduced the parameter set in which mutual deterrence was an equilibrium. Furthermore, the consular system did not render clans politically or socially less important. On the contrary, mutual deterrence fostered Genoa's clan structure by encouraging clan members to strengthen their military might and internal organization. The consular system was built on and reinforced clan structure. An individual's welfare depended on the strength of his clan, particularly because of the expectation that other clans also sought to benefit their own members.[35] "Far from loosening family bonds, urban association strengthened them . . . lineage ties became more clearly defined, more firmly patrilineal and more frequently invoked" (D. Hughes 1978, p. 107). Individuals may have been socialized as clan members first and citizens of Genoa second. In particular, the consular system motivated clans to instill the norm of

---

[32] See *Annali* 1155–61, vol. I; *CDG*, vol. I, particularly nos. 266, 268, 269, 270, 271; Krueger (1949, pp. 127–8); Lisciandrelli (1960, pp. 11–12); Byrne (1920); Vitale (1955, 1:36–8); de Negri (1986, pp. 275–81); and G. Day (1988, pp. 86–99).

[33] Based on Giovanni Scriba, the only surviving Genoese cartulary from this period. No pre-1155 cartulary was preserved, nor is there one for the years immediately after 1164.

[34] Piracy did continue, however (see *CDG*, vol. III, nos. 104–7).

[35] The historical records rarely describe friction within clans, although it sometimes occurred. For example, in May 1144 Ugo Embriaco swore not to commit any hostile acts against Willielmus Embriaco and to discipline himself in order to restore good relations between them (*CDG*, vol. I, no. 133).

protecting their clans by force and the appropriateness of using violence to achieve political and economic ends. A mutual-deterrence equilibrium is by definition based on deterrence – an opponent's expected violent response increases the expected cost of using violence against him. The institution thus strengthened a culture of violence.

This undermining process became prominent when the external threat suddenly seemed to recede permanently. In 1162 Barbarossa appeared strong, and Genoa agreed to provide the emperor with a fleet to conquer Sicily in 1164. In that year, however, civil war resumed in Germany and the Veronese League was established in Lombardy to fight the emperor. The fleet the Genoese had prepared for the Sicilian campaign was ready but, to the apparent surprise of the Genoese, the emperor failed to come with his army (*Annali* 1162, vol. I, pp. 88–90; 1164, 1165, vol. II, *CDG*, vol. I, no. 308, vol. II, nos. 3–5).

By 1164 Genoa's external threat could no longer constrain its clans by decreasing the benefit of gaining in an interclan conflict. At the same time, Genoa now had more privileges than it had in the past, implying that controlling the consulate was more profitable than it had been in 1155.

Theoretically, a weakened external threat and a larger gain from controlling the consulate implied a higher payoff to becoming a controlling clan. In other words, a change in an exogenous parameter led to a change in the number of privileges, a quasi-parameter. The change in the quasi-parameter meant that once the exogenous parameter returned to its original level, returning to the previous institution could no longer have been feasible. A higher level of privileges implies a smaller set of parameters for which interclan deterrence is an equilibrium (annex 8.2) for a given division of gains from privileges among the clans. This would not have been the case had the consular system altered other quasi-parameters – such as the identity affiliation of clan members or their patronage networks – to reinforce itself. In fact, the consular system had the opposite impact on these quasi-parameters.

If a mutual-deterrence equilibrium no longer exists (for a given allocation of income between the clans), the model predicts that clans would confront each other militarily. This conclusion does not change qualitatively if the model is extended so that the interclan division of income is determined endogenously. Such a model must include the possibility that if a particular mutual-deterrence equilibrium no longer exists, one clan may find it more profitable to agree to a smaller share of the income, avoiding the cost of a military confrontation. The problem is that an allocation of income for which another mutual-deterrence equilibrium exists is unlikely to be acceptable to both clans.[36] The new allocation has to be both acceptable to both clans ex ante and self-enforcing ex post, despite the link between income and military strength. If, for example, clan 1 finds it profitable to challenge at the existing income allocation, it will not accept a new allocation that gives it a lower income share. Clan 2, however, will not accept any new allocation that gives it a share that is so low that it prefers military confrontation. There may not be a new allocation that is acceptable ex ante and self-enforcing ex post, especially given the relationship between military strength and income. Any allocation that gives clan 1 a higher income share will add to its military strength relative to clan 2. Hence although clan 1 will have less to gain from challenging given the new allocation, it will also be more likely to have the upper hand in a military confrontation. In the context of Genoa, the clans could not restore a mutual-deterrence equilibrium by abandoning privileges and returning to a piracy-based economy. A clan advocating such a strategy would have aligned the Genoese at large with its opposing clan, because the common Genoese benefited from trade.

Theory predicts that Genoa's clans were more likely to challenge each other militarily in 1164, the year that a civil war broke out. The same families that had shared the consulate from 1154 to 1164 and cooperated in acquiring privileges fought one another in these civil wars.[37] Fighting occurred mainly in 1164–9 and 1189–94; between 1171 and 1189 the victorious Manecianos assumed control over the consulate.[38]

The annals reflect on the causes and extent of the civil war. "Civil discords and hateful conspiracies and divisions had arisen in the city on account of the mutual envy of the many men who greatly wished to hold office as consuls of the commune" (*Annali* 1190, vol. II, pp. 219–20). The extent of the fighting was such that "in our city the evil increased and the civic contentions flared up more as the flame of the fire ... [and] rarely is it possible to see a citizen ... without any kind of armor, walking in the city" (*Annali* 1160, vol. II, p. 63).

---

[36] For a theoretical analysis in this spirit, see Fearon (1997).

[37] See, for example, *Annali*, various years, vol. II, pp. 16, 28, 104.

[38] On fighting, see *Annali*, various years, vols. I, II. When the main clans fought, smaller ones (such as the Albericis and Roza) took charge. Genoa neither gained nor lost privileges between 1164 and 1189. Trade does not seem to have expanded (Giovanni Scriba; Obertus Scriba; Guglielmo Cassinese). Genoa's weakness is reflected in its near defeat by Pisa (see Greif 1998c and 2004a for details).

Genoa's civil wars reveal the limited ability of the consular system to maintain a privilege-based economy in the absence of an external threat. Instead of advancing the commune's economy, Genoa's main clans fought over the distribution of the spoils from past successes. Fostering Genoa's economic development and establishing political order required appropriate institutional development.

8.5 SELF-ENFORCING LIMITED STATE: THE GENOESE *PODESTERIA*, 1194–1339

In 1194 an institutional development occurred that enabled the Genoese to end the civil war, further mobilize their resources, and attain a new level of economic prosperity. At the center of the new institution was a *podestà* (power), a non-Genoese who governed the city as its military leader, judge, and administrator, usually for one year.

Understanding this new self-enforcing political institution requires identifying several key factors: the agents and circumstances that led to the change, the options that were cognitively understood at that point, and the implications of institutional elements inherited from the past on possible new self-enforcing institutions. Indeed, the transition to the new institution reflects local learning that past institutions entailed and the coordination and inclusion effects of past institutional elements.

The transition to the *podesteria* occurred when Genoa faced a severe external threat that increased the cost of the rivalry between the Carmadinos and Manecianos for both. In 1194 Emperor Henry VI, the son of Frederick Barbarossa, demanded that Genoa provide naval assistance to help him attack Sicily. Failure to do so would have alienated the emperor, jeopardizing Genoese claims to the privileges the emperor had promised them in Sicily. It would also have allowed Genoa's rival, Pisa, to grow stronger by gaining these privileges. To stand up to this external threat without incurring the high costs of refusing the emperor's request, the Genoese clans needed to mobilize their resources jointly.

The threat by the emperor, most likely, made such mobilization possible. As in 1154, the external threat implied that joint mobilization was an equilibrium for a larger set of parameters than before. In 1154 the imperial threat shifted the Genoese into an equilibrium whereby the Carmadinos and Manecianos jointly mobilized their resources. In 1194 the Carmadinos refused to mobilize their resources, withdrew from the commune, and threatened to establish a rival one (*Annali* 1194, vol. II). The collapse of the consular system in 1164 seems to have made them leery of relying on external threats to sustain political order. As a result, this time they conditioned their participation on an institutional change. Such change came about in 1194, when the emperor's seneschal (agent) proposed that the consulate accept an imperial *podestà* to rule the city.[39]

The idea of ruling cities through *podestàs* also reflects institutional learning. During the first half of the twelfth century, Italian communes experimented with relying on a single administrator to manage their affairs. After Barbarossa's attempt to control the Italian cities failed, many communes continued to nominate civil officials, called *rectores, dominatores,* and *podestàs,* to act as administrators. These administrators, who were bound by the law, had police and judicial authorities.[40] In this respect, they were similar to the dictators of ancient Rome (Spruyt 1994, p. 143). In the 1190s Emperor Henry VI used nonlocal imperial vicars, or *podestàs,* to administer Italian cities on his behalf and secure his control.[41]

In Genoa the consulate, which was dominated by the Manecianos – Genoa's elite – agreed to accept an imperial *podestà,* and the Maneciano and the Carmadino clans participated in the conquest of Sicily. Subsequent events, however, reflect the divergence in interests between the emperor, who aspired to control Genoa through his *podestà,* and the Genoese, who wanted to retain their independence. During the Sicilian campaign, the imperial *podestà* died. Without consulting the emperor, the Genoese nominated another *podestà* (*Annali* 1194, vol. II, p. 239). The emperor refused to recognize this *podestà* and threatened to treat Genoa as a rebellious city (*Annali* 1194, vol. II, pp. 240–1). Unintimidated, the Genoese successfully confronted the emperor; they continued to nominate their own *podestà* and to use a *podestà* even when the emperor did not require them to do so.

Under the *podesteria* system, Genoa enjoyed a long period of relative political order, in which clans jointly mobilized their resources and the economy expanded rapidly. Political historians have long debated how the *podestà* was able to pacify and unite Genoa. Vito Vitale, Genoa's eminent historian, argues that the *podestà* was merely an administrator, hired to meet the need for professional administration and the desire

---

[39] See *Annali* 1194, vol. II, pp. 231–2; Vitale (1955, 1:51–5); Abulafia (1977, pp. 204–12); and G. Day (1988, p. 149).
[40] See Hyde (1973, pp. 100–1); Heywood (1921, p. 262); and Waley (1988, p. 42).
[41] See G. Day (1988, p. 147) and Heywood (1921, pp. 214 , 220).

to limit competition over consular posts (Vitale 1951, p. 9). According to him, internal tranquillity under the *podesteria* was sustained by the gains from cooperation. Other scholars, such as Heers (1977, p. 206), consider the *podestà*'s military power, which allowed him to impose peace on Genoa's rival clans, as the key to enabling cooperation.

Both of these positions have weaknesses. If the *podestà* was simply an administrator and political order was sustained by the gains from jointly mobilizing resources, why didn't these gains guarantee cooperation under the consulate? If the *podestà*'s superior military ability fostered cooperation, why didn't he become a dictator or assume political control?

8.5.1 Creating a Balance of Power

Hiring the *podestà* was an organizational change: it altered the relevant intertransactional linkages by introducing an additional strategic player. The change altered the rules of Genoa's political game and hence the set of self-enforcing beliefs in the central transaction among the Genoese clans.

Understanding the nature and the implications of this change requires a contextual refinement (Chapter 7). Given the fundamental asymmetry, it is likely that the *podesteria* incorporated institutional elements inherited from the past – specifically, clans and their shared norms and beliefs. We can therefore develop a conjecture regarding the impact of the *podestà* by considering a game whose rules and analysis recognize the impact of these institutional elements. We can then ask whether the introduction of the *podestà* can entail interclan cooperation and political order as an equilibrium outcome without subjecting Genoa to dictatorship. (For the formal analysis, see annex 8.3.)

Three conditions needed to be met to ensure interclan cooperation and political order as an equilibrium outcome without subjecting the city to a dictatorship. First, the *podestà* had to be militarily deterred from attempting to become a dictator and gaining political control. Second, the *podestà* had to be deterred from siding with one clan against another.[42] Third, the *podestà* had to deter each clan from challenging another in a larger set of situations than otherwise would be the case. In other words, the *podestà* should reinforce interclan cooperation.

---

[42] Failed institutional refinement (section 7.2) after 1154 probably made the Genoese aware of this problem. Interclan cooperation after 1154 was facilitated by having the della Volta clan to balance the two viscountal clans. The della Volta clan married into both clans and was active in the consulate. Eventually, it became part of the Carmadino clan faction (see Greif 2004a).

To prevent the *podestà* from becoming a dictator, he had to be too weak militarily to be able to fight Genoa's clans (and the Genoese more generally).[43] Making the *podestà* weaker than each clan also deterred him from siding with one clan against another. This type of collusion, in which the *podestà* provides military assistance to one clan in return for a pecuniary reward, is possible only if the clan can commit to reward the *podestà* after he assumes power. The stronger a clan is relative to the *podestà*, the less able it is to commit to do so, since the clan would never pay the *podestà* more than the cost of confronting him militarily. The weaker the *podestà*, the less the clan can commit to reward him for colluding against another clan. If the amount a clan can commit to pay the *podestà* is less than he would receive by not colluding, collusion is not an equilibrium outcome.

But how can a *podestà* who is weaker than each clan deter any single clan from attacking another? Limiting the *podestà*'s military ability relative to that of a clan implies that he can neither become a dictator nor collude with one clan against another. But such a limitation also reduces the *podestà*'s military ability to deter one clan from challenging the other.

To see how each clan can nevertheless be deterred from challenging the other, we need to consider the incentives for a defending clan and the *podestà* to fight alongside one another against an attacking clan. More generally, we need to consider the conditions under which particular beliefs will be self-enforcing. These are the beliefs supporting the behavior that no clan attacks the other and the *podestà* does not collude with a clan that attacks another, fights against the other clan, and is assisted by the clan that was attacked.

The strategy combination associated with these beliefs is a subgame perfect equilibrium, if the reward to the *podestà*, his military strength, and the other parameters are such that the following conditions hold. First, the *podestà* is sufficiently weak militarily and his wage sufficiently high that he is better off getting paid than colluding. Second, the *podestà* is sufficiently strong and clans are sufficiently equal in terms of military strength that he is better off fighting against a clan that attacked another than colluding, but only if the clan that was attacked also fights. Third, the *podestà*'s strength and the relative strength of the clans is such that each clan would fight alongside the *podestà* if attacked, and each clan would find it optimal not to challenge.

---

[43] If these other Genoese were strong enough to deter the *podestà* by themselves, however, they would not have needed him to subdue the clans.

These conditions and the equilibrium strategy indicate how the *podesteria* system can provide the appropriate incentives – entail the required self-enforcing beliefs – to be effective in mitigating all of these problems. If the *podestà*'s military strength is reduced enough relative to his wage, the maximum reward that any clan can credibly commit to giving him following collusion will not be enough to induce him to collude. The *podestà*, expecting a clan that had been attacked by another to fight with him, prefers to confront the attacking clan rather than collude with it. The attacked clan is motivated to fight alongside the *podestà*, because if it does not, the *podestà*'s strategy implies that he will not confront the other clan. At the same time, the combined forces of the *podestà* and the clan fighting alongside him are such that it is optimal for a clan to fight with the *podestà*.

This analysis illustrates the delicate balance of power that must be maintained for the *podesteria* to promote political order. On the one hand, the *podestà* cannot be strong enough militarily to gain control himself or collude with a clan. On the other hand, he must be strong enough so that his threat to fight alongside a clan if necessary eliminates any clan's motivation to challenge another.

8.5.2 *The* Podesteria *System in Action*

Theoretically, introducing the *podestà* could have been a self-enforcing institutional change that weakened the link between political order and the mobilization of clan resources. To address whether this was actually the case, we have to examine the rules and regulations governing the *podesteria* to determine if they match the theoretical conditions required for the *podesteria* to enhance cooperation and order.

To compensate the *podestà* for fighting if the need arose, the commune paid him generously (Vitale 1951, p. 25). Soldiers and judges whom the *podestà* brought with him supported him. His military force (possibly supported by Genoese who were unaffiliated with the main clans) was neither negligible nor considerable (Vitale 1951, p. 27). In the words of the annals, it was sufficient for the *podestà* to perform "the revenges against all those who were in anything rebellious in [the] Genoese republic ... he made all the guilty succumb. His shade and his boldness made the escort and the walk of everyone sure" (*Annali* 1196, vol. II, p. 253).

At the same time, the Genoese *podestà* was kept sufficiently militarily weak relative to the Genoese as a whole to prevent him from becoming a dictator. Indeed, no *podestà* ever attempted to gain control over the city. Arguably, the *podestà* was kept sufficiently weak militarily in order to prevent collusion with a clan. Theoretically, a militarily powerful clan can credibly commit to provide only a small reward. Yet a clan and a *podestà* might adopt other commitment devices, such as marriages and joint economic ventures, that do not depend on relative military strength.

To prevent this from happening, various rules sought to prevent the *podestàs* from getting involved in Genoese society and politics. The *podestà* was selected by a council consisting of members chosen on a geographical basis to prevent any clan from gaining control. The outgoing *podestà* supervised the selection process. Neither the *podestà* himself nor his relatives (to the third degree) were allowed to socialize with the Genoese, buy property, marry, or manage any commercial transactions for themselves or others in Genoa. The *podestà*, as well as the soldiers who came with him, had to leave the city at the end of the term and agree not to return for several years. To avoid developing special relations with any clan, each of which dominated a particular part of the city, the *podestà* rotated his residence among different quarters until special housing was built for him.

The *podesteria* was constantly refined, as local institutional learning revealed its deficiencies. To increase flexibility in administrative and political decisions and to align the *podestà*'s actions and Genoa's interests, after 1196 eight *rettori* or *consiglieri* (one per district) functioned as part of the administration and control. These officials were chosen to isolate the *podestà* from the influence of Genoa's main clans. Very few rectors were identified with one of the major families involved in the interclan wars of the twelfth century.[44] Shortly after this change, it was institutionalized that the *podesteria's* regulations had to be approved by a larger forum (a council). Major policy decisions had to be approved by the *parlamentum* of Genoese with "full rights." In 1229 Genoa's legal rules were codified to further reduce discretion and limit the clans' ability to establish patronage networks through their hold over legal matters (Vitale 1951, pp. 32–40; 1955, 1:56).

A *podestà* was not given a free hand to mismanage the city. After the end of his term, a *podestà* had to remain in the city for fifteen days, during which auditors assessed his conduct. Deviations from the set of prespecified rules were punished by fines to be paid before his departure (Vitale 1951, pp. 27–8). A *podestà*'s concerns about his reputation probably gave

---

[44] See Olivieri (1861), years 1196, 1199, 1202, 1203, 1205, and 1206; Vitale (1951, p. 11); and G. Day (1988, pp. 150–1).

him an additional incentive to prevent interclan confrontation, because many communes hired *podestàs* and a good reputation could help a *podestà* secure another post.[45] Similarly, the Genoese concerns with being able to hire a high-quality *podestà* in the future rendered their promise to pay him credible. *Podestàs* were recruited from a handful of Italian cities, and their contracts were read in front of each city's "parliament."[46]

In Genoa the end of the civil war and the increased ability to mobilize resources under the *podesteria* fostered political order and economic ascendance. The *podesteria* led to a period that was "indeed the Golden Age of Genoa" (Vitale 1955, 1:69). The *podesteria* lasted for about 150 years (to 1339), during which time it was challenged by temporary imbalances between clans, the political rise of the *popolo* (nonnobles), and the conflict between the pope and the emperor. Still, the *podesteria* retained the same basic structure throughout its history, functioning as a nonpartisan balance of power and administrative and judicial authority.

In 1195 Genoa was peaceful for the first time in many years, and the Genoese reaffirmed their control over the smaller cities around them. In the next hundred years, Genoa freed itself from the rule of the Holy Roman Empire; defeated Pisa, its commercial rival in the western Mediterranean; and was on the verge of defeating Venice, its commercial rival in the eastern Mediterranean (Vitale 1955; Donaver 1990 [1890]). It acquired extensive privileges in the Mediterranean and the Black Sea (Vitale 1951, chaps. 2–3).

During this period, Genoa enjoyed spectacular economic growth. In the years immediately following the introduction of the *podesteria* (1191–1214), the value of long-distance trade grew at an annual rate of at least 6 percent a year compared with an annual growth of 3 percent between 1160 and 1191. By 1314 the value of Genoa's trade was more than forty-six times that in 1160.[47] A contemporary source estimated that Genoa was the richest city in northern Italy (Hyde 1973).

---

[45] The *podesterias* of various cities differed in some important respects. In Pisa the *podesteria*, established in 1190, was not aimed at creating a balance of power (Rossetti et al. 1979; Christiani 1962; Heywood 1921). The first *podestà* (1190–9) was the Count of Gherardesca, who served on behalf of Emperor Henry VI. By 1199 the Visconti clan, which dominated Pisa before 1190, had reestablished its control and subsequently controlled the *podesteria*. Only after a war in 1237 between the Viscontis and the de Gherardescas were non-Pisan *podestàs* nominated.

[46] The community responsibility system, discussed in Chapter 10, also strengthened the credibility of the promise.

[47] These calculations are based on all the available cartularies from this period: Giovanni Scriba, Obertus Scriba, Guglielmo Cassinese, Lanfranco Scriba, and Giovanni

Genoa's population also exploded during this period. Between 1050 and 1200 the population doubled in size. Between 1200 and 1300 it increased by 230 percent (Bairoch et al. 1988, pp. 43, 49).[48] During the same periods, the population of Venice grew about 50 percent. By 1300 Genoa was second in size only to Venice, whose population was about 10 percent greater than Genoa's.

8.6 THE *PODESTERIA* AS A SELF-UNDERMINING INSTITUTION

The *podesteria* fostered interclan cooperation, political stability, and economic growth. It was a self-enforcing institution: the belief that any attempt by a clan to gain political dominance by using force was futile deterred clans from doing so, and the belief that a clan could gain from cooperation without the risk of losing its rewards through military confrontation motivated cooperation.

Yet like the consular system, the *podesteria* was also self-undermining and hence, it came under strain at the end of the thirteenth century. It restrained interclan warfare but did not eliminate interclan rivalry. Central to the success of the institution was the fact that clans had roughly similar military strength, so that a relatively weak *podestà* could be pivotal to one clan's victory over another. No clan could afford to become too weak relative to another, while each could have gained from being strong if another clan became temporarily weak. The *podestà* himself was motivated not to allow one clan to become weak either, as his compensation was conditional on no clan dominating Genoa at the end of his term. As we have seen, the system was set to ensure that no clan would be able to commit to pay to a *podestà* his promised remuneration if that clan gained control over Genoa. Hence as the city grew more prosperous, the punishment that would be imposed on a rebellious clan was bounded, while the gains from rebelling were increasing.

Under the *podesteria*, clans were still motivated to invest in acquiring the military capability to attack other clans, fortifying their residences, establishing patronage networks, and socializing their members to internalize the norm of revenge.[49] The Genoese continued to retain

di Guiberto. See also Sieveking (1898–9, p. 67); J. Day (1963, p. XVI). See Greif (1994c, 1998c, 2004a).
[48] No population estimates for either city are available for 1100.
[49] Mutual deterrence makes a culture of revenge – socializing a norm of revenge – rational ex ante, but the resulting feuds are costly ex post. A vendetta may be rational ex post, however, if a clan's failure to take revenge induces other clans to

their clan identity rather than identifying themselves with the city as a whole. Indeed, the *podesteria* had no mechanism for reversing the legacy of the civil war, which fostered interclan animosity and cycles of feuds or vendettas.

These feuds, which began after the civil wars, curtailed interclan interactions that might have weakened the bonds among clan members or strengthened interclan social and economic ties.[50] They were so violent that clans approached the pope for the right to build family churches, arguing that it was too dangerous for them to frequent public churches. Indeed, vendetta killings took place even in churches (D. Hughes 1978, p. 112). Business transactions, like prayers, were increasingly conducted in private. In the cartulary of Giovanni Scriba (1154–64), 88 percent of overseas contracts were written in public places, such as churches and markets. In contrast, in the cartulary of Obertus Scriba (1186), 90 percent of such contracts were written in private places, mainly merchants' residences.[51]

As Chapter 6 notes, the incentive for each clan to develop a patronage network and the access of all city residents to Genoa's lucrative overseas trade also contributed to undermining the *podesteria*. It entailed more wealth accumulation by nonclan members than otherwise would have been the case. Over time these families organized themselves to form their own armed political factions. Similarly, clans sought to increase their power by creating *alberghi*. *Alberghi* were clanlike social structures whose purpose was to strengthen ties among members of various families through formal contracts and the adoption of common surnames, usually that of the *albergo*'s most powerful clan. By the fifteenth century, the city's politics and economics were dominated by about thirty *alberghi*, each containing five to fifteen lineages.

In the short run, these changes did not render Genoa's *podesteria* ineffective, but over time it became self-enforcing over a smaller range of situations. After 1311 the city attempted to restore political stability by

---

believe that it is easy "prey," leaving it worse off than if it had participated in a costly vendetta. Indeed, termination of a feud was a public matter (see, e.g., *Annali* 1169, vol. II, p. 112).

[50] See, for example, *Annali* 1190, II, p. 220; 1193, II, p. 228; 1203, III, pp. 28–9; 1187, II, pp. 204–5; 1203. For a first-rate account of the experiences of other Italian cities in constraining their violent nobles, see Martines (1972).

[51] This distinction does not reflect a composition effect in the sense of capturing the activities of merchants who differ from each other along such attributes as wealth. Greif (2004a).

having a strong military ruler, either an external one, such as the king of Germany, to whom the city submitted itself in 1311, or an internal one (a doge). After 1339, however, the *podesteria* was no longer self-enforcing. The city was torn by intense interclan strife, or one Genoese clan (with or without the support of Genoa's external foes) waged war against Genoa from abroad. In the next 200 years there were thirty-nine revolts and civil wars (S. A. Epstein 1996, appendix). Genoa declined economically, because it was unable to offer naval and military support to its commercial outposts abroad or prevent the devastation of its own agricultural hinterland.

In 1381 Genoa was defeated by Venice. In a sense this defeat was preordained, although not sealed, during the twelfth century. It was then that particular self-enforcing yet self-undermining institutions established themselves. They had a lasting impact on the city's political, economic, and social history.

Ironically, the defeat led to organizational changes that brought about institutional development that isolated property from the peril of political military conflicts within Genoa. This organizational development reflects an unintended consequence of Genoa's economic progress and interclan competition. Economic prosperity and wealth transfer to nonclan members in return for support implies that various families, which did not belong to Genoa's main clans, were able to acquire substantial economic and military resources. Genoa, before being defeated by Venice in 1381, borrowed heavily from these families, which probably differed from the old feudal clans by being more interested in economic success than political control. Unable to pay its debt after the defeat, Genoa ceded control over various tax-bearing sources to its local creditors. These creditors organized themselves in a self-governed entity, the Bank of San Giorgio, which over time came to administer most of the towns and cities in the Genoese dominion.

Like the merchant guild examined in Chapter 3, the Bank of San Giorgio was an organization that linked transactions among Genoa's many internal creditors. It enabled them to coordinate their responses and impose their decisions on one another. Over time the bank became so powerful that it was able to secure the property rights of its members even in periods of political violence. Niccolò Machiavelli, writing in 1532, noted that whoever gained political control over Genoa had to respect the rights of the bank, "as it possesses arms, money, and influence," and abusing its rights entailed "the certainty of a dangerous rebellion" (1990, p. 352).

Only in 1528, when Andrea Doria established an aristocratic republic similar to that of Venice, was Genoa able to achieve lasting political stability. At that late date, however, the political and economic situation around the Mediterranean prevented Genoa from restoring its past glory. Ironically, this very inability may have made a Genoese republic feasible again.[52]

8.7 CONCLUDING COMMENTS

This conclusion discusses the two central issues of the chapter: Genoa's historical experience and the processes of state building. It then turns to the general insight the analysis provides regarding distinct trajectories of state development in Europe and the Muslim world. Specifically, it notes that in Europe the large, kin-based social structures that hinder the formation of effective states were already declining by the late medieval period. This was not the case in the Muslim world, however.

8.7.1 *The Genoese Experience: Institutions and Building Effective States*

Understanding Genoa's political, economic, and social history required considering the institutions that constrained violence within the city and fostered growth-enhancing policies. Genoa's history was shaped by these institutions whose details, and hence effectiveness, reflected more than the functions they fulfilled. The details of these institutions also reflected institutional elements inherited from the past. Clans, and the beliefs and norms that shaped their objectives and motivated their behavior, exerted coordination and inclusion effects on Genoa's institutional development, which was based on the need to maintain mutual deterrence among clans and motivate them to mobilize their resources to advance Genoese commerce.

In the early days of the commune, the consulate provided a means for coordinating the behavior of the clans, but it had no power to impose its decisions on them. Peace prevailed but prosperity was curtailed because mutual deterrence implied a wedge between the level of privileges that was economically efficient and the level that was an equilibrium outcome. For a period following 1154, an external threat promoted an interclan mobilization of resources. The threat implied that each clan had less to gain from militarily challenging others so that all clans could better commit

---

[52] See, for example, Donaver (1990 [1890], pp. 86ff.) and S. A. Epstein (1996, chap. 5).

to refrain from attack following commercial expansion. Genoa's economic structure was thus transformed into one based on privileged trade.

Economic prosperity and the other implications of the consulate, however, undermined the self-enforceability of Genoa's institutional foundations. Clans were motivated to invest in coercive power, and individuals identified more with their clans than with the city of Genoa. Mutual deterrence gradually became an equilibrium in a smaller set of parameters. Once the external threat unexpectedly subsided, peace was no longer an equilibrium outcome, and Genoa descended into civil war.

It took thirty years and a particular historical circumstance for a new self-enforcing political institution – the *podesteria* – to be established. The transition to the *podesteria* reflects a recognition of institutional failure, the increased external threat, the process of learning about possible alternatives, and, most likely, appropriate leadership. The relationship between the old and the new institution, however, reflects the fundamental asymmetry and the consequent impact of past institutions on subsequent ones. The *podesteria* was built around institutional elements inherited from the past, incorporating Genoa's clan structures and their beliefs and norms.

Yet, for the first time the Genoese state had independent power over the clans. The *podesteria* was a self-enforcing institutional change that increased the set of parameters in which interclan mutual deterrence was self-enforcing. Because the *podestà* had coercive power and decision-making ability, however, he needed to be appropriately motivated to imply the desired outcome. The *podesteria* endogenously motivated him to confront a challenging clan, forgo colluding with any single clan, and refrain from using his coercive power to abuse rights or gain control over the city. The *podesteria* system thus represented a form of limited government.

In the long run, however, the *podesteria* failed to sustain political order. Like the consular system, the *podesteria* was self-undermining. Clans still had an incentive to acquire military power and shape their members' identities as clan members rather than as Genoese citizens. Military power remained the means by which various social groups advanced their causes, and the *podestà* had no incentive to change Genoa's underlying clan structure. Eventually he failed to keep the balance of power among Genoa's various rival groups and the system collapsed.

To understand Genoa's political, economic, and social history, we had to examine its polity as self-enforcing. Arguably, a similar analysis is required for understanding the relative success or failure of other past and present polities. Thus, we have to move beyond the common political economy analysis that takes the state as given and focuses on rules governing elections, collective decision making, and the behavior of the state's agents. We similarly have to move beyond assuming that the state is endowed with coercive power. Instead, we have to study the factors influencing the acquisition and use of coercive power in the society. More generally, we have to study polities and political outcomes as self-enforcing and recognize that agents' choices among various economic, social, and political actions are influenced by their impact on this self-enforceability.

8.7.2 *Violence, Institutions, and Prosperity*

Both the predator-ruler and the neo-Hobbesian perspectives assume that the existence of a state implies that it has a monopoly over coercive power. Genoa's historical experience highlights the limits of this premise. Institutions influencing the acquisition and use of coercive power – coercive constraining institutions – are central to the process of building a state and its economic implications. In an effective, welfare-enhancing state, these institutions render coercive power productive as it is being applied to prevent the use of coercive power for the purpose of welfare-reducing redistribution of resources. In Genoa, this was achieved by having a *podestà* with the coercive power to check the Genoese clans whose coercive power, in turn, limited his ability to abuse rights using his power. As we have seen, however, this was insufficient to guarantee long-term prosperity as the *podesteria* failed to undermine the clan structure. Studying processes of state building, while explicitly specifying the relationships between violence, institutions, and prosperity, will enhance greater understanding of the failures and successes of these processes.

Indeed, the analysis of Genoa highlights the limitation of even the intuitive assertion, implicit in both the predator-ruler and neo-Hobbesian perspectives, that peace always promotes economic prosperity, whereas violence always undermines it. The impact of order or its absence depends on the institutions rendering peace or violence as equilibrium outcomes.

Peace prevailed under the consulate in Genoa. Yet, analyzing the mutual deterrence that underpinned it reveals that it was only partially successful in fostering prosperity. The beliefs associated with mutual deterrence discouraged the clans from taking economically productive actions because to do so would have undermined the self-enforceability of peace. Peace came at the price of limiting prosperity. (For a general analysis of this phenomenon, see Bates et al. 2002.)

Conversely, political violence in Genoa was not always detrimental to economic prosperity. The Bank of San Giorgio provided coordination and aligned the interests of Genoa's debt holders who directly controlled much of the city's private and public assets. The bank enhanced the ability of asset holders to credibly commit to use their economic and coercive power to retaliate following abuse of their property rights. The bank seems to have been a component of an institution, possibly similar to the one examined in Chapter 4, that deterred abuse of rights by those who fought for political control over Genoa.

More generally, Genoa's experience supports the claim that a central challenge to state building is the ability to motivate the preexisting social structures to mobilize their military and economic resources to create an effective state. Providing motivation is challenging because the process of state building can undermine the institutions that maintain political order among these social structures, as well as the social structures themselves. It may not be coincidental that contemporary states with major ethnic and tribal cleavages find it difficult to establish democratic, peaceful, and egalitarian polities (Collins 2004).

An external threat can increase the set of parameters in which cooperation among social structures is self-enforcing, thereby facilitating beneficial cooperation (Greif 1998c). The lack of an external threat in the postcolonial period may well have helped thwart the foundation of effective states in contemporary Africa (Bates 2001). Genoa illustrates, however, that the politically beneficial implications of such threats depend on two factors: first, the inability of one social structure to collude with the external power against the another social structure; and, second, the need for the institutions prevailing during the period of threat to undermine, rather than reinforce, these social structures, so that political order will be maintained once the threat recedes.

Genoa's history also underscores that processes of state building involve more than reforming political institutions by implementing the rules that prevail in effective Western states for electing leaders and for collective decision making. When and where such rules emerged endogenously, they reflected an equilibrium in the relationships among the political actors. They were followed by the political agents because they were part of a corresponding self-enforcing institution (Greif 2004b). Attempts to transplant Western political rules elsewhere for the purpose of building effective, welfare-enhancing states is therefore insufficient. Building effective, welfare-enhancing states requires making a transition to new self-enforcing institutions. Creating institutions associated with such states amounted to replacing one self-enforcing institutional equilibria with another.

One can postulate that the role model provided by the European experience increasingly facilitates meeting this challenge. The relative success of the Western state has influenced beliefs, norms, and aspirations elsewhere in the world in a manner that makes it easier for Western political rules to become an equilibrium outcome. Similarly, economic globalization and urbanization have undermined kin-based social structures that often obstruct building an effective state.

In any case, successful transitions to new institutional equilibria are challenging. Those whose support is crucial must be motivated to do so and this requires an assurance that they will be better off, ex post, than if they objected to it (e.g., Fernandez and Rodrik 1991; Roland 2000; Lau, Qian, and Roland 2000). A state capable of influencing payoffs ex post can potentially provide these assurances. Such a powerful state, however, can provide them credibly only if its power is limited in the sense that it can credibly commit not to abuse it. In addition, to enhance welfare, such a state has to be an equilibrium outcome without resorting to economically inefficient distribution policies. Finally, for an effective, welfare-enhancing state to persist, its institutional foundations must become self-enforcing in a larger set of parameters and able to adapt efficiently to changing circumstance. This is a tall order.

8.7.3 Social Structures and States in Europe and the Muslim World

The ease of and means for beneficial institutional transitions, as the histories of Genoa and Venice illustrate, depend on institutional elements – particularly social structures and the associated beliefs and norms – inherited from the past. In the case of Genoa, kin-based social structures limited the ability to build an effective state. More generally, such structures contributed greatly to the failure of the late medieval European experiment of creating effective states (Tabacco 1989; Waley 1988). In the long run, however, the emergence of effective states in Europe may have been facilitated by the relative weakness of kin-based social structures. Tribes or clans were not central to European political and economic institutions after the late medieval period.

Indeed, even by the late medieval period, Europe had already evolved toward a society with weak kin-based organizations. The tribes that had existed in the medieval period, for example, were no longer effective social structures. This is well reflected in the observation that the dominant response to the absence of an effective state in late medieval Italy was not to resort to a societal organization based on tribal or other innate groups. Instead, Italy established city-states, or communes of individuals unrelated by blood.

This relative decline of a kin-based organization of society began in the medieval period and reflected the actions of the church, an interest-based social structure. For ideological or self-serving reasons, the church, from as early as the fourth century, weakened European kin-based social structures. This was achieved by such policies as prohibiting marriages among kin (sometimes up to the seventh degree), encouraging the donation of one's inheritance to the church, advocating consensual marriages, and condemning practices that enlarged the family, such as polygamy, divorce, and remarriage (Goody 1983).[53] Such policies remained in force for centuries. In 1059, for example, an encyclical required that "if anyone had taken a spouse within the seventh degree, he will be forced canonically by his bishop to send her away; if he refuses, he will be excommunicated" (Goody 1983, p. 135). Many of these policies, such as monogamy, remained characteristics of the European family.

By the late medieval period, kin-based social structures were no longer at the center of European institutional complexes. The rise of alternative, non-kin-based social structures in such forms as communes, guilds, fraternities, and universities is a hallmark of this time, reflecting the already substantial relative decline of kin-based social structures. To achieve various goals and fulfill various functions that were traditionally performed by kin-based social structures (or the state), the Europeans increasingly, and perhaps uniquely, relied on self-governed, interest-based social structures. More broadly, as further elaborated in Chapter 12, the relative absence of both kin-based social structures and an effective state in late medieval Europe led the Europeans to progressively rely on corporations: non-kin-based, self-governed, interest-based social structures.

The rise of these social structures, in turn, further undermined those that were kin-based by offering alternatives. For example, there was less need to rely on an extensive family for a social safety net or protection. Moreover, like the church, other interest-based social structures

---

[53] For an extensive analysis of the relative importance of the extended family in the past and the present in various parts of the world, see Goody (1983); Mitterauer and Sieder (1982); Korotayev (2003); Bittles (1994). For the profitability of these prohibitions to the church, see Goody (1983) and Ekelund et al. (1996). See also Stark (1996) for other means the church employed. In addition, as is well known, the process through which, and policies adopted by the tribes that conquered the Western Roman Empire encouraged social integration.

undermined kin-based structures that threatened them. The Italian city-states, for example, sought with greater success than Genoa to limit the strong noble clans still present from the past (Tabacco 1989; Waley 1988). Because the church had an interest in constituting itself as a corporation, it promoted a legal scholarship to define and sanction the legal status of corporations (Berman 1983).

Historical development similar to Europe's did not seem to have occurred in the Muslim world. Although data are difficult to come by, it seems that large-scale, kin-based social structures remained prominent. Islam, as is well known, created a strong sense of common Muslim identity by advocating the ideal of a community of believers with equal rights, the *umma*. Indeed, by the eighth century, membership in this religious community no longer depended on particular political, ethnic, or tribal affiliations. Kin-based social structures in the form of tribes, clans, and lineages nevertheless remained central in the Muslim world (e.g., Watt 1961; Cahen 1990; Rahman 2002; Rippin 1994; Crone 2004).

Initially the Muslim community, composed mainly of members of Arab tribes, was particularly segregated along tribal lines. Over time, members of other ethnic groups less segregated than the Arabs along tribal lines, accepted Islam, leading to a relative decline in the importance of tribalism in the Muslim Middle East as a whole. Yet large-scale, kin-based social structures, particularly tribes, ethnic groups, clans, and extended families, have remained important institutional elements.

Indeed, the political and military history of the Muslim Middle East reflects the continuous importance of tribes and ethnic groups (e.g. Saunders 1965; M. Hodgson 1974, vol. 1; Kennedy 1986; Lapidus 1989; Greif 2002; Crone 2003, 2004). This outcome reflects this region's historical heritage and the initial weakness of the state. "The tribal tradition [that dominated the Muslim world during its first two centuries] . . . owed its character to the absence of a state . . . kinsmen hung togther so as not to hang separately" (Crone 2004, p. 51).

Ironically, however, tribalism also reflected the strategy that the early caliphs adopted for the purpose of preserving the *umma*. It was initiated by the first caliph, Abu Bakr, who faced revolts known as the Wars of Apostasy following Muhammad's death in 632. Abu Bakr fought the successionists into submission with the support of the Arab tribes that remained loyal to him. In addition, however, he initiated a policy that strengthened tribal affiliation.

Abu Bakr and his successor, the caliph 'Umar I (634–44), began a Muslim military expansion outside the Arabian Peninsula and divided the spoils of war among various members of the *umma*. The perpetual yearly reward for supporting the *umma* was given to individuals, but within their tribal context, meaning that a man was rewarded according to his tribal affiliation. Moreover, a system was set up to retain separation between the conquered non-Arab population and their Arab rulers and among various Arab tribes. The Arabs established garrison towns where they settled, and each neighborhood was inhabited by a particular tribe (AlSayyad 1991). Separation from the local population was fostered by prohibiting Arabs from buying land outside southern Arabia.

The first ruling dynasty of the Muslim empire, the Umayyads, continued this policy but complemented it by treating various ethnic groups within the Muslim world differently. Although conversion to Islam was encouraged by a preferential tax treatment, for example, new converts were institutionally discriminated against. They could not hold positions of power, could not serve in the respectable cavalry, and were treated unequally when the spoils of war were distributed. Even the term used to refer to new, non-Arab converts to Islam reveals the extent to which the *umma* was associated with the Arab ruling elite at this point. A convert was called *mawla* (freed slave, literally "reborn"), a term of pre-Islamic origin that was used in southern Arabia to denote individuals who were latecomers to the tribe, not ascribed members.

This strategy of "divide along social lines, compensate for support, and rule" took advantage of the existing social differentiations within the emerging Islamic Empire to create a militarily strong coalition. It differentially rewarded members of distinct social structures such as ethnic groups, tribes, and clans. At the same time, the strategy also strengthened existing social divisions and hindered social integration of the *umma*. Social differences, even among Arab tribes, remained intact and were expressed in constant internal military conflicts during the Umayyad period (which lasted until 751). Non-Arabs retained their separate social identities, and in some cases this social differentiation was expressed and regenerated through religious division. Non-Arab Muslims, such as the Berbers and Persians, adopted particular versions of Islam that expressed their dissatisfaction with the system and allowed them to find religious justification for their objections.

More generally, the later political history of the Muslim world is characterized by conflicts among groups of distinct ethnic origins, such as Arabs, Persians, Berbers, Turks, and Kurds. Rulers found it difficult to gain support outside their ethnic or tribal groups, as is reflected in their large reliance on slaves (*mamaluks*) bought as children and raised to be soldiers and administrators. "The exclusive personal loyalty of the slave or client-soldier," who was not a member of the existing innate social structures, was "vital to the political supremacy of rulers" in the premodern Muslim world (Lapidus 1989, p. 148).

Marriage patterns are perhaps the best indication of the differences in social structures in the two societies. In general, consanguineous marriages – those among individuals of the same blood – constitute a means for preserving the clans, lineages, and the extended family. These marriages were and still are very common in the Muslim Middle East and North Africa. In this region, the number of marriages contracted between persons who are related as second cousins or closer is the highest in the world. In this generation and in each country in the region such marriages number from 20 to 50 percent of the total (Bittles 1994; this rate is currently less than 1 percent in the West).[54] The practice may have predated Islam, reflecting tribal heritage and the desire to preserve control over family wealth, but it was encouraged by the Muslim inheritance law (M. Hodgson 1974, 2:124). Under it, an individual has relatively little control over the distribution of his assets after his death. In this context, consanguineous marriages enabled keeping the family wealth intact. The Muslim inheritance law also strengthened the extended family in general by mandating that one's assets be divided among many relatives (Schacht 1982 [1964], pp. 169–74).

Innate, kin-based social structures larger than the nuclear family – such as ethnic groups, tribes, and clans – still dominate many countries in the Middle East but the tribal divisions and clan associations that prevailed in Europe in the medieval period disappeared long ago. Given the relationships between social structures and the process of state building, it may not be surprising that political developments in these two societies has been remarkably different.[55]

ANNEX 8.1: A FORMAL MODEL OF GENOA'S POLITICAL INSTITUTION

Consider two clans, C^i and C^j with infinite life-spans and a discount factor of $\delta \in (0, 1)$. Suppose for the moment that the number of privileges

---

[54] English court rolls indicates that in late medieval England cousins were not even likely to interact much with each other. See Razi (1993).

[55] Different sources of political legitimacy also played an important role. See Greif (2002) and Chapter 6.

is $T \in [0, \overline{T}]$ and that they generate total, per period income of I(T). The stage game of this complete information game has two substages. In the first, both clans simultaneously decide whether to cooperate in piracy. Cooperation by both yields the gain of R(T) and total income of $I(T) + R(T)$.[56] At the end of this substage, each clan k gets the share $\lambda^k \in (0, 1)$ of total income. In the next substage, each clan (sequentially) has to decide on a sunk investment in military strength, ψ^k. This investment replaces that which was made in the previous period and which becomes obsolete when the new investment is made. This investment is subject to the clan's budget constraint, $\psi^k \leq \lambda^k[I(T) + R(T)]$. Investment in military strength is observable and is henceforth equated, for simplicity, with recruiting supporters.[57] After investing in military strength, and before the other clan's past military investment amortized, a clan can decide whether to "challenge" the other clan or not.

If neither clan challenges, the period ends, clan $k \in \{i, j\}$ gets a payoff of $\lambda^k[I(T) + R(T)] - \psi^k$, and the stage game is repeated. If either clan challenges, an interclan war transpires. Each clan bears the cost of war, c, and stands to win with probability $s^{k,w}(\psi^k, \psi^{-k})$. The probability of winning is nondecreasing in the clan's own investment and nonincreasing in the opponent's investment.[58] The winning clan becomes a "controlling" clan, gaining all the subsequent per period income from privileges, I(T).[59] The losing clan receives a continuation value of zero.

Following an interclan war, war against an external threat may transpire. To capture the impact of this external threat on interclan equilibrium relationships in a simple manner, I assume that before interclan military conflict the clans' joint military strength and their expectations

---

[56] The analysis is robust – indeed strengthened – if we extend a clan's utility functions to include benefits from social prestige and political control.

[57] For recent works on military deterrence, see Powell (1993); Bates, Greif, and Singh (2002); Grossman and Kim (1995); and Skaperdas (1992).

[58] All functions are assumed to be continuous and differential. For a general discussion and examples of contest success functions, see Skaperdas (1996). The possibility of a tie within a given period can easily be incorporated into the model without changing its insights. Specifically, denote clan k's per period probability of winning as $S^{k,w}(\psi^k, \psi^{-k})$, which is the per period probability that clan k will win, allowing for ties. Define $s^{k,w}(\psi^k, \psi^{-k}) = S^{k,w}/(1 - \delta(1 - S^{k,w})(1 - S^{-k,w}))$. This function captures the probability that clan k will ever win and the implied reduction in the value of winning due to delay. An example for $S^{k,w}(\psi^k, \psi^{-k})$, which implies that $s^{k,w}(\psi^k, \psi^{-k})$ increases in the first argument and decreases in the second, is $S^{k,w}(\psi^k, \psi^{-k}) = f(\psi^k)/(f(\psi^k) + f(\psi^{-k})) - \epsilon$, where ϵ is in the interval $[0,1]$, and $f(\psi^t) = \alpha(\psi^t)^m$, where $\alpha > 0$, $m > 0$, $t = k, -k$.

[59] In equilibrium, clans do not cooperate in piracy following a challenge.

of cooperation against the external threat are such that the impact of the external threat can be ignored. An external threat affects the net expected gains from being a controlling clan, which depend on its military investment, the likelihood of war, and the outcomes of such a war.[60]

Formally, assume that in every period after an interclan war (if one occurs), the controlling clan can invest in military strength after receiving that period's payoff. Following this investment, war against the threat may occur. The probability of such a war depends on the magnitude of the external threat, $\theta \in [0, \bar{x}]$ and the military strength of the controlling clan. Accordingly, we can define $\omega(\psi^k, \theta)$ as the probability of war when ψ^k is invested in military ability and $s(\psi^k, \theta)$ as the ex ante probability that either a war did not occur or that it occurred and the clan won. The probability $\omega(\psi^k, \theta)$ decreases in Ψ^k and increases in θ, whereas $s(\psi^k, \theta)$ increases in ψ^k and decreases in θ. At the limit, as $\theta \to 0$, $s(\cdot) \to 1$ and $\omega(\cdot) \to 0$. War against the threat costs c. If war does not occur or if the controlling clan wins, the game proceeds as before. Defeat implies a zero continuation payoff.

Consider a controlling clan k's time-discounted average expected payoff (henceforth, average payoff), $V^{k,c}(T, \theta)$,[61] which is the value function of

$$(\text{OP}) \text{Max}_{\psi^k}(1 - \delta) \sum_{t=0}^{\infty} \delta^t [s(\Psi^k, \theta)]^t [I(T) - \psi^k - c\omega(\psi^k, \theta)]^{62}$$

subject to the clan's participation constraint, $(1 - \delta)\sum\delta^t s(\cdot)^t[I(T) - \psi^k - c\omega(\cdot)] \geq 0$, and the clan's budget constraint, $I(T) - \psi^k - c\omega(\cdot) \geq 0$.

Because OP involves maximizing a continuous function over a compact set, a solution exists. I assume that the solution is an interior solution. Establishing that $V^{k,c}(T, \theta)$ is increasing in T and decreasing in θ

---

[60] Indeed, a joint Carmadino-Maneciano front was a strong deterrent. As reported in the annals, in 1155 the emperor destroyed the Italian city of Tortona, "so that the [Italian] cities ... [will] pay a large homage to [him]. But the Genoese consuls ... did not want to give or to promise him even the value of one mite and meanwhile fortified all the castles.... As soon as [the emperor] learned that the Genoese had prepared to war with such fierce expedience," he did not attack the city (*Annali* 1155, vol. I, pp. 54–5.) This suggests that the emperor could not have employed a divide-and-conquer strategy in Genoa, as the clans were united in opposing his rule.

[61] For simplicity of presentation, I omit parameters not relevant to this stage of the analysis.

[62] Clans can differ in their military strength and in their investment in it. Hence the function s(). is not necessarily the same for both clans. For ease of presentation, I ignore this issue.

is straightforward and intuitive. A controlling clan's payoff increases in its gross income, namely, its number of privileges, T, and declines in the magnitude of the external threat, θ. Clearly, a clan prefers to control a city with more profitable privileges and face less risk and investment for maintaining this control. Assume that a controlling clan finds it profitable to confront an external threat, that is, $\delta V^{k,c}(T, \theta; \psi^k) > c$. (Henceforth the endogenous variable ψ^k in $V^{k,c}(T, \theta; \psi^k)$ is not explicitly denoted.)

Mutual-Deterrence Equilibrium with a Fixed Number of Privileges

A clan is deterred from challenging its opponent if the other clan's military investment is such that the net expected gain from challenging is less than that from not challenging. In a mutual-deterrence equilibrium, neither clan can gain from reducing its military investment or challenging the other clan.

To consider the necessary and sufficient conditions under which a mutual-deterrence equilibrium can exist, suppose that no challenge has ever occurred, neither clan is expected to challenge, and clan $k \in \{i, j\}$ invests ψ^k in each period. In this case, clan k's average payoff, $V^k(\lambda^k, T; \psi^k)$, equals its net per period income, namely, $\lambda^k[I(T) + R(T)] - \psi^k$. If clan k expects to obtain this payoff each period, it would be deterred from challenging if this payoff is higher than the expected payoff from initiating interclan war.

Formally, clan k will not challenge if and only if the following inequality holds:

$$\delta V^{k,d}(\lambda^k, T; \psi^k) \geq \delta s^{k,w}(\psi^k, \psi^{-k})V^{k,c}(T, \theta; \psi^k) - c(1 - \delta)$$

where $\delta V^{k,d}(\lambda^k, T; \psi^k)$ is the present value of the clan's average payoff under mutual deterrence in the next period and $\delta s^{k,w}(\psi^k, \psi^{-k})V^{k,c}(T, \theta; \psi^k) - c(1 - \delta)$ is its net present value if it becomes a controlling clan in the next period, discounted by the probability that it would win the interclan war $(s^{k,w}(\psi^k, \psi^{-k}))$ minus the (time-discounted average) cost of the war.

We are interested in the situation in which this inequality holds for both clans and neither can gain by reducing its investment in military strength. For this to prevail, condition 8.1 must be satisfied:

Condition 8.1: There exists $(\psi^{i,d}, \psi^{j,d})$ such that for $k \in \{i, j\}$,

A. The investments are feasible: $\psi^{k,d} \leq \lambda^k[I(T) + R(T)]$ and
B. they maximize payoffs: $\psi^{k,d} \in \arg\max V^{k,d}(\lambda^k, T; \psi^k)$ subject to

C. achieving deterrence: $\forall \cdot \psi^{-k} \leq \lambda^{-k}[I(T) + R(T)]$, $\psi^{-k} \geq \psi^{-k,d}$,
$\delta V^{-k,d}(\lambda^{-k}, T; \psi^{-k,d}) \geq \delta s^{-k,w}(\psi^{-k}, \psi^{k,d})V^{-k,c}(T, \theta) - (c + (\psi^{-k} - \psi^{-k,d}))(1 - \delta)$ $[ICC^{-k}]$

If condition 8.1 is satisfied, there is a feasible investment for each clan (A) that is the lowest investment (B) that will deter the other clan from challenging for any possible investment the other clan can make (C). If a (subgame perfect) mutual-deterrence equilibrium (λ^k, T) exists, condition 8.1 must hold. If it holds, this directly implies that such an equilibrium exists.[63] Specifically, if condition 8.1 is satisfied, the following strategy combination is a mutual-deterrence equilibrium (λ^k, T): if a challenge has never occurred, clan $k \in \{i, j\}$ cooperates in piracy and invests $\psi^{k,d}$ in military strength. The clan does not challenge if $\psi^{-k} \geq \psi^{-k,d}$ and challenges otherwise. Neither clan cooperates in piracy following a challenge. If clan k has ever won a challenge, it invests $\psi^{k,c}$ in preparation to confront the external threat.[64]

Efficiency Attributes of Mutual-Deterrence Equilibrium When the Number of Privileges Is Endogenous

Assume that income from privileges, $I(T)$, increases and income from piracy, $R(T)$, decreases in the number of privileges, T. (Specifically, $I'(T) \geq 0$ and $R'(T) \leq 0$.) Assume that the function $I(T) + R(T)$ is strictly concave and has a unique maximum, which is the (economically) efficient number of privileges $\tau \in (0, \overline{T})$, $I'(\tau) + R'(\tau) = 0$. Hence the (economically) efficient mutual-deterrence equilibrium is τ. Clan k's optimal mutual-deterrence equilibrium maximizes its average payoffs, namely, $V^{k,d}(\lambda^k, T; \psi^k)$.

To evaluate if peace was achieved at the cost of commercial expansion, we need to determine whether the *efficient* mutual-deterrence equilibrium

---

[63] Because the forms of the utility and winning functions as well as the order of other parameters are unknown, I do not provide a general existence theorem.

[64] Neither clan cooperates in piracy with the other following a challenge, because it expects that the other would not do so either. This aspect of the mutual-deterrence equilibrium strategy is not essential to the main results. A more complicated analysis, based on a belief-dependent utility function, suggested by Geanakopolos et al. (1989), indicates that a fear of revenge that endogenously emerges would have given the clans an additional motivation to avoid joint piracy if joint piracy provided one clan with a better opportunity to assault the other (a realistic assumption). Indeed, feuds characterized interclan relationships in Genoa after a military confrontation between them.

is also the *optimal* mutual-deterrence equilibrium for each individual clan. In other words, is cooperating to acquire the economically efficient number of privileges (that which maximizes total surplus) the best each clan can do?[65] If the answer is no, we can conclude that, theoretically, the need to sustain political order in Genoa hindered economic efficiency. We can then use the model to identify the source of this inefficiency.

The interesting case is the one in which the efficient number of privileges entails a positive investment in military strength. Formally, a necessary condition for mutual-deterrence equilibrium (λ^k, T) to be characterized by a positive investment in military ability is the following: there exists a feasible investment for one clan that makes it profitable for that clan to challenge if the other does not invest, that is, for $k = i$ or j, $\exists \psi^k \leq \lambda^k[I(T) + R(T)]$ such that $\delta s^{k,w}(\psi^k, 0)V^{k,c}(T, \theta) - (c + \psi^k)(1 - \delta) > \delta V^{k,d}(\lambda^k, T; 0)$. This condition is more likely to hold if the value of θ is lower (since $V^{k,c}$ increases in θ), c is lower, or δ is higher.

Proposition 8.1 establishes that when the efficient mutual deterrence equilibrium is characterized by a positive investment in military ability, it maximizes a clan's gross average payoff but not its net average payoff.[66]

Proposition 8.1

a. Assume that mutual-deterrence equilibrium (λ^k, τ) exists, the clans' equilibrium investment in military strength, $\psi^{k,*}(\tau)$, is strictly positive (without loss of generality), $\partial^2 s(\cdot)/\partial \psi^{k2} < 0$, and $\partial^2 \omega(\cdot)/\partial \psi^{k2} > 0$ for $k = i, j$ (namely, $k = i$ and $k = j$). Then each clan's net average payoff is not maximized at τ.

b. Assume that mutual-deterrence equilibrium (λ^k, T) exists for every T and the implied investment in military strength, $\psi^{k,d}(T)$, is strictly positive for $k = i, j$ (without loss of generality). Then if

---

[65] The question and analysis assumes that acquiring more privileges entails a transition from one mutual-deterrence equilibrium to another. It ignores possible hindrances to efficiency from the difficulties of such a transition.

[66] The result also holds qualitatively when $\psi^{k,*}(\lambda^k, \tau)$ is strictly positive to only one clan and there is no piracy. When piracy does not take place, the marginal political cost is positive for any mutual-deterrence equilibrium (T) with a positive investment in military strength if and only if $(1 - \delta)/(1 - \delta s(\cdot)) > \lambda^k$. In other words, for any δ and λ^k, if $s(\cdot)$ (i.e., the probability of survival as a controlling clan is sufficiently close to one), the result holds. The marginal political cost is positive, since a high $s(\cdot)$ implies that the gains from taking control increase by more than the expected loss from a failed challenge.

a clan's optimal number of privileges is not zero, its net average payoff is maximized in a mutual deterrence equilibrium (λ^k, T*) such that T* < τ and $\lambda^k \, \partial I(T^*)/\partial T = \partial \psi^{-k,d}(T^*)/\partial T - \lambda^k \partial R(T^*)/\partial T$.

Proof: At a mutual deterrence equilibrium (λ^k, T), clan k's optimal investment is such that the incentive constraint in condition 8.1, ICC^{-k}, is binding at the largest feasible investment for clan $-$k, that is, $\lambda^{-k}[I(T) + R(T)]$. This locally binding constraint implicitly defines ψ^{-k} as a function of T, that is, $\psi^{-k,d}(T)$. The most profitable mutual-deterrence equilibrium (T) for clan k is the one that maximizes its per period income in a mutual deterrence equilibrium, that is, $H(T) = \lambda^k[I(T)) + R(T)] - \psi^{k,d}(T)$. The first-order condition for maximization is

$$\lambda^k \left[\frac{\partial I(T)}{\partial T} + \frac{\partial R(T)}{\partial T} \right] - \frac{\partial \psi^{k,d}(T)}{\partial T} \geq 0.$$

Evaluated at $T = \tau$, this first-order condition holds if and only if $\frac{\partial \psi^{k,d}(\tau)}{\partial T} \leq 0$. The equilibrium investment in military strength, $\psi^{k,*}(\tau)$, increases in T if $\partial V^{-k,c}/\partial T > \partial V^{-k,d}/\partial T$. By the envelope theorem,

$$\frac{\partial V^{-k,c}}{\partial T} = \frac{(1 - \delta)}{(1 - \delta s(\cdot))} \frac{\partial I(T)}{\partial T}.$$

Similarly,

$$\frac{\partial V^{-k,d}}{\partial T} = \lambda^{-k} \left[\frac{\partial I(T)}{\partial T} + \frac{\partial R(T)}{\partial T} \right].$$

Hence $\partial V^{-k,c}/\partial T > \partial V^{-k,d}/\partial T$ if and only if

$$\frac{(1 - \delta)}{(1 - \delta s(\cdot))} \frac{\partial I(T)}{\partial T} > \lambda^{-k} \left[\frac{\partial I(T)}{\partial T} + \frac{\partial R(T)}{\partial T} \right].$$

Evaluated at $T = \tau$, the right-hand side of the inequality equals zero, and the left-hand side is strictly positive. Hence the equilibrium investment in military strength increases at $T = \tau$, that is, $\partial \psi^{k,d}(\tau)/\partial T > 0$, implying that the clans' expected utility is not maximized with the efficient number of privileges.

As for the second claim, clan k's expected utility is maximized in a mutual-deterrence equilibrium in which

$$\lambda^k \frac{\partial I(T)}{\partial T} = \left[\frac{\partial \psi^{k,d}(T)}{\partial T} - \lambda^k \frac{\partial R(T)}{\partial T} \right],$$

which is the required condition.   Q.E.D.

This proposition implies that an inefficient mutual-deterrence equilibrium is more likely to exist if the external threat is weaker. Specifically, the expected value of being a controlling clan increases as the external threat weakens, implying a larger parameter set for which the efficient mutual-deterrence equilibrium is characterized by a positive investment in military strength, equivalent to having a positive number of supporters (recall that investing in military strength is equated with recruiting supporters).

Formally, at the limit, when $\theta \to 0$ (and hence $s(\cdot) \to 1$ and $\omega(\cdot) \to 0$ for $\psi^k = 0$), $c(1 - \delta) \to 0$, and $R(T) \to 0$ the equilibrium number of supporters must be positive if for $k = i$ or j, $\exists\, \psi^k \le \lambda^k[I(T) + R(T)]$ such that $s^{k,w}(\psi^k, 0) > \lambda^k$, that is, there is a feasible number of supporters that makes clan k's probability of winning, $s^{k,w}(\cdot)$, larger than its share of the gains, λ^k, when the other clan has no supporters.

Proposition 8.2: Suppose that for $\forall\, T \in [0, \tau]$, a mutual-deterrence equilibrium (λ^k, T) with a positive equilibrium investment in military strength exists. For both clans, the number of optimal privileges, $T^*(\theta)$, is nondecreasing in θ.

Proof: Any reduction in $V^{k,c}(\cdot)$ relaxes the mutual-deterrence constraints and makes more privileges optimal for both clans. Since θ directly affects only $V^{k,c}(\cdot)$, to prove the proposition, it is sufficient to show that a controlling clan's expected utility decreases in θ. A controlling clan's expected utility is the value function of problem OP above defined earlier. To see that it is decreasing in θ, define $g(\cdot) = I(T) - \psi - c\omega(\cdot)\ (> 0)$ and recall that $\partial s(\cdot)/\partial\theta < 0$ and $\partial\omega(\cdot)/\partial\theta > 0$. These relations and the envelope theorem imply that

$$\frac{\partial V^{k,c}}{\partial\theta} = \frac{(1 - \delta)\delta}{(1 - \delta S(\cdot))^2} \frac{\partial s(\cdot)}{\partial\theta} g(\cdot) - \frac{(1 - \delta)}{(1 - \delta s(\cdot))} \frac{\partial\omega}{\partial\theta} c < 0. \quad \text{Q.E.D.}$$

ANNEX 8.2: EXISTENCE OF A MUTUAL-DETERRENCE EQUILIBRIUM

What are the conditions under which a mutual-deterrence equilibrium does not exist? Condition 8.1 implies that such an equilibrium (λ^k, T) does not exist if one clan finds it profitable to challenge when the other clan invests all its resources in enhancing its military strength. That is, if for k = i or j, $\exists \psi^k \leq \lambda^k[I(T) + R(T)]$ such that for $\psi^{-k} = \lambda^{-k}[I(T) + R(T)]$, $\delta V^{k,d}(\lambda^k, T, \psi^{k,d}) < \delta s^{k,w}(\psi^k, \psi^{-k})V^{k,c}(T, \theta) - (c + (\psi^k - \psi^{k,d}))(1 - \delta)$.

The left-hand side of this inequality equals $\delta\{\lambda^k[I(T) + R(T)] - \psi^{k,d}\}$ and thus decreases with R(T), while the right-hand side increases with θ, since $\partial V^{k,c}/\partial\theta < 0$ (as established in the proof to proposition 8.2). Hence as R(T) and θ decrease, this condition is more likely to be satisfied.

At the limit, as $R(T) \to 0$, $\theta \to 0$ (implying that $s(\cdot) \to 1$ and $\omega(\cdot) \to 0$) and $\delta \to 1$, a mutual-deterrence equilibrium (λ^k, T) does not exist if and only if for k = i or j, $\lambda^k < s^{k,w}(\cdot)$ for some feasible ψ^k and all feasible ψ^{-k}. That is, a mutual-deterrence equilibrium (λ^k, T) for the allocation λ^k does not exist if one clan has enough supporters so that its probability of winning a challenge is higher than its share in the income.

ANNEX 8.3: THE COLLUSION AND *PODESTERIA* GAMES

The Collusion Game

To what extent can a clan commit ex ante to reward ex post a *podestà* who provides it with military assistance? Denote by $v_i(m_j, m_k; m_i)$ the probability that player i (a clan or the *podestà*) will win a war against j and k, given respective military strengths of m_j, m_k, and m_i. The probability of i winning is declining in m_j and m_k and increasing in m_i. (For ease of presentation, I omit the parameter m_i in the following equations.) If a player participates in a military confrontation, he has to bear a cost, c. V_i is the net present value to player i of controlling Genoa. Assume that local clans gain more than a *podestà* does from controlling the city, that is, $V_i > V_p$ if player i is a clan.[67]

---

[67] This assumption, as well as the one that the cost of war is the same for all players, is not essential to the result but simplifies the presentation. For simplicity, I ignore the clans' ability to invest resources in military strength, since this ability does not qualitatively alter the results.

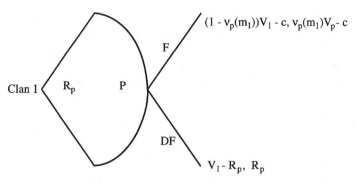

Figure 8.2. The collusion game

Consider what happens after a clan (say clan 1) and a *podestà* collude against the other clan and gain control over the city (Figure 8.2). The controlling clan has to decide what reward, $R_p > 0$, to give the *podestà*. Once this reward is announced, the *podestà* can either accept it or reject it and fight the clan for control of the city. If he accepts, the payoffs are $V_1 - R_p$ to the clan and R_p to the *podestà*. If he rejects it and fights, the expected payoff to each is the probability of winning times the value of gaining control minus the cost of war, namely, $(1 - v_p(m_1))V_1 - c$ and $v_p(m_1)V_p - c$.

The clan will not find it profitable to offer an R_p higher than the one required to make it indifferent between fighting or not, that is, $V_1 - R_p \geq (1 - v_p(m_1))V_1 - c$. Hence it will offer $R_p \leq v_p(m_1)V_1 + c$. If the *podestà* receives a payment as great as the net expected value of fighting against a clan, namely, $R_p \geq v_p(m_1)V_p - c$, he will find it optimal not to fight. Thus in any subgame perfect equilibrium, the clan will not offer more than the amount required to make the *podestà* indifferent between fighting or not, namely, $R_p = v_p(m_1)V_p - c$. This implies that the only subgame perfect equilibrium is the one in which the clan offers $R_p = v_p(m_1)V_p - c$, while the *podestà*'s strategy is to fight if paid less than that amount and not to fight if paid at least that amount. The payoffs associated with this equilibrium are $V_1 - V_p^c$ to the clan and V_p^c to the *podestà*, where $V_p^c = \text{Max}\{0, v_p(m_1)V_p - c\}$.

The analysis implies that after collusion occurs, the *podestà*'s reward depends on his military ability.[68] Specifically, in any equilibrium, the

---

[68] A similar commitment problem prevails in the relationship between clans and their supporters. In that case, their ongoing relations could help mitigate such a problem, something that is not feasible with an outsider.

podestà will not receive more than the net present value of militarily confronting the clan. Thus ex ante – before collusion occurs – a clan cannot credibly commit to ex post reward the *podestà* more than this amount. When $v_p(m_1)V_p - c \leq 0$, for example, the clan cannot make any credible promise to reward the *podestà*. The weaker the *podestà*, the weaker the ability of the clan to make its ex ante promise of a reward credible.[69]

The Podesteria *Game*

Limiting the *podestà*'s military ability (relative to that of a clan) implies that his military might, in and of itself, becomes less effective in deterring one clan from challenging the other. To see how a clan still can be deterred from challenging, consider two other problems: motivating the *podestà* to help a clan that stands to lose in an interclan confrontation and motivating a clan to fight alongside the *podestà*.

Let I_i be the per period income for clan i if no interclan military confrontation takes place, W the *podestà*'s wage, and δ the time discount factor.[70] The *podesteria* game reveals how the interclan game can be altered by introducing a *podestà*, despite the need to limit his military strength (Figure 8.3).

This repeated game begins, without loss of generality, with clan 1 having to decide whether to challenge clan 2. If clan 1 challenges, clan 2 must choose between fighting and not fighting. In either case the *podestà* can respond by preventing clan 1 from taking control (an action denoted by p), by not preventing clan 1 (dp), or by colluding with clan 1 (co). If the *podestà* colludes with clan 1, I assume, for ease of exposition, that clan 2 cannot gain control over the city and that the *podestà* and clan 1 are playing the collusion game (Figure 8.2). Because the collusion game has a unique subgame perfect equilibrium, Figure 8.3 presents only the payoffs associated with this equilibrium.

The payoffs to this game are as follows:

• If clan 1 does not challenge, the payoffs are (I_1, I_2, W) to clan 1, clan 2, and the *podestà* respectively, and the same game is played in the next

---

[69] Introducing asymmetric information can strengthen this result. Suppose that there is asymmetric information between the *podestà* and the clan regarding the clan's military strength. In this case, a generous offer to the *podestà* will be made by a militarily strong clan, which will not have to compensate the *podestà* ex post. Hence the *podestà* is further deterred from colluding.

[70] It is implicitly assumed that the *podestà*'s reservation utility after assuming office is zero.

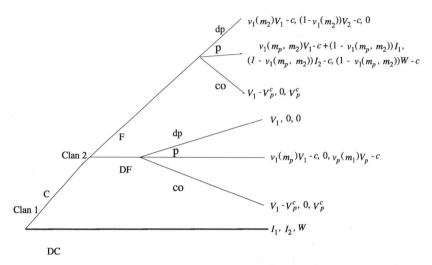

Figure 8.3. The *podesteria* game

period. If clan 1 challenges and clan 2 does not fight, clan 1 becomes the controlling clan. The associated payoffs are as follows: If the *podestà* does not prevent, the payoffs are $(V_1, 0, 0)$. If the *podestà* colludes, clan 1 rewards him with V_p^c (namely, the *podestà*'s payoff in the equilibrium of the collusion game). The payoffs are $(V_1 - V_p^c, 0, V_p^c)$. If the *podestà* attempts to prevent clan 1 from taking over, his payoff equals the net expected value of an attempt to gain control. The payoffs are $(\nu_1(m_p)V_1 - c, 0, \nu_p(m_1)V_p - c)$.

- If clan 1 challenges and clan 2 fights, the associated payoffs are as follows: if the *podestà* does not prevent the fight, each clan's payoff equals the net expected value of being a controlling clan, while the *podestà* gets zero, that is, $(\nu_1(m_2)V_1 - c, (1 - \nu_1(m_2))V_2 - c, 0)$.[71] If the *podestà* colludes, as before, clan 1 assumes control. The payoffs are $(V_1 - V_p^c, 0, V_p^c)$.

- If the *podestà* prevents the fight, clan 1 will either gain control and get V_1, or fail to gain control and get only its share in that period's income, I_1. If clan 1 fails to gain control, clan 2 gets its share of that period's income, I_2, while the *podestà* gets his wage, W. The payoffs are thus $(\nu_1(m_p, m_2)V_1 - c + (1 - \nu_1(m_p, m_2))I_1, (1 - \nu_1(m_p, m_2))I_2 - c, (1 - \nu_1(m_p, m_2))W - c)$.

---

[71] The analysis holds if a *podestà* who did not prevent an interclan confrontation could challenge the clan that won it.

266

Consider the following strategy combination: clan 1 does not challenge, clan 2 fights if it is challenged, and the *podestà* prevents the fight if and only if clan 1 challenges and 2 fights. If clan 1 challenges but clan 2 does not fight, the *podestà* colludes if $V_p^c > 0$, and does not otherwise. This strategy combination is a subgame perfect equilibrium if the following conditions hold:

a. $(1 - v_1(m_p, m_2))W - c \geq V_p^c$. The *podestà* prevents and does not collude if clan 2 fights.

b. $(1 - v_1(m_p, m_2))I_2/(1 - \delta) \geq c$. Clan 2 fights if challenged.

c. $c + \frac{\delta I_1}{1-\delta} \geq v_1(m_p, m_2)(V_1 - I_1)$. Clan 1 does not challenge.

Intuitively, condition (a) implies that the *podestà* is better off preventing if clan 2 fights and that he colludes otherwise. Condition (b) guarantees that clan 2 fights. Because the *podestà* does not prevent unless 2 fights, and because condition (b) implies that 2 prefers to fight rather than not fight if the *podestà* prevents, fighting if challenged represents clan 2's best response. Condition (c) then implies that clan 1, expecting clan 2 and the *podestà* to fight together, finds it optimal not to challenge.

These conditions and the equilibrium strategy indicate how the *podesteria* system can provide the appropriate incentives to overcome the problems that could render it ineffective. Condition (a) and clan 2's strategy prevent collusion between clan 1 and the *podestà* by sufficiently reducing the *podestà*'s military strength relative to his wage, so that the most clan 1 can credibly commit to reward the *podestà* following collusion is not enough to induce him to collude. The *podestà*, expecting clan 2 to fight with him, prefers to prevent clan 1 from challenging rather than colluding. Clan 2 is motivated to fight alongside the *podestà* because if he does not (the *podestà*'s strategy implies), the *podestà* will not confront clan 1. At the same time, condition (b) implies that the combined forces of clan 2 and the *podestà*, relative to clan 2's share in the gain (I_2), are such that it is optimal for clan 2 to fight with the *podestà*.

A delicate balance of power must thus be maintained for the *podesteria* to promote political order. On the one hand, the *podestà* cannot be strong enough militarily to gain control himself or collude with clan 1. (Both sides of condition (a) decline in m_p, but the right-hand side increases in W.) On the other hand, he must be strong enough so that his threat to fight alongside clan 2 if necessary eliminates clan 1's incentive to challenge. (The left-hand side of condition (b) increases in m_p.) This balance provides the *podestà* with an important incentive that is not explicitly captured in the model. The more equal the clans are in military strength, the more likely the equilibrium is to hold, and the *podestà* is more likely to gain W without being involved in a war. The *podestà* is thus motivated to prevent fighting, but not at the cost of severely weakening either clan. The *podestà* can therefore credibly commit to maintain the relative strength of each clan.

9

On the Origin of Distinct
Institutional Trajectories

Cultural Beliefs and the Organization of Society

Societal organization – complexes of economic, legal, political, social, and moral institutions – is highly correlated with per capita income in contemporary societies: most developing countries are "collectivist," whereas the developed West is "individualist."[1] In collectivist societies the social structure is "segregated," in the sense that each individual interacts socially and economically mainly with members of a particular religious, ethnic, or familial group. Within these groups, contract enforcement is achieved through informal economic and social institutions. Little cooperation exists between members of different groups, but members of collectivist societies feel involved in the lives of other members of their group.

In individualistic societies, the social structure is "integrated," in the sense that economic transactions are conducted among people from different groups, and individuals frequently shift from one group to another. Contract enforcement is achieved mainly through specialized organizations, such as courts. Self-reliance is highly valued.

Sociologists and anthropologists believe that the organization of society reflects its culture, an important component of which is cultural beliefs. Cultural beliefs are the shared ideas and thoughts that govern interactions among individuals and between them, their gods, and other groups. Cultural beliefs differ from knowledge in that they are not empirically discovered or analytically proved. Cultural beliefs become identical and

---

[1] All societies have both individualistic and collectivist elements; categorizing societies in this way is based on the relative importance of each. See Bellah et al. (1985); Reynolds and Norman (1988); and Triandis (1990), who also document the evidence regarding the correlation between societal organization and per capita income.

commonly known through the socialization process, by which culture is unified, maintained, and communicated.[2]

That cultural beliefs influence outcomes is intuitive, but formal examination of the relations between cultural beliefs and societal organization is subtle. If cultural beliefs are defined arbitrarily, a variety of phenomena can be generated. How should cultural beliefs be restricted? What are the sources of cultural beliefs? Should cultural beliefs be considered rational? Do cultural beliefs influence the trajectory of institutional change?

The perspective developed in the previous chapters suggests the merit of using game-theoretic equilibrium analysis to restrict analytically the set of admissible cultural beliefs. Furthermore, we can study the impact of cultural heritage on institutional development by examining how particular cultural features exert coordination, inclusion, and refinement effects. The historical and game-theoretic analysis in this chapter supports this claim. It presents a historical and game-theoretical analysis of the relations between culture and societal organization by examining the cultural factors that have influenced the evolution of two premodern societies along distinct trajectories of societal organization. The analysis particularly indicates the importance of cultural beliefs in influencing selection among alternative institutions, in becoming an integral part of the resulting institutions, and in directing subsequent organizational and institutional development. Culture is an important factor for determining societal organizations, influencing institutional development, and rendering intersocietal institutional borrowing challenging. At the same time, the behavior institutions generate reproduces the culture that led to these institutions to begin with.

The game-theoretic framework is useful in restricting the admissible set of cultural beliefs that capture individuals' expectations with respect to actions others will take in various contingencies. Because cultural beliefs are identical and commonly known, when each player plays his best response to these cultural beliefs, the set of permissible cultural beliefs is restricted to those that are self-enforcing. This subset of cultural beliefs can be formalized as a set of probability distributions over an equilibrium strategy combination. Each probability distribution reflects the expectation of a player with respect to the actions that will be taken on and

---

[2] On cultural beliefs in general, see, for example, K. Davis (1949, in particular pp. 52ff., 192ff.) and Bandura (1971). On their importance in influencing institutional change, see Greif (1994a) and Nee and Ingram (1998).

off the path of play. In this regard, cultural beliefs do not differ from institutionalized beliefs in general (Chapter 5).

Although equilibrium analysis is used to restrict admissible cultural beliefs in a particular game, the analysis of their dynamic implications recognizes that they are attributes of individuals, not games or institutions. Due to the fundamental asymmetry between beliefs inherited from the past and technologically feasible alternatives, cultural beliefs inherited from the past affect decisions in subsequent strategic situations. Past cultural beliefs provide focal points and coordinate expectations, thereby influencing equilibrium selection and the new institutions of which they become an integral part.

Furthermore, distinct cultural belief induce different trajectories of endogenous institutional change. Individuals attempt to improve their lot by reinforcing and refining institutions, particularly by establishing new organizations. These organizations, as was already discussed, alter the relevant rules of the game by, for example, introducing a new player (the organization itself), changing the information available to players, or changing the payoffs associated with particular actions. The introduction of a new organization reflects an increase in the stock of knowledge, which may be the outcome of an intentional pursuit or unintentional experimentation.

A necessary condition for an intentional organizational change is that those able to initiate it expect to gain from it. Because their expectations depend on their cultural beliefs, different cultural beliefs lead to distinct trajectories of organizational development. The subsequent process of modifying and refining the new institutions further contributes to the distinctiveness of each trajectory. Once a specific organization is introduced, it influences the rules of subsequent games, leading to diverse paths of organizational and institutional development and hence to different societal organizations.

Diverse cultural beliefs can also lead to differential economic behavior toward individuals with various social characteristics, such as wealth or membership in a specific social group. For example, different cultural beliefs can imply different social patterns of economic interactions, each of which entails different dynamics of wealth distribution. Different cultural beliefs can also imply different relations between efficiency and profitability in intrasociety and intersociety economic interactions. Some cultural beliefs can render efficient intersociety relations unprofitable, leading to an economically inefficient social structure.

Various social patterns of economic interactions further affect societal organization by leading to distinct institutions based on social and moral propensities (see section 5.3). Frequent economic interactions between the same individuals entail social networks and relationships that facilitate informal collective economic and social punishments for deviant behavior. Social and economic patterns of interactions also affect intrinsic motivation (motivation based on the utility derived from acting according to internalized norms). Intrinsic motivation seems to be universal, but different patterns of social and economic interactions lead to the development of distinctive normative systems; over time, individuals consider the behavior they follow to be the behavior they ought to follow. Different internalized norms, in turn, reinforce distinct behavior.

Chapter 8 has already lent support to the conjecture that cultural beliefs, norms, and organizations inherited from the past influence trajectories of institutional development. It exposed the interrelationships between Genoa's political institutions and its initial social structures and cultural beliefs. This chapter further substantiates this conjecture by presenting a comparative analysis of the relations between culture and societal organizations. It examines the cultural factors that led two premodern societies – the eleventh-century Maghribi traders from the Muslim world and the twelfth-century Genoese traders from the European (Latin) world – to evolve along distinct trajectories of societal organization. The chapter models the agent-merchant transaction (Chapter 3) in order to examine the relations between culture and societal organization in the related multiple-equilibria game. It then demonstrates that differences in the institutions of the two societies and their dynamics can be consistently accounted for as reflecting diverse cultural beliefs and their dynamic implications. Past cultural beliefs regarding off-the-equilibrium-path behavior influenced institutional selection, became an integral part of the resulting institutions, affected various economic and social outcomes, influenced the dynamic of institutional change, and led to distinct organizational and contractual innovations. In this analysis, features that are usually invoked to explain distinct observed outcomes (social groups, social patterns of economic employment, the distribution of wealth, the availability of courts) are accounted for endogenously, as reflecting distinct underlying cultural beliefs.

The analysis further supports the thesis advanced in Chapter 7 that beliefs and the associated organizations (social structures) inherited from the past constitute initial conditions in processes leading to new institutions; exert environmental, coordination, and inclusion effects;

become elements in the new institutions; and direct processes of institutional refinement, innovation, and adoption. Societies advance along distinct institutional trajectories; they can fail to adopt the organization of more economically successful ones because the fundamental asymmetry between institutional elements inherited from the past and technologically feasible alternatives implies that the past, encapsulated in institutional elements, directs institutional dynamics.

Interestingly, the analysis reveals that the societal organization of traders from the Muslim world resembles modern collectivist societies, whereas that of the traders from the Latin world resembles contemporary individualistic societies. These findings suggest the theoretical and historical importance of culture in determining societal organizations, in leading to institutional path dependence, and in forestalling successful intersociety adoption of institutions.

Section 9.1 begins the analysis, providing relevant information on agency relationships among the Genoese and using the analytical framework developed in Chapter 3 to explore distinct possible institutions. Section 9.2 discusses the origin and manifestations of diverse cultural beliefs in the two societies and shows how they relate to different institutions; it argues that diverse beliefs led to distinct institutions in the two groups. Section 9.3 comparatively explores the relationships among cultural beliefs, social patterns of agency relations, and wealth distribution in the two societies. Sections 9.4 and 9.5 present the institutional, organizational, and contractual dynamics that each of the institutions and their cultural beliefs entailed.

9.1 AGENCY RELATIONS AND CULTURAL BELIEFS

Overseas trade was central to Genoa's economy, as the maxim *genuensis ergo mercator* (Genoese, therefore merchant) suggests. In this sense, Genoese society was similar to that of the eleventh-century Maghribi traders. The Genoese and Maghribis operated in the same areas, had similar naval technology, and traded similar goods.

Like their Maghribi counterparts, Genoese merchants had much to gain from employing overseas agents. Doing so required supporting institutions, because agents can embezzle merchants' capital abroad. Without such institutions, merchants, anticipating opportunistic behavior, will not operate through agents, and mutually beneficial exchanges in agency service cannot be carried out. To surmount this commitment problem, an institution is needed through which an agent can commit himself ex ante, before receiving the merchant's capital, to be honest ex post, after receiving the merchant's goods.

Historical records indicate that the Genoese had institutions that enabled agents to commit themselves ex ante to be honest ex post. The Genoese employed agents extensively and established agency relationships outside the family. The first Genoese historical source reflecting agency relations, the cartulary of Giovanni Scriba (1154–64), contains 612 trade-related contracts. These documents reveal that only about 5 percent of total trade investment did not entail agency relations and only about 6 percent of the funds sent abroad through agents was entrusted to family members.[3]

Cartularies and the contracts they contain may overstate the extent of trade conducted through agency relationships and understate agency relationships outside the family. Other, unbiased sources are needed to confirm what they reveal. Fortunately, we have such a source. A document from 1174 lists all the Genoese traders in Constantinople in 1162, the value of the goods each brought to trade, and the owner of the capital. It indicates that merchants invested about 76 percent of their capital through overseas agents and that only about 30 percent of all capital sent by merchants was handled by agents who were family members.[4]

To compare the institutions that prevailed among the Maghribis and the Genoese, I build on the model presented in Chapter 3. This model considers an economy in which there are M merchants and A agents, where $M < A$, and all merchants and agents live an infinite number of periods. Agents have a time discount factor δ, and an unemployed agent receives a per period reservation utility of $\bar{w} \geq 0$. In each period, an agent can be hired by only one merchant, and a merchant can employ only one agent. Matching is random, but a merchant can restrict the matching to a subset of the unemployed agents containing agents who, according to the

---

[3] Later cartularies (e.g., Obertus Scriba 1186, 1190; Giovanni di Guiberto 1200–11; Lanfranco Scriba 1203) show that at the end of the twelfth century, about 16 percent of agency relations involved family members. Two individuals are considered to be family members if the contract mentions that they are relatives, if they have the same surname (unless the surname indicates a place of birth or occupation), or if there is any evidence (such as a marriage contract) indicating they were relatives. I have traced the genealogy of all the families mentioned in the cartulary of Giovanni Scriba based on Belgrano (1873) and all available twelfth-century cartularies.

[4] For a Latin transcription of this list, see Bertolotto (1896, pp. 389–97).

information available to the merchant, have previously taken particular sequences of actions.[5]

A merchant who does not hire an agent receives a payoff of $\kappa > 0$. The gross gain from cooperation is γ. A merchant who hires an agent decides what wage ($W \geq 0$) to offer the agent. An employed agent can decide whether to be honest or to cheat. If he is honest, the merchant's payoff is $\gamma - W$, and the agent's payoff is W. If the agent cheats, his payoff is $\alpha > 0$ and the merchant's payoff is $\gamma - \alpha$. It is assumed that $\gamma > \kappa + \bar{w}$ (cooperation is efficient); $\gamma > \alpha > \bar{w}$ (cheating entails a loss, and an agent prefers cheating over receiving his reservation utility); and $\kappa > \gamma - \alpha$ (a merchant prefers not to hire an agent and receive κ over being cheated). After the allocation of the payoffs, each merchant can decide whether to terminate his relations with his agent. There is a probability τ, however, that a merchant is forced to terminate agency relations due to exogenous factors such as wars.

Suppose that the history of the game is common knowledge. What is the minimum (symmetric) wage offered by all merchants for which an agent's best response is to be honest, given that he will be fired if he cheats and rehired if he is honest (unless forced separation occurs)? Determining this wage requires fully specifying the merchants' strategies. To analyze the impact of different strategies in the same framework, however, the analysis initially focuses on probabilities that are a function of the strategies themselves.

Denote an unemployed agent who was honest in the last period he was employed as an *honest agent*, and let h_h be the probability that he will be hired in the current period. Denote as an unemployed agent who ever cheated in the past as a *cheater*, and let h_c be the probability that he will be hired in the current period. Proposition 9.1 specifies the minimum wage that supports honesty.

Proposition 9.1: Assume that $\delta \in (0, 1)$ and $h_c < 1$. The *optimal wage*, the lowest wage for which an agent's best response is to play honest, is $W^* = w(\delta, h_h, h_c, \tau, \bar{w}, \alpha) > \bar{w}$, and w is monotonically decreasing in δ and h_h and monotonically increasing in h_c, τ, $\bar{w}$, and α. (This proposition is identical to proposition 3.1 and for the proof, see annex 3.1 in Chapter 3.)

---

[5] What follows assumes that the probability of rematching with the same agent equals zero for all practical purposes.

A merchant induces honesty by offering the carrot of a wage higher than the agent's reservation utility and the stick of terminating their relations. For a high enough wage, the difference between the present value of the lifetime expected utility of an unemployed and an employed agent is higher than what an agent can gain from cheating in one period. Hence the agent's best response is to be honest. The minimum wage that ensures honesty decreases in factors that increase the lifetime expected utility of an honest agent relative to that of a cheater (δ and h_h) and increases in factors that increase the relative lifetime expected utility of a cheater (h_c, τ, $\bar{w}$, α).

How can differences between collectivist and individualistic societies manifest themselves in agency relations? Intuitively, in a collectivist society everyone is expected to respond to whatever transpires between any merchant and agent;[6] in an individualistic society this may well not be the case. Two strategy combinations formalize this difference: the individualistic and the collectivist (multilateral) strategies. In each strategy a merchant hires, for a wage W^*, an unemployed agent, whom he rehires as long as cheating or forced separation does not occur. Under the individualistic strategy, a merchant randomly hires an unemployed agent. Under the collectivist strategy, a merchant never employs a cheater and randomly hires only from among the unemployed agents who have never cheated. An agent's strategy is to be honest if and only if he is offered at least W^*. Each of these strategies is a subgame perfect equilibrium, as established in proposition 9.2.

Proposition 9.2: Assume that under both the individualistic and the collectivist strategy combinations $\gamma - \kappa \geq W^*$ (although note that W^* is lower under the collectivist strategy). Then each strategy combination is a subgame perfect equilibrium of the one-sided prisoner's dilemma game. (The proof appears in annex 9.1.)

The individualistic strategy is a subgame perfect equilibrium, because merchants are not expected to take into account the agent's past behavior when making hiring decisions. Hence each merchant perceives the probability that an unemployed agent who cheated in the past will be hired to be equal to the probability that an unemployed honest agent will be hired. By proposition 9.1 this implies that each merchant is indifferent between hiring a cheater and hiring an honest agent. (As discussed later, when the decision to acquire information is endogenous, in an individualistic equilibrium the merchant would not have the related information.)

---

[6] Timur Kuran has suggested that it may better to refer to such beliefs as *communalist*.

Under a collectivist equilibrium, because each merchant expects others not to employ a cheater, the perceived probability of being hired is lower for a cheater than for an honest agent. By proposition 9.1, this implies that a higher wage is required to keep a cheater honest. The merchant thus strictly prefers hiring an honest agent. The merchant's expectations are self-enforcing: although cheating conveys no information about future behavior, the agent's strategy does not call for cheating any merchant who violates the collective punishment, and merchants do not "punish" any merchant who hires a cheater.

This analysis so far assumed that the history of the game is common knowledge. In fact, acquiring and transmitting information during the late medieval period was costly. The model should thus incorporate a merchant's decisions to acquire information. Merchants gathered information by belonging to informal information-sharing networks. Suppose, therefore, that a merchant can either "invest" or "not invest" in "getting attached" to a network before the game begins and that his action is common knowledge. Investing requires paying Δ each period, in return for which the merchant learns the private histories of all the merchants who also invested. If he does not pay Δ each period, he knows only his own history. Intuitively, under the individualistic equilibrium, history has no value, since an agent's wage does not depend on it. Hence no merchant will invest in information. In contrast, under the collectivist equilibrium, history has value, because the optimal wage is a function of an agent's history. Merchants will invest, because an agent who cheated in the past will cheat if hired and paid the equilibrium wage. Although on the equilibrium path cheating never occurs, merchants are motivated to invest, because this action is common knowledge and a merchant who does not invest is cheated if he pays W^*. This intuition is verified in proposition 9.3.

Proposition 9.3: W^*_{-i} is the minimum wage that merchant i has to pay his agent if only he does not invest. W^*_c is the equilibrium wage under the collectivist strategy in the full information game. If the merchant invests, the collectivist strategy is an equilibrium if and only if $W^*_{-i} - W^*_c \geq \Delta$. Not Invest and the individualist strategy is an equilibrium, whereas Invest and the individualist strategy is not an equilibrium. (The proof is by inspection.)

In the real world, information is often incomplete. Some agents may have an unobservable "bad" attribute and thus be more likely to cheat. The analysis here holds when the proportion of bad types is high or low.

Under a collectivist equilibrium, incomplete information reinforces investment in information. Under an individualistic equilibrium, the value of information may still be zero (if the proportion of bad types is high), or it may be insufficient to induce investment in information (if the proportion of bad types is low). In the intermediate case, demand for information would be lower in the individualistic society than in the collectivist society. This analysis thus relies on the complete information model, which highlights the role of expectations with respect to actions and ignores the potentially important expectations with respect to types.

The preceding analysis relates two institutions and different cultural beliefs – that is, different expectations with respect to actions that will be taken off the path of play. In an individualistic equilibrium, players are expected to be indifferent; in a collectivist equilibrium, players are expected to respond to whatever transpires between others. Because these cultural beliefs correspond to an equilibrium, they are self-enforcing, and each entails a different wage, enforcement institution (second-party versus third-party enforcement), and investment in information.

On the equilibrium path, individualistic and collectivist cultural beliefs entail the same actions with respect to agents: merchants randomly hire unemployed agents, and agents never cheat. Assuming perfect monitoring allows us to concentrate on cultural beliefs concerning actions that never actually transpire, thereby emphasizing the institutional and other implications of diverse expectations regarding actions (rather than the actions themselves). The analysis in section 9.2 identifies cultural beliefs with probability distributions over the off-the-path-of-play portion of a strategy combination generating an observed path of play. Historically, it is not feasible to distinguish between cultural beliefs relating to on-the-path and off-the-path of play, as imperfect monitoring is a likely cause of the observed punishment phases. For this reason, no attempt to do so is made here.[7]

9.2   THE ORIGIN AND MANIFESTATIONS OF DIVERSE CULTURAL
BELIEFS AMONG THE MAGHRIBIS AND THE GENOESE

Are there historical reasons to believe that the Maghribis and the Genoese held diverse cultural beliefs? The historical records provide no reason to

---

[7] For a discussion of imperfect monitoring models, see Appendix A. The fact that under imperfect monitoring, agents will be punished on the equilibrium path does not qualitatively alter the results presented here.

believe that a particular theory of equilibrium selection is relevant in this case. They do indicate, however, that cultural "focal points," as well as social and political events in the early development of these societies, were probably instrumental in shaping different cultural beliefs and the related equilibria in these groups.

By the time the Maghribis began trading in the Mediterranean (early in the eleventh century) and the Genoese began trading (toward the end of that century), they had internalized different cultures and were in the midst of different social and political processes. Their cultural heritage and the nature of these processes suggest that the natural focal point was a collectivist equilibrium for the Maghribis and an individualistic equilibrium for the Genoese.

The Maghribis were *mustarbin*, non-Muslims who adopted the values of the Muslim society, including the view that they were members of the same *umma*. The term, which is translated as "nation," is derived from the word *umm* (mother). It reflects the basic value of mutual responsibility among members of that society (Cahen 1990; Rahman 2002). Each member of the *umma* has a fundamental duty to personally "right wrong" done by any member of the community (e.g., B. Lewis 1991; Cook 2003). The Muslim tradition attributes to Muhammad the statement that "whoever sees a wrong, and is able to put it right with his hand, let him do so; if he can't, then with his tongue; if he can't, then with his heart, and that is the bare minimum of faith" (Cook 2003, p. 4).

The Maghribis were also part of the Jewish community, which shared the idea that all the people of Israel were responsible for one another. During the late medieval period, the idea of the centrality of a community of equal members was prominent in both the Muslim and Jewish societies. Indeed, the "congregational forms of religious organization became the template for the newly forming Muslim religious communities" (Lapidus 1989, p. 120). As is common among immigrant groups, the Maghribis, who migrated from Iraq to Tunisia, retained social ties that enabled them to transmit the information required to support a collectivist equilibrium. The associated collectivist cultural beliefs in turn encouraged the Maghribis to retain their affiliation with this information network.

By the time the Genoese began trading, they had already internalized different cultures and were in the midst of different social and political processes. Evidence regarding Western individualism dates from before the late medieval period. Europe had a long individualistic tradition, which some scholars have traced to the ancient world. They argued that ancient Greek literature and Western novels celebrate the individual, in contrast to Eastern novels, which celebrate "doing one's duty" (e.g., Hsu 1983). Whatever the origin of individualism, by 1200 Europe had already "discovered the individual," according to Morris (1972).[8]

In the medieval period, the individual, rather than his social group, was at the center of Christian theology.[9] Chapter 8 already discussed how the church fostered the decline of large-scale, kin-based social structures. It advanced the creation of "a new society based not on the family but on the individual, whose salvation, like his original loss of innocence, was personal and private" (D. Hughes 1974, p. 61; see Matthew 10:35–6, 4:21–2, 8:21–2, 2:47–50, 23:8–9). In Catholicism, praying requires a priest; in Judaism, it requires a sufficient number of cobelievers. In Islam, praying in the company of others is considered more meritorious, and praying with the congregation is mandatory for the noon prayer on Friday, the Muslim holy day. During the twelfth century, the confession, long confined to the monastic world, became widespread among Christian laypeople.[10]

Individual and bilateral relations were also at the center of twelfth-century feudal culture, of which Genoa was an integral part. The feudal world was based on contractual, hierarchical relations that defined the obligations of one individual to another.[11] It was a world in which material and political conditions were not based on the general obligations of individuals toward their larger community but on the well-defined obligations of individuals to their lord. Even battles were not fought between armies per se but between individual knights within armies (Gurevich 1995, pp. 178–80).

Legal developments also reflect distinct cultural beliefs in late medieval Muslim and Christian societies. In Europe, the appropriateness of

---

[8] Macfarlane (1978) developed a method for quantifying individualism during this period based on land market transactions. He found that England was more individualistic in the thirteenth century than previously assumed, although French and Hoyle (2003) recently qualified his findings.

[9] Although medieval Christianity did not lack collectivist elements; such elements were simply less important than in Islam. On relative levels of individualism and collectivism in contemporary societies, see Bellah et al. (1985); Reynolds and Norman (1988); and Triandis (1990).

[10] For a general discussion and survey of the literature, see Gurevich (1995). See also Bloch (1961, 1:106–8). On Muslim prayer, see Qur'an 62:7.

[11] Paradoxically, the individualistic obligation inherent in Christianity also called for anonymous contributions to charity, which the Genoese made. See the discussion in S. A. Epstein (1996, particularly pp. 91–4, 112–20, 129–30).

customary law was challenged, and eventually marginalized, on the grounds that the customs might be wrong. In contrast, according to the dominant jurisprudential theory of (Sunni) Islam, the consensus of the community was recognized as a legitimate source of law.[12]

Indeed, although clans were central to Genoa's politics, the contract through which the Genoese established their commune around 1096 was a contract between individuals, not clans. Treaties between Genoa and other political units were signed by as many as 1,000 members of the commune rather than by only the consuls or clan leaders. After the establishment of the *podesteria*, the number of Genoese active in trade rose dramatically. Instead of the few dozen traders previously active in each trade center abroad, hundreds of Genoese were trading by the end of the twelfth century. At the same time, Genoa experienced a high level of immigration. In the absence of appropriate social networks for information transmission beyond clan boundaries and among the multiple families of newcomers, an individualistic equilibrium was likely to be selected.[13] Once it was, individualistic cultural beliefs discouraged investment in information. In the absence of a coordinating mechanism, a switch to a collectivist equilibrium was unlikely.

Collectivist cultural beliefs were a focal point among the Maghribis, and individualistic cultural beliefs were a focal point among the Genoese. Does the historical evidence indicate the existence of the related institutions? Was there high investment in information and collective punishment among the Maghribis and low investment in information and individualistic punishment among the Genoese?

The Maghribis shared information and practiced collective punishment (see Chapter 3). In contrast, the Genoese tried to conceal information. According to Lopez (1943, p. 168), the "individualistic, taciturn, and reserved Genoese" were not "talkative" about their businesses and were even "jealous of their business secrets." For example, when, in 1291, the Vivaldi brothers attempted to sail from Genoa directly to the Far East, their commercial agreements were drawn for trade in "Majorca, even for the Byzantine Empire" (p. 169). Genoa's historical records are not explicit

---

[12] See, for example, Bloch (1961, 1:113–16); Kelly (1992, p. 185); Rippin (1994, pp. 80–1); Schacht (1982 [1964]); and Rahman (2002).

[13] No society is purely individualistic. In Genoa information about agents probably circulated among families and clans. In some families, only one member invested in trade, suggesting that he may have been investing on behalf of others. It is nevertheless notable that in the cartulary of Giovanni Scriba, even members of the same family are found constantly to hire different agents.

about the nature of punishment, but they suggest the lack of collective punishment and informal communication (Lopez 1943, p. 180, and de Roover 1965, pp. 88–9).

Cultural factors that coordinated expectations and social and political factors that slightly altered the relevant games in the formative period seem to have directed the Maghribis and the Genoese toward different institutions. As the related cultural beliefs were a part of the institutional framework of each group, they determined the costs and benefits of various actions and hence efficiency. For example, because collectivist cultural beliefs reduce the optimal wage, they can sustain cooperation in situations in which individualistic cultural beliefs cannot sustain them (Greif 1993; Chapter 3). Even if each member of the society recognizes the inefficiency caused by individualistic cultural beliefs, a unilateral move by an individual or a (relatively) small group would not induce a change. Because expectations about expectations are difficult to alter, cultural beliefs can make Pareto-inferior institutions and outcomes self-enforcing. More generally, cultural beliefs influence the motivation and ability to introduce various changes.

9.3 CULTURAL BELIEFS, SOCIAL PATTERNS OF AGENCY RELATIONS, AND THE DISTRIBUTION OF WEALTH

What are the implications of different cultural beliefs for social patterns of economic relations and the dynamics of wealth distribution? Can different cultural beliefs manifest themselves in distinct social structures? Examining this issue requires extending the theoretical analysis to allow each merchant to serve as an agent for another merchant.

In this extended game, two social patterns of agency relations and associated dynamic patterns of wealth distribution can emerge. The first is a vertical social structure, in which merchants find it optimal to hire and therefore employ only agents; individuals thus function as either merchants or agents. The second is a horizontal social structure, in which merchants employ only other merchants, and individuals function as agents and merchants, providing and receiving agency services. What are the relations between cultural beliefs and these social patterns of agency relations?

Under collectivist cultural beliefs, traders have information about everyone's past conduct. Their strategies can therefore be conditional on this information. Accordingly, the collectivist cultural beliefs are redefined to include the expectations that merchants will not retaliate against an agent who cheats a merchant who has cheated any other merchant. The historical evidence indicates that the Maghribis shared such expectations.[14]

It is now possible to examine the relations between cultural beliefs and social patterns of agency relations. Intuitively, under collectivist cultural beliefs, a merchant's capital functions as a bond that reduces the optimal wage required to keep him honest. If a merchant cheats while acting as an agent, he is no longer able to hire agents under the threat of collective punishment. Hence cheating by a merchant while he functions as an agent reduces the future rate of return on his capital. This implies that a merchant who had cheated while acting as an agent has to bear a cost that an agent (who cannot act as a merchant) would not have to bear. Hence a lower wage is required to keep a merchant honest, and each merchant is motivated to hire another merchant as his agent, leading to a horizontal social structure.

Under individualistic cultural beliefs, however, past cheating does not reduce the rate of return on a merchant's capital. But having capital to invest de facto increases a merchant's reservation utility relative to that of an agent, thereby increasing the wage required to keep him honest. Merchants are discouraged from hiring other merchants as their agents, leading to a vertical social structure.

To see this formally, consider the optimal wage required to ensure the honesty of a merchant who functions as an agent (under the assumption that each merchant is risk-neutral and has the discount factor δ). If a merchant is always honest, the present value of his lifetime expected utility is the sum of the present value of his expected utility from being an agent, V_h^a, plus the present value of his expected utility from being a merchant, $(\gamma - W^*)/(1 - \delta)$. That is, $V_h^a + (\gamma - W^*)/(1 - \delta)$. If this merchant cheats while providing agency services, the present value of his expected utility from being an agent is the sum of his current gain from cheating, α, plus the lifetime expected utility of a cheater V_c^a. In addition, he receives $\gamma - W^*$ from being a merchant in the current period plus the present value of the future periods' expected utility from being a merchant who had cheated, V_c^m. Hence the present value of his lifetime expected utility is

---

[14] The words of a Tunisian merchant who was accused, in 1041–2, of cheating exemplify that if an agent who had been accused of cheating were to receive agency services from other Maghribi traders, his agents could cheat him without being subject to community retaliation. That merchant complains that when it became known that he had cheated, "people became agitated and hostile to [me] and whoever owed [me money] conspired to keep it from [me]" Bodl. MS Heb., a2, f. 17, sect. D. Goitein (1973, p. 104). See also Greif (1989).

$\alpha + \gamma - W^* + V_c^m + V_c^a$. For a merchant to be honest when providing agency services, he should not be able to gain from one period of cheating, that is, it must be that $V_h^a + (\gamma - W^*)/(1 - \delta) \geq \alpha + \gamma - W^* + V_c^m + V_c^a$. For a person who can act only as an agent and is not a merchant, the equivalent honesty condition is $V_h^a \geq \alpha + V_c^a$.

These honesty conditions enable us to examine the relations between different cultural beliefs and hiring decisions. Under collectivist cultural beliefs, a merchant who cheated in the past can no longer rely on collective punishment to deter his agent from cheating him and therefore has to pay a higher wage to keep him honest. This implies that under a collectivist strategy, a merchant's lifetime expected utility from being a merchant decreases if he cheats when acting as an agent – that is, $(\gamma - W^*)(1 - \delta) > \gamma - W^* + V_c^m$. Since, everything else being equal, an agent's honesty condition is $V_h^a \geq \alpha + V_c^a$, a merchant strictly prefers to employ another merchant as his agent.

In contrast, under individualistic cultural beliefs, a merchant who cheats while providing agency services does not have to pay his agents more in the future – that is, $(\gamma - W^*)/(1 - \delta) = \gamma - W^* + V_c^m$. Hence, everything else being equal, a merchant is not motivated to employ another merchant.

This analysis does not take into account that it is likely that a merchant's reservation utility is higher than that of an agent. If the higher reservation utility is merely a reflection of the merchants' investment in trade, it encourages the employment of merchants under collectivist cultural beliefs but discourages their employment under individualistic cultural beliefs. If the merchants' higher reservation utility is unrelated to investment in trade, it increases the optimal wage required to keep them honest, independent of any cultural beliefs.

Merchants' capital thus serves as a bond that encourages their employment under collectivist cultural beliefs. Merchants' higher reservation utilities, however, discourage their employment under individualistic cultural beliefs (and possibly collectivist cultural beliefs). Hence, under individualistic cultural beliefs a society reaches a vertical social structure for a larger set of initial conditions than under collectivist cultural beliefs, whereas under collectivist cultural beliefs a society reaches a horizontal social structure for a larger set of initial conditions than under individualistic cultural beliefs.

Different social structures among the Maghribis and the Genoese are indeed evident. The Maghribi traders were, by and large, merchants who invested in trade through horizontal agency relations. Each trader served as an agent for several merchants while receiving agency services from them or other traders. Sedentary traders served as agents for those who traveled and vice versa; wealthy merchants served as agents for poorer ones and vice versa.

Traders did not belong to a "merchant class" or an "agent class." The extent to which the Maghribis' social structure was horizontal can be quantified by examining what can be referred to as agency measure. *Agency measure* is defined as the number of times a trader operated as an agent divided by the number of times a trader operated as either a merchant or an agent. It equals one if the trader was only an agent, zero if he was only a merchant, and some intermediate value if he was both a merchant and an agent. In 175 letters written by Maghribi traders, in which 652 agency relations are reflected, 119 traders appear more than once and almost 70 percent of them have an agency measure between zero and one. The more times a trader appears in the documents, the more likely he is to have an intermediate agency measure.[15]

The horizontal social structure of the Maghribis is also reflected in the forms of business associations through which they established agency relations. They mainly used partnership and "formal friendship." In a partnership, two or more traders invested capital and labor in a joint venture, sharing the profit in proportion to their capital investment. In "formal friendship," two traders operating in different trade centers provided each other with agency services without pecuniary compensation.[16]

In contrast, agency relations among the Genoese traders were vertical. Wealthy merchants who rarely (if ever) functioned as agents hired relatively poor agents who rarely (if ever) functioned as merchants (de Roover 1965, p. 51). "As a rule," Genoese agents in the twelfth century were

---

[15] This measure was calculated for all the letters available regarding trade with Sicily and the area within contemporary Israel during the mid-eleventh century and the trade of Naharay ben Nissim (Michael 1965; Gil 1983a, 1983b; Greif 1985; Ben-Sasson 1991). The nature of the sources precludes calculating a value-based agency measure for the Maghribis.

[16] See discussion in Maimonides (1951, p. 220); Goitein (1967, pp. 164–9, 173, 183); Stillman (1970, p. 388), Gil (1983b, 1:200ff.). Goitein (1964, p. 316) concludes that about half of the business dealings reflected in the geniza are formal friendships. The Maghribis referred to such partnership as *shirka* ("partnership" in Arabic) or *shuthafuth* ("partnership" in Hebrew), *khulta* ("mixing" in Arabic), *kis wahid* ("one purse" in Arabic), *baynana* ("between us" in Arabic), or *lilwasat* ("into the midst" in Arabic). Formal friendship is *suhba* ("companionship" in Arabic), *sadaqa* ("friendship and charity" in Arabic), or *bida'a* ("goods" in Arabic). The term *bida'a* also appears in Muslim juridical literature; see Udovitch (1970, pp. 101ff., 134).

"not men of great wealth or of high position" (Byrne 1916–17, p. 159). Only 21 percent of the 190 trader families mentioned more than once in the cartulary of Giovanni Scriba (1154–64) have an agency measure between zero and one, and these traders accounted for just 11 percent of the value of trade.

The vertical character of the Genoese social structure is also reflected in the forms of business associations through which agency relations were established. Particularly from the end of the twelfth century, the Genoese used mainly *commenda* contracts, in which one party usually provided capital and the other provided labor, in the form of traveling and transacting overseas.[17] The difference in forms of business associations between the two merchant groups does not reflect different knowledge. Members of both groups were familiar with the same types of contracts, and neither was legally, politically, or morally barred from using them (Krueger 1962).[18]

Diverse cultural beliefs not only affect social patterns of economic interactions; they also lead to diverse dynamics of wealth distribution. Everything else being equal, a vertical society provides better opportunity for upward mobility to wealthless individuals (in a partial equilibrium framework). Because under individualistic cultural beliefs an agent's ability to commit is negatively related to his wealth, wealthless individuals

---

[17] Between 1154 and 1164, 80 percent of investment (by value) through agents utilized *societas* contracts, in which the agent contributed a third of the capital (Giovanni Scriba). Later cartularies reflect a shift to the *commenda* contract. The shift was completed in Genoa by 1216, when only 2 of the 299 (trade-related) contracts that have survived were *societas* contracts (Krueger 1962, p. 421). Krueger conjectures that the change in the form of business association reflects the increasing role of relatively poor individuals as merchants. Yet examining all the cartularies from 1200 to 1226 reveals that societas contracts represented only 6 percent of the contracts entered into by the families that dominated Genoa's commerce and politics in the mid-twelfth century (the Ventus, della Volta, Castro, Filardus, Mallonus, Spinula, Ususmaris, and de Albericis) (see Lanfranco Scriba 1202–26 and Giovanni de Guiberto 1200–11). In subsequent centuries changes in wealth distribution and other factors seem to have blurred the clear distinction between agents and merchants in Genoa. The situation in the twelfth century is therefore particularly revealing. In Jewish law, the term for the commenda is '*eseq* (Maimonides 1951, pp. 299–30; Goitein 1967, pp. 169–80). The Arabic term is *qirad* and "*mudaraba*" (Udovitch 1970). Although we lack good measures, the *mudaraba* was probably widely used in the Islamic world for various purposes. For a reference to Jewish commenda reflected in the *geniza*, see Oxford MS Heb. b.11, f.8, Mann 1970, 2:29–30.

[18] For a general discussion, see de Roover (1965); Goitein (1973; 11ff.) Gil (1983b, 1:216ff.); and Greif (1989). For a evidence of knowledge, see Lieber (1968) and Greif (1989).

are better able to capture the rent (above the reservation utility) available to agents. In a horizontal society, wealthless individuals are not able to capture this rent, because under collectivist cultural beliefs the ability to commit is positively related to one's wealth.

The historical sources are mute with respect to the dynamics of wealth distribution among the Maghribis, but the Genoese sources reflect a dynamic of wealth distribution that is consistent with the theoretical prediction. Wealth transfer is reflected in a declining concentration of trade investment and the increase over time of trade investment made by commoners. The cartulary of Giovanni Scriba (1154–64) reveals that trade was concentrated largely in the hands of a few noble families, with less than 10 percent of the merchants investing 70 percent of the total. The cartulary of Obertus Scriba (1186) reflects a decline in the share of the top families, with 10 percent of the them investing less than 60 percent of the total. In 1376 the number of commoners who paid customs in Genoa exceeded the number of nobles (295 versus 279), and nobles accounted for just 64 percent of the total invested (Kedar 1976, pp. 51–2).[19] That agency relations contributed to shifting wealth distribution is reflected in the affairs of Ansaldo Baialardo, who was hired by the noble Genoese merchant Ingo della Volta in 1156. Between 1156 and 1158, Ansaldo sailed abroad as Ingo's agent. By investing only his retained earnings, he accumulated 142 lire, more than three and a half times the cost of a house at the time.[20]

As suggested in Chapter 8, the growing wealth of commoners is indirectly reflected in the political history of Genoa. A relative increase in the wealth of a subgroup within a society is likely to lead it to demand a greater say in political matters. Hence, as wealth distribution changes, attempts to change the political organization of the society are likely to be made. This was indeed the case in Genoa: the *popolo* revolted against the nobility during the thirteenth century, changing the political organization of Genoa to reflect and protect their growing wealth (Vitale 1955).[21]

---

[19] De Roover (1965) argues that agency relations in Italy facilitated the transfer of wealth. The year 1376 is the only year for which, to the best of my knowledge, data are available in the secondary literature. Chapter 8 points to a complementary process; patronage reflecting interclan conflict also shifted wealth distribution in Genoa.

[20] On Ansaldo, see de Roover (1965, pp. 51–2). On the cost of a house, see Giovanni di Guiberto (1200–11), nos. 260, 261.

[21] In Venice, however, this has not been the case due to the lesser reliance on reputation mechanism. See Chapter 8.

9.4 TRANSCENDING THE BOUNDARIES OF THE GAME: SEGREGATED AND INTEGRATED SOCIETIES

Over time the merchant-agent game faced by the Maghribis and the Genoese changed for reasons exogenous to each merchant. Following various military and political changes in the Mediterranean, both groups had the opportunity to expand their trade to areas previously inaccessible to them (A. R. Lewis 1951; Chapter 8). Commercially, both groups responded similarly, expanding their trade to encompass the area that spanned from Spain to Constantinople. From the perspective of institutional analysis, however, their responses differed. The Genoese responded in an "integrated" manner, whereas the Maghribis responded in a "segregated" manner.

The Maghribis expanded their trade by employing other Maghribis as agents. As Chapter 3 discusses, they emigrated from North Africa to other trade centers; for generations, the descendants of these emigrants cooperated with the descendants of other Maghribis. This segregated response was not a result of the Maghribis' status as a religious minority, as they did not establish agency relations with other Jewish traders, even when such relations were (ignoring agency cost) perceived by the Maghribi traders as very profitable. That this segregation is endogenous is reflected in the Maghribis' later history: when, toward the end of the twelfth century, they were forced due to political reasons to cease trading, they integrated with the larger Jewish communities.

The Genoese also responded to the new opportunities by emigrating, and their cartularies document the dominance of agency relations with other Genoese. But although the cartularies were written in Genoa and are hence biased toward reflecting agency relations among Genoese, they nevertheless clearly indicate the establishment of agency relations between Genoese and non-Genoese. In the cartulary of the Genoese Giovanni Scriba (1154–64), for example, at least 18 percent of all funds sent abroad through agents were sent to or carried by non-Genoese.[22]

The rationale behind the different responses by the Maghribis and the Genoese to the same exogenous change in the rules of the game becomes clear once one considers the impact of cultural beliefs on equilibrium

---

[22] For non-Genoese in other cartularies, see Obertus Scriba (1186, nos. 9, 38; 1190, nos. 138, 139); Guglielmo Cassinese (1190–2; nos. 418, 1325); and Lanfranco Scriba (1202–6, no. 524). The ease of hiring a non-Genoese is reflected in the fact that they were used to circumvent a politically unfavorable situation in Sicily (Abulafia 1977, pp. 201ff.).

selection. The change altered the basic model in a specific manner. As trade with more remote trade centers became possible, a merchant could hire either an agent from his own economy who would sail or move abroad or an agent native to the other trade center. Inter-economy agency relations are likely to be more efficient than intra-economy agency relations, because they enhance commercial flexibility; a native agent would not need to emigrate and would also likely possess a better knowledge of local conditions.

In deciding whether to establish inter-economy agency relations, however, a merchant's concern is profitability, not efficiency. The relations between efficiency and profitability are influenced by cultural beliefs that crystallize before inter-economy agency relations become possible. Individualistic cultural beliefs lead to an "integrated" society in which inter-economy agency relations are established if they are efficient. Collectivist cultural beliefs create a wedge between efficient and profitable agency relations, leading to a "segregated" society in which efficient inter-economy agency relations are not established. Whenever uncertainty exists about whether collectivist or individualistic cultural beliefs will be practiced in inter-economy agency relations, these (more efficient) agency relations become less profitable to collectivist merchants, because agents' wages increase.

To see why this is the case, suppose that two identical economies, within which either individualistic or collectivist cultural beliefs prevail, become a joint economy in which players can identify members of their previous economy but inter-economy agency relations are possible. What will the patterns of hiring agents in the joint economy be, as a function of the players' cultural beliefs? (For ease of presentation, I assume that past actions are common knowledge. Letting players invest in information greatly strengthens the results presented subsequently.)

Intuitively, when players project their cultural beliefs on the new game – that is, when their expectations concerning others' actions in the postchange game are the prechange expectations – these prechange cultural beliefs constitute the initial conditions for a dynamic adjustment process. For example, if the prechange economies were collectivist, players expect each merchant to hire agents from his own economy, and they expect that merchants of the same economy will retaliate against an agent who has cheated one of them. Yet the prechange cultural beliefs are insufficient to calculate best responses in the postchange game. They do not stipulate a complete strategy for a player, because the same prechange behavior implies off-the-path-of-play situations in the postchange game that did not exist before. For example, the prechange cultural beliefs do not specify how merchants from one economy would react to actions taken by an agent from their economy in inter-economy agency relations. As the others' strategies are not specified, a player cannot find his best response.

To find his best response, a merchant has to form expectations about the response of the merchants from the other economy to actions taken in inter-economy agency relations. Although the merchants from the agent's economy can be expected to respond in various ways, two responses predominate. Given any agent's action in inter-economy agency relations, the merchants from the agent's economy can regard him either as one who cheated one of them or as one who did not cheat one of them. For example, in a collectivist economy, merchants may consider an agent who cheated in inter-economy agency relations as a cheater subject to collective retaliation, or they may ignore his cheating. Nothing in the prechange cultural beliefs indicates which of these responses will be selected for each action. Accordingly, the best that can be done analytically is to assume that in inter-economy agency relations any probability distribution over these two responses is possible.[23] Considering the prechange cultural beliefs and any such probability distributions as initial conditions allows us to examine the merchants' best response (while not imposing any differences between the prechange economies apart from their cultural beliefs).

What would merchants' best response be as a function of their cultural beliefs? Assume initially that there is no efficiency gain from inter-economy agency relations. Intuitively, when inter-economy agency relations become possible between two collectivist economies, the initial cultural beliefs specify collective punishment in intra-economy agency relations. If there is doubt over whether collective punishment also governs inter-economy agency relations, the optimal wage is higher in inter-economy agency relations than in intra-economy relations. It is higher because the uncertainty about collective punishment in inter-economy relations reduces the probability that an agent who cheats in such relations will be punished, which, as established in proposition 9.1, increases the optimal wage. As the merchants' cost of establishing inter-economy agency relations is higher than the cost of establishing

---

[23] This probability distribution can also be thought of as reflecting a merchant's uncertainty regarding the agent's expectations concerning the responses of merchants from the agents' economy.

intra-economy agency relations, only intra-economy agency relations will be initiated, and segregation will result. If inter-economy agency relations are more efficient, merchants will initiate them only if the efficiency gains are sufficiently large.

This analysis does not hold when inter-economy agency relations become possible between two individualistic economies. Although similar uncertainty is likely to exist, the optimal inter-economy and intra-economy wages are the same. Individualistic cultural beliefs make this uncertainty irrelevant for determining the optimal wage. Hence any efficiency gains from inter-economy agency relations will motivate merchants to establish them.

Proposition 9.4, which requires some additional definitions, formalizes the analysis. A joint economy is *segregated* if, given the initial conditions, merchants from each economy strictly prefer to hire agents from their own economy. It is *integrated* if, given the initial conditions, merchants from at least one economy are indifferent with respect to the original economy of their agents. Denote a merchant from economy s by M^s and by A^t an agent from economy t, where s, t $\in \{K, J\}$. Denote by μ the perceived probability that merchants from economy s will consider an A^s last employed by M^t as a cheater if he cheated when employed by M^t. Denote by η the perceived probability that merchants from economy s will consider an A^s, last employed by M^t, as a cheater if he was honest when employed by M^t.

> **Proposition 9.4:** Suppose that inter-economy agency relations do not entail efficiency gains and that the two economies are identical in their parameters. If the prechange economies are collectivist, the joint economy is segregated for any $\mu \in [0, 1)$ and $\eta \in (0, 1]$ and integrated only if $\mu = 1$ and $\eta = 0$. If the prechange economies are individualistic, the joint economy is integrated for $\mu \in [0, 1]$ and $\eta \in [0, 1]$. (The proof appears in annex 9.1.)

When inter-economy agency relations become possible between a collectivist and an individualistic economy, a collectivist merchant will not initiate inter-economy agency relations, regardless of the uncertainty regarding the individualistic merchants' responses.[24] The wage the merchant has to pay to keep the agent honest is higher than the wage in

---

[24] To focus on the asymmetry in responses due to diverse cultural beliefs, I ignore the possible implications of vertical and horizontal social structures on agents' reservation utility.

the collectivist economy, because the collectivist economy's wage is lower than the individualistic economy's wage. Hence collectivist cultural beliefs create a wedge between efficient and profitable agency relations, and inter-economy agency relations will be initiated by collectivist merchants only if the efficiency gains are high enough.

In contrast, because the collectivist economy's wage is lower, individualistic merchants may find it optimal to establish inter-economy relations, even if such relations *do not* imply efficiency gains, thereby inducing (asymmetric) integration. To see why, consider the uncertainty regarding the collectivist merchants' responses that most decreases the profitability of inter-economy relations. Suppose that the collectivist merchant would not impose a collective punishment on a cheater ($\mu = 0$) but would impose punishment on an agent who was honest in inter-economy relations ($\eta = 1$). The expectation that collectivist merchants would not collectively punish a cheater in inter-economy relations cannot by itself (i.e., when $\eta = \mu = 0$) decrease the profitability of inter-economy relations enough to prevent integration. This implies that if a collectivist agent who was employed by an individualistic merchant becomes unemployed, his lifetime expected utility equals that of any unemployed collectivist agent. The wage in the individualistic economy is more than that required to keep the agent honest, because the lifetime expected utility of an unemployed collectivist agent is lower than that of an individualistic agent. Hence it is profitable for an individualistic merchant to hire a collectivist agent.

If collectivist merchants are also expected to consider an agent who was honest in inter-economy agency relations to be a cheater ($\eta > 0$), the wage that has to be paid to a collectivist agent by an individualistic merchant increases further. An unemployed collectivist agent who was honest in inter-economy agency relations has a lower lifetime expected utility than other unemployed collectivist agents. Hence a higher wage (than when $\eta = 0$) is required to induce honesty. Integration may still follow, because an honest agent will become unemployed only in the future. Thus these expected responses by the collectivist merchants will forestall inter-economy agency relations only if the agent's time discount factor is high enough.

Individualistic (but not collectivist) merchants are likely to induce integration. They may find it profitable to initiate inter-economy agency relations even without efficiency gains, regardless of uncertainty about the collectivist merchants' responses. Segregation can result, however, if the expected response of the collectivist merchants erects "barriers to exit" for collectivist agents.[25] Furthermore, because integration increases the wage in the collectivist economy, collectivist merchants may strive to use social or political actions to try to prevent inter-economy agency relations. Proposition 9.5 establishes the necessary and sufficient conditions for integration and segregation.

> **Proposition 9.5:** (a) For any $\mu \in [0, 1]$ and $\eta \in [0, 1]$, a collectivist merchant will not initiate inter-economy agency relations. (b) A sufficient condition for integration is $\mu \geq \eta$. A necessary condition is $\mu + (1 - \delta)(V_h^{u,I} - \mu V_c^{u,c} - (1 - \mu)V_h^{u,c})/\delta\tau(V_h^{u,c} - V_c^{u,c}) \geq \eta$. (Superscript c [or I] means a collectivist [individualistic] economy.) (c) A necessary condition for segregation is $\mu < \eta$. If μ is close enough to zero and η close enough to one, then $\exists \tilde{\delta} \in (0, 1)$, s.t. $\forall \delta \geq \tilde{\delta}$ the economy is segregated. (The proof appears in annex 9.1.)

The preceding analysis reveals the relations between different cultural beliefs, the endogenous emergence of segregation and integration, and economic efficiency. Pareto-inferior segregation may prevail because of the structure of expectations and the absence of a mechanism able to alter them in a manner that makes this alteration common knowledge. Thus the extent of trade expansion of a collectivist society is limited by the initial expectations regrading the boundaries of the society. Different cultural beliefs determine the direction of trade expansion, as individualistic merchants are likely to penetrate collectivist societies but collectivist merchants are not likely to penetrate individualistic societies. Indeed, during the period under consideration, trade expansion was based on the penetration of the Muslim world by merchants from the Latin world. As discussed in section 9.5, segregation and integration influence the relations between individuals and their society and hence affect the evolution of organizations that govern collective actions and facilitate exchange.

9.5 TRANSCENDING THE BOUNDARIES OF THE GAME: ORGANIZATIONAL EVOLUTION

Among the Maghribis, collectivist cultural beliefs led to a collectivist society with economic self-enforcing collective punishment, horizontal agency

---

[25] If integration is sequential and a collectivist agent who had been hired by an individualistic merchant "joins" the pool of individualistic agents, these expectations and the decrease in the number of collectivist agents may lead to a new equilibrium in which the two economies differ in size.

relations, segregation, and an in-group social communication network. In a collectivist society, the credible threat of informal collective economic punishment can induce individuals to forgo "improper" behavior. Suppose, for example, that every Maghribi expects every other Maghribi to consider a specific behavior "improper" and punishable in the same manner as cheating in agency relations. This punishment is self-enforcing, for the same reason that self-enforcing collective punishment in agency relations is self-enforcing. It is feasible, because there is a network for information transmission. This punishment is likely to be reinforced by social and moral enforcement mechanisms that, as discussed previously, emerge as a result of frequent economic interactions within a small segregated group. To make the threat of collective punishment credible, expectations need to be coordinated by defining what constitutes "improper" behavior. In a collectivist society, this coordination is likely to be based on informal mechanisms, such as customs and oral tradition.

Among the Genoese, individualistic cultural beliefs led to an individualistic society with a vertical and integrated social structure, a relatively low level of communication, and no economic self-enforcing collective punishment. In such a society, a relatively low level of informal economic enforcement can be achieved, because of the absence of economic self-enforcing collective punishment and networks for information transmission. Furthermore, the integrated social structure and the low level of communication hinder social and moral enforcement mechanisms. To support collective actions and facilitate exchange, an individualistic society needs to develop formal – legal and political – enforcement organizations. A formal legal code is likely to be required to facilitate exchange by coordinating expectations and enhancing the deterrence effect of formal organizations.

During the period under consideration, both the Genoese and the Maghribis were establishing self-governance systems. The Maghribis emigrated to and operated within the Fatimid Caliphate, in which "the administration of their own affairs was left to themselves" (Goitein 1971, p. 1). Genoa had just been incorporated into a city and liberated de facto from the rule of the Holy Roman Empire.[26] Hence both groups were in a position to devise their own form of authority and jurisdiction, but their responses differed. The Maghribis did not develop formal organizations to support collective actions and exchange, and they seem not

---

[26] See Chapter 8 and, for evidence on this particular point, *Annali* 1162, vol. I, and the discussions in Airaldi (1986) and Vitale (1955).

to have used the ones available to them; the Genoese developed such organizations.

Despite the existence of a well-developed Jewish communal court system (and access to the Muslim legal system), the Maghribis entered contracts informally, used or adopted an informal code of conduct, and attempted to resolve disputes informally (see Goitein 1967; Greif 1989, 1993). In contrast, during the twelfth century the Genoese ceased to use the ancient custom of entering contracts by a handshake and developed an extensive legal system for registering and enforcing contracts. The customary contract law that governed the relations between Genoese traders was codified, as permanent courts were established (Vitale 1955). After 1194, to a large extent, the law was in the hands of the *podestà* and his judges.

In an individualistic society, agents are not expected to be subject to collective punishment. An agent who embezzled goods would not be recruited by the cheated merchant again, but he could become a merchant himself, hiring agents under the same conditions as the merchant he had cheated. Hence agency relations can be established only if agents' wages are so high that everyone prefers being an agent to being a merchant. In other words, for agents to be employed, merchants have to pay them all the profit and part of the capital. Clearly, there cannot be an equilibrium at such a wage. Thus for agency relations to be established in an individualistic society, an external mechanism – such as a legal system backed by the state – is needed to limit agents' ability to embezzle merchants' capital. A legal system complements an institution based on individualistic cultural beliefs; it does not replace the associated bilateral reputation institution. Where a legal system has only a limited ability to restrict cheating (e.g., from misreporting profit expenses), a reputation mechanism still has to be used. The extensive writing of agency contracts suggests that this was indeed the case among the Genoese.

The relations between cultural beliefs and organizational development are reflected not only in these general processes but also in organizations that served specific economic aims. For example, in medieval trade the need for enforcement organizations to support collective action was likely to manifest itself in relations between traders and rulers (Chapter 4). As long as the number of traders was low, the relatively high value to the ruler of each trader's future trade was sufficient to motivate the ruler to respect the trader's rights. When the number of traders was large, this was no longer the case. One way in which protection could be provided at the higher volume of trade would be for a sufficiently large number of traders to respond – in the form of a trade embargo – to transgressions by the ruler against any trader. Once an embargo is declared, however, some traders can benefit from ignoring it and selling their goods in the prohibited area in times of shortage. Some enforcement mechanism is required to ensure that each trader will respect a collective decision to impose an embargo. In collectivist societies, one would expect that informal enforcement mechanisms would be sufficient to ensure traders' compliance with embargo decisions. In individualistic societies, one would expect organizations specializing in embargo enforcement to emerge.

The historical evidence on the Maghribis and the Genoese is consistent with this prediction. Among the Maghribis compliance was ensured through informal means. After the Muslim ruler of Sicily abused the rights of some Maghribi traders, the Maghribis responded by imposing, circa 1050, an embargo on Sicily. The embargo was organized informally. Maymun ben Khalpha wrote a letter to Naharay ben Nissim of Fustat (old Cairo) from Palermo (Sicily) in which he informed Naharay about the tax increase and asked him to "hold the hands of our friends [the Maghribi traders] not to send to Sicily even one dirham [a low-value coin]." Indeed, the Maghribis sailed to Tunisia instead of to Sicily; a year later the tax was abolished.[27] There is no evidence that compliance was supported by any formal enforcement organization, although the Maghribis could have used the Jewish court system or a communal organization to enforce the embargo.

In sharp contrast, as we have seen in Chapter 4, in Genoa a formal enforcement organization worked to make the threat of collective retaliation credible. After the authorities declared a commercial embargo (*devetum*) on a particular locality, any merchant found in violation was subject to legal prosecution.

The history of the modern bill of lading provides another example of the development of formal organizations and distinct contractual forms among the Genoese but not the Maghribis. This bill combined an earlier version of the bill of lading with a so-called bill of advice. The original bill of lading was the ship's scribe's receipt for the goods the merchant deposited on the ship. This receipt was sent by the merchant to his overseas agent, who then claimed the goods on the basis of the scribe's signature.

---

[27] DK 22, a, lines 29–31, b, lines 3–5, Gil (1983a, pp. 97–106); TS 10 J 12, f. 26, a, lines 18–20, Michael (1965, 2:85).

The bill of advice was sent after the ship arrived at its destination by the ship's scribe to the consignee, who did not come to claim the goods. The bill of lading and the bill of advice surmounted an organizational problem related to the shipping of goods abroad.

The earliest known European bill of lading and letter of advice date from the 1390s and relate to the trade of Genoa. In contrast, the Maghribi traders hardly ever used bills of lading, although the device was known to them.[28] Why did the Genoese advance the use of the bill and the Maghribis abandon it? The Maghribis rejected the bill because they had solved the related organizational problem by using their informal collective enforcement mechanism. Maghribis entrusted their goods to other Maghribis traveling on board the ship that carried their merchandise. To exemplify this, consider a letter sent early in the eleventh century by Ephraim, son of Isma'il from Alexandria, to Ibn 'Awkal, a prominent merchant who lived in Fustat (old Cairo). Ephraim mentions the names of the men on four different ships entrusted "to watch carefully the 70 bales and one *barqalu* [containing the goods] until they will deliver them safely into the hands of Khalaf son of Ya'qub."[29]

Instead of solving the organizational problem between the merchant and the ship's operator, the Maghribis circumvented it. This fact is forcefully illustrated in a letter sent from Sicily in 1057. It describes what happened to loads of merchandise whose covers were torn during a voyage. After the ship arrived in port, the operator of the ship started to steal the merchandise. The writer of the letter remarked that "unless my brother had been there to collect [the goods], nothing that belonged to our friends [the Maghribi traders] would have been collected."[30] The letter makes clear that the ship's operator did not consider himself – and the traders did not consider him – responsible for protecting the goods. Similarly, if goods of unknown ownership were unloaded from the ship, or if the ship did not reach its destination, it was not the captain but the Maghribi traders who took care of their fellow traders' goods.[31] The Genoese traders, lacking an equivalent informal enforcement mechanism,

---

[28] For information on Genoa, see Bensa (1925). For the use of the bill of lading by the Maghribi traders and possible bias in the historical records, see Goitein (1973, pp. 305ff.).

[29] TS 13 J 17, f. 3, Goitein (1973, p. 313). On the generality of this practice, see Goitein (1967).

[30] Bodl. MS Heb., c28, f. 61, a, lines 12–14, Gil (1983a, pp. 126–33).

[31] See, for example, Bodl. MS Heb., c28, f. 61, a, lines 9–17, Gil (1983a: 126–33).

could not rely on fellow traders. They solved the organizational problem associated with shipping goods by using bills of lading, letters of advice, and the legal responsibility they entail.

The differences between collectivist and individualistic societies are also likely to manifest themselves in the development of organizations related to agency relations. Proposition 9.1 established that the more likely it is that there will be future relations between a specific agent and merchant, the less that merchant has to pay his agent. (A reduction in the probability of forced separation, τ, reduces the optimal wage.) The magnitude of this reduction is a function of cultural beliefs, because the gains from reducing the probability of forced separation depend on the probabilities that a cheater and an honest agent will be rehired. The lower the probability that a cheater will be rehired and the higher the probability that an honest agent will be rehired, the lower the gain from changing the probability of forced separation. Furthermore, when an unemployed honest agent is rehired with probability one, the gain from changing the probability of forced separation is zero.[32]

Collectivist cultural beliefs and the resulting segregation and collective punishment increase, possibly to one, the probability that an honest agent will be rehired. These factors are likely to reduce to zero the probability that a cheater will be rehired. Thus under collectivist beliefs and segregation, a merchant's incentive to reduce the probability of forced separation is marginal, or even absent. In contrast, under individualistic cultural beliefs and the resulting integration and second-party punishment, merchants are motivated to establish an organization that reduces the likelihood of forced separation.

The evolution of family relations and business organization among the Maghribis and the Genoese suggests that the Genoese, but not the Maghribis, introduced an organization that changed the probability of forced separation. When the Maghribi and the Genoese merchants first began trading in the Mediterranean, it was common in both groups for a trader's son to start operating independently during his father's lifetime. The father would typically help the son until the son was able to operate on his own. After the father's death, his estate was divided among his heirs, and his business dissolved.[33]

---

[32] Formally, $\partial^2\, W(.)/\partial h_c d\tau > 0$ (for $\delta > h_c$), $\partial^2\, W(.)/\partial h_h \partial \tau < 0$, and $\partial W/\partial \tau = 0$ when $h_h = 1$.

[33] On the Maghribis, see Goitein (1967, pp. 180ff.) and Gil (1983b, 1:215ff.). On the Genoese, see Giovanni Scriba (nos. 236, 575, 1047) for father's help and Giovanni Scriba (no. 946) for a will.

Later development of family relations and business organization, however, differ substantially. During the thirteenth century, the Genoese traders adopted the family firm, the essence of which was a permanent partnership with unlimited and joint liability. This organization preserved family wealth undivided under one ownership, with the trader's son joining the family firm.[34] The Maghribi traders, who had been active in trade at least as long as the Genoese, did not establish a similar organization.

Why did the two societies develop differently in this regard? Given the collectivist cultural beliefs of the Maghribis and the resulting segregation, collective punishment, and horizontal relations, a merchant could not gain much by introducing an organization that reduced the likelihood of forced separation. Among the Genoese traders, individualistic cultural beliefs motivated merchants to increase the security of the employment they offered their agents. The family firm seems to have been the manifestation of this desire. In the Genoese family firm, several traders combined their capital to form an organization with an infinite life-span and a lower probability of bankruptcy. Agency relationships were now with the organization rather than with individual merchants.[35]

These historical examples suggest that collectivist and individualistic cultural beliefs are likely to motivate the introduction of different organizations. Once an organization is introduced, it is likely to lead to other organizational innovations (through learning and experimentation), as existing organizations direct responses to subsequent contractual problems. For example, the organizational "macroinvention" of the family firm led to organizational "microinventions" among the Italians. Family firms began to sell shares to nonfamily members. The capital of the Bardi Company consisted of fifty-eight shares: six members of the family owned the majority of the shares, five outsiders owned the rest. In 1312 the capital of the Peruzzi Company was distributed among eight members of the family and nine outsiders. In 1331 the Peruzzi family lost control of the company when more than half the capital belonged to outsiders (de Roover 1963, pp. 77–8; see additional examples in de Roover 1965). Tradable shares required a suitable market, which led to the development of "stock markets." The separation between

---

[34] See de Roover (1965, pp. 70ff.) and Rosenberg and Birdzell (1986, pp. 123–4).

[35] Additional theoretical and historical work is required to establish whether and how the family firm achieved a level of commitment greater than that of each of its members.

ownership and control introduced by the family firm led to the introduction of organizations and procedures able to surmount the related contractual problems, such as improvement in information-transmission techniques, accounting procedures, and the incentive scheme provided to agents.

9.6 CONCLUDING COMMENTS

The Maghribis and the Genoese were constrained by the same technology and environment, and they faced the same organizational problems. But their different cultural heritages and political and social histories gave rise to different cultural beliefs. Theoretically, their distinct cultural beliefs are sufficient to account for the diverse institutional trajectories of the two groups. Cultural beliefs may thus have had a lasting impact despite their temporary nature. The analysis demonstrates how the interactions between institutions, exogenous changes, and the process of organizational innovation govern the historical development of institutions and the related economic, political, legal, and organizational developments.

Collectivist cultural beliefs constituted part of the Maghribis' collective enforcement mechanism and induced investment in information, segregation, horizontal economic interactions, and a stable pattern of wealth distribution. The endogenous partition of society restricted economic and social interactions to a small group and facilitated in-group communication and economic and social collective punishments. Collectivist cultural beliefs led to institutions based on the group's ability to use economic, social, and, most likely, moral sanctions against deviants.

Individualistic cultural beliefs constituted a part of the Genoese' second-party enforcement mechanism. These beliefs induced a low level of communication, a vertical social structure, economic and social integration, and the transfer of wealth to the relatively poor. These manifestations of individualistic cultural beliefs weakened the dependence of each individual on any group, limiting the ability of each group to use economic, social, and moral sanctions against individual members. Individualistic cultural beliefs led to institutions based on legal, political, and (second-party) economic organizations for enforcement and coordination.

Each of the two systems has different efficiency implications. The collectivist system is more efficient in supporting intra-economy agency relations and requires less costly formal organizations (such as lawcourts), but it restricts efficient inter-economy agency relations. The individualistic system does not restrict inter-economy agency relations, but it is less efficient in supporting intra-economy relations and requires costly formal organizations.

Each system also entails different patterns of wealth distribution, each of which is likely to have different efficiency implications. This implies that the relative efficiency of individualistic and collectivist systems depends on the magnitude of the relevant parameters. Although the Italians eventually drove the Muslim traders out of the Mediterranean, the historical records do not allow the relative efficiency of the two systems to be tested. Furthermore, as the comparison between Genoa and Venice highlights, different outcomes are possible given the same cultural heritage.

Yet, it is intriguing to note that the Maghribis' institutions resemble those of contemporary underdeveloped countries, whereas the Genoese institutions resemble the developed West, suggesting that the individualistic system may have been more efficient in the long run. The analysis presented here enables conjecturing about the possible long-run benefits of the individualistic system. To the extent that the division of labor is a necessary condition for long-run, sustained economic growth, formal enforcement institutions that support anonymous exchange facilitate economic development. Individualistic cultural beliefs foster the development of such institutions, enabling society to capture these efficiency gains. An individualistic society also entails less social pressure to conform to social norms of behavior, thus fostering initiative and innovation. Indeed, Genoa was well known among the Italian city-states for its individualism, and it was a leader in commercial initiative and innovation.

Although further historical research is needed to substantiate the importance of individualism, the analysis here highlights the importance of cultural heritage, particularly cultural beliefs and organizations (social structures), in leading to particular institutional elements and thereby making institutional trajectories – and hence economic growth – a historical process. The capacity of an institution to change is thus a function of its history, particularly because uncoordinated cultural beliefs about what others believe are difficult to change, organizations reflect the cultural beliefs that led to their adoption, and these organizations and cultural beliefs influence the historical evolution of strategic situations and institutions.

ANNEX 9.1

Proof of Proposition 9.1

See the proof of proposition 3.1 in Chapter 3.

Proof of Proposition 9.2

Under both strategies the merchants act in accordance with the strategy assumed in proposition 9.1.[36] Under the individualistic strategy, $h_c = h_h > 0$ while under the collectivist strategy $h_h > 0$ and $h_c = 0$ after every history. Hence proposition 1 holds, and given W^*, an agent cannot do better by deviating. This implies that on the equilibrium path a merchant's strategy is a best response.

The only nontrivial part of the proof regarding off-the-path-of-play events is verifying the optimality of the merchant's hiring procedures after cheating under the collectivist strategy. Denote the probability that a cheater (honest agent) will be hired by h_c^c (h_h^c) under the collectivist strategy. Under this strategy h_c^c equals zero (because a cheater is not expected to be rehired), but h_h^c equals $\tau M/(A - (1 - \tau)M) > 0$ along the equilibrium path (because an honest agent will be hired in the future). According to proposition 9.1, the optimal wage for a cheater is $W_c^* = w(., h_h^c = 0, h_c^c = 0)$, and the optimal wage for an honest agent is $W_h^* = w(., h_h^c > 0, h_c^c = 0)$. Because the function w decreases in h_h, $W_c^* > W_h^*$, implying that a merchant strictly prefers to hire an agent who has always been honest rather than an agent who has cheated. Firing a cheater and hiring only from the pool of honest agents are thus optimal for the merchant. This implies that in another off-the-path-of-play event in which a merchant does not fire an agent who cheated him, there is no wage at which it is profitable for the merchant to employ the agent. The merchant should pay the agent at least W_c^*, implying that even if this agent is honest, the best response of the merchant is to fire him in the next period. Hence for any $W \neq \alpha$, the agent's best response is to cheat. Q.E.D.

---

[36] For technical reasons, I assume that if a merchant offers $W = 0$, employment is de facto not taking place and the merchant receives κ and the agent receives $\overline{w}$; the collectivist strategy also calls for ignoring cheating by more than one agent, and under the individualistic strategy in the off-the-path-of-play event in which a merchant did not fire an agent who cheated him, the agent's strategy specifies cheating for every wage, and the merchant's strategy specifies offering $W = 0$.

Proof of Proposition 9.4

The first subscript or superscript in what follows denotes the merchant's economy and the second the agent's economy. For any $\mu \in [0, 1]$ and $\eta \in [0, 1]$, the implications of the corresponding beliefs with respect to the probability of future employment of A_t last employed by M_s are as follows: $h_c^{s,t}(\mu) = \mu h_c^{t,t} + (1 - \mu)h_h^{t,t}$ is the probability that A_t will be hired if he is a cheater; $h_h^{s,t}(\eta) = \eta h_c^{t,t} + (1 - \eta)h_h^{t,t}$ is the probability that A_t will be hired if he is honest. Denote by $W_{s,t}^*$ the optimal wage that M_s pays A_t, $s \in \{K, J\}$, $t \in \{K, J\}$. Suppose that an unemployed agent from economy s was last employed by a merchant from economy t, and denote by $h_I^{t,s}$ the probability that this agent will be rehired if he took action I when he was last employed, where I is either h for honest or c for cheat. Assume that the two economies are collectivist. Taking the prechange paths of play and cultural beliefs as given, will a merchant hire an agent from the other economy? Clearly, M_s will not hire A_t if $W_{s,t}^* > W_{s,s}^*$, that is, if M_s has to pay A_t more than he has to pay to A_s to keep him honest. Given the cultural beliefs, the symmetry of the two economies, and the collective strategy held in each of them, it follows that

$$\eta h_c^{t,t} + (1 - \eta)h_h^{t,t} = h_h^{s,t} < h_h^{s,s} \quad \forall \eta \in (0, 1). \tag{*}$$

$$\mu h_c^{t,t} + (1 - \mu)h_h^{t,t} = h_c^{s,t} > h_c^{s,s} \quad \forall \mu \in (0, 1). \tag{**}$$

Inequality (**) states that if A_t may not be punished by the merchants from economy t for having cheated M_s, then the perceived probability that he is hired after cheating M_s is higher than the probability that an agent from economy s is hired. Simply stated, after cheating M_s, A_t has an employment option not available to A_s, namely, to be hired by merchants from his own economy.

Proposition 9.2 established that the function w increases in h_c and decreases in h_h. Thus for s = K and t = J: $W_{s,t}^* = w(h_h^{s,t}, h_c^{s,t}) > w(h_h^{s,s}, h_c^{s,s}) = W_{s,s}^* \, \forall \, \mu \in [0, 1), \eta \in (0, 1]$.

By symmetry the same result holds for s = J and t = K. The best response of a merchant from one economy is never to hire an agent from the other economy unless $\mu = 1$ and $\eta = 0$. If this condition does not hold, the joint economy is a segregated one in which merchants from one economy hire only agents from their own economy and play the collectivist strategy with respect to them.

Assume now that two individualistic economies interact. Following the line of argument above and using the fact that $h_h^{s,s} = h_c^{s,s}$ in individualistic economies, it is easy to demonstrate that within each economy a merchant is indifferent between hiring an agent from his own economy and hiring one from the other economy, because the optimal wage (W^*) of an agent is identical. (Clearly, this assumes that the number of P and A in each economy is "large.") If all the merchants are indifferent (and hence may as well hire randomly from both economies), the joint economy is an integrated one in which an individualistic strategy is played. Q.E.D.

Proof of Proposition 9.5

Suppose that economy s is collectivist and t is individualistic. (a) A^t who cheated M^s will be rehired with probability $h_c^{s,t} = \mu h_c^{t,t} + (1 - \mu)h_h^{t,t} > h_c^{s,s} \ \forall \ \mu \in [0, 1]$. A^t who was honest when employed by M^s will be rehired with probability $h_h^{s,t} = \eta h_c^{t,t} + (1 - \eta)h_h^{t,t}$, which is equal to $h_h^{s,s} \ \forall \ \eta \in [0, 1]$. Since W^{*c} (the collectivist society wage) is lower than the wage offered in the individualistic society, $\forall \ \mu \in [0, 1]$, $\eta \in [0, 1]$, $h_c^{s,t} > h_c^{s,s}$ and $h_h^{s,t} = h_h^{s,s}$, a wage higher than W^{*c} is required to keep the agent honest. (b) The minimum wage for which $A^{t,s}$ is honest is W^* s.t. $(W^* + \delta\tau V_h^u)/(1 - \delta + \delta\tau) = \alpha + V_c^u$, where the superscript u represents unemployed, $V_h^u = \eta V_h^{u,c} + (1 - \eta)V_h^{u,c}$, $V_c^u = \mu V_c^{u,c} + (1 - \mu)V_h^{u,c}$. The minimum wage for which $A^{t,t}$ is honest is $W^{*,I}$ s.t. $(W^{*,I} + \delta\tau V_h^{u,I})/(1 - \delta(1 - \tau)) = \alpha + V_c^{u,I}$. $W^{*,I} - W^* = (1 - \delta)[V_h^{u,I} - V_c^u] + \delta\tau(\mu - \eta)[V_h^{u,I} - V_c^{u,I}]$. All the terms in $W^{*,I} - W^*$ are positive except for $(\mu - \eta)$. Integration occurs if and only if $W^{*,I} - W^* \geq 0$, implying the sufficient and necessary conditions. (c) The necessary condition follows directly from the analysis in (b). Continuity implies that to prove the sufficient condition, it is enough to consider $\mu = 0$ and $\eta = 1$. From (b), $W^{*,I} - W^* \geq 0$ if and only if $[1 - \delta(1 - \tau)][V_c^{u,I} - V_h^{u,c}] \geq \delta\tau[V_h^{u,I} - V_h^u]$. Because $V_c^{u,I} - V_h^{u,c} < V_h^{u,I} - V_h^u \ \forall \ \delta$ and the limit of $(1 - \delta + \tau\delta)/\delta\tau$ equals 1 as δ goes to 1, $\exists \ \tilde{\delta} \in (0, 1)$, s.t. $\forall \ \delta \geq \tilde{\delta}$, the inequality above fails to hold. Q.E.D.

PART IV

The Empirical Method of Comparative and Historical Institutional Analysis

The inherent indeterminacy and context-specificity of institutions challenge our ability to study them using the traditional social science empirical methods. These methods rest on the premise that, given a set of exogenous and observable features of a situation, deductive theory can sufficiently restrict the outcome set to render a positive analysis meaningful. In the case of endogenous institutions, we lack such a theory.

Parts I–III highlight several reasons why it may be impossible to develop a deductive theory of institutions. Institutions are inherently indeterminate and context-specific. Various transactions can be linked to a central one, and multiple equilibria – and hence institutions – can prevail in the repeated situations that are essential to institutional analysis. Different institutions embodying distinct cognitive models and information can be self-enforcing. Institutional change is a function of the prevailing institutions, while its direction is influenced by institutional elements inherited from the past. Whether or not a deductive theory of institutions will ever be developed, our current state of knowledge is such that we cannot understand institutions relevant in a particular time and place by relying solely on deductive theory.

Inductive analysis à la Bacon, which identifies and classifies institutions based on their observable features alone, is similarly deficient for studying institutions. Pure induction is insufficient because various institutional elements, such as beliefs and norms that motivate behavior, are not directly observable. Moreover, the same observable elements can be part of different institutions; identical rules and organizations can be components of institutions that differ in their beliefs and norms and hence implications. Finally, over time, institutional change can cause the same rule or organization to be part of distinct institutions with different welfare implications.[1]

Genoa and Pisa, for example, appear to have had the same *podesteria* system, but they had very distinct institutions. In Genoa the podestá created a balance of power, whereas in Pisa he represented the domination of one group over another. The merchant guild was initially a welfare-enhancing institution that protected property rights. Over time, however, guilds such as the Hanseatic League began to use their power to reduce welfare by preventing competition.

Multiple institutions can prevail in a given situation, institutions have unobservable components, and the same observable elements can be part of different institutions. Furthermore, the impact of an institution depends on the details of these components and the broader context. Econometric analysis of institutions is therefore plagued by problems of having to cope with too many endogenous and unobservable variables whose causal relationships are not well understood and whose implications depend on the context. Empirical studies that identify an institution with macro-level proxies of the institution's implications, such as political violence, peace, or the protection of property rights, are similarly problematic. Without recognizing the institutional foundations of outcomes and the broader context, an attempt to evaluate the welfare implication of these outcomes is bound to be misleading. As the case of Genoa reveals, peace may not be conducive to economic growth, and political violence may not endanger property rights. Similarly, protecting property rights may reduce welfare and slow economic growth. In Europe, the decline in slavery – de facto prohibiting property rights in humans – contributed to growth by fostering labor-saving technological innovations.

Part IV responds to the challenge posed by the inability to study institutions using the traditional methods of social science by introducing a complementary case study method. Rather than focusing on predicting institutions, this method focuses on *identifying* them, understanding their details and origins, and examining the factors that render them self-enforcing. It then evaluates an institution's impact based on comprehending its micro-details and the broader context. Such an analysis is crucial for comprehending past and present institutions, identifying the factors that lead to distinct institutional trajectories, and foreseeing the

---

[1] Conversely, although a rule may no longer be supposed to influence behavior, it may nevertheless do so. Indeed, the community responsibility system, described in Chapter 10, was effective for a long time after it was formally abolished.

direction of institutional change in response to, say, institutional reform or an exogenous environmental change.

This empirical method – a theoretically informed case study method – is based on *interactive, context-specific analysis*. Its objective is both to identify and understand institutions relevant in a given situation and to foster the understanding of institutions in general. Central to this method is a context-specific analysis that interactively uses deductive theory, contextual knowledge of the situation and its history, and context-specific modeling to develop and evaluate conjectures about the relevance of particular institutions.

Because institutional dynamics are historical processes, relying on the contextual knowledge of the situation and its history responds to the context-specificity and historical contingency of institutions. Combined with theory and context-specific modeling, such knowledge helps the researcher to form a conjecture about the relevant institutions, to expose why particular institutions were more likely to emerge in the particular historical setting under consideration, and to understand how they were rendered self-enforcing.

The method can be crudely summarized as follows. Theory and contextual and comparative information are used to identify important issues, transactions, and possible causal relationships in the episode under consideration. They are also used to determine which institutional factors can be treated as exogenous and which are to be treated as endogenous. Contextual analysis, generic theoretical insights, and empirical evidence are used to develop a conjecture about the relevant institution: which transactions were (or were not) linked, why and in what way, and how and why the resulting game and the beliefs within it led to particular behavior.

The conjecture is formalized and evaluated using a context-specific model in which the exogenous, historically determined technological and institutional factors define the rules of the game. Combining analysis of the game, which recognizes the role of historical factors in influencing equilibrium selection, with evidence enables us to evaluate – reject, refine, or "accept" (i.e., not reject) – the conjecture and thereby to understand the relevant endogenous institutions. This conjecturing and evaluating process is interactive: we repeatedly use theory, contextual knowledge, and evidence to develop a conjecture; we then present and analyze the conjecture using an explicit context-specific model; and finally we use predictions and other insights from the model to evaluate and modify the conjecture.

The analyses of historical institutions presented in Parts I–III relied on such interactive, context-specific analysis. The empirical study in Chapter 10 more explicitly illustrates the need for, and benefit of, this method and its main assertion, that induction, deduction, and context-specific analysis are complementary in institutional analysis. Theory and context-specific modeling discipline the historical accounts, whereas induction and contextual-knowledge discipline the theoretical arguments.

Chapter 10 makes this argument by examining the institutions that supported impersonal exchange in Europe before the territorial state provided (relatively) impartial justice. It analyzes the historical transition from economies based on personal exchange to those in which progressively more impersonal exchange is also possible. The analysis thus touches on an issue central to economic history and development: the transition of economies and societies from ones in which personal relationships limit economic and social interactions to ones in which impersonal economic exchange and social mobility prevail.

Chapter 11 argues the generality of the assertion that neither deduction nor induction is sufficient for analyzing endogenous institutions. It then introduces the mechanics of conducting an interactive, context-specific analysis, focusing on the role of contextual, historical knowledge and context-specific modeling. Appendix C, which examines private-order, reputation-based institutions, complements this discussion by elaborating on the role of theory in an interactive, theoretically informed, context-specific analysis.

10

The Institutional Foundations of Impersonal Exchange

This chapter illustrates the merit of interactive, theoretically informed, context-specific analysis by examining a central question in economic history and development economics. This question concerns the institutional evolution that enabled increasingly more impersonal exchange in some economies but not in others (see North 1990; Greif 1994a, 1997a, 1998b, 2000, 2004b, 2004c; Rodrik 2003; Shirley 2004). We often assert that such institutional evolution facilitates specialization, efficiency, and growth. Yet we know little about the historical development of the institutional foundations of impersonal exchange.

This historical development is the focus of the chapter. It examines the nature and dynamics of institutions that supported impersonal exchange characterized by separation between the *quid* and the *quo* across jurisdictional boundaries in premodern Europe. Commerce expanded particularly during the three hundred years prior to the mid-fourteenth century even though there were no impartial courts with geographically extensive judicial powers to support exchange among traders from various corners of Europe. What were the institutions, if any, that supported interjurisdictional exchange characterized by separation between the *quid* and the *quo* over time and space? Specifically, were there institutions that enabled such exchange that was also impersonal, in the sense that transacting did not depend on expectations of future gains from interactions among the current exchange partners, or on knowledge of past conduct, or on the ability to report misconduct to future trading partners?

The theoretical and historical analysis presented here substantiates that in premodern Europe impersonal exchange characterized by separation between the *quid* and the *quo* across jurisdictional boundaries was facilitated by a self-enforcing institution: the community responsibility system. Central to this system were the particularly European, self-governed communities known as communes, which occupy the gray area between communities and states as we usually conceptualize them. The communes were similar to communities in that they were characterized by intracommunity personal familiarity. Like states, however, they had a (geographically) local monopoly over the legal use of coercive power. The courts of these self-governed communes, however, were partial and represented the interests of the community.

Under the community responsibility system, a local, community court held all members of a different commune legally liable for default by any one involved in contracts with a member of the local community. If the defaulter's communal court refused to compensate the injured party, the local court confiscated the property of any member of the defaulter's commune present in its jurisdiction as compensation. A commune could avoid compensating for the default of one of its members only by ceasing to trade with the other commune. When this cost was too high, a commune court's best response was to dispense impartial justice to nonmembers who had been cheated by a member of the commune. Expecting ex post dispensation of impartial justice, traders were motivated to enter into impersonal, intercommunity exchange. Intercommunity impersonal exchange was possible not despite the partiality of the court but because of it; the court cared about the community's collective reputation.

More generally, the strategy and organizational structure associated with the community responsibility system enabled impersonal exchange among traders with finite life-spans in the absence of partial legal contract enforcement. The community responsibility system turned communities into ongoing organizations with infinite life-spans that internalized the cost of a default by each of their members on other members. Partial communal courts were thereby motivated to administer impartial justice.

The system also motivated communities to establish the organizational structure enabling one to reveal credibly his personal and communal identity to his trading partner and motivating one who was cheated to reveal misconduct to the court. This ex post information, rather than ex ante knowledge of past conduct or the ability to communicate misconduct to future trading partners, enabled exchange to be an equilibrium outcome.

Two intertransactional linkages were therefore central to the community responsibility system. First, the linkages of information-sharing, coercive, and economic transactions among particular groups of traders – the communes' members – made it possible to believe a commune would punish a member for default in intercommunity exchange. Second, the intercommunity economic transaction between particular traders was linked to future transactions between all members of their respective communes. A commune was thereby motivated to punish a member who defaulted in intercommunity exchange.

The community responsibility system constitutes the missing link in our understanding of the institutional development that led to modern markets. Theoretically, the development of law-based institutions supporting impersonal exchange is puzzling. Arguably, reputation-based institutions that support personal exchange have a low fixed cost but a high marginal cost of exchanging with unfamiliar individuals. Law-based institutions, which enable impersonal exchange, have a high fixed setup cost but a low marginal cost for establishing new exchange relationships (Li 1999; Dixit 2004).

If exchange was initially personal, why was a legal system established to support impersonal exchange despite the high fixed cost, and how was knowledge about the benefit of impersonal exchange generated?[1] In Europe the community responsibility system constituted an intermediary institution that was neither purely law based nor purely reputation based. It enabled intercommunity impersonal exchange based on communities' partial legal systems and reputational considerations.

The community responsibility system was a self-enforcing institution in which incentives to both courts and traders were provided endogenously as an equilibrium outcome. Over time, however, trade expansion and growth in the size, number, and economic and social heterogeneity of merchants' communities reduced its economic efficiency and intracommunity political viability. By the late thirteenth century, the system was declining, at least in the areas examined here, due to the impact of trade and urban growth on the very factors that had rendered it an equilibrium outcome. Ironically, the community responsibility system may have undermined itself as the processes that it fostered increased trade and urban growth – the causes of its decline.

The ability to effectively replace the community responsibility system reflected the environmental effect, because it depended on political governance. When and where the appropriate institutional environment prevailed, its demise fostered the gradual development of the institutions

---

[1] Other factors apart from the expenses of setting up the system can hinder the transition from reputation-based to law-based institutions, even when law-based institutions are more efficient. These factors include coordination failure (Greif 1994a; Kranton 1996), collective action problems (Li 1999; Dixit 2004), and the inability of the state to commit to respect property rights (Greif 1997b, 2004b).

supporting impersonal exchange based on territorial law and individual legal responsibility that are common today.

This analysis also relates to a question central to international trade (trade across jurisdictional boundaries). This question concerns the institutional determinants of trade, the impact of domestic institutions on these trade flows, and their impact on domestic institutions (see Greif 1992; Staiger 1995; Maggi 1999; Grossman and Helpman 2002, 2003). The community responsibility system was a domestic institution that fostered trade across jurisdictional boundaries. Furthermore, the institutional transition that the decline of the system entailed highlights the importance of studying the causal relationships between international trade and the development of domestic institutions.

Despite numerous studies on the impact of international trade on growth, very little conclusive causal evidence has emerged (Helpman 2004). The history of the community responsibility system supports the conjecture that institutional change is an important channel through which trade influences growth.[2] Indeed, the decline of the system and the subsequent institutional development fostered the institutional distinction between domestic and international trade. Under the community responsibility system, there was little, if any, distinction between the institutions that governed impersonal exchange within and outside states. Indeed, *nation* is the term frequently used during the premodern period to refer to communes. The uneven demise of the system within and across national boundaries, however, rendered state boundaries relevant to trade.

The historical analysis presented here draws on the rich historical sources available from Florence and England. Together with secondary sources, these sources are sufficient to establish the centrality of the community responsibility system in Europe as a whole, although there is much room for additional historical and comparative research.

An earlier generation of scholars (e.g., Wach 1868; Santini 1886; Arias 1901; Maitland and Bateson 1901; Planitz 1919; Patourel 1937) noted the wealth of historical documents reflecting aspects of the community responsibility system. This chapter builds on the works of these prominent scholars who, lacking an appropriate analytical framework, could not account for the system details, development, implications, and interrelationships between various institutional and organizational features.

---

[2] I am indebted to Elhanan Helpman for pointing out the general importance of this issue. Acemolglu et al. (2002) conjecture that premodern Atlantic trade fostered institutional development.

The importance of studying the institutional foundation of impersonal exchange during the late medieval period did not escape more recent scholarly attention. But scholars have relied either on theory (and formal modeling) alone or on history alone to assert the relevance of particular institutions. Neither line of research succeeded in establishing that impersonal exchange prevailed or in identifying its institutional foundations. I compare these researches and conclusions with the one derived here to highlight the merit of theoretically informed, context-specific analysis.

Section 10.1 provides a historical background. Then sections 10.2 and 10.3 critique analyses based on either theory or history claiming that particular institutions governed impersonal exchange in premodern Europe. Section 10.4 presents a context-specific analysis of the community responsibility system. Section 10.5 discusses the system's endogenous decline and subsequent institutional developments.

10.1 EXCHANGE IN WHICH THE *QUID* IS SEPARATED FROM THE *QUO*

Exchange characterized by a separation between the *quid* and the *quo* over time and space was common in Western Europe during the late medieval commercial expansion, perhaps for the first time since the fall of the Roman Empire. In towns, fairs, and marketplaces, merchants from distant parts of Europe provided and received credit, used contracts to buy and sell goods for future delivery, and insured cargo they shipped overseas.[3]

What institutions generated these regularities of behavior among merchants from distant parts of Europe? Did they enable impersonal exchange characterized by separation between the *quid* and the *quo*? Or was exchange confined to impersonal spot exchange (supported by local courts) or personal exchange (supported by repeated interactions or social relationships)?[4]

---

[3] For a general discussion, see Lopez and Raymond (1955, pp. 157–238) and de Roover (1963, pp. 42–118). For evidence on exchange among merchants from distinct parts of Europe, see R. Reynolds (1929, 1930, 1931); Face (1958); Postan (1973); Moore (1985); and Verlinden (1979). For historical examples, see Obertus Scriba (1190, nos. 138, 139, 669); Lanfranco Scriba (1202–26, vol. 1, no. 524); Guglielmo Cassinese (1190–2, no. 250).

[4] The historical evidence does not allow us to address these questions by tracing the exchange relationships of individual merchants over time. Discovering whether impersonal exchange was possible in premodern Europe requires determining whether there was an institution that enabled it.

Institutions that support impersonal exchange characterized by a separation between the *quid* and the *quo* over time and space have to mitigate the contractual problem intrinsic to it: the need to commit ex ante not to breach contractual obligations ex post despite the separation between the *quid* and the *quo*. A borrower, for example, can enrich himself after obtaining a loan by not repaying his debt. Expecting such behavior ex post, a lender will not lend ex ante in the absence of institutions that enable the borrower to commit to repay the loan. For such commitment to be undertaken in impersonal exchange, trading partners have to be able to commit to one another even though they do not expect to trade again, lack information about their partners' past conduct, and are not able to credibly commit to report misconduct to future trading partners.

10.2 THE INADEQUACY OF DEDUCTION ALONE TO IDENTIFY INSTITUTIONS

Scholars who have studied the institutional foundations of impersonal exchange have noted the absence of an effective, national, and impartial legal system in the early stages of the late medieval commercial expansion in Europe. They drew on theoretical arguments – deduction – to conjecture about whether and which alternative institutions prevailed. In the absence of contextual and historical analysis, different scholars reached surprisingly different conclusions. Those who view contract enforcement by the state as the cement of economic activity conclude that impersonal exchange did not take place. Impersonal exchange was infeasible, according to this view, because the "personal ties, voluntaristic constraints, and ostracism" that supported exchange during this period were not "effective" in supporting impersonal exchange (North 1991, p. 100). According to this view, the rise of impersonal exchange in premodern Europe had to wait for the rise of the state and its legal system.

Other scholars reach the opposite conclusion. Those who object to state intervention in economic affairs claim that the prevalence of impersonal exchange during the late medieval period supports their view that state intervention is unnecessary even for contract enforcement. Thus, Benson (1989) argues that during this period a private-order institution, that of the law merchant, enabled "thousands of traders [who] traveled to fairs and markets all over Europe exchanging goods which they knew little about with people they knew little about" (p. 648). "Merchants formed their own courts to adjudicate disputes in accordance with their own laws. These courts' decisions were accepted by winners and losers alike, because they were backed by the threat of ostracism by the merchant community at large – a very effective boycott sanction" (p. 649). This was a "voluntarily produced, voluntarily adjudicated, and voluntarily enforced mercantile law" (p. 647).

The validity of this assertion, like the validity of the claim that impersonal exchange did not take place, is questionable, given the lack of empirical support and the internal logical contradictions. Benson's only reference to historical support is a study by Trackman (1983, p. 10), but that study examined the content of law during the premodern period, not how it was enforced. Although Trackman suggests that reputation probably supported impersonal exchange, he does not substantiate the assertion.

Logically, the argument is not very convincing either. How could the fear of ostracism influence behavior if interaction was with individuals about whom "they knew little" (Benson 1989, p. 641)? For an argument about ostracism to hold water, it is necessary to articulate how information about past behavior is diffused among traders and how they are motivated to participate in collective punishment.

10.3 THE INADEQUACY OF THEORY ENRICHED WITH A MICROANALYTIC MODEL

Recognition of the need to endogenously account for information flows and enforcement is at the heart of the article on this issue by Milgrom, North, and Weingast (1990), who use a microanalytic model to lend support to the deductive assertion that a private-order institution supported impersonal exchange. Their analysis focuses on contract enforcement at the Champagne fairs, arguably the most important interregional trading fair in Europe during the twelfth and thirteenth centuries (Verlinden 1979). During this period, much of the trade between Northern and Southern Europe was conducted at these fairs, where merchants from different localities entered into contracts, including contracts for future delivery, that required enforcement over time (Verlinden 1979). How could a merchant from one community commit to honor contractual obligations toward a member of another?

In the large merchant community that frequented the fairs, Milgrom et al. argue, a reputation mechanism based on familiarity could not have surmounted this commitment problem, because the traders lacked the social networks required to make past actions known to all. Noting the operation of judges at the fairs, they pose the following question: "What prevents a merchant from cheating by supplying lower quality goods than promised, and then leaving the fairs before being detected? In these circumstances the cheated merchant might be able to get a judgment against his supplier, but what good would it do if the supplier never returned to the fairs? Perhaps ostracism by the other merchants might be an effective way to enforce the payment of judgments. However, if that is so, why was a legal system needed at all?" (pp. 5–6).

To address this question, Milgrom et al. present a formal model, the essence of which is as follows. Suppose that each pair of traders is matched only once and each trader knows only his own experience. The fairs' court is modeled as capable only of verifying past actions and keeping records of traders who cheated in the past. Acquiring information and appealing to the court is costly for each merchant. Despite these costs, there exists a (symmetric sequential) equilibrium in which cheating does not occur. The court's ability to activate a multilateral reputation mechanism by controlling information provides the appropriate incentives. Each merchant is motivated to pay the fee and check on the past conduct of his partner with the court, because only then will the court record the exchange. Without this record, the court will not make the occurrence of cheating known to others in the future. Expecting not to be punished in the future, one's best response is to cheat. Anticipating that this will be the case, a trader finds it best to pay the court and make a record to begin with, thereby ensuring that a cheating is recorded. A trader who was cheated is motivated to complain, because the cheater will then compensate him. The cheater will do so because otherwise the court will inform each of his future partners that he cheated in the past. These future partners will cheat a trader who cheated before (if he did not make amends), knowing that the court will not inform future partners of their actions.

Hence a court can ensure contract enforcement through time, even if it cannot use coercive power against cheaters. Milgrom et al. suggest that the role of the Champagne fairs' court was similar to that described in their theoretical analysis. This theoretical analysis thus supports the assertion that the law merchant system could have provided contract enforcement at the fairs. This analysis is theoretically insightful, but is it empirically relevant? Was the law merchant system central to late medieval trade in general and the fairs in particular?

Milgrom et al. bring two arguments to support the relevance of their analysis. First, the analysis explains exchange characterized by separation between the *quid* and the *quo* among traders from distinct parts of Europe at the fairs. Put differently, the analysis gains support from accounting for the behavior it seeks to explain. Second, the authors argue that "key characteristics" of the "model correspond to practices found at the Champagne fairs. Although merchants at the fairs were not required to query before any contract, the institutions of the fair provided this information in another manner. As noted previously, the fairs closely controlled entry and exit. A merchant could not enter the fair without being in good standing with those who controlled entry, and any merchant caught cheating at the fair would be incarcerated and brought to justice under the rules of the fair. So anyone a merchant met at the fair could be presumed to have a 'good reputation' in precisely the sense of our model" (p. 20).

The analysis – using a microanalytic model – identifies a theoretical possibility but does not establish that it corresponds to a historical reality. It devotes little attention to substantiating the relevance of the analysis. The weight of substantiation is on the argument that the model can explain the behavior that motivated its formulation to begin with. But many models can generate this pattern of behavior. As a matter of fact, Milgrom et al.'s assertion that the authorities at the fairs had the ability to capture one who would then be "incarcerated and brought to justice at the fair" (p. 20) suggests the need to examine the role of coercive power rather than commercial sanctions in the operation of the fairs. Indeed, if one accepts their assertion that the fair's court could have verified a cheater's identity and known about his past transgression, a cheater would not have returned to the fair for fear of coercive retribution rather than commercial sanctions. In short, because context and theory are not interactively used to form and evaluate a conjecture, their analysis is unsatisfactory.

The analysis suffers from three additional problems. First, the historical context is essentially ignored in attempting to identify the relevant institution. As a result, the hypothesis and the model incorporate assumptions that are questionable given our historical knowledge. The model assumes that the identities of traders could have been verified by the court and that merchants traded with their own capital. But just how did the authorities of the fairs verify that a merchant was in good standing? No reliable form of identification was available during that period (there were no picture IDs), and forgeries of documents were common. Moreover, during this period merchants throughout Europe used agents. Merchants could have cheated anonymously by sending agents to trade on their behalf.

Second, the analysis does not make use of relevant historical details. For example, the analysis assumes that there is a group of players, the traders. But traders during the late medieval period were only a subset of the population. This is a relevant aspect of the historical context, because it raises the issue of how the "fly-by-night" problem was mitigated. What prevented a peasant near the fair from coming to it once, taking out a loan, and disappearing forever?

Third, in developing their hypothesis, Milgrom et al. ignore relevant theoretical insights. For example, game theory highlights the importance of a sufficiently long horizon in sustaining cooperation (Appendix C, section 2.1). Given the relatively short life expectancy in the medieval period, claiming that the law merchant system was the institution that governed impersonal exchange among individuals ignores this problem. It is inconsistent with the analysis to argue, as they do, that trade was actually conducted among members of the same families for generations. If this had been the case, trade would not have been impersonal and could have been based on families' concerns with their reputations.

Theory, then, even theory combined with a microanalytic model, fails to explain convincingly whether an institution supporting impersonal exchange prevailed in premodern Europe and to identify it if it did. As I show later, relying only on induction – observable historical evidence – to identify this institution failed as well.

10.4   THE COMMUNITY RESPONSIBILITY SYSTEM

In attempting to identify the institution, if any, that supported impersonal exchange during the late medieval period, it is useful to note first the absence of one institution: a state with a legal system capable of effectively supporting impersonal exchange between individuals from distant localities. Local courts existed throughout Europe and had a legal monopoly over the use of coercive power in rather limited territorial areas. Even within a relatively well-organized political unit, such as England, there was no legal system that could provide the required enforcement.[5]

The law was absent in yet another sense. By and large, local courts were not unbiased agents of a central legal authority or impartial dispensers of justice. More often than not, they were partial; controlled by and reflected the interest of the local elite. In the countryside as well as in cities, local courts were controlled by the local landed or urban elite. An English charter concerning the imperial German city of Lübeck noted, for

---

[5] See Plucknett (1949, p. 142); Ashburner and Walter (1909); Postan (1973); and *Select Cases Concerning the Law Merchant, A.D. 1239–1633*, vol. 2.

example, that the city is "governed" by its "burgesses and merchants," who are responsible for dispensing justice.[6]

According to many economic historians, because no impartial legal system was effective over a large geographical area, personal exchange predominated, and impersonal exchange was either absent or confined to spot exchange supported by local courts (see North 1990). But this conclusion overlooks that European medieval trade was conducted in the social and institutional context of communes, self-governed communities.[7] During the late medieval period, most of the towns west of the Baltic Sea in the North and the Adriatic Sea in the South acquired this status. Although marked regional differences across communes existed, they shared much in common. As in a community, members of communes knew one another; like states, however, the communes had local enforcement institutions, often based on legitimate use of coercive power.[8] There were entry barriers to communes; gaining affiliation with one was usually a lengthy and costly process. Although local, rural to urban migration was common, migration from one commune to another meant losing the benefits of citizenship. Throughout Europe, immigration was expensive and risky; in the extreme case of Venice, acquiring citizenship meant one had to pay taxes for at least ten years. In Genoa, it took three years to acquire.

Is it theoretically possible that despite the partiality of the courts and their limited geographical scope, these communes provided the

---

[6] *Calendar of the Patent Rolls* 1266–72, 20.

Substantiating the assertion that such courts were partial and that their judgments reflected the interests of the local elite is subtle. Particularly problematic is finding evidence about partiality with respect to foreign merchants, because, as I argue, under the community responsibility system these courts provided – as an equilibrium phenomenon – impartial justice exactly because they were partial.

Yet many documents from the period, discussed shortly, reflect distrust of the impartiality of courts. In England local courts provided partial justice to local peasants (Hanawalt 1974); it is reasonable that, in the absence of a countervailing force, they would not have dispensed equal justice to nonlocals. Court deliberations in Italy reflect the fact that the profitability of local businesses, not impartial justice, motivated legal rulings in disputes with nonlocals (English 1988). In Germany nonlocal merchants, peasants, and even lower-ranked nobles were considered foreigners. They were formally called *guests* and were widely discriminated against in courts of law (Volckart 2001).

[7] While some will use the term *commune* to refer to the Italian city-states that were independent, it is also used, as here, to refer to autonomously governed communities in general.

[8] While the communal structure underpinned the community responsibility system, organizations representing the communes, such as guilds, were those actually involved in intercommunal commercial disputes.

foundation for an institution that supported intercommunity impersonal exchange characterized by distance between the *quid* and the *quo*? If so, did this institution prevail in late medieval Europe?

10.4.1 A Theory of the Community Responsibility System

The following complete-information, repeated-game model indicates that, under certain conditions, a community responsibility system can support, as an equilibrium outcome, impersonal exchange characterized by separation between the *quid* and the *quo*.[9] Consider a game in which N_L lenders and N_B borrowers ($N_L > N_B$) are engaged (without loss of generality) in credit transactions. Each player lives for T periods: T – 1 periods of trading and one period of "retirement." The time discount factor is δ. At the beginning of a period, the oldest cohort of borrowers and lenders dies and is replaced. At the beginning of each period, a borrower can decide whether or not to initiate exchange. Every borrower who initiates an exchange is randomly matched with a lender.

A lender who was matched with a borrower can decide whether or not to lend the finite amount l. A borrower who does not travel receives a payoff of 0 and lenders who do not lend receive a payoff of r > 0. A borrower who receives a loan can repay it or not. If he repays, the lender receives the principle, l, and an interest of i > r. The borrower receives goods valued at g > 0. If the borrower does not repay the loan, the lender receives a payoff of 0, and, because he lost his capital, he leaves the game. The borrower reaps G > g from not paying and G < g + i + l. By these assumptions lending is efficient but is profitable to both parties only if the borrower pays his debt. The borrower is better off, however, not paying and cheating is inefficient.

Because we want to capture situations in which there are no expectations for future exchange, assume that the probability of matching between a particular lender and borrower is zero.[10] To capture exchange, which is impersonal in the sense that a lender does not know a borrower's past conduct nor can he inform other lenders of misconduct, assume that

---

[9] Fearon and Laitin (1996) explore how communities can be motivated to discipline their members to achieve interethnic political cooperation.

[10] For the following analysis to hold it is sufficient to assume that the probability of a particular pair rematching is sufficiently low, relative to the time discount factor and gains from exchange and cheating, to render the bilateral reputation mechanism ineffective.

past conduct is private information known only to transacting agents. Whatever transpired between a particular lender and borrower can be observed only by them.

In this game there is no equilibrium with lending on the equilibrium path. The assumption that borrowers have finite life-spans is sufficient for this outcome. A borrower's unique best response in the last period is to cheat, implying that the lender would not lend in this period and the game unravels. Furthermore, even if we were to assume that the players have infinite life-spans, the impersonality of exchange implies that there is still no equilibrium with lending. Because past conduct is private information and repeated interaction is lacking, lenders, as individuals or a group, cannot credibly threaten to punish a borrower who has cheated in the past.[11] The analysis thereby reveals the problems that any institution fostering impersonal exchange has to mitigate.

When we add communities to the game, however, an equilibrium with lending can exist despite the borrowers' finite life-spans and the impersonality of exchange. Assume that there are two communities:[12] all borrowers are members of community B, and all lenders are members of community L. Each community has a territory, and all lending and repayment is made in the lenders' territory. Each community has an enforcement institution – a monopoly over coercive power – within its territory. Historically, each self-governed community has its own courts. Accordingly, let the lenders'

---

[11] Multilateral reputation mechanism (e.g., Greif 1989, 1993; Kandori 1992) can support lending if future lenders can condition their behavior on a borrower's past conduct. In models of incomplete information about traders' types, there are equilibria in which the implied costs of building relationships with a new trader of unknown type sufficiently increases the cost of cheating one's current trade partner to support exchange, even in the absence of information about identities and past history (Ghosh and Ray 1996; Kranton 1996). Consistent with the focus here on exchange that is impersonal in the sense that there is also no expectation of future trade, the low frequency of bilateral interactions assumed here precludes such equilibria. Contagious equilibria (Kandori 1992; Ellison 1994) do not exist in this one-sided prisoner's dilemma game as a cheated player leaves the game. The analysis is also robust in assuming that a borrower can use the capital he embezzled. See Appendix C.

[12] Assuming more communities does not qualitatively change the analysis as such an assumption does not fundamentally change the strategic interactions between two communities. The community responsibility system provides a disincentive for communities to get involved in a conflict between two foreign merchants. Having more communities increases each community's outside options, however, implying that the necessary conditions for the community responsibility system are less likely to hold. I argue later that increasing number of communes contributed to the decline of the community responsibility system.

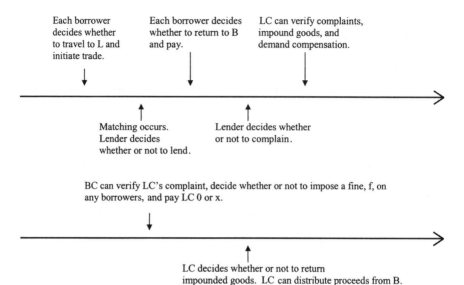

Figure 10.1. Time-action line. *Note*: LC denotes the lenders' court; BC, the borrowers' court.

court denote the lenders' enforcement institution and borrowers' court the borrowers' enforcement institution.

Because these courts represented the interests of each community's members, assume that a community court's payoff is the net present value of the sum of the payoffs of the community's living members (i.e., members of cohorts 0 to T).[13] Two assumptions are implicit in this specification. First, each community member's payoff has an equal weight in the court's objective function. This clearly does not hold at all times and places; it is used here as a benchmark case. Second, courts do not care about the welfare of future members or respect the "honor" of the commune. Relaxing this assumption only strengthens the results presented here.[14]

---

[13] The court's value function at the end of a period is the same as at the beginning of the next period.

[14] I assume away the possibility of bribes, because decisions about disputes in intercommunity exchange were made by a community's representatives and involved many decision makers. In Florence before 1250, for example, initiating actions over disputes in intercommunity exchange was the responsibility of the city administrator and his council. By 1325, in order to take such actions, the city administrator had to make two requests to the commune to get approval. In 1415 the statute detailing the rules for such actions specified that they were under the authority of consuls responsible for crafts and trade and no longer under the authority of the city's administrator. For these consuls to initiate actions in intercommunity disputes, the actions had to be approved by two additional bodies, the Consuls of the Popolo

Figure 10.1 presents the time line of actions. Each period, t, begins with the previous game between borrowers and lenders. A lender can then complain, at personal cost $c > 0$, to the lenders' court that he was cheated. The lenders' court can verify the validity of the complaints at cost C_L.[15] The court can also impound the goods of the $I_B(t)$ borrowers present in its territory.[16] By impounding a borrower's goods, the lenders' court gains $g > 0$, but impounding causes the goods to lose value, for example, due to the inability to sell them on time or through damage during the storage period. Denote this damage by $d > 0$, and assume $g - d > 0$ to ensure that impounding is profitable. The most a lenders' court can gain by impounding is therefore $I_B(t)(g - d)$. The borrowers' court can then verify the validity of the complaint at cost C_B, impose a fine, $f \geq 0$, on a borrower who cheated, and transfer the amount x (which is no larger than the fine collected) to the lenders' court. (The implicit assumption, relaxed below, is that the probability of disagreement between the lenders' court and the borrowers' court is zero.) Finally the lenders' court decides whether to distribute the proceeds from the impounded goods or the sum provided by the borrowers' court and to whom.

A court's actions are common knowledge. Analytically, this assumption is justified, because, in the equilibrium studied later, lenders and borrowers are motivated to discover the courts' actions.[17] Historically, the courts' actions were indeed made public (in Florence decisions regarding intercommunal disputes were recorded in a publicly displayed book [Vecchio and Casanova 1894, pp. 137–9, 265]).

The reader may be wondering at this point the about rationale for assuming here that a lender can prove cheating at the court, because a similar assumption was not made in the game without communities. Even in the absence of a court, a lender who was cheated can arguably convey, at some cost, this fact to others. In the game without communities, however,

and the Consuls of the Commune (Santini 1886, pp. 168–72). Bribes arguably made arbitration of disputes problematic.

[15] Historically, courts verified complaints by considering the contracts, questioning witnesses, and approaching the borrower for proof of payment. In particular, a lender buttressed a claim that a debt was not paid by furnishing the debt contract. Normally the borrower would take possession of the contract after paying the debt.

[16] The terms *to impound* (to take legal or formal possession of goods to be held in custody of the law) and *to confiscate* (to seize by or as if by authority) seem appropriate here. *Distraint* and *witheram* are often used in medieval documents.

[17] In the perfect monitoring version of the model, cheating does not transpire and hence lenders are not motivated to acquire information, but this is no longer the case when (as we will see) the model is expanded to include imperfect monitoring.

there is no equilibrium in which a lender is motivated to inform others of cheating because he does not recover the cost of doing so. Threatening to reveal cheating to others is not credible. Even if we ignore this strategic consideration in order to deter cheating in the game without communities, a lender must convey the information to a sufficient number of a cheater's future lenders. The cost of doing so was arguably prohibitively high in the late medieval period given the communications and transportation technology, the large number of merchants, and the large geographical area in which they operated.[18] The cost of informing a stationary court, however, was much lower and, as the subsequent analysis establishes, the community responsibility system endogenously motivated a lender to furnish a valid complaint, thereby making the threat to reveal cheating credible.

Is there a subgame perfect equilibrium with lending on the equilibrium path in this game? For one to exist, the appropriate motivation should be provided to the economic agents and the courts. In particular, the penalty for cheating imposed by the borrowers' court should be credible and sufficiently high to deter cheating, and a lender should receive a sufficient reward only for a valid complaint, so that information about cheating is solicited. The borrowers' court should be better off compensating the lenders' court than letting the cheater keep the spoils and forgoing future gains from borrowing. The lenders' court should be better off if lending continues than if it confiscates all goods and forgoes future lending.

The following definitions are helpful in exposing the strategies that provide such motivation and the conditions under which they are equilibrium. The game is in a *cooperation state* if there has been no impounding without default; the borrowers' court has never refused to pay compensation after default or paid in the absence of default; and the lenders' court has never failed to verify a complaint, request compensation for a valid complaint, or refused to return impounded goods after receiving compensation from the borrowers' court. If any of these conditions fail to hold, the game is in *conflict state*. Note that because I assume, so far, that all complaints are perfectly verifiable, the probability of disagreement between the lenders' court and the borrowers' court is zero.

Proposition 10.1: If (1) $gN_B \sum_{t=0}^{T-1}(T-t)\delta^{t+1} + I_B(t)(g-d) \geq i+l+c+C_L+C_B$ (the net present value of the borrowers' court payoff

---

[18] Information costs were probably low within merchants' communities, but the focus here is on impersonal exchange outside one's community.

from future trade is higher than the cost of settling a dispute), and (2) $(i - r)N_B \sum_{t=0}^{t-1}(T - t)\delta^{t+1} \geq (g - d)N_B$ (the net present value of the lenders' court payoff is higher from continuing trade than from impounding all goods), then the following strategy is a subgame perfect equilibrium with lending on the equilibrium path.

In conflict state, a borrower neither trades nor returns and pays if given a loan. A lender does not lend or complain. The lenders' court impounds the goods of every lender in its territory and neither validates complaints nor requests compensation. The borrowers' court neither validates complaints nor imposes a fine or furnishes compensation.

In cooperation state, a borrower travels, and if offered a loan, he borrows, returns, and pays his debt. A lender lends if he is matched with a borrower and complains if he is cheated. The lenders' court verifies every complaint and, if it is valid, it impounds the goods of all borrowers present in its territory and demands that the borrowers' court pay a compensation of x. This equals the total cost of default to the lender $(i + l)$ plus the cost to the lenders for complaining and verifying $(c + C_L)$, that is, $x = i + l + c + C_L$. If the borrowers' court provides compensation, the lenders' court compensates the lender who was cheated and returns the impounded goods. The borrowers' court verifies any complaint. If it is found to be valid, the borrowers' court imposes a fine of $f = x + C_B$ on the defaulter and pays x to the lenders' court.[19] If either court takes any other action in cooperation state, the game reverts to a conflict state.

Proof of proposition 10.1: For the above strategies to be an equilibrium, no player should be able to gain from a one-time deviation after any history. If the game is in a conflict state, no player can gain from such a deviation because the strategies constitute a Nash equilibrium in the stage game. In cooperation state, a borrower's best response is to travel, return, and repay. Traveling, borrowing, and paying yields $g > 0$, whereas not traveling yields 0 and cheating implies a net penalty of $-c - C_L - C_B < 0$.

Because the lenders' court will transfer $i + l + c$ to a lender who was cheated complaining is profitable. A lender's best response to

---

[19] Budget constraints are ignored. Bankruptcy under the community responsibility system introduces a difficult state verification problem, which was recognized during this period. Communities had to pay.

cheating is to complain; c > 0 implies that an invalid complaint is not profitable; and because i − r > 0, a lender's best response is lending. Inequality (1) implies that the net present values of future lending and of the impounded goods to the living members of the borrowers' community exceed the value of x, the amount demanded by the lenders' court, and the verification cost, C_B.[20] Hence the borrowers' court cannot gain from taking an action leading to a conflict state. Its best response in cooperation state is to verify any complaint, impose a fine on a cheater, and compensate the lenders' court if the complaint is valid. Inequality (2) implies that the lenders' court is better of in cooperation state than in conflict state. Its best response in cooperation state is therefore verifying complaints, returning the impounded goods, paying the lender who was cheated, and not impounding without a valid complaint.   Q.E.D.

Theoretically, then, the community responsibility system can support impersonal exchange by endogenously providing all the appropriate incentives. It is optimal for a borrower to repay rather than default even in his last period because defaulting implies punishment by his community court. Anticipating such an outcome, lenders find it optimal to lend. Moreover, anticipating compensation for a valid complaint, a lender is motivated to provide the court with information regarding cheating, making it possible for the court to condition its behavior on this information. Public information is endogenously generated, because a lender who was cheated is motivated to complain, a lender does not benefit from furnishing false claims, and courts are motivated to examine their validity.

The credible threat to have a defaulting borrower punished by his own community is at the crux of the community responsibility system. A community's concern with its reputation motivates its partial court to dispense impartial justice. The community, although it aggregates only the payoffs of its living members, becomes a de facto substitute for a single player with an infinite horizon. The end-game problem is mitigated by placing a community's reputation as a bond for the behavior of each of its members. The borrowers' court finds it optimal to punish a cheater,

---

[20] If coordinated cheating by all the borrowers is possible, the condition would be

$$gN_B \sum_{t=0}^{T}(T - t)\delta^{t+1} \geq N_B(G - g).$$

The net present value of future borrowing is larger than the gains from collectively cheating. As done with respect to g, it is assumed that a borrower has no future income from G − g.

because doing so serves the younger cohorts best. Although an individual borrower cannot be punished by the lenders if he cheats in period $(T-1)$, impounding, as well as the lenders' credible threat not to lend again to the other borrowers, implies that the borrowers' court is better off imposing a fine on the defaulters and compensating the lenders' community.

The community responsibility system simultaneously mitigates the end-game problem implied by the merchants' finite life-spans and the strategic and technological problems of generating information about cheating. An institution based on intracommunity familiarity and enforcement institutions enables intercommunity exchange characterized by separation between the *quid* and the *quo* over time and space. This exchange can also be impersonal in the sense that an individual does not expect to gain from future exchange with his current partner and has neither knowledge of his past conduct nor the ability to report misconduct to future trading partners.

The preceding discussion has ignored an important aspect of the community responsibility system: making a borrower's communal and personal identity (name) known to a lender. For the system to support exchange, a lender has to know the identity of the borrower so that the court can punish cheaters. In personal exchange, this knowledge is available, by definition, to the economic agents. When trading with strangers in situations in which knowledge of their identity (i.e., their name) is crucial for contract enforcement, one cannot rely on them to reveal their identities truthfully. As revelation renders one punishable, a borrower intending to cheat will falsify his identity. A borrower faces the difficulty of credibly revealing his identity so that he can be punished if he cheats. Additional institutional features are required for credibly revealing identity. In the modern economy, this is the role of the driver's license, passport, and other forms of identification, which rely on printing and photographic technologies that did not exist in the medieval period.[21]

The community responsibility system can theoretically mitigate this problem by relying on intracommunity personal familiarity to enable an individual to reveal his communal identity (affiliation) and personal

---

[21] For similar reasons, the ability of medieval actors to retaliate collectively against a cheater not personally known to all of them was difficult due to the challenge of describing him to those who were not cheated. A physical description would be of limited use, and new names could be assumed after cheating. Most commoners did not even have last names during this period, and the surnames that did exist were often descriptive (usually reflecting one's physical features or place of birth). See Emery (1952) and Lopez (1954).

identity (name) credibly to nonmembers, rendering him vulnerable to punishment. To capture this possibility in the model, assume that the borrowers' community can first establish, at cost C_0, an organization in the lender's territory. This organization can certify the communal and personal identity of a borrower. Assume that

$$gN_B \sum_{T=0}^{T-1}(T - t)\delta^{t+1} \geq C_0,$$

namely, the gain from borrowing is more than the cost of establishing a certifying organization. In this case, it is profitable for the borrowers' community to establish a certifying organization. In this extended game, exchange can be sustained as an equilibrium outcome under the conditions discussed previously. The community responsibility system can endogenously generate the information regarding the communal and personal identity of the cheater required for its operation. It can support exchange that is impersonal in the sense that the economic agents do not know, prior to the exchange, each other's identities.

10.4.2 The Historical Evidence on the Community Responsibility System

Theoretically, the community responsibility system can foster intercommunity impersonal exchange. This possibility, however, does not imply that such an outcome had occurred during the late medieval period. Historical evidence, however, supports the claim that the community responsibility system prevailed throughout Europe.[22]

The strategy of holding every member of a community liable for each member's default in intercommunity exchange is apparent even in documents related to intercommunity exchange within the same political unit. In a charter granted to London in the early 1130s, King Henry I announced that "all debtors to the citizens of London discharge these debts, or prove in London that they do not owe them; and if they refuse either to pay or to come and make such proof, then the citizens to whom the debts are

---

[22] Yet to be established are what other institutions, if any, may have also facilitated exchange that was impersonal to some degree and their relative importance. (In later periods intermediaries were widely used. See Hoffman et al. 2000.) The community responsibility system was also used to protect a community's merchants from abuse abroad (e.g., from robberies and tolls). It thus complemented the merchant guild examined in Greif et al. (1994). I ignore this issue here.

due may take pledges within the city either from the borough or from the village or from the county in which the debtor lives."[23]

This charter is representative; evidence from other charters, treaties, and regulations reveals that the community responsibility system was the law of the land in England. Charters for English towns reveal that by 1256 cities that were home to 65 percent of the urban population had clauses in their charters allowing for and regulating "distrain" (impounding) of goods under the community responsibility system.[24] The centrality of the community responsibility system in supporting English trade among members of various towns is also revealed in the surviving correspondence of the mayor of London for the years 1324–33. In this correspondence, 59 of the 139 letters dealing with economic issues (42 percent) explicitly mention community responsibility.[25] They indicate that the mayor was motivated and expected the authorities of other towns to be motivated by the threat that all members of a community would be held liable if certain actions were not taken.

Charters regulating the relationships between English communities and their main international trading partners also reflect the strategy of holding community members liable for a member's default in intercommunity exchange. Charters reveal that the community responsibility system governed exchange between English merchants and merchants in Germany, Italy, France, Poland, and Flanders (whose cities were England's largest trade partners).[26] Similar evidence is reflected in the same 139 letters of

---

[23] *English Historical Documents*, vol. 2: 1012–13; see discussion by Stubbs 1913. English legal documents indicate that one's merchant guild – which in many cases was also the governing body of the borough – was his relevant community (Maitland 1889, p. 134). Yet the charter suggests that a community de facto was the smallest unit (borough, village, or county) that could be pressed to penalize a culprit.

[24] This is a lower bound. There were about 500 chartered towns in England by the end of the thirteenth century (Beresford and Finberg 1973); 247 charters from the twelfth and thirteenth centuries have survived (Ballard and Tait 1913, 1923). The calculations are for cities with populations of at least 5,000 people by 1300, the year for which we have population figures (Bairoch et al. 1988). A learning process is suggested by the observation that charters of 35 cities explicitly refer to the earlier charter of Lincoln.

[25] *Calendar of Plea and Memoranda Rolls,* vol. 1. A quarter of these letters relate to commercial transactions. The rest relate to stolen goods or disputes over the legality of tolls.

[26] The following sources provide additional independent evidence that the strategy associated with the community responsibility system governed the relationships between English and non-English communes: *Calendar of the Patent Rolls* 20: 1266–72 (regarding Lübeck) and 460: 1232–1339 (regarding Ypres); Vecchio and

the mayor of London, 50 extant letters deal with international commercial matters, and of these 15 (30 percent) refer to the strategy of the community responsibility system

Thirteenth-century treaties between Flanders, German towns, and the Hanseatic League also reflect the importance of holding community members liable for a member's default in intercommunity exchange (Verlinden 1979, p. 135; Dollinger 1970, pp. 187–8; Planitz 1919; Volckart 2001). Florentine historical records provide ample evidence of agreements and treaties regulating the community responsibility system, reflecting its role as the default arrangement in Italy during the twelfth and thirteenth centuries. The earliest preserved Florentine commercial treaties are from the early twelfth century. From then until 1300, thirty-three of the forty-four surviving treaties (75 percent) mention the strategies associated with the community responsibility system and regulate its operation. In addition to Florence, the treaties mention at least twenty-three other Italian towns as ones in which the system prevailed. These treaties and other sources include references to all the large Italian cities (Genoa, Venice, Milan, Pisa, Rome) as well as to numerous smaller ones (e.g., Siena, Padua, Cremona, Lucca, St. Miniato, Montepulcino, Montalcino, Prato, Arezzo, and Massa Trebaria).[27]

Evidence also reflects the strategy of holding an individual liable for the cost his default in intercommunity exchange imposed on his community. Internal regulations in Florence from the late thirteenth century reveal that the commune intended to make a merchant pay the damages when found guilty of cheating a member of another community (Santini 1886, p. 166). It had the right to sell the property of a merchant who refused to pay and to banish him from the commune (Vecchio and Casanova 1894, pp. 248–9).

In England the charters of Pontefract (1194), Leeds (1208), and Great Yarmouth (1272) explicitly specified that if the default by one community member caused the goods of another member to be impounded, the party at fault had to compensate the injured party. If he did not, his property would be confiscated and he would be expelled from the community (Ballard and Tait 1913, 1923). In various English boroughs, once a foreign creditor established that a member of the borough had failed to repay

---

Casanova (1894) (court cases in various Italian cities). See also *Calendar of Plea and Memoranda Rolls*, vol. 1.

[27] See Arias (1901) and Vecchio and Casanova (1894) regarding these treaties. Regarding Italy, see Wach (1868).

a debt, the borough would compensate him with its own funds and seek double indemnity from the debtor (Plucknett 1949, p. 137).

Evidence from charters, treaties, and regulations supports the claim that the strategies associated with the community responsibility system were *supposed* to be followed. But did the community responsibility system involve more than rules and regulations? Did belief in the causal relationships captured by the model, and behavior in various circumstances, prevail as well? Were these rules and regulations expected to be followed and did they influence behavior? Was the community responsibility system indeed an institution? The historical evidence indicates that it was.

To buttress the claim that the community responsibility system was a relevant contract enforcement institution, it is useful to extend the model to capture explicitly that commercial disputes can arise, that courts have only a limited ability to verify past actions, and that different courts can reach different conclusions based on the same evidence.

Assume that lender-borrower relations are characterized by imperfect monitoring – that is, the lender receives a signal that is a random variable that depends on the action taken by the borrower. Even if cheating has not occurred, the lender's signal may indicate that he was cheated.[28] Further assume that each court has an independent imperfect monitoring ability; verifying complaints implies receiving a publicly observed signal indicating whether cheating occurred. The signals are not perfectly correlated implying that courts can sincerely disagree about whether cheating took place.[29]

Under conditions intuitively similar to those examined in the perfect monitoring case, there is a perfect Bayesian equilibrium with lending. Two additional characteristics of this equilibrium, however, are that disputes about past conduct will occur and that they will be followed by conflicts

---

[28] The historical records suggest that disputes were more likely to occur when one of the contracting parties died, the debt was old, the contract was not clearly defined, or the contracting obligations were allegedly fulfilled by the agents of one of the parties rather than by one of the principals.

[29] Technically, the main assumptions are as follows: Let $\alpha_B(t)$ denote a borrower's action in period t with $\alpha_B(t) \in \{R, D\}$ where R denotes repay and D denotes not repaying. Let $\alpha_j(t) \in \{RC, NRC\}$ denote agent j's action in period t, where $j \in \{\text{lender, lenders' court, borrowers' court}\}$ and RC and NRC denote requesting and not requesting compensation, respectively. Let $\theta_L(t)$, $\theta_{LC}(t)$, $\theta_{BC}(t)$ denote three random variables, each representing a signal about a borrower's action in period t (to the lender, the lenders' court, and the borrowers' court respectively). Each of them could be R or D. Conditional on a borrower's action, $\theta_L(t)$, $\theta_{LC}(t)$, and $\theta_{BC}(t)$ are iid across time and transactions. θ_L is observed only by L. θ_{LC} and θ_{BC} are publicly observed.

of finite durations. During conflict, impounding will occur and lending will cease. This retaliation will be finite in length; once it is over, lending will resume.

The intuition behind these results is well known.[30] Although on the equilibrium path no cheating occurs (in the sense that a borrower chooses not to pay), finite periods of conflict are required to provide communities and contracting individuals with the appropriate incentives. If the borrowers' court's strategy calls for compensating the lender, even if it concludes that cheating did not occur, the lenders' court's best response is to claim that a dispute occurred even if it did not. Similarly, if the lenders court's strategy calls for not confiscating property when it maintains that cheating occurred, the borrowers' court's best response is not to furnish compensation even if its signal indicates that cheating occurred, thereby motivating borrowers' to cheat. Misrepresenting information has to be costly; forgone gains from exchange are the means of generating these costs.

If the community responsibility system prevailed, we should find court cases and other sources reflecting the strategy of holding community members liable; confiscating their property; and, in case of disagreement over whether a default had occurred, ceasing to trade for a finite period of time. Such evidence is available, from England, Italy, and elsewhere.[31] In Florence alone, between 1280 and 1298 (a period for which we have particularly good data), we know of thirty-six cases of dispute, confiscation, or trade cessation involving as many as twenty-five different cities. Later court cases involved Spain (Aragon) and England. Another indication that disputes were common is that even university students, who were not directly involved in credit transactions, were hold liable for default by members of their community. Students asked the authorities for immunity from confiscation as early as 1155 in Bologna and 1171 in Florence.[32]

To illustrate such cases, consider the request by one Beatrice, who in 1238 asked the Florentine court for retaliation against the Commune

---

[30] These results are generic in imperfect monitoring models (Green and Porter 1984; Abreu, Pearce, and Stacchetti 1986).

[31] See Moore (1985), Plucknett (1949) regarding England; Santini (1886), Vecchio and Casanova (1894), Catoni (1976) regarding Italy; and see Pro SC 2/178/93: 14 May 1270, published in *Select Cases Concerning the Law Merchant*, 1:8–10, regarding Flanders.

[32] Data for 1280–98 were collected from the documents contained in Santini (1886). See Vecchio and Casanova (1894) regarding the operation of the community responsibility system in the relations between Florence, England, and Spain. See Munz (1969, p. 77) and Santini (1886, pp. 20–4) regarding students' requests.

of Pisa for a sum she claimed was owed to her by the heirs of Ubaldo Viscount. Her request was granted after the Commune of Pisa denied payment. Such a denial, according to the model, would occur when the two courts differed in their assessment of the situation. Various commercial treaties indeed reflect that contemporaries considered retaliation unavoidable in cases of disagreements between courts. A treaty between Pisa and Florence signed in 1214 specifies that retaliation would follow if the judges were unable to settle the dispute (Santini 1886, pp. 165–8).[33]

That retaliation was a calculated response aimed at providing proper incentives and fostering exchange rather than an act of revenge is suggested by attempts to confine retaliatory acts to intercommunity commercial matters and by the fact that retaliation lasted for a finite number of periods, after which a "suspension" was announced and trade resumed, without making this suspension conditional on full compensation.[34] Theory highlights the logic behind this practice: retaliations arguably lasted long enough to make misrepresentation of information sufficiently costly to make it unprofitable.[35]

That the community responsibility system was aimed at fostering exchange gains further support by observing that in commercial matters it could have been legally applied only when it could theoretically be effective – namely, when default could be verified. Verification is easier in transactions in which one party assumes a specific obligation (such as repaying a debt); it is more difficult to show in transactions in which one party has wide latitude in choosing actions (e.g., as in agency relationships). I find no evidence that the community responsibility system governed such transactions.

The conjecture about the importance of the community responsibility system gains support from its ability to account for puzzling organizational details of premodern trade. Consider, for example, the Champagne fairs, the main international fair in Europe at the time. The fairs were not organized as a meeting place for individual merchants

---

[33] As this case illustrates, a legal procedure generally preceded the impoundment of goods. Vecchio and Casanova (1894) and Arias (1901) discuss this process in Italy, Maitland and Bateson (1901, pp. 14–15) in England.

[34] A Florentine statute from 1325 identified losses in currency or goods, damage to property, tax extortion, and personal detention as cases in which it was appropriate to grant retaliation (Santini 1886). No retaliation was allowed in cases involving bodily offenses.

[35] See Arias (1901, pp. 177–88); Santini (1886, p. 165); and Vecchio and Casanova (1894, pp. 216–23, 237–42).

from different localities but as a meeting place for traders from different *communities*, who often had their own places of residence, storage facilities, permanent representatives, and scribes, as well as a consul who had legal authority over members of its own community at the fairs. Although the authorities of the fairs contracted with rulers in the surrounding areas to secure the right of passage for merchants and safeguarded their property rights at the fair, they relinquished legal rights over the merchants once they were there. One was subject to the laws of his community, not the laws of the locality in which a fair was held. Law was personal rather than territorial.

The rationale behind these arrangements is clear once one recognizes that they were part of the organizational features of the community responsibility system. These arrangements enabled a trader to establish his communal and personal identity in interactions with merchants who did not know him personally. Living in the quarters of a particular community represented a way of demonstrating ones' communal identity. A contract written by the scribe of a particular community was proof that a member of that community assumed an obligation in intercommunity exchange.[36]

If a community is held liable for the actions of its members, it has to be able to verify who its members are and to discipline them when necessary. Personal law was compatible with the community responsibility system. Similarly, the fairs' authorities had to have the ability to identify members of a particular community and its representatives in order to approach them when necessary. Indeed, the Florentine statutes very often explicitly warned merchants attending the fairs not to act in way that would invoke a dispute and a reprisal (Vecchio and Casanova 1894, pp. 248–9).

That the community responsibility system prevailed in the fairs is also clear from regulations passed in 1260 that empowered the fairs' authorities to pronounce a sentence of exclusion from the fairs following a default. This exclusion was extended to the defaulter's compatriots if the judicial authorities of their own towns or principalities did not compel them to fulfill their obligations. Later in the century the king of France transferred legal authority at the fairs to royal bailiffs. In 1326, however,

---

[36] We have only one piece of evidence about the content of these scribes' cartularies (Verlinden 1979). The fifteen contracts, written by an Italian scribe in 1296, mention individuals from twelve communities, revealing that communal affiliation was important to the contracting individuals and suggesting that there was an institutionalized way to verify it.

he concluded that doing so had led to a decline in trade and restored the community responsibility system at the fairs (Thomas 1977).

In smaller fairs and within cities, less extensive arrangements provided the means to identify one's communal and personal identity. Certifying organizations, in terms of the theoretical analysis, were common. Merchants of the same community traveled together, lodged together (often in their own special residences), and witnessed one another's contracts.[37] Communal identification was facilitated by the fact that, even within the same political entity, members of distinct communities had different dialects and customs. Contracts and court cases reflect the large extent to which medieval merchants knew one another's communal affiliations.

In regions with a relatively strong central political system, a fair's authorities were motivated to follow the procedures of the community responsibility system so that they would not be sued in the courts of the central authorities if they broke the rules.[38] More generally, however, authorities at fairs were arguably motivated to follow the strategy of a lenders' court – holding a community liable for the contractual obligations of each of its members – because running a successful fair was a profitable business. Providing intercommunity impersonal contract enforcement increased the fair's attractiveness, and the ability to do so critically depended on the community responsibility system, without which fair authorities were unable to extend their reach beyond their limited geographical areas. The threat of excluding a particular individual from the fair was ineffective, because it could not deter cheating in old age or cheating and then trading through agents or family members.

Incentives provided by the community responsibility system shaped the characteristics of premodern international trade centers, particularly fairs, because it impacted comparative advantage in contract enforcement. Theoretically, under this system, trade centers without affiliated trading communities have an advantage over trade centers with such communities. In trade centers with affiliated trading communities, incentives to provide intercommunity enforcement are weakened, because the community's own merchants may have to bear the cost of retaliation in case of

---

[37] Communal lodging facilities for foreign merchants were a feature of premodern trade (e.g., Constable 2003). An exception was the city of Bruges, where merchants rented houses and landlords were liable for their tenant's contractual obligations (de Roover 1948).

[38] For an example involving an Englishman and merchants from Brussels at the fair of St. Botulph in England, see *Selected Cases Concerning the Law Merchant*, 2:11–12, no. 7.

intercourt disputes. If a merchant from community A sued a member of community B in the court of community C, the resulting dispute would hurt the merchants from community C when visiting community B. Community C could thus lose from adjudicating such disputes. This is not the case in trade centers that do not have an affiliated community of long-distance traders, implying that they have an advantage over trade centers that have such a community in providing contract enforcement in impersonal exchange.

Indeed, historically, trade centers with a community of long-distance traders adjudicated only disputes between one of their members and a foreign trader, not disputes between foreign traders. Trade centers without such communities, however, did adjudicate disputes between foreign traders. Under the English charters, a town was allowed to impound goods only in cases involving local citizens. Court cases from English fairs, which did not have a community of long-distance traders, however, reflect the impoundment of goods belonging to members of various communities (Moore 1985). This state of affairs is not unique to England, suggesting that it did not reflect royal discretion. In Florence, only Florentines had the right to ask a Florentine court to impound the goods of foreign merchants (Vecchio and Casanova 1894, pp. 14–15). The courts of the Champagne fairs, which did not represent any community of long-distance traders, adjudicated disputes between any foreign merchants.

More generally, the comparative advantage in contract enforcement entailed by the community responsibility system provides a rationale behind a puzzling phenomenon: the fact that, by and large, the main medieval fairs did not have affiliated communities of long-distance traders (i.e., the localities in which the fairs were held did not have a domestic community of long-distance traders). The merchants of the communities in which large fairs, such as the Champagne fairs, were held were mainly local traders who did not travel to other trade centers.

If the community responsibility system governed intercommunity exchange, we would expect organizational details and rules to change to facilitate it in a manner consistent with the functioning of this institution. In particular, we would expect that it would respond to opportunities to avoid the wastefulness associated with impounding goods. In the perfect monitoring case, the role of impounding is captured in condition 1 in proposition 10.1. This condition was that:

$$gN_B \sum_{t=0}^{T-1}(T-t)\delta^{t+1} + I_B(t)(g-d) \geq i + l + c + C_L + C_B$$

for the borrowers' court to be motivated to compensate following a default, the net present value of future trade and the impounded goods should be higher than the cost of verifying the complaint and compensating if it is valid. Theoretically, as long as trade is limited, impounding goods may be necessary for this condition to hold. As trade expands – as the size of the borrowers' community increases – the net present value of future trade is sufficient to provide the appropriate incentives.[39]

Consistent with this theoretical prediction, evidence from twelfth- and thirteenth-century Italy and Germany reflects a transition away from impounding. Treaties from twelfth-century Florence include the threat of impounding goods. By the early thirteenth century, members of one community were often allowed to leave the other community during a grace period between the time the right to confiscate was granted and the time it was executed (e.g., Arias 1901, p. 52). By the early fourteenth century, there was a grace period of one month, during which merchants were allowed to leave after the right to confiscate was granted; this became the default, at least in Florence (Santini 1886, pp. 68–72, 165). A German law of 1231 established a mandatory grace period throughout the Holy Roman Empire, reflecting the broad transition away from confiscation (Planitz 1919, p. 177).

That the community responsibility system was regulated by an imperial law in Germany suggests that it predominated in that region of Europe as well. More generally, the evidence presented in this chapter indicates that by the thirteenth century the community responsibility system prevailed in the most heavily populated and commercial areas of Europe (Italy and Flanders), in the better-organized monarchies of Europe (such as England), and in the largest political units (France and the Holy Roman Empire).

The origin of the system is unknown: it has neither a clear Roman law nor customary Germanic law antecedents (Wach 1868).[40] It may be best explained as a response to the absence of a state with an effective legal

---

[39] In this case, it is also sufficient for equilibrium with exchange that first only the borrowers' court verifies complaints, and only if cheating isn't discovered, then the lenders' court independently verifies as well. Historically, as discussed later, when communities agreed not to impound goods following a complaint but to verify it first, they also agreed that verification will first be done by the borrowers' court.

[40] The legality of collective responsibility was deliberated in countless premodern European legal treatises from as early as Monk Bartolommeo (d. 1347); to Giovanni De Brelgel (d. 1778).

system. The particularities of the response reflect the combined impact of institutional elements inherited from the past and the interests of communities' members. Specifically, they were the self-governance of cities by their mercantile elite, the European legal tradition of man-made (rather than divine) laws, and the Roman legal tradition that did not rule out corporate liability. Whether or not the community responsibility system rose spontaneously or was designed, it clearly became an explicit, well-regulated, and integral part of formal legal procedures.

10.5 INSTITUTIONAL DECLINE AND TRANSITION: TOWARD INDIVIDUAL LEGAL RESPONSIBILITY

The community responsibility system enhanced efficiency by supporting intercommunity impersonal exchange. Why, then, do thirteenth-century records at least from Italy and England provide abundant evidence of attempts to abolish the system rather than limit the harmful effects of disputes as was done previously?[41] The decline of the system in the late thirteenth century is puzzling, given that it transpired in various European regions in the absence of common social, political, or economic upheavals. What led to the decline of the community responsibility system?

Addressing this question suggests that the system was self-undermining. The same processes it fostered – an increase in intercommunity interactions, the number and size of communities, and intracommunity heterogeneity – diminished the system's effectiveness, increased its economic costs, and undermined its intracommunity political viability.[42]

In particular, theory suggests that the processes fostered by the community responsibility system will reduce the range of situations in which it enables commitment and increases the frequency and cost of intercommunity conflicts.[43] Growth in the number of traders and communities, the locations of trade, and intercommunity interactions reduces the cost of falsifying one's community affiliation and increases the cost of

---

[41] Historical documents from before the thirteenth century indicate changes and refinements in the community responsibility system. The thirteenth century seems nevertheless to have been a turning point. For the first time wholesale attempts were made to abolish the system and, at least within some territorially large political units, to provide a relatively effective alternative.

[42] This growth is very well documented (see Bairoch et al. 1988 and Beresford and Finberg 1973).

[43] This discussion is intuitively based on the model presented in the text. Extending it to incorporate these considerations explicitly is possible. For simplicity it is not done here.

verifying one's identity. This was the case because members of one community learn about other communities, and members of the same community are less likely to know each other. Furthermore, an increase in trade makes it more likely that disputes will transpire, leading to more – and potentially more costly – trade cessations. More trade also increases the costs of traders' strategic responses to expected disputes: because courts can impound goods only from traders present in their jurisdictions, merchants will respond to expected disputes by ceasing trade.

By the second half of the thirteenth century, the ease of falsification and the difficulty of verification seem to have hindered the operation of the community responsibility system in England. Based on evidence from the important English fair of St. Ives, Moore (1985) concludes that during the thirteenth century the community responsibility system "worked well enough in many cases, but it could be cumbersome and time consuming, both for the creditor and the court: it usually seems to have involved long disputes over whether or not the original debtor and/or the men actually being sued for the debt were truly members of their town, community or guild, with everyone scurrying to disclaim responsibility for the obligation" (p. 119). Plucknett (1949) notes that the growth of English towns reduced the costs of falsification. The legal authority of these towns did not extend to the adjacent countryside. People living near towns were apparently able to present themselves as being members of the town when dealing with nonmembers, cheat their trading partners, and leave the town's jurisdiction. During the thirteenth century "there seems to have been much trafficking between foreign merchants and natives whose mercantile status was doubtful, and whose assets and persons were by no means entirely within the territorial jurisdiction of a local court" (pp. 137–8).[44]

---

[44] One example of the ability to falsify communal identity and its strategic use is reflected in a case brought before the court of the St. Ives fair (1275). Merchants from the community of Leicester were summoned to the court and held liable for the debt of Thomas Coventry of Leicester. They argued, however, that "the said Thomas Coventry was never peer... of theirs... or a member of the commonality of Leicester." Shortly after the court hearing, Thomas Coventry appeared at the fair, admitted that he was from Leicester, and sued the original plaintiffs, arguing that their false accusation caused him "no small damage." The original plaintiffs could not defend themselves but claimed not to be under the jurisdiction of the court since they were from London (which by that time had gained an exemption from the community responsibility system). This court case is contained in Pro. SC 2/178/94: 8 May 1275. Parts of the document appeared in the *Select Pleas in Manorial and Other Seigniorial Courts, Reigns of Henry III and Edward I*, ed. Maitland (1889), no. 155: 145–6.

Decreasing falsification costs and increasing verification costs imply that the community responsibility system could support exchange in fewer situations. That this was increasingly the case is suggested by evidence from the English Close Rolls. Throughout the period under consideration, English merchants could have chosen to register debts in these chancery rolls, thereby placing their transactions under the jurisdiction of the common law. Doing so would have implied that property and goods could have been placed as bonds for repaying debts (Moore 1985, n. 105). Registration, however, was costly, and before 1271 few if any debts were enrolled. As long as the community responsibility system functioned well, traders could avoid the cost of registration. Between 1257 and 1271, however, the number of registered debts increased by a factor of forty-three, suggesting that the system may have been failing.[45]

Evidence from Italy suggests that increasing social mobility between communities undermined the effectiveness of the community responsibility system, which critically depends on a community's ability to locally punish its members. Treaties from late thirteenth-century Florence reflect that in Italy this ability had been eroding and defaulters were fleeing their communities.[46] The response was to move away from personal law and toward territorial law. Between 1254 and 1298, Florence entered into at least twelve treaties with other Italian cities in which each commune ceded to the other the right to detain any of its merchants who were fleeing the community to avoid paying a penalty under the community responsibility system (Arias 1901).

By the end of the thirteen century the number of disputes in Florence was high. Between 1302 and 1314, Florence granted at least thirty-six concessions (rights to impound) and at least thirteen suspensions (moratoria on impoundment), and it was subject to at least six retaliations (cases in which the other community responded to impoundment in kind). At least thirty other communities or polities were involved.[47] The number

---

[45] These data are based on all the available records in the *Close Rolls of the Reign of Henry III 1227–72*, years 1256–72. There is only one entry for 1257, four for 1269, and forty-three for 1271. See Plucknett (1949, p. 137) on the cost of using the common law. The rising costs of commercial disputes is also suggested by evidence of a transition in Italy from the use of impoundment to the imposition of a toll, which allowed trade to continue during disputes and reduced uncertainty (Vecchio and Casanova 1894).

[46] It is not likely that this reflects lax punishment of defaulters prior to that period. Had this been the case, lenders would not have lent, and potential debtors would have had no need to flee.

[47] Calculations are based on evidence from Barbadoro (1921).

of disputes increased between 1302 and 1314, but we have no data to determine whether disputes were less common prior to 1302.

That the community responsibility system became less efficient and more costly would not necessarily have led to its decline. What seems to have induced attempts to abolish the system was the reduction in its intra-community political viability. The intracommunity social and economic heterogeneity to which the community responsibility system contributed implied that within a community the costs and benefits of the community responsibility system became less evenly distributed. Those who had negative gains from the system sought to abolish it.

This assertion has three implications that we can bring to the evidence. First, larger – and hence arguably more heterogeneous – communities are more likely to attempt to abolish the community responsibility system. The community's nonmercantile population will favor abolishing the system, because it bears the cost of conflicts (which leads to an absence of foreign merchants) but does not directly gain from the system. Furthermore, in larger cities, the net economic benefit of the system may be negative, due to the high frequency of disputes. Second, rich, well-established merchants – members of the mercantile elite – are likely to attempt to abolish the system for governing exchange. These merchants gain relatively little, if anything, from it because they have the connections, reputations, and wealth to conduct trade based on their personal reputation and collateral abroad. However, they bear the system's cost because they have wealth abroad that can be impounded. Third, because wealthy merchants have goods abroad, they are likely to attempt to retain the community responsibility system in governing the security of foreign merchants' property rights. They will seek to continue the system to protect their property rights abroad from abuses through robberies, excess taxation, and the like.

The historical evidence is consistent with these predictions. The Italian cities grew larger earlier than the English towns, and treaties of Florence reflect an attempt to abolish the community responsibility system early in the thirteenth century (Arias 1901). During this time, charters routinely authorized the smaller towns in England to employ the system. The largest English city, London, however, was an exception. In the 1130s its merchants were exempted from the system, although the city retained the right to impound non-Londoners' goods. Flemish towns, which were also larger than English towns, seem to have gained an exemption from the community responsibility system in England: between 1225 and 1232, the king assured the merchants of Ypres, the largest city in Flanders, that none of them "will be detained in England...nor will they be partitions for another's debts."[48] Larger cities attempted to abolish the community responsibility system early.

Italian historical records reveal a reduction in the intracommunity political viability of the community responsibility system due to the different gains and losses to various segments of the population within a commune. In 1296 some Florentine merchants appealed to the city authorities about a conflict with Bologna. The livelihoods of these merchants depended on being able to pass through Bologna. They proposed setting up a toll (*pedaggio*) to be levied almost exclusively on their goods, just to settle a dispute in which they were probably not directly involved (Arias 1901, p. 165). The city as a whole did not seem to have been interested in paying for resolving the dispute. Similarly, distinct interests of different segments of the population are reflected in a Florentine regulation from 1415 that forbade retaliation against foreign rectors, officials, or traders selling edibles (Santini 1886, pp. 168–72).

The desire of the wealthy merchants to abolish the system is reflected in the political economy of the community responsibility system in Florence. During the thirteenth century, affluent Florentine merchants, known as *mercatores*, conducted business throughout most of Europe. While they may have had the ability to exchange based on their own reputations, they had a great deal to lose from retaliations. Indeed, once they secured political control over Florence in the second half of the thirteenth century, they entered into a sequence of treaties aimed at moving Florence away from the community responsibility system. In 1279, not only Florence but the cities of Venice and Genoa, as well as most of the cities of Tuscany, Lombardy, Romagna, and Marca Trivigiana, agreed to its abolition (Arias 1901, pp. 170–6, 400–1).[49] Similar factors probably contributed to the decline of the community responsibility system in various parts of Europe.

---

[48] See *English Historical Documents*, vol. 2, no. 270: 1012–13 regarding London and *Calendar of the Patent Rolls*, 460: 1232–1339, regarding Ypres.

[49] In England and France we find similar but less clear evidence. In England, in the second half of the thirteenth century there "was an increasing number of individuals...able to respond to...suits by producing royal licenses of immunity from prosecution for any debts [under the community responsibility system] except those for which they were principal debtors or pledges" (Moore 1985, p. 119). Arguably, wealthy merchants bought immunities. Thomas (1977) provides similar evidence regarding France. This evidence is also consistent with an attempt to free-ride on the community responsibility system.

The ability to devise an alternative system depended on the institutional environment, particularly that of political institutions. In Italy, no third party – such as a king – existed to devise an impartial legal system. Consistent with the theoretical prediction, however, retaliations continued in Italy for centuries but mainly occurred in cases involving the abuse of property rights rather than commercial disputes (Vecchio and Casanova 1894; Barbadoro 1921). As the Italian communes were shifting from republics to oligarchies, their institutions were altered to serve different interests. A community responsibility system securing property rights abroad was valuable for the wealthy merchants; one that enabled less fortunate merchants to enter into impersonal exchange was not. At the same time, the wealthy Italian merchants began relying on large-scale family firms with collateral abroad to better commit to their contractual obligations. It is no coincidence that large firms with branches abroad emerged during the late thirteenth century when the community responsibility system was declining.

The disintegration of the empire in Germany during the thirteenth century also meant that there was no central ruler with the power to provide an effective alternative to the community responsibility system. As late as the fifteenth century, collective responsibility was still widely practiced, despite attempts dating back to the thirteenth century to abolish it (Planitz 1919, pp. 176ff.). The lack of local monopoly over coercive power enabled the simultaneous operation of a "feud system," until at least the sixteenth century. A merchant would hire a feudal lord with a mercenary army to force a community to compensate him for defaults. Frankfurt-am-Main, which held a major annual international fair, was involved in at least 229 such feuds between 1380 and 1433. Between 1404 and 1438, the important city of Nuremberg was involved in no fewer than 200 feuds (Volckart 2001). It was a costly system in terms of ex ante incentives and the ex post cost of disputes.[50]

In England, by contrast, the state facilitated the replacement of the community responsibility system with one based on individual legal responsibility and the coercive power of the state. When, toward the end of the thirteenth century, the community responsibility system was declining,

---

[50] The Hundred Year's War (1337–1453) and the earlier wars with England and Flanders meant that the political situation in France during this period was not conducive to providing impartial justice. Raising revenues was probably a top priority for the Crown.

the political power of the commercial urban sector was on the rise, as reflected in the transfer in 1295–7 of the right to approve taxes from the Great Council (which represented the nobles) to a parliament with representatives from the urban commercial sector. The increase in wealth, population, and military importance of the urban commercial sector that this transition reflects and the political representation it entailed implied that the commercial sector had the voice required to coordinate the institutional transition, mitigate the collective action problem, and enable the Crown to commit not to abuse property rights through the legal system (Greif 2004b).

The Statute of Westminster I (1275) officially abolished the community responsibility system in England with respect to debt. Subsequent statutes recognized that this led to a decline in commerce because "merchants who in the past have lent their substance to various people are impoverished because there was no speedy law provided by which they could readily recover their debts on the day fixed for payment" (Statute of Acton Burnell 1283). Such statutes gradually articulated on an alternative contract enforcement institution based on territorial law, individual responsibility, central administration of justice, and collateral.[51]

The corresponding contract enforcement institution based on individual responsibility, however, developed slowly and became effective gradually, as participants learned about its deficiencies and invented new ways to improve it, particularly by learning how to control agents of the state more effectively.[52] Indeed, some royal charters granted after 1275 still allowed towns to impound goods based on collective responsibility.[53] We have

---

[51] See the Statute of Westminster I in *English Historical Documents*, vol. 3: 404 and the decline in trade in the Statute of Acton Burnell (1283), ibid., no. 54: 420–2. The alternative contract enforcement institution established by the king is described in the Statute of Acton Burnell. The Statute of Westminster II (1285), ibid., no. 57: 428–57; the Statute of Merchants (1285), ibid., no. 58: 457–60; Plucknett (1949, pp. 138–50); and Moore (1985, p. 120) provide a discussion. The English Crown may have been imitating the French system. See the discussion of Patourel (1937, p. 97).

[52] For administrative changes to curtail corruption, see the Statute of Merchants (1285), *English Historical Documents*, vol. 3, no. 58: 457–60. In 1352 common creditors were ranked with the Crown's creditors insofar as imprisonment of the defaulted debtors was concerned, and outlawry covered debt and actions of account (Plucknett 1949, pp. 324–6, 343). Administrative procedures and cross-checks were used to reduce corruption and bribery; legal procedures and sanctions were slow to be developed and made more effective.

[53] This was true in the charters of Rhuddlan (1284) and Blakewell (1286) (Ballard and Tait 1923).

already seen that the correspondence of the mayor of London from 1324 to 1333 reflects the use of the strategies associated with the community responsibility system. A comparable set of letters is also available for 1360–70. In this source, 55 of 159 of the mayor's domestic and international economic letters (35 percent) reflect the operation of the community responsibility system, and half of these cases are about contract enforcement.

Interestingly, in the early period the number of domestic and international cases was almost the same, although more were domestic than international. Later this was not the case, as the subsequent data set has 45 percent more international cases. An institutional distinction between trade inside and outside national boundaries was in the process of emerging.[54] International trade was born.

10.6 CONCLUDING COMMENTS

Impersonal exchange characterized by a separation between the *quid* and the *quo* over time and space are the hallmark of the modern market economy. Comparative and historical analysis of the nature and dynamics of contract enforcement institutions that supported exchange that was impersonal to various degrees in different economies is likely to enhance our understanding of the historical process of economic development and contemporary impediments to the expansion of markets.

Neither a law-based institution provided by an impartial third party nor one based on the interacting parties concerned with maintaining their personal reputation supported such exchange during the late medieval period. Instead, impersonal exchange was supported by an institution central to which were self-governed communities, intracommunity (partial) courts, and collective reputation Noncontractual, joint, communal liability and communal reputation endogenously motivated partial courts to provide impartial justice.

The community responsibility system was a self-enforcing institution; all incentives – to individual traders and their communal courts – were provided endogenously. Beliefs regarding communes' responses to cheating and beliefs in the value of future trade turned each community into

---

[54] *Calendar of Letters from the Mayor and Corporation of the City of London.* More evidence of the continuation of the system is reflected in a long series of reprisals between England and Florence that last until 1460 (Vecchio and Casanova 1894, p. 262).

an ongoing organization with an infinite life-span. Each community internalized the cost of a default by each of its members on other members and whose future trade served as a bond for contractual performance.[55] Communal liability, which was neither contractual nor voluntary for an individual merchant, supported intercommunity impersonal exchange. Exchange did not require that the interacting merchants have knowledge about past conduct, share expectations about trading in the future, have the ability to transmit information about a merchant's conduct to future trading partners, or know a priori the personal identity of each other.

Initially, the community responsibility system was a self-reinforcing institution, in that it led to processes that increased the range of parameters within which it was self-enforcing. It reinforced the communal structure on which it was based, motivating communities to define communal membership clearly, to establish the organizations required to indicate who their members were to the rest of the society, and to strengthen their intracommunity enforcement institutions.

In the long run, however, the community responsibility system was undermined by the growth of long-distance trade and the increase in the size, number, and heterogeneity of communities. These changes reduced the system's effectiveness, economic efficiency, and intracommunity political viability. For example, they made it easier to falsify one's community affiliation, hindered verification of affiliation, reduced the cost of intercommunity mobility, and made some members of the community worse off than they otherwise would have been. By the late thirteenth century, wealthy members of communities sought exemptions from the community responsibility system, and communities were laboring to abolish it.

The ability to replace the community responsibility system with an alternative institution depended on the institutional environment, particularly on political institutions. In England the political system was conducive to a transition to legal contract enforcement based on individual legal responsibility. Where the state stepped in to provide an effective alternative, economic institutions moved closer, albeit slowly, to the enforcement system that prevails today, in which individual liability is the rule,

---

[55] See Bull (1987); Cremer (1986); Kreps (1990b); and Tadelis (1999, 2002) on the roles of ongoing organizations in fostering cooperation among agents with finite life-spans and how the separation between personal and economic identities mitigates the unraveling problem. The analysis of the community responsibility system highlights the importance of an ongoing organization in mitigating the unraveling problem and supporting cooperation between its members and nonmembers.

much impersonal exchange is supported by the legal system, and collective responsibility is consensual and contractual. The asymmetry in the ability to provide alternative institutions within and outside polities created the institutional distinction between national and international trade.

This history calls into question the conventional wisdom that the rise of the European state was a precondition for the rise of markets. The community responsibility system suggests the importance of the opposite line of causation: the institutional demand created by the market influenced the development of state-governed, law-based institutions. When and where the state could respond to this challenge while being constrained from abusing rights, markets subsequently prospered.

The influence of the community responsibility system on the development of contractual and organizational forms in Europe, how and to what extent it evolved differently in various European areas, and what these distinctions implied for subsequent market expansion are yet to be examined. Similarly, the extent to which institutions similar to it prevailed in other premodern societies has not yet been examined. It may well be that the system was unique to Europe, because it rested on two pillars – self-governed mercantile communities and man-made law, which these communities participated in formulating – that were not common in other premodern market societies. In the Muslim world, for example, communities were not self-governed (e.g., Cahen 1990, p. 520) and the prevailing religious law rejected the notion of collective responsibility central to the community responsibility system (e.g., Schacht 1982 [1964], p. 125). If the community responsibility system was unique to Europe, it is likely to have been among the factors accounting for Europe's subsequent commercial development.

The community responsibility system demonstrates the dynamic causal relationship between institutions and international trade.[56] A multitiered, interjurisdictional (and, in this sense, international) institution provided both individuals and domestic legal jurisdictions with the appropriate incentives. On the one hand, like institutions mitigating a sovereign's debt problem, the community responsibility system was a precondition for exchange.[57] In both cases, institutions that induce those with domestic legal authority to enforce or follow international contractual obligations

---

[56] Interestingly, collective responsibility is not practiced in contemporary international trade. Only the assets of the individuals (or corporations, including the state) who defaulted can be captured.

[57] Regarding the sovereign's debt problem, see, for example, Bulow and Rogoff (1989) and Wright (2002).

are crucial. On the other hand, the community responsibility supports the conjecture about the importance of studying the reverse causality from international trade to the development of domestic institutions. Its history reflects the fact that institutional change is an important causal channel between trade and growth.

The community responsibility system also highlights the importance of some neglected aspects of the micro-foundations of contract enforcement institutions. It combined aspects of law-based and reputation-based institutions, revealing the importance of enforcement institutions combining coercive power and reputation (Greif and Kandel 1995; Dixit 2004).[58] It also highlights the importance of departing from the assumption common in analyses of reputation mechanisms that identities are common knowledge. One of the central components of the community responsibility system was the mechanism for credibly revealing one's personal and communal identity. Arguably, an important part of a society's contract-enforcement institutions consist of the ways in which people can credibly commit to transmit information about their identity. The community responsibility system also highlights the importance of departing from focusing on reputation-based institutions in which behavior is conditioned on ex ante (before transacting) information about past conduct. Underpinning the community responsibility system was the ability to substantiate ex post that one had been cheated by a particular person rather than verifying that this particular person had never cheated before.

Only recently have the economic implications of collective responsibility gained attention.[59] In contemporary economies, collective responsibility plays a role in microfinance in developing countries (Besley and Coate 1995; Bouman 1995) and in business associations with joint and unlimited liability (Bernstein 1992). The community responsibility system and the nineteenth-century German cooperatives (Guinnane 1997) illustrate the importance of collective responsibility in the development of industrial economies. Indeed, the community responsibility system reveals that collective responsibility was central to the functioning of European markets

---

[58] In studying the institutional foundations of exchange, economists have concentrated on those based on impartial third-party enforcement in the form of the law or those based on individuals' concern with their economic reputation (see surveys in Greif 1997b, 2000, and McMillan and Woodruff 2000). For the interrelationships between legal and reputation-based institutions, see Greif (1994a); Kranton (1996); and Johnston et al. (2002).

[59] For theoretical analyses, see Varian (1990); Tirole (1996); and Ghatak and Guinnane (1999).

in the past, calling attention to the possibly important, yet neglected, role of collective responsibility in modern market economies. The community responsibility system suggests that an important role of modern firms is to provide collective responsibility.

The centrality of collective responsibility in premodern Europe underscores the fact that the contemporary tendency to consider only individual legal responsibility (or contractual joint liability) as morally and legally acceptable means imposing the result of a long process of European institutional evolution in places where a similar process did not necessarily occur (Levinson 2003). The community responsibility system reveals how important the social and political context is in determining the set of feasible, efficiency-enhancing institutions. Institutional policy has to take account of the fact that, while all institutions supporting impersonal exchange have to mitigate the same contractual problem, the institutions most appropriate for doing the job differ across settings. They depend on the institutional environment and the institutional elements inherited from the past.

11

Interactive, Context-Specific Analysis

To identify and understand the operation of the community responsibility system, the analysis in Chapter 10, like all of the empirical analyses in this book, used a particular case study method. Specifically, it employed a theoretically informed, case study method that extensively relied on contextual knowledge of the situation and its history, and context-specific modeling. This chapter first argues that this method usefully responds to the challenge that institutional analysis presents to the traditional empirical methods of the social sciences; it then presents this method in detail.

The challenge that institutions present to the traditional empirical methods of social science has two sources. First, although institutions are not random – those that fulfill a particular function or interest respond to the same forces and considerations – they are inherently indeterminate, historically contingent, and context-specific. We don't have a theory of institutions to guide their empirical analysis, and what we know about them suggests that seeking such a theory is likely to be a futile exercise (section 11.1). Second, we cannot generally study institutions by considering only their observable features (section 11.2).

The method presented here responds to institutions' inherent indeterminacy, their context-specificity, and the need to coexamine institutions' observable and unobservable components. This method interactively combines theory, contextual knowledge of the situation and its history, and context-specific modeling. A case study approach such as this is promising for several other reasons. Institutions' inherent indeterminacy and context-specificity imply that we often need to study an institution as a historically unique phenomenon. The influence of past institutions on subsequent ones means that taking the historical context into account is empirically useful. We can use knowledge of the context to eliminate some theoretically possible but contextually implausible institutions. The limits of our theory of institutions render case studies an important source for evaluating and developing general propositions regarding them. Finally, the case study method is essential in meeting the interest in comprehensively understanding particular institutions for policy purposes.

The motivating question of an interactive, context-specific analysis is what are the behavioral outcomes – such as exchange or its absence – whose institutional underpinnings are important to understand? Theory plays an important role in formulating and attempting to address this question (section 11.3). It directs attention to theoretically important behavioral outcomes, facilitates the delineation of the general forces that shape various institutions, describes the conditions required for their functioning, and identifies what evidence one must confirm when considering the relevance of various institutions. Appendix C elaborates in detail on theory's contributions to the case of reputation-based institutions.

Contextual knowledge of the situation – of its history and of comparable situations – also contributes to identifying important issues and formulating a conjecture about the relevant institution (section 11.4). Contextual knowledge is used to identify what behavioral outcomes are important in the episode under consideration, what the relevant central and auxiliary transactions and the related institutional elements are, and what institutional and other factors can be treated as exogenous. Historical information is particularly useful in formulating a conjecture regarding the relevant institution because institutional dynamics are a historical process. Knowledge of the institutional heritage is therefore critical in focusing attention to a subset of the theoretically possible institutions.

Context-specific modeling helps to formulate, present, and evaluate alternative conjectures about the institutions we seek to identify (sections 11.5). A context-specific model recognizes that various historically determined, technological and institutional factors should be taken as exogenous in studying a particular institution. Analyzing the model and solving for various equilibria enable the researcher to evaluate – modify, reject, or accept – the conjecture that a particular institution prevailed.[1] Equilibrium analysis helps the researcher evaluate a conjecture by exposing the conditions under which particular beliefs and behavior can be self-enforcing, generating predictions under the assumption that some self-enforcing beliefs prevailed, and facilitating a counterfactual and comparative analysis (section 11.6).

---

[1] I use the term *accept* in its econometric sense of *inability to reject*.

This evaluation process entails the interactive use of context-specific analysis and evidence. The model identifies evidence that can be used to evaluate the conjecture, and the context is then searched to verify its presence or absence. The absence of supporting evidence indicates the need to reformulate the conjecture and evaluate a new one. The challenge in this interactive process is to avoid ending up with a tautology by adjusting the model to fit the data. The model and the conjecture it captures have to be tested based on evidence that was not used in formulating the conjecture.

11.1 INSUFFICIENCY OF DEDUCTION

In studying endogenous institutions, we cannot generally rely on deductive theory (an inference in which the conclusion about particulars follows necessarily from general or universal premises). Theory enables predicting endogenous variables – in our case, institutions – based on the exogenous features of a situation. In general, the fewer the exogenous features of the situation and the greater the number of endogenous variables, the less powerful (although more general) a theory is likely to be and the less likely it will be able to predict a single outcome. Institutional analysis, however, is about situations in which there are few exogenous features and a large number of endogenous variables. It seems that the lack of a deductive institutional theory does not reflect a lack of scholarly input but rather the inherent nature institutions.

To appreciate the sources of the limits of our deductive theory of institutions, recall the relationship between theory and empirical analysis in neoclassical economics that studies the allocation of goods and services. The general equilibrium model provides a theory of allocation: given the endowments of all economic agents, their preferences, and technology, the model predicts equilibrium price vectors and the allocation associated with each. It reveals the general conditions under which a unique price vector is an equilibrium. The limitations of this theory for positive analyses are well known. But it provides a useful deductive theory linking any vector of the exogenous variables (endowment, preferences, and technology) with a unique endogenous outcome (a price vector). To study allocations using this theory, we need only identify the agents' endowments, preferences, and technology at the time and place under study. It is consistent with the theory to ignore other – contemporary or historical – features of the situation.

Classical, evolutionary, and learning game theory suggests that seeking an equivalent comprehensive, deductive theory of institutions may be futile. In situations of interest to institutional analysis – strategic, recurrent situations with large action spaces – multiple equilibria, and hence institutions, usually exist. In a repeated prisoners' dilemma game, for example, defection every period and cooperation every period are both equilibria for a large parameter set; both the rule of behavior of perpetual defection and the rule of conditional cooperation can prevail. In fact, an infinite number of equilibria are associated with even such simple games as an infinitely repeated prisoners' dilemma game (Appendix A).[2]

This multiplicity of equilibria is not an artifact of a particular feature of the prisoners' dilemma game. Multiple equilibria are more likely to prevail in exactly the kinds of situations of interest to institutional analysis.[3] If the analysis takes as exogenous only noninstitutional aspects of the situation, multiple self-enforcing behaviors are bound to exist. The failure to develop a deductive theory of institutions reflects an inherent institutional indeterminacy: the fact that multiple behavior and beliefs can be self-enforcing in a given environment. Game theory thus suggests that even in a world in which individuals are perfectly rational and share common knowledge of their rationality and the situation, deduction is insufficient for generating a unique outcome. This is even more likely to be the case in the real world. Game theory thus rejects the ahistorical view that the same environment will lead to the same institutions in all historical episodes.

Furthermore, there is no theory to indicate which game is relevant to a given transaction at a given time and place. Consider institutions governing the provision of credit, for example. For credit to be provided,

---

[2] See the discussion of evolutionary and learning game theory in Chapters 1 and 5, respectively.

[3] Economists' acceptance of the game-theoretic framework as opposed to the lukewarm reception in political science and sociology may reflect the distinct questions the two groups ask. Economists usually examine situations in which the players' action sets are rather restricted and arguably known to them and the analyst. In these situations the interacting agents are more likely to share common knowledge of the relevant rules of the game, and many institutions can be taken as exogenous to the analysis. The textbook discussion of oligopoly theory, for example, does not even mention that it is assumed that the rivaling firms cannot resort to violence. In contrast, other social scientists are often concerned with situations in which it is not clear what is known, and more institutions must be explained rather than assumed.

a borrower must credibly commit ex ante to repay his debt ex post. Many technologically feasible and nonmutually exclusive institutions can enable a creditor to do so. Social exchange within the family can constrain its members sufficiently to enable credit relations. Expected social and economic sanctions by members of the business community following a transgression can facilitate lending within the group. The expectation that a court of law will punish a cheater or moral beliefs (such as fear of God's punishment) can support impersonal lending. We have no theory to inform us which, if any, of these possible institutions is relevant in a particular historical episode. We have no theory regarding which game-theoretic model we should use. Game theory can be used to consider a meta-game in which each of these institutions can be studied as an equilibrium, but doing so exacerbates the problem of multiple equilibria and hence equilibrium selection.

One response to the problem of institutional selection, noted in Chapter 2, has been to impose on the analysis the deductive postulate that institutions are selected based on their function (efficiency, fairness, the interests of a particular group). But functionalist accounts of this nature are generally valid only when it is possible to establish a causal link between the origin of the institution and its presumed effect (see, e.g., Stinchcombe 1968, pp. 87–93; Elster 1983). In the case of institutions, the causal link itself depends on existing institutions, which determine what individuals are able and motivated to do (Chapter 7).

Other scholars have responded to the problem of institutional selection by considering it as a "second-order coordination" problem, the problem of coordinating on one equilibrium. This coordination is provided by such mechanisms as leadership, culture, authority, bargaining, negotiation, and collective decision-making organizations (Calvert 1992; Knight 1992; Miller 1993; Greif 1994a). The discussion in Part III highlights the importance of these mechanisms. But we have no deductive theory regarding which mechanism is important under what conditions. Deduction alone is therefore insufficient.

Deduction alone is also insufficient because history matters. We cannot study institutions while considering only environmental factors (Field 1981). There is a fundamental asymmetry between institutional elements inherited from the past and alternative, technologically feasible ones. The initial rules of the game are therefore historically determined and cannot be deduced (Chapter 7).

In particular, games reflect and embody people's cognitive models, knowledge, and norms, which are products of, and embodied in, a society's institutions (Chapter 5). These historically inherited features influence the process of institutional selection and hence new institutions. Thus even if we know the objective structure of the situation, we cannot deductively predict institutions. If we begin the analysis by specifying a game that captures our perception of the situation, we ignore the fact that the players may have a different cognitive understanding of it. If we impose our own cognitive understanding on the players, then instead of learning how the prevailing internalized beliefs influenced and were embodied in institutions, we are likely to end up examining or predicting irrelevant alternatives.

In short, one cannot begin an institutional analysis by considering an environment devoid of any institutions and deductively proceed to identify the relevant institution. Classical, evolutionary, and learning game theory lends support to the claim that institutional analysis cannot be approached deductively. Institutions are not environmentally determined – multiple equilibria are often possible in the formation of institutions in given circumstances – and hence they cannot be deduced.

11.2 THE INSUFFICIENCY OF INDUCTION

Like pure deduction, the purely inductive method associated with Francis Bacon of classifying and generalizing without necessarily understanding the lines of causation is insufficient for studying endogenous institutions.[4] Some institutional elements, particularly beliefs and norms that provide motivation, are unobservable, and the same observable features, such as rules and organizations, can be part of different institutions. The premise of induction, that enough endogenous variables are observable to render classification useful, does not hold in the case of endogenous institutions.

Consider the common practice of identifying and classifying institutions based on their observable features, which are rules and organizations. Focusing on these observable features is sufficient for positive analysis only if the unobservable institutional elements associated with them – beliefs and norms – do not matter. But game theory indicates that these unobservable institutional elements do matter and that ignoring them provides an incomplete picture of the institution. The multiple equilibria result reveals that many unobservable institutional

---

[4] Any inductive analysis, however, rests on some deductive assertions regarding what is important to classify.

elements – each potentially motivating different behavior – can be associated with observable ones. Observable institutional elements are generally insufficient for deducing unobservable ones, and hence the institution in its entirety. Studying institutions based only on their observable features implies considering distinct institutions as identical.

Observable institutional elements – rules and organizations – often provide little information about the relevant institution. Formal legal rules, for example, sometimes convey little information about the institution in question, because observable legal rules can be empty words that have no bearing at all on behavior. In the case of the merchant guild, for example, laws guaranteeing property rights to foreign merchants sometimes represented no more than empty promises aimed at luring merchants to travel to foreign lands where their property could be abused. Even legal rules that would be enforced if invoked might not be part of the institutions that influence behavior. Both the Jewish and the Muslim legal systems to which the Maghribi traders had access would have enforced the law stating that one was not legally liable to pay compensation if a family member breached a contract. But this law was not part of the institution that governed the relationships among the Maghribis. Fear of collective punishment, not fear of enforcement of the law, motivated Maghribis to pay compensation if a family member defaulted.

Similarly, a legal rule, even a constitutional rule, can be behaviorally irrelevant because it is unenforceable. In Mexico after the revolutions of 1910–17, a constitutional rule nationalized the oil industry. But nationalization was not implemented for many years. The de facto institution that supported ownership patterns and behavior in the oil industry reflected the power relationships between Mexico, the United States, and the large oil companies, as well as the scarce human capital possessed by the employees of these companies. Mexico's constitutional rule was not part of the relevant institution (Haber et al. 2003). The rule was arguably a means of mobilizing popular support rather than part of an institution assigning property rights.

But laws can also be a component of an institution, even if the behavior they dictate is not followed. Consider building code regulations, which are aimed at ensuring housing safety in the event of an earthquake. In California, these regulations are, by and large, adhered to. In Turkey, adherence is much more lax. The regulations may be a part of a different institution in each place. Presumably in Turkey the regulations only change the division of the surplus from not building according to code by enhancing the bargaining power of inspectors and increasing the level of bribes that they can collect.[5]

Similarly, the existence of a specific organization does not imply that a particular institution prevails. The same organization can be part of distinct institutions with different implications, each of which differs from the others in its unobservable components, such as beliefs. Guild organizations could have been part of an institution that protected property rights, but they could also have been part of one that created monopoly rights. Indeed, they can even be part of both institutions at the same time.

In short, we cannot rely only on induction and study endogenous institutions by examining their observable features, such as rules and organizations. Ironically, the game-theoretic insight regarding multiplicity that supports the assertion that deduction is insufficient for positive analysis of endogenous institutions also implies the insufficiency of induction based on observable aspects of the institutions. Multiple institutions can be associated with the same observable institutional elements.

The traditional empirical methods of the social sciences rest on two premises: first, that theory can sufficiently restrict – *predict* – the endogenous outcomes for a given set of the exogenous and observable features of the situation; and, second, that sufficiently many endogenous variables are observable to render classification based on inspection meaningful. These premises, however, do not hold in the case of endogenous institutions.

11.3 INITIATING INSTITUTIONAL ANALYSIS

That neither deduction nor induction is sufficient to study endogenous institutions implies that their study can begin from neither the institution nor the game. If an institution is the endogenous factor we want to identify and is not entirely directly observable, it cannot be the starting point of the analysis. Similarly, we cannot begin the analysis by formulating the situation as a game, as doing so would entail assuming much of what should be empirically identified and analytically understood. We seek to understand how a particular game became and remained relevant and what beliefs and norms established themselves within the rules of the game.

---

[5] Indeed, following the disastrous consequences of the 1999 Izmit earthquake, it has been widely claimed that the failure to enforce building codes contributed greatly to the number of casualties. See, for example, the press release at http://www.geohaz. org/press/izmit99.htm.

To begin the analysis, we use contextual analysis and deductive theory to identify the substantive issues that merit examining at the time and place under consideration. Contextual knowledge of the society under consideration, including its economic, political, and social features, is necessary. There is no point in asking, for example, what institutions facilitated the employment of agents in long-distance trade if the economy under consideration was a subsistence economy that did not trade. Similarly, there is no point in considering how impersonal exchange was facilitated in a small village in which anonymity does not prevail. In such cases, the historical context implores us to pose other questions, such as why long-distance trade did not prevail or larger settlements were not established. The analysis thus begins by recognizing the context specificity and historical contingency of institutions. In other words, one needs to be familiar with the society under consideration.

Given such contextual knowledge, theoretical considerations foster our ability to identify important issues. Theories of economic growth, for example, highlight the importance of institutions that motivate technological innovations and transform savings into investment. Cultural analysis highlights the importance of institutions that motivate individuals to consider the pursuit of profit and material welfare as morally appropriate. Property rights theory highlights the importance of institutions securing property rights for the operation of markets. Transaction cost economics highlights the importance of reducing transaction costs to a level at which exchange is possible. Political economy theories highlight the importance of institutions that maintain political order, enable rulers to commit to request property rights, and influence the use of the coercive and regulatory powers of the state.

Using theoretical considerations to identify the relevant issues is important, because observed behavior does not always directly reflect the importance of the institutions to which that theory directs us. The behavior that an institution generates may well be off the equilibrium path and therefore not observable. As Greif et al. (1994) note with respect to contract enforcement institutions, "The effectiveness of institutions for punishing contract violations is sometimes best judged like that of peacetime armies – by how little they must be used. Thus, in reading the historical record to determine whether a major role of merchant institutions was to ensure contract compliance, the numbers of instances of enforcement is not a useful indicator" (p. 746).

Combining contextual knowledge and deductive reasoning is imperative. For example, property rights theory highlights the importance of property rights security to encourage investment, production, and exchange. Yet we have to look at the context to identify which specific property rights were important and whether the central government, the neighboring tribe, the local elite, the landlord, the army, or one's relatives threatened them.

Theory and contextual knowledge should therefore be combined to identify welfare-related central transactions and the related regularities of behavior, such as the employment of agents, the establishment of large corporations, the lending of money in the absence of a legal system, the pursuit of a healthy or unhealthy life-style, and the investment of resources in inventive activities. Alternatively, we can begin the analysis by identifying some outcomes of interest, such as the rule of law, economic growth, social stability, political order, property rights security, or a particular income distribution. In this case, we ask: What regularities of behavior in which transactions manifested themselves in, or contributed to, these outcomes of interest? Which transactions are crucial to achieving the outcomes of interest (such as efficiency, political order, resource mobilization, or equity)?

The analysis can also begin by exploring why the dog did not bark – why behavior that could have led to a particular outcome did not occur. What are the auxiliary transactions that are or could have been linked to that central transaction? What are the transactions that could have been entered into but were not, and why? We try to determine what generated the behavior we observe in the central transaction or what could have prevented generating the behavior whose absence we seek to understand.

In twelfth-century England, for example, agency relationships were apparently not established, despite the fact that long-distance trade prevailed. Godric of Norfolk, a seafaring merchant, did not employ agents, although he recognized the danger of traveling overseas. His late medieval biographer noted that in the course of sailing "to and fro between Scotland and Britain" to conduct his trade, Godric "fell into many perils of the sea" (Coulton 1918, pp. 415–20). Merchants recognized the risk of trading without agents, but they did not adopt technologically feasible behavior that could have mitigated it. Why weren't agency relationships established? What institution, if any, prevented agency relationships from being formed?

By concentrating on central transactions, behavior, and outcomes, we avoid functionalism as well. The analysis does not begin by considering an institution's observable features, such as organizations and rules, and attempt to account for them based on the function they are postulated to serve. Rather, it begins by considering behavior and outcomes that did or did not transpire, and only then exploring the institutions leading to these outcomes. Considering institutions as self-enforcing implies that there is no need to invoke a function to account for the prevalence of a particular institution.

11.4 TOWARD A CONJECTURE: ASSEMBLING THE PIECES

Once we have identified the issue to be examined, we lay the foundation for forming a conjecture about a relevant institution by defining the scope of the analysis, gathering empirical information, examining the historical context, and relying on generic theoretical insights. The objective is to develop a conjecture about the relevance of one among the many alternative institutions that can generate the behavior we seek to understand.[6] In developing a conjecture, we have to avoid the pitfall of asserting that producing a model generating the observed behavior is sufficient to account for this behavior. In studying the merchant guilds, I could have built a model supporting the assertion that international interactions provided the foundations for an institution securing property rights. The historical context, however, indicates the futility of such analysis.

In any institutional analysis, various institutional (and noninstitutionalized) aspects of the situation must be taken as exogenous: we cannot study every man-made aspect of the situation endogenously at the same time, nor is there a conceptual need to do so, for the reasons elaborated in Part III. It is conceptually sound and analytically useful to take some endogenous institutions as given while studying the other institutions and the forces rendering them self-enforcing. Deciding which institutions to consider endogenous and which exogenous is determined by the central transaction of interest and those conjectured to be linked to it.

To identify exogenous and endogenous institutional features and, more generally, to limit the scope of the analysis, we rely on contextual knowledge and empirical analysis aimed at identifying the relevant transactions and actors. Indeed, identifying the relevant auxiliary transactions is key to developing a conjecture about the relevant institution. In Chapter 3, for example, the key to identifying the Maghribi traders' coalition was recognizing the auxiliary transaction of information sharing. After all, given the technology of the period, other transactions could have been

---

[6] It is often sufficient to develop a conjecture about the class of the relevant institution, that is, the institution's general attributes rather than their exact details.

linked to the merchant-agent transaction to support agency relationships. The merchant-agent transaction could have been linked to transactions among family members, to transactions with the legal system, even to the perceived transaction with a divine entity. Central to identifying the Maghribi traders' coalition was recognizing that agents' behavior was not influenced by these possible intertransactional linkages. Likewise, in Chapter 4 identifying the relevant transactions as those between merchants and their guilds – rather than, say, the transactions between nation-states – was crucial.

Once we have identified the relevant transactions and actors, we can differentiate between the institutional elements we can take as exogenous and endogenous. We take as exogenous historically determined institutions beyond the control of all the individuals interacting in the transactions of interest. In studying the Maghribi traders or the merchant guild, for example, I considered such man-made aspects of the situation as language, money, product markets, political units, and a transportation system as exogenous. Given the central transactions of interest and the related institutions – those governing agency relationships and those governing the relationships between foreign merchants and local rulers – there was no need to consider these man-made factors as endogenous. I simply accepted them as part of the context, an exogenous, historically inherited feature of the situation.

We can similarly consider as exogenous some institutions that are endogenous to all the interacting individuals whose behavior we study. This is appropriate if the transactions in which these institutions generate behavior are "farther away" from those of interest (see section 7.2). We focus on the institutional elements that directly influence behavior in the central and auxiliary transactions and create the link among them, ignoring institutions related to other transactions. In studying Genoa's political institutions, for example, I took the institutions governing marriages in the city as given.

We have to consider as endogenous, however, the institutional elements linking the central transaction with the auxiliary ones and generating the related behavior. In the impersonal exchange examined in Chapter 10, the central transaction was the transaction between traders; the auxiliary transactions were those among the courts and between each court and individual traders. The analysis therefore had to consider the institutional elements linking these transactions and generating behavior in them. In the agency relationships among the Maghribis, the central transaction was that between each merchant and agent; the auxiliary transactions were those between each agent and his potential future merchants and those related to information sharing among the traders.

In the process of identifying relevant transactions, we use inductive analysis to identify aspects of the situation that are relevant to forming and later evaluating a conjecture about possible institutions. Of particular importance are organizations, rules, and beliefs about the structure of the situation. Recognizing the importance, and legal independence, of the European communes was crucial to identifying the community responsibility system (Chapter 10). Explicit statements in the primary (historical) sources, interviews, surveys, and other sources can reveal individuals' beliefs, strategies, knowledge, technology, and the magnitude of potentially relevant parameters such as a community's size, demography, and wealth. In analyzing the community responsibility system, I used treaties and charters as a guide to identifying the institution. Patterns of behavior can also provide important clues. The observation that agency relationships were multilateral among the Maghribis but bilateral among the Genoese was important in directing attention to institutions based on multilateral and bilateral reputation mechanisms (Chapter 9).

Historical information is indispensable in generating a conjecture about the relevant institution, because institutional dynamics constitute a historical process. That history is encapsulated in past institutional elements and new institutions emerge in the context of existing ones implies that we can benefit from contextual refinement (Chapter 7). We can use historical information to narrow the set of conjectures about possible institutions, because new institutions reflect the fundamental asymmetry between institutional elements inherited from the past and alternative, technologically feasible ones. Historical knowledge directs our attention to the institutional elements more likely to be complementary to, to coordinate on, and to be part of the institution we are trying to identify. Knowing that communes prevailed in Europe before market expansion took place, for example, directed attention to their possible role in contract enforcement institutions that supported impersonal exchange. Recognizing that clans became important social entities in Italy before the establishment of the Republic of Genoa directed attention toward institutions incorporating clans as institutional elements.

Deductive theory also has an important role to play in developing a conjecture about the relevant institution. Theory fosters our ability to develop a conjecture by identifying the causal mechanisms underpinning various institutions, the problems institutions of a particular type (e.g., reputation-based or legal) have to overcome to be effective, and the general conditions under which a particular institution can be self-enforcing. Generic theoretical insights thus point to evidence that helps identify the relevant institution and even to sort among alternative institutions within that class.

In developing the conjecture that reputational considerations induced behavior among the Maghribis, theory highlighted the importance of establishing whether merchants perceived an agent who cheated to be a "bad type," who would continue to cheat in the future or not. Generic theoretical insights identified the evidence required to do so. Once the combined theoretical and empirical analysis substantiated the relative irrelevance of the incomplete information model with bad type, theory indicated other problems that reputation-based institutions have to mitigate in this case. It drew attention, for example, to the need to mitigate the end-game problem and retain the credibility of transmitting information about cheating, even when cheating does not transpire. (Appendix C illustrates the general use of deductive theory in developing a conjecture about relevant institutions in the particular case of reputation-based institutions.)

All models of behavior endow interacting individuals with some preferences. In studying institutions, it is useful to gain a sense of the preferences of the relevant actors without succumbing to the fallacy of asserting that behavior necessarily reveals preference. Preferences, however, are unobservable. They differ across historical episodes and are often endogenous to the institution under consideration. Furthermore, institutions drive a wedge between preferences and behavior, making it difficult to distinguish them from observed behavior without identifying the related institutions. Identifying the institutions, however, may well require knowing the preferences.

No good empirical strategy to deal with this problem has yet been developed. In general, preferences have to be either identified inductively based on knowledge of the broader context or based on some deductive assertion. In either case, verifying the appropriateness of the assertion about the appropriate preferences is part of the process of verifying the conjecture about the institution. In studying the merchant guilds, I assumed that rulers were not deterred from using coercive force to achieve economic ends. Historical evidence supported this assertion. In studying political institution in Genoa, I assumed that norms did not preclude the use of coercive power to achieve political aims. The analysis then noted that the political institutions both reflect norms sanctioning the use of violence and reinforced these norms.

11.5 CONJECTURE AND CONTEXT-SPECIFIC MODELS

A conjecture about the relevant institution consists of a statement about the transactions that were or were not linked (and hence the relevant decision makers and their possible actions), the institutional elements that link and influence behavior in these transactions, the important environmental features on which these institutional elements depend, and the causal relationships between the exogenous and endogenous features. Although in some cases we can evaluate a particular conjecture based on deductive, inductive, and contextual knowledge without explicit modeling, a context-specific model is often useful for presenting and evaluating a conjecture.

The justification for using models that rest on the deductive assumption that individuals act as if they are rational, as I do here, is that institutions provide the micro-foundations required for decision making (Chapter 5). It is exactly because rationality is contextual that individuals can act rationally in pursuing well-defined goals within the confines spanned by institutions, which reflect, embody, and structure the sphere that the decision makers comprehend and in which they have well-defined goals.

When game theory is used to capture the conjecture, we present it by specifying the rules of the game (the actors, their actions and information, and the relationships between actions and outcomes), the beliefs that prevailed within these rules, and various causal relationships. A conjecture about a contract enforcement institution, for example, must specify what rewards desirable behavior implies, what sanctions are to be used to deter undesirable behavior, who is to apply the sanction, how the sanctioners learn when to apply sanctions or decide what sanctions to apply, why they do not shirk from their duty, and why offenders do not flee to avoid the sanction. In any case, the model recognizes that the game relevant to the interacting actors and their behavior in it is contingent on what transactions had been linked, how, and to what effect.

The model should be as simple as possible, capturing the exogenous features of the situation and allowing the researcher to investigate the feasibility, rationale, and implications of the endogenous features postulated in the hypothesis. To the extent possible, its details should be based on evidence, and they should not integrate unobservable features of the situation (unless their relevance can be empirically substantiated, as discussed later).[7] A specification based on observable features serves two purposes. First, it constrains the set of possible models, reducing the likelihood of generating a model that has nothing to do with the relevant institution but can still explain its relevant endogenous features. Second, selecting assumptions based on evidence limits the ability (or temptation) to account for the observed phenomenon with ad hoc assumptions about unobservable features of the situation.

I could have argued, for example, that trust among the Maghribi traders was based on their religiosity, communal affinity, or unobservable personal attributes, such as honesty.[8] Although each of these factors may have played a role in the operation of the Maghribi traders' coalition, the context-specific analysis supports the centrality of a reputation mechanism based on economic sanctions.

The challenge, in other words, is to use the model to evaluate a conjecture. It is easy enough to present a game with the behavior we want to explain as an equilibrium outcome. We are not interested in ad hoc modeling, however; we want to *identify* the relevant institutions, not *assert* that a feasible one was relevant. Accordingly, the context-specific model is structured for the purpose of evaluating the hypothesis that a particular institution prevailed. Whenever possible, the analysis should attempt to refute the importance of other institutions whose relevance is reasonable. But attempts to identify theoretically the set of all possible institutions can divert attention to irrelevant alternatives, given the knowledge of the individuals under consideration and the manner in which these institutions were selected. Accordingly, the model is used mainly to substantiate a conjecture about the relevance of a particular institution rather than proving that all other feasible institutions did not.

Before elaborating on the usefulness of a context-specific model, I should note the limitations of modeling in evaluating a conjecture.[9] The need to preserve analytical tractability and models' underlying mathematical techniques restricts the conjectures that can be expressed and analyzed using an explicit model. Game-theoretic models, particularly

---

[7] This follows the Ockham's razor principle of keeping conjectures simple and of selecting among alternative hypotheses that generate the same predictions as the one making the least number of assumptions.

[8] In the modern context we can sometimes get measures of such unobservable attributes using surveys and experiments.

[9] For discussions of the virtues and pitfalls of modeling in empirical analysis, see Kreps (1990a); Scharpf (1997); Bates et al. (1998); and Powell (1999).

dynamic game-theoretic models with large action sets, can easily become very complicated. Of course, the right conjecture is preferable to an elegant but irrelevant model. In some cases the best we can do is to use a model that captures only some aspects of the conjecture we want to evaluate. In other cases the problem can be mitigated by conducting the analysis sequentially. In studying organizations, for example, it may be easier first to consider an organization as exogenous to the institution under consideration and only later to extend the analysis to consider the organization as endogenous.

11.6   EVALUATING A CONJECTURE THROUGH INTERACTIVE, CONTEXT-SPECIFIC ANALYSIS

Once a conjecture about the relevant institution has been formed and presented using a context-specific model, it is evaluated through an interactive analysis. The model – and the context-specific conjecture it captures – is evaluated based on the evidence, while evidence is used to reject, accept, or alter the conjecture. What is to be avoided in this interactive analysis is the tautology in which the model is adjusted to fit the evidence. The challenge is to put the model and the conjecture it captures to an empirical test. This can be achieved in several, complementary ways.

A model and its analysis provides an explicit statement of the aspects of the situation the researcher claims are important or unimportant – a statement that can be confronted with the evidence and alterative statements. To evaluate the conjecture and enrich our understanding of the institution, we use the model in various ways. Subjecting the model to game-theoretic equilibrium analysis restricts the set of admissible institutions (by restricting possible beliefs, as elaborated in Chapter 5). Equilibrium analysis subjects the conjecture to the test of logic. If there is no equilibrium that generates the behavior we seek to explain, it may be that the assertion that individuals behave in a manner captured by the logic of game theory is wrong. Alternatively, the model may have been misspecified (important aspects of the situation may have been overlooked). In this case, it will need to be reevaluated. I recognized the importance of the threat to Genoa's political institutions posed by Frederic Barbarossa, for example, only after a model ignoring this factor failed to account for the patterns of Genoa's political and economic history.

An additional check on the admissibility of a conjecture is considering whether the complexity or other attributes of the equilibrium render it unreasonable given our knowledge of the actors and the situation. For example, if the beliefs associated with the equilibrium are very complex, is it reasonable to assume that they prevailed in a particular episode? Does the model reasonably approximate the situation in which the actors are playing against the rule rather than against the rules of the game? Is the analysis robust, particularly with respect to aspects of the situation that are not well reflected in the historical records? Is it reasonable given the coordination and inclusion effects of institutional elements inherited from the past? Is it complementary to existing institutions and the related institutional complex?

If there is an equilibrium corresponding to the behavior we seek to explain, it reveals the internalized beliefs, norms, and on- and off-the-equilibrium-path beliefs associated with it. We can then return to the evidence to evaluate which of the possible equilibrium beliefs (or, more precisely, the types of beliefs) prevailed.[10] Private correspondence, diaries, questionnaires, public correspondence and debates, and rules are likely to reflect the beliefs interacting individuals hold. Such *direct evidence* was central to the study of the Maghribi traders, the merchant guild, and the community responsibility system.

Equally important is *indirect evidence:* the confirmation of qualitative and quantitative predictions generated under the assumption that the conjecture – captured in the game and an equilibrium in it – is correct. By generating predictions – exposing causal relationships between exogenous and endogenous, observable and unobservable features of the situation – the model enables us to further evaluate the conjecture by exposing it to the risk of failing to account for the historical evidence and hence being falsified.

The premise of evaluating whether a conjecture should be rejected based on predictions generated under the assumption that it is correct is the same premise used in econometric analysis. In an econometric analysis, we reject a hypothesis by testing for predictions generated under the assumption that it is correct. The best we can do is fail to reject it; this does not imply that we should either accept it or that every other hypothesis will be rejected. Here, too, a conjecture is evaluated by considering the predictions it generates. Hence econometric analysis and the qualitative, case study, prediction-based evaluation conducted here are compatible. This compatibility implies that econometric analysis is an integral part of the method advocated here and that we can use it to test various predictions

---

[10] It is often useful to group beliefs by their qualitative nature (e.g., those entailing a finite punishment) rather than their details (e.g., the length of the punishment).

statistically. In some cases it may indeed be best to specify only a reduced-form econometric model that captures our conjecture and to evaluate its implications statistically.[11]

The qualitative, case study, prediction-based evaluation of a conjecture and statistical evaluation differ, however, in two important ways. First, unlike statistical evaluation, qualitative, case study, prediction-based evaluation is conducted without the benefit of a confidence interval. Second, econometric analysis is used only to evaluate whether a theoretically induced conjecture should be rejected. The interactive, context-specific analysis adopted here uses evidence to *develop* as well as to evaluate the relevant conjecture. Doing so is required to avoid the fallacy of ad hoc theorizing.

In evaluating predictions, care has to be taken not to endow the interacting individuals with knowledge they may not have had. In Chapter 9, for example, the theoretical analysis implied that the choices of contractual forms by the Maghribi and Genoese traders should be a function of cultural beliefs and that each group should therefore choose different forms. The first step in evaluating the historical relevance of this prediction was to establish that both groups were indeed familiar with all relevant forms of business associations. After establishing that this was the case, I compared the prediction of the model with the historical evidence.

Predictions can be generated using equilibrium analysis, counterfactual analysis, and comparative statics. Equilibrium analysis generates predictions by indicating the observable implications associated with various equilibria. Some of these predictions are straightforward. The model of the merchant guild, for example, predicted that trade expansion would follow the establishment of a guild organization in a particular location. Other predictions are more subtle and can be difficult to reach without a formal model. The prediction that collective punishment of overseas agents, not individualistic punishment, encourages the use of particular contractual forms and a horizontal social network required a model that highlighted the associated line of causation.

A particularly useful feature of game theory is that it generates equilibrium predictions based on off-the-equilibrium-path beliefs – that is, beliefs

---

[11] Okazaki (2005) conjectures that in eighteenth- and nineteenth-century Japan, the organization of the merchant coalition (*Kabu Nakama*) was the organizational manifestation of a reputation-based contract enforcement institution. To evaluate this conjecture, he expresses it as a reduced-form econometric model, which he estimates using data from periods in which the coalition was and was not politically barred from functioning.

about behavior in situations that would not actually transpire given the prevailing beliefs. The analytical power of predictions regarding off-the-equilibrium-path beliefs is evident in Chapter 9, where I considered the institutional ramifications of distinct cultural beliefs among the Maghribis and Genoese.

A game-theoretic model facilitates counterfactual analysis of off-the-equilibrium-path beliefs. By exposing the observable implications of various off-the-equilibrium-path beliefs, a model generates refutable predictions. Such counterfactual analysis was indispensable in studying Genoa's political institutions. In this case, it was crucial to distinguishing whether interclan peace reflected mutual deterrence or peaceful neighborly relations.

Counterfactual analysis can also be used to evaluate a conjecture in other ways. The self-enforceability of institutions often depends on unobservable features of the situation, and institutions exhibit indeterminacy in the sense that more than one institution can prevail in a given environment. An explicit model exposes the relationships between the exogenous parameters and various endogenous variables as well as the relationships between observable and unobservable variables. This facilitates counterfactual analysis. We can consider the observable implications of changing an observable or unobservable feature of the situation. The evidence on agency relationships among the Maghribi traders did not reveal the importance of incomplete information about agents' honesty. The issue was resolved by considering the observable implications of a model with and without such incomplete information.

Comparative statics analysis examines the change in the equilibrium level of the endogenous (equilibrium) variables following a marginal change in the value of a parameter, an exogenous variable. In considering the relationships between city size, the distribution of wealth, and incentive to adopt the community responsibility system, I conducted a comparative statics analysis. In game-theoretic models, such analysis has to be conducted with care, because the models usually do not have a unique equilibrium. Conducting a comparative statics analysis may be misleading, as the equilibrium itself may change with the parametric change. Comparative statics can nevertheless be conducted in one of two ways. The first is appropriate when there are good reasons to assert that the same equilibrium will prevail before and after the marginal parametric change. This assertion is usually appropriate because of institutional persistence, discussed in Chapter 6. Individuals draw on knowledge of past institutions in considering behavior in marginally different environments. Marginal parametric changes are not likely to lead to equilibrium change.[12]

In studying the community responsibility system, I conducted such a comparative statics analysis in exploring the implication of the increasing sizes and heterogeneity of communities on the institution. In studying the merchant guild, I conducted such an analysis to study cross-sectional changes. I noted that given the prevailing equilibrium, marginal traders – those from relatively small cities – are more likely to be abused.

The second way to conduct a comparative statics analysis is to consider changes in the equilibrium set (the set of all possible equilibria) due to parametric change. I conducted such an analysis in examining Genoa's political institutions, arguing that under the consular system, once the number of commercial privileges abroad and the wealth of the city increased, there was no equilibrium with mutual deterrence.[13]

Organizations are institutional elements that change the equilibrium set. We can evaluate a conjecture about the implications of a particular organization by comparing the implied equilibrium sets with and without this organization. In studying the impact of organizations on outcomes by enabling intertransactional linkages, we change the "relevant" rules of the game. We first consider a "benchmark" game that captures the essence of the central transaction, ignoring the organization whose impact we want to explore. We then consider an augmented game in which an organization – as an institutional element – is incorporated. Organizations are modeled as constituting a new player (the organization itself), changing the information available to players, or changing payoffs associated with certain actions (Greif 1994a, pp. 915–16). We can then repeat the analysis and consider the change in the set of self-enforcing rules, beliefs, and outcomes.[14]

---

[12] However, the exceptions to this rule are difficult to identify ex ante because, for example, leadership can play a role (see Chapter 7).

[13] Monotone comparative statics, which studies the change in the equilibrium set due to a change in the exogenous parameters, is a useful technique for such an analysis (Milgrom and Shannon 1994), although it is not always necessary.

[14] Many of the technical aspects of analyzing the linkage among games (see Bernheim and Whinston 1990; Aoki 2001) can be applied here as well. These analyses examine situations in which a player's choice variable is to link one game with another. By linking games in such a manner, the equilibrium set in one game can be expanded. Here, although organizations are exogenous to each of the interacting players, they influence (limit or expand) the equilibrium set in the central (original) interaction.

Such an analysis was implicit in Chapter 3 and explicit in Chapter 4. The Maghribi traders' coalition changed the rules of the "original" game governing the transaction between merchants and their potential agents. By providing information, the Maghribi traders' group linked the transaction between each merchant and agent to future transactions between that agent and all other member merchants. The guild organizations changed the rules of the game between a ruler and each foreign merchant. The merchant guild organization linked the transaction between a ruler and each merchant to the transactions by all merchants and the ruler and between the merchants and their communal authorities.

From the perspective of each individual in the original game, these organizations (composed of rules, beliefs, and norms beyond the individual's control) are exogenous. Sometimes, as in the analysis of the merchant guild, it is possible to evaluate a conjecture while considering the organization and its behavior as exogenous. But studying the motivation of members of an organization is often required to evaluate a conjecture, particularly because although organizations can change the set of possible self-enforcing beliefs in the central transaction, the basic structure of repeated, strategic interactions – and hence the multiplicity of possible equilibria – is not changed. The introduction of a police force may lead to law-abiding behavior or corruption. Having a legal system with the ability to impose its judgment does not necessarily lead to the rule of law. For the rule of law to take hold, appropriate beliefs must influence the behavior of the individuals who are members of the relevant organizations, such as the court and police. An organization leads to a particular behavior only if it is complemented by appropriate beliefs and norms; studying organizations as an integral part of institutions must take this into consideration.

Hence, to evaluate a conjecture about the impact of an organization, it is often necessary to examine whether the organization itself and its postulated behavior could have been an equilibrium. Such a need arose in analyzing why Maghribi merchants and agents retained their affiliation with the Magrhibi community and why traders were motivated to transfer information and to participate in collective punishment. The analysis considered as endogenous what motivated the Maghribis to retain their affiliation with their group and what enabled and motivated them to take the actions required to render a multilateral reputation mechanism effective. More generally, a conjecture about the institutional elements that generate behavior by an organization and its members has to be evaluated in the same manner that we evaluate a conjecture about an institution in general.

The more qualitative and quantitative predictions support a conjecture, the greater is the confidence in it. That the model predicts the observation motivating the analysis (e.g., agents' honesty, peace, or impersonal exchange) confers very limited empirical validity on the conjecture the model captures. It is important to generate several falsifiable predictions. I evaluated the conjecture about the community responsibility system based on predictions about observable features, such as the relationship between the size of a community and participation in intercommunity lending, lenders' behavior, the legal authority over merchants abroad, and the relationship between the expected value of future trade and the actions taken following accusation of default. The more predictions the analysis can account for, the greater the confidence in its validity. Yet we always have more confidence in rejecting a conjecture than in accepting it.

Whether or not we use an explicit, context-specific model to evaluate a conjecture, recognizing that institutional dynamics is a historical process and knowing the general properties of this process provide an important means of evaluating a conjecture about the relevance of a particular institution. Institutions reflect knowledge entailed by past institutions, the fundamental asymmetry between institutional elements inherited from the past and alternative ones, the impact of existing institutions on the extent of this asymmetry, institutional refinement, and institutional interrelatedness. Because current institutions are a function of past ones, historical information is necessary in evaluating a conjecture about them. In asserting that a particular institution generated behavior in some period, we go beyond pointing to its function and the factors that make it an equilibrium.

A conjecture about the relevance of a particular institution gains support by identifying the historical origins of its institutional elements and the knowledge of its feasibility, details, and implications. In considering institutional historical origin we ask: Can we identify the historical origin of the institutional elements central to the institution? How was the knowledge underlying the institution gained? Were past institutions such that the knowledge they imply would have led to the postulated institution? Were the institutional elements central to the postulated institutions inherited from the past?

Recognizing the Maghribis' cultural beliefs and the fact that they were initially an immigrant group lends support to the claim about the practice of collective punishment among them. The observation that Europe's urban population was concentrated in self-governed communes within which members' identities were known supports the relevance of the community responsibility system. The conjecture about the nature of the *podestà* gained support from identifying the historical processes leading to knowledge regarding its implications.

A conjecture similarly gains support from examining the plausibility of a process leading to it, given the historical context. Distinguishing five issues is useful. The first is the motivation and ability to establish the institution (if it was intentionally established). Does the institution serve the interests of those who have the ability and power to influence institutional selection? Given existing institutions, what motivated and enabled them to implement this institution or refine existing ones to form it? The conjecture regarding the community responsibility system gains support from noting that it used the communes' courts, which were controlled by the same merchants who benefited from the system. They were motivated and able to institute that system. We can use extensive-form games to capture the details of this historical process. Who are the decision makers at each point in time, what did they know, and what options were available to them?

The second issue regards an unintentional process that may have led to the postulated institution. Can we identify a plausible evolutionary process through which the conjectured institution could have emerged given the institutional environment and institutional elements inherited from the past? Here we can use evolutionary and learning models while capturing the influence of existing institutions.[15] Knowledge that such models can be constructed in a particular case lends support to the conjecture. Indeed, the conjecture regarding the Maghribi traders' coalition gains support from observing that it is easy to construct a learning model leading to the behavior captured in the repeated-game model used to study them. This observation lends support to the repeated-game formulation and the analysis as a whole.

The third issue regards the fundamental asymmetry and contextual refinement: Do the institutional elements in the new institutions reflect institutional asymmetry? Can we reconcile the conjectured institution with the environmental, coordination, and inclusion effects of previous ones? The conjecture regarding the community responsibility system gained support from noting that it was complementary to the environment in which no state had effective means to enforce contracts. The conjecture is also consistent with coordination provided by existing communal

---

[15] As done, for example, in Gintis 2000, sec. 11.8.

organizations, including these communes' courts. That this institution reflects the environmental, coordination, and inclusion effects of institutional elements inherited from the past lends support to the conjecture that it was relevant.

The fourth issue regards institutional interrelatedness. Is the postulated institution likely to have emerged given the influence of the existing institutional complexes? Is the new institution complementary to existing ones? Were the existing complexes conducive to an institution of this form? What were the transaction cost implications of the existing institutions on the ability to attain or establish the postulated one? The conjecture regarding the community responsibility system gained support from its compatibility with the existing institutional complex. Like the communal system itself, it was based on man-made law, self-governance, explicit coordination, and use of the communes' legal authorities.

The fifth issue regards the process of institutional decline and its ramifications. An assertion that a particular institution prevailed in the past gains support from identifying the exogenous and endogenous processes leading to the institutional decline. It similarly gains support from finding that subsequent institutions reflect the refinement, coordination, and inclusion effects of the previous institutions' components.

The discussion so far implicitly considered equilibrium, counterfactual, and comparative-statics predictions with respect to the case under study. Evaluating such predictions with respect to "out of the sample" cases further validates the analysis and its generality. My analysis of the community responsibility system initially focused on England; Italy generated out-of-sample predictions. The analysis suggested that this institution could have prevailed in other European regions with relatively large communes but could not have prevailed where this was not the case; and could not have prevailed in the Muslim world, despite its large urban communities, because of the religious rejection of collective responsibility. The historical records confirm these predictions. Similarly, the analysis of the Maghribis suggests that multilateral punishment is more likely to exist in relatively small and closed communities with internal information flows, a prediction confirmed in various studies (see, e.g., Clay 1997).

In evaluating out-of-sample predictions, however, it is important to keep in mind the context specificity of the analysis. The inherent indeterminacy of institutions implies that there is no one-to-one mapping from the exogenous features of a situation to its endogenous ones. Situations with identical exogenous aspects can have different institutions. We need to consider the compatibility and distinction in the contemporary and historical contexts to evaluate the appropriateness of comparisons across cases.

The structure of the method suggested here is such that it facilitates comparative institutional analysis over time and societies that furthers our ability to identify an institution in a given historical episode. Focusing on the central and auxiliary transactions lets us consider what distinct auxiliary transactions were linked to the same central transactions in different episodes. Considering the context also facilitates comparative analysis, by revealing the historical contexts that are sufficiently similar to make an examination of the institutional foundations of distinct outcomes constructive. These features of the method allow us to compare, for example, the institutions that governed agency relationships among the Maghribis and the Genoese (Chapter 9) as well as the political institutions in Genoa and Venice (Chapter 6).

In short, a conjecture gains support to the extent that the associated context-specific analysis

- is based on the simplest possible assumptions that can be supported by the historical evidence;
- indicates the existence of an equilibrium that captures the essence of the conjecture, particularly with respect to its unobservable elements, such as beliefs;
- is robust to different specifications, particularly with respect to aspects of the situation that are not well reflected in the historical evidence;
- indicates that the expectations and behavior associated with the equilibrium are not unreasonably complex given the historical episode, and/or there is an empirically plausible evolutionary and learning process that could have led to their emergence;
- is confirmed by direct evidence;
- is confirmed by indirect evidence, that is, predictions that can be falsified either by evidence from the historical episode under consideration or through a comparative study over time and space;
- reflects the influence of past institutional elements and institutional refinement;
- highlights the factors and processes that could have led to the conjectured institution in that particular context;
- accounts for the institution's subsequent decline (if it is observed) and reveals the institution's impact on subsequent institutions;
- is confirmed by comparative and out-of-sample analysis.

The more ways we can support a conjecture, the more confidence we have in its validity. Because different conjectures may be supported by distinct evidence, a partial ordering between analyses is thus possible. It may well be the case that we will not be able to reject two conjectures. In such cases, we learn about the limits of our possible knowledge.

11.7 CONCLUDING COMMENTS

Interactively using contextual knowledge, deduction, induction, context-specific modeling, and evidence while benefiting from comparative and counterfactual analyses is the hallmark of the empirical method proposed in this chapter. Deduction and induction complement each other and are complemented by a context-specific analysis. Theory highlights the issues to be explored and the general considerations and evidence that have to be examined; knowledge of the historical and current context is used to develop a conjecture regarding the relevant institution – what transactions were linked, by what institutional elements, how, and why – while this conjecture is evaluated, refined, and even overhauled through the interactive use of a context-specific model and evidence. This empirical method thereby recognizes and takes advantage of the context specificity and historical contingency of institutional analysis.

PART V

Concluding Comments

12

Institutions, History, and Development

This chapter reflects on four issues central to this book. Two are methodological: the nature of institutions and the analytical and empirical method with which to study them. Two are substantive: the insights from the comparative institutional analysis of institutions in the European and Muslim worlds and the policy implications of the perspective on institutions presented in this book.

Institutions are the engine of history because, as I argue in section 12.1, they constitute much of the structure that influences behavior, including behavior leading to new institutions. Their independent impact and their interrelations with social and cultural factors imply that we cannot study them as reflecting only environmental factors or the interests of various agents. Although institutions are not random and all institutions generating the same behavior respond to the same forces, their details and implications are not determined by these forces. Comparative and historical institutional analysis – the central aspects of which are reviewed in section 12.2 – fosters our ability to capture and study institutions from the required broader perspective.

Section 12.3 dwells on the insights from the comparative and historical analysis of institutions in the European and Muslim worlds during the late medieval commercial expansion. It emphasizes that many of the elements and features of modern, welfare-enhancing Western-style institutions were already present or in the process of emerging during the late medieval period: individualism, man-made formal law, corporatism, self-governance, and rules reflecting an institutionalized process in which those who were subject to them had a voice and influence. Institutions may well be the engine of history, and to the extent that the Rise of the West is due to its underpinning institutions, the roots of this rise may have begun to take hold as early as the late medieval period.

Section 12.4 examines the implications of the perspective proposed here for the developmental challenges that so many countries still face. Socially beneficial policy aimed at beneficial institutional change has to accommodate the context, recognize that institutional dynamics are a historical process, and take into account the importance of institutional elements inherited from the past. Policy must rely on these three pillars to create institutions that are compatible with the context and to direct institutional dynamics toward better institutional equilibria.

12.1 INSTITUTIONS AND BLACK BOXES: THE GOOD, THE BAD, AND THE MESSY

Whether a society's institutions achieve socially good or bad outcomes, they cannot be studied independently from the broader society of which they are an integral part. The components of institutions reflect and constitute the cultural and social world that members of a society share and internalize. Institutions are shaped by a society's social and cultural heritage, and they contain norms and internalized and behavioral beliefs. These norms and beliefs, in turn, reflect the cognitive models, knowledge, and coordination that were generated through a historical process of interactions, socialization, learning, experimentation, and leadership. Institutions also determine social positions and manifest themselves in formal and informal organizations, such as communities, ethnic groups, schools, firms, political lobbies, and bodies for collective decision making. Institutionalized rules, transmitted culturally, socially, and formally, convey and foster processes of norm and belief formation while reflecting norms and beliefs regarding the world around us, our interests, legitimacy, and human attributes.

Institutions do not merely influence behavior and outcomes – including policies – at a given moment in time. They are also the engine of history as they shape change. Institutions affect the timing and nature of institutional change and influence the details of new institutions. Institutions impose constraints and provide opportunities for intentional institutional change, as well as unleash processes of unintentional changes. Moreover, because the institutional elements inherited from the past are the properties of societies and individuals, history – encapsulated in institutional elements – influences selection among alternative institutions in new – not yet institutionalized – situations.

Existing institutions influence how institutional change can be effected and hence how and what interests can be pursued by altering institutions.

Institutions determine whether or not it is easy to adjust them to serve a particular function, such as efficiency or the welfare of a particular group. Institutionalized rules, beliefs, norms, and the associated organizations influence the motivation and ability of various interests and functions to shape institutional development. The institutional histories of Genoa, Venice, and Pisa are different, not because of distinct functional needs or interests, but because of their different institutional heritages.[1] The Maghribi traders' coalition and the Genoese bilateral contract-enforcement institution were two distinct institutional responses to the same need.

Institutions serving the same needs are not random. They all reflect the same forces and considerations. Yet distinct institutions entail different dynamics. The mechanism for institutional change is a function of opportunities, constraints, and processes that the prevailing institutions imply. Once established as equilibria, institutions do not necessarily have built-in mechanisms to efficiently respond to changing circumstances as we have seen, for example, in the case of the Maghribi traders' coalition. Institutions do not necessarily induce a beneficial institutional change. Indeed, an institution can remain self-enforcing even if the behavior it generates is no longer efficiency-enhancing. We have seen just that in the case of Genoa's political institutions. Similarly, an institution can undermine itself, even though a better alternative is not available, as the community responsibility system did in various parts of Europe. Finally, the function of an institution can change even if its form does not. The merchant guild, initially a welfare-enhancing institution that protected property rights, later used its abilities to reduce welfare by preventing competition.

Hence, whether the society under consideration is a nation, an ethnic group, or a business enterprise and whether the institution under study is good or bad in generating a particular behavior, its analysis is likely to be messy. We have to leave the comfortable arena of traditional economic inquiry in which the economy is assumed as isolated from the broader society and its history. It is generally inappropriate to assume that a society's institutions are determined only by environmental factors to serve a particular function or the interests of individuals unconstrained by

---

[1] The establishment of the Commune of Genoa reflected interests, but Genoa's institutional foundations were built on and influenced by the heritage of particular shared beliefs, norms, and social structures, which prevented these clans from advancing the welfare of their members to the extent technologically possible. The opposition to abolishing slavery in the Muslim world likewise reflects internalized beliefs and illustrates the impact of institutional complexes on the direction of change.

institutional heritage. Understanding the impact, origin, and persistence of distinct institutional trajectories necessitates recognizing the dynamic interplay between institutions, interests, and the nature of institutional dynamics as a historical process.

The complex nature of institutions implies that a superficial study is likely to be misleading. Even with seemingly identical organizations, rules, and outcomes, institutions may differ by, for example, their underpinning behavioral beliefs. Genoa and Pisa appear to have had the same *podesteria* system, yet they had very distinct institutions. In the former the *podestà* provided a balance of power, whereas in the latter it represented the domination of one group over another. For markets to function, property rights must be secure, but we have to know the context to recognize potential predators. For example, the government, the local elite or bureaucracy, the police, the army, the neighbors, or even relatives are possibilities. Context-specific analysis going beyond studying institutions as rules is necessary.

Indeed, invoking distinct rules was found insufficient to account for why some economies are rich and others are poor, why some have effective markets and polities, why some societies fail or succeed in adopting new institutions, and why the same political rules entail different welfare-related outcomes. To account for such outcomes, students of institutions have argued the importance of complementing the study of formal rules with that of informal institutions (North 1990), social capabilities (Abramovitz 1986), social capital (Putnam 1993), social infrastructure (Hall and Jones 1999), and civil capital (Djankov et al. 2003). Advancing institutional analysis requires going beyond invoking these concepts parametrically in our models or using proxies to study their impact empirically. Comparative and historical institutional analysis contributes to achieving just that by studying the institutional elements influencing behavior on the micro-level of the interacting individuals.

12.2 COMPARATIVE AND HISTORICAL INSTITUTIONAL ANALYSIS

To cut through the Gordian knot of institutional analysis, comparative and historical institutional analysis advances a pragmatic definition that accommodates the variety in origins, functions, and manifestations of institutions. It encompasses, but goes beyond, various definitions commonly used by economists, sociologists, and political scientists. *An institution is a system of social factors that conjointly generate a regularity of behavior.* These factors are social in being man-made, nonphysical factors

382

that are exogenous to *each* individual whose behavior they influence. The various social factors that constitute an institution – in particular, rules, beliefs, norms, and organizations – motivate, enable, and guide individuals to follow one behavior among the many that are technologically feasible in social situations.

The institutionalized rules, beliefs, and norms that generate behavior in social situations are exogenous to *each* individual whose behavior they influence, and they constitute and are formed by intertransactional linkages. A transaction is an action taken when an entity, such as a commodity, social attitude, or piece of information, is transferred between individuals or other social units and has an external effect on the recipient. Institutional elements generating behavior in the central transaction of interest (e.g., economic exchange) reflect the actual and expected behavior in auxiliary transactions. The institutional elements influencing behavior in auxiliary transactions imply the norms and beliefs that enable, motivate, and guide behavior in the central transaction. Behavior and expected behavior in auxiliary transactions make institutionalized rules commonly known, render particular beliefs possible and relevant, and lead individuals to internalize particular norms. These rules, beliefs, and norms, in turn, constitute the institutional elements that conjointly generate behavior in the central transaction.

The games we use to study institutions constitute statements regarding the intertransactional linkages underpinning the institutional elements that generate behavior in the central transaction of interest. Analyzing the game that captures these intertransactional linkages enables examination of their underpinning institutional elements. It further enables limiting the self-enforcing and reproducing institutional elements that generate behavior in the central transaction.

Institutions have a pervasive influence on behavior, because individuals seek cognitive, coordinative, normative, and informational guidance for their behavior. In situations in which institutions generate behavior, they find this guidance in institutionalized rules. Such rules provide shared cognition, articulate expected behavior, frame the situation, and specify normatively appropriate actions. Institutions span the domain that individuals understand, within which they can predict others' behavior, determine their interest, and specify the morally appropriate. Rule following is motivated by belief in the validity of these cognitive models, belief that others will follow the prescribed behavior, and the intrinsic motivation provided by the internalization of these behavioral standards. At the same time, because each individual responds to the commonly known rules and beliefs about behavior based on his private information and knowledge, institutionalized rules aggregate this information and knowledge and reflect the trade-off between the psychological and social benefits of following normatively sanctioned and socially appropriate behavior and its materialistic cost.

Endogenous institutions are self-enforcing and reproducing in the sense that each individual, using his private knowledge and information, follows the behavior expected of him, while the implied behavior does not refute the validity of the beliefs motivating behavior or erode its motivating norms. In situations in which institutions generate behavior, institutions and the behavior they generate constitute an equilibrium. Institutions reflect the actions of the interacting agents but constitute the structure influencing each agent's behavior.

Institutionalized rules, beliefs, and norms also generate behavior in transactions within and across organizational boundaries. They generate behavior among members of organizations (social structures) and among them and nonmembers. Organizations differ from other institutions, however, in that the associated beliefs and norms lead to differential behavior toward members and nonmembers. As institutional elements, however, organizations are means for and a reflection of the ways that the set of self-enforcing beliefs and behavior in various central transactions are altered. Organizations specify, store, and distribute rules; facilitate the internalization of norms; and link the central transaction to auxiliary ones. The games relevant to a particular central transaction and behavior are conditional on the transactions that were linked to it.

Recognizing that institutions provide the cognitive, coordinative, informational, and normative micro-foundations of behavior highlights the factors causing institutions to persist in marginally changing environments. The cognitive content of institutions implies that even if the situation changes, regularities of behavior will remain unchanged as long as those who recognize the change do not convey it to others through action. The coordinative content of institutionalized rules similarly implies that following them is the best predictor of others' behavior in marginally changing or similar situations. Norms render institutionalized behavior robust to environmental changes, while the scarcity of cognitive resources and attention transforms institutionalized behavior into habits.

Behavior generated by an institution will therefore prevail as long as the relevant parameters are within its *institutional support*, the range of parameters within which this behavior is self-enforcing and reproducing. Exogenous parametric change causing an institution to be outside this support will lead to its demise. *Endogenous institutional change* reflects institutions' influence on the ability and motivation to experiment, to create organizations, and to develop new knowledge. Endogenous changes also reflect the influence of institutions on various aspects of the situation beyond generating behavior in the central transactions they govern. Often this influence is on *quasi-parameters* – aspects of the situation that are endogenously changed by the institution and impact the parameter set in which the institution is self-enforcing. When the impact of an institution on quasi-parameters increases the range of parametric values in which the institution is self-enforcing, the institution is *reinforcing*. If an institution reinforces itself, more individuals in more circumstances adhere to the associated behavior. When an institution is *self-reinforcing* – self-enforcing and reinforcing – exogenous changes in the underlying situation that otherwise would have led an institutional change do not have this effect.

Yet an institution can also undermine itself, causing it to be self-enforcing in a smaller set of parameters. A self-enforcing institution can thereby cultivate the seeds of its own demise. When an institution undermines itself, exogenous changes in the underlying situation that otherwise would not have led to institutional change can have this effect. Furthermore, endogenous institutional change will occur when the self-undermining process reaches such a critical level that past patterns of behavior are no longer self-enforcing. Whether the mechanism that brings about institutional change is unintentional or intentional depends on the nature of the quasi-parameters that delimit self-reinforcement.

Societies face new situations when an institution that governed a transaction is no longer self-enforcing, when it is perceived to be losing its self-enforcing characteristics, or when technological, organizational, and other changes bring about new transactions. In such situations, new institutions do not reflect merely interest and environmental factors but also the impact of institutional elements inherited from the past. History, encapsulated in institutional elements, influences the process leading to new institutions and influences their details.

The influence of past institutional elements on institutional selection reflects that they, rather than technologically feasible alternatives, are part of the initial conditions in processes leading to new institutions.[2] There is

---

[2] Various implications of past institutions, such as the pattern of personal relationships, wealth distribution, military ability, or knowledge, are also part of these initial conditions.

a *fundamental asymmetry* between institutional elements inherited from the past and technologically feasible alternatives. Creating new shared cognition, providing coordination by alternate means, generating new commonly known beliefs, and establishing a new morality is a time-consuming, uncertain, and costly undertaking. More consequentially, past institutional elements constitute what people perceive to be and desire to hold as the true, the expected, and the appropriate. Seeking to create alternative systems of the correct, the normatively appropriate, and the expected are inherently contradictory. If people believe that something is true and normatively appropriate, they do not seek to alter it. The extent of this fundamental asymmetry – the *transaction costs* of creating new institutional elements – depends on the details of existing institutions.

In contrast, as the social-level manifestations of the cognitive, coordinative, normative, and informational foundations of behavior, institutional elements inherited from the past are properties of societies and their constituting members. They are part of what individuals bring with them and carry within them when facing new situations. In these situations, one's optimal action depends on the actions taken by others, implying that in new situations individuals will attempt to predict others' behavior. Past institutionalized beliefs – particularly cultural beliefs that emerge without centralized coordination – are a natural "focal point" in new situations. Formal and informal organizations, such as clans, religious groups, firms, or parliaments inherited from the past constitute actors in the processes leading to new institutions and resources that these new institutions will draw upon. Even institutional elements that were central to institutions that are no longer effective in influencing behavior can influence behavior in new situations. Past institutional elements constitute part of the historical – cultural, social, and organizational – heritage that influences selection among alternative institutions in new situations, integrates into them, and propagates as a result.

The impact of past institutional elements on new institutions expresses itself in the *environmental, coordination, and inclusion effects*. New institutions reflect the institutional environment within which they establish themselves, reflect coordination by past institutional elements, and include institutional elements inherited from the past. New institutions recombine existing institutional elements or reflect the refinement of existing institutions by marginally changing them. The sequentiality in institutional development implies that a society's institutions will *complement* one another, reflect common sources of coordination, and share institutional elements. A society's institutions will therefore be grouped in *institutional complexes* of such interrelated institutions, and this interrelatedness further influences institutional persistence and the direction of institutional change.

We do not have a single analytical framework to study endogenous institutions and their dynamic. But classical game theory enriched by insights developed elsewhere has proved useful. In a game-theoretic representation, the cognitive models regarding the structure of the situation, norms, and internalized beliefs are captured in the rules of the game, while behavior and behavioral beliefs are represented as strategies and the probability distributions over them. Game-theoretic analysis restricts the admissible set of institutional elements that can prevail as a system in equilibrium. It also reveals the institutional support of a particular behavior, namely, the parameter set in which the behavior is self-enforcing. We can also capture the fundamental asymmetry between institutional elements inherited from the past and technologically feasible alternatives by considering institutional heritage as part of the initial conditions in processes leading to new institutions. We study new institutions using *contextual refinement* in which game theory and history complement each other in restricting the set of admissible institutions.

The absence of a one-to-one mapping from the environment, interest, or function to institutions and the fact that some institutional elements are not observable challenges the use of traditional empirical methods in the social sciences. Econometric analysis, which relies on such deductive analysis to postulate causal relationships and on inductive study for classification, should therefore be conducted with care. A theoretically informed, case study approach based on interactive, context-specific analysis aimed at *identifying* institutions, is therefore particularly promising. Contextual knowledge of the situation and its history, together with deductive reasoning and inductive analysis, facilitates the interactive process of formulating and evaluating a conjecture regarding a relevant institution.

It is often useful to present and evaluate the conjecture with the assistance of a context-specific model, whose details are based on evidence that constrains the set of possible models and whose appropriateness should be evaluated. Such a model has to recognize that the game relevant to the interacting actors and their behavior in it is contingent on what transactions had been linked, how, and to what effect. Equilibrium analysis, comparative statics, counterfactual analysis, and other predictions are used to evaluate – modify, reject, or accept – the conjecture. The process continues to use interactively contextual knowledge, theory, and modeling to evaluate evidence and evidence to evaluate the conjecture until theoretical comprehension and empirical confirmation of a conjecture are reached.

Historical knowledge is particularly important in such empirical analysis. The historicity of institutions implies that we can further develop and evaluate a conjecture, avoid "just so" explanations, and sort among observationally equivalent conjectures by tracing an institution's origins. New institutions incorporate knowledge gained in the past and reflect the environmental, coordination, and inclusion effects. We can therefore further develop and evaluate conjectures about relevant institutions using context-specific refinement. We refine the set of admissible institutions by requiring that they be self-enforcing, but we also build on the knowledge from history to rule out those that are possible yet contextually irrelevant. History mitigates the failure of the game-theoretic refinement literature, while game theory delimits claims regarding the influence of history.

Emphasizing the context-specificity of institutions and their historical contingency does not imply aborting the social-scientific tradition of seeking generalizations. In fact, the accumulation of comparative and historical institutional analyses has the promise of fostering our understanding of which institutions matter and why, which are conducive to generating welfare-enhancing outcomes, and which are more likely to adapt efficiently to changing needs. The reasons for and processes through which societies and economies develop along particular institutional trajectories and to what effect will be better understood.

12.3 THE LATE MEDIEVAL COMMERCIAL EXPANSION AND THE RISE OF THE WEST: THE ORIGIN OF THE MODERN ECONOMY

Indeed, each analysis of a particular institution presented in this book yielded general insights regarding the institutional foundations of markets and polities and related factors, mechanisms, and processes. The discussion here, therefore, focuses on the broader conclusion these analyses provided regarding European institutional development.

First, these analyses highlighted that the institutional foundations of the late medieval commercial expansion did not depend on enforcement provided by a centralized state that dispensed impartial justice. The common assertion (e.g., by North 1990) that market expansion and economic development require an effective state is not confirmed by the experiences reported here. Private-order, self-enforcing institutions were the hallmark of the late medieval expansion. Yet, this private order was not, as advocates such as Friedrich A. von Hayek and Milton Friedman would have us believe, a result of "spontaneous order" among economic agents. Rather, it was a product of intentional and coordinated efforts by many individuals – who were often economic as well as political agents with coercive capabilities.

The second general conclusion is the particularities of the social structures central to these intentional and coordinated efforts. Historically, the social structures that substituted for an effective state had been kin-based, such as lineages or tribes. In late medieval Europe, however, at least in the towns, which were the center of economic and political change and the forerunner for future developments, this had not been the case. The dominant social structures were self-governed, interest-based, and intentionally established organizations (whose existence did not depend on the participation of a particular member) among individuals unrelated by blood. They were self-governed in the sense that their members participated in specifying the rules that regulated their activities. Participation rendered rules legitimate. In other words, economic and political *corporations* were central to the institutional underpinning of the late medieval European commercial expansion. Corporations and the subsidiary organizations they established, such as courts, were central to all the European institutions examined here, the merchant guild institution, the political institutions of Genoa and Venice, and the community responsibility system.

Corporations reflect the intentional and coordinated effort to create institutions as well as a means for doing so. They produced legitimate rules and altered self-enforcing beliefs in a central economic or political transaction by linking them to other economic and coercive – legal or otherwise – transactions. Incentives were often provided by both economic reputation and coercion. This was also the case in the many other medieval corporations not examined in this work, such as monastic orders, military orders of knighthood, associations for mutual insurance, and universities.

One could argue that concluding that the state was of limited importance and corporations were central to the institutional foundations of the late medieval commercial expansion is biased by the focus on long-distance, interstate commerce. But self-governed corporations were also central to the merchant guilds and the community responsibility system, which were private-order institutions within existing states. Indeed, during this period, corporations such as craft guilds, merchant guilds, and towns were also central to production, exchange, taxation and providing the state with other services, even within the large European states.

Indeed, even the European states of this period are best studied as institutions central to which are self-governed, non-kin-based corporations. Projecting the image of the later, more centralist and absolutist European state on the late medieval one is misguided.[3] The late medieval polities were, to a surprising degree, self-governed, political corporations; laws and rules were man-made; and citizens – albeit often not all of them – had a political voice and representation. Effective representation was backed by the economic importance and coercive power of the citizens who were often organized into corporations within the state. The general nature of these earlier European politics as self-governed, non-kin-based corporations is reflected in the rise of bodies for political representation throughout Europe, from England in the west to Hungary and Poland in the east, from Sicily and Spain in the south to Germany in the north. Even the Holy Roman Empire officially became a constitutional monarchy in 1356 (Ertman 1997; Spruyt 1994; Herb 2003; Greif 2004b).

The conjoined influence of several factors contributed to the rise of corporations. Centuries of invasions and internal defragmentation weakened the European states. The weakness of the state in the late medieval period provided an *opportunity* for economic agents to self-organize, but this does not *explain* the *particularities* of their responses. Why corporations? A kin-based organization of society or a theocracy were possible alternatives. Historically such societal organizations often emerged in the absence of an effective state. This was the case, for example, in the Islamic world during its first two hundred years when the weakness of the state, and other factors that will be discussed later, fostered tribal bonds. The particularities of the European response – the rise of interest-based, non-kin-based corporations – reflect various institutional elements inherited from the past.

The church had weakened kin-based social structures (such as clans and tribes) in Europe, as discussed in section 8.7 and contributed to cultural beliefs associated with individualism, as discussed in section 9.2. This hindered the establishment of institutions based on large-scale, kin-based social structures and collectivist cultural beliefs. The church itself, however, was not in a position to provide an effective alternative to the state in the late medieval period. Its administrative structure was

---

[3] S. R. Epstein (2000) has similarly argued that projecting the nineteenth-century European state on earlier periods is misleading.

weakened by the medieval warfare and upheavals and the later con-flicts with the Holy Roman Emperor and various kings. Furthermore, the church had legitimacy to set rules only in a limited number of situations, as discussed in section 5.4.

The result was not, as Hobbes would have us believe, a war of all against all. Rather, the weakness of large-scale, kin-based social structures and individualism enabled and motivated commoners to self-organize to gain from cooperation (although this cooperation was sometimes at the expense of others). This enabled them to gain economic and polit-ical power alongside feudal lords and kings. Political development was marked by a republican movement and the increasingly corporate nature of the polity (Greif 2004b). In doing so, the Europeans built on the beliefs and norms inherited from the Roman and Germanic legal traditions, which made explicit man-made (rather than divine) laws, self-governance, and formal decision-making processes a focal point (indeed, even Euro-pean canon law is man-made). They also built on the idea of corporations, which, after all, date back to the Roman time (e.g., Kuhn 1912).

The feudal view that political authority was contractual and nonter-ritorial also facilitated the creation of self-governed corporations with coercive power within the confines of existing political units. Even the establishment of the Hansa was not considered a revolt by the feudal lords in whose territory the Hanseatic cities were located.

The cultural beliefs and norms associated with individualism, corpo-ratism, and the implied legitimacy of man-made law in which those who are governed by them have an influential voice became central to European societal organization. Individualism and corporatism were the hallmark of institutions that supported the late medieval commercial expansion and political changes.

Rubeus de Campo, mentioned in Chapter 1, lived in a period of remark-able economic growth due to this particular organization of society. For a long period of time, this organization of society supported impersonal markets and effective polities, thereby fostering economic prosperity. The efficiency implications of particular insitutions, however, depended on their details and the broader context. The associated institutions were effective when those with coercive power cared about their economic reputations and were constrained from abusing their power by others with economic and coercive powers. They were socially beneficial when there was an intra-corporation uniformity of economic interests, and the distribution of intra-corporation resources was such that coercion could have been used only to discipline members whose actions undermined cooperation and economic gains. Finally, they were efficient when inter-corporation interactions were confined to economic, rather than military, competition and when economic resources could not be used to forestall competition.

When these conditions did not hold, the associated institutions were not socially beneficial. The failure to create an effective, socially beneficial monopoly over coercive power in Genoa, for example, cost the Genoese dearly. When the German Hansa's economic and military might sufficiently increased, it was used to restrict competition. The comparison between England and Italy illustrates another general force at work. In England, the monarchy was sufficiently effective to imply that inter-corporate competition among guilds and communes, for example, could not be conducted using coercion; inter-corporation economic competition was induced. At the same time, the English king had limited administrative and coercive powers relative to those of chartered towns, for example. Property rights were relatively secure. This was not the case in Italy. Once rents from overseas expansion declined, in the absence of centralized authority inter- and intra-communal conflicts over it ensued. (See Greif 2004b for further details, references, and discussion of other cases.)

More generally, although efficiency enhancing and self-enforcing, late medieval institutions were inherently self-undermining. Reputation was central to their operation, but the effectiveness of reputation mechanisms depended on rents (surpluses above and beyond those possible under perfect competition). The progression of the commercial expansion that the late medieval institutions enabled eventually eroded the rents that rendered the institutional foundations of these markets self-enforcing. Similarly, time, commercialization, and specialization eroded the homogeneity of interests within merchant communities and altered the distribution of coercive and economic resources. The economic process as a whole was self-undermining.

This institutional decline probably contributed a great deal to the fourteenth-century crisis that expressed itself in widespread economic, social, demographic, and political upheavals.[4] Europe had to create new institutions to regulate its commerce, production, and polity. It was a lengthy process, in which many of the organizations established during the late medieval period (the Hanseatic League, various merchant and

---

[4] As Hatcher and Bailey (2001) note in their beautiful survey, theories of this decline – such as neo-Malthusian and Marxist theories – fail to account for it adequately.

craft guilds) were used to restrict competition, innovation, and expansion in order to maintain rents and increase profits. The decline provided an opportunity for the territorial state to use these organizations and establish new institutions to serve its interests.

Some of the state-centered institutions were efficiency enhancing, as the state was arguably in a better position to provide protection (North and Thomas 1973) and coordinate economic activities on a larger scale than it had been (S. R. Epstein 2000). However, the state and its institutions also imposed large inefficiencies, including destructive interstate warfare (Hoffman 1991), mercantilism and rent seeking (Ekelund and Tollison 1981; Root 1994), and absolutism and institutional rigidity (Rosenthal 1992). In any case, on the eve of their second growth phase during the modern period, European institutions seem to have been very distinct from those of the late medieval period.

There is nevertheless a striking commonality between the economic and political institutions that were central to Europe's late medieval commercial expansion and those that currently prevail in its modern economy. In both periods, the cultural beliefs and norms associated with individualism and corporatism have prevailed. The basic social unit is the individual or nuclear family, rather than larger, kin-based social structures, such as clans or tribes. The predominate social structure is the economic and political self-governing corporation with legitimate institutionalized processes for setting rules, laws, in which those who are governed by them have an influential voice.[5] These institutional elements were and are central to the European institutions enabling impersonal exchange and motivating the state to serve its citizens.[6]

---

[5] Corporations in the modern West are everywhere. In the economic sphere the most notable ones are the business corporations, but there are others, such as business associations and not-for-profit organizations. Similar to the new polities of the late medieval period, the state in the modern West is a self-governed, political corporation. The organizational foundations of the polity are such that – unlike in an absolute monarchy, a dictatorship, a fascist regime, or a theocracy – it does not have an independent objective function. Like various medieval corporations, the modern state also provides individuals with social safety nets beyond those provided by the family and private and religious charities.

[6] Interestingly, the institutions of both periods also reflect secularism, although the moral authority of the church influenced social development as discussed in previous chapters. Commerce-related evidence reveals a shift toward religiosity following the crisis of the fourteenth century. This shift is reflected, for example, in the names ships were given following the Black Death (e.g., from such names as the Lion or Glory to such names as Santa Maria or Faith) (Kedar 1976). Platteau (1994) and Lal (1998) argued that the church was important in setting basic moral standards.

In particular, individualism and corporations with statelike authority among non-kin were central to the late medieval institutions that supported increasingly complex and impersonal exchange. Individualism and economic corporations, albeit without coercive power, have remained central to European economic institutions to the present. Similarly, bodies for political representation, the legitimacy of rule setting by corporations, and the concept of a state as a corporation were central to the institutional foundations of the state in the late medieval period. This is also the case in the modern European state.

Is the similarity between the late medieval and modern European societal organizations a coincidence? Do modern institutions reflect the influence of the institutional elements inherited from the late medieval period, which, in turn, incorporated deeper cultural and social features? Were the late medieval institutions instrumental in reproducing these features through the institutional elements, knowledge, and history they implied? Was the late medieval period thus crucial to the subsequent institutional development of Europe? If the answer to these questions is yes, the age of absolutism and mercantilism may have been an exception rather than the rule in the path of European institutional development during the last millennium.

No one has evaluated whether this was the case or traced exactly how earlier institutional heritage influenced later outcomes. But there is much to suggest that the late medieval institutional development had direct impact on later institutions. The modern business corporation grew out of the traditional legal form of the corporation, as developed for medieval guilds, municipalities, monasteries, and universities. The operation of the late medieval corporations led to the development of particular knowledge, laws, and other institutional elements that manifested in current practices such as trading in shares, limited liability, auditing, apprenticeships, and double-entry bookkeeping. European commercial law, insurance markets, patent systems, public debt, business associations, and central banks were developed in the context of medieval institutions.

In the political sphere, the medieval rise of the corporative form of societal organization contributed to the development that led to the modern European states. Corporations contributed to diminishing the challenge that large-scale, kin-based social structures present to the state and to development central to the institutional foundations of the modern, effective European state, which is, after all, a corporation. Among these are the concept of corporations as legal personalities, the separation between personal and corporate property, the belief that corporations are to serve the interests of their members, and processes of collective decision making. (These features are also central to modern economic corporations.) More generally corporations fostered both norms and beliefs in the appropriateness and possibility of self-governance, decision making through majority vote, and man-made law (e.g., Berman 1983 and Korotayev 2003).

Furthermore, states in Europe were established during the premodern period through a process of bottom-up, organic formation. In building their states, rulers had to rely on the corporate bodies they inherited from the past, the local governance they enabled, and the resources they could provide. These corporations therefore had the ability to constrain the state from abusing its power and directing its policies. This institutional heritage thereby contributed to the rise of an effective state (Ertman 1997; Tilly 1990; Greif 2004b). More generally, the manifestations of the late medieval republican movement – its underpinning norms, beliefs, and organizations – have survived to modern times. The Hanseatic League, the Republic of Venice, and the Swiss Confederation lasted until the eve of the modern period. The causal relationships between the institutional foundation of the medieval and modern European states are well reflected in the many cases (notably the Dutch Republic, England, and France) in which medieval representative organizations and the associated shared beliefs and norms provided the institutional elements central to the later transition to more-democratic, growth-oriented states.

The rise of the Dutch Republic and the political supremacy of England's Parliament during and after the seventeenth century rest on their late medieval organizational and institutional foundations. The composition, form, and powers of the English Model Parliament, summoned in 1295, provided the springboard and mold for the modern one; the French Estates-General, which played a central role in the French Revolution, was established in 1302. Constitutional monarchy – which encompasses the idea that a ruler is subject to the law and members of the state pledge their loyalty to abstract principles rather than the person who led them – prevailed in the late medieval period, in which the modern theory of voting also originated. Legitimacy in the late medieval period and in the modern European state resides in the hands of surprisingly similar bodies, and institutional complexes in the two periods bear striking likeness.

The sources of modern European economic growth differ from those of its medieval predecessor. Medieval economic expansion relied on Smithian growth, which takes advantage of specialization and trade. Growth in the modern era relies on science and technology to alter production functions and transform useless resources into endowments. Changes in cultural beliefs about the nature, role, and possibilities of useful knowledge – science and technology – in the hundred years before 1750 directly contributed to this transition (Mokyr 2002). Interestingly, however, individualistic pursuit and self-governed, non-kin-based corporations (similar to the medieval universities, such as the Lunar and the Royal Societies) were central to propagating these beliefs, mobilizing the resources to act on them, and rendering them effective in influencing outcomes. The objectives of these corporations were different from most of their medieval predecessors, but the institutional means were surprisingly similar.

Whether the similarities between European institutions in the late medieval and modern periods reflect a historical process or a common condition has yet to be evaluated. Be the result of this evaluation as it may, Europe seems to have been evolving along a *particular* institutional trajectory since at least that time.[7] Indeed, the limited comparative analysis between the European and the Muslim worlds conducted here suggests that Europe has been evolving along a *distinct* institutional trajectory; institutional distinctions between the two prevailed from at least the late medieval period.

The collectivism of the Maghribis reflects a broader cultural trait in Muslim society, in which large kin-based social units, such as clans, lineages, and tribes also have remained central until today and segregation along religious and ethnic lines is still common. Corporations did not emerge endogenously, nor were they recognized as legal entities. Europe has always had its share of institutions based on networks, communities, and kin, but corporations increase the range of possible institutions.

Similarly, the relationship between the Maghribi traders and the state is representative. Laws and regulations of commercial activities were specified either by the religious authorities or by a state or both. Merchants in the Muslim world could not amend the law in a manner that combined private- and public-order institutions in the same way that European merchants could, nor could they use the resources of the state to

---

[7] If the conjecture regarding the importance of individualism and collectivism is substantiated, it would provide an important complement to Weber's (1958 [1904–5]) thesis regarding the importance of the Protestant ethic in Europe's economic growth. It would indicate the rationale for the particular organizational and institutional developments of Europe that differentiated it from other regions of the world before the rise of Protestantism. At the same time, it would account for why, despite Weber's assertion about the uniqueness of the Protestant ethic, non-Protestant economies developed as well, albeit within a distinct organizational and institutional framework.

formulate policies to advance their economic interests. Cities were not self-governed, and merchants had no political representation or voice. "True urban autonomies would have been unthinkable in [the Muslim] world" during the medieval period (Cahen 1990, p. 520), and, more broadly, there was no interest-based organization of society along corporate lines (Crone 2004, pp. 335–6). Indeed, "the authority of the universal Shari'a was likely to invalidate any local corporate convention" (M. Hodgson 1974, 2: 122; and see also Kuran 2005). Furthermore, "there was very little contact between the world of the [Muslim or other] traders and that of the government" (Goitein 1973, p. 10).

Similar institutional complexes prevailed in the Muslim Mediterranean world in later centuries. Processes of rule making were not participatory, formal rules governing economic life were not in the hands of the economic agents, and the ability to incorporate was very limited. Surveying the extensive literature regarding the Ottoman Empire, Pamuk (2000) noted that "the influence of various social groups, not only of landowners but also of merchants and moneylenders, over the policies of the central government remained limited" (p. 10). Policies were shaped to a large degree by the priorities and interests of a central bureaucracy and the structure of the private economic sector was not dictated by its needs but by those of the state. Social segregation along innate, religious, ethnic, and other lines prevailed in Muslim cities at least until the early modern period.[8]

Do these differences in institutional complexes help explain different trajectories of economic prosperity and growth in these two great civilizations? This question is not easy to answer, as different institutions can fulfill the same function with equal efficiency. Furthermore, an institution often has a multidimensional influence on efficiency and welfare, making interinstitutional comparison difficult. Finally, we have no good measure for comparing an institution that is less efficient in the short run but more efficiently adaptive in the long run. Hence the extent to which the late medieval European institutions were more or less efficient than alternative ones at the time and the value of their contributions to distinctions in subsequent institutional development and outcomes remains to be examined.

---

[8] On segregation, see Chapters 8 and 9, Lapidus (1984), and Hodgson (1974, pp. 105ff.). On institutions more generally, see Kuran (2004); Cahen (1990); B. Lewis (1991); and Lapidus (1984, 1989). Çizakça (1996), however, emphasizes the similarity in business partnerships in the European and the Muslim worlds.

There are, however, at least four theoretical reasons why intentionally created institutions based on individualism, corporatism, and self-governance are particularly conducive to efficiency, including adaptive efficiency. To the extent that the division of labor is a necessary condition for long-run sustained economic growth, formal enforcement institutions that support anonymous exchange facilitate economic development. Individualism fosters the development of such institutions, thereby enabling society to capture these efficiency gains. Similarly, economic prosperity requires institutions that lead to socially beneficial policies and the specification, protection, and adjustments of property rights. Individualism, corporatism, and self-governance on the level of the polity foster the development of such institutions, thereby enabling society to capture gains from cooperation. Third, an individualist society entails less social pressure to conform to social norms of behavior while the corporations are better able to mobilize resources and diversify risk than the individual or the family. Together, therefore, risk taking, initiative and organizational and technological innovations are encouraged.[9]

Finally, intentional institutions centered around corporations foster beneficial institutional dynamics. No one institution is most efficient under all circumstances, implying that even those that were relatively efficient will gradually cease being so. Intentional institutional creation increases awareness of the operation of these institutions and the need for change. The flexibility of corporate structure, self-governance, man-made laws, and institutionalized processes of rule making with input from those governed by these rules provide the means for beneficial change.

The European institutions and institutional dynamics that emerged as early as the late medieval period may have been more efficient than other societal organizations. To the extent that the particularities of the European institutions were instrumental in shaping economic, political, and social outcomes and reflect a historical process, late medieval society may have cultivated the seeds of the Rise of the West.[10]

---

[9] This flexibility may have been crucial for the new ideas and beliefs that emerged during the Enlightenment, leading to the technological and scientific breakthroughs that made modern growth possible (Mokyr 2002).

[10] Hamilton (1991, pp. 1–2) is among the many scholars who have noted the institutional distinctions between Europe and China consistent with the preceding argument. "In the West, commercial organizations in the private sphere rested upon legal institutions and upon individualism, neither of which had central importance in China," he writes. "Kinship and collegiality in China play roles analogous to those played by law and individuality in the West, but with very different developmental trajectories and outcomes."

While an evaluation of this assertion has yet to be conducted, it is interesting to note that within Europe, the areas that experienced medieval institutional development were also early to embark on modern economic growth. The late medieval institutional revolution did not transpire in much of Eastern Europe, southern Italy, the Balkans, or various parts of Spain, the very areas that were late to industrialize. In contrast, the areas that became the Dutch Republic, Germany, and England led Europe in commercialization, industrialization, and the move toward centralized but limited government. As the experiences of France and northern Italy remind us, however, these outcomes were not historically determined. In France absolutism triumphed for a long period; Italy was devastated by civil wars and by conflicts with external foes.[11] Unlike areas that did not experience the late medieval institutional revolution, however, both northern Italy and France found it relatively easy later to adopt institutions that were conducive to modern growth.[12]

Whether the institutional roots of the Rise of the West go back to the late medieval period remains an open issue. So, too, does the issue of whether these institutions were more efficient than those of other societies. Yet claims that the Rise of the West is due to either predetermined factors (such as endowment) or later events (such as colonialism or the Industrial Revolution) face the challenge of demonstrating that the implications of these exogenous factors and these particular events were not reflections of the institutional particularities of Europe at the time.

More generally, the historical analysis offered here lends support to the claim that institutions are the engine of history. Institutions shape a society's historical development. They influence behavior and outcomes at a given moment in time, affect the timing and nature of their change, and shape the details of new institutions. Institutions impose constraints, provide opportunities for intentional institutional change, and unleash processes of unintentional institutional changes. The fundamental asymmetry between institutional elements inherited from the past and technologically feasible alternatives, in turn, implies that institutional elements inherited from the past influence the direction of the subsequent institutional change and the implied historical developments.

---

[11] England and the Dutch Republic may have been particularly fortunate in having institutions that restricted their corporations to competing only economically and not militarily, while the central authorities had limited ability to create institutions to extract rent for their own objectives (see Greif 2004b).

[12] Mokyr (2002) traces the origin of the institutions linking science and technology in the modern period to these areas.

This conclusion – that institutions are the engine of history – goes beyond the common, more limited assertion that institutions influence economic, political, and social outcomes. Reaching this conclusion required extending institutional analysis beyond the study of rules to the study of institutions as self-enforcing systems of rules, norms, beliefs, and organizations.

12.4 THE CHALLENGE AHEAD: CONSTRUCTING WELL-FUNCTIONING MARKETS AND POLITIES

Understanding the late medieval commercial expansion – where, when, why, and among whom trade expanded – requires considering the micro-level institutions that enabled, guided, and motivated behavior in particular economic and political transactions. When successful, these institutions increased gains and reduced the costs of respecting property rights, mobilizing resources for commercially beneficial policies, employing the polity and its organizations to foster welfare, and adhering to contractual obligations in personal and impersonal exchange.

Whether enabling, motivating, and guiding economic exchange, political behavior, or coercive actions – legal or not – and whether welfare-enhancing or not, these institutions were based on the same principle. Intertransactional linkages created reward (economic, political, social, or normative) for a particular behavior and a penalty for failing to comply. The details of these intertransactional linkages, the related institutions, and hence the resulting extent of the markets and the effectiveness of polities reflected economic and political interests, as well as the social and cultural factors that provided initial institutional elements. These factors provided networks for information transmission, formal and informal organizations with various capacities and interests, and systems of norms and beliefs regarding expected behavior. When the resulting institutions were self-enforcing and reinforcing, they incorporated and perpetuated these social and cultural features.

The effectiveness of the resulting institutions depended on the broader context and institutional details. In Europe this effectiveness was enhanced by external military threats and economic competition among states and corporations on the one hand and institutions that created a relative internal uniformity of interests within corporations on the other hand. This effectiveness was further enhanced by the ability of the economic agents to link economic and coercive – legal or not – transactions.

Economic reputations complemented by the ability to inflict coercive punishments fostered institutional effect-iveness.

Coercive power was rendered economically productive, however, when and where the context and institutional details prevented those who controlled coercion from using it for their personal advantage. The weakness of the centralized state in Europe and of the large kin-based social units, and the wide distribution of military ability among the economic agents, contributed to this situation. The process of institutional and state development was done from below. Political actors and judges had limited ability to structure the market and the polity for their exclusive benefit. To enrich themselves, they had to contribute to welfare more generally.[13] When an institution motivated those courts, communes, clans, and individuals with coercive power to use it in a manner that was economically productive, markets expanded and welfare-enhancing policies were pursued.

The process of institutional development in Europe has been conducted in a context and through a process that was distinct from what has been experienced in most less-developed countries since World War II and at the end of colonialism. In modern developing countries, kin-based social structures predominated and the process of development has been conducted with the intention of first building an effective centralized state. This attempt was taken in the context of a world order, in which external threats were relatively muted, and a global economy, in which those who controlled the state could raise capital in the international capital markets and sell domestic minerals and other local products without relying on domestic economic agents.

When the state construction effort was successful, politicians, unconstrained by domestic economic agents or external threat and competition, used their power to construct institutions and pursue policies to serve their private – economic and political – gains (Easterly 2001). When the effort failed, politicians were either unable to pursue or found it personally unrewarding to pursue welfare-enhancing policies or establish welfare-enhancing institutions.

More recent attempts have concentrated on development that circumvented the state and provided resources directly to the poor and to local communities. Often, however, resources provided by external,

---

[13] In particular, they catered for the welfare of those with coercive and economic power to the exclusion of others.

international agencies ended up serving the interests of community leaders who had access to them rather than contributing to social welfare more generally (Platteau and Gaspart 2003). State-centered and community-centered development faced the same challenges of providing governments, politicians, agents of the state, and representatives of communities with appropriate incentives. In the absence of institutions motivating them to take welfare-enhancing actions and pursue policies aimed at facilitating welfare-enhancing institutional change, development has been lagging.

Such institutions are seemingly not necessary for promoting welfare, however. A period of economic growth, in fact, can be initiated without institutional reform – by little more than "an attitudinal change on the part of the top political leadership towards a more market-oriented, private-sector-friendly policy framework" (Rodrik 2003, p. 15) – but without an institutional reform growth runs out of steam quickly. Reforming institutions, however, is difficult. Attempts to reform them by imposing the West's "best practices," its rules and regulations, have accomplished less than was hoped for.

From the perspective developed here, this result is not surprising. European growth was neither state-centered nor based on communities embodied within effective states that benefited from international aid. Furthermore, institutions are not rules. They are self-enforcing systems of rules, beliefs, norms, and organizations. Institutional development is a sequential process in which some institutions are prerequisites for others, an institution's implications depend on various conditions, and distinct institutions can achieve the same outcome. Successful reform requires much more than a change of rules; it requires creating new systems of interrelated institutional elements that motivate, enable, and guide individuals to take particular actions. Reform must first empirically identify, rather than assume, the transactions that are important for improving welfare, as they depend on local conditions and institutions. We need to discover empirically, rather than assert deductively, whether, for example, the abuse of property rights by the police, the army, rebels, or the government is the source of property rights insecurity. Only then can we consider what institutional reform would be beneficial and feasible.

Such considerations entail recognizing that institutions are not rules, that institutional development is a sequential process in which past institutional elements matter, that an institution's implications depend on various conditions, and that different institutions are better in different circumstances. Successful reform requires much more than changing rules; it requires creating new systems of interrelated institutional elements that motivate, enable, and guide individuals to take particular actions.

In pursuing institutional reforms by altering self-enforcing institutions, developmental assistance will have to shift its focus. Rather than focusing only on helping countries specify rules, it will have to seek to change organizations, beliefs, and intertransactional linkages. The challenge is to create new self-enforcing institutions so that when aid ceases, the institutions will persist. At the same time, these institutions have to be amenable to endogenous change when they are no longer beneficial.

Institutional reform involves replacing one set of self-enforcing institutions with another. Not only do new institutions have to be created but existing ones have to be changed, because institutional reform does not begin with a *tabula rasa*. What we consider a state of anarchy, for example, is not devoid of institutions. Those involved share beliefs regarding expected behavior and related outcomes, hold particular norms, and often are organized into well-defined social structures. Initial conditions in processes of institutional change include existing self-enforcing institutions and their undesired outcomes.[14] Economies in need of institutional reform are not without institutions. Unless we understand the institutions that are generating outcomes, our ability to develop appropriate reform strategies will be limited. A prerequisite to successful institutional reform is understanding existing institutions, the complexes of which they are part, the forces that render them self-enforcing, and the transactions costs of institutional change they imply. The reform strategy itself has to learn from, work with, build on, and potentially undermine existing institutions while recognizing that institutional development is a historical process that may well be time-consuming.

When pursuing reforms, however, we have to recall that the very same cognitive, coordinative, normative, and informational factors that make institutions important determinants of behavior forestall devising institutional reforms. Given a particular context, it is difficult to know what institutions are beneficial or what the long-term implications are of introducing new institutional elements. Furthermore, we know little about how to devise institutions that are conducive to beneficial dynamic adaptability. An institution that represents a better fit with existing ones may be

---

[14] The ability of those with political power to block institutional reforms is well recognized, but little attention has been given to the impact of beliefs, norms, formal and informal organizations inherited from the past, or the implications of past institution on interests.

easier to implement, but it may reinforce other institutions that are better undermined.

Conducting context-specific institutional analysis; building on existing institutional elements; learning, experimenting, and measuring the impact of various changes are indispensable. The promise of an institutional reform strategy based on a context-specific analysis is suggested by the findings of Berkowitz, Pistor, and Richard (2003), who found that countries that developed their formal legal order internally and adapted imported codes to local conditions ended up with much better legal institutions than those that adopted codes verbatim from the West.

The historical analyses in this book lend support to the claim that the institutional forms best fitted to achieving a particular outcome depend on the particularities of the situation and can differ from those currently prevailing in the West. In fact, current Western institutions are themselves different from those that prevailed there in the past (although as stressed already, they share much in common). The late medieval commercial expansion, the longest period of economic expansion Europe ever experienced, rested on a set of institutions that were distinct in form – although they shared much in essence – from those that support modern growth in Europe. There was no democracy, no constitutional or balance-of-power restrictions on rulers, no effective territorial states, no universal protection of property rights, no independent judiciary.

Late medieval institutions, in Europe and elsewhere, may well have been better suited for their tasks than their modern counterparts, given the broader context and institutional heritage. The Maghribi traders' coalition was a beneficial institution given the state's inability to enforce contracts abroad. The merchant guilds secured property rights from the grabbing hand of the state by taking advantage of Europe's political fragmentation and communal organization. In Genoa the existing social structures and the associated beliefs and norms implied that the *podesteria* was better able to promote order and prosperity than the elected consuls, a seemingly more democratic system. Establishing an independent, territorial judiciary was well beyond the organizational and financial capacity of the late medieval state. The community responsibility system nevertheless provided impartial justice because of – not despite – its reliance on partial judges and localized law.

The challenge of fostering welfare through institutional reform is to build on institutional elements inherited from the past and the existing institutional environment to foster welfare in the short run while creating institutions conducive to beneficial endogenous change. Whatever form such institutions take, if they are to enhance material welfare, they must fulfill the same functions that the European institutions fulfilled in the late medieval period. They must render coercive power economically productive in securing property rights and provide contract enforcement while allowing for economic reputation to contribute to such security and enforcement. They must encourage beneficial economic behavior, such as saving, investment, and innovations, and discourage rent-seeking behavior. They must reinforce socially beneficial institutions while allowing other institutions to undermine themselves. And they must reduce the transaction costs of institutional change in a manner that enables institutional development that takes advantage of past institutional elements without being captive of them.

* * * *

Multiple institutions can prevail in a given environment; institutional dynamics is a nondeterministic historical process. The theory that this book advances therefore constitutes a conceptual, analytical, and empirical framework for fostering understanding and the positive analysis of institutions.

Because institutional development is not deterministic, there is no unique history of institutions; there are many institutional histories. Learning about and from these histories will improve our understanding of distinct developmental trajectories and increase our appreciation of the many forms they can take, the forces that shape them, and the ways in which they can be harnessed.

A

A Primer in Game Theory

This presentation of the main ideas and concepts of game theory required to understand the discussion in this book is intended for readers without previous exposure to game theory.[1]

A game-theoretic analysis starts by specifying the rules of the game. These rules identify the decision makers (the players), their possible actions, the information available to them, the probability distributions over chance events, and each decision maker's preference over outcomes – specifically, the set of all possible combinations of actions by the players. A game is represented, or defined, by the triplet of the players' set, the action set (which specifies each player's actions), and the payoff set (which specifies each player's payoffs as a function of the actions taken by the players). The rules of the game are assumed to be common knowledge.[2] The situations considered are strategic in the sense that each player's optimal strategy depends on the actions of other players. (Nonstrategic situations constitute a special case.)

---

[1] For a relatively nontechnical introduction to game theory, see Dixit and Nalebuff (1991); Gibbons (1992, 1998); and Watson (2001). For a more technical analysis, see Fudenberg and Tirole (1991) and Gintis (2000). See Aumann and Hart (1994, 2002) for an extensive review of the application of game theory to economics and political science; Milgrom and Roberts (1995) on organizational theory; Hart and Holmstrom (1987) and Hart (1995) on contract theory; and Weingast (1996), Sened (1997), and Bates et al. (1998) on political science.

[2] S is common knowledge if all players know S, all players know that all players know S, and so on ad infinitum (D. Lewis 1969). In games of complete information, the rules of the game are common knowledge. In games of incomplete information, the probability distribution of the aspect of the game that is not common knowledge is common knowledge. The strategy set in a game in the set of all possible plans of actions by all the players when each conditions his action on the information available to him.

Appendix A

The objective of game-theoretic analysis is to predict behavior in strategic situations – to predict an action combination (an action to each player) for any given rules of the game. The difficulty of finding such solutions stems from the fact that because the action optimal for each player depends on others' actions, no player can choose his optimal action independently of what other players do. For player A to choose behavior, he has to know what B will do, but for B to choose behavior, he has to know what A will do. The classical game-theoretic concepts of Nash equilibrium and its refinements, such as subgame perfect equilibrium, mitigate this infinite loop problem and eliminate some action combinations as implausible in a given game.

The basic idea of the Nash restriction is not to consider the dynamic problem of choosing behavior but to consider behavior that constitutes a solution to the problem of choosing behavior. Nash equilibria restrict admissible solutions (action combinations) to those that are self-enforcing: if each individual expects others to follow the behavior expected of them, he finds it optimal to follow the behavior expected of him.

To keep the discussion simple, I concentrate, without loss of generality, on two-player games, although the analysis applies to games with more players as well. Sections A.1 and A.2 examine static games in which the players move simultaneously and dynamic games in which the players move sequentially, respectively. Section A.3 then discusses repeated game theory, which examines situations in which a particular stage game, either static or dynamic, is repeated over time. Knowledge of games with incomplete information, in which players have different information regarding aspects of the structure of the game, is not essential for reading the book. Short discussions of such games are provided in Chapter 3 and Appendix C, section C.1. Chapter 5 discusses learning game theory, while Appendix C, section C.2.7, discusses imperfect monitoring.

A.1 SELF-ENFORCING BEHAVIOR IN STATIC GAMES: THE NASH EQUILIBRIUM

Consider first static (or simultaneous-move) games – games in which all players take actions simultaneously. Assume that all players have the same information about the situation. The structure of such games is as follows: Player 1 chooses an action a_1 from the set of feasible actions A_1. Simultaneously, player 2 chooses an action a_2 from the set of feasible actions A_2. After the players choose their actions, they receive the following payoffs: $u_1(a_1, a_2)$ to player 1 and $u_2(a_1, a_2)$ to player 2.

		Player 2's actions	
		C	D
Player 1's actions	C	1, 1	−15, 5
	D	5, −15	−8, −8

Figure A.1. The Prisoners' Dilemma Game

The prisoners' dilemma game is perhaps the best-known and most-explored static game. It is so well known because it illustrates that in strategic situations, rationality alone is insufficient to reach a Pareto-optimal outcome. Unlike in market situations, in strategic situations one's desire to improve his lot does not necessarily maximize social welfare. In the prisoners' dilemma game, each player can either cooperate with the other or defect. If both cooperate, each player's payoff will be higher than if they both defect. But if one cooperates and the other defects, the defector benefits, receiving a higher payoff than if both cooperate. Meanwhile, the cooperator receives a lower payoff than he would have had he also defected.

Figure A.1 presents a particular prisoners' dilemma game. The players' actions are denoted by C (cooperate) and D (defect). Each cell corresponds to an action combination, or a pair of actions. The payoffs associated with each action combination are represented by two numbers, the payoff to player 1 and the payoff to player 2.

In this game, the best each player can do is defect. Player 1 cannot expect player 2 to play C, because no matter what player 1 does, player 2 is better off playing D. If player 1 plays C, then player 2 gains 1 playing C but 5 playing D. If player 1 plays D, then player 2 gains −15 from playing C and only −8 from playing D. The same holds for player 1, who is always better off playing D. In the language of game theory, defecting is each player's dominant strategy: it is the best that he can do, independent of what the other player does. Hence the action combination (D, D) will be followed if the game captures all aspects of the situation.

In the particular case of the prisoners' dilemma, one's expectations about the behavior of the other player do not matter when choosing an action. Playing D is the best one can do regardless of the other's choice of action. But in strategic situations in general, a player's optimal choice of action depends on the other player's choice of action.

		Player 2's actions	
		Left	Right
Player 1's	Left	2, 2	0, 0
actions	Right	0, 0	2, 2

Figure A.2. The Driving Game

Consider, for example, the driving game presented in Figure A.2. This game represents a situation in which two drivers are heading toward each other. Both players can choose to drive on the left or the right side of the road. If they both choose the same side, a collision is avoided and each receives a payoff of 2. If they choose opposite sides, either (right, left) or (left, right), they collide, and each receives a payoff of 0.

In this game the situation is strategic: the best action for one player depends on the action of the other. If player 1 is expected to choose left, for example, player 2's optimal response is to play left, thereby earning 2 instead of 0 from playing right. But if player 1 is expected to play right, player 2 is better off playing right as well. Player 2's optimal choice depends on player 1's actual choice. To choose an action, player 2 has to know the action of player 1. But the same holds for player 1. As each player's choice of action depends on that of that of the other, neither can choose an action.

This interrelatedness of decisions implies that we cannot find out what the players will do by examining the behavior of each of them separately, as we did in the prisoners' dilemma game. The ingenuity of the Nash equilibrium concept is that instead of attempting to find out what the players will do by examining the players' decision processes, we find possible outcomes by considering what outcomes if expected will be followed.

Suppose that it is common knowledge that both players hold the same expectations about how the game will be played. What expectation about behavior can they hold? They can expect only that self-enforcing behavior will be followed. Behavior is self-enforcing if, when players expect it to be followed, it is indeed followed because each player finds it optimal to do so expecting the others to follow it. An action combination (often referred to also as a strategy combination) satisfying this condition is called a Nash equilibrium. A Nash equilibrium fulfills a mutual best-response condition:

		Player 2's actions	
		Head	Tail
Player 1's	Head	−1, 1	1, −1
actions	Tail	1, −1	−1, 1

Figure A.3. The Matching Pennies Game

each player's best response to his correct beliefs regarding the others' behavior is to follow the behavior expected of him.[3]

To illustrate that not all behavior satisfies this condition, consider behavior that, if expected, will not be followed. In the driving game, this case occurs with respect to the action combination (right, left). This combination would not be followed if each player expected the other to follow it. If player 2 expects player 1 to play right, her best response is to play right, receiving 2 instead of 0. Hence player 1 cannot hold the belief that player 2 will play left in this case. We can continue to consider whether various action combinations are self-enforcing in this manner. This analysis yields that the driving game has two Nash equilibria, (left, left) and (right, right).[4] If, for example, (left, left) is expected, both players will find it optimal to drive on the left because, expecting the other to do so, it is each driver's best response. Indeed, each of these Nash equilibria prevails in different countries. This analysis also illustrates that a game can have multiple Nash equilibria.

Some games do not have an action combination that satisfies the Nash condition. Consider the matching pennies game in Figure A.3. Each of the two players simultaneously chooses either head or tail. If their choices do not match, player 2 loses receiving −1 while player 1 receives 1. If they do match, player 1 loses receiving −1 while player 2 receives 1. In this game, there is no Nash equilibrium, as defined previously. This lack of an equilibrium reflects that this game captures a situation in which each

---

[3] In static games an action combination (a_1^*, a_2^*) is a Nash equilibrium if a_1^* is a best response for player 1 to a_2^* and a_2^* is a best response to a_1^*. That is, a_1^* must satisfy $u_1(a_1^*, a_2^*) \geq u_1(a_1, a_2^*)$ for every a_1 in A_1, and $u_2(a_1^*, a_2^*) \geq u_2(a_1^*, a_2)$ for every a_2 in A_2.

[4] There is also a third, mixed-strategy Nash equilibrium, in which each player chooses which side to drive on with probability 0.5. See the discussion of this notion later in this appendix.

player tries to outguess the action of the other. If player 1 expects player 2 to play heads, his best response is to play tails. Yet, if player 2 expects player 1 to play tails, his best response is to play tails. If 1 expects 2 to play tails, his best response is to play heads. If 2 expects 1 to play heads, his best response is to play heads as well, and the cycle begins again.

It is reasonable, in such situations, that peoples' expectations about behavior will be probabilistic in nature. People will expect others to play heads some of the time and tails some of the time. Game theory defines Nash equilibrium in such cases as well. This is done by referring to the actions in a player's action set (A_i) as pure strategies and defining a mixed strategy as a probability distribution over the player's pure strategies. We can then solve for the so-called mixed-strategy Nash equilibrium.[5] In the matching pennies game and the driving game, for example, playing each action with a probability of 0.5 for each player is a mixed-strategy Nash equilibrium.

Any game with a finite number of players, each of whom has a finite number of pure strategies, has a Nash equilibrium, although possibly only in mixed strategies. By restricting action combinations (i.e., plans of behavior) to those that are self-enforcing in the Nash equilibrium sense, game theory restricts the set of admissible behavior in such games.

Although the situations described here are very simple, the same analysis can be applied to more complicated ones, in which players move sequentially and there is asymmetric information or uncertainty. The equilibrium notions used for such situations are, by and large, refinements of the Nash equilibrium – that is, they are Nash equilibria that fulfill some additional conditions. The following discussion of dynamic games illustrates the nature of these refinements and the usefulness of imposing further restrictions on admissible self-enforcing behavior.

A.2 SELF-ENFORCING BEHAVIOR IN DYNAMIC GAMES: BACKWARD INDUCTION AND SUBGAME PERFECT EQUILIBRIA

Consider a dynamic situation in which the players move sequentially rather than simultaneously. It is easier to present dynamic games in extensive (tree-diagram) form than in the normal (matrix) form used in Figures A.1–3. In extensive form a game is presented as a graph or a tree in which a branching point is a decision point for a player and each branch

---

[5] Harsanyi provided an interpretation of this mixing as reflecting one's uncertainty about the other player's choice of action. For an intuitive account, see Gibbons (1998).

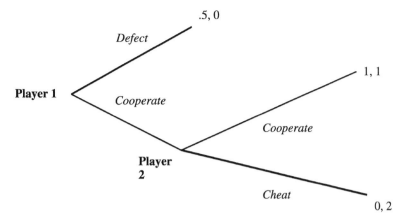

Figure A.4. The One-Sided Prisoner's Dilemma Game

is associated with a different action. The payoffs associated with different actions are denoted at the end of the tree.

Although dynamic games can have many branches and decision points, their basic structure can be illustrated in the case of a game with two decision points. In this game player 1 chooses an action a_1 from the set of feasible actions A_1. After observing player 1's choice, player 2 chooses an action a_2 from the set of feasible actions A_2. After the players choose their actions, they receive payoffs $u_1(a_1, a_2)$ to player 1 and $u_2(a_1, a_2)$ to player 2.

The one-sided prisoner's dilemma game is an example of a dynamic game with this structure (Figure A.4). First, player 1 chooses either to cooperate or defect. If he chooses to defect, the game ends and the players' payoffs are $(.5, 0)$. If player 1 chooses to cooperate, player 2 can choose an action. If he chooses to cooperate, both players' payoffs are 1, but if he chooses to cheat, he receives the higher payoff of 2, while player 1 receives a payoff of 0.[6] In this game, player 1 can gain from cooperating, but only if player 2 cooperates. If player 2 cheats, player 1 receives a lower payoff than if he had not cooperated.

Dynamic games such as the one-sided prisoner's dilemma are of interest in the social sciences because they capture an essential part of all exchange relationships – personal, social, economic, and political. Exchange is

[6] This game is also known as the game of trust (Kreps 1990a). Player 1 can either not trust (defect) or trust (cooperate). If player 1 does not trust, the game is over. If he trusts, player 2 can decide whether to honor the trust (cooperate) or to renege (cheat).

	Player 2's actions		
		Cooperate	Cheat
Player 1's actions	Cooperate	1, 1	0, 2
	Defect	.5, 0	**.5, 0**

Figure A.5. One-Sided Prisoner's Dilemma Game in Matrix Form

always sequential: some time elapses between the *quid* and the *quo* (Greif 1997a; 2000). More generally, in social relationships one often has to give before receiving; at the moment of giving, one receives only a promise of receiving something in the future.

Can player 1 trust player 2 to cooperate? To find out, we can work backward through the game tree, examining the optimal action of the player who is supposed to move at each branching point. This method is known as backward induction.[7]

Consider player 2's decision. He receives a payoff of 2 from cheating and a payoff of 1 from cooperating, implying that cheating is his optimal choice. Expecting that, player 1 will choose to defect and receive .5 rather than cooperate and receive 0. (These branches are in bold in the game tree diagram in Figure A.4.) This action combination is self-enforcing, because player 1's best response to cheating is to defect, while player 2's best response to defecting is to cheat. Backward induction reveals the self-enforcing action combination of (defect, cheat). This action combination is a Nash equilibrium.

As this analysis indicates, Nash equilibria can be Pareto-inferior. The payoffs associated with (cooperate, cooperate) leave each player better off than if player 1 defects; cooperation is thus profitable and efficient. But if player 1 cooperates, the payoff to player 2 from cheating is higher than from cooperating. Cooperation is not self-enforcing.

In the one-sided prisoner's dilemma game, backward induction yields the only Nash equilibrium. This can easily be seen if we present the game in matrix form (Figure A.5). In matrix form, player 1 chooses between cooperating and defecting, while player 2 chooses between cooperating and cheating. The payoffs associated with each action combination are

---

[7] For experimental evidence on people's use of backward induction, see Appendix B. For the theoretical weaknesses of backward induction and subgame perfection, see Fudenberg and Tirole (1991); Binmore (1996); and Hardin (1997).

the same as those in Figure A.4. The Nash equilibrium outcome is in boldface.

When backward induction is possible, it always leads to action combinations that are Nash equilibria, but the opposite does not hold. If we represent an extensive (tree-diagram) form in the associated matrix (normal) form, not every Nash equilibrium in the game's matrix form can be reached through backward induction in the original tree form. This is because analyzing the game in tree form using backward induction captures that the players move sequentially, something that is not captured in the matrix form representation of the game. That the tree form captures more information about the structure of the game allows us to eliminate some Nash equilibria that we cannot eliminate in the normal form. Specifically, we can eliminate Nash equilibria that are based on noncredible threats or promises. The tree representation thus assists in deductively restricting – refining – the set of admissible self-enforcing behavior.

To see this advantage of backward induction, consider the following tree and matrix presentations of the same game (Figure A.6). In this game, player 1 chooses between playing left (L) or right (R), while player 2, who moves second, chooses between playing up (U) or down (D). If player 1 plays L, the payoffs are 1 to player 1 and 2 to player 2. If player 1 plays R and player 2 plays D, the payoffs are (2, 1) but if player 2 plays U, the payoffs are (0, 0.) The analysis of this game illustrates how backward induction eliminates Nash equilibria based on noncredible threats.

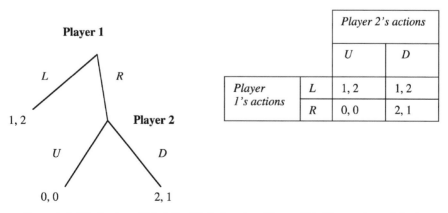

			Player 2's actions	
			U	D
Player 1's actions		L	1, 2	1, 2
		R	0, 0	2, 1

Figure A.6. Elimination of Nash Equilibria Based on Noncredible Threats through Backward Induction

415

The matrix form presentation of this game shows two Nash equilibria: (L, U), with payoff (1, 2,) and (R, D), with payoff (2, 1). Backward induction yields only (R, D). (L, U) did not survive backward induction, because it relies on a noncredible threat that is concealed by the normal form presentation. In this equilibrium, player 1 is motivated to choose L because player 2 is supposed to play U, while player 2's best response to player 1's choice of L is indeed U. Given that player 1 chose L, player 2's payoff does not really depend on choosing between U and D, because given that player 1 chose L neither of these actions would be taken. Hence the equilibrium (L, U) depends on a noncredible threat off the equilibrium path – that is, it relies on player 2 taking an action in a situation that would never occur if the players play according to this action combination. Had the need for player 2 to take this action actually risen, he would not have found it optimal to do so. Backward induction enables us to call player 2's bluff and restrict the set of admissible self-enforcing behavior accordingly. If player 1 played R and hence player 2's choice of action influences the payoffs, playing D and receiving 1 (instead of playing U and receiving 0) is optimal for player 2. Backward induction captures that player 1, anticipating that response, would choose R and receive 2 rather than choose L and receive 1.

Backward induction can be applied in any dynamic finite-horizon game of perfect information. In such games the players move sequentially and all previous moves become common knowledge before the next action has to be chosen. In other games, such as dynamic games with simultaneous moves or an infinite horizon, however, we cannot apply backward induction directly. The notion of subgame perfect equilibrium enables us nevertheless to restrict the set of admissible Nash equilibrium by eliminating those that rely on noncredible threats or promises. Indeed, when backward induction can be applied, the resulting Nash equilibrium is a subgame perfect equilibrium – it is a refinement of Nash equilibrium in the sense that it is a Nash equilibrium that satisfies an additional requirement.

To grasp the concept of subgame perfect equilibrium intuitively, note that in the examples presented here, the action combinations yielded by backward induction satisfied the mutual-best-response requirement of Nash equilibrium. It also satisfied the requirement that player 2's action be optimal in the game that begins when he has to choose an action. Beginning at this decision point, backward induction restricts the admissible action of player 2 to be optimal.

In dynamic games with simultaneous moves, however, we cannot, in general, follow this procedure, because an optimal action depends on

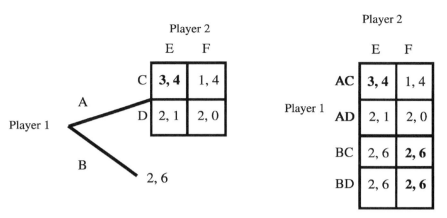

Figure A.7. Subgame Perfection

the action of the other player. To see why this condition limits the use of backward induction, consider the following game, presented in both extended and normal form (Figure A.7). Player 1 moves first, choosing between A and B. If player 1 chooses B, the game is over and the payoffs are (2, 6). If player 1 chooses A, both players play the simultaneous move game presented in the two-by-two matrix. In the two-by-two game that follows player 1's choice of action A, backward induction cannot be applied by considering the optimal moves of either player 1 or player 2. Each player's optimal action depends on the action of the other. In other words, no player moves last, as in a sequential move game.

We can still, however, follow the logic of the backward induction procedure by finding the Nash equilibrium in the two-by-two game and considering player 1's optimal choice between A and B, taking this Nash equilibrium outcome into consideration. The Nash equilibrium in the two-by-two game is (C, E), which yields the payoffs (3, 4). Player 1's optimal choice between A and B is therefore A. The action combination that this procedure yields is (AC, E), which is a subgame perfect equilibrium.

To see that this procedure eliminates Nash equilibria that rely on non-credible threats, note that there are three Nash equilibria in the game: (AC, E), (BC, F), and (BD, F). (BC, F) and (BD, F) yield payoffs of (2, 6), making player 1 worse off and player 2 better off than the (AC, E) subgame perfect equilibrium. Both of these equilibria, however, rely on noncredible threats off the equilibrium path. Consider (BC, F). While considering the game as a whole, the choice of C or F does not affect payoffs, because these actions are off the path of play. But if the need to actually take these actions arises, they would not constitute a mutual best response. If player 2 chooses F, player 1's best response is D rather than C, which yields player 1 a payoff of 2 instead of 1. Similarly, in (BD, F), if player 1 chooses D, player 2's best response is E instead of F, which yields him a payoff of 1 instead of 0.

The notion of a subgame perfect equilibrium applies the mutual-best-response idea that is the essence of Nash equilibrium to subgames. Intuitively, a subgame is part of the original game that remains to be played, but a subgame begins only at points at which the complete history of how the game was already played is known to all players. A Nash equilibrium (in the game as a whole) is a subgame perfect equilibrium if the players' strategies constitute a Nash equilibrium in every subgame. Every finite game has a subgame perfect equilibrium.

A.3 SELF-ENFORCING BEHAVIOR IN REPEATED GAMES: SUBGAME PERFECT EQUILIBRIA, THE FOLK THEOREM, AND IMPERFECT MONITORING

So far we have examined games in which players interact only once. Institutional analysis, however, is concerned with recurrent situations, in which individuals interact over time. One way to examine such situations is to use dynamic games with more complicated game trees. A subset of such games – repeated games – has been found to be particularly amenable to formal analysis and useful for institutional analysis (Chapter 6).

Repeated-game theory examines situations in which the same (dynamic or static) stage game (such as a prisoners' dilemma or one-sided prisoner's dilemma game) is repeated every period. At the end of each period, payoffs are allocated, information might be revealed, and the same stage game is repeated again. Future payoffs are discounted by a time discount factor (often denoted by δ). A history in a repeated game is the set of actions taken in the past; a strategy specifies action combination in every stage game after every possible history. A strategy combination specifies a strategy for each player.[8]

To examine self-enforcing behavior in such games, suppose that the stage game is the prisoners' dilemma game presented in Figure A.1. If this stage game is repeated only once, the only subgame perfect equilibrium is (defect, defect); (cooperate, cooperate) is not an equilibrium. A comparable subgame perfect equilibrium in the repeated game is that

---

[8] For ease of presentation, I often refer to an action combination as a strategy.

after every history both players always defect. This equilibrium is also the unique equilibrium if the game is repeated a finite number of times. The reasons for this and the implied important implications for institutional analysis are discussed in Appendix C, section C.2.1. The discussion here focuses on situations in which the stage game is repeated for an infinite number of periods.

When the stage game is infinitely repeated, the preceding strategy is still a subgame perfect equilibrium. Each player's best response to this strategy is always to defect. But other equilibria are also possible.[9] Consider, for example, the following strategy to each player: In the first period, cooperate. Thereafter cooperate if all moves in all previous periods have been (cooperate, cooperate); otherwise defect. Each player's strategy thus calls for initiating exchange in the first period and cooperating as long as the other also cooperates. It calls for no cooperation if either player ever defects. This threat of ceasing cooperation forever is credible because (defect, defect) is an equilibrium.

A credible threat of such a trigger strategy can motivate the players to cooperate if they are sufficiently patient. The strategy implies that a player has to choose between present and future gains. Defection implies a relatively large immediate gain (5 in the game presented in Figure A.1), because the other player cooperates. But doing so implies losing future gains from cooperation because, following defection, both players will defect forever (and hence each will receive -8). The net present value of following the trigger strategy is $1/(1 - \delta)$. Deviating from it implies receiving a one-time payoff of 5, followed by -8 each period thereafter. This yields the net present value of $5 - \delta/(1 - \delta)$, which declines as the players' time discount factor increases: if the players are sufficiently patient – if they value future gains enough – the preceding strategy is an equilibrium.

One of the most useful features of repeated-game theory is that verifying that a particular strategy combination is a subgame perfect equilibrium is often easier than verifying that a strategy is a Nash equilibrium. Roughly speaking, in any repeated game a strategy combination is a subgame perfect equilibrium if no player can gain from a one-period deviation after any history. In other words, to check if a particular strategy combination is a subgame perfect equilibrium, it is sufficient to substantiate that after any history – any sequence of actions that can transpire, given the

---

[9] Experimental evidence indicates that people do indeed understand the strategic difference between one-shot and repeated games. See Appendix B.

strategy – no player can gain from a one-period deviation after which he will return to follow the strategy.[10]

In strategic dynamic situations, multiple equilibria often exist. The Folk theorem of repeated games established that in infinitely repeated games there is usually an infinite number of subgame perfect equilibria.[11] Given the rules of the game, more than one pattern of behavior can prevail as an equilibrium outcome, and this is more likely to be the case in dynamic games with large actions set.

By revealing the general existence of multiple equilibria, game theory raises the problem of equilibrium selection. The "refinement" literature in game theory has attempted to refine the concept of the Nash equilibrium to restrict the set of admissible outcomes deductively. Subgame perfect equilibrium is one such restriction. But so far game theory has not offered a suitable deductive refinement for infinite repeated games leading to a unique equilibrium (Van Damme 1983, 1987; Fudenberg and Tirole 1991).

---

[10] The formal analysis is due to Abreu (1988). Definition: Consider a strategy combination s, and denote the set of players by N and a player by i. The strategy is made up of s_i, the strategy for player i, and s_{-i}, the strategy for the other players. The strategy s_i is unimprovable against s if there is no $t - 1$ period history (for any t) after which i could profit by deviating from s_i in period t only (and conforming to s_i from $t + 1$ and on). Proposition: Let the payoffs of a stage game G be bounded. In each finitely or infinitely repeated version of the game with time discount factor $\beta \in (0, 1)$, a strategy σ is a subgame perfect equilibrium if and only if for $\forall$ i (i.e., every player), σ_i is unimprovable against σ.

[11] The original Folk theorem of repeated games (Friedman 1971) established that any average payoff vector that is better for all players than the (static, one-period game) Nash equilibrium payoff vector can be sustained as the outcome of a subgame perfect equilibrium of the infinitely repeated game if the players are sufficiently patient. Later analyses established that the equilibrium outcome set is even larger (see, e.g., Fudenberg and Maskin 1986).

B

Is Homo Sociologicus Strategic?

The analysis in this book accepts the notion that people tend to respect the socially expected and normative sanctions (Chapter 5). It also rests on a particular notion of rationality, maintaining that when institutions generate behavior, socially articulated and disseminated rules regarding the situation span the domain that people understand and within which they can act rationally. Are these two premises consistent with each other? Is it appropriate to consider individuals as strategic while recognizing that social and normative considerations influence behavior? Or should we model people as *homo sociologicus*, as passive rule followers? Specifically, is it appropriate to model individuals who have such social and normative inclinations as rational decision makers when they are guided by socially articulated and disseminated rules?[1] Do they have stable preferences regarding outcomes?[2] Are they motivated by the consequences of their actions? In other words, do they act strategically? This appendix presents evidence to support the claim that, although people have social and normative propensities, it is nevertheless

---

[1] The literature on the issue of rationality is immense. For a recent discussion and survey, see Mantzavinos (2001, pp. 50–4).

[2] For a survey of psychological evidence indicating that individuals do not always have stable preferences, see Rabin (1998), who identifies two main reasons for this to be the case. First, people have difficulty evaluating their own preferences: they do not always accurately predict their own future preferences or even accurately assess the well-being they have experienced from past choices. Second, research on framing effects, preference reversals, and related phenomena reveal that people may prefer option x to y when the choice is elicited one way but prefer y to x when the choice is elicited another way. The first issue is more relevant to what people want to exchange and less relevant to the issue here, namely, how institutions enable actions. The second issue is consistent with the argument made here – that institutions frame the context within which individuals choose actions.

appropriate and necessary to consider them as rational in the above sense.

Experimental game theory is a promising analytical framework to address these questions, particularly because participants share common knowledge of the rules of the game and many experiments were explicitly designed to reveal individuals' social and normative inclinations. These experiments provide three ways to address the foregoing questions: considering whether nonrational explanations better fit the data, testing whether the observed behavior is consistent with some well-behaved preference ordering, and using experimental results to determine whether people are motivated by consequences and behave strategically. The evidence is inconsistent with nonrational accounts, consistent with a well-behaved preference ordering, and reflective of consequential and strategic behavior.[3]

Consider, for example, the ultimatum game, which has been used to study altruism. In this game, a proposer suggests a potential division of a fixed amount of money. The responder can either agree to the proposal (in which case the amount is divided accordingly) or disagree (in which case both get nothing). If players are motivated only by self-interest and monetary income, the unique subgame perfect equilibrium is one in which the proposer makes the smallest possible offer, which the responder accepts. Numerous experiments conducted in different countries with different monetary amounts and different experimental procedures reveal that this is not what actually happens. Fehr and Schmidt (1999) report that in 71 percent of the cases, the proposers offered between 40 and 50 percent of the total to the other player. Moreover, individuals often reject low offers, revealing that they prefer that both parties end up with nothing to receiving what they perceive as an inadequate allocation.

Although this evidence is usually considered as reflecting of altruism or aversion to inequality, a nonrational explanation for this behavior has been advanced. Roth and Erev (1995) and Binmore, Gale, and Samuelson (1995) try to explain the existence of fair offers and the rejection of low offers in this game using an irrational learning model.[4] The central idea

---

[3] See E. Hoffman et al. (1996a, 1996b); Fehr and Schmidt (2001); Henrich et al. (2001); and Falk and Fischbacher (2000).

[4] Another possible explanation is that because most real-life interactions are repeated, subjects in a laboratory mistake one-time games for repeated games. Even if this is true, it cannot account for many of the results reported, such as the tendency to cooperate when interactions are anonymous and behavior is known to be of short duration.

is that proposers and responders have distinct incentives to learn. The rejection of low offers is not costly for responders, who are irrational in terms of slowly learning, rather than deducting, not to reject them. In contrast, rejections are very costly to proposers, who therefore quickly learn to avoid making low offers. Hence behavior may not converge to the subgame perfect equilibrium in which the lowest possible offers are made.

The validity of such learning arguments with respect to simple games such as the ultimatum game seems doubtful. Furthermore, in many studies (as discussed later), proposers do anticipate responders' reactions.[5]

Are altruistic individuals rational? Using the dictator game, Andreoni and Miller (2002) demonstrate that behavior exhibiting social preference is consistent with a well-behaved preference ordering. The dictator game resembles the ultimatum game, except that the proposer acts as a dictator who can divide the fixed amount in any way he pleases (including assigning the full amount to himself). Andreoni and Miller constructed dictator game experiments in which they manipulated the "exchange rate" between what the dictator gives and the other player receives. For every dollar the dictator gave up, the other person received an amount smaller than, equal to, or greater than one dollar. Changing the dictator's budget constraint in this way enabled the behavior of the same individual to be examined under different constraints. It is therefore possible to test whether behavior satisfies the necessary and sufficient conditions required for the existence of well-behaved preferences.[6]

The results were unambiguous, leading the authors to conclude that preferences are predictable and well behaved at the aggregate level and that individuals exhibit a significant degree of rationally altruistic behavior. Indeed, more than 98 percent of the subjects made choices that were consistent with utility maximization. It is possible to capture altruistic choices with quasi-concave utility functions for individuals; altruism

---

[5] The merit of an alternative theory – that individuals act in a one-shot game as they do in repeated games – is discussed later.

[6] Specifically, they have examined whether individuals reveal a preference ordering that satisfies the generalized axiom of revealed preference (GARP). A is directly revealed as preferred to B if B was in the choice set when A was chosen. If A is directly revealed as preferred to B, B is directly revealed as preferred to C and Y is directly revealed as preferred to Z, then A is indirectly revealed as preferred to Z. The GARP is as follows: if A is indirectly revealed as preferred to B, then A is not strictly within the budget set when B is chosen, that is, B is not strictly directly revealed as preferred to A. Satisfying GARP is both a necessary and sufficient condition for the existence of well-behaved preferences, given linear budget constraints.

reflects rational behavior, given the underlying preferences.[7] Furthermore, Andreoni and Miller found that a model capturing the preference revealed in one experiment consistently accounts for behavior in other experiments.[8]

Many experiments reveal that individuals respond as postulated in game theory to the strategic environment in which they interact.[9] In hundreds of double-auction experiments, prices and quantities quickly converged to the competitive equilibrium predicted by standard self-interest theory.[10] In the case of the two games discussed previously, Forsythe et al. (1994) hypothesize that if people are motivated only by altruism or aversion to inequality, the outcome in both games should be the same. However, individuals could also be reciprocators – conditional cooperators who are willing to take materially costly actions that raise or lower others' payoffs depending on others' past actions and their perceived intentions. In particular, if people are willing to punish others for what they consider to be unfairly low offers and if the proposers anticipate this through backward induction, higher offers should be made in the ultimatum game than in the dictator game. In fact, offers were significantly higher in the ultimatum game, suggesting that many proposers do apply backward induction. In a ten-dollar dictator game, 21 percent of the proposers gave the other player nothing, and 21 percent gave the other at least an equal share. In a ten-dollar ultimatum game, however, all proposers offered the responder something, and 75 percent offered at least an equal amount.

---

[7] As they note, however, their analysis did not explore the influence of the changing environment – the rules of the game, level of anonymity, the gender or age of the participants, or the framing of the decision – on the preference ordering.

[8] Fehr and Schmidt (1999) report similar results.

[9] Ostrom (1998), however, argues that "what is clearly the case from experimental evidence is that players do not use backward induction in their decisionmaking plans in an experimental laboratory" (p. 5). The context of these words, however, suggests that what she might have had in mind is that the results are inconsistent with backward induction in finitely repeated games, under the assumption that people are motivated only by self-interest. Ostrom cites Rapoport (1997) and McKelvey and Palfrey (1992) to support her position. But Rapoport's analysis is not concerned with rejecting backward induction. His focus and main conclusion regard the importance of the framing effect on behavior, captured by information about the order of play (p. 133). He notes that the order of moves influences equilibrium selection. McKelvey and Palfrey (1992) examine the centipede game, which is problematic as far as backward induction is concerned, as Fudenberg and Tirole (1991, pp. 96–100) note. They conclude that a game of incomplete information based on reputation explains their data.

[10] See surveys in Davis and Holt (1993) and Hagel and Roth (1995).

Similar results are reported in cross-country analysis. Henrich et al. (2001) conducted experiments in 15 very different settings, ranging from modern urban to hunter-gatherer societies. They concluded that in all of these societies, individuals exhibited stable preferences and behavior motivated by consequences. In each society, people by and large correctly anticipated the responses of others.[11]

Fehr and Schmidt (1999) also found evidence of backward induction. They report that in twelve public good games without punishment, in which free-riding is a dominant strategy, average and median contributions in the first period were 40–60 percent of the endowment, but 73 percent of participants contributed nothing in the last period.

Fehr and Gächter (2000) conducted experiments with an extended public good game in which individuals have the option to participate in the (costly) punishment of others after contributions are made. They found that the behavior of reciprocators who are willing to punish free riding is anticipated by at least some potential free riders and that the expectation that free-riding will be punished prevents its occurrence from the beginning. Individuals who deviated more from the average contribution were punished more severely, and they responded to this punishment by increasing their contributions. Some individuals inflicted punishments to generate an increase in average contributions and were successful in achieving this.

Fehr and Fischbacher (2001) explicitly tested the ability of individuals to understand the strategic difference between one-shot and repeated games. The evidence indicates that, by and large, they understand it very well. Fehr and Fischbacher ran two sets of ultimatum game experiments. In both experiments, subjects played the game ten times, each time with a different opponent. In one set of experiments, the proposers knew nothing about the past behavior of their current responders. In the other set a "reputation" condition was imposed, as past behavior of the responders was made known. In theory, if individuals understand the distinction between one-shot and repeated interactions, responders would be motivated to build up reputations for "toughness" and rejection of low offers. Hence the acceptance threshold (the lowest acceptable offer for the responder) should increase. Slightly more than 80 percent of the responders increased their acceptance thresholds under the reputation condition.[12]

---

[11] See also Roth et al. (1991).

[12] For similar results in gift exchange games, see Gächter and Falk (2002). Their findings undermine the suggestion that individuals exhibit dispositional social

Gächter and Falk (2002) found behavior consistent with the insight of incomplete information models – that is, individuals act "as if" they are of a particular type in order to cause others to identify them as such. They examined behavior in gift exchange games in which the proposer offers a wage to the responder, which the responder can accept or reject. If the responder rejects the offer, both players receive a zero payoff. If he accepts, he is paid the offered wage but has to make a costly "effort" choice. Clearly, if the responder maximizes only his monetary payoff, his best response is always to accept any offer and to choose the lowest possible effort level.

Gächter and Falk studied two versions of this game. In the one-shot experiment, the parties were informed that they would never play against each other again. In the repeated-game experiment, the parties knew that they would play ten times. Reciprocity, or a significant and positive wage-effort relationship, was found in both experiments. Consistent with game-theoretic analysis, reciprocity and incentives provided by repeated interactions seemed to complement each other. The positive wage-effort relationship was steeper and effort levels higher in the repeated-game treatment. About half of the individuals who revealed themselves as selfish in the last period by providing the selfish amount of labor imitated the reciprocators in all other periods of the repeated-game experiment.[13] Individuals act "as if" they are of a particular type in order to cause others to identify them as such.

Experimental evidence thus lends support to the claim that individuals are rational, in the sense of having stable preferences and being motivated by the consequences of their actions. They behave strategically, trying to anticipate others' responses to their actions, adjusting their responses to others' actions, and using backward induction.[14] The experimental evidence reinforces the view of the great sociologist, Talcott Parsons, that "action remains rational in the sense that it comprises the quasi-intentional pursuit of gratification by reasoning humans who balance complex and multifaceted evaluative criteria" (DiMaggio and Powell 1991a, p. 17).

These experimental results fit well with recent empirical findings in institutional sociology. In facing new situations, individuals actively seek

preferences because they mistake the one-shot laboratory experiments with repeated, real-life situations.

[13] For similar findings, see Fischbacher, Gächter, and Fehr (2001).

[14] Lindbeck (1997) elaborates on why it is appropriate to assume that individuals act rationally given the values they have internalized.

to improve their lot. DiMaggio and Powell note, for example, that "early adopters of organizational innovations are commonly driven by a desire to improve performance" (1991b, p. 65). At the same time, they emphasize the importance of mimetic behavior: individuals mimic the behavior of others in situations in which institutions generate behavior. This response is consistent with the argument developed in Chapter 7 that individuals with social propensities act rationally when facing a new situation, but that once an institutionalized equilibrium behavior establishes itself, each individual best acts mimetically.

Individuals have the propensity to respond to social and moral considerations. Yet, as the experimental and sociological evidence indicates, even such individuals have stable preferences regarding outcomes and act strategically to achieve them.

C

The Role of Theory

Reputation-Based Private-Order Institutions

Theory is unavoidable in positive institutional analysis. Implicitly or explicitly, a student of institutions resorts to theory to guide the selection of issues and to identify relevant factors and causal relationships. Theoretical assertions about the importance of exchange, polities, and the harnessing of coercive power direct the investigation of the institutional foundations of agency relationships, property rights security, impersonal exchange, and the mobilization of resources for collective action. The investigation itself is directed by a concept of institutions central to which are intertransactional linkages and the associated institutional elements, self-enforceability, and the nature of institutional development as a historical process. Game theory tells us what to look for in considering and evaluating the self-enforceability of institutional elements in a given environment.

Theory also makes another important contribution. By pointing to the general principles that underpin the operation of institutions that can lead to a particular outcome, theory indicates that institutions – and the history they induce – are not random. Context and contingency are important, but institutions generating similar behavior in the same central transactions are subject to the same forces and have to respond to the same considerations regardless of the particularities of time and place. Institutions that achieve the same outcomes have to mitigate the same problems that are implied by the inherent attributes of the central transaction under consideration and by the general context. Hence theory is useful in directing our search for evidence that facilitates forming a conjecture about and evaluating whether a particular institution prevailed at a particular time and place.

This appendix delineates the forces that shape the general attributes of reputation-based private-order economic institutions prominent in the historical examples analyzed in this book. It emphasizes the generic implications of these forces in directing a context-specific analysis aimed at identifying the relevant institution. The discussion highlights the distinction between a game-theoretic and an institutional analysis: game theory considers possible equilibria in a given game; institutional analysis considers the man-made, nonphysical factors that generate regularities of behavior while being exogenous to each individual whose behavior they influence.

Consider a situation in which the inherent characteristics of the central transaction can be captured as a version of the one-period repetition of a prisoners' dilemma or one-sided prisoner's dilemma game (both games are described in Appendix A). In such games a weakly dominant strategy is for at least one player to take an action to which the other player's best response causes the game to reach a Pareto-inferior outcome. These actions are usually referred to as "cheating" and the alternatives that lead to better outcomes as "cooperating" or "playing honest." Such situations are everywhere in the economic, political, and social spheres. In the economic sphere, they are inherent in voluntary exchanges of goods and services (see Greif 2000) and involuntary exchanges, such as the poaching of a firm's workers by another firm (see Kambayashi 2002). They are inherent in the relationship between the government and economic agents (see Kydland and Prescott 1977), as well as the relationships between owners of common resources (see Ostrom 1990). In short, such situations are central to what we model as voluntary or involuntary exchange, agency relationships, collective action, and free-riding problems. The theory behind this simple game can therefore be generalized to study multiple real-world situations.

In the absence of exogenous enforcement, can an individual be endogenously induced to take actions that are not in his short-term economic interest? In the game-theoretic formulation, how are individuals motivated to take action off the equilibrium path of the (unique) one-period game? Why would one cooperate or be honest despite the fact that cheating is economically rational if the game is repeated just once?

Two lines of analysis consider ways through which the social norms of cooperation and honesty can be sustained when at least some individuals care only about their material well-being.[1] The first examines situations

---

[1] For surveys of these lines of analysis and reputation-based institutions, see Greif and Kandel (1995); Klein (1996); Greif (2000); Hart (2001); and Dixit (2004). For important contributions and insights, see Milgrom and Roberts (1982); Shapiro and

in which there is *asymmetric information* regarding the propensity of various agents to cheat. In the current context, in these situations there is a probability that a player is "good," in the sense that he would not cheat (e.g., under any circumstances), despite economic temptation. Whether a particular individual is "good," however, is private information. Each player knows if he is "good," but the others do not. Cooperation can be curtailed by what is referred to as *adverse selection*; one's decisions depend on privately held information in a manner that adversely affects those who are uninformed. The analysis thus focuses on why and how individuals can be motivated to cooperate in aspiring to gain reputations as players of the "good" type.

The second line of analysis examines situations in which there is a moral-hazard problem in which there are only "bad" agents who always maximize their material well-being. The focus of the analysis is on why and how the expectation of future interactions can motivate such individuals to cooperate. In either line of analysis, a player's reputation is a function from the history of the game to a probability distribution over his strategies.

These two lines of analysis are not mutually exclusive, but the distinction between them is analytically useful. The game-theoretic analysis of reputation-based private-order institutions in these situations focuses mainly on particular intertransactional linkages – the same transaction over time or the same transaction among different individuals. Accordingly, this is also the focus of the subsequent discussion, although I note that focusing on these particular linkages highlights the potential roles of various others, through social exchange, organizations, and the use of violence.

C.1   ADVERSE SELECTION: INCOMPLETE INFORMATION

Incomplete information models are useful in studying situations with asymmetric information and adverse selection. It is assumed that at least one of the interacting individuals knows his type, while the others do not. Nature moves first and selects with some probability the types of the various players. The ex ante probability distribution over types is common knowledge, but the selection itself is private information. The game is repeated for a finite or infinite number of periods. In this case, even if

Stiglitz (1984); Kreps et al. (1982); Kreps (1990a); O. Williamson (1985); Joskow (1984); Nelson (1974); Klein and Leffler (1981); Shapiro (1983); and Akerlof and Yellen (1986).

the actual number of "good" players is very small, they can nevertheless have a large impact on the equilibrium behavior of all agents. Particularly, cooperation can often be achieved even if many of the players are bad types (Kreps et al. 1982).

To grasp the intuition, consider a one-sided prisoner's dilemma game in which agents and merchants are randomly matched each period and past actions are observed by all players. A "bad" agent may find it optimal to mimic the behavior of a "good" agent for a period of time and refrain from cheating. Cheating in the first period implies losing gains from future cooperation or the ability to cheat again (because merchants will update their beliefs about that agent's type and not rehire him). A strategy of acting like a "good" type for some periods and then cheating later implies gaining from cooperation for some period as well as from cheating. But because cheating is postponed, this strategy implies a higher payoff only when the agent's time discount factor and the gain from cooperation are sufficiently high relative to the gain from cheating. If this is the case, a "bad" type finds it optimal to mimic, at least for a period, the behavior of a "good" type. Given this behavior, it is optimal to interact with him, although, with some probability, he may cheat in the future. Incomplete information and the conditioning of future behavior on past conduct implies the possibility of a "pooling equilibrium" in which "bad" types and "good" types behave the same way – honestly – for many periods. Indeed, even if the probability that an individual is honest is very low, if the game is played for a sufficiently large number of periods, the extent of cooperation progressively approaches the first best (a situation in which a Pareto-optimal outcome is achieved by everyone behaving honestly).[2]

By highlighting the exact way that cooperation can prevail and the conditions required for this to be the case, theory facilitates the evaluation of its relevance to the institution we seek to identify. Among the questions that the theory highlights are the following: Does the broader historical context reflect such factors as religious beliefs and a culture of guilt that could have led people to believe that some agents are inherently good? How are expectations for future interactions generated? If a player

---

[2] A similar result follows when we assume that all agents are trustworthy in the sense that each incurs some intrinsic psychic cost if he cheats. The distribution of these costs is common knowledge, but one's intrinsic cost is private information. Cooperation can be sustained on the equilibrium path as low-cost ("bad") agents mimic the behavior of high-cost ("good") agents for some periods to acquire reputations that they will eventually exploit by cheating (Hart and Holmstrom 1987).

plays the stage game with different partners in different periods, how do future partners learn about his past conduct? Why are agents who cheated unable to assume a new identity (as is done in modern economies when an owner changes the name of his firm), allowing him to reestablish agency relationships despite having cheated in the past?[3]

Similarly, we can evaluate a conjecture about the relevance of an incomplete-information, reputation-based institution by looking for the generic implication of this theory. In the absence of other considerations, individuals should cheat in their old age. Is this the case? That merchants update their beliefs about each agent's type implies an economic payoff to an agent who acted in a manner that caused merchants to update their beliefs favorably. Do we see agents attempting to signal their types by taking such costly actions as contributing to charity or acting as though they were religious? In a pooling equilibrium, a player conditions his actions toward another player only on the other player's past conduct, not on other considerations, such as his ethnicity. Is this actually the case? Is it the case that agents who cheated in the past are never rehired?

Asserting that reputation reflects incomplete information is intuitively appealing. But a general theoretical insight highlights the inherent difficulty of empirically substantiating the relevance of cooperation based on it. Incomplete-information models are very sensitive to the specification of incomplete information, but the researcher cannot observe the details and nature of incomplete information in a particular setting. Hence we can usually account for particular behavior, as well as its absence, as reflecting some unobserved diversity of types in the population.[4]

C.2 MORAL HAZARD: COMPLETE INFORMATION

When all agents are "bad" types, motivating them to be honest can be achieved based on the lure of future reward. Conditioning future reward from cooperation on past conduct is used to motivate behavior. The basic theoretical insight highlights the importance of increasing the reward for honesty and decreasing the payoff following dishonest behavior. The larger the discrepancy between the two, the more honest behavior can be generated.

---

[3] In Tadelis's (1999, 2002) model of a firm's reputation, described later, in equilibrium agents who change their identities earn a lower income.

[4] For a discussion and an example, see Hart (2001).

The basic intuition is captured in the Folk theorem of repeated games, which can be illustrated by considering an infinitely repeated prisoners' dilemma game (see Appendix A, section A.3). Assume that for each player the net present value if both players cooperate in every future period is higher than the net present value for a player if he cheats in the current period (while the other cooperates) and subsequently gets the payoff associated with cheating by both players every period. If this is the case, there is an equilibrium in which cooperation is achieved. In this equilibrium, future cooperation is made conditional on past conduct: following cheating by either player, both players' strategies call for cheating forever. The threat of cheating is credible – it is part of a subgame perfect equilibrium – because cheating is each player's best response to the expected behavior of cheating by the other.

That the promise of future reward can potentially support cooperation is the starting point rather than the conclusion of institutional analysis. Theory informs us about the conditions required for cooperation based on the long hand of the future. Institutional analysis is about the particularities of the institutional elements that made, or failed to make, these conditions a reality at a particular time and place. It is concerned with understanding how expectations for repeated interactions were generated and among whom. Why did an individual stand to gain more from cooperation than from cheating? Why could someone who cheated one partner not establish an equally profitable cooperative relationship elsewhere? Why, and how, was a cheated individual motivated and able to circulate this information? How were those supposed to respond to cheating to gain this information? What made the threat of punishment credible?

Generic theoretical insights provide a valuable guide when attempting to identify the relevant institutional elements and other factors. The following discussion considers such insights about the endogenous construction of future rewards. It then analyzes the credibility of maintaining relationships and the credibility of threats of future bilateral and multilateral punishment and renegotiation following cheating. It also provides insights into the generation and distribution of information, imperfect monitoring, the cost of reputation-based institutions, and endogenous intertransactional linkages and organizations.[5]

---

[5] Within an institution, all these considerations are interrelated. Although discussing them sequentially focuses attention on each, it comes at the cost of commenting only on these interrelations.

Appendix C

C.2.1 The End-Game Problem

Conditioning future reward on past conduct influences decisions about current behavior. Such conditioning, however, requires generating the belief that a future reward will be forthcoming. The distinction in the equilibrium set between finite- and infinite-horizon games reveals a fundamental difficulty in doing so.

Consider a stage game with a unique equilibrium, such as the prisoners' dilemma game. The Folk theorem establishes that if the game is repeated an infinite number of periods and the players are sufficiently patient (i.e., if they place a high weight on future periods' rewards), cooperation can be sustained by conditioning future cooperation on past cooperation. Cheating implies gaining today but losing all gains from future cooperation.

If such a stage game is repeated a finite number of periods, cooperation based on the promise of future reward from cooperation cannot be sustained – it is not an equilibrium outcome. Intuitively, the best one can do in the last period is to cheat. After all, a player cannot be punished for cheating in the future if the game ends. Expecting cheating, the other player will not cooperate either. Anticipating that neither player will cooperate in the last period, the best each player can do is to cheat in the next-to-last period. Following this logic, the equilibrium continues to unravel backward in this manner, implying that cooperation in any period is not an equilibrium outcome. This is the end-game problem.

In general, uncertainty can mitigate the end-game problem, because the infinite-horizon game is analytically equivalent to a game with an uncertain final period. Specifically, when there is a constant or sufficiently low per-period probability that the repeated game will be terminated at the end of each period, the repeated game is analytically equivalent to one in which the stage game is infinitely repeated. The only impact of the uncertainty is to decrease the time discount factor (Telser 1980). In this case, although the game will certainly end at some point, uncertainty about the final period implies that there are always (expected) gains from future cooperation that can be lost due to cheating.

The possible importance of this factor in sustaining cooperation based on the long hand of the future notwithstanding, individuals' horizons tend to become shorter in their old age – and old age is difficult to conceal. Hence the end-game problem becomes relevant when we model interactions among individuals. Institutions based on the future have to guarantee that the future is long enough. Understanding an institution based on future reward therefore requires identifying why there is still enough of a future reward to motivate honesty whenever one has to decide whether to cheat.

Theory suggests several ways to achieve this. The first, relevant particularly to one-sided prisoner's dilemma games, is altering the time profile of gains from cooperation.[6] The strategy specifies that, if one does not cheat, his share in the gains from cooperation will increase as time goes by, or he will get a bonus upon retirement. If commitment to such payments can be made, this strategy can be an equilibrium with cooperation. Such an endogenous alteration of the division of gains from cooperation can be done either by distributing the gains in the transaction under consideration (such as through wage payment in agency relationships) or by linking it to other transactions (such as social exchange).[7] In late medieval Genoa, for example, noble merchant families rewarded agents who had served them for years with marriage into the nobility.

Another way to mitigate the end-game problem in either one-sided prisoner's dilemma or prisoners' dilemma games is by endogenously linking the reputational considerations of individuals from different generations. Intertemporal linking of utility streams can create the equivalent of entities with infinite life-spans, or at least entities whose per period probability of survival is high enough to allow cooperation. When others condition their behavior on an individual's past conduct and the individual's welfare depends on this behavior, it is possible to motivate the individual to cooperate even in his last period. Families, dynasties, family firms, and other innate social units served as entities with infinite life-spans that mitigated the end-game problem for their members in many historical episodes. Among the Maghribi traders, a reputation-based institution was based on intergenerational linkages that took advantage of an individual's concern about his descendants' well-being despite his own finite life-span. In modeling the relationships between merchants and rulers in Chapter 4, I assumed that the ruler had an infinite horizon in order to capture the dynastic nature of the state during the period.

In modern economies, other endogenous entities, such as firms with identities distinct from that of their owners, play a similar role. Tadelis (1999, 2002) uses a model combining moral hazard and adverse selection to explore how organizations that separate identities from entities can

---

[6] This can also be done in asymmetric prisoners' dilemma games with transferable utilities.

[7] Technically, we study such linkages using finitely repeated games with complete information in which (unlike the prisoners' dilemma game) there are multiple equilibria in the stage game. For a classical analysis, see Benoit and Krishna (1985).

motivate individuals to cooperate in their old age. He assumes that a firm's reputation reflects the past ability and actions of its owner, who can sell the firm without the knowledge of the firm's clients. When buyers of the firms' products are willing to pay more for a product from a reputable firm than from another, reputation is valuable. Hence an owner of a reputable firm can find it optimal not to cheat in his old age, because the loss of reputation would decrease the value of the firm's name, an asset he can sell. The analysis also implicitly highlights the role of auxiliary organizations and the associated beliefs, such as those ensuring that a firm cannot adopt the name of another.

The end-game problem is an issue only with respect to players who can cheat. If a player who can cheat lives a long time and is sufficiently patient, there can be an equilibrium with cooperation even if the other players have short life-spans. Cooperation is based on the players with short lives conditioning their behavior on the other players' actions toward their predecessors.

To understand this causal effect, consider a game between a firm with an infinite life-span and its workers. Each worker is known to live for several periods, after which he dies and is replaced by another. This game is a version of the one-sided prisoner's dilemma game. In each period the workers can first decide whether to provide their labor as an input to the firm. If they do, the firm can decide whether to pay the promised wages. When each worker knows only his private history, the end-game problem implies that there is no equilibrium with the provision of labor input and wage payments, because the firm's optimal strategy is to not pay a worker in his last period. An equilibrium with the provision of labor and wage payment exists, however, if the firm's past conduct is public information among the workers and if the firm's expected future gains from production (after paying wages) is sufficiently high. In this equilibrium, the threat of future workers punishing the firm (by not working if it ever fails to pay a worker) motivates the firm to pay (see Bull 1987; Cremer 1986; Kreps 1990b; and Tadelis 1999, 2002).

Intergenerational links within an organization composed of overlapping generations of members can also mitigate the end-game problem in relationships among its members. Consider a situation in which individuals have a predetermined life-span. Every year the organization recruits a new member to replace one who just died. Members of the organization interact in a prisoners' dilemma type of situation by either contributing effort or not. Actions are observable. The best a member can do is to provide no effort in the period just before retiring. But in the last period, the member can still be rewarded or punished based on his effort. Hence a strategy in which young members work hard and older ones do not but are nevertheless compensated can support some (albeit not an optimal) level of cooperation. Younger workers are motivated to work hard and reward older workers who do not contribute effort because otherwise the play of the game will revert to no cooperation (Cremer 1986).

Organizations can also mitigate the end-game problem in interactions between organizations, as the analysis of the community responsibility system illustrates. Intergenerational relationships within communities were part of an institution that enabled these communities to commit to act as if they had infinite life-spans, even though they were concerned only with the welfare of their finitely lived members.

C.2.2   Endogenous Payoffs

A necessary condition for the promise of future reward to foster cooperation is that the net present value of the gain from cheating and the implied utility stream in the following periods be less than the net present value from cooperating. Understanding a reputation-based institution requires identifying the way in which this condition has been fulfilled endogenously. Reputation-based institutions manipulate one's gains from various actions and outside options to enable cooperation. Theory suggests various ways in which payoffs can be endogenously manipulated and the relationship between these payoffs and the environment.

Consider a situation in which employers and employees are randomly matched to play a one-sided prisoner's dilemma game. Past actions are private information, and there is some exogenous probability that the relationship between any employer and employee will terminate at the end of each period, even if the employee was honest. Hence in each period some merchants randomly hire agents from the pool of unemployed agents. Because there are more employees than employers, one can remain unemployed for some periods before being rehired.

In equilibrium with cooperation in which an employer fires an employee who cheated, each employer has to pay workers a wage that is high enough that the gain from cheating and then joining the pool of unemployed agents is lower than the expected wage from being honest and continuing to receive the wage. Wages and the unemployment rate are thus endogenously adjusted to create the right incentives. In equilibrium some employees are involuntarily unemployed, in the sense that they are willing to work for less than the equilibrium wage but are nevertheless not hired (Shapiro and Stiglitz 1984). Organizations that distribute information about employees' past conduct, however, can alter employees' outside options (following cheating in a particular relationship) by reducing the probability that a worker who cheated in the past will be hired (Greif 1989, 1993).

If the environment is such that there are more employers than employees and if wage contracts are legally enforceable, an employer cannot punish an employee by firing or not paying him. Because wages are legally enforceable, as long as past conduct is private information, an unemployed employee will be hired. In such cases an equilibrium with cooperation requires a different manipulation of utility streams. One option is to pay employees bonuses rather than wages (MacLeod and Malcomson 1989).

Another option is to create an endogenous sunk cost by "building relationships" among the two players interacting in a prisoners' dilemma game. Various means, such as posting bonds and exchanging gifts, can be used ex ante to increase the ex post cost of cheating implied by the need to establish new relationships.[8] While theory affirms this intuition, it also highlights the important role that incomplete information plays in making an investment in building relationships an equilibrium outcome.

To see why this is the case, suppose that the endogenous sunk cost of building relationships is achieved in the following way. Once two particular players are matched, they can choose whether to play a high-payoff or low-payoff prisoners' dilemma game in each period. In the high-payoff game, a player can lose more if cheated. The players can thus invest in their relationships by playing the low-payoff game for some period. After these periods of reduced utility to both players, they begin to cooperate to the fullest possible extent. If the players' strategies call for such investment whenever new relationships are formed, cheating entails having to invest in building a relationship with another player.

These intuitive strategies are not part of an equilibrium, because two newly matched agents have an incentive to forgo paying this bond, given that everyone else in the population requires it. After all, it is the need to pay the bond in the next new relationship following cheating that contributes to deterring cheating in the present relationship. But because

---

[8] Note, however, that posting a bond creates a one-sided prisoner's dilemma situation. Once an employee posts a bond, the employer can expropriate it and hire another agent. In many cases bonds are placed in the hands of a third party (such as an escrow company), whose actions are disciplined by either the legal system or reputational concerns.

this is true for everyone, no one has the incentive to post the bond. Hence there is no equilibrium with an endogenous cost of building relationships. This problem disappears, however, if there is a sufficiently high probability that an individual is a "bad" type, who will cheat in either game. If one's type is unobservable, this uncertainty motivates each player to first verify the other's type by playing the lower-payoff game (Kranton 1996; see also Ghosh and Ray 1996 and Watson 1999).

Organizations also play a part in endogenously altering payoffs. In the late medieval period, nonrefundable entry fees to merchant and other guilds, which had a monopoly over certain trade and crafts, arguably enabled intraguild cooperation that otherwise would not have been possible. Regulations for entry and exit play a similar role in modern economies. In modern economies, organizations manipulate the ownership of resources to enable them to commit to provide high-quality service. This is possible when this ownership fosters the ability of the organization's clients to punish it when necessary. Hotel chains, for example, purchase independent hotels, thereby increasing their clients' ability to punish them if they fail to provide good service. Following mediocre performance by one hotel in the chain, the client can refrain from using the other hotels in the chain (Ingram 1996).

More generally, manipulation of payoffs can be achieved by linking the central transaction – modeled as a prisoners' dilemma or a one-sided prisoner's dilemma game – with other transactions. Social exchange, norms, and violence often play a role in achieving this. Social, psychological, and physical harassment of a cheater can be a means to alter payoffs to deter cheating.[9]

The details of the underlying transaction have another important ramification for the manipulation of payoffs required for cooperation. The preceding discussion implicitly assumed that cheating in one period does not directly influence an individual's utility or possible actions in future periods. In particular, it was implicitly assumed that a cheater "consumes" the gains from doing so at the end of the period in which he cheats. But cheating often implies obtaining an investment good that can be used to change one's payoffs in subsequent periods. Among the Maghribis, for example, an agent who cheated gained capital, which he had the ability, knowledge, and opportunity to invest in future periods. Reputation-based institutions supporting cooperation in such situations therefore have to

---

[9] See Wiessner (2002) for the role of gossip among African bush women of low social rank in disciplining high-ranked men who deviate from the groups' norms.

ensure that honesty is profitable, despite the higher gain from cheating. The Maghribis did so by having agents invest their own capital through other agents, who, in turn, were not expected to be punished for cheating an agent who had himself cheated in the past.

C.2.3 Credibility

Understanding the effectiveness of a reputation-based institution requires understanding how the promise and threat of various actions are made credible. Unless the (implicit) promise to continue hiring an honest agent is credible, the best thing for the agent to do is cheat. Symmetrically, if the agent cannot commit to refrain from cheating and establishing new relationships, no merchant will hire him. Most of the generic theoretical insights about how the credibility of continuing relationships is achieved were discussed earlier in connection with the endogenous manipulation of payoffs.

As we have seen in the case of the Maghribis, understanding this credibility is an integral part of the analysis. Among the Maghribis, merchants could have committed to continue hiring intragroup agents, because the collective punishment entailed that the wage premium required to keep an agent honest was lower within the group than outside. Arguably, agents could have committed to retain their affiliation with the group because of the higher expected income from agency relationships (due to the higher probability of being employed) and the capital premium.[10]

Game theory is very useful in identifying the conditions under which the threat of punishment following cheating is credible, because it highlights the distinction between the Nash equilibrium and the subgame perfect equilibrium. A subgame perfect equilibrium is a Nash equilibrium that satisfies the additional condition that it is a Nash equilibrium in every proper subgame. In particular, for threats and promises to be credible, behavior off-the-equilibrium-path has to constitute a Nash equilibrium (see Appendix A, section A.3).

A generic insight of game theory is that punishment is credible if the players' strategies entail a transition to an equilibrium in the stage (one-period) game in the case of punishment.[11] In the case of a prisoners'

---

[10] As noted in Chapter 3, this assertion cannot be empirically substantiated, but the theoretical possibility that this was the case increased confidence in the identification of the coalition.

[11] More generally, the punishment is credible and may deter cheating if it entails a transition to an equilibrium with a lower payoff for one who is to be punished.

dilemma game, this is the (unique) equilibrium, in which both players cheat. The credibility of a promise to be honest can also be fostered by the nature of the goods exchanged. Indeed, in contemporary international trade, barter is commonly used for exactly this purpose (Marin and Schnitzer 1995).

C.2.4 Credibility and Multilateral (Third-Party) Punishment

Of particular interest and importance to institutional analysis is the credibility of punishments and rewards in reputation-based institutions in which punishments and rewards are provided by a third party, namely, an individual who is not a party to the central transaction the institution governs. Such reputation-based institutions are usually able to support more cooperation than bilateral relationships, as we have seen in the case of the Maghribi traders. Multilateral punishment usually implies a harsher punishment than a bilateral one, enabling cooperation in a wider range of parameters.[12]

The problem of credibility of punishment is more severe in cases of multilateral punishment. Why would one punish an individual who had not hurt him? How is a threat of collective punishment made credible? Without denying the possible importance of such motivational factors as contempt, disgust, and desire to punish one who acted unfairly toward others, game theory draws attention to additional factors. In the case of incomplete information, one is motivated to participate in collective punishment because cheating reveals that an individual is a "bad" type. An employer would not hire a worker who had already revealed himself as a "bad" type, because he would expect the worker to cheat him as well. When collective punishment is based on incomplete information, individuals are motivated to acquire information about who has cheated in the past.

Complete-information models reveal other ways to motivate individuals to participate in collective punishments. In prisoners' dilemma games, individuals can be motivated to participate in punishing individuals who did not cheat them by the threat that failing to do so will invoke punishment from others. The equilibrium strategy is not to cooperate with a

---

[12] For an exception, see Bendor and Mookherjee (1990). When a player is simultaneously involved in many bilateral games, if all games are identical, multilateral punishment cannot support cooperation if it cannot be supported in each of the separate games based on bilateral punishment.

player who has either cheated in the past or has failed to punish someone who cheated in the past. This "second-order punishment" has to be supported by yet higher punishment orders for cheating someone who failed to punish someone who failed to punish and so forth.

Second-order punishment is not effective in one-sided prisoner's dilemma games, which – unlike the prisoners' dilemma game – have an asymmetric structure. In a one-sided prisoner's dilemma game, there are two types of players (e.g., merchants and agents), and matching is always between individuals of different types. Hence in the merchant-agent game, a merchant always plays with an agent. A merchant therefore cannot directly punish another merchant by refusing to cooperate with him.

Multilateral punishment in such situations can be achieved in two other main ways. The first is by not punishing an agent who cheated a merchant who failed to punish an agent. The second is by linking the basic transaction, which we capture in the one-sided prisoner's dilemma game, with another transaction. The merchant guild provides a historical example of this strategy and linkage. A merchant who did not participate in punishing someone who did not respect the merchant's property rights abroad was excluded from using the guild's ships for transporting his goods; another merchant who carried the excluded goods in these ships as if they were his own was subject to fine. Theory thus reveals the relationships between the features of the underlying central transaction and the feasibility and nature of a reputation-based institution based on collective punishment.

Other strategies can also be used to make the threat of collective punishment credible. A difficulty in inducing collective punishment in prisoners' dilemma games (without relying on second-order punishment) is that punishment based on reverting to the stage-game equilibrium in which both parties cheat is costly to the one who inflicts the punishment. One way to mitigate this problem is through a strategy in which an individual participates in his own punishment (Kandori 1992; Ellison 1994). In such a strategy, an individual who cheated in the past is supposed to cooperate with the one who punishes him by cheating. Hence the one who punishes is motivated to do so because it is profitable. Punishing entails receiving the payoff associated with cheating while the other cooperates. But why would a cheater cooperate in his punishment rather than continue to cheat? Motivation can be provided by making the punishment phase finite in length. After participating in his own punishment for a while, a cheater is "forgiven," and the players' strategies call for cooperating with him as if he had never cheated. He is induced to participate in his own punishment by the expected gains from future forgiveness. Others are motivated to participate in punishing him because they directly benefit from doing so, as they cheat while he cooperates in the punishment phase.

These analytical results were in games without transferable utilities – that is, in situations in which the distribution of the gains from cooperation (within a stage game) cannot be determined by the interacting individuals. These games assume that matching is random – individuals cannot choose whom they interact with and can thus not decide whether they want to be matched with someone who had previously cheated.

Greif (1989, 1993) considers a one-sided prisoner's dilemma game in which utilities are transferable and individuals have some control over whom they interact with. In addition, the analysis incorporated the assumption that the relationship between a particular merchant and agent can end exogenously even if the agent was honest. In this case, as we have seen in Chapter 3, there is yet another way to support collective punishment. In equilibrium, the wage required to keep an honest agent is lower under the threat of collective punishment than under bilateral punishment. This is the case because the worst punishment that can be inflicted on any agent is the same: total exclusion from future interactions. But one who has been honest in the past has more to gain from future interactions. Once his relationship with the current merchant ends, he will be hired by another merchant with a positive probability, earning the equilibrium wage. Because the equilibrium wage is higher than an agent's income if he is unemployed, an agent who has never cheated in the past has more to lose from cheating. But if the wage that has to be paid to an agent who cheated someone else in the past is higher than that paid to an agent who did not cheat, every merchant has an incentive to hire an agent who has been honest in the past.

C.2.5 Renegotiation

The discussion of the credibility of punishments ignores another important theoretical insight into the nature of reputation-based institutions – renegotiation by the interacting individuals. It might intuitively be assumed that renegotiation, in which the players decide on how the game will be played after a given history, would improve welfare. In fact, theory indicates that it can undermine it. To see why this is the case, consider a prisoners' dilemma game and recall that to induce cooperation, punishment from cheating requires a transition to an equilibrium in the stage game in which the total payoff is lower than when the players cooperate. When renegotiation during this punishment phase is possible, both parties have a strong incentive to let bygones be bygones and resume cooperation. But if this is known ex ante, it decreases the punishment from cheating, implying that the original cooperative equilibrium cannot be sustained. If cooperation will be resumed after cheating, why not cheat?

Theory suggests that attention should be given to why the possibility of renegotiation does not undermine cooperation to begin with. The historical analyses illustrate two basic reasons why this can be the case. Among the Maghribis, renegotiation was not an issue for two interrelated reasons. First, because the "market" for agents was thick – many agents were active in each trade center and they were substitutes for each other – a merchant could switch agents at little cost. Second, a merchant had to pay a strictly higher wage to an agent who had cheated in the past than to an agent who had never cheated, because every merchant's strategy specified that no one would hire an agent who had cheated in the past and because agency relationships between a particular merchant and agent could have been terminated for exogenous reasons. This was the case because an agent who did not expect to be hired by others would not expect to lose future gains from serving them as an agent in the future. Because the punishment is lower, a higher wage premium had to be paid to keep an agent honest.

The merchant guild reflects another response to the problem of renegotiation. In this case, the problem of renegotiation expressed itself as a free-rider problem, in which some merchants would trade with a ruler during an embargo. The maximum punishment that could be inflicted upon the ruler following an abuse of rights was switching to the one-stage-game equilibrium of no trade and abuse of rights if a merchant traded. But this equilibrium yields lower payoffs to both the ruler and the merchants than an equilibrium in which some merchants do trade while their property rights are secured because of the low level of trade during an embargo. This low level of trade implies that the ruler's gain from taxing merchants is sufficiently high to motivate him to respect their property rights under the threat that they would not return to trade if their rights were abused. Switching to this equilibrium, however, undermines the severity of the punishment that can be inflicted on a ruler following an abuse of rights in the optimal level of trade. The response to this problem was an organizational change that linked the ruler-merchant transaction with one among the merchants themselves. The organization of the merchant guild used coercive power to punish a merchant who traded during an embargo.

C.2.6 *Endogenous Information*

Theory also highlights the details of the information required for a reputation mechanism to function. Multilateral punishment depends critically on the ability of those who are supposed to punish to identify the one who is to be punished. Theory indicates that sufficient information for collective punishment can be contained in a "label" indicating whether one's status is that of one who has to be punished or not (Kandori 1992). In addition, a cheated agent must be motivated to make the cheating known and those who punish must be motivated to acquire this information, even though both actions are likely to be costly. The endogenous generation and transmission of such information and motivation is an integral part of how an institution functions.

Such information may be readily available to the interacting individuals if interactions are confined to a relatively small group, particularly if these individuals also interact socially. Throughout most of history interactions within such groups, intertransactional linkages within them, and the associated beliefs and norms provided information and provided motivation to transmit, acquire, and act on it. But when such information is based on personal familiarity, as existed among the Maghribis, for example, cooperation is limited by the extent to and speed at which the social network can transmit information.[13]

More generally, the manner in which such information is circulated and motivation is provided influences the extent (in terms of the number of interacting individuals and the amount one is willing to entrust to the other) to which the threat of collective punishment is credible. One of the main institutional transitions in the modern, economically developed world has been the introduction of institutional elements that enabled more impersonal exchange to prevail among more individuals. The regulations of personal identities by the state, identification cards, passports,

---

[13] Reputation-based institutions face a trade-off between the benefits of a larger network, which enables more benefit from cooperation, and the delay and cost of information transmission that this larger size entails. Technically, we can capture the additional information cost of the larger size by making the time discount factor a decreasing function of size: the larger the group, the more time it takes for the information about cheating to be diffused.

credit bureaus, and credit cards are among the institutional innovations that enabled individuals to identify themselves credibly to strangers and provide information regarding their past conduct.

For a multilateral reputation mechanism to function, individuals have to be induced to transmit information. Why would an individual who has been cheated in the past inform others that someone had cheated him? Knowing that no one would cheat on the equilibrium path, why would anyone invest in gaining access to an information network or gathering current information?

The motivation to inform others that an individual had cheated depends critically on the relationships among the players who are supposed to punish a cheater. Competition among those who are supposed to punish reduces the motivation to provide such information. The Maghribis were not in competition with one another. Because they sold their goods in competitive markets, one merchant's loss was not another's gain. Because informing others that a particular agent cheated did not lower the payoff of the merchant who informed, a merchant had nothing to lose from informing on a cheater. The thick information networks and constant business communication among the traders made the cost of supplying this information negligible. This would not be the case among producers or merchants competing with one another in a "thin" market in which a reduction in the economic activity of one is another's gain.

Similarly, for collective punishment to be credible, individuals have to be motivated to acquire the necessary information. If people do not know whom to punish, the threat of punishment is not credible. Motivating individuals to acquire information is trivial when the situation is one of incomplete information and they are motivated to acquire information about a new partner's past conduct. Motivating individuals to acquire information is more problematic in situations in which cheating is not supposed to occur on the equilibrium path or the probability of its occurring is so low that investing in information is not worthwhile.

These considerations highlight the importance of what can be called a secondary information network – namely, an information network to which one is motivated to acquire access, irrespective of considerations about cheating. Among the Maghribis, traders were motivated to retain an information network because it was valuable to gather commerce-related information in general. Geographical proximity and constant interactions in social or religious activities are among the other reasons why an independent network may exist. Both factors are present in the case of the Jewish diamond traders of New York (Bernstein 1992).

Organizations specializing in soliciting and distributing information can also provide individuals with the incentive to acquire the information required for multilateral punishment. The article by Milgrom et al. (1990) discussed in Chapter 10 analyzes the role of such organizations. The authors consider an infinitely repeated game in which two players are matched only once to play a prisoners' dilemma game and the players do not share the social network required to make past actions known to all. They then enrich the game by introducing an organization capable of verifying past actions and keeping records of those who cheated in the past. Acquiring information and appealing to the organization is costly for each player. Despite these costs, there exists a (symmetric sequential) equilibrium in which cheating does not occur and players are induced to provide the court with the information required to support cooperation. The court's ability to activate a multilateral reputation mechanism by controlling information provides the appropriate incentives. Hence an organization can ensure contract enforcement over time even if it cannot use coercive power against cheaters by supplementing the operation of a reputation mechanism.[14]

Not all situations require information flows for the threat of multilateral punishment to be effective. Kandori (1992) and Ellison (1994) consider a situation in which players with infinite life-spans are randomly matched each period to play a prisoners' dilemma game. Bilateral punishment cannot sustain cooperation, and past cheating is private information. Nevertheless, cooperation may be possible based on a contagious equilibrium. The strategy in this equilibrium is for every player to cheat subsequently if he either cheated or was cheated in the past. Cheating thus leads to a total collapse of cooperation.

Equilibria constructed in this manner are not very reasonable, because any unintentional or perceived cheating or cheating by one "bad apple" leads to a transition to a punishment phase.[15] Furthermore, such equilibria do not exist in one-sided prisoner's dilemma games. For the fear of punishment to prevent cheating, a player's utility during the punishment phase has to be lower than it would have been had cooperation taken place during this phase. So why would an individual start cheating after having been cheated? In the prisoners' dilemma game, a player

---

[14] Today such organizations as credit bureaus and Verisign fulfill such functions (Greif 2000).

[15] It is possible to get out of this state if everyone switches to cooperating again at some future time. This requires coordination among players who lack the ability to communicate, however.

cheats after having cheated or having been cheated because he expects the other player to continue cheating as well; if this is the case, the best he can do is to cheat. In one-sided prisoner's dilemma games, however, only one individual can cheat.[16] Thus no individual can be motivated to continue cheating by the expectation that the other player will do so as well.

C.2.7 Imperfect Monitoring

The discussion so far has assumed perfect monitoring in which, in particular, one knows ex post with certainty the actions of the person one played against. Those who are supposed to punish a cheater can verify if cheating indeed occurred. Reality, however, is often characterized by imperfect monitoring.

Imperfect monitoring is a situation in which actions are not directly observed (see Appendix A, section A.3). One can deduct others' actions from a signal that is not perfectly correlated with these actions. If one player took a particular action, the signal indicates that it was taken with a higher probability than if it was not taken. But because the signal is only probabilistic, it can still indicate that this action was not taken. Players can thus receive a false impression about others' past behavior.[17]

The basic insights of games with perfect monitoring are relevant to games with imperfect monitoring, with one important addition. On the path of an equilibrium with cooperation, although no one actually cheats, (finite) periods of punishment nevertheless occur when cheating is signaled. The intuition is that if one's strategy does not specify punishment after observing cheating, then the best response of other players is to cheat, implying that cooperation cannot be sustained. To support cooperation, after observing a signal that cheating has occurred, each player has to punish the specified player, even if it is known that he did not cheat.

---

[16] The assumption is that the one who was cheated drops out of the game.

[17] The classical work on imperfect monitoring games is Green and Porter (1984). See also Abreu et al. (1986); Abreu, Milgrom, and Pearce (1991); and Fudenberg, Levine, and Maskin (1994). For recent surveys, see Pearce (1995) and Kandori (2002) and the articles by Bhaskar, van Damme, Piccione and Ely, Valimaki, Compte, Mailath, Morris, and Aoyagi in the January 2002 issue of the *Journal of Economic Theory*. For applications for institutional analysis, see Clay (1997) and Maurer and Sharma (2002).

C.2.8 *Endogenous Intertransactional Linkages and Organizations*

The preceding discussion focused on a particular intertransactional link: that among the same central transaction in different time periods. In reputation-based institutions, the interacting individuals can link other transactions, thereby changing the set of beliefs in the central transaction under consideration. This is the case, for example, when one harasses or uses violence against someone who cheated him. Organizations also play an important role in facilitating the operation of reputation-based institutions by linking transactions. Organizations – either informal ones, such as social networks and communities, or formal ones, such as credit bureaus and guilds – change the set of self-enforcing beliefs in the central transaction in various ways. We have seen that organizations representing infinite-horizon players enable individuals to commit despite their finite life-spans. Organizations can also increase the frequency of interactions and internalize the cost of cheating inflicted by one player on others. In addition, they acquire, store, and distribute information; produce and propagate the meaning of various actions; provide a uniform interpretation of past actions; and coordinate behavior by providing public signals.

Organizations can also reduce the expected cost of imposing and participating in a punishment. They can be an appropriately motivated third party required to verify past actions, to arbitrate, and to enable the players to compensate one another during disputes in a Pareto-improving manner (by avoiding costly punishment). Indeed, within an institution organizations can be relevant for the endogenous construction of future rewards and payoffs, enhancing the credibility of maintaining relationships and threats of future punishment, preventing renegotiation following cheating, generating and distributing information, and improving monitoring.

An important class of organizations not mentioned so far comprises those which serve as intermediaries with a greater ability to commit. In modern economies, credit card companies, escrow accounts, cash against document contracts, and cashier's checks are among the organizations and instruments used for this purpose. The implied enhanced ability to commit is endogenously achieved because the organization both increases the frequency of interactions and creates an infinite-horizon player. Instead of transacting with other players, each player involved in the original transaction interacts with the organization.

Consider the operation of a credit card company. The exchange between a seller and a buyer is replaced by an exchange between the seller and the credit card company and between the credit card company and the buyer. The credibility of the payment from the credit card company to the seller is based on the public institutions that enable it to commit. The credibility of the payment from the buyer to the credit card company is based partly on the company's ability to taint the buyer's credit rating.

Organizations, however, are made up of individuals. Understanding their behavior and implications therefore requires considering the motivation and ability of these individuals to take various actions (see Chapter 5). An important generic theoretical insight is that in reputation-based institutions, an organization's motivation to act in a manner that fosters cooperation may reflect its concern with its own profitability and reputation. *Consumer Reports* commits to provide dependable information, because otherwise readers would not continue to buy it. Stock exchanges are motivated to monitor the accuracy of the information provided by the firms that trade in them, because otherwise people may be less willing to purchase stocks.

C.2.9   *The Costs of Reputation-Based Institutions*

Reputation-based institutions are not free. Their operation often depends on costly organizations, and their capacities and operation rely on and create barriers to engaging in various activities.

The following examples illustrate such costs. In an institution based on the expectation of multilateral punishment, a player will be honest, fearing the response of all members of the group. The expected length of his relationship with any particular individual within that group is thus less important than under bilateral punishment. If there are efficiency gains from frequently changing the people with whom one interacts, these changes will occur only within the group. In contrast, in an institution based on investment in the sunk cost of establishing bilateral relationships, once these costs are sunk one would refrain from establishing new relationships, even if they were more efficient and therefore generated a larger surplus to divide. Sunk costs create a wedge between efficient and profitable relationships. If a new seller arrives offering a potential buyer the same goods at a lower price, the buyer may nevertheless refrain from establishing a relationship with him, because doing so would require making another sunk investment in establishing a relationship.[18]

The discussion here, however, is not directly concerned with the costs of reputation-based institutions. Instead, the concern is with the ability to use the observable implications of such costs, as revealed by generic theoretical insights, to help identify an institution. Indeed, the distinct behavioral implications of the costs associated with each of these two institutions fosters the ability to identify them empirically.

C.3 CONCLUDING COMMENTS

The preceding discussion highlights the contributions of theoretical insights in facilitating the forming and substantiating of conjecture regarding the relevance of a particular institution. The basic game-theoretic insights that cooperation, for example, is possible if interactions are of an infinite duration and the players are sufficiently patient, is the institutional analysis's initial observation rather than its conclusion. It sets the stage for evaluating whether the conditions required for the operation of this mechanism are in place and in what form. In conducting an interactive analysis aimed at such an evaluation, there is a constant feedback from evidence to theory and from theory to evidence. We use theory to delineate various possibilities and the conditions conducive to the existence and functioning of a particular institution; we use evidence to direct the analysis toward particular issues and possibilities rather than others.

In using theory to consider various possibilities, it is imperative to be attentive to the possible importance of factors outside that theory. In the case of private-order, reputation-based institutions, there are often complementarities between them and public-order (and, more generally, coercion-based) institutions. Institutions based only on reputation are particularly important when actions cannot be verified by the court (as was the case among the Maghribis) or when the interacting individuals involved are also those who control the court (as was the case with the merchant guild). But even in such circumstances public-order institutions can nevertheless play an important role in the operation of private-order institutions. In the case of the merchant guild, for example, a ruler's

---

[18] Fafchamps (2004) reports such behavior in contemporary Africa. For analyses of the costs of reputation-based institutions, see Kranton (1996); Kali (1999); Dasgupta (2000); and Annen (2003).

ability to control the use of violence in his domain was crucial for the operation of a reputation-based institution between him and foreign merchants. The theory of such complementarities is not well developed, however. In attempting to identify an institution generating behavior in a particular central transaction, it is therefore important to keep in mind that its institutional elements may have both private-order, reputation-based and public-order, coercion-based components. In identifying reputation-based private-order institutions in particular, it is useful to consider their possible reliance on and interactions with public-order institutions.

References

Abercrombie, Nicholas, Stephen Hill, and Bryan S. Turner. 1994. *The Dictionary of Sociology*. 3rd ed. London: Penguin Group.

Abou El Fadl, Khaled. 2001. *Rebellion and Violence in Islamic Law*. Cambridge: Cambridge University Press.

Abramovitz, M. 1986. "Catching Up, Forging Ahead, and Falling Behind." *Journal of Economic History* 46 (2): 385–406.

Abreu, Dilip. 1988. "On the Theory of Infinitely Repeated Games with Discounting." *Econometrica* 56: 383–96.

Abreu, Dilip, Paul R. Milgrom, and David G. Pearce. 1991. "Information and Timing in Repeated Partnerships." *Econometrica* 59 (6): 1713–33.

Abreu, Dilip, David G. Pearce, and Ennio Stacchetti. 1986. "Optimal Cartel Equilibria with Imperfect Monitoring." *Journal of Economic Theory* 39 (June): 251–69.

Abulafia, David. 1977. *The Two Italies*. Cambridge: Cambridge University Press.

——— 1985. "Catalan Merchants and the Western Mediterranean, 1236–1300: Studies in the Notarial Acts of Barcelona and Sicily." *Viator* 16: 209–42.

Abu-Lughod, Janet. 1991. *Before European Hegemony: The World System, A.D. 1250–1350*. Oxford: Oxford University Press.

Acemoglu, Daron, Simon Johnson, and James A. Robinson. 2001. "The Colonial Origins of Comparative Development: An Empirical Investigation." *American Economic Review* 91 (Dec.): 1369–1401.

——— 2002. "The Rise of Europe: Atlantic Trade, Institutional Change and Economic Growth." Memo, MIT.

Acemoglu, Daron, and James A. Robinson. 2000. "Political Losers as a Barrier to Economic Development." *AEA Papers and Proceedings* 90: 126–30.

Airaldi, Gabriella. 1983. "Groping in the Dark: The Emergence of Genoa in the Early Middle Ages." *Miscellanea di Studi Storia* 2: 7–17.

——— 1986. *Genova e la Liguria nel Medioevo*. Turin: Utet Libreria.

Akerlof, George A. 1986. *An Economic Theorist's Book of Tales*. Cambridge: Cambridge University Press.

Akerlof, George A., and R. E. Kranton. 2000. "Economics and Identity." *Quarterly Journal of Economics* 115 (3): 715–53.

Akerlof, George A., and Janet L. Yellen. 1986. *Efficiency Wage Models of the Labor Market.* Cambridge: Cambridge University Press.

AlSayyad, Nezar. 1991. *Cities and Caliphs: On the Genesis of Arab Muslim Urbanism.* New York: Greenwood.

Andreoni, James, and John Miller. 2002. "Giving According to GARP: An Experimental Test of the Consistency of Preferences for Altruism." *Econometrica* 70 (2): 737–53.

Annali Genovesi di Caffaro e dei suoi Continuatori. 1099–1240. Trans. Ceccardo Roccatagliata Ceccardi and Giovanni Monleone. 4 vols. Genoa: Municipio di Genova, 1923–29.

Annen, Kurt. 2003. "Social Capital, Inclusive Networks, and Economic Performance." *Journal of Economic Behavior and Organization* 50 (4): 449–63.

Aoki, Masahiko. 1994. "The Contingent Governance of Teams: Analysis of Institutional Complementarity." *International Economic Review* 35 (3): 657–76.

2001. *Toward a Comparative Institutional Analysis.* Cambridge, MA: MIT Press.

Arias, G. 1901. *I trattati commerciali della Repubblica Fiorentina.* Florence: Successori le Monnier.

Aron, J. 2000. "Growth and Institutions: A Review of the Evidence." *World Bank Research Observer* 15 (1): 99–135.

Arrow, Kenneth J. 1974. *The Limits of Organization.* New York: Norton.

1981. "Optimal and Voluntary Income Redistribution." In Steven Rosenfield (ed.), *Economic Welfare and the Economics of Soviet Socialism: Essays in Honor of Abram Bergson,* 267–88. Cambridge: Cambridge University Press.

Arthur, Brian W. 1988. "Self-Reinforcing Mechanisms in Economics." In K. J. Arrow and P. Anderson (eds.), *The Economy as an Evolving Complex System,* 9–33. New York: Wiley.

1994. *Increasing Returns and Path Dependence in the Economy.* Ann Arbor: University of Michigan Press.

Ashburner, M., and A. Walter. 1909. *The Rodian Sea-Law.* Oxford: Clarendon Press.

Aumann, Robert J. 1987. "Game Theory." In J. Eatwell, M. Milgate, and P. Newman (eds.), *The New Palgrave: A Dictionary of Economics* 2: 460–82. London: Macmillan.

Aumann, Robert J., and Adam Brandenburger. 1995. "Epistemic Conditions for Nash Equilibrium." *Econometrica* 65 (5): 1161–80.

Aumann, Robert J., and Sergiu Hart (eds.). 1994, 2002. *Handbook of Game Theory with Economic Implications.* Vols. 2, 3. North Holland: Elsevier Science Publishers.

Bairoch, Paul, Jean Batou, and Pierre Chèvre (eds.). 1988. *The Population of European Cities from 800 to 1850.* Geneva: Center of International Economic History.

Baliga, Sandeep, and Ben Polak. 2004. "The Emergence and Persistence of the Anglo-Saxon and German Financial Systems." *Review of Financial Studies* 17 (1): 129–63.

Ball, R. 2001. "Individualism, Collectivism, and Economic Development." *Annals of the American Academy of Political and Social Science* 573 (Jan.): 57–84.

Ballard, Adolphus, and James Tait (eds.). 1913. *British Borough Charters, 1042–1216*. Cambridge: Cambridge University Press.

(eds.). 1923. *British Borough Charters, 1216–1307*. Cambridge: Cambridge University Press.

Bandura, A. 1971. *Social Learning Theory*. Englewood Cliffs, NJ: Prentice-Hall.

Banerjee, A. V., and A. F. Newman. 1993. "Occupational Choice and the Process of Development." *Journal of Political Economy* 101 (2): 274–98.

Banks, Jeffrey S., and Randall L. Calvert. 1989. "Communication and Efficiency in Coordination Games." Working Paper No. 196. Department of Political Science, University of Rochester.

Barbadoro, Bernardino. 1921. *Consigli della Reppublica Fiorentina*. Bologna: R. Accademia dei Lincei, Forni Editore.

Bardhan, Pranab. 1991. "Alternative Approaches to the Theory of Institutions in Economic Development." In Pranab Bardhan (ed.), *The Economic Theory of Agrarian Institutions*, 3–17. Oxford: Clarendon Press.

Barzel, Yoram. 1989. *Economic Analysis of Property Rights*. Cambridge: Cambridge University Press.

2002. *A Theory of the State*. Cambridge: Cambridge University Press.

Bates, Robert H. 2001. *Prosperity and Violence: The Political Economy of Development*. New York: Norton.

Bates, Robert H., R. J. P. de Figueiredo, and B. R. Weingast. 1998. "The Politics of Interpretation: Rationality, Culture, and Transition." *Politics & Society* 26 (4): 603–42.

Bates, Robert H., Avner Greif, Margaret Levi, Jean-Laurent Rosenthal, and Barry Weingast. 1998. *Analytic Narrative*. Princeton, NJ: Princeton University Press.

Bates, Robert H., Avner Greif, and Smita Singh. 2002. "Organizing Violence." *Journal of Conflict Resolution* 46 (5): 599–628.

Becker, Gary S. 1974. "A Theory of Social Interactions." *Journal of Political Economy* 82: 1963–93.

Belgrano, Luigi T. 1873. *Tavole genealogiche a corredo della illustrazione del registro arcivescovile de Genova*. Genoa: Atti della Società Ligure di Storia Patria.

Bellah, Robert N., Richard Madsen, William M. Sullivan, Ann Swidler, and Steven M. Tipton. 1985. *Habits of the Heart: Individualism and Commitment in American Life*. Berkeley: University of California Press.

Bellamy, John. 1973. *Crime and the Courts in England, 1660–1800*. Princeton, NJ: Princeton University Press.

Benabou, R. 1994. "Education, Income Distribution, and Growth: The Local Connection." Working paper, Department of Economics, Massachusetts Institute of Technology.

Bendor, Jonathan, and Dilip Mookherjee. 1990. "Norms, Third-Party Sanctions, and Cooperation." *Journal of Law, Economics, & Organization* 6 (Spring): 33–63.

References

Benjamin of Tudela. 1159–1173. *Itinerary.* Trans. Michael Singer, Marcus N. Adler, and A. Asher. Malibu, Calif.: Joseph Simon/Pangloss Press, 1987.

Ben-Ner, Avner, and Louis Putterman (eds.). 1998. *Economics, Values and Organization.* Cambridge: Cambridge University Press.

Benoit, Jean-Pierre, and Vijay Krishna. 1985. "Finitely Repeated Games." *Econometrica* 53 (4): 905–22.

Bensa, Enrico. 1925. *The Early History of Bills of Lading.* Genoa: Stabilimento D'arti Grafiche.

Ben-Sasson, Menahem. 1991. *The Jews of Sicily, 825–1068* (in Hebrew and Judeo-Arabic). Jerusalem: Ben-Zevi Institute.

Benson, Bruce L. 1989. "The Spontaneous Evolution of Commercial Law." *Southern Economic Journal* 55 (3): 644–61.

Beresford, M., and H. P. R. Finberg. 1973. *English Medieval Boroughs: A Handlist.* Newton Abbott: David and Charles.

Berger, Peter L. 1977. *Invitation to Sociology.* Harmondsworth: Penguin Books.

Berger, Peter L., and Thomas Luckmann. 1967. *The Social Construction of Reality.* New York: Anchor Books.

Berkowitz, Daniel, Katherian Pistor, and Jean-François Richard. 2003. "Economic Development, Legality, and the Transplant Effect." *European Economic Review* 47 (1): 165–95.

Berman, Harold J. 1983. *Law and Revolution: The Formation of the Western Legal Tradition.* Cambridge, MA: Harvard University Press.

Bernheim, B. Douglas. 1984. "Rationalizable Strategic Behavior." *Econometrica* 52 (4): 1007–28.

Bernheim, B. Douglas, and Debraj Ray. 1989. "Collective Dynamic Consistency in Dynamic Games." *Games and Economic Behavior* 1 (4): 295–326.

Bernheim, B. Douglas, and Michael D. Whinston. 1990. "Multi-market Contract and Collusive Behavior." *Rand Journal of Economics* 21 (1): 1–26.

Bernstein, L. 1992. "Opting Out the Legal System: Extralegal Contractual Relations in the Diamond Industry." *Journal of Legal Studies* 21 (Jan.): 115–57.

Bertolotto, Gerolamo. 1896. "Nuova serie di documenti sulle relazioni di Genova coll' Impero Bizantino." In *Atti della Società Ligure de Storia Patria, XXVIII.* Genoa: Società Ligure di Storia Patria.

Besley, Tim, and Stephen Coate. 1995. "Group Lending, Repayment Incentives and Social Collateral." *Journal of Development Economics* 46 (1): 1–18.

Bester, H., and W. Güth. 1998. "Is Altruism Evolutionarily Stable?" *Journal of Economic Behavior and Organization* 34: 193–209.

Binmore, Kenneth. 1996. "A Note on Backward Induction." *Games and Economic Behavior* 17 (1): 135–7.

Binmore, Kenneth, John Gale, and Larry Samuelson. 1995. "Learning to be Imperfect: The Ultimatum Game." *Games and Economic Behavior* 8: 56–90.

Bittles, Alan H. 1994. "The Role and Significance of Consanguinity as a Demographic Variable." *Population and Development Review* 20 (3): 561–84.

Blau, Joshua, 1961. *A Grammar of Medieval Judaeo-Arabic.* Jerusalem: Magnes Press.

1965. *The Emergence and Linguistic Background of Judaeo-Arabic.* London: Oxford University Press.

Bloch, Marc. 1961. *Feudal Society.* Vol. 1. Trans. L. A. Manyon. Chicago: University of Chicago Press.

Bohnet, Iris, and Bruno S. Frey. 1999. "Social Distance and Other-Regarding Behavior in Dictator Games: Comment." *American Economic Review* 89 (1): 335–9.

Bolton, Gary E., and Axel Ockenfels. 2000. "A Theory of Equity, Reciprocity and Competition." *American Economic Review* 90 (1): 166–93.

Bouman, F. J. A. 1995. "Rotating and Accumulating Savings and Credit Associations: A Development Perspective." *World Development* 23 (3): 371–84.

Bowles, Samuel, and Herbert Gintis. 1976. *Schooling in Capitalist America: Educational Reform and the Contradictions of Economic Life.* New York: Basic Books.

1998. "The Evolution of Strong Reciprocity." Santa Fe Institute Working Paper, 98-08-073E.

Brinton, Mary, and Victor Nee (eds.). 1998. *The New Institutionalism in Sociology.* New York: Russell Sage Foundation.

Britnell, R. H. 1996. *The Commercialisation of English Society, 1000–1500.* 2nd ed. New York: Manchester University Press.

Buchanan, James M. 1999. *The Collected Works of James M. Buchanan.* Fairfax, VA: Liberty Fund.

Bull, Clive. 1987. "The Existence of Self-Enforcing Implicit Contracts." *Quarterly Journal of Economics* 102 (1): 147–59.

Bulow, Jeremy, and Kenneth Rogoff. 1989. "A Constant Reconstracting Model of Sovereign Debt." *Journal of Political Economy* 97 (1): 155–78.

Byrne, Eugene H. 1916–17. "Commercial Contracts of the Genoese in the Syrian Trade of the Twelfth Century." *Quarterly Journal of Economics* 31: 128–70.

1920. "Genoese Trade with Syria in the Twelfth Century." *American Historical Review* 25: 191–219.

1928. "The Genoese Colonies in Syria." In L. J. Paetow (ed.), *The Crusade and Other Historical Essays*, 139–82. New York: F. S. Crofts.

Cahen, Claude. 1990. "Economy, Society, Institutions." In P. M. Holt, Ann K. S. Lambton, and Bernard Lewis (eds.), *The Cambridge History of Islam*, 511–38. Cambridge: Cambridge University Press.

Calendar of Letters from the Mayor and Corporation of the City of London. Circa A.D. 1350–60. Ed. Reginald R. Sharpe. London: Corporation of the City of London, 1885.

Calendar of Plea and Memoranda Rolls Preserved among the Archives of the Corporation of the City of London at the Guild Hall. 1926–61. Corporation of London. 6 vols. Cambridge: Cambridge University Press.

Calendar of the Patent Rolls Preserved in the Public Record Office. English Historical Documents. 1893–1910. 14 vols. London: His Majesty's Stationery Office.

References

Calvert, Randall L. 1992. "Leadership and Its Basis in Problems of Social Coordination." *International Political Science Review* 13 (1): 7–24.

——— 1995. "Rational Actors, Equilibrium, and Social Institutions." In Jack Knight and Itai Sened (eds.), *Explaining Social Institutions*, 57–93. Ann Arbor: University of Michigan Press.

Camerer, Colin, and Ari Vespsalaninen. 1987. "The Efficiency of Corporate Culture." Paper presented at the Colloquium on Strategy Content Research, The Wharton School, University of Pennsylvania.

Campos, N. F., and J. B. Nugent. 2002. "Who Is afraid of Political Instability?" *Journal of Development Economics* 67 (1): 157–72.

Cardini, Franco. 1978. "Profilo di un Crociato Guglielmo Embriaco." *Acrchivo Storico Italiano* 2–4: 405–36.

Carus-Wilson, E. M. 1967. *Medieval Merchant Venturers*. London: Butler and Tanner.

Casella, A., and J. E. Rauch. 2002. "Anonymous Market and Group Ties in International Trade." *Journal of International Economics* 58 (1): 19–47.

Catoni, Giuliano. 1976. "La brutta avventura di un mercante senese nel 1309 e una questione di rappresaglia." *Archivo Storico Italiano* 479: 65–77.

Cavalli-Sforza, Luigi L., and Marcus W. Feldman. 1981. *Cultural Transmission and Evolution*. Princeton, NJ: Princeton University Press.

Chamley, Christophe P. 2004. *Rational Herds: Economic Models of Social Learning*. Cambridge: Cambridge University Press.

Charness, Gary, and Brit Grosskopf. 2001. "Relative Payoffs and Happiness: An Experimental Study." *Journal of Economic Behavior and Organization* 45: 301–28.

Charness, Gary, and Matthew Rabin. 2002. "Understanding Social Preferences with Simple Tests." *Quarterly Journal of Economics* 117 (3): 817–69.

Christiani, Emilio. 1962. *Nobilta' e popolo nel Comune di Pisa*. Instituto Italiano per gli Studi Storici, 13. Milan: Casa Editrice Einaudi.

Chwe, Michael Suk Young. 2001. *Rational Ritual: Culture, Coordination, and Common Knowledge*. Princeton, NJ: Princeton University Press.

Cipolla, Carlo M. 1993. *Before the Industrial Revolution*. 3rd ed. New York: Norton.

Çizakça, Murat. 1996. *A Comparative Evolution of Business Partnerships*. Leiden: E. J. Brill.

Clark, Andy. 1997a. "Economic Reason: The Interplay of Individual Learning and External Structure." In John Drobak and John Nye (eds.), *The Frontiers of the New Institutional Economics*, 269–90. San Diego, CA: Academic Press.

——— 1997b. *Being There: Putting the Brain, Body, and World Togther Again*. Cambridge, MA: MIT Press.

Clark, Gregory. 1991. "Yields per Acre in English Agriculture, 1250–1860: Evidence from Labour Inputs." *Economic History Review* 44 (3): 445–60.

Clay, Karen. 1997. "Trade, Institutions, and Credit." *Explorations in Economic History* 34 (4): 495–521.

Close Rolls of the Reign of Henry III. 1227–72. 14 vols. London: His Majesty's Stationery Office, 1902–38.

Coase, Ronald H. 1937. "The Nature of the Firm." *Economica*, n.s., 4: 386–405.

Codice diplomatico della Repubblica di Genova dal MCLXIIII [sic] al MCL XXXX [sic]. 1936, 1938, 1942, Ed. Cesare Imperiale di Sant'Angelo. Vols. I–III. Rome: Tipografia del Senato.

Cole, Harold L., George J. Mailath, and Andrew Postlewaite. 1992. "Social Norms, Saving Behavior and Growth." *Journal of Political Economy* 100 (6): 1092–1125.

Coleman, James S. 1990. *Foundations of Social Theory*. Cambridge, MA: Harvard University Press.

Collier, David, and Ruth Collier. 1991. *Shaping the Political Arena*. Princeton, NJ: Princeton University Press.

Collins, Kathleen. 2004. "The Logic of Clan Politics – Evidence from Central Asian Trajectories." *World Politics* 56 (2): 224–61.

Colvin, Ian D. 1971. *The Germans in England, 1066–1598*. London: Kennikat Press.

Commons, John R. 1924. *Legal Foundations of Capitalism*. New York: Macmillan.

Conlisk, J. 1996. "Why Bounded Rationality?" *Journal of Economic Literature* 34 (2): 669–700.

Constable, R. Olivia. 2003. *Housing the Stranger in the Mediterranean World: Lodging, Trade, and Travel in Late Antiquity and the Middle Ages*. Cambridge: Cambridge University Press.

Cook, Mechael. 2003. *Forbidding Wrong in Islam*. Cambridge: Cambridge University Press.

Coulton, G. G. (ed.). 1918. *Social Life in Britain from the Conquest to the Reformation*. Cambridge: Cambridge University Press.

Crawford, S., and Elinor Ostrom. 1995. "A Grammar of Institutions." *American Political Review* 89 (3): 582–600.

Cremer, Jacques. 1986. "Cooperation in Ongoing Organizations." *Quarterly Journal of Economics* 101 (1): 33–49.

Crone, Patricia. 2002. *Roman, Provincial and Islamic Law*. Cambridge: Cambridge University Press.

　　2003. *Slaves on Horses*. Cambridge: Cambridge University Press.

　　2004. *God's Rule: Government and Islam*. New York: Columbia University Press.

D'Andrade, R. G. 1984. "Cultural Meaning Systems." In R. A. Shweder and R. A. LeVine (eds.), *Culture Theory: Essays on Mind, Self, and Emotion*, 88–122. Cambridge: Cambridge University Press.

Dasgupta, Partha. 2000. "Economic Progress and the Idea of Social Capital." In Partha Dasgupta and Ismail Serageldin (eds.), *Social Capital: A Multifaceted Perspective*, 325–424. Washington, DC: World Bank.

Dasgupta, Partha, and Ismail Serageldin (eds.). 2000. *Social Capital: A Multifaceted Perspective*. Washington, DC: World Bank.

David, Paul A. 1985. "Clio and the Economics of Qwerty." *American Economic Review* 75 (2): 332–37.

——— 1994. "Why Are Institutions the 'Carriers of History'?: Path-Dependence and the Evolution of Conventions, Organizations and Institutions." *Structural Change and Economic Dynamics* 5 (2): 205–20.

Davis, Douglas D., and Charles A. Holt. 1993. *Experimental Economics*. Princeton, NJ: Princeton University Press.

Davis, Kingsley. 1949. *Human Society*. New York: Macmillan.

Dawes, Robyn M., and Richard H. Thaler. 1988. "Anomalies: Cooperation." *Journal of Economic Perspectives* 2 (3): 187–97.

Day, John. 1963. *Les douanes de genes, 1376–1377*. Paris: S.E.V.P.E.N.

Day, Gerald W. 1984. "The Impact of the Third Crusade upon Trade with the Levant." *International History Review* 3 (Apr.): 159–68.

——— 1988. *Genoa's Response to Byzantium, 1154–1204*. Urbana: University of Illinois Press.

De Figueiredo, Rui, Jack Rakove, and Barry R. Weingast. 2001. "Rationality, Inaccurate Mental Models, and Self-Confirming Equilibrium: A New Understanding of the American Revolution." Memo, Stanford University.

Dekel, E., D. Fudenberg, and D. K. Levine. 1999. "Payoff Information and Self-Confirming Equilibrium." *Journal of Economic Theory* 89 (2): 165–85.

de Negri, Teoflio Ossian. 1986. *Storia di Genova*. Florence: G. Martello.

Denzau, A., and D. C. North. 1994. "Shared Mental Models: Ideologies and Institutions." *Kyklos* 47: 3–30.

de Roover, Raymond. 1948. *Money, Banking and Credit in Mediaeval Bruges*. Cambridge, MA: Mediaeval Academy of America.

——— 1963. *The Rise and Decline of the Medici Bank, 1397–1494*. Cambridge, MA: Harvard University Press.

——— 1965. "The Organization of Trade." In M. M. Postan, E. E. Rick, and M. Miltey (eds.), *Cambridge Economic History of Europe*, 3:42–118. Cambridge: Cambridge University Press.

Diamond, Jared. 1997. *Guns, Germs, and Steel: The Fates of Human Societies*. New York: Norton.

DiMaggio, Paul. 1994. "Culture and Economy." In Neil Smelser and Richard Swedberg (eds.), *The Handbook of Economic Sociology*, 27–57. Princeton, NJ: Princeton University Press; New York: Russell Sage Foundation.

——— 1997. "The New Institutionalism: Avenues of Collaboration." *Journal of Institutional and Theoretical Economics* 154: 1–10.

DiMaggio, Paul, and W. Powell. 1991a. Introduction. In W. Powell and P. DiMaggio (eds.), *The New Institutionalism in Organizational Analysis*, 1–40. Chicago: University of Chicago Press.

——— 1991b. "The Iron Cage Revisited: Institutional Isomorphism and Collective Rationality in Organizational Fields." In W. Powell and P. DiMaggio (eds.), *The New Institutionalism in Organizational Analysis*, 63–82. Chicago: University of Chicago Press.

Dixit, Avinash. 2004. *Lawlessness and Economics: Alternative Modes of Governance*. Princeton, NJ: Princeton University Press.

Dixit, Avinash, and Barry Nalebuff. 1991. *Thinking Strategically: The Competitive Edge in Business, Politics and Everyday Life*. New York: Norton.

Djankov, Simeon, Edward L. Glaeser, Rafael La Porta, Florencio Lopez-de-Silanes, and Andrei Shleifer. 2003. "The New Comparative Economics." *Journal of Comparative Economics* 31 (4): 595–619.

Dobbin, F. 1994. *Forging Industrial Policy: The United States, Britain and France in the Railroad Age*. Cambridge: Cambridge University Press.

Dollinger, Philippe. 1970. *The German Hansa*. Stanford, CA.: Stanford University Press.

Donaver, Federico. 1990 [1890]. *Storia di Genova*. Genoa: Nuova Editrice Genovese.

Duby, Georges. 1974. *The Early Growth of the European Economy*. Ithaca, NY: Cornell University Press.

Duffy, Bella. 1903. *The Tuscan Republics (Florence, Siena, Pisa and Lucca) with Genoa*. New York: G. P. Putnam's Sons.

Dugger, William M. 1990. "The New Insitutionalism: New but Not Insitutionalist." *Journal of Economic Issues* 24 (2): 423–31.

Durkheim, Emile. 1950 [1895]. *The Rules of Sociological Method*. New York: Free Press.

——— 1953. *Sociology and Philosophy*. New York: Free Press.

Easterly, William. 2001. *The Illusive Quest for Growth*. Cambridge, MA: MIT Press.

Easterly, William, and R. Levine. 2002. "Tropics, Germs, and Crops: How Endowments Influence Economic Development." Mimeo, Center for Global Development and Institute for International Economics.

Eggertsson, Thráinn. 1990. *Economic Behavior and Institutions*. Cambridge: Cambridge University Press.

Ekelund, Robert B., Jr., Robert F. Hébert, Robert D. Tollison, Gary M. Anderson, and Audrey B. Davidson. 1996. *Sacred Trust: The Medieval Church as an Economic Firm*. New York: Oxford University Press.

Ekelund, Robert B., Jr., and Robert D. Tollison. 1981. *Mercantilism as a Rent-Seeking Society*. College Station: Texas A&M University Press.

Ellickson, Robert C. 1991. *Order without Law*. Cambridge, MA: Harvard University Press.

Ellison, Glenn. 1993. "Learning, Local Interaction, and Coordination." *Econometrica* 61 (5): 1047–71.

——— 1994. "Cooperation in the Prisoner's Dilemma with Anonymous Random Matching." *Review of Economic Studies* 61 (3): 567–88.

Elster, Jon. 1983. *Explaining Technical Change: A Case Study in the Philosophy of Science*. Cambridge: Cambridge University Press.

——— 1989a. *The Cement of Society: A Study of Social Order*. Cambridge: Cambridge University Press.

——— 1989b. "Social Norms and Economic Theory." *Journal of Economic Perspectives* 3 (4): 99–117.

——— 2000. "Rational Choice History: A Case of Excessive Ambition." *American Political Science Review* 94 (3): 685–95.

461

Ely, J., and O. Yilankaya. 1997. "Evolution of Preferences and Nash Equilibrium." Mimeo, Northwestern University.

Emery, R. 1952. "The Use of the Surname in the Study of Medieval Economic History." *Medievalia et Humanistica* 7: 43–50.

Engerman, Stanley L., and Kenneth L. Sokoloff. 1997. "Factor Endowments, Institutions, and Differential Paths of Growth among New World Economies." In Stephen Haber (ed.), *How Did Latin America Fall Behind?*, 260–304. Stanford, CA: Stanford University Press.

English, Edward D. 1988. *Enterprise and Liability in Sienese Banking, 1230–1350*. Cambridge, MA: Medieval Academy of America.

English Historical Documents, 1042–1189. 1968. Ed. D. C. Douglas and G. W. Greenaway. Vol. 2. London: Eyre and Spottiswoode.

English Historical Documents, 1189–1327. 1975. Ed. H. Rothwell. Vol. 3. London: Eyre and Spottiswoode.

Ensminger, Jean. 1997. "Changing Property Rights: Reconciling Formal and Informal Rights to Land in Africa." In John N. Drobak and John V. C. Nye (eds.), *The Frontiers of the New Institutional Economics*, 165–96. New York: Academic Press.

Epstein, Steven A. 1984. *Wills and Wealth in Medieval Genoa, 1150–1250*. Cambridge, MA: Harvard University Press.

1991. *Wage Labor and Guilds in Medieval Europe*. Chapel Hill: University of North Carolina Press.

1996. *Genoa and the Genoese, 958–1528*. Chapel Hill: University of North Carolina Press.

Epstein, Steven. R. 1998. "Craft Guilds, Apprenticeship and Technological Change in Preindustrial Europe." *Journal of Economic History* 53 (4): 684–713.

2000. *Freedom and Growth: The Rise of States and Markets in Europe, 1300–1750*. New York: Routledge.

Ertman, Thomas. 1997. *Birth of the Leviathan: Building States and Regimes in Medieval and Early Modern Europe*. Cambridge: Cambridge University Press.

Eysenck, M. W., and M. T. Keane. 1995. *Cognitive Psychology: A Student's Handbook*. Hillsdale, MI: Lawrence Erlbaum.

Face, Richard D. 1952. "The Embriaci: Feudal Imperialists of the Twelfth-Century Genoa." M.A. thesis, University of Cincinnati.

1958. "Techniques of Business in the Trade between the Fairs of Champagne and the South of Europe in the Twelfth and Thirteenth Centuries." *Economic History Review* 10 (3): 427–38.

1980. "Secular History in Twelfth Century Italy: Caffaro of Genoa." *Journal of Medieval History* 6 (2): 169–84.

Fafchamps, Marcel. 2004. *Market Institutions in Sub-Saharan Africa*. Cambridge, MA: MIT Press.

Falk, Armin, and Urs Fischbacher. 2000. "A Theory of Reciprocity." Working Paper No. 6, University of Zurich.

Farrell, Joseph, and Eric Maskin. 1989. "Renegotiation in Repeated Games." *Games and Economic Behavior* 1 (3): 327–60.

Fearon, James D. 1991. "Counterfactuals and Hypothesis-Testing in Political-Science." *World Politics* 43 (2): 169–95.

1997. "Bargaining over Objects That Influence Future Bargaining Power." Working paper, Department of Political Science, University of Chicago.

Fearon, James D., and David D. Laitin. 1996. "Explaining Interethnic Cooperation." *American Political Science Review* 90 (4): 715–35.

Fehr, Ernst, and Urs Fischbacher. 2001. "Reputation and Retaliation." Mimeo, University of Zürich.

Fehr, Ernst, and Simon Gächter. 2000. "Cooperation and Punishment in Public Good Experiments." *American Economic Review* 90 (4): 980–94.

Fehr, Ernst, and Klaus M. Schmidt. 1999. "A Theory of Fairness, Competition, and Cooperation." *Quarterly Journal of Economics* 114 (3): 817–68.

2001. "Theories of Fairness and Reciprocity – Evidence and Economic Applications." Working Paper 75, Institute for Empirical Research in Economics, University of Zürich.

2003. "Theories of Fairness and Reciprosity: Evidence and Economic Applications." In Mathias Dewatripont, Lars Peter Hansen, and Stephen Turnovsky (eds.), *Advances in Economics and Econometrics: Theory and Applications, Eighth World Congress*, 1:208–56. Cambridge: Cambridge University Press.

Fernandez, Raquel, and Dani Rodrik. 1991. "Resistance to Reform: Status Quo Bias in the Presence of Individual-Specific Uncertainty." *American Economic Review* 81 (5): 1146–55.

Fershtman, Chaim, and Yoram Weiss. 1993. "Social Status, Culture and Economic Performance." *Economic Journal* 103 (July): 946–59.

Field, Alexander. 1981. "The Problem with Neoclassical Institutional Economics: A Critique with Special Reference to the North-Thomas Model of Pre-1500 Europe." *Explorations in Economic History* 18 (2): 174–98.

2002. *Altruistically Inclined?: The Behavioral Sciences, Evolutionary Theory, and the Origins of Reciprocity*. Ann Arbor: University of Michigan Press.

Fischbacher, Urs, Simon Gächter, and Ernst Fehr. 2001. "Are People Conditionally Cooperative? Evidence from a Public Goods Experiment." *Economic Letters* 71: 397–404.

Fischel, Walter J. 1958. "The Spice Trade in Mamluk Egypt." *Journal of Economic and Social History of the Orient* 1 (2): 157–74.

Fligstein, Neil. 1990. *The Transformation of Corporate Control*. Cambridge, MA: Harvard University Press.

Forsythe, Robert, Joel Horowitz, N. S. Savin, and Martin Sefton. 1994. "Fairness in Simple Bargaining Games." *Games and Economic Behavior* 6: 347–69.

Frank, Andre Gunder. 1998. *Reorient: Global Economy in the Asian Age*. Berkeley: University of California Press.

Frank, Robert H. 1987. "If Homo Economics Could Choose His Own Utility Function, Would He Want One with a Conscience?" *American Economic Review* 77 (4): 593–604.

French, H. R., and R. W. Hoyle. 2003. "English Individualism Refuted – and Reasserted: The Land Market of Earls Clone (Essex), 1550–1750." *Economic History Review* 4 (Nov.): 595–622.

References

Frey, Bruno S. 1997. *Not Just for the Money: An Economic Theory of Personal Motivation*. Cheltenham: Edward Elgar Publishing.

Friedman, James W. 1971. "Noncooperative Equilibrium for Supergames." *Review of Economic Studies* 38 (8): 1–12.

Friedman, Jeffrey (ed.). 1996. *The Rational Choice Controversy: Economic Models of Politics Reconsidered*. New Haven: Yale University Press.

Friedman, Milton. 1984. *The Methodology of Positive Economics*. Cambridge: Cambridge University Press.

Fudenberg, D., and D. Kreps. 1988. "A Theory of Learning and Nash Equilibrium." Mimeo, Stanford University.

Fudenberg, Drew, and David K. Levine. 1993. "Self-Confirming Equilibrium." *Econometrica* 61 (3): 523–45.

———. 1998. *The Theory of Learning in Games*. Cambridge, MA: MIT Press.

———. 2003. "Steady State Learning and the Code of Hammurabi." Working paper, University of California, Los Angeles.

Fudenberg, Drew, David K. Levine, and Eric Maskin. 1994. "The Folk Theorem with Imperfect Public Information." *Econometrica* 62 (5): 997–1039.

Fudenberg, D., and E. Maskin. 1986. "The Folk Theorem for Repeated Games with Discounting and Incomplete Information." *Econometrica* 54 (3): 533–54.

Fudenberg, Drew, and Jean Tirole. 1991. *Game Theory*. Cambridge, MA: MIT Press.

Fukuyama, Francis. 1995. *Trust: The Social Virtues and the Creation of Prosperity*. New York: Free Press.

Furnivall, John S. 1956. *Colonial Policy and Practice: A Comparative Study of Burma and Netherlands India*. New York: New York University Press.

Furubotn, Erik G., and Rudolf Richter. 1997. *Institutions and Economic Theory*. Ann Arbor: University of Michigan Press.

Gächter, Simon, and Armin Falk. 2002. "Reputation and Reciprocity: Consequences for the Labour Relation." *Scandinavian Journal of Economics* 104 (1): 1–26.

Galor, O., and J. Zeira. 1993. "Income-Distribution and Macroeconomics." *Review of Economic Studies* 60 (1): 35–52.

Garfinkel, Harold. 1967. *Studies in Ethnomethodology*. Englewood Cliffs, NJ: Prentice-Hall.

Geanakoplos, John, David Pearce, and Ennio Stacchetti. 1989. "Psychological Games and Sequential Rationality." *Games and Economic Behavior* 1 (1): 60–79.

Ghatak, M., and T. W. Guinnane. 1999. "The Economics of Lending with Joint Liability: Theory and Practice." *Journal of Development Economics* 60 (1): 195–228.

Ghosh, Parikshit, and Debraj Ray. 1996. "Cooperation in Community Interaction without Information Flows." *Review of Economic Studies* 63 (3): 491–519.

Gibbons, Robert. 1992. *Game Theory for Applied Economists*. Princeton, NJ: Princeton University Press.

1998. "Game Theory and Garbage Cans: An Introduction to the Economics of Internal Organization." In R. Stern and J. Halpern (eds.), *Debating Rationality: Nonrational Elements of Organizational Decision Making*, chap. 2. Ithaca, NY: ILR Press.

2001. "Trust in Social Structures: Hobbes and Coase Meet Repeated Games." In K. Cook (ed.), *Trust in Society*, chap. 11. New York: Russell Sage Foundation.

Gibbons, Robert, and Andrew Rutten. 1997. "Hierarchical Dilemmas: Social Order with Self-Interested Rulers." Working paper, Cornell University.

Giddens, Anthony. 1997. *Sociology*. London: Polity Press.

Gil, Moshe. 1971. *The Tustars, the Family and the Sect*. Tel Aviv: Tel Aviv University Press.

1983a. "The Jews in Sicily under the Muslim Rule in the Light of the Geniza Documents." Unpublished manuscript, Tel Aviv University.

1983b. *Palestine during the First Muslim Period (634–1099)* (in Hebrew and Arabic). Vols. 1–3. Tel Aviv: Ministry of Defense Press and Tel Aviv University Press.

Gilboa, Itzhak, and David Schmeidler. 2001. *Theory of Case-Based Decisions*. Cambridge: Cambridge University Press.

Gintis, Herbert. 2000. *Game Theory Evolving*. Princeton, NJ: Princeton University Press.

Giovanni di Guiberto. 1200–11. *Cartolare* (in Latin and Italian). Ed. M. W. Hall-Cole and R. G. Reinert. Documenti, XVII–XVIII. Turin: Editrice Libraria Italiana, 1939–40.

Giovanni Scriba. 1154–64. *Cartolare* (in Latin and Italian). Ed. Mario Chiaudano and Mattia Moresco. Vols. 1, 2. Turin: S. Lattes & C. Editori, 1935.

Glaeser, Edward L., Rafael La Porta, Florencio Lopez-de-Silanes, and Andrei Shliefer. 2004. *Do Institutions Cause Growth?* Memo, Harvard University.

Glaeser, Edward L., and Andrei Shleifer. 2002. "Legal Origin." *Quarterly Journal of Economics* 117 (4): 1193–1230.

Goitein, Shelomo Dov. 1957. "The Beginning of the Karim Merchants and the Character of Their Organization." *Journal of Economic and Social History of the Orient* 1: 175–84.

1964. "Commercial and Family Partnerships in the Countries of Medieval Islam." *Islamic Studies* 3: 315–37.

1967. *A Mediterranean Society: Economic Foundations*. Los Angeles: University of California Press.

1971. *A Mediterranean Society: The Community*. Los Angeles: University of California Press.

1973. *Letters of Medieval Jewish Traders*. Princeton, NJ: Princeton University Press.

1978. *A Mediterranean Society: The Family*. Los Angeles: University of California Press.

Gonzalez de Lara, Yadira. 2002. "Institutions for Contract Enforcement and Risk-Sharing: From Debt to Equity in Late Medieval Venice." Memo, Ente Einaudi, Bank of Italy.

References

2004. "The State as an Enforcer in Early Venetian Trade: A Historical Institutional Analysis." Memo, University of Alicante, Spain.

Goodin, Robert, and Hans-Dieter Klingemann (eds.). 1996. *A New Handbook of Political Science*. New York: Oxford University Press.

Goody, J. 1983. *The Development of the Family and Marriage in Europe*. Cambridge: Cambridge University Press.

Gould, S. J., and N. Eldredge. 1977. "Punctuated Equilibria: The Tempo and Mode of Evolution Reconsidered." *Paleobiology* 3: 115–51.

Grantham, George. 1992. "The Manse, the Manor and the Market: New Perspectives on the Medieval Agricultural Revolution." Memo, McGill University.

1993. "Economic Growth without Causes: A Reexamination of Medieval Economic Growth and Decay." Presented at the annual meeting of the American Economic History Association, Tucson, AZ.

Granovetter, Mark S. 1985. "Economic Action, Social Structure, and Embeddedness." *American Journal of Sociology* 91 (3): 481–510.

2002. "A Theoretical Agenda for Economic Sociology." In Mauro Guillen, Randall Collins, Paula England, and Marshall Meyer (eds.), *The New Economic Sociology: Developments in an Emerging Field*, 35–59. New York: Russell Sage Foundation.

Gras, N. S. B. 1939. *Business and Capitalism: An Introduction to Business History*. New York: F. S. Crofts.

Green, Donald P., and Ian Shapiro. 1994. *Pathologies of Rational Choice Theory*. New Haven: Yale University Press.

Green, Edward, and Robert Porter. 1984. "Noncooperative Collusion under Imperfect Price Information." *Econometrica* 52 (Jan.): 87–100.

Greif, Avner. 1985. "Sicilian Jews during the Muslim Period (827–1061)" (in Hebrew and Arabic). M.A. thesis, Tel Aviv University.

✓ 1989. "Reputation and Coalitions in Medieval Trade: Evidence on the Maghribi Traders." *Journal of Economic History* 49 (4): 857–82.

1992. "Institutions and Commitment in International Trade: Lessons from the Commercial Revolution." *American Economic Review* 82 (2): 128–33.

1993. "Contract Enforceability and Economic Institutions in Early Trade: The Maghribi Traders' Coalition." *American Economic Review* 83 (3): 525–48.

1994a. "Cultural Beliefs and the Organization of Society: Historical and Theoretical Reflection on Collectivist and Individualist Societies." *Journal of Political Economy* 102 (5): 912–50.

1994b. "Trading Institutions and the Commercial Revolution in Medieval Europe." In Abel Aganbegyan, Oleg Bogomolov, and Michael Kaser (eds.), *Economics in a Changing World*, 1: 115–25. Proceedings of the Tenth World Congress of the International Economic Association. London: Macmillan.

1994c. "On the Political Foundations of the Late Medieval Commercial Revolution: Genoa during the Twelfth and Thirteenth Centuries." *Journal of Economic History* 54 (4): 271–87.

1995. "Political Organizations, Social Structures, and Institutional Success: Reflections from Genoa and Venice during the Commercial Revolution." *Journal of Institutional and Theoretical Economics* 151 (4): 734–40.

1996a. "A Comment on the 'Evolution of Economic Systems: The Case of Japan' by Tetsuji Okazaki and Masahiro Okuno-Fujiwara." In Y. Hayami and Masahiko Aoki (eds.), *The Institutional Foundation of Economic Development in East Asia*, 522–6. London: Macmillan.

1996b. "Microtheory and Recent Developments in the Study of Economic Institutions through Economic History." Working Paper No. 96-001, Stanford University, Department of Economics.

1997a. "Microtheory and Recent Developments in the Study of Economic Institutions through Economic History." In David M. Kreps and Kenneth F. Wallis (eds.), *Advances in Economic Theory*, 2: 79–113. Cambridge: Cambridge University Press.

1997b. "Institutional Structure and Economic Development: Economic History and the New Institutionalism." In John N. Drobak and John Nye (eds.), *Frontiers of the New Institutional Economics*, 57–94. Volume in honor of Douglass C. North. New York: Academic Press.

1997c. "Cultural Beliefs as a Common Resource in an Integrating World: An Example from the Theory and History of Collectivist and Individualist Societies." In P. Dasgupta, K.-G. Mäler, and A. Vercelli (eds.), *The Economics of Transnational Commons*, 238–96. Oxford: Clarendon Press.

1997d. "Contracting, Enforcement, and Efficiency: Economics beyond the Law." In Michael Bruno and Boris Pleskovic (eds.), *Annual World Bank Conference on Development Economics*, 239–66. Washington, DC: World Bank.

1998a. "Historical and Comparative Institutional Analysis." *American Economic Review* 88 (2): 80–4.

1998b. "Historical Institutional Analysis: Game Theory and Non-market Self-Enforcing Institutions during the Late Medieval Period" (in French). *Annales*, no. 3 (May–June): 597–633.

1998c. "Self-Enforcing Political Systems and Economic Growth: Late Medieval Genoa." In Robert H. Bates, Avner Greif, Margaret Levi, Jean-Laurent Rosenthal, and Barry R. Weingast, *Analytic Narratives*, 23–63. Princeton, NJ: Princeton University Press.

2000. "The Fundamental Problem of Exchange: A Research Agenda in Historical Institutional Analysis." *Review of European Economic History* 4 (3): 251–84.

2001. "Impersonal Exchange and the Origin of Markets: From the Community Responsibility System to Individual Legal Responsibility in Pre-modern Europe." In M. Aoki and Y. Hayami (eds.), *Communities and Markets in Economic Development*, 3–41. Oxford: Oxford University Press.

2002. "The Islamic Equilibrium: Legitimacy and Political, Social, and Economic Outcomes." Working paper, Stanford University.

2004a. "State Building and Commercial Expansion: Genoa's Experience." Memo, Stanford University.

2004b. "Commitment, Coercion, and Markets: The Nature and Dynamics of Institutions Supporting Exchange." In Claude Menard and Mary M. Shirley (eds.), *The Handbook for New Institutional Economics*. Norwell, MA: Kluwer Academic Publishers.

2004c. "Impersonal Exchange without Impartial Law: The Community Responsibility System." *Chicago Journal of International Law* 5 (1): 109–38.

Greif, Avner, and Eugene Kandel. 1995. "Contract Enforcement Institutions: Historical Perspective and Current Status in Russia." In Edward P. Lazear (ed.), *Economic Transition in Eastern Europe and Russia: Realities of Reform*, 291–321. Stanford, CA: Hoover Institution Press.

Greif, Avner, and David Laitin. 2004. "A Theory of Endogenous Institutional Change." *American Political Science Review* 98 (4): 1–20.

Greif, Avner, Paul R. Milgrom, and Barry R. Weingast. 1994. "Coordination, Commitment and Enforcement: The Case of the Merchant Gild." *Journal of Political Economy* 102 (4): 745–76.

Gross, Charles. 1890. *Gild Merchant*. Oxford: Clarendon Press.

Grossman, Gene M., and Elhanan Helpman. 2002a. *Special Interest Politics*. Cambridge, MA: MIT Press.

2002b. "Integration versus Outsourcing in Industry Equilibrium." *Quarterly Journal of Economics* 117: 85–120.

2003. "Outsourcing in a Global Economy." *Review of Economic Studies* 1: 300–16.

Grossman, Herschel, and Minseong Kim. 1995. "Swords or Plowshares? A Theory of the Security of Claims to Property." *Journal of Political Economy* 103 (6): 1275–88.

Grossman, Sanford J., and Oliver D. Hart. 1986. "The Cost and Benefits of Ownership: A Theory of Vertical and Lateral Integration." *Journal of Political Economy* 94 (4): 691–719.

Guglielmo Cassinese. 1190–2. *Carlolare* (in Latin and Italian). In Margaret W. Hall, Hilmar C. Krueger, and Robert L. Reynolds (eds.), *Notai Liguri Del Sec. XII*. Turin: Editrice Libraria Italiana, 1938.

Guinnane, T. W. "Cooperatives as Information Machines: German Rural Credit Cooperatives, 1883–1914." *Discussion Papers 97–20*. University of Copenhagen, Department of Economics.

Gurevich, Aaron. 1995. *The Origins of European Individualism*. Oxford: Blackwell.

Gustafsson, Bo. 1987. "The Rise and Economic Behaviour of Medieval Crafts Guilds. An Economic-Theoretical Interpretation." *Scandinavian Economic History Review* 35 (1): 1–40.

Güth, W. 1992. "An Evolutionary Approach to Explaining Cooperative Behavior by Reciprocal Incentives." *International Journal of Game Theory* 24: 323–44.

Güth, W., and M. Yaari. 1992. "Explaining Reciprocal Behavior in Simple Strategic Games: An Evolutionary Approach." In U. Witt (ed.), *Explaining Forces and Change: Approaches to Evolutionary Economics*, 23–34. Ann Arbor: University of Michigan Press.

Haber, Stephen. 1997. "Institutional Change and TFP Growth: Brazil and Mexico, 1860–1940." Working Paper, Stanford University.

Haber, Stephen, Armando Razo, and Noel Maurer. 2003. *The Politics of Property Rights: Political Instability, Credible Commitments, and Economic Growth in Mexico, 1876–1929*. Cambridge: Cambridge University Press.

Hagel, John H., and Alvin Roth (eds.). 1995. *Handbook of Experimental Economics*. Princeton, NJ: Princeton University Press.

Hall, Peter A., and Rosemary C. R. Taylor. 1996. "Political Science and the Three New Institutionalisms." *Political Studies* 44 (4): 936–57.

——— 1998. "The Potential of Historical Institutionalism: A Response to Hay and Wincott." *Political Studies* 46 (4): 958–62.

Hall, Robert E., and Charles I. Jones. 1999. "Why Do Some Countries Produce So Much More Output per Worker Than Others?" *Quarterly Journal of Economics* 114 (Feb.): 83–116.

Hamilton, Gary G. 1991. "The Organizational Foundations of Western and Chinese Commerce: A Historical and Comparative Analysis." In Gary G. Hamilton (ed.), *Business Networks and Economic Development in East and Southeast Asia*, 48–65. Hong Kong: University of Hong Kong, Centre of Asian Studies.

Hanawalt, B. 1974. "The Peasant Family and Crime in Fourteenth-Century England." *Journal of British Studies* 13 (2): 1–18.

Hardin, Russell. 1989. "Why a Constitution." In Bernard Grofman and Donal Wittman (eds.), *The Federalist Papers and the New Institutionalism*, 100–20. New York: Agathon Press.

——— 1997. "Economic Theories of the State." In Dennis C. Mueller (ed.), *Perspectives on Public Choice: A Handbook*, 21–34. Cambridge: Cambridge University Press.

Hart, Oliver. 1995. *Firms, Contracts, and Financial Structure*. Oxford: Clarendon Press.

——— 2001. "Norms and the Theory of the Firm." *University of Pennsylvania Law Review* 149 (6): 1701–15.

Hart, Oliver, and Bengt Holmstrom. 1987. "The Theory of Contracts." In Truman F. Bewley (ed.), *Advances in Economic Theory, Fifth World Congress*, 71–157. Cambridge: Cambridge University Press.

Hart, Oliver, and J. Moore. 1999. "Foundations of Incomplete Contracts." *Review of Economic Studies* 66 (1): 115–38.

Hatcher, John, and Mark Bailey. 2001. *Modeling the Middle Ages: The History and Theory of England's Economic Development*. Oxford: Oxford University Press.

Hayek, Friedrich A. von. 1937. "Economics and Knowledge." *Economica* 4: 33–54.

——— 1973. *Law Legislation and Liberty*. Vol. 1. Chicago: University of Chicago Press.

——— 1976. *Law Legislation and Liberty*. Vol. 2. Chicago: University of Chicago.

——— 1979. *Law Legislation and Liberty*. Vol. 3. Chicago: University of Chicago.

Hearder, H., and D. P. Waley (eds.). 1963. *A Short History of Italy from Classical Times to the Present Day*. Cambridge: Cambridge University Press.

Hechter, M. 1992. "The Insufficiency of Game Theory for the Resolution of Real World Collective Action Problems." *Rationality and Society* 4 (1): 33–40.

Heers, Jacques. 1977. *Parties and Political Life in the Medieval West*. Oxford: Oxford University Press.

Helpman, Elhanan. 2004. *The Mystery of Economic Growth*. Cambridge, MA: Harvard University Press.

Henrich, Joseph, Robert Boyd, Samuel Bowles, Colin Camerer, Ernst Fehr, and Hebert Gintis. 2004. *Foundations of Human Sociality: Experimental and Ethnographic Evidence from Fifteen Small-Scale Societies*. Oxford: Oxford University Press.

Henrich, Joseph, Robert Boyd, Samuel Bowles, Colin Camerer, Ernst Fehr, Hebert Gintis, and Richard McElreath. 2001. "In Search for Homo Economicus: Behavioral Experiments in 15 Small-Scale Societies." *American Economic Review* 74 (May): 73–8.

Herb, Michael. 2003. "Taxation and Representation." *Studies in Comparative International Development* 38 (3): 3–31.

Herlihy, David. 1958. "The Agrarian Revolution in Southern France and Italy, 801–1150." *Speculum: A Journal of Mediaeval Studies* 33 (1): 23–42.

1969. "Family Solidarity in Medieval Italian History." In David Herlihy, R. S. Lopez, V. Slessarev (eds.), *Economy Society, and Government in Medieval Italy: Essays in Memory of Robert L. Reynolds*, 173–84. Kent, OH: Kent State University Press.

Heyd, W. 1868. *Le colonie commerciali degli Italiani in Oriente nel Medio Evo*. 2 vols. Venice: G. Antonelli.

1885. *Histoire du commerce du Levant au Moyen-âge*. 2 vols. Leipzig: Otto Harrassowitz.

Heywood, William. 1921. *A History of Pisa, Eleventh and Twelfth Centuries*. Cambridge: Cambridge University Press.

Hicks, John. 1969. *A Theory of Economic History*. Oxford: Oxford University Press.

Hickson, Charles R., and Earl A. Thompson. 1991. "A New Theory of Guilds and European Economic Development." *Explorations in Economic History* 28 (2): 127–68.

Hirshleifer, Jack. 1985. "The Expanding Domain of Economics." *American Economic Review* 75 (6): 53–70.

Hodgson, Geoffrey M. 1998. "The Approach of Institutional Economics." *Journal of Economic Literature* 36 (1): 166–92.

Hodgson, Marshall G. S. 1974. *The Venture of Islam*. Vols. 1, 2. Chicago: University of Chicago Press.

Hoffman, Elizabeth, Kevin McCabe, Keith Shachat, and Vernon Smith. 1994. "Preferences, Property Rights, and Anonymity in Bargaining Games." *Games and Economic Behavior* 7 (3): 346–80.

Hoffman, Elizabeth, Kevin McCabe, and Vernon Smith. 1996a. "On Expectations and the Monetary Stakes in Ultimatum Games." *International Journal of Game Theory* 125 (3): 289–301.

1996b. "Social Distance and Other-Regarding Behavior in Dictator Games." *American Economic Review* 86 (3): 653–60.

Hoffman, Philip T. 1990. "Taxes, Fiscal Crises, and Representative Institutions: The Case of Early Modern France." Unpublished manuscript, Washington University, Center for the History of Freedom.

470

1991. "Land Rents and Agricultural Productivity – the Paris Basin, 1450–1789." *Journal of Economic History* 51 (4): 771–805.

1996. *Growth in a Traditional Society: The French Countryside, 1450–1815.* Princeton, NJ: Princeton University Press.

Hoffman, Philip T., Gilles Postel-Vinay, and Jean-Laurent Rosenthal. 2000. *Priceless Markets: The Political Economy of Credit in Paris, 1660–1870.* Chicago: University of Chicago Press.

Höllander, Heinz. 1990. "A Social Exchange Approach to Voluntary Cooperation." *American Economic Review* 80 (5): 1157–67.

Homans, George C. 1950. *The Human Group.* New York: Harcourt.

1961. *Social Behavior.* New York: Harcourt, Brace & World.

Hsu, F. L. K. 1983. *Rugged Individualism Reconsidered.* Knoxville: University of Tennessee Press.

Huck, S., and J. Oechssler. 1999. "The Indirect Evolutionary Approach to Explaining Fair Allocations." *Games and Economic Behavior* 28: 13–24.

Hughes, Diane Owen. 1974. "Toward Historical Ethnography: Notarial Records and Family History in the Middle Ages." *Historical Methods Newsletter* 7 (2): 61–71.

1977. "Kinsmen and Neighbors in Medieval Genoa." In Harry A. Mistiming, David Herlihy, and A. L. Udovitch (eds.), *The Medieval City*, 95–111. New Haven: Yale University Press.

1978. "Urban Growth and Family Structure in Medieval Genoa." In Philip Abrams and E. A. Wrigley (eds.), *Towns in Societies*, 105–30. Cambridge: Cambridge University Press. Previously published in *Past and Present* 66 (1975): 3–28.

Hughes, Everett C. 1937. "Institutional Office and the Person." *American Journal of Sociology* 43 (3): 404–13.

Hyde, John K. 1973. *Society and Politics in Medieval Italy: The Evolution of Civil Life, 1000–1350.* London: Macmillan.

Ingram, Paul. 1996. "Organizational Form as a Solution to the Problem of Credible Commitment: The Evolution of Naming Strategies among US Hotel Chains, 1896–1980." *Strategic Management Journal* 17 (Summer): 85–98.

Jacoby, David. 1997. *Trade, Commodities, and Shipping in the Medieval Mediterranean.* Aldershot: Variorum.

Johnston, Simon, John McMillan, and Christopher Woodruff. 2002. "Courts and Relational Contracts." *Journal of Law, Economics, and Organization* 18 (Spring): 221–77.

Jones, W. J. 1976. *The Foundations of English Bankruptcy: Statutes and Commissions in the Early Modern Period.* Philadelphia: Transactions of the American Philosophical Society.

Joskow, Paul L. 1984. "Vertical Integration and Long-Term Contracts: The Case of Mine-Mouth Coal Plants." Paper presented at the Economic and Legal Organization Workshop, Department of Economics, Massachusetts Institute of Technology.

Kalai, E., and E. Lehrer. 1993a. "Rational Learning Leads to Nash Equilibrium." *Econometrica* 61 (5): 1019–45.

1993b. "Subjective Equilibrium in Repeated Games." *Econometrica* 61 (5): 1231–40.

1995. "Subjective Games and Equilibria." *Games and Economic Behavior* 8: 123–63.

Kali, R. 1999. "Endogenous Business Networks." *Journal of Law, Economics, and Organization* 15 (3): 615–36.

Kambayashi, Ryo. 2002. "The Registration System and the Grade Wage System, Coordination and Relative Performance Evaluation." Memo, Tokyo University.

Kandori, Michihiro. 1992. "Social Norms and Community Enforcement." *Review of Economic Studies* 59 (1): 63–80.

1997. "Evolutionary Game Theory in Economics." In David M. Kreps and Kenneth F. Wallis (eds.), *Advances in Economic Theory* 1: 243–77. Cambridge: Cambridge University Press.

2002. "Introduction to Repeated Games with Private Monitoring." *Journal of Economic Theory* 102 (1): 1–15.

2003. "The Erosions and Sustainability of Norms and Morals." *Japanese Economic Review* 54 (1): 29–48.

Kandori, Michihiro, George Mailath, and R. Rob. 1993. "Learning, Mutation, and Long Run Equilibria in Games," *Econometrica* 61 (1): 29–56.

Kaneko, Mamoru, and Akihiko Matsui. 1999. "Inductive Game Theory: Discrimination and Prejudices." *Journal of Public Economic Theory* 1 (1): 1–37.

Kantor, Shawn E. 1998. *Politics and Property Rights: The Closing of the Open Range in the Postbellum South*. Chicago: University of Chicago Press.

Kedar, Benjamin Z. 1976. *Merchants in Crisis: Genoese and Venetian Men of Affairs and the Fourteenth-Century Depression*. New Haven: Yale University Press.

Kelly, J. M. 1992. *A Short History of Western Legal Theory*. Oxford: Clarendon Press.

Kennedy, Hugh. 1986. *The Prophet and the Age of the Caliphates*. New York: Longman.

Klein, Benjamin, and Keith B. Leffler. 1981. "The Role of Market Forces in Assuring Contractual Performance." *Journal of Political Economy* 89 (4): 615–41.

Klein, Daniel (ed.). 1996. *Reputation: Studies in the Voluntary Enforcement of Good Behavior*. Ann Arbor: University of Michigan Press.

Knight, Jack. 1992. *Institutions and Social Conflict*. Cambridge: Cambridge University Press.

Kockesen, L., E. A. Ok, and R. Sethi. 2000a. "The Strategic Advantage of Negatively Interdependence Preferences." *Journal of Economic Theory* 92: 274–99.

2000b. "Evolution of Interdependent Preferences in Aggregative Games." *Games and Economic Behavior* 31: 303–10.

Korotayev, A. V. 2003. "Unilineal Descent Organization and Deep Christianization: A Cross-Cultural Comparison." *Cross-Cultural Research* 37 (1): 133–57.

Kranton, Rachel E. 1996. "Reciprocal Exchange: A Self-Sustaining System." *American Economic Review* 86 (4): 830–51.

Kranton, Rachel E., and D. F. Minehart. 2001. "A Theory of Buyer-Seller Networks." *American Economic Review* 91 (3): 485–508.

Krasner, S. D. 1984. "Approaches to the State: Alternative Conceptions and Historical Dynamics." *Comparative Politics* 16 (2): 223–46.

Kreps, David, M. 1990a. *A Course in Microeconomic Theory.* Princeton, NJ: Princeton University Press.

1990b. "Corporate Culture and Economic Theory." In James Alt and Kenneth Shepsle (eds.), *Perspectives on Positive Political Economy*, 90–143. Cambridge: Cambridge University Press.

Kreps, David M., Paul Milgrom, John Roberts, and Robert Wilson. 1982. "Rational Cooperation in the Finitely Repeated Prisoners' Dilemma." *Journal of Economic Theory* 27: 245–52.

Kritkos, Alexander, and Friedel Bolle. 1999. "Approaching Fair Behavior: Self-Centered Inequality Aversion versus Reciprocity and Altruism." Discussion Paper 143. Frankfurt/Oder.

Kroeber, A. L., and Clyde Kluckhohn. 1952. *Culture: A Critical Review of Concepts and Definitions.* Cambridge, MA: Peabody Museum.

Krueger, Hilmar C. 1932. "The Commercial Relations between Genoa and Northwest Africa in the Twelfth Century." Ph.D. diss., University of Wisconsin, Madison.

1933. "Genoese Trade with Northwest Africa in the Twelfth Century." *Speculum* 6 (July): 377–95.

1949. "Post-War Collapse and Rehabilitation in Genoa (1149–1162)." In *Studi in onore di Gino Luzzatto*, 4: 117–28. Milan: Istituto di Storia Economica dell'Universita di Napoli.

1957. "Genoese Merchants, Their Partnerships and Investments, 1155 to 1164." In Editoriale Cisalpina (eds.), *Studi in onore di Armando Sapori*, 257–72. Milan: Instituto Editoriale Cisalpino.

1962. "Genoese Merchants, Their Associations and Investments, 1155 to 1230." In D. A. Graffre (ed.), *Studi in onore di Amintore Fanfani*, 1: 415–26. Milan: Multa Paucis.

1987. "The Genoese Exportation of Northern Cloths to Mediterranean Ports, Twelfth Century." *Revue Belge de Philologie et d'Histoire* 65 (4): 722–50.

Kuhn, Arthur K. 1912. *The Law of Corporations.* New York: Columbia University Press.

Kuran, Timur. 1993. "The Unthinkable and the Unthought." *Rationality and Society* 5 (4): 473–505.

1995. *Private Truths, Public Lies: The Social Consequences of Preference Falsification.* Cambridge, MA: Harvard University Press.

1998. "Moral Overload and Its Alleviation." In Avner Ben-Ner and Louis Putterman (eds.), *Economics, Values, and Organization*, 231–66. Cambridge: Cambridge University Press.

2004. "Why the Middle East Is Economically Underdeveloped: Historical Mechanisms of Institutional Stagnation." *Journal of Economic Perspective* 18 (2): 71–90.

2005. "Why the Islamic Middle East Did Not Generate an Indigenous Corporate Law." Memo, University of Southern California.

Kydland, Finn E., and Edward C. Prescott. 1977. "Rules Rather than Discretion: The Inconsistency of Optimal Plans." *Journal of Political Economy* 85 (3): 473–92.

Lal, Deepak. 1998. *Unintended Consequences: The Impact of Endowments, Culture, and Politics on Long-Run Economic Performance.* Cambridge, MA: MIT Press.

Landa, Janet T. 1978. "The Economics of the Ethnically Homogeneous Chinese Middleman Group: A Property Rights–Public Choice Approach." Ph.D. diss., Virginia Polytechnic Institute and State University.

1988. "A Theory of the Ethnically Homogeneous Middleman Group: Beyond Markets and Hierarchies." Working paper, Hoover Institution, Stanford University.

Lane, Frederic C. 1944. "Family Partnerships and Joint Ventures in the Venetian Republic." *Journal of Economic History* 4: 178–96.

1973. *Venice: A Maritime Republic.* Baltimore: Johns Hopkins University Press.

Lanfranco Scriba. 1202–26. *Cartolare* (in Latin and Italian). In H. C. Krueger and R. L. Reynolds (eds.), *Notai Liguri Del Sec. XII e Del XIII.* Genoa: Societa Ligure di Storia Patria, 1952–4.

Langum, David J. 1987. *Law and Community on the Mexican California Frontier: Anglo-American Expatriates and the Clash of Legal Traditions, 1821–1846.* Norman: University of Oklahoma Press.

Lapidus, Ira M. 1984. *Muslim Cities in the Later Middle Ages.* Cambridge: Cambridge University Press.

1989. *A History of Islamic Societies.* Cambridge: Cambridge University Press.

Lau, Lawrence J., Yingyi Qian, and Gérard Roland. 2000. "Reform without Losers: An Interpretation of China's Dual-Track Approach to Transition." *Journal of Political Economy* 108 (1): 120–43.

Levi, Margaret. 1988. *On Rules and Revenues.* Berkeley: University of California Press.

1997. *Consent, Dissent, and Patriotism.* Cambridge: Cambridge University Press.

2004. "An Analytic Narrative Approach to Puzzles and Problems." In Ian Shapiro, Rogers Smith, and Tarek Masoud (eds.), *Problems and Methods in the Study of Politics*, 201–26. Cambridge: Cambridge University Press.

Levin, Jonathan. 2003. "Relational Incentive Contracts." *American Economic Review* 93 (3): 835–57.

Levinson, Daryl J. 2003. "Collective Sanctions." *Stanford Law Review* 56 (253): 345–428.

Lewis, Archibald R. 1951. *Naval Power and Trade in the Mediterranean, A.D. 500–1100.* Princeton, NJ: Princeton University Press.

Lewis, Bernard. 1982. *The Muslim Discovery of Europe.* New York: Norton.

1990. *Race and Slavery in the Middle East.* Oxford University Press.

1991. *The Political Language of Islam.* Chicago: University of Chicago Press.

Lewis, D. 1969. *Convention: A Philosophical Study*. Cambridge, MA: Harvard University Press.

Li, Shuhe. 1999. "The Benefits and Costs of Relation-Based Governance: An Explanation of the East Asian Miracle and Crisis." Memo, City University of Hong Kong.

Lieber, A. E. 1968. "Eastern Business Practices and Medieval Europe Commerce." *Economic History Review* 21: 230–43.

Lindbeck, Assar. 1997. "Incentives and Social Norms in Household Behavior." *American Economic Review* 87 (2): 370–7.

Lisciandrelli, Pasquale. 1960. "Trattati e negoziazioni politiche della Repubblica di Genova (958–1797)." *Atti della Societa Ligure de Storia Patria*, n.s., 1 (old series, 75). Genoa: Societa Ligure di Storia Patria.

Lloyd, T. H. 1991. *England and the German Hansa, 1157–1611*. Cambridge: Cambridge University Press.

Loewsenstein, George, Max Bazerman, and Leigh Thomson. 1989. "Social Utility and Decision Making in Interpersonal Context." *Journal of Personality and Social Psychology* 57: 426–41.

Lopez, Robert Sabatino. 1937. "Aux origines du capitalisme gènois." *Annales d'Histoire Economique et Sociale* 47: 429–54.

 1938. *Storia delle colonie genovesi nel Mediterraneo*. Bologna: Nicola Zanichelli.

 1943. "European Merchants in the Medieval Indies: The Evidence of Commercial Documents." *Journal of Economic History* 3 (1): 164–84.

 1952. "The Trade of Medieval Europe in the South." In M. M. Postan and E. Miller (eds.), *The Cambridge Economic History of Europe*, 2: 257–354. Cambridge: Cambridge University Press.

 1954. "Concerning Surnames and Places of Origin." *Medievalia et Humanistica* 8: 6–16.

 1967. *The Birth of Europe*. Trans. J. M. Dent & Sons. London: M. Evans.

 1976. *The Commercial Revolution of the Middle Ages, 950–1350*. Cambridge: Cambridge University Press.

Lopez, Robert Sabatino, and I. W. Raymond. 1955. *Medieval Trade in the Mediterranean World*. New York: Columbia University Press.

Luzzatto, Gino. 1961. *An Economic History of Italy: From the Fall of the Roman Empire to the Beginning of the Sixteenth Century*. Trans. Philip Jones. London: Routledge & K. Paul.

Macaulay, Stewart, 1963. "Noncontractual Relations in Business: A Preliminary Study." *American Sociological Review* 28: 55–70.

Macfarlane, Alan. 1978. *The Origins of English Individualism*. Oxford: Basil Blackwell.

Machiavelli, Niccolò. 1990 [1532]. *Florentine Histories* (also known as *History of Florence*). Introd. Harvey C. Mansfield Jr. Trans. Laura F. Banfield and Harvey C. Mansfield Jr. Princeton, NJ: Princeton University Press.

MacLeod, W. Bentley, and James M. Malcomson. 1989. "Implicit Contracts, Incentive Compatibility, and Involuntary Unemployment." *Econometrica* 57 (2): 447–80.

Macy, Michael W. 1997. "Identity, Interest and Emergent Rationality – an Evolutionary Synthesis." *Rationality and Society* 9 (4): 427–48.

Maggi, Giovanni. 1999. "The Role of Multilateral Institutions in International Trade Cooperation." *American Economic Review* 89 (1): 190–214.

Mahoney, James. 2000. "Path Dependence in Historical Sociology." *Theory and Society* 29 (4): 507–48.

Maimonides, Moshe. 1951. *Mishne Torah*. Vol. 12. Trans. I. Klein. New Haven: Yale Judaica Series.

1957. *Responda* (in Judeo-Arabic and Hebrew). Ed. J. Blau. Jerusalem.

Maitland, Frederick William (ed.). 1889. *Select Pleas in Manorial and Other Seigniorial Courts, Reigns of Henry III and Edward I*. Vol. 2. London: Seldon Society Publications.

Maitland, Frederick William, and Mary Bateson. 1901. *The Charters of the Borough of Cambridge*. Cambridge: Cambridge University Press.

Mann, Jacob. 1919. "Responsa of the Babylonian Geonim as a Source of Jewish History." *Jewish Quarterly Review* 20: 139–72, 309–65.

1970. *The Jews in Egypt and in Palestine under the Fatimid Caliphs*. Vol. 2. New York: Katav Publishing House.

Mantzavinos, Chris. 2001. *Individual, Institutions and Markets*. Cambridge: Cambridge University Press.

March, G. James, and Johan P. Olsen. 1989. *Rediscovering Institution: The Organizational Basis of Politics*. New York: Free Press.

Margolis, Howard. 1987. *Pattern, Thinking, and Cognition: A Theory of Judgement*. Chicago: University of Chicago Press.

1994. *Paradigms and Barriers: How Habits of Mind Govern Scientific Beliefs*. Chicago: University of Chicago Press.

Marimon, Ramon. 1997. "Learning from Learning in Economics." In David M. Kreps and Kenneth F. Wallis (eds.), *Advances in Economic Theory*, 1: 278–315. Cambridge: Cambridge University Press.

Marin, Dalia, and Monika Schnitzer. 1995. "Tying Trade Flows: A Theory of Countertrade with Evidence." *American Economic Review* 85 (5): 1047–64.

Martines, Lauro (ed.). 1972. *Violence and Civil Disorder in Italian Cities, 1200–1500*. UCLA Center for Medieval and Renaissance Studies. Los Angeles: University of California Press.

Maurer, Noel, and T. Sharma. 2002. "Enforcing Property Rights through Reputation: Mexico's Early Industrialization, 1878–1913." *Journal of Economic History* 61 (4): 950–73.

McKelvey, Richard D., and Thomas Palfrey. 1992. "An Experimental Study of the Centipede Game." *Econometrica* 60 (July): 803–36.

McMillan, John. 2002. *Reinventing the Bazar: A Natural History of Markets*. New York: Norton.

McMillan, John, and Christopher Woodruff. 1999. "Interfirm Relationships and Informal Credit in Vietnam." *Quarterly Journal of Economics* 114 (4): 1285–1320.

2000. "Private Order under Dysfunctional Public Order." *Michigan Law Review* 98: 2421–45.

Mead, George Herbert. 1967 [1934]. *Mind, Self, and Society: From the Standpoint of a Social Behaviorist.* Ed. Charles W. Morris. Chicago: University of Chicago Press.

Menger, Carl. 1871 [1976]. *Principles of Economics.* New York: New York University Press.

Meyer, J. W., and B. Rowen. 1991. "Institutionalized Organizations: Formal Structure as Myth and Ceremony." In W. Powell and P. DiMaggio (eds.), *The New Institutionalism in Organizational Analysis*, 41–62. Chicago: University of Chicago Press.

Michael, Murad. 1965. "The Archives of Naharay ben Nissim, Businessman and Public Figure in Eleventh Century Egypt" (in Hebrew and Arabic). Ph.D. diss., Hebrew University, Jerusalem.

Milgrom, Paul, Douglass C. North, and Barry R. Weingast. 1990. "The Role of Institutions in the Revival of Trade: The Medieval Law Merchant, Private Judges, and the Champagne Fairs." *Economics and Politics* 1 (March), 1–23.

Milgrom, Paul, Yingyi Qian, and John Roberts. 1991. "Complementarities, Momentum, and the Evolution of Modern Manufacturing." *American Economic Review* 81 (2): 84–8.

Milgrom, Paul, and John Roberts. 1982. "Predation, Reputation, and Entry Deterrence." *Journal of Economic Theory* 27 (2): 280–312.

1990. "Rationalizability, Learning, and Equilibrium in Games with Strategic Complementarities." *Econometrica* 58 (6): 1255–77.

1992. *Economics, Organization and Management.* Englewood Cliffs, NJ: Prentice-Hall.

1995. "Complementarities and Fit: Strategy, Structure, and Organizational Change in Manufacturing." *Journal of Accounting and Economics* 19 (2–3): 179–208.

Milgrom, Paul, and Chris Shannon. 1994. "Monotone Comparative Statics." *Econometrica* 62 (1): 157–80.

Miller, Gary J. 1993. *Managerial Dilemmas: The Political Economy of Hierarchy.* Cambridge: Cambridge University Press.

Mitchell, C. Wesley. 1925. "Quantitative Analysis in Economic Theory." *American Economic Review* 15 (1): 1–12.

Mitterauer, Michael, and Reinhard Sieder. 1982. *The European Family.* Oxford: Basil Blackwell.

Mokyr, Joel. 1990. *The Lever of Riches.* Oxford: Oxford University Press.

2002. *The Gift of Athena.* Princeton, NJ: Princeton University Press.

Moore, Ellen Wedemeyer. 1985. *The Fairs of Medieval England.* Toronto: Pontifical Institute of Medieval Studies.

Moriguchi, Chiaki. 1998. "Evolution of Employment Systems in the US and Japan: 1900–60. A Comparative Historical Analysis." Unpublished manuscript, Stanford University.

Morris, Colin. 1972. *The Discovery of the Individual, 1050–1200.* London: S.P.C.K. for the Church Historical Society.

Moser, Peter. 2000. *The Political Economy of Democratic Institutions.* Cheltenham: Edward Elgar.

Munck, Gerardo L. 2001. "Game Theory and Comparative Politics." *World Politics* 53 (Jan.): 173–204.

Munz, Peter. 1969. *Frederick Barbarossa.* Ithaca, NY: Cornell University Press.

Muthoo, Abhinay, and Kenneth A. Shepsle. 2003. "Agenda-Setting Power in Organizations with Overlapping Generations of Players." Typescript, Harvard University.

Nee, Victor, and Paul Ingram. 1998. "Embeddedness and Beyond: Institutions, Exchange and Social Structure." In M. Brinton and V. Nee (eds.), *The New Institutionalism in Sociology*, 19–45. New York: Russell Sage Foundation.

Nelson, Philip. 1974. "Advertising as Information." *Journal of Political Economy* 82 (4): 729–54.

Nelson, Richard R. 1994. "The Co-evolution of Technology, Industrial Structure, and Supporting Institutions." *Industrial and Corporate Change* 3: 47–63.

1995. "Recent Evolutionary Theorizing about Economic Change." *Journal of Economic Literature* 33 (1): 48–90.

Nelson, Richard R., and Sidney G. Winter. 1982. *An Evolutionary Theory of Economic Change.* Cambridge, MA: Harvard University Press.

North, Douglass C. 1981. *Structure and Change in Economic History.* New York: Norton.

1990. *Institutions, Institutional Change and Economic Performance.* Cambridge: Cambridge University Press.

1991. "Institutions." *Journal of Economic Perspectives* 5 (1): 97–112.

1993. "Institutions and Credible Commitment." *Journal of Institutional and Theoretical Economics* 149 (1): 11–23.

2005. *Understanding the Process of Institutional Change.* Princeton, NJ: Princeton University Press.

North, Douglass C., and Robert P. Thomas. 1973. *The Rise of the Western World.* Cambridge: Cambridge University Press.

North, Douglass C., and Barry R. Weingast. 1989. "Constitutions and Commitment: The Evolution of Institutions Governing Public Choice in Seventeenth-Century England." *Journal of Economic History* 49: 803–32.

Norwich, John Julius. 1989. *History of Venice.* New York: Random House.

Obertus Scriba de Mercato. 1186, 1190. *Cartolare* (in Latin and Italian). Ed. R. Mario Chiaudano and Morozzo Della Rocca. Documenti, XI and XVI. Turin: Editrice Libraria Italiana, 1940.

Okazaki, Tetsuji. 2005. "The Role of the Merchant Coalition in Pre-modern Japanese Economic Development: An Historical Institutional Analysis." *Explorations in Economic History* 42 (2): 184–201.

Okazaki, Tetsuji, and Masahiro Okuno-Fujiwara. 1998. "Evolution of Economic Systems: The Case of Japan." In Y. Hayami and Masahiko Aoki (eds.), *The Institutional Foundation of Economic Development in East Asia*, 482–521. London: Macmillan.

Okuno-Fujiwara, Masahiro, and Andrew Postlewaite. 1990. "Social Norms and Random Matching Games." CARESS Working Paper #90-18, University of Pennsylvania.

Olivieri, Agostino. 1861. *Serie dei consoli del comune di Genova*. Genoa: Forni Editore Bologna. Originally published in *Atti della Ligure di Storia Patria* 1 (1858): 155–479.

Olson, Mancur. 1982. *The Rise and Decline of Nations*. New Haven: Yale University Press.

——— 1993. "Dictatorship, Democracy, and Development." *American Political Science Review* 87 (3): 567–76.

Ostrom, Elinor. 1990. *Governing the Commons: The Evolution of Institutions for Collective Action*. Cambridge: Cambridge University Press.

——— 1998. "A Behavioral Approach to the Rational Choice Theory of Collective Action." *American Political Science Review* 92 (1): 1–22.

Otto of Freising and His Continuator. 1152–8. *The Deeds of Frederick Barbarossa*. Translated and annotated by Charles Christopher Mierow with collaboration of Richard Emery. New York: Columbia University Press, 1953.

Pagano, Ugo, and Maria Alessandra Rossi. 2002. "Incomplete Contracts, Intellectual Property and Institutional Complementarities." Memo, University of Siena.

Pamuk, Şevket. 2000. *A Monetary History of the Ottoman Empire*. Cambridge: Cambridge University Press.

Parker, Geoffrey. 1990. *The Military Revolution (1500–1800)*. Cambridge: Cambridge University Press.

Parsons, Talcott. 1951. *The Social System*. London: Routledge and Kegan Paul.

——— 1990. "Prologomena to a Theory of Social Institutions." *American Sociological Review* 55 (3): 319–33.

Patourel, J. H. le. 1937. *Medieval Administration of the Channel Islands, 1199–1399*. Oxford: Oxford University Press.

Pearce, David G. 1984. "Rationalizable Strategic Behavior and the Problem of Perfection." *Econometrica* 52 (4): 1029–50.

——— 1987. "Renegotiation-Proof Equilibria: Collective Rationality and Intertemporal Cooperation." Unpublished manuscript, Department of Economics, Yale University.

——— 1995. "Repeated Games: Cooperation and Rationality." In Jean-Jacques Laffont (ed.), *Advances in Economic Theory*, 1: 132–74. Sixth World Congress. Cambridge: Cambridge University Press.

Persson, Karl Gunnar. 1988. *Pre-industrial Economic Growth, Social Organization, and Technological Progress in Europe*. New York: Blackwell.

Pertile, Antonio. 1966. *Storia del diritto italiano dalla caduta dell'Impero Romano alla codificazione*. 2nd ed. 2 vols. Bologna: Arnaldo Forni Editore.

Peters, Guy. 1996. "Political Institutions, Old and New." In Robert Goodin and Hans-Dieter Klingemann (eds.), *A New Handbook of Political Science*, 205–20. New York: Oxford University Press.

Pierson, Paul. 2000. "Increasing Returns, Path Dependence, and the Study of Politics." *American Political Science Review* 94 (2): 251–67.

Pierson, Paul, and Theda Skocpol. 2002. "Historical Institutionalism in Contemporary Political Science." In Ira Katznelson and Helen V. Milner (eds.), *Political Science: State of the Discipline*, 693–721. New York: Norton.

Pirenne, Henri. 1939. *Mohammed and Charlemagne*. New York: Norton.
    1956. *A History of Europe*. New York: University Books.
Planitz, H. 1919. "Studien zur Geschichte des Deutschen Arrestprozesses, II. Kapital, der Fremdenarrest." *Zeitschrift de Savigny-Stifung fuer Rechtsgeschichte* (Germanistische Abteilung) 40: 87–198.
Platteau, Jean-Philippe. 1994. "Behind the Market Stage Where Real Societies Exist. Part II: The Role of Moral Norms." *Journal of Development Studies* 30 (3): 753–817.
    2000. *Institutions, Social Norms and Economic Development*. Amsterdam: Harwood Academic Publishers.
Platteau, J. P., and F. Gaspart. 2003. "The Risk of Resource Misappropriation in Community-Driven Development." *World Development* 31 (10): 1687–1703.
Platteau, Jean-Philippe, and Y. Hayami. 1998. "Resource Endowments and Agricultural Development: Africa versus Asia." In M. Aoki, and Y. Hayami (eds.), *The Institutional Foundations of East Asian Economic Development*, 357–410. London: Macmillan.
Plucknett, Theodore Frank Thomas. 1949. *Legislation of Edward I*. Oxford: Clarendon.
Pollock, Frederick, and Frederic William Maitland. 1968. *The History of the English Law before the Time of Edward I*. 2nd ed. 2 vols. Cambridge: Cambridge University Press.
Pomeranz, Kenneth. 2000. *The Great Divergence: China, Europe and the Making of the Modern World Economy*. Princeton, NJ: Princeton University Press.
Posner, R. A. 1997. "Social Norms and the Law: An Economic Approach." *Papers and Proceedings from the 104th Meeting of the American Economic Association. American Economic Review* 87 (2): 333–8.
Postan, Michael M. 1973. *Medieval Trade and Finance*. Cambridge: Cambridge University Press.
Pounds, Norman John Greville. 1994. *An Economic History of Medieval Europe*. 2nd ed. New York: Longman.
Powell, Robert. 1993. "Guns, Butter, and Anarchy." *American Political Science Review* 87 (1): 115–32.
    1999. *In the Shadow of Power: States and Strategies in International Politics*. Princeton, NJ: Princeton University Press.
Powell, W., and P. DiMaggio (eds.). 1991. *The New Institutionalism in Organizational Analysis*. Chicago: University of Chicago Press.
Poznanski, S. 1904. "Ephraim ben Schemria de Fustat" (in French and Hebrew). *Revue des Etudes Juives* 48: 146–75.
Pryor, F. L. 1977. *The Origins of the Economy: A Comparative Study of Distribution and Peasant Economies*. New York: Academic Press.
Pryor, John. 1988. *Geography, Technology, and War*. Cambridge: Cambridge University Press.
Przeworski, Adam. 1991. *Democracy and the Market: Political and Economic Reforms in Eastern Europe and Latin America*. Cambridge: Cambridge University Press.

Putnam, Robert D. 1993. *Making Democracy Work*. Princeton, NJ: Princeton University Press.

——— 2000. *Bowling Alone*. New York: Simon and Schuster.

Rabin, Matthew. 1993. "Incorporating Fairness into Game Theory and Economics." *American Economic Review* 83 (5): 1281–1302.

——— 1994. "Cognitive Dissonance and Social Change." *Journal of Economic Behavior and Organization* 23 (2): 177–94.

——— 1998. "Psychology and Economics." *Journal of Economic Literature* 36 (1): 11–46.

Rahman, Fazlur. 2002. *Islam*. 2nd ed. Chicago: University of Chicago Press.

Rapoport, Amnon. 1997. "Order of Play in Strategically Equivalent Games in Extensive Form." *International Journal of Game Theory* 26 (1): 113–36.

Rashdal, Hastings. 1936. *The Universities of Europe in the Middle Ages*. Vol. 1. Ed. F. M. Powicke and A. B. Emden. Oxford: Oxford University Press.

Rauch, J. E. 2001. "Business and Social Networks in International Trade." *Journal of Economic Literature* 39 (Dec.): 1177–1203.

Razi, Zevi. 1993. "The Myth of the Immutable English Family." *Past & Present* 140 (Aug.): 3–44.

Rey, E. 1895. "Les seigneurs de giblet." *Revue de l'Orient Latin* 3:398–422. Paris: Presses Universitaires de France.

Reynolds, Charles H., and Ralph V. Norman, eds. 1988. *Community in America*. Berkeley: University of California Press.

Reynolds, Robert L. 1929. "The Market for Northern Textiles in Genoa 1179–1200." *Revue Belge Philologie et d'Historie* 8: 831–51.

——— 1930. "Merchants of Arras and the Overland Trade with Genoa in the Twelfth Century." *Revue Belge Philologie et d'Histoirie* 9: 495–533.

——— 1931. "Genoese Trade in the Late Twelfth Century, Particularly in Cloth from the Fair of Champagne." *Journal of Economic and Business History* 3: 362–81.

Richardson, Gary. 2002. "Craft Guilds and Christianity in Late-Medieval England: A Rational-Choice Analysis." Memo, University of California, Irvine.

Riker, William. 1964. *Federalism: Origins, Operations, and Significance*. Boston: Little Brown.

Rippin, Andrew. 1994. *Muslims: Their Religious Beliefs and Practices*. Vol. 1: *The Formative Period*. Reprint, London: Routledge.

Rodrik, Dani. 2003. "Growth Strategies." Memo, Harvard University. [Forthcoming in *The Handbook of Economic Growth*.]

Rodrik, Dani, Arvind Subramanian, and Francesco Trebbi. 2003. "Institutions Rule: The Primacy of Institutions over Geography and Integration in Economic Development." Memo, Harvard University.

Roland, Gérard. 2000. *Transitions and Economics: Politics, Markets, and Firms*. Cambridge, MA: MIT Press.

Romer, Paul. 1996. "Preferences, Promises, and the Politics of Entitlement." In Victor R. Fuchs (ed.), *The Individual and Social Responsibility*, 195–220. Cambridge: Cambridge University Press.

481

Root, Hilton L. 1989. "Tying the King's Hands: Credible Commitments and Royal Fiscal Policy during the Old Regime." *Rationality and Society* 1 (Oct.): 240–58.

———. 1994. *The Fountain of Privilege: Political Foundations of Markets in Old Regime France and Englands.* Berkeley: University of California Press.

Rorig, Fritz. 1967. *The Medieval Town.* Berkeley: University of California Press.

Rosenberg, Nathan. 1982. *Inside the Black Box: Technology and Economics.* Cambridge: Cambridge University Press.

Rosenberg, Nathan, and L. E. Birdzell Jr. 1986. *How the West Grew Rich.* New York: Basic Books.

Rosenthal, Jean-Laurent. 1992. *The Fruits of Revolution.* Cambridge: Cambridge University Press.

Ross, Lee, and Richard E. Nisbett. 1991. *The Person and the Situation.* Boston: McGraw-Hill.

Rossetti, G., M. C. Pratesi, G. Garzella, M. B. Guzzardi, G. Guglie, and C. Sturmann. 1979. *Pisa nei secoli XI e XII: Formazione e caratteri di una classe di governo.* Pisa: Pacini Editore.

Roth, Alvin E., Vesna Prasnikar, Masahiro Okuno-Fujiwara, and Shmuel Zamir. 1991. "Bargaining and Market Behavior in Jerusalem, Ljubljana, Pittsburgh, and Tokyo: An Experimental Study." *American Economic Review* 81 (5): 1068–95.

Roth, Alvin E., and I. Erev. 1995. "Learning in Extensive-Form Games: Experimental Data and Simple Dynamic Models in Intermediate Term." *Games and Economic Behavior*, special issue: Nobel Symposium, 8: 164–212.

Rothstein, Bo. 1996. "Political Institutions: An Overview." In Robert Goodin and Hans-Dieter Klingemann (eds.), *A New Handbook of Political Science*, 133–66. New York: Oxford University Press.

Rubinstein, Ariel. 1991. "Comments on the Interpretation of Game Theory." *Econometrica* 59 (4): 909–24.

———. 1998. *Modeling Bounded Rationality.* Cambridge, MA: MIT Press.

Sachs, Jefrey D. 2001. "Tropical Underdevelopment." NBER Working Paper No. 8119.

Salzman, L. F. 1928. "A Riot at Boston Fair." *History Teachers' Miscellany* 6: 2–3.

Samuelson, Paul A. 1993. "Altruism as a Problem Involving Group versus Individual Selection in Economics and Biology." *American Economic Review* 83 (2): 143–8.

Santini, Pietro. 1886. "Appunti sulla vendetta privata e sulle rappresaglie." *Archivo Strico Italiano* 18: 162–76.

Saunders, J. J. 1965. *A History of Medieval Islam.* New York: Routledge.

Savage, Leonard J. 1954. *The Foundations of Statistics.* New York: Wiley & Sons.

Schacht, Joseph. 1982 [1964]. *An Introduction to Islamic Law.* Oxford: Clarendon Press.

Scharpf, F. W. 1997. *Games Real Actors Play.* Boulder, CO: Westview.

Schelling, Thomas. 1960. *The Strategy of Conflict.* Cambridge, MA: Harvard University Press.

Schneider, G., T. Plumper, and S. Baumann, 2000. "Bringing Putnam to the European Regions – on the Relevance of Social Capital for Economic Growth." *European Urban and Regional Studies* 7 (4): 307–17.

Schotter, Andrew. 1981. *The Economic Theory of Social Institutions*. Cambridge: Cambridge University Press.

Schumann, Reinhold. 1992. *Italy in the Last Fifteen Hundred Years*. 2nd ed. Lanham, MD: University Press of America.

Scott, W. Richard. 1998. *Organizations: Rational, Natural, and Open Systems*. Englewood Cliffs, NJ: Prentice-Hall.

——— 1995. *Institutions and Organizations*. Thousand Oaks, CA: Sage Publications.

Scott, W. Richard, John W. Meyer, et al. 1994. *Institutional Environments and Organizations*. London: Sage Publications.

Searle, John R. 1995. *The Construction of Social Reality*. New York: Free Press.

Segal, Ilya. 1999. "Complexity and Renegotiation: A Foundation for Incomplete Contracts." *Review of Economic Studies* 66 (1): 57–82.

Segal, Ronald. 2001. *Islam's Black Slaves*. New York: Farrar, Straus and Giroux.

Segal, Uzi, and Joel Sobel. 2000. "Tit for Tat: Foundations of Preferences for Reciprocity in Strategic Settings." Memo, University of California, San Diego.

Select Cases Concerning the Law Merchant, A.D. 1270–1638. Vol. 1: *Local Courts*. 1908. Ed. Charles Gross. Selden Society Publications, 23. London: B. Quaritch.

Select Cases Concerning the Law Merchant, A.D. 1239–1633. Vol. 2: *Central Courts*. 1930. Ed. H. Hall. Selden Society Publications, 46. London: B. Quaritch.

Sen, Amartya K. 1995. "Moral Codes and Economic Success." In Samuel Brittan and Alan P. Hamlin (eds.), *Market Capitalism and Moral Values*. Aldershot: Edward Elgar.

Sened, Itai. 1997. *The Political Institution of Private Property*. Cambridge: Cambridge University Press.

Sewell, William H. 1992. "A Theory of Structure: Duality, Agency, and Transformation." *American Journal of Sociology* 98 (1): 1–29.

Shapiro, Carl. 1983. "Premiums for High Quality Products as Return to Reputation." *Quarterly Journal of Economics* 98 (4): 659–79.

Shapiro, C., and J. E. Stiglitz. 1984. "Equilibrium Unemployment as a Worker Discipline Device." *American Economic Review* 74 (3): 433–44.

Shepsle, Kenneth A. 1979. "Institutional Arrangements and Equilibrium in Multidimensional Voting Models." *American Journal of Political Science* 23: 27–59.

——— 1992. "Institutional Equilibrium and Equilibrium Institutions." In H. F. Weisberg (ed.), *Political Science: The Science of Politics*, 51–82. New York: Agathon Press.

Shirley, Mary M. 2004. "Institutions and Development." In Claude Menard and Mary M. Shirley (eds.), *Handbook on New Institutional Economics*. Norwell, MA: Kluwer Press.

Shiue, Carol H., and Wolfgang Keller. 2003. "Markets in China and Europe on the Eve of the Industrial Revolution." Memo, University of Texas.

References

Sieveking, Heinrich. 1898–9. *Genueser Finanzwesen mit Besonderer Berücksichtigung de Casa di S. Giorgio.* 2 vols. Leipzig: Freiburg.

Simon, Herbert A. 1955. "A Behavioral Model of Rational Choice." *Quarterly Journal of Economics* 69: 99–118.

1976. *Administrative Behavior.* 3rd ed. New York: Macmillan.

1987 [1957]. *Model of Man, Social and Rational.* New York: John Wiley.

Skaperdas, Stergios. 1992. "Cooperation, Conflict, and Power in the Absence of Property Rights." *American Economic Review* 84 (4): 720–39.

1996. "Contest Success Functions." *Economic Theory* 7: 283–90.

Smelser, Neil, and Richard Swedberg. 1994. "The Sociological Perspective on the Economy." In N. Smelser and R. Swedberg (eds.), *The Handbook of Economic Sociology*, 3–26. Princeton, NJ: Princeton University Press; New York: Russell Sage Foundation.

Sobel, Joel. 2002. "Can We Trust Social Capital?" *Journal of Economic Literature* 40 (March): 139–54.

Sonn, Tamara. 1990. *Between Qur'an and Crown.* Boulder, CO: Westview Press.

Spruyt, Hendrik. 1994. *The Sovereign State and Its Competitors.* Princeton, NJ: Princeton University Press.

Staiger, Robert. 1995. "International Rules and Institutions for Trade Policy." In Gene M. Grossman and Kenneth Rogoff (eds.), *The Handbook of International Economics*, vol. 3, chap. 29. North Holland: Elsevier Science Publishers.

Stark, R. 1996. *The Rise of Christianity: A Sociologist Reconsiders History.* Princeton, NJ: Princeton University Press.

Stein, Peter. 1999. *Roman Law in European History.* Cambridge: Cambridge University Press.

Stewart, Hamish. 1992. "Rationality and the Market for Human Blood." *Journal of Economic Behavior and Organization* 1 (2): 125–43.

Stiglitz, J. 1994. *Whither Socialism?* Cambridge, MA: MIT Press.

Stillman, Norman Arthur. 1970. "East-West Relations in the Islamic Mediterranean in the Early Eleventh Century." Ph.D. diss., University of Pennsylvania.

Stinchcombe, Arthur L. 1968. *Constructing Social Theories.* Chicago: University of Chicago Press.

Stubbs, W. (ed.). 1913. *Selected Charters and Other Illustrations of English Institutional History from the Earliest Times to the Reign of Edward the First.* 9th ed. Oxford: Clarendon.

Sugden, Robert. 1986. *The Economics of Rights, Cooperation and Welfare.* Oxford: Basil Blackwell.

1989. "Spontaneous Order." *Journal of Economic Perspective* 3 (4): 85–97.

Sutton, John. 1991. *Sunk Costs and Market Structure: Price Competition, Advertising, and the Evolution of Concentration.* Cambridge, MA: MIT Press.

Swidler, Ann. 1986. "Culture in Action." *American Sociological Review* 51 (Apr.): 273–86.

Tabacco, Giovanni. 1989. *The Struggle for Power in Medieval Italy.* Cambridge: Cambridge University Press.

Tadelis, Steve. 1999. "What's in a Name? Reputation as a Tradeable Asset." *Economic Review* 89 (3): 548–63.

———. 2002. "The Market for Reputations as an Incentive Mechanism." *Journal of Political Economy* 110 (4): 854–82.

Telser, L. G. 1980. "A Theory of Self-Enforcing Agreements." *Journal of Business* 53: 27–43.

Thelen, Kathleen. 1999. "Historical Institutionalism in Comparative Politics." *Annual Review of Political Science* 2 (June): 369–404.

Thomas, H. 1977. "Beitraege zur Geschichte der Champagne-Messen im 14. Jahrhundert." *Vierteljahrschrift fuer Sozial-und Wietschaftsgeschichte* 64 (4): 433–67.

Thrupp, Sylvia L. 1965. "The Gilds." In M. M. Postan, E. E. Rick, and M. Miltey (eds.), *Cambridge Economic History of Europe*, 3: 230–79. Cambridge: Cambridge University Press.

Tilly, Charles. 1990. *Coercion, Capital, and European States, AD 990–1992.* Cambridge, MA: Blackwell.

Tirole, Jean. 1996. "A Theory of Collective Reputation (with Applications to the Persistence of Corruption and to Firm Quality)." *Review of Economic Studies* 63 (1): 1–22.

Tooby, John, and Leda Cosmides. 1992. "The Psychological Foundations of Culture." In Jerome H. Barkow, Leda Cosmides, and John Tooby (eds.), *The Adapted Mind: Evolutionary Psychology and the Generation of Culture*, 19–136. New York: Oxford University Press.

Topiks, D. 1998. *Supermodularity and Complementarity*. Princeton, NJ: Princeton University Press.

Townsend, Robert M. 1979. "Optimal Contracts and Competitive Markets with Costly State Verification." *Journal of Economic Theory* 21 (2): 265–93.

Trackman, Leon E. 1983. *The Law Merchant: The Evolution of Commercial Law.* Littleton, CO: Fred B. Rothman.

Triandis, Harry C. 1990. "Cross-Cultural Studies of Individualism and Collectivism." In J. Berman (ed.), *Nebraska Symposium on Motivation, 1989*, 41–133. Lincoln: University of Nebraska Press.

Tversky, A., and D. Kahneman. 1981. "The Framing of Decisions and the Psychology of Choice." *Science* 211: 453–58.

Udovitch, Abraham L. 1962. "At the Origins of Western Commenda: Islam, Israel, Byzantium." *Speculum* 37: 198–207.

———. 1970. *Partnership and Profit in Medieval Islam.* Princeton, NJ: Princeton University Press.

Ullmann-Margalit, Edna. 1977. *The Emergence of Norms.* Oxford: Clarendon Press.

Van Damme, Eric. 1983. *Refinements of the Nash Equilibrium Concept.* Berlin: Springer-Verlag.

———. 1987. *Stability and Perfection of Nash Equilibria.* Berlin: Springer-Verlag.

Van der Vee, Herman. 1977. "Monetary, Credit, and Banking Systems." In E. E. Rich and C. H. Wilson (eds.), *The Cambridge Economic History of Europe*, 5: 290–391. Cambridge: Cambridge University Press.

Varian, H. R. 1990. "Monitoring Agents with Other Agents." *Journal of Institutional and Theoretical Economics* 146 (1): 153–74.

Veblen, Thorstein. 1899. *The Theory of the Leisure Class.* New York: Macmillan.

Vecchio, A. del, and E. Casanova. 1894. *Le rappresaglie nei comuni medievali e specialmente in Firenze.* Bologna: R. Forni.

Verlinden, C. 1979. "Markets and Fairs." In M. M. Postan, E. E. Rick, and M. Miltey (eds.), *The Cambridge Economic History of Europe*, 3: 119–53. Cambridge: Cambridge University Press.

Vitale, V. 1951. *Il comune del podestà a Genova.* Milan: Ricciardi.

1955. *Breviario della storia di Genova.* 2 vols. Genoa: Societa Ligure di Storia Patria.

Volckart, Oliver. 2001. "The Economics of Feuding in Late Medieval Germany." Working paper, Institut fur Wirtschaftsgeschichte, Berlin.

Wach, A. 1868. *Der Arrestprozess in seiner geschichtlichen Entwicklung.* 1. Teil: *De Italienische Arrestprozess.* Leipzig: Haessel.

Waley, Daniel. 1988. *The Italian City-Republics.* 3rd ed. London: Longman.

Watson, Joel. 1999. "Starting Small and Renegotiation." *Journal of Economic Theory* 85 (1): 52–90.

2001. *Strategy: An Introduction to Game Theory.* New York: Norton.

Watt, Montgomery W. 1961. *Muhammad: Prophet and Statesman.* Oxford: Oxford University Press.

1987. *The Influence of Islam on Medieval Europe.* Edinburgh: At the University Press.

Watts, R. W., and J. L. Zimmermann. 1983. "Agency Problems, Auditing and the Theory of the Firm: Some Evidence." *Journal of Law and Economics* 26 (Oct.): 613–33.

Weber, M. 1947. *The Theory of Social and Economic Organization.* Reprint, New York: Free Press, 1964.

1949. *The Methodology of the Social Sciences.* Glencoe, IL: Free Press.

1958 [1904–5]. *The Protestant Ethic and the Spirit of Capitalism.* New York: Charles Scribner's Sons.

Weibull, Jörgen. 1995. *Evolutionary Game Theory.* Cambridge, MA: MIT Press.

Weiner, A. 1932. "The Hansa." In J. R. Tanner, C. W. Previté-Orton, and Z. N. Brooke (eds.), *The Cambridge Medieval History*, 7: 216–69. Cambridge: Cambridge University Press.

Weingast, Barry R. 1993. "Constitutions as Governance Structures: The Political Foundations of Secured Markets." *Journal of Institutional and Theoretical Economics* 149 (1): 286–311.

1995. "Institutions and Political Commitment: A New Political Economy of the American Civil War Era." Memo, Stanford University.

1996. "Political Institutions: Rational Choice Perspectives." In Robert Goodin and Hans-Dieter Klingemann (eds.), *A New Handbook of Political Science*, 167–90. New York: Oxford University Press.

1997. "The Political Foundations of Democracy and the Rule of Law." *American Political Science Review* 91 (2): 245–63.

Weingast, B., and W. Marshall. 1988. "The Industrial Organization of Congress; or, Why Legislatures, Like Firms, Are Not Organized as Markets." *Journal of Political Economy* 96 (1): 132–63.

White, Lynn. 1964. *The Medieval Technology and Social Change*. London: Oxford University Press.

Wiessner, Polly. 2002. "Hunting, Healing, and Hxaro Exchange. A Long-Term Perspective on !Kung (Ju/'hoansi) Large-Game Hunting." *Evolution and Human Behavior* 23: 407–36.

Williamson, Dean V. 2002. "Transparency and Contract Selection: Evidence from the Financing of Trade in Venetian Crete, 1303–1351." Memo, U.S. Department of Justice.

Williamson, Oliver E. 1975. *Markets and Hierarchies: Analyses and Antitrust Implications*. New York: Free Press.

————. 1985. *The Economic Institutions of Capitalism*. New York: Free Press.

————. 1993. "Transaction Cost Economics and Organization Theory." *Industrial and Corporate Change* 2 (2): 107–56.

————. 1996. *The Mechanisms of Governance*. Oxford: Oxford University Press.

————. 1998. "Transaction Cost Economics: How It Works; Where It Is Headed." *De Economist* 146 (1): 23–58.

————. 2000. "The New Institutional Economics: Taking Stock, Looking Ahead." *Journal of Economic Literature* 38 (Sept.): 595–613.

Wilson, Edward O. 1975. *Sociobiology*. Cambridge, MA: Belknap Press, Harvard University Press.

Witt, Ulrich. 1986. "Evolution and Stability of Cooperation without Enforceable Contracts." *Kyklos* 39, fasc. 2: 245–66.

Woolcock, Michael. 1998. "Social Capital and Economic Development: Toward a Theoretical Synthesis and Policy Framework." *Theory and Society* 27 (2): 151–208.

Wright, Mark. 2002. "Reputations and Sovereign Debt." Working paper, Stanford University.

Wrong, Dennis H. 1961. "The Oversocialized Conception of Man in Modern Sociology." *American Sociological Review* 26 (2): 183–93. Reprinted as chapter 2 in Dennis H. Wrong, *The Oversocialized Conception of Man* (New Brunswick, NJ: Transaction Publishers, 1999).

————. 1999. *The Oversocialized Conception of Man*. New Brunswick, NJ: Transaction Publishers.

Yang Li, Mu. 2002. "Essays on Public Finance and Economic Development in a Historical Institutional Perspective." Ph.D. diss., Stanford University.

Young, H. Peyton. 1993. "The Evolution of Conventions." *Econometrica* 61 (1): 57–84.

————. 1998. *Individual Strategy and Social Structure*. Princeton, NJ: Princeton University Press.

Young, H. Peyton, and Mary A. Burke. 2001. "Competition and Custom in Economic Contracts: A Case Study of Illinois Agriculture." *American Economic Review* 91 (3): 559–73.

Zak, Paul J., and Stephen Knack. 2001. "Trust and Growth." *Economic Journal* 111 (470): 295–321.

Zhang, Jiajie. 1997. "Nature of External Representations in Problem Solving." *Cognitive Science* 21 (2): 179–217.

Zucker, L. G. 1983. "Organizations as Institutions." In S. B. Bacharach (ed.), *Research in the Sociology of Organizations*, 1–42. Greenwich, CT: JAI.

    1991. "The Role of Institutionalization in Cultural Persistence." In W. Powell and P. DiMaggio (eds.), *The New Institutionalism in Organizational Analysis*, 83–107. Chicago: University of Chicago Press.

Index

absolutism, 393, 394
Abu Bakr, 253
accounting system, 85, 204, 300
agency relations, 273–4
  and efficiency, 62
  honesty in, 65, 66, 68, 75, 215,
    276
  intercoalition, 81–3
  inter-economy, 289–94
  intra-economy, 289–93
  modeling, 429
agents, overseas, 61
  coordination of, 69
alberghi, 175, 245
al-Mawardi, 150
altruism, 144, 422
aman, 101
analogy, 213
arms race, 173
attention, 166
auditing, 204
Austrian Economics, 154
authority, *see* cultural, authority; power

backward induction, 414–16
  and experimental evidence of, 414–20,
    425
Bacon, Francis, 19, 355
Bank of San Giorgio, *see* Genoa
bankruptcy, 325
barriers to entry and exit, *see* institutions,
  reputation-based
behavior, 8, 13–15, 124–38
  altruistic, 423
  consequential, 422
  mimetic, 427
  morally appropriate and socially
    accepted, 36, 127, 143-7, 421–2
  opportunistic, 62, 273
  regularities of, 32–3

satisficing, 152
  situationally contingent, 144
behavior, micro-foundations of, 16, 125–38
  cognitive, 125
  coordinative, 125
  informational, 125
  normative, 125, 143–7
  social, 143–7
beliefs, 10–14, 36–7, 133, 139–40
  admissible set of behavioral, 139
  admissible set of internalized, 140,
    141–2 (*see also* cognitive modes;
    models, mental)
  behavioral, 36–7, 46, 139
  institutionalized, 30, 34, 36–7, 48, 124
  internalized, 31, 36, 46, 124–8
  religious, 202, 431
  subjective, 132
  See also fundamental asymmetry
bill of lading, 296–8
bonuses, and motivation, 438
bribes, 322
Bruges, 100, 104, 106–8
business
  associations, forms of, 285, 286
  organization, family relations and, 298
  See also networks
Byzantine Empire, 96
  See also Rums

Caliphate
  Abbasid, 77
  Fatimid, 61, 294
capital
  as bond, 283, 284
  See also civil capital; social capital
case-study method, 21, 307, 350–1, 387
  See also context-specific analysis
Catalan merchants, 100
Champagne fairs, 315, 333–5, 336